In the Company
of Others

D1500930

In the Company of Others

of Others

An Introduction to Communication

J. Dan Rothwell
Cabrillo College

MAYFIELD PUBLISHING COMPANY

Mountain View, California
London • Toronto

Library of Congress Cataloging-in-Publication Data

Rothwell, J. Dan.
   In the company of others : an introduction to communication / J. Dan Rothwell.
      p.cm.
   Includes bibliographical references and index.
   ISBN 1-55934-738-4
    1. Communication. I. Title.

   P90 .R665 1999
   302.2—dc21   99-046763

Manufactured in the United States of America
10   9   8   7   6   5   4   3   2   1

Mayfield Publishing Company
1280 Villa Street
Mountain View, California 94041

Sponsoring editor, Holly J. Allen; developmental editor, Kathleen Engelberg; production editor, Linda Ward; manuscript editor, Kay Mikel; design manager, Jean Mailander; art editor, Robin Mouat; text and cover designer, Ellen Pettengell; cover art, Kevin Ghiglione; illustrators, John Waller and Judy Waller, Line Works, Inc., Cartographics, John Nelson, and Robin Mouat; photo researcher, Brian Pecko; manufacturing manager, Randy Hurst. The text was set in 9.5/12 Palatino by Progressive Publishing Alternatives and printed on 45# Somerset Matte 800 by R. R. Donnelley & Sons Company.

Text and photo credits appear on page 527, which constitutes an extension of the copyright page.

This book is printed on acid-free paper.

To my family,
Marcy, Hilary, Geoff, Barrett, and Clare

Preface

Lord Byron once remarked, "Who would write, who had anything better to do?" During the three years I spent preparing this textbook, there were moments when watching a sitcom rerun for the fifth time seemed preferable to writing another word, sentence, paragraph, or page. I gained stamina, however, from reminding myself of Samuel Johnson's comment, "What is written without effort is in general read without pleasure." Throughout this challenging task, my desire to write an interesting work that addressed some important themes and issues often ignored in other textbooks provided the driving incentive to complete this work. There are dozens of competent textbooks on human communication. There is little point in adding to the pile unless *In the Company of Others* has something new to offer. I believe it does.

Features

While covering all the standard topics in substantial detail, remaining faithful to the core material almost all instructors agree is essential, *In the Company of Others* differs from other texts in significant ways. In addition to covering the basic skills of communication, this text is built on the themes of cooperation and competence.

Cooperation: A Unifying Theme

Cooperation is a unifying theme of this book. One of the great potential contributions of the communication discipline is that we not only can discuss cooperation knowledgeably, but we can also provide specific advice on how to structure human transactions so cooperation can become a reality. Many textbooks in several disciplines pay lip service to the need for human cooperation, but they are noticeably devoid of informed suggestions regarding how to make it happen. This does little more than frustrate students who are looking for concrete ideas and specific advice to help them work together with others. *In the Company of Others* thoroughly addresses the issue of cooperation in interpersonal relationships, in group transactions, even in public speaking. This book as a whole is based on the assumption that cooperation should be embraced, nurtured, and cultivated.

Communication Competence Model: A Foundation for Students

The communication competence model is one of our discipline's unique contributions to understanding and improving human behavior. One of the premises of this book is that communication competence, whether in the interpersonal, small-group, public-speaking, or communication technology arena, is critical to student success and achievement. The five components of the model—*knowledge, skill, sensitivity, commitment,* and *ethics*—highlight the complexity of the communication process and provide direction and guidance for students. The model is integrated throughout the text, not merely discussed in the first chapter, then dropped entirely or mentioned briefly in later chapters. Most topics and issues in the text, including perception of self and others, intercultural communication, language use, listening, transacting power, managing conflict, using communication technologies, and many others are analyzed from the model's perspective.

Integration of Gender and Culture

Gender and culture are important themes because we live in a world of increasing diversity. *In the Company of Others* treats gender and culture as integral parts of the overall discussion of communication. Gender receives special attention early in the text in Chapter 2, and culture is the subject of Chapter 3. Additional coverage, based on the material in these two chapters, appears throughout the text. Topics related to gender and culture include cultural differences in nonverbal meanings, the role of gender and culture in powerful/powerless language, cross-cultural friendships and romantic relationships, gender and cultural bias in the workplace, the effects of communication technologies on cultural transactions, and many others.

Emphasis on Power

Power is inherent in every human transaction. It is perplexing that many textbooks give so little attention to the integral role power plays in all human relationships. The communication discipline has many valuable insights to offer on this important subject. Chapter 7 gives special focus to the subject of power in relationships, and later chapters include additional discussions and applications. Such topics as the effects of power imbalances in relationships, sources of personal power, strategies for transacting power competently and cooperatively, and ways to empower oneself and others are addressed.

Focus on Critical Thinking

Asking students to think critically and determine which ideas and conclusions make more sense than others may strike some students as promoting closed-mindedness. "Shouldn't all ideas be given an equal hearing?" Chapter 6 explores the issue of open- and closed-mindedness. The point is made that open-mindedness is following where the evidence and reasoning leads, and closed-mindedness is accepting or rejecting an idea or conclusion despite what the evidence and reasoning suggests. Criteria for evaluating evidence and reasoning are provided in the chapter to help students sort out the sensible from the not-so-sensible ideas and conclusions. Chapters 14, 15, and

16 offer further coverage of critical thinking, with a focus on using sound reasoning and concrete evidence to build both informative and persuasive speeches.

Focus on Controversy Boxes Communication theory separated from the realities of a complex and not always pleasant world can seem sadly irrelevant to students faced with vexing problems. Addressing important controversies directly can provide significant opportunities for student learning. Special boxes called *Focus on Controversy* present current, controversial issues. The aim is to show students how to weigh evidence and draw conclusions supported by research. Examples of topics include the ethics of hypercompetitiveness, excessive self-esteem, universal standards of beauty, verbal obscenity, crying in the workplace, and plagiarism of public speeches. Every controversy receives a balanced treatment, with conclusions drawn and thought-provoking questions posed. Treatment of relevant controversies are certain to spark interesting discussion in the classroom and, more importantly, trigger critical thinking from students.

A Fresh Look at Communication Technologies

No one can doubt the enormous impact communication technologies are having on our lives. How we cope with these technologies and the huge changes that they bring to our lives is a vital issue. Chapter 17 addresses the trends and issues associated with these changes. Students should learn not only how to evaluate the accuracy of information and the credibility of sources but also how to handle the sheer volume of information that technology makes available. The chapter gives students concrete suggestions for coping with information overload and balancing their real lives and face-to-face relationships with their time in the virtual worlds of the Internet and the World Wide Web.

Readability

Readability is a vital concern to me. Textbooks should not induce a coma, although it is understandable why some might cause eyelids to slam shut. Textbooks are not meant to read like the latest Stephen King novel, but they don't need to be a horror by reading like instructions for programming your VCR. Similarly, an overly dense, theoretical text written in technical language can impede clarity and understanding for students and create the kind of frustration many people experience when reading manuals for using the latest computer software. Consequently, obvious and not-so-obvious places have been searched to provide the precise example, the amusing illustration, the poignant event, and the dramatic instance to engage readers, enhance enjoyment, and improve clarity. Colorful language and lively metaphors have been sprinkled throughout the text to provide vividness. Additionally, a recurring segment called *Sharper Focus* uses extended examples to illustrate important points and ignite student interest. Sample topics include stereotyping of Asian students, jargon of the computer world, cultural differences in perception of the "nanny trial," dialectics applied to the Meg Ryan-Dennis Quaid relationship, dealing with a Bill Gates temper tantrum, challenging the "glass ceiling" in the workplace, teamwork and the U.S. women's Olympic basketball team, stage fright among great speakers and performers, and China and the Internet.

Finally, the readability of *In the Company of Others* has been enhanced by extensive classroom testing of the book. More than 200 students offered constructive comments, which were used to improve the readability of the final product. If this textbook is successful in gaining and maintaining the interest of readers, I owe a debt to those students who provided helpful advice.

Organization of the Text

In the Company of Others is divided into four parts. Part One, Fundamentals of Communication, lays the groundwork for the other three parts. Chapters 1 through 6 discuss the communication competence model, the role of perception in human transactions, intercultural communication, the use and misuse of language, nonverbal communication, and listening. Each of these subjects crosses into every arena of communication. These arenas are treated in Parts Two through Four.

Part Two, Interpersonal Communication, discusses power, interpersonal dialectics, strategies for making relationships work, and conflict management techniques (Chapters 7–9). Part Three, Group Communication, explains the anatomy of small groups and teambuilding and teamwork (Chapters 10–11). Part Four, Public Communication, addresses preparing to speak, developing and presenting the speech to an audience, and constructing an effective informative or persuasive speech (Chapters 12–16). Chapter 17, Technology and Communication, discusses the influence communication technologies have on our communication with others.

Instructor Support Package

Mayfield Publishing Company offers a support package for those who adopt *In the Company of Others*.

Instructor's Manual

The Instructor's Manual was developed and written in consultation with the author by Char Morrison, an instructor at Cabrillo College. Outlines of each chapter, transparency masters, speech evaluation forms, numerous classroom-tested activities and exercises, and suggestions for video clips and Internet resources are included.

We also offer an extensive test bank, with a complete explanation of how to conduct a cooperative exam, grade it, and present the results to students. Cooperation is a unifying theme of *In the Company of Others,* so cooperative exams are an appropriate and innovative option. The complete test bank is also available in computerized format, allowing you to edit the questions from the test bank and to incorporate your own questions. The computerized test bank is available in both Windows and Macintosh formats.

Instructor's CD-ROM

An Instructor's CD-ROM contains an Image Bank, PowerPoint slides, and other instructor's materials. Full-color images from the book are included on the CD in a format suitable for classroom presentation, either with an LCD overhead projector or as part of a PowerPoint presentation. Lecture outlines for each chapter are also included on PowerPoint slides. The Instructor's Manual can be downloaded from the CD and customized to fit any course organization, and the transparency masters can be printed out or projected from the CD-ROM. This complete package of presentation resources can be used with both IBM-compatible and Macintosh computers.

Mayfield Communication Acetates

A set of 48 acetates, half in full color, enhance lecture presentations. They present important communication concepts but do not duplicate images from the text.

Web Site

An interactive Web site (**http://www.mayfieldpub.com/rothwell**) has been developed to accompany *In the Company of Others*. Among the instructor's resources are a syllabus builder, which allows instructors to construct and edit a syllabus that can then be accessed online with a unique Internet address or printed for distribution, and downloadable instructor's materials, including electronic transparencies, PowerPoint slides, and the Instructor's Resource Guide (password-protected). To obtain the password, check the copyright page of the instructor's manual or call your Mayfield representative at 800-433-1279. Student resources include interactive quizzes for each chapter that provide immediate feedback to the student, an extensive set of links for research and further information, and guidelines for evaluating the credibility and reliability of information found on the Internet.

Student Resources

The following guides can be shrinkwrapped with the textbook at no additional cost to students.

Student Worksheets

Many professors already assign activities and/or critical-thinking exercises. These worksheets, prepared by Robert Mild, Fairmont State College, provide practical activities in an easy-to-use format to help students grasp key concepts discussed in the textbook.

Quick Guide to the Internet

The Mayfield Quick View Guide to the Internet for Communication Students, authored by John Courtright and Elizabeth Perse, provides instruction on using the Internet.

Acknowledgments

I owe a great debt to my colleagues who reviewed this textbook. Several reviewed the manuscript numerous times, demonstrating that they haven't learned the fine art of assertiveness by saying no. Those who deserve my special thanks are Debbie Analauren, Cabrillo College, Mark Murphy, Everett Community College; and Char Morrison, Cabrillo College. Additionally, I am grateful to the many reviewers across the county who provided feedback to help make this a better teaching tool: Ruth H. Aurelius, Des Moines Area Community College; Robbin D. Crabtree, New Mexico State University; Bonnie Creel, Tarrant County Community College; Jeanine Fassl, University of Wisconsin, Whitewater; Laura A. Fleet, Howard University; Laurie H. Fluker, Southwest Texas State University; Lawrence A. Galizio, Portland Community College; Randal J. Givens, York College; Mark T. Morman, Johnson County Community College; Susanna G. Porter, Kennesaw State University; Rachelle C. Prioleau, University of South Carolina, Spartanburg; Thomas E. Ruddick, Edison Community College; Marilyn M. Shaw, University of Northern Iowa; Edwina Stoll, DeAnza College; Nancy Street, Bridgewater State College; Curt VanGeison, St. Charles County Community College; Michelle T. Violanti, University of Tennessee; Ruth A. Wallinger, Frostburg State University; and David W. Worley, Indiana State University.

A special thanks goes to Topsy Smalley and Georg Romero, crack reference librarians at Cabrillo College. They located references and critical material that would have remained forever hidden from me. I am wowed by their skills, unflagging energy, and cheerful attitudes.

This project couldn't have been done without the amazing editorial and production team at Mayfield Publishing Company. Kate Engelberg, Linda Ward, Jean Mailander, Robin Mouat, Brian Pecko, and Randy Hurst define what it means to be professional. I very much enjoyed working with them. Their attention to detail was reassuring. Holly Allen, the senior editor, deserves special mention. She solicited this book from me and was a hands-on editor from start to finish. Holly was a driving force behind this book. We had a few disagreements along the way, but she challenged me to think in new ways, and *In the Company of Others* is a better book as a result.

About the Author

J. Dan Rothwell is chair of the Cabrillo College Speech Communication Department. He has a B.A. in American History from the University of Portland in Oregon, an M.A. in Rhetoric and Public Address, and a Ph.D. in Communication Theory, both from the University of Oregon. He has written *In Mixed Company: Small Group Communication* and *Telling It Like It Isn't: Language Misuse and Malpractice,* and he is the co-author (with James Costigan) of *Interpersonal Communication: Influences and Alternatives.*

Professor Rothwell encourages feedback from both students and instructors. He can be reached by mail in care of the Speech Communication Department, Cabrillo College, Aptos, CA 95003, or by e-mail at darothwe@cabrillo.cc.ca.us.

Brief Contents

Contents

Part Four *Public Communication* 331

Fundamentals of Communication

Chapter 1

Communication Competence

A captain spots a light in the distance, directly in the path of his ship. He orders his signalman to send the message, "Turn 10 degrees south." A message is transmitted back to the ship, "*You* need to turn 10 degrees north." Irritated, the captain orders a second message transmitted, "I am this ship's captain, and I order you to turn 10 degrees south." An immediate reply is sent, "I am a seaman second class, and I am telling you to turn 10 degrees north." Exasperated, the captain responds, "This is a battleship coming right at you; turn 10 degrees south." This prompts an immediate response, "This is a lighthouse; turn 10 degrees north."

This simple story illustrates the enormous complexity of human communication. Issues of status and power, leadership and followership, competition and cooperation, communication styles of conflict management, the transactional nature of human communication, and negotiation strategies are all contained in this brief encounter. In this textbook we will explore these issues plus many more.

Human communication is an extremely complex process. If you want to do it well, you need a useful map to guide your exploration. The purpose of this chapter is to describe that map, namely, the communication competence model. This chapter has four objectives:

1. to discuss why communication is important,
2. to explain what communication is and is not,
3. to develop the communication competence model, and
4. to explore the connection between competition, cooperation, and communication competence.

Importance of Communication

Communication is a central focus of our lives. Few things absorb more of our time each day than communication in one form or another. One study (Verderber et al., 1976) found that college students spend, on average, 61% of their waking hours communicating. The quality of your life is directly linked to your ability to communicate effectively.

Stories of feral or "wild" children growing up without any apparent human contact and horrific instances of children imprisoned in closets or basements reveal that social interaction with other people is critically necessary for normal human development. Extreme isolation from human contact has tragic results (Box 1-1). Despite intensive training, these unfortunate children do not learn to communicate normally unless their plight is discovered within the first 6 years of life. After age 6, language learning is very difficult, and shortly after puberty the capacity to learn language virtually disappears (Pinker, 1994).

Social isolation, with few opportunities to communicate, also exacts a physical toll on us (Ornish, 1990). Socially isolated individuals have a four times greater risk of death from heart disease than those who have strong social support from relatives and friends. Their risk of an early death is greater than the risk of death from smoking (Ornish, 1990).

Unhappy relationships also diminish physical well-being. Marital arguments adversely affect our immune system (Kiecolt-Glaser et al., 1987). One study revealed that the more college roommates disliked each other the more likely they were to contract colds and flu and to visit a doctor (as cited in Goleman, 1995).

Box 1-1   Sharper Focus

The Story of Genie

Genie was 13 years old when she was discovered in a suburb of Los Angeles in 1970. From the time she was 2 years old, Genie had been confined in a bare room with the curtains drawn. She was strapped naked to a potty chair and sometimes tied in a makeshift straitjacket by her abusive father. Genie had minimal human contact. If she made noise, her father literally barked or growled, or beat her with a stick. Genie's mother, almost blind, finally escaped from the house with Genie (Rymer, 1993).

When Genie was discovered, she could not walk, talk, stand erect, chew solid food, or control her bodily functions. Despite years of intensive training, Genie never lost her unnatural voice quality, and she never learned to master more than an immature, pidgin-like language. She constructed sentences such as:

"Mike paint."

"I like elephant eat peanut."

"Genie have Momma have baby grow up."

Genie was incapable of mastering the full grammar of the English language (Pinker, 1994). Her ability to communicate—a vital link to other human beings—had been profoundly impaired by her early isolation.

Communication is the means by which we establish social connection. The quality of that social connection is directly linked to the quality of our communication with others. A primary distinction between relationships that endure and thrive and those that do not is effective communication (Gottman, 1994a, 1994b). Partners who learn to express their love and respect for each other and who manage conflict in constructive ways nurture their relationships. Unremarkable day-to-day small talk cements the feelings two people have for each other. Individuals in long-distance relationships suffer the most from fewer opportunities to share small talk, especially face to face (Gerstel & Gross, 1985).

Communication also serves practical purposes. Communication skills can help you get a job, receive a promotion, and perform successfully in the workplace. A survey of 253 personnel interviewers at businesses large and small reported that 98% thought that oral communication skills had a significant impact on hiring decisions (Peterson, 1997). In a survey of 480 companies and public organizations, communication abilities were ranked first among personal qualities of college graduates deemed desirable by employers. Work experience was second and academic credentials sixth (as cited in Morreale, 1999). The most common reasons jobs are *not* offered to some applicants are "inability to communicate" and "poor communication skills" (Endicott, 1979). Moreover, once people are hired, communication skills are the determining factor in their success or failure on the job (Downs & Conrad, 1982; Schmidt, 1991).

Despite the critical importance of communication skills to our lives, there is strong evidence that communication deficiencies abound. Numerous national reports emphasize the need for college students to upgrade their oral and written communication skills (see Berko & Brooks, 1994). One study of 402 companies found that 80% of their employees *at all levels* need improvement in communication skills such as public speaking, listening, and interpersonal communication (as cited in "Workers Lack," 1992). This is why more than a thousand faculty members surveyed from a wide variety of academic disciplines and colleges identified these *essential skills* for every college graduate: speaking, listening, problem solving, interpersonal skills, working in groups, and leading groups (R. Diamond, 1997).

humans have natural desire to communicate

Communication Myths

Before discussing what communication is and, more specifically, what competent communication is, let's dispel some common myths about communication.

Myth 1: Communication Is a Cure-All

people are constantly communicating – can't help it

Gurus, con artists, pop psychologists, and self-appointed experts fill the shelves of bookstores and line up to appear on talk shows. They offer communication as the magic elixir that will solve all relationship problems, but communication is not a cure-all. Relationships can't always be fixed by better communication. Sometimes communicating clearly reveals just how far apart individuals in a relationship have grown. Skillful communication may ease the pain of breaking up, but it may not sufficiently heal the wounds of a bruising relationship. Similarly, despite its importance to your employment future, improving your interviewing skills may not be sufficient to land a job. You also need the necessary background and experience to be hired.

Communication is a very important tool. When employed skillfully, communication can help solve numerous problems. Communication, however, is a means to an end, not an end in itself. Communication is not the basis of all human problems. Thus, not all problems can be solved even by textbook-perfect communication.

Myth 2: Communication Quantity Equals Quality

Jimmy Stewart and Henry Fonda, both movie stars and gifted actors, had opposing viewpoints on politics. Stewart was a strong conservative, Fonda a steadfast liberal. In their early acting days they roomed together in New York. One day a political argument between them turned into a fistfight in the street. "Thank God it was snowing," recalled Stewart. "I went down on my face more than he did." They subsequently agreed never to discuss politics, and they never did throughout their close, 30-year friendship (as cited in Ansen, 1997, p. 78).

More communication isn't always better communication. Couples who argue sometimes try to resolve disagreements by engaging in communication marathons. They keep resurrecting points of contention, and, like someone picking a scab, they reopen old wounds again and again. Time apart—not more direct communication—is sometimes the best remedy. Occasionally, as Stewart and Fonda discovered, agreeing to disagree and not discussing an issue at all is the best solution.

Myth 3: Communication Is an Automatic Transmission

Transmitting a message does not mean communication has automatically occurred: "But I *told* them I couldn't go to the ceremony" assumes that telling constitutes communication. Like sending a distress signal at sea and no one receiving it, communication requires much more than sending messages. You can express your ideas to others, but if others don't understand the ideas or aren't listening, communication does not take place.

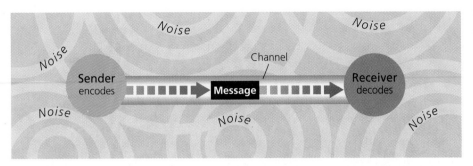

Figure 1-1 Linear Model of Communication

Communication Defined

The *Oxford English Dictionary* (*OED*) includes a 1,200-word definition of communication. Communication scholars and researchers have contributed more than 100 different definitions of their own. There is no ideal, nor sacred, definition of communication. Authors, scholars, and students of human communication offer definitions suitable to their perspectives on the subject.

The definition that best fits the perspective presented in this textbook is this: *Communication is a transactional process of sharing meaning with others* (Rothwell, 1998). This definition should be easier to remember than the *OED*'s version since it has 1,191 fewer words. The remainder of this section will be devoted to explaining each part of this seemingly simple definition.

Communication as Transaction

Many communication models have been developed over the years, and each attempts to describe communication in concrete terms. In this section you will learn about three communication models: linear, interactive, and transactional. As you will see, each of these models provides building blocks for understanding the next model.

Linear Model   The communication process has been described as a linear, one-way phenomenon (Figure 1-1). Communication, from this perspective, involves a **sender** (initiator and encoder) who sends a **message** (stimulus that produces meaning) through a **channel** (medium through which a message travels, such as oral or written) to a **receiver** (decoder of a message) in an atmosphere of **noise** (interference with effective transmission and reception of a message).

When the President of the United States addresses the nation on television, all the components of the linear model are present. The president is the *sender* who encodes (puts ideas into a spoken language) the *message*. The message is composed of the ideas the president wishes to express (for example, what this country should do about gun violence). The *channel* is the medium of television and is oral, aural (hearing), and visual. The *receivers* are members of the television audience who tune into the address and decode the message (translate the president's spoken ideas). *Noise* might be static in the television transmission or, perhaps, family members fighting over the remote control.

This is an unusual channel for a marriage proposal. The choice of channel can have a great effect on how a message will be received.

The linear model provides insight into the communication process, especially by highlighting the concepts of "channel" and "noise." The choice of channel can make an enormous difference in the way a message is received. Do you ask your partner to marry you, for example, by sending an e-mail message? By having a banner pulled across the sky by an airplane? Face to face on bended knee? By registered mail with a prenuptial agreement attached?

John Robinson learned that he had been fired from his position as football coach at the University of Southern California when USC athletic director Mike Garrett left a message on Robinson's answering machine. Robinson felt that "dignity was not shown" by this choice of an impersonal channel to inform him of such bad news ("At the Beep," 1997). Imagine how you would feel in Robinson's position, or if your boyfriend or girlfriend dumped you via the answering machine.

Actor Daniel Day-Lewis actually chose both the answering machine and the fax to deliver bad news. In 1996 he notified Isabelle Adjani, the mother of their child who was pregnant with their second child, that their relationship was over.

He communicated this devastating news by fax machine. Then he informed Adjani on her answering machine that he had gotten married. Later he felt remorse for his thoughtlessness, so he apologized to Adjani—on her answering machine (as cited in Locke, 1998). Communicating a personal message via an impersonal channel makes the choice of channel as much an issue as the message itself.

Identifying the influence of noise on the transmission and reception of messages is another important contribution of the linear model. **Physical noise,** or external distractions, such as startling sounds, poorly heated rooms, or the unfortunate periodic reappearance of bellbottom trousers and paisley ties, all divert our attention from the message sent by a source. **Physiological noise,** or biological influences, such as sweaty palms, pounding heart, and butterflies in the stomach induced by speech anxiety, can have a dramatic effect on both senders and receivers of messages. **Psychological noise,** in the form of preconceptions, biases, and assumptions, also interferes with effective message transmission and reception. One poll found that 40% of African Americans and Latinos questioned and 27% of White Americans agreed with the statement, "Asian Americans are unscrupulous, crafty, and devious in business." Nearly 50% of these same respondents from all three groups agreed that "Muslims belong to a religion that condones or supports terrorism" (Goldberg, 1994). Such preconceived biases make effective transmission and reception of messages between ethnic groups extremely difficult. **Semantic noise** in the form of word choice that is confusing or distracting also creates interference. Racist, sexist, and homophobic references, even if unintended, easily derail productive conversation.

Despite its insights, the linear model is quite limited. Its most glaring weakness is the absence of **feedback,** or the receiver's verbal and nonverbal responses to a message. The linear model assumes that communication consists of the transmission of a message from a sender to a receiver with no receiver response; listeners are merely passive containers waiting to be filled with information. This assumption is a serious flaw because all of us constantly adjust our communication with others based on the feedback we receive. The inability to read feedback accurately and to make appropriate adjustments is a serious communication competence issue, as you will see in the next section.

Interactive Model Two components have been added to the linear model to form the interactive model of communication (Figure 1-2). They are feedback and fields of experience.

The addition of feedback clearly indicates that communication is not a one-way but a two-way process. Receivers are actively involved in the process; they are not inert vessels. Receivers become senders and senders become receivers of messages.

The second component, **fields of experience,** identifies a possible source of misunderstanding. Fields of experience include our cultural background, ethnicity, geographic location, extent of travel, and general personal experiences accumulated over the course of a lifetime. Fields of experience overlap, but often they don't overlap enough for understanding to occur. Parents, who know from their own experience how important education was to their attainment of important goals, want the same for their children. Their kids, however, don't have the experience yet that might give them that same perspective. Languishing in a math or chemistry class may seem very remote from accomplishing life goals for many

Figure 1-2 Interactive Model of Communication

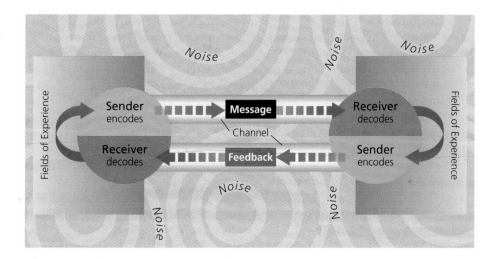

teenagers. The more experiences we have in common, the better the likelihood that misunderstandings can be avoided.

Transactional Model The transactional perspective further advances our understanding of human communication in two ways (Figure 1-3). First, it recognizes that each party in the communication process is simultaneously both a sender and a receiver. Communicating is a transaction. Each of us is a *sender-receiver,* not merely a sender *or* a receiver. You may be the speaker in a conversation, but your listeners are sending feedback to you constantly, mostly nonverbally. This feedback may encourage you to speak as you've been speaking or to make adjustments.

Second, the transactional perspective recognizes that communication has an impact on all parties involved. We are defined *in relation to each other* as we send and receive messages. Thus, transactional communication is not merely two-way interaction. Something more than movement of information back and forth occurs when humans communicate. We continuously influence each other and develop a relationship one to the other as we communicate (Anderson & Ross, 1994). An interviewer cannot exist without an interviewee. A leader must have followers. Parents must have children or they can't be defined as parents. The roles we play in life result from how we are defined in relation to others.

We can see the influence we have on each other during communication more clearly by examining the two dimensions of every message—content and relationship (Watzlawick et al., 1967). The **content dimension** refers to what is actually said and done. The **relationship dimension** refers to how that message defines or redefines the association between individuals.

A teenage son might say to his father either "Give me $20; I need it for gas" or "May I please have $20 to pay for gas?" Both messages have the same essential content, but the relationship dimension is different. The first statement exhibits disrespect for the father. An order is given, not a request. The second statement, by contrast, is a request and shows respect. Of course, nonverbal aspects of these messages must also be considered. If the first statement was said jokingly or the second statement was delivered in a sarcastic tone of voice, the nature of the relationship would be the opposite of what the words themselves indicate.

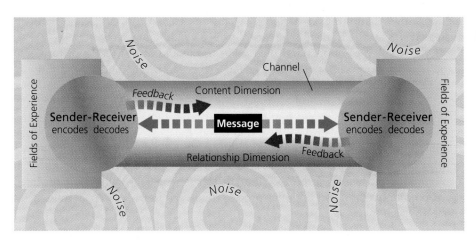

Figure 1-3 Transactional Model of Communication

[Handwritten margin notes:]
sender — what is the best way I can send this message?
— through medium, construct message

receiver — hopes message was clear. Sends feedback

Message content can also differ while the relationship dimension stays the same. "May I go to the movies with Cathy?" and "May I borrow the car?" are messages that display different content but essentially the same relationship. Although the specific requests differ, respect is shown to the person receiving the request in both instances.

These illustrations of the content and relationship dimensions of messages show one-way transmission. They are not transactional because we don't see the reaction to the message and the impact it has on each party. Here is an example that shows transactional communication:

> Everyone's favorite visitors were my great-grandparents. [My] Scottish grandmother called her grandchildren "wee bairns." When she was well into her seventies, her Irish husband would remark on her lovely complexion: "She had skin like a peach when I married her and she still does today." In fact, she was wrinkled as a prune, but no one contradicted him. Great-Grandmother was nearly blind, but Great-Grandfather maintained that only she could cook eggs properly. Because she couldn't see well, she often poured pepper in the eggs, which he dutifully ate, his eyes reddening and filling with tears. (as cited in Pipher, 1996, p. 40)

The message content is simply a dry recitation of what is said and done. If content were the primary focus, the husband's comment, "skin like a peach," might be a subject of dispute among family members. Yet no one disagrees because the point of the message is not the literal truth of it but what it says about the husband's relationship with his wife, his tenderness toward her, and the respect and affection family members accord both great-grandparents. Likewise, the husband eats his eggs covered with pepper (nonverbal message content) without comment even though he feels substantial discomfort. His selfless act communicates his considerable love for his wife. The transactional model recognizes not merely what is said but also the way messages influence our associations with others.

Communication as Process

Communicating is a process of adapting to the inevitable changes that affect any relationship. The process view of communication recognizes "events and relationships as dynamic, ongoing, ever-changing, continuous" (Berlo, 1960, p. 24). In a relationship, "nothing never happens" (Johnson et al., 1974), or, as the bumper sticker says, "Change is inevitable, except from a vending machine."

If you wanted to understand the ocean, you wouldn't just take a picture of a single wave or scoop up a cupful of water. The ocean can be understood only in terms of its entirety—the tides and currents, waves, plant and animal life, and so forth. Likewise, to understand communication, you have to focus not on single words, sentences, or gestures but on how currents of thought and feeling are expressed by both verbal and nonverbal means in the context of change.

Relationships can't be frozen in time, even though our memories of the "way we were" sometimes have this effect. Every conversation is a foothold on our next conversation, and we bring our accumulated experiences to each new conversation. Communication is an ongoing process, and each new experience influences future transactions.

Communication as Shared Meaning

Communicating is sharing meaning with others. Our world becomes meaningful through communication with others. Sharing our ideas, feelings, and experiences is all part of the process of *constructing meaning*, that is, making connections and patterns in our minds and making sense of our world. When we seek help from friends or counselors about problems we are experiencing in our romantic relationships, we are trying to make sense of what may be too confusing for us to sort out by ourselves.

We share meaning with others verbally and nonverbally. Our language, eye contact, posture, gestures, facial expressions, and so forth communicate meaning to others. We "make sense" of our relationships by talking to and about others.

Sometimes meaning doesn't get shared verbally even though words are transmitted from one person to another. For example, there is a story of a Catholic nun teaching religion to her third-graders and conducting standard catechism drills. She repeatedly asked her students, "Who is God?" Her students were to respond in unison, "God is a supreme being." Finally, she decided to test the fruits of her patient labor and called on one of the boys in the class. When asked "Who is God?" he promptly and proudly replied, "God is a string bean." Words were transmitted, but meaning was not shared.

Sharing meaning cross-culturally poses its own unique problems and requires more than a word-for-word translation between languages. Electrolux, a Scandinavian manufacturer, discovered this when it tried selling its vacuum cleaners in the United States with the slogan, "Nothing sucks like an Electrolux." As Ray Gordon, a sociologist and expert on Latin America, puts it, "If you know the language but not the culture in a country you visit, you will be able to make a fluent fool of yourself" (as cited in Brembeck & Howell, 1976, p. 205).

Sharing meaning nonverbally can be equally problematic. A woman in one of my classes recounted an experience she had when traveling in Greece. Used to sticking her thumb out and hitching a ride in the United States, she tried thumbing a ride in Greece. Motorists honked and waved at her repeatedly, smiling as they passed her walking along the roadside. She walked for $2\frac{1}{2}$ hours before she arrived at her destination, never once receiving the offer of a ride. She discovered later that the hitchhiking gesture used so prominently in the United States roughly means "good job" or "way to go" in Greece. Had she used the same gesture in

The "thumbs up" sign translates as an offensive message in some cultures, making an international sporting event a potential source of embarrassment, as can the mullet.

Italy, the response from motorists might have been quite different. In Italy this gesture belittles and depreciates a person.

Communication is a transactional process of sharing meaning with others. We are sender-receivers trying to make sense of our dynamic, ever-changing relationships with others. These relationships define who we are and what roles we play in life.

Communication Competence Model

Defining communication does not tell us how to communicate in a competent manner. For that we need a map, or a theoretical model, to guide us. This section explains what competent communication is and is not and provides a model for analyzing our own communication with others.

Competence Defined

Littlejohn and Jabusch (1982) define **communication competence** as "the ability and willingness of an individual to participate responsibly in a transaction in such a way as to maximize the outcomes of shared meanings" (p. 30). Trenholm and Jensen (1988) define communication competence as "the ability to communicate in a personally effective and socially appropriate manner" (p. 11). Communication competence has about as many different definitions as does communication. Nevertheless, there are several points of agreement among most communication theorists concerning its nature. Let's look at some of these factors.

Matter of Degree   Communication competence is not an either-or concept. Our competence varies by degrees from highly proficient to severely deficient, with gradations in between. Thus, we are sometimes more and sometimes less competent, not either competent or incompetent.

All of us have communication strengths and weaknesses, which depend on the situation and the circumstances. Labeling someone a "competent communicator" makes a judgment of that individual's degree of proficiency in a particular set of circumstances but does not identify who that person is as a human being. Some people are proficient at establishing intimate relationships with a few individuals but feel awkward and ill at ease in large gatherings of strangers. Others would rather body surf a tidal wave or eat a live toad than give a public speech. Thus, you may be perceived to be "highly proficient" in social gatherings, "moderately skillful" in leadership positions in groups, and "woefully inadequate" in public speaking situations. Any one or all of these designations could change for better or worse on any given day or change of circumstance.

We- Not Me-Oriented   Because communication is transactional, competence is ascertained by looking at how we work together with others, not merely how we work separately from others. The focus has to be on "We" (what makes transactions with others successful), not "Me" (what makes me successful). For a marriage to work, for example, the goals of the relationship have to be given greater priority than personal goals that interfere with the success of the marriage. When you enter into an intimate relationship, interdependence (a We-orientation) is primary, and independence (a Me-orientation) is secondary. A 20-year study by Gottman (1994b) of why marriages succeed and fail found that the more marriage partners, especially husbands, viewed their marriage as a joint undertaking, the more likely the marriage would succeed. Gottman cites one couple from his study whose communication clearly expresses the partners' apparent interdependence:

DEXTER: When we moved in we kept the house together, we handled the money togcther, everything. We shared cooking, cleaning.

MIDGE: There's never been a time when I've had a problem and thought, "Well, this is my problem, I'll take care of it." We've always divvied them up. (p. 131)

When children enter the equation, family goals assume greater importance than individual goals. Commitment in a relationship doesn't mean using the relationship for selfish ends. Commitment means putting the relationship first and individual needs, goals, and desires second. This does not mean that individual goals can never be met in an intimate relationship or in a family situation. Not all individual goals clash with relationship or group goals, and some individual goals (for example, intimacy) can only be accomplished in a context of interdependence. Nevertheless, trying to achieve individual goals at the expense of relationship or group goals usually produces unsatisfactory outcomes for both you and others.

Effectiveness How well you progress toward the achievement of your goals defines the **effectiveness** of your communication style (Spitzberg & Cupach, 1989). If your cynical humor provokes hostility from your roommate, you may need to modify your humor if your goal is to remain roommates.

In the context of communication competence, effectiveness is *relational*, not individualistic. Individual effectiveness may be deemed deficient if such effectiveness prevents others from accomplishing their own goals when a more cooperative, We-orientation could have been chosen (Spitzberg & Cupach, 1989).

Effectiveness is not the sole determinant of communication competence, however. Sometimes, despite your best efforts and highly proficient communication, you may not achieve your goals. Your lack of effectiveness may be due to forces beyond your control, not the quality of your communication. A person can exhibit exemplary communication and still have relationships with family, friends, spouses, and coworkers fail. Sometimes the chemistry between people doesn't work well.

Appropriateness Spitzberg and Cupach (1989) define **appropriateness** as "the avoidance of violating social or interpersonal norms, rules, or expectations" (p. 7). Appropriateness of your communication cannot be ascertained simply by considering a message separated from the abundant complexity of context, however. **Context** is the environment where communication occurs: *who* (sender-receiver) communicates *what* (message) to *whom* (receiver-sender), *why* a message is sent (purpose), *where* (setting) it is sent, and *when* (timing) and *how* (channel) it is transmitted. We determine the appropriateness of our communication by analyzing all of these elements.

Every communication context is governed by rules. A **rule** "is a followable prescription that indicates what behavior is obligated, preferred, or prohibited in certain contexts" (Shimanoff, 1980, p. 57). A family, for example, is a rule-governed group (Yerby & Buerkel-Rothfuss, 1982). Rules govern who takes out the trash, who cooks the meals, who pays the bills, and so forth. There are also rules governing communication transactions within the family unit, such as "We never go to bed angry" and "Children will address a parent or stepparent in a respectful way at all times."

Rules create expectations regarding appropriate behavior. Some rules are explicitly stated (directly expressed), but most rules are merely implied (indirectly indicated) by patterns of behavior. A violation of an implicit rule often leads to an explicit statement of the rule. College instructors take for granted that students will not interrupt the flow of a lecture or class discussion by conversing inappropriately with fellow students. On occasion, however, this implicit rule has to be made explicit to students whose enthusiasm for casual conversation outweighs their enthusiasm for the classroom task.

Although appropriateness of communication is determined by context, which is governed by rules, rules are not sacred. Some rules may need to be modified. When students share a dorm room or an apartment, rule modification is almost inevitable if communication is to remain competent. If one person expects a spotlessly clean, orderly environment and the other person expects a more casual environment, difficulties living together will occur. When rules clash, a modification of the rules will have to be negotiated unless one person is willing to completely accept the other's rules.

No matter how bizarre a rule may seem to outsiders, the appropriateness of our communication is maintained as long as those most affected abide by the rule. Two guys that I knew, for instance, lived in an apartment together, and both agreed never to do any dishes (explicit rule). This may sound like a health hazard in the making, but they concocted a unique idea for avoiding dishes without turning their apartment into a roach motel. They threw away their dishes after using them and purchased cheap replacement dishes from Goodwill. Most people would find this rule oddball to say the least, but it worked for them. They negotiated the rule when they first moved into the apartment, and both were happy with the result. Their communication was appropriate because they both abided by the rule that they had negotiated.

Communication becomes inappropriate if it violates rules when such violations could be averted without sacrificing a goal by choosing alternative communication behaviors (Getter & Nowinski, 1981, p. 303). If one of the guys in the previous example began violating the dishes rule by refusing to pay for replacement dishes, this would be inappropriate communication. The violation is premature when no attempt to renegotiate the rule is attempted. Renegotiation might produce a mutually satisfactory alternative. Recognizing which rules thwart communication effectiveness and learning ways to change these rules appropriately is an important task if you hope to improve your relationships with others.

Elements of Communication Competence

Five elements can be extracted from the definition of communication competence: knowledge, skills, sensitivity, commitment, and ethics. These elements provide a framework for analyzing communication (Figure 1-4). Let's look at each of these elements in more detail.

Knowledge We cannot determine appropriate and effective communication without knowledge of the rules that create behavioral expectations. **Knowledge** is an understanding of what is required by the communication context. Knowledge in any communication situation is critical.

Communication is both appropriate and effective when there is mutual satisfaction (We-orientation) with the process and the outcomes. That mutual satisfaction begins with knowledge of the rules that govern our transactions with others.

Competent communication is . . .

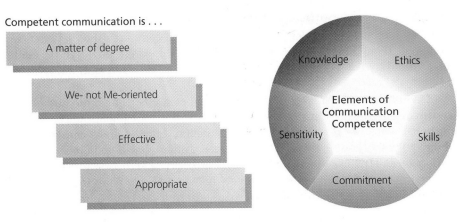

Figure 1-4 Communication Competence Model

You're not likely to be satisfied with the process if you expect cordial communication (courtesy rule) but receive adversarial, antagonistic treatment. If, however, you know in advance that initially you will be treated as an adversary to test your mettle, then you might be less unsatisfied with your treatment. You might even look forward to the challenge. Knowing the communication rules prepares you to adapt your communication so it is appropriate for the context and likely to be effective in achieving the desired results.

Mutual satisfaction, however, does not mean that you always get what you want. Again, it is a matter of degree, not either-or. The more satisfied both parties are with both the process and the outcomes, the more competent the communication. You may find satisfaction in negotiating with another person because both of you listened carefully to each other's views, even disagreed, but exhibited mutual respect. Compromise may be the result, but this can be mutually satisfying if there was relatively equal give-and-take on both sides.

Skills Communication competence encompasses the skill to apply your knowledge in actual situations. A study of undergraduate women (Christensen et al., 1980) found that all participants recognized nonverbal cues that signaled discomfort of the person being interviewed at the same time. All participants were instructed to change topics immediately if the interviewee signaled discomfort. Nevertheless, half of the participants continued to ask questions on the topic long beyond what was appropriate. All participants who acted inappropriately in this manner had scored poorly on a "social competence" (communication appropriateness) questionnaire given earlier. Even when participants were informed in advance what the appropriate behavior was, they still exhibited skill deficiency in reacting to the situation.

A **communication skill** is "the successful performance of a communication behavior . . . [and] the ability to repeat such a behavior" (Spitzberg & Hecht, 1984, p. 577). Clearly, fluently, concisely, eloquently, and confidently communicating messages are examples of skills. Knowledge about communication without communication skill will not produce competence. You can read stacks of books about public speaking, but there is no substitute for skill gained by practice and experience speaking in front of an audience.

Conversely, skill without knowledge is equally unproductive. Learning to "express your feelings honestly" can be an important communication skill in many situations. Expressing your honest feelings indiscriminately, however, no matter what the likely consequences, mimics the act of an innocent child, not a mature adult.

One key to achieving communication competence is using a mixture of both knowledge and skills. Lack of knowledge constrains your understanding regarding what skills are required in a given situation. Limited skills constrain your ability to respond appropriately even if you know what is required. Having a variety of skills allows you to make choices appropriate to the specific context. The ability to communicate a message concisely and precisely is an important skill. Lacking fluency—speaking with long pauses and disfluencies (uhms and ahs)—can nullify an individual's effectiveness despite concision and precision.

Sensitivity   A We-orientation puts the focus on others, not on ourselves. Consequently, a third element of communication competence is sensitivity. **Sensitivity** is defined in two ways.

1. *Sensitivity means having your antenna extended to pick up signals coming from others.* These signals may indicate disharmony, conflict, frustration, anger, concern, fear, anxiety, and so forth. Failure to recognize these signals can have severe repercussions for a relationship. If you are obviously angry but your partner doesn't have a clue that this is how you feel, you will likely perceive this cluelessness as insensitivity to your needs. Competent communicators develop a sensitivity to nuances and subtleties of communication transactions and respond to them.

2. *For the competent communicator, sensitivity means treating others as you would have them treat you.* Don't expect friendship from others if you are unprepared to be friendly. Love, friendship, loyalty, and concern each operates on a two-way street, not a one-way street pointing toward you.

Commitment   Knowledge, skills, and sensitivity are important elements of communication competence. The We-orientation also requires commitment to others. **Commitment** is a conscious decision to invest in another person in order to nourish and sustain a relationship.

Love is important in romantic relationships, but love is not enough. Lund (1985) studied 129 heterosexual college seniors and found that commitment, more than love, binds together two people in a romantic relationship. Couples who exhibited high degrees of love but low degrees of commitment were less likely to stay together than couples who were highly committed to the future of the relationship.

The degree of investment in a relationship exhibits the level of commitment. Investing time, energy, feelings, thoughts, and effort in a relationship shows commitment. The happiest dating and married couples exhibit a relatively equal investment in the relationship (Hecht et al., 1994). Investment is We-oriented. It shows we care about the relationship, not just about ourselves. Our relationships with friends and coworkers likewise require an investment. Friends drift apart when little investment is made to maintain the friendship. Relationships with coworkers can become tense and contentious when energy is focused on completing mutual tasks with little energy given to the relationship itself.

Similarly, making groups successful requires commitment to the group. When you put yourself first, ahead of the group, and invest little time, energy, thought, and effort in the group, you diminish the effectiveness of the group. Group accomplishments can be remarkable when all members work together at a high level of commitment.

Ethics   A few years ago a national poll ("Amoral Majority," 1991) asked 5,500 Americans whether they would kill a stranger for $10 million; 7% said they would. Applied to the total adult population of the United States, this response means that about fifteen million people would be willing assassins for a big chunk of cash. Here is the Me-orientation gone mad. How do we decide whether behavior is right or wrong? Should personal gain serve as the primary criterion?

note p. 15

Communication appropriateness inherently (by its nature) involves questions of right and wrong behavior and how we decide such issues. Competent communicators must concern themselves with more than merely what works to achieve personal or group goals. A person may be quite effective at accomplishing goals, but if these goals produce bad outcomes for others, their appropriateness must be questioned. **Ethics** provides a set of standards for judging the moral correctness of communication behavior. For example, when might lying be permissible, and when is lying wrong?

Human communication behavior is so complex that any list of standards for judging the ethics of communication, applied absolutely, is bound to run into difficulty. Communication appropriateness is determined within a context, and judging right and wrong communication behavior is also contextual. Nevertheless, some basic values can be applied to human behavior to *guide* our communication choices. These values act as standards for communication competence. They are:

1. *Respect.* "Some form of the Golden Rule is embraced by virtually all of the major religious and moral systems" (Jaksa & Pritchard, 1994, p. 101). Treating others as you would want to be treated is a central guiding ethical standard. Johnstone (1981) argues from a humanistic perspective that "to be humane suggests that one's conduct is guided by a respect for and a tenderness towards others" (p. 177). Respect shows concern for others (We-orientation) not just concern for self (Me-orientation).

2. *Honesty.* Ethically responsible communicators try to avoid intentionally deceptive messages. Honesty is a cultural expectation. Bok (1978) claims that there is a "presumption against lying" (p. 32). Winch (1959) argues that learning to speak "involves at the same time learning that speaking truthfully is the norm and speaking untruthfully a deviation" (p. 242). Margaret Farley, professor of Christian ethics at Yale University Divinity School, notes that all ethical systems condemn lying (as cited in "Lying Is Part," 1996). One poll found that honesty was the most prized attribute in a friend ("Lying in America," 1987).

3. *Fairness.* Prejudice has no place in the communication arena. Racism, sexism, homophobia, ageism, and all the other "isms" that plague the human spirit and divide nations and peoples would diminish if we applied the standard of fairness in our communication with diverse groups.

4. *Choice.* Our communication should strive to allow people to make their own choices, free of coercion (Jaksa & Pritchard, 1994). Persuasion allows free

Ethical values of respect, honesty, fairness, and choice were all called into question by Linda Tripp's secret taping of telephone conversations she had with her "friend" Monica Lewinsky, which triggered the impeachment of President Bill Clinton.

choice among available options. Coercion forces choice without permitting individuals to think or act for themselves.

In the abstract, these standards may seem straightforward and noncontroversial, but almost nothing in human communication is absolute and clear cut. Free choice, for example, collides with parents' responsibility to insist that their children behave in certain ways and make certain choices that may ultimately depend on coercion (the threat of punishment). In some cases two or more ethical standards may collide. For instance, what if being honest shows disrespect and lack of concern for another person's feelings (for example, "Yes, you *are* fat and unattractive")? Despite these difficulties, all four of these ethical standards are strong values in our culture, and they serve as important guidelines for our communication behavior.

Competition and Cooperation

My students were assigned a group symposium presentation. Although I had not indicated that groups had to choose different topics, the students assumed this without checking with me. When two groups discovered they had chosen the same topic, their communication became openly hostile. One group tried to preempt the other by negotiating with me to present its symposium first, thereby stealing the thunder of the other group. The group left out of this negotiation cried foul. Tempers flared. I tried to resolve the conflict by instituting a random drawing to designate the order of presentation. I assured both groups that they could work on the same topic because grades were determined on specific criteria, not by a comparison between groups. The groups were unmollified.

Outside class, the competitive communication persisted. Members of the two groups engaged in a nasty verbal confrontation during lunch in the cafeteria.

Voices were raised, threats were made, and menacing gestures were exchanged. Two individuals almost came to blows, so I was told later. Members of one group swarmed the library and checked out every source on the topic they could locate. They hoarded these resources, giving themselves an advantage while handicapping the opposing group.

The competition between these two groups was completely unnecessary and counterproductive. Neither group did the assignment well. Each was busy trying to hurt the other instead of focusing on doing a high-quality presentation.

Competitiveness can produce incompetent communication. The next sections will explore the effects of competition and cooperation on communication competence.

Definitions

Although the terms "competition," "cooperation," and "individual achievement" seem straightforward, there can be some confusion regarding the differences between these three terms. **Competition** (Kohn, 1992) is a process of mutually *exclusive* goal attainment (MEGA); for you to win, others must lose. In the fall of 1996 the city of San Francisco advertised 50 new firefighter positions in a competitive job search. The city received more than 10,000 applications. That's 200 disappointed applicants, on average, for each firefighter job.

Examples of competitive communication include waging battles to win arguments with friends, spouses, or partners; fighting over material possessions and child custody during a divorce; interrupting a conversation to seize the floor and the attention of listeners; insisting that your opinion is correct and another person's is incorrect; demanding obedience from employees who have less power; trying to win recognition at work as the best performer; criticizing and diminishing others to look superior to rivals at work. In all of these acts, communication is a vehicle to defeat others and to establish yourself as best at others' expense.

Unlike competition, **cooperation** is a process of mutually *inclusive* goal attainment (MIGA); for me to achieve my goal, you must also achieve your goal. We sink or swim together. Examples of cooperative communication include negotiating problems to the mutual satisfaction of all parties in a conflict; engaging in teamwork to solve problems and make decisions; encouraging participation from those who have not had a chance to be heard in a group discussion; teaching those with deficient skills to improve and become more capable; and expressing support to those who are discouraged. The spirit and essence of cooperation is to raise everyone up to a high standard for the benefit of all, not to drag anyone down to defeat for the sake of individual glory.

Individual achievement is the realization of personal goals without having to defeat an opponent. Although we sometimes refer to setting increasingly higher standards for ourselves and attempting to attain a previously unrealized goal as "competing with ourselves," no loser is required. Thus, no competition occurs. Giving a speech better the second time you perform it is an individual achievement. It becomes competitive when you try to outperform someone else, not when you attempt to improve on your own previous performance.

Competing and cooperating are wholly different processes. When we compete, we try to prevent others from achieving their goals so we can achieve our goal. *The single inescapable fact that defines competition is that the system of rewards is*

Winning is exhilarating, but losing can be heartbreaking.

structured to benefit the victorious. Even the runner-up position may brand you a loser. Tim Montgomery, a sprinter on the 1996 U.S. Olympic 4 × 100 relay team, put it this way when faced with the prospect of earning a silver, not a gold medal: "Second place is first place for losers" (as cited in Killion, 1996). Legendary coach Vince Lombardi left no doubt about the importance of winning when he said this: "There is no room for second place. I have finished second twice at Green Bay and I never want to finish second again. There is a second place bowl but it is a game for losers played by losers. It is and always has been an American zeal to be first in anything we do and to win and to win and to win" (as cited in Eitzen, 1996, p. 182).

Competitive communication, however, is not without its benefits—even when you lose. Psychological, spiritual, or emotional benefits can be derived from competing and knowing that you tried your best, even though you lost. Such secondary rewards, however, are just that—secondary. Even a terrific performance during a job interview doesn't entirely numb the sting of losing to another applicant. Moral victories, even personal bests, almost always pale in comparison to the principal focus of competition—winning—and the rewards that come with it.

Cooperation, unlike competition, requires the attainment of our goals by *working with others*, not against them. The two symposium groups in my class could have used cooperative communication. They could have coordinated their efforts, shared resources, pooled information, and negotiated a way to minimize repetition in their presentations. Both groups might have benefited by using this approach.

Competitive communication can be tumultuous, but cooperative communication also can be difficult, at times contentious, even frustrating. Cooperative communication is a process, not an outcome. Parties in a conflict, for example, may communicate cooperatively yet still not reach an agreement because they seek very different outcomes.

The cooperative communication process doesn't mean yielding to others' demands. Although yielding to pressure and intimidation from others may be mistaken for "being cooperative," giving in to pressure is a win-lose process. They win, you lose. Cooperative communication requires working together with those who may disagree with you, adopting communication patterns that encourage cooperation from others, and finding solutions that satisfy all parties to the greatest extent possible. Cooperative communication will be explored in detail in Chapters 6 through 11.

The Extent of Hypercompetitiveness

Hypercompetitiveness is an excessive emphasis on beating others to achieve one's goals. Hypercompetitiveness is prevalent in U.S. culture. Social psychologist Elliot Aronson (1976) claims that Americans "manifest a staggering cultural obsession with victory" (p. 154). Kevin Daugherty, youth sports specialist for the American Sport Education Program, says, "Our culture bombards us with messages that winning is everything" (as cited in Krucoff, 1998). Nathan Miller bitingly asserts that "conversation in the United States is a competitive exercise in which the first person to draw a breath is declared the listener" (as cited in Bolton, 1979, p. 4).

In the United States, competition is everywhere. Our economic, judicial, educational, and political systems are based on competition. Economists Frank and Cook (1995) observe that "global and domestic [economic] competition have never been more intense than now" (p. 6). The legal arena is inherently adversarial. Attorney Alan Dershowitz bluntly states that a criminal trial is not a search for truth: "The only goal is to win, not to do justice. I admit that. I am proud of that. Though I want to win fairly. Still, as an advocate, the only master I serve is winning" (as cited in Frymer, 1996). In education, students compete against each other for grades, scholarships, awards, and admission to prestigious colleges. Faculty compete for academic awards, grants, promotions, perks, and parking places. In politics, too, the principal focus, and sometimes the exclusive aim, is to beat your opponent by whatever means are deemed necessary.

No discussion of human communication can ignore competition—"the common denominator of American life" (Kohn, 1992, p. 1)—without being woefully incomplete. Competition saturates our society and influences our relationships with others. We will compete over almost anything. Brian Krause won the 25th annual International Cherry Pit Spit contest in 1998 by defeating his dad, Rick Krause, 10-time winner and holder of the North American pit spit record since 1988. Brian launched a cherry pit 72 feet, 11 inches, more than 3 feet farther than Rick. Then there is the annual hot-dog-eating contest in Coney Island, New York. Defending champion Hirofumi Nakajima, "The Tokyo Terror," retained his world title in 1998 by defeating American Ed "The Animal" Krachie in a "grudge match." The 135-pound Nakajima consumed 19 hot dogs complete with buns in a mere 12 minutes to retain his title. The 380-pound Krachie accused Nakajima of cheating, alleging that he must have used muscle relaxants to help gorge himself to victory. We take even silly contests very seriously in a competitive society.

We try to best others in board games and in boardrooms. We are weekend warriors battling on the playgrounds and playing fields, vying for victory in "leisure time activities." We compete for trophies or bragging rights. Even suffering can become a competitive issue. As Kushner (1981) observes, some of us enter the "Suffering Olympics" where we compete to establish which person has suffered the most in life: "You think you've had problems? That's minor league stuff compared to the major league pain I've had to endure."

The pervasiveness of competition, not competition itself, is the chief problem. Our single-minded resolve to defeat others and claim victory for ourselves often leaves little room for an alternative approach to human communication. Psychologist Bruce Ogilvie warns, "We have to be careful in our country about ever attacking winning. It's a deeply embedded ethic in our culture" (as cited in Kutner, 1994). This is sage advice. It is appropriate to challenge this dogma, not by advocating that we replace one extreme perspective (hypercompetitiveness) with another (ultracooperativeness), however, but simply by encouraging substantially greater cooperation than currently occurs.

Hypercompetitiveness and Communication Competence

The mutually inclusive nature of cooperation reflects the Me-orientation of competent communication. But is Me-oriented competition always incompetent communication?

First, communication competence is a matter of degree. A small amount of competitiveness does not make for incompetent communication. It is only when the goal must be achieved at any cost that competition becomes destructive. It is *excessive* competition, not competition itself, that produces incompetent communication.

Second, although competent communication requires a We- not Me-orientation, it does not exclude all competitive communication. Orientation implies primary, not exclusive, focus. The emphasis matters, not the mere presence of occasional competitive communication patterns. Trying to win an argument with your relationship partner can be challenging and fun as long as this verbal jousting isn't taken seriously and doesn't involve a sensitive issue.

Third, a cooperative option doesn't always exist. Interviewing for a job is unavoidably competitive whenever more than one applicant is vying for a single position. Encouraging individuals to hone their oral communication skills so that they might compete more effectively in situations where no cooperative alternative exists should be applauded. Presenting yourself in the best possible light to "win the job" is a useful skill.

Competitive and cooperative communication can coexist within the communication competence model. Because our culture is already hypercompetitive, we often lack the requisite knowledge and skills to communicate cooperatively in situations that don't require a competitive style. Skill-building emphasis should be placed on developing cooperative communication because cooperation is a primary path to communication competence. In the remainder of this chapter, and discussions in later chapters, I will explain why this is so.

Consequences of Competition and Cooperation

If competition produced mostly positive effects, we would want to use it as much as possible in our communication with others. Hypercompetitiveness would then be the primary path to communication competence. A competitive communication

Table 1-1 Effects of Cooperation Compared to Hypercompetitiveness	
Cooperation	**Hypercompetition**
Enhances self-esteem	Creates "failure factory"
Builds interpersonal relations	Damages interpersonal relations
• creates empathy	• creates hostility/aggression
• develops connection	• disconnects
• encourages trust	• encourages distrust
Develops teamwork/cohesiveness	Teamwork occurs when winning
Improves achievement/performance	Impedes achievement/performance
Reduces incentive to cheat	Encourages cheating

style has many unintended consequences, however. Let's examine the evidence on the consequences of competition and cooperation (Table 1-1).

Self-Esteem   Your self-appraisal, your perception of your worth, attractiveness, and social competence, is called **self-esteem.** Self-esteem affects your communication in several ways. Individuals with high self-esteem are more likely to accept feedback, even if it is critical, than those who have low self-esteem (Lefton, 1991). People with low self-esteem are more reluctant to communicate than are people with high self-esteem. They manifest greater communication apprehension and shy away from engaging in interpersonal conversation and from speaking in front of a group (Infante et al., 1997). They expect to fail because their confidence in themselves and in their communication skills is low. People with low self-esteem tend to avoid placing themselves in situations that might reveal their communication deficiencies. Individuals with high self-esteem usually dominate persons with low self-esteem. Consequently, leaders in groups are not usually drawn from the ranks of those who have a low opinion of themselves.

The effects of competition on an individual's self-esteem depend largely on whether a person is victorious or suffers defeat (Box 1-2). Those who can and do win usually feel bolstered by competition. Losers often feel diminished. Competition permits few winners and requires abundant losers, so it is not surprising that the research on competition shows that it has a mostly negative effect on the self-esteem of most individuals (Deutsch, 1985; Johnson & Johnson, 1989). This same research shows that cooperation usually enhances self-esteem.

Interpersonal Relationships   Competition is not structured to enhance interpersonal relationships. Rivals try to prevent each other from achieving desired goals. As Tom Glavine, pitcher for the Atlanta Braves, put it when he had just defeated the San Francisco Giants in an important game in the 1993 pennant race, "I don't feel pity for them. It's not the business to feel sorry for them. Jumping on people when they are down—it's what the sport is about" (as cited in Sexton, 1993).

It is difficult to feel close to a person when he or she actively tries to achieve success at your expense. Rubin (1985) describes how competition affects friendship:

> To win for his team a boy beats his best friend . . . [so] winning means also losing something precious in the relationship with a friend. For it is not likely that the two will compete on the football field and . . . share their fears and vulnerabilities after it.

Box 1-2 Sharper Focus

The Case of Amy Van Dyken

In a competitive environment it is the best who are valued. The less capable just make defeat more probable and thereby burden the team. Olympic swimming sensation Amy Van Dyken—winner of four gold medals in the 1996 games—spent 7 years losing races before she finally won. During high school, she overheard her relay teammates grumbling that "with Van Dyken anchoring [the race], we're not even going to get second." Van Dyken recalls that "I found out later that some of them had gone to our coach several times and said they would refuse to be in the relay with me because I was so terrible." To her credit, Van Dyken persevered. Most people under similar circumstances would quit, and Van Dyken at one point in college did quit, but later returned "because of how greasy my hair got when I wasn't in the pool two times a day" (as cited in Meacham, 1996).

In the minds of Van Dyken's teammates, her value was in direct proportion to her contribution to overall victory. This is understandable in a competitive system where primary rewards go only to the winners. A person's self-esteem is a secondary, if not an altogether unimportant, consideration. Sports psychologist Terry Orlick (1978) notes, "For many children competitive sports operate as a failure factory which not only effectively eliminates the 'bad ones' but also turns off many of the 'good ones'" (p. 129). One study found that children quit 5 times more often when their Little League coach communicated hypercompetitiveness than when their coach emphasized skill building, not winning ("Put Enjoyment," 1994).

Not very different, is it, from the world of work for which he is destined? . . . Not very good training, is it, for the kind of sharing of self and emotional support friendship requires? (pp. 81–82)

Competition reduces empathy (Kohn, 1993). **Empathy** is "thinking and feeling what you perceive another to be thinking and feeling" (Howell, 1982, p. 108). Empathy is other directed. It is the We-orientation of communication competence. When you have empathy, you experience another person's perspective. Trying to win an argument clouds your ability to empathize. Your focus is on yourself, not on the other person or on what damage winning the argument might produce. *The more empathy you feel, the more difficult it becomes to view another person as a rival to be vanquished.*

Competition also incites hostile communication between opponents (Van Oostrum & Rabbie, 1995). Hostile communication drives people apart. Cooperation, in contrast, is structured to enhance interpersonal attraction, trust, and empathy (Kohn, 1992, 1993). Individuals become partners, working together to accomplish goals.

Teamwork/Cohesiveness The degree of liking we have for members of a group, and the level of commitment to the group that this liking produces, is called **cohesiveness.** Cohesiveness nurtures teamwork.

A common notion is that intergroup (between groups) competition promotes intragroup (within a group) cohesiveness and teamwork. There is some validity to this claim. Van Oostrum and Rabbie (1995) found "weak indications" that intergroup competition generates intragroup cohesion. This is primarily true, however, for winning, not losing, teams. Losing teams typically fall apart as members look for someone to blame (Van Oostrum & Rabbie, 1995). Communication within the group often becomes hostile when defeat becomes common.

Teamwork doesn't require competition. In fact, hypercompetitiveness is often counterproductive. Teamwork is best created by

1. a challenging goal that
2. is highly valued by all group members and
3. requires a team effort to attain. (Larson & LaFasto, 1989)

Members of a mountain climbing team must work together cohesively and communicate cooperatively to achieve the common, much desired goal of reaching the summit. Mountain climbing teams typically do not compete against each other. The goal is to conquer the mountain, not vanquish another team. In fact, competing against other teams in this instance or becoming too Me-oriented would increase the risk of accidents and fatalities and diminish the spiritual experience of climbing.

Achievement and Performance When George Bush was president, he called for "a new spirit of competition between students, between teachers and between schools" (as cited in Jacobs, 1989) to improve student achievement and performance. Republican presidential hopeful Bob Dole echoed Bush's viewpoint in his 1996 convention speech. Bush and Dole were articulating a widely accepted assertion in the United States—that competition enhances achievement and performance in schools, in the workplace, in virtually every walk of life—but the evidence does not support this assertion. Almost 200 studies show cooperative learning is superior to either competitive or individualistic modes of teaching when student achievement and performance are measured (Johnson & Johnson, 1987). David Johnson concludes, "There's almost nothing that American education has seen with this level of empirical support" (as cited in Kohn, 1987, p. 54).

Studies of scientists, academic psychologists, businesspeople, and airline pilots also show that cooperation boosts and competition diminishes achievement and performance (see Helmreich in Kohn, 1992). One study found that even the *worst* cooperative groups, those relatively weak on task accomplishment, on average outperformed the *best* competitive groups in an organization (Van Oostrum & Rabbie, 1995).

Kohn (1992) cites three substantial reasons cooperation promotes, and competition dampens, achievement and performance:

1. *Beating others is not the same goal as achieving excellence and performing well.* We can defeat a rival and still exhibit mediocre performance (Van Oostrum & Rabbie, 1995). We usually refer to this as "winning ugly."
2. *Cooperation promotes efficient utilization of resources, and competition typically induces inefficient utilization of resources.* When individuals work cooperatively to achieve a common goal, there is likely to be less duplication of effort, better utilization of individual skills, and greater pooling of information and knowledge.
3. *Focusing on beating others typically produces antagonistic, hostile, and unpleasant communication.* Such communication is not conducive to achieving excellence (Van Oostrum & Rabbie, 1995).

All three of these reasons applied to the two warring symposium groups in my class: the groups focused on beating each other instead of performing well, they hoarded resources, and their communication with each other was hostile and

Box 1-3   Focus on Controversy

Ethics and Hypercompetitiveness

Competent communication involves ethical considerations, and hypercompetitiveness raises serious ethical concerns. Lying and deception clearly violate the ethical criterion of *honesty,* and hypercompetitiveness encourages dishonesty. As Sissela Bok (1978), in her widely acclaimed book, *Lying,* explains: "The very stress on individualism, on competition, on achieving material success which so marks our society also generates intense pressures to cut corners . . . such motives impel many to participate in forms of duplicity they might otherwise resist" (p. 258).

Cheating, in addition to being dishonest, violates the ethical criterion of *fairness* because it gives an unfair advantage to the cheater. Cheating has become widespread in the United States, and hypercompetitiveness is the driving force behind it. In 1985 the American Association for the Advancement of Science reported that "highly competitive pressures" were responsible for widespread scientific fraud (as cited in Boffey, 1985). In education, cheating among students has become widespread. On February 18, 1999, NBC News reported that 70% of college students cheat on tests, and 84% cheat on term papers, usually by buying them off the Internet. Intense competition for grades is cited as a primary reason students cheat. As William Zuspan states, "Some students feel pressured into going against their own moral beliefs purely as a matter of survival" (as cited in Jaksa & Pritchard, 1994, p. 55). When much is at stake and few can be winners, cheating and dishonesty flourish.

Another ethical standard, *respect* for others, is shown by sportsmanship, empathy, and compassion. How does hypercompetitiveness, which glorifies the victors and is indifferent to or even contemptuous of losers in a contest, teach any of these elements of respect? What ethical lessons are taught when in order for me to feel good about myself (a winner) I must make you feel bad about

yourself (a loser)? How does rooting for an opponent's failure so we can be successful, even cheering when it happens, show respect? As Alice Walker so eloquently notes, we live in a culture where "the only way I can bloom is if I step on your flower, the only way I can shine is if I put out your light" (as cited in Lanka, 1989, p. 24). Respect, not in the sense of being impressed by someone's talent as a potential rival but of valuing someone as a person, doesn't blossom in a hypercompetitive environment.

This is all well and good, you may be saying, but we live in a hypercompetitive society. Our children will have to face the disappointment of losing throughout their lives, and so will we. They'll lose in love; they'll lose arguments with parents and teachers; they may even lose custody of their children in a divorce. Is it not the responsibility of parents to teach children how to lose?

Teaching a child how to lose with grace and dignity is an important communication lesson, but just as important is teaching them how to communicate cooperatively with others. Our children will be afforded many opportunities to practice losing without any encouragement from us. Does it not make more sense to offer cooperative experiences for our children to counterbalance the competitive exposure they most surely will face without our assistance?

Questions for Thought

1. Are the ethical questions raised here merely misplaced idealism that ignore the unavoidable realities of American society? Don't we have to deal with what is, not with what we might like our society to be?
2. Are the ethical questions raised here an indictment only of hypercompetitiveness, or can the same questions be raised about competition in general?

unpleasant. (See Box 1-3 for more on the consequences of hypercompetitiveness in our society.)

Summary

Communication is the transactional process of sharing meaning with others. The communication competence model acts as a map that can guide your transactions with others. Studying the human communication process increases your knowledge of how to behave appropriately and effectively in a specific context. Communication skill development allows you to use your knowledge of communication in useful ways. Knowledge and skills, however, don't automatically improve relationships. Being sensitive to the needs of others increases effective communication. Sensitivity means monitoring your communication so you can improve. Being committed to improving your communication style by investing time, energy, feelings, thoughts, and effort into nurturing and sustaining your relationships will also improve your relationships. Finally, the primary path to communication competence is through cooperation. The We-orientation is best exemplified by learning cooperative communication skills. The communication competence model, with a special emphasis on cooperation, will serve as the map directing your journey into a variety of communication environments that will be explored in subsequent chapters.

Suggested Readings

Butler, S. (1986). *Everyone's a winner: Non-competitive games for all ages.* Minneapolis, MN: Bethany House. Butler provides a wonderful compendium of games that require no winners and losers, just fun for everyone.

Etzioni, A. (1993). *The spirit of community.* New York: Crown. The author makes a strong case for cooperation.

Frank, R., & Cook, P. (1995). *The winner-take-all society.* New York: The Free Press. Two economists offer an excellent discussion of the economic disadvantages of hypercompetitiveness.

Kohn, A. (1992). *No contest: The case against competition.* New York: Houghton Mifflin. This is the best single source of research on competition and cooperation. Kohn is a hardcore critic of competition.

Nelson, M. (1998). *Embracing victory: Life lessons in competition and compassion.* New York: William Morrow. A former star athlete presents the positive effects of competition, especially for women, with some cautionary notes on excessive competitiveness.

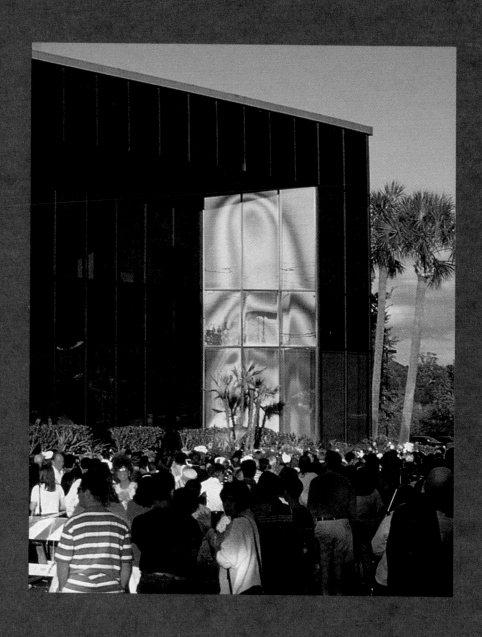

Chapter 2

Perception of Self and Others

Michael Watson tastes the sauce he had prepared for the roast chicken. "Oh, dear," he says, "there aren't enough points on the chicken." He tries to explain his odd ability to "taste shapes." As he puts it, "Flavors have shape. I wanted the taste of this chicken to be a pointed shape, but it came out all round. Well, I mean it's nearly spherical. I can't serve this if it doesn't have points" (as cited in Cytowic, 1993, p. 4). Michael Watson has synesthesia, a rare condition in which perceptions commonly confined to one sense overlap with two or more senses.

Rachel also has synesthesia, but her perceptions are somewhat different from Watson's. She describes it this way: "I most often see sound as colors, with a certain sense of pressure on my skin. . . . One of the things I love about my husband are the colors of his voice and his laugh. It's a wonderful golden brown, with a flavor of crisp, buttery toast" (as cited in Cytowic, 1993, p. 118). Synesthetes' perception of the physical world departs dramatically from the version of reality you might describe. Their brains are wired differently. Thus, they perceive differently from other people. Most synesthetes are women, and the majority enjoy their unusual perceptual ability (Goode, 1999).

Many individuals perceive the physical world in astoundingly bizarre ways. Some have reversed and inverted vision, making the world look as though the person is standing on his or her head (Cytowic, 1993). One individual, identified as Dr. Richard, sometimes saw the different parts of a person as separate parts not belonging together in a single form. At other times he might hear someone singing and see their mouth moving, but the sound and movement were disjointed, like a badly dubbed foreign film (see Marcel, 1983).

What do these strange cases tell us about perception? They dramatically illustrate the key point that no two people perceive exactly the same reality. There are always individual differences, oftentimes subtle, sometimes glaringly obvious.

A memorable scene from Woody Allen's Oscar-winning movie *Annie Hall* illustrates how subjective our perceptions can be in a relationship. When Annie is asked by her therapist how often she and Alvie have sex, she replies, "Constantly. Three times a week." When Alvie's therapist asks him the same question, he responds, "Never. Three times a week." Both characters have the same physical experience, but they have a markedly different perception of that experience.

As you will see in this chapter, perception is not an unbiased process. The biases inherent in our subjective perception of self and others make communicating competently a challenge of no small proportions.

The primary purpose of this chapter is to explain the complex perception process and its relationship to self and others. This chapter has three objectives:

1. to describe the perceptual process in general,
2. to discuss the process of perception of self and others, and
3. to identify the relationship between perception and communication competence.

We all behave as we do largely because of our perceptions of the world and the people inhabiting it. The way we communicate and the effectiveness with which we engage others in the process of sharing meaning begins with our perceptions of self and others.

"Man, you're big. You must be in fourth grade, huh?" said 7-year-old Sonny Santiago to General Colin Powell. Perception is relative.

The Perceptual Process

Perception is the process of selecting, organizing, and interpreting data from our senses. It is an active process, not a passive one, whereby we make sense of the world and give meaning to our experience. The eye is not a camera, nor the ear a tape recorder. Sight, sound, touch, taste, and smell are sensations, but sensation and perception, although related, are not the same. Our sense organs (eyes, ears, nose, skin, and tongue) contain sense receptors that change physical energy (light, sound waves, and so forth) into neural impulses. Perception is the processing of these neural impulses so we go beyond merely sensing and begin to *make sense of them*, or build meaningful patterns from them. "We sense the presence of a stimulus, but we perceive what it is" (Levine & Shefner, 1991, p. 1). Sound waves, for instance, are the raw materials of hearing, but they are not hearing itself.

Sensory Limitations

What sensory data we select and how it will be organized and interpreted are influenced greatly by the capacity of our sensory receptors to be stimulated in the first place. "We experience everything in the world not as it is—but only as the world comes to us through our sensory receptors" (Singer, 1987, p. 9).

As sensitive as these receptors are, they have a limited capacity to receive stimuli. Table 2-1 indicates the average threshold, or minimal amount of energy, that triggers a sensation for each human sensory system.

The sensitivity of our five sense organs is impressive, but there are many stimuli that our senses are incapable of receiving. Vision is our primary sense organ, but we do not see ultraviolet rays, X rays, gamma rays, or cosmic rays, nor do we see heat waves, radar, or long radio waves. If we could see light energy of slightly longer wavelengths than we do, we would see warm-blooded animals glowing in the dark (Rathus, 1990). Compared to an eagle's, our vision is not very acute. Listening to a radio interview one day, I heard a caller ask a forest ranger to compare the vision of an eagle with that of humans. According to the ranger, a human can discern a taxi from 18 stories above the street but cannot see much detail about the taxi. An eagle, however, can see a ladybug from the same height—and can even discern the black spots on the back of the ladybug.

Human hearing, likewise, is sensitive yet limited. The human ear registers sound from about 20 cycles per second up to about 20,000 cycles per second. This may seem impressive, but it is not when compared to a dog that can hear up to

Table 2-1 Threshold of Human Senses

Sense	Stimulus	Receptors	Threshold
Vision	Electromagnetic energy	Rods and cones in the retina	A candle flame viewed from a distance of about 30 miles on a clear night
Hearing	Sound pressure waves	Hair cells on the basilar membrane of the inner ear	The ticking of a watch from about 20 feet away in a quiet room
Touch	Mechanical displacement or pressure on the skin	Nerve endings located in the skin	The wing of a bee falling on a cheek from a distance of one-half inch
Smell	Chemical substances in the air	Receptor cells in the upper part of the nasal cavity	One drop of perfume diffused throughout a small apartment
Taste	Chemical substances	Taste buds on the tongue	About one teaspoon of sugar dissolved in two gallons of water

Source: Adapted from Galanter (1962).

50,000 cycles per second, a mouse that can hear up to 90,000 cycles per second, or a bat that can hear up to 100,000 cycles per second (Roediger et al., 1991).

Even within the normal range of human sensory ability, the volume of stimuli bombarding each of us is enormous. Birdwhistell (1970) claims that up to 10,000 bits of "minimally discernible" sensory data are available to an individual *each second*. No one could attend to and process all available sensory data. Our senses have the potential to receive a wide range of data, but the channel capacity of our senses is finite.

Perception is inherently subjective and selective. We perceive what we can sense. Much of our world is hidden from us by the limitations of our senses. Individual human differences in **sensory acuity,** the level of sensitivity of our senses, add another element to the subjective perception of our world. The tongue may have as many as 10,000 taste buds or as few as 500 (Plotnik, 1996). About 25% of the population have more abundant taste buds and are "supertasters." If you are a supertaster, sugar seems twice as sweet to you as it does to average tasters.

Differing taste perceptions can be a source of repetitive conflict at mealtime. Contentious communication issues such as control ("You're telling me what I should like and not like to eat; butt out") and concern for others ("I know it tastes bland to you, but it's good for you and you need to keep up your strength") can center around differing taste perceptions.

Individual differences in tasting ability are also greatly affected by an individual's sense of smell. Flavor is the combination of taste and smell. Your sense of smell is about 10,000 times more sensitive than your sense of taste (Reyneri, 1984). Sophia Grojsman is one of only a dozen master perfumers in the United States. She earns more than $100,000 annually identifying and mixing fragrances for perfumes. At this time, no scientific or computer system is capable of replacing her especially acute sense of smell (Plotnik, 1996).

Recently, the issue of smell perception has become a source of interpersonal communication conflict. I have observed some rather nasty verbal exchanges between people in movie theatres, on elevators, and in other public places that were triggered by one person wearing "offensive" perfume. Signs have even begun appearing in some public facilities asking people not to wear strong smelling perfumes or colognes that might provoke allergic reactions from some individuals. Some people with a clearly diminished sense of smell do not perceive that saturating themselves in potent perfume, aftershave, or cologne can be troublesome.

If you could see, hear, taste, touch, and smell all there is to be sensed, imagine how different your perceptions would be. If you had the eyes of an eagle, the ears of a bat, and the nose of a dog, aside from how odd you would look, wouldn't your perception of the world be radically different? Recognizing this should make us all less arrogantly self-satisfied that our perceptions are totally reliable, whereas those of others, if they differ from our own, are unreliable and invalid. Greater humility in this regard can help construct bridges (cooperation) between people instead of creating chasms to divide us (competition).

Perceptual Set

A **perceptual set** is a tendency to perceive a stimulus in a fixed way as the result of an expectation. Mothers are perceptually set to hear the cries of their babies. Students are sometimes perceptually set to like or dislike a teacher. Negotiators for management and labor are usually perceptually set for the "other side to be unreasonable." This perceptual set is often competitive and adversarial, focused on beating an opponent.

Try this demonstration of a perceptual set on your unsuspecting friends to see how easily they fall victim to it. Have a friend spell the word "shop" out loud. Now ask that person to respond immediately to the question, "What do you do when you come to a green light?" Almost everyone will automatically reply "stop." Why? Spelling the word "shop" establishes an expectation that the answer will rhyme, even though the correct answer does not. Our perception is fixed on a single type of answer. You may be surprised by the power of perceptual sets. Follow the shop/stop demonstration with this version of the same illustration: spell "joke" out loud. "What do you call the white of an egg?" A surprising number of people, although usually far fewer than the first demonstration, will be victimized a second time and answer "yolk." Perceptual sets are not always bad, but they are often the source of perceptual distortion, which can produce serious consequences.

Our previous experiences can create perceptual sets. In one experiment (Fucci et al., 1993) the perception of whether rock music was loud or soft was markedly influenced by whether the 40 college students tested already liked or disliked rock music. If you have had an ugly experience in the dentist's chair, you are set to have a similarly painful experience on your next visit. You may experience pain far in excess of what the dentist's procedure normally causes. This is not unlike when parents take their kids to get shots and are stunned to hear sounds closely approximating a dog caught in a bear trap coming from their children's mouths, even before the shot is administered.

We're accustomed to seeing men as presidents and women as first ladies. Former First Lady Barbara Bush played on this perception when she gave a commencement speech at Wellesley College in June 1990 and said, "Someone out in this audience may even be someone who will one day follow in my footsteps and preside over the White House as the president's spouse. I wish *him* well!" See Box 2-1 for more on perceptual sets and how we see ourselves.

Gender and Perception

In *Women's Reality: An Emerging Female System in a White Male Society*, Anne Wilson Schaef (1985) argues that we live in a sexist White male system. In *The Myth of Male Power: Why Men Are the Disposable Sex*, Warren Farrell (1993) argues that it is a myth to think that men have most of the power and that women are relatively powerless. These authors have distinctly different perceptions of reality, but both profess to want the same thing—to bring men and women together, not divide the sexes. Whatever their merits or demerits, these books illustrate the larger issue that gender matters when perception is an issue.

Let's distinguish between sex and gender before proceeding with this discussion. **Sex** is biological (female-male), and **gender** is social role behavior (feminine-masculine) (Stewart et al., 1996). Maleness gives a man a deep voice, but this sex characteristic doesn't require men to behave in dominant, overpowering ways. Most communication behavior is learned within the rules of a culture. Unger and Crawford (1992) explain that "gender is what culture makes out of the 'raw material' of biological sex" (p. 18). Communication behaviors considered appropriate

Box 2-1   Sharper Focus

Beauty or the Beast?

Samantha is 5 ft 6 in. tall and is wafer thin at 99 pounds. Her eyes are sunken and her light brown hair is brittle. Diagnosed by her doctor as anorexic, 16-year-old Samantha is terrified of gaining weight. When asked to comment on her mother's description of her eating habits, she replies, "I eat plenty. Just last night I had pizza and ice cream" (as cited in Pipher, 1994, p. 176). Her mother explains that Samantha consumed a mere teaspoon of ice cream and less than a slice of pizza with the cheese removed. A typical meal consists of lettuce and a few grapes.

Anorexics have a perceptual set that "fat is my enemy," and this distorts the image they have of themselves. Some anorexic girls (only about 10% of anorexics are boys) can be full height yet weigh as little as 60 pounds. Bruch (1978) cites one case of a young woman who thought she was gorging herself when she ate more than one cracker with peanut butter. She even avoided licking postage stamps because she thought the sweet tasting glue on the stamps contained calories.

Despite exaggerated reports in the popular press, anorexia nervosa is a relatively rare disorder, occurring in less than 1% of the population (Walters & Kendler, 1995). Nevertheless, anorexics illustrate the strong perceptual distortion that can occur when a certain expectation is created. Anorexics tend to come from families governed by very rigid rules (Bruch, 1980). Desperate to stop their child's suicidal starvation, parents may adopt controlling communication when trying to force their child to eat. Showering their troubled child with support and encouragement, however, may be a far more effective communication strategy.

Anorexia is the extreme example of a wider perceptual set permeating our society. Social standards dictating what constitutes "overweight" and "thin" have changed drastically in the last few decades. Miss Sweden of 1951 was 5 ft 7 in. tall and weighed 151 pounds, hefty by today's beauty pageant standards. By 1983 Miss Sweden had slimmed down considerably, weighing in at a scant 109 pounds on a 5 ft 9 in. frame. Since 1979, the majority of Miss America contestants have been at least 15% below recommended body weight for their height, coming alarmingly close to a medical definition of anorexia (Schneider et al., 1996). In the past 30 years, the voluptuous size-12 Marilyn Monroe image of beauty has been downsized to the size-2 Teri Hatcher of *Lois & Clark*

TV fame. The average size of a professional model is 5 ft 9 in. and 110 pounds. An average woman in the United States is 5 ft 4 in. and 142 pounds.

What is the result of this disparity between fantasy and reality? Eighty percent of women diet at some time, and 50% are on a diet at any specific time (Schneider et al., 1996). Almost half of all female college students describe themselves as overweight (Drewnowski & Yee, 1987). More than 95% of women who have no eating disorder *overestimate* their actual body size, on average by 25% (Thompson, 1986).

Body image distortion is not confined to women. In one study, 28% of college men described themselves as overweight (Drewnowski & Yee, 1987). For men, however, the perceptual set is often that they are too skinny and need to be more muscular. In the same study, 40% of college men reported that they wanted to gain weight (presumably in muscular development). Up to 11% of high school boys use anabolic steroids to increase muscle size (Schneider et al., 1996).

A study by Harrison Pope, chief of the Biological Psychiatry Laboratory at McLean Hospital, and his colleagues found that of 276 bodybuilders 33 men and 32 women had muscle dysmorphia. Muscle dysmorphia is a preoccupation with one's body size and a perception that, though very muscular, one actually looks puny. It is the opposite of the anorexic perceptual set. Muscle dysmorphs give up jobs, careers, and social engagements so they can spend hours every day lifting weights to "bulk up." They may refuse to appear in public in a bathing suit, fearing that people will see their bodies as tiny and out of shape ("Body Builders," 1998).

Our body image plays an important role in our self-concept, and communication begins with our self-concept. The image we have of ourselves imposes itself on every aspect of our relationships with others. Hamachek (1992) maintains that body image is "the foundation of our self-image. . . . Our body image does not constitute the whole of the self, but it is a highly significant aspect of it" (p. 159). Body image is largely influenced by society's conception of an ideal body. So consumed are we by body image that in one study 11% of the participants claimed they would abort a fetus if they thought the fetus had a tendency toward obesity (as cited in Pipher, 1994).

for males and females are socially constructed. There are norms and rules established in every culture that define what it is to be feminine or masculine.

Consider these behaviors and decide which ones seem more typically masculine or feminine:

- Crying in a public meeting
- Hugging same-sex friends to express concern
- Killing large spiders crawling on the ceiling
- Checking suspicious noises in the house late at night
- Cooking meals for the family
- Replacing a faulty light switch
- Shopping for groceries for the family
- Repairing a broken water pipe

Despite gratifying gains in gender equality in our society, these behaviors tend to be performed more often by either males or females depending on the behavior in question. We don't perceive masculinity and femininity as identical.

Perceived gender differences produce substantial differences in communication behavior (Coates, 1993). In *You Just Don't Understand,* Deborah Tannen (1990) explains that every conversation has two dimensions: status and connection. **Status** is hierarchical, and conversation perceived from this dimension is a "negotiation in which people try to achieve and maintain the upper hand if they can" (p. 24). **Connection** is nonhierarchical, and conversations perceived from the standpoint of connection view talk between self and others as a "negotiation for closeness" (p. 25). When status is the focus, an individual asks, "Am I one-up or one-down?" When connection is the focus, an individual asks, "Are we closer or farther apart?" Figure 2-1 includes several additional comparisons that help clarify the two primary dimensions of every conversation.

An individual whose conversational style focuses on status will view interpersonal talk as an exercise to exhibit an independent spirit or viewpoint—to stand out from the crowd. Conversation is seen as a contest where arguments can be won, viewpoints changed, and control over others can be gained. An individual whose conversational style focuses on connection will view interpersonal talk as a consensus-seeking activity, an opportunity to cement alliances, establish friendships, engage in pleasant interaction, and support others in their efforts to expand their choices in life. According to Tannen, men and women are concerned with both status and connection, but men typically give more focus and weight to status and women typically give more focus and weight to connection (see also Coates, 1993; Wood, 1996).

Checking with your partner before confirming plans to see a friend for the evening is often perceived in dramatically different ways by men and women in relationships. The man is likely to view it as having to ask permission, which signifies loss of status and independence. A woman, however, is likely to perceive that the man is showing sensitivity to her (Tannen, 1990). After all, their lives are intertwined, so what happens to one affects the other. Separate needs for independence and intimacy conflict here.

Men usually see conversation as a contest, a competitive opportunity to increase status (Coates, 1993; Wood, 1996). Thus, men typically display their knowledge and expertise on a subject for all to appreciate. They impart infor-

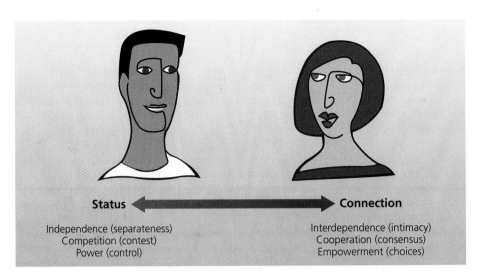

Figure 2-1 The Status-Connection Dimensions of Conversation

mation and advice and offer solutions to problems. Why?—because this spotlights their expertise (status enhancing). Conversely, women typically make references to personal experiences, share feelings, and listen intently to establish cooperative rapport with others. Men use *report talk,* and women use *rapport talk* (Tannen, 1990).

Perceptual misunderstandings between genders often result from style differences in communication (Box 2-2). The preference men have for cruising the globe rather than stopping to ask for directions when lost (status diminishing) and the perception by men that women "chatter" when they talk on the phone to each other for seemingly endless periods of time (connection enhancing) are two common examples. If one person is concerned with the internal question "Do you respect me?" (status), but the other is concerned with the internal question "Do you like me?" (connection), gross misperceptions of common conversations will often ensue.

You can point fingers of blame, accusing men of being insensitive jerks (which they sometimes are). You can accuse women of being passive and "touchy-feely" (which they sometimes can be). Or you can try to understand that men and women often approach simple conversation from conflicting perspectives. *This means that conversation is often a negotiation between individuals with two different perceptions.* This negotiation can be a competitive, adversarial contest of wills, or it can be a cooperative effort to find areas of agreement and to work out areas of disagreement.

Not all women and men follow the patterns outlined by Tannen. Some women adopt more typically male patterns of communication, especially in the workplace, and some men adopt more typically female patterns, especially at home. In fact, the Tannen model is useful even if gender is removed entirely from consideration because in normal conversation individuals have a tendency to emphasize either status or connection. Recognizing that you are communicating with a person who focuses on status and that you focus on connection can give you insight into why your communication may falter.

Box 2-2

Focus on Controversy

Tannen's Viewpoint Criticized

Deborah Tannen's model of gender communication has been criticized for supporting the status quo by urging understanding instead of change. "Tannen is an apologist for men. She repeatedly excuses the insensitivities of the men in her examples and justifies their outright rudeness as just being part of their need for independence" (Freed, 1992, p. 23). Tannen is accused of encouraging women to adjust to the male communicative style, but not vice versa.

This criticism requires a rather narrow reading of Tannen's work. In *You Just Don't Understand,* Tannen (1990) clearly states at the outset that "women and men should both make adjustments" in their conversational styles. She further notes that both male and female conversational styles are "equally valid" (p. 15). Viewing one style as superior to the other encourages warfare. As Tannen explains:

> Sensitivity training judges men by women's standards, trying to get them to talk more like women. Assertiveness training judges women by men's standards and tries to get them to talk more like men. No doubt, many people can be helped by learning to be more sensitive and more assertive. But few people are helped by being told that they are doing everything all wrong. (p. 297)

Failure to see style differences can provoke misunderstandings. Consider a simple example. Does inviting someone into a conversation in a group show sensitivity? When viewed from the standpoint of connection, it may seem to be sensitive because connection is enhanced by talking. "Maybe he just needs a little encouragement to talk." Silence is perceived as disconnecting. When viewing this act from the standpoint of status, however, inviting a man into a conversation when he has been steadfastly quiet could be perceived as very insensitive. It spotlights the man's nonparticipation and may be seen as status diminishing. It also may require the man to reveal that he knows nothing about the topic of conversation (also status diminishing and potentially embarrassing).

Recognizing style differences doesn't require preservation of the status quo. It merely allows for "no-fault negotiation" whereby "you can ask for or make adjustments without casting or taking blame" (p. 298).

A second criticism is that Tannen seriously underemphasizes the role of power imbalances as a cause of gender differences in communication (see Freed, 1992; Tavris, 1992). "The fact that women are the outsiders, not that they have some universal conversational style, is what creates differences between the sexes" (Tavris, 1992, p. 300). Men's concern for status, and their clear advantage in the power hierarchy, places women in a relatively powerless position. Women who strive for status are rebuked for being "unfeminine." Thus, apparent differences in communication styles are more often the "artifacts of a power imbalance" (Tavris, 1992, p. 299). Women communicate in ways typical of most people in a relatively powerless position.

Tannen (1990) does not ignore the obvious power differences between men and women. She clearly states, "No one could deny that men as a class are dominant in our society, and that many individual men seek to dominate women in their lives" (p. 18). Part of her model notes that dominance flows from the status dimension of conversation and that empowerment flows from connection. She simply offers the *difference* perspective as an additional view, not a substitute for the *dominance* perspective. She explains that "male dominance is not the whole story. It is not sufficient to account for everything that happens to women and men in conversations—especially in conversations in which both are genuinely trying to relate to each other with attention and respect" (p. 18). Her point of view is supported by Mulac and Bradac (1995) who found distinctly different male and female linguistic styles but could not explain these communication differences by looking at unequal power distribution.

Tannen (1990) calls for greater empathy between men and women. "Understanding the other's ways of talking is a giant leap across the communication gap between women and men, and a giant step toward opening lines of communication" (p. 298).

The dominance perspective on male-female communication emphasizes power imbalances. The difference perspective emphasizes conversational styles. Both perspectives provide insights, and they can be complementary. The dominance perspective will be discussed at length in Chapter 7.

Questions for Thought

1. In your estimation, does difference or dominance better explain gender differences in communication?
2. In what ways can the difference and dominance perspectives complement rather than contradict each other?

Perception of Self

From the moment you are welcomed into the world, you begin the process of becoming who you are, a person separate from others. In this section you will learn more about the perception of self and the role it plays in human communication.

Self-Concept

Each one of you has a sense of who you are and what makes you a person distinct from other persons. This **self-concept** is the sum total of everything that encompasses the self-referential term "me." It is your identity or self-perception. As Kilpatrick (1975) explains, it is "a conviction of self-sameness—a bridge over the discontinuities which invariably creep or crash into our lives. It is the link between the child of seven and that same person at seventeen; between the seventeen-year-old and the seventy-year-old to come" (p. 31).

Your self-concept is not formed in isolation. Self-concept is a social construction, a product of interpersonal communication. We discover who we are partly by contrasting ourselves with others. "You find out who you are by meeting who you aren't" (Anderson & Ross, 1994, p. 116). Parents, teachers, friends, relatives, coworkers, bosses, even strangers are instrumental in shaping our concept of self. We learn to think of ourselves as humorous if others laugh at our jokes. We see ourselves as leaders if we notice that others follow us. We see ourselves as quiet if others seem much more talkative in social circumstances. As you will see later, self-concept influences competent communication in many ways.

Self-Esteem

Self-concept is the descriptive element of self-perception. *Self-esteem* is the evaluative element of self-perception (Hamachek, 1992). It is self-appraisal: your perception of self-worth, attractiveness, and social competence. "I am a quiet person" describes your perception of self without attaching an evaluation to the perception. "I'm *too* quiet," however, attaches an evaluation to the perception. If you want to be more talkative and outgoing because you see being quiet as a personal flaw, then this is a self-esteem matter.

How smart, attractive, capable, and loving you think you are is influenced by two principal processes: feedback from others and social comparison with others. Regarding feedback, it is difficult for us to perceive ourselves as smart if every important person in our lives is telling us that we are slow-witted or just average. As Eric Hoffer once remarked, "It is thus with most of us; we are what other people say we are. We know ourselves chiefly by hearsay." This is especially true when the feedback comes from our significant others—those whose opinions we value highly such as parents, teachers, friends, and loved ones.

How we feel about ourselves is also a product of social comparison. An interesting study by Morse and Gergen (1970) shows what happens to self-esteem when individuals compare themselves to others. Male applicants for a summer job were seated alone in a room and asked to fill out several forms, including a self-esteem test. When each applicant was half-finished filling out the self-esteem test, an accomplice of the experimenters was sent in posing as another job applicant. In half the cases the accomplice was an impressive looking person—attractive

Box 2-3 Focus on Controversy

Self-Esteem: More Is Not Always Better

The *Final Report of the California Task Force to Promote Self-Esteem and Personal and Social Responsibility* (1990) asserts, "The lack of self-esteem is central to most personal and social ills plaguing our state and nation as we approach the end of the twentieth century" (p. 4). It claims, "People who esteem themselves are less likely to engage in destructive and self-destructive behavior, including child abuse, alcohol abuse, abuse of other drugs (legal and illegal), violence, crime, and so on" (p. 5).

The conclusions of the task force report were based on what to most people may seem to be self-evident truths. California state assemblyman John Vasconcellos, a member of the task force, recently had to admit, "We didn't claim to have proven it all. The science was not very far advanced" (as cited in Bauer, 1996).

Nevertheless, "the hope that raising everyone's self-esteem will prove to be a panacea for both individual and societal problems continues unabated today, and indeed . . . may even be gaining in force" (Baumeister et al., 1996, p. 30). High self-esteem, so goes the reasoning of the task force, should provide a "social vaccine" that inoculates individuals against attacks on their self-concept from criticism, insults, and demonstrations of disrespect. A recent review (Baumeister et al., 1996) of more than 150 studies on self-esteem contradicts this reasoning. The most aggressively violent individuals, whether neo-Nazi skinheads, terrorists, Ku Klux Klan members, juvenile delinquents, gang members, psychopaths, or spouse abusers, do not suffer from low self-esteem. Rather, they exhibit superiority complexes, and their "self-appraisal is unrealistically positive" (p. 28). Nazis thought of themselves as members of the "master race" and vilified Jews as "vermin." The image of a Mafia godfather suffering from low self-esteem as he orders the assassinations of rivals is difficult to visualize. Bullies and psychopaths seem contemptuous of the unfortunate victims they torment.

Perhaps bullies, godfathers, gang members, and the like simply camouflage their low self-esteem, as is often asserted, beneath the veneer of bluster and self-assertion. Maybe favorable self-appraisals mask deep-seated insecurities. If this sounds reasonable to you, then try arguing the reverse proposition: that timid, reticent individuals don't suffer from low self-esteem. They simply mask their enormous self-confidence and deep-seated security. Both claims require us to ignore persuasive evidence to the contrary without providing supportive evidence for the validity of the assertions.

A major cause of aggression in human relations seems to be not low self-esteem, masked or otherwise, but "high self-esteem combined with an ego threat" (Baumeister et al., 1996, p. 8; see also Bushman & Baumeister, 1998). In other words, aggression, with its emphasis on competitive, adversarial communication,

suit and shoes, with an attaché case containing, among other things, a book by Plato. In the other half of the cases the accomplice wore a dirty shirt, torn pants, had an unkempt beard, and carried a dog-eared copy of a sleazy best-seller. There was no verbal exchange between the applicants and the accomplices. After the accomplice came into the room, the applicants finished the second-half of the self-esteem test.

When applicants were in the presence of the impressive accomplice, their scores on the self-esteem test declined. In the presence of the unimpressive accomplice, however, their self-esteem scores increased significantly. Social comparison influences self-esteem.

Two dimensions of social comparison are relevant to self-esteem: one dimension asks how *inferior or superior* am I, and the second dimension asks how *similar to or different from* others am I (Adler & Towne, 1999). Images of beautiful, successful people presented in the mass media can reduce the self-esteem of those who do not feel they measure up to the unrealistic standards depicted.

If people think well of themselves, they are likely to think well of others (but see Box 2-3 for an exception). Conversely, if individuals have a negative view of themselves, they are likely to disapprove of others (Hamachek, 1992). Oscar Wilde

(*continued*)

results from a discrepancy between two views of self: favorable self-appraisal but an unfavorable appraisal from others. When others do not communicate "proper respect" worthy of a "superior person"—and instead criticize, insult, or show disrespect—an aggressive response is likely. Aggressive acts are often "communicative responses to unwelcome, disputed appraisals" by others (Baumeister et al., 1996, p. 27).

Arrogance and self-absorbed narcissism (excessive love of self) are manifestations of inflated self-esteem. Elitists and bullies do not need a boost in self-esteem. They already feel entitled to special treatment. Failure to accord them special treatment is perceived as insulting, and insults often produce violent responses. "The higher the self-esteem, the greater the vulnerability to ego threats. Viewed in this light, the societal pursuit of high self-esteem for everyone may literally end up doing considerable harm" (Baumeister et al., 1996, p. 30).

Is our society's emphasis on bolstering self-esteem completely misguided? If we are looking for a cure-all in raised self-esteem, the answer is "yes." Raising self-esteem is not always a desirable goal, especially if it is indiscriminate. When children's self-esteem is inflated by effusive praise for relatively trivial accomplishments, the potential for later disillusionment and deflated egos increases. As psychologist Robert Brooks of Harvard explains, "There are well-meaning parents who have seen self-esteem as 'every little thing your kid does, praise them to the sky.' [But] if [teaching self-esteem] is done wrong, you can raise a generation of kids who cannot tolerate frustration" (as cited in Begley, 1998, p. 69). Conversely, ignoring low self-esteem of our children and even adults is not desirable either. What good can possibly come from people feeling bad about themselves?

The answer lies in moderation. Modesty and humility should be part of the mix. When we see professional athletes strutting and posturing before their fans, insisting that they receive thunderous applause and accolades for relatively insignificant athletic accomplishments, modesty and humility are missing. Our goal should not be to create a society of egomaniacs inflated with their own self importance. Such self-centeredness (Me-orientation) doesn't fit the model of communication competence. Constructive self-esteem comes from accomplishing significant things without expecting a coronation (Kohn, 1994).

Questions for Thought

1. In your estimation, how much should improving self-esteem be emphasized in our schools?
2. Do you agree with the conclusion that overemphasizing self-esteem can lead to egomaniacal self-centeredness?

remarked that "all criticism is a form of autobiography." We see in others what we see in ourselves. We interpret the world through the lens of self-concept.

The publicity given to self-esteem as an issue in our society and the concerns about body image already discussed suggest that as a rule we suffer from inadequate self-esteem, but research indicates otherwise. One study (Kamprath, 1997) found that most sixth- and eighth-graders rated themselves as having moderately high self-esteem. Most of us feel quite accomplished, even more so than statistically makes sense. When male participants in another study were asked to rank themselves on their ability to get along with others, *all* of them ranked themselves in the top half of the population. Sixty percent ranked themselves in the top 10% of the population, and 25% were convinced they qualified for the top 1% (Gilovich, 1991). The same study found that 70% of the male participants ranked their leadership abilities in the top 25% of the population, and only 2% thought they had below average leadership abilities. Ninety-four percent of university professors believe they outperform their colleagues (as cited in Gilovich, 1991).

Our self-appraisals also tend to be more flattering than the appraisals others have of us. On a host of communication abilities, individuals consistently rated themselves more highly than did their superiors, subordinates, and peers in large

Calvin and Hobbes

by Bill Watterson

corporations (Sypher & Sypher, 1984). Summarizing several studies on self-appraisals, Gilovich (1991) concludes that "a large majority of the general public thinks that they are more intelligent, more fair-minded, less prejudiced, and more skilled behind the wheel of an automobile than the average person" (p. 77).

There is a cultural component to our self-appraisals and feelings of self-worth. We live in a hypercompetitive culture that encourages self-promotion. A common question at most job interviews in the United States is "Why should we hire you?" You are asked to promote yourself for the position. You are, after all, competing against other candidates, and the hiring committee is presumably looking for the best. In contrast, Asian cultures encourage the denial of self-importance. Reticence, not self-assertion, is valued. Promoting yourself is thought to be boastful. Your possible contribution to the group is important, as well as your likely conformity to the norms of the group or organization (Brislin, 1993).

Self-Serving Bias

We protect our self-concept and our self-esteem by exercising a self-serving bias. The **self-serving bias** is the tendency to attribute our successes or good fortune to ourselves but to assign our failures or bad fortune to external circumstances. Gilovich (1991) summarizes a large body of research on this phenomenon. Athletes tend to attribute their victories to personal prowess but blame their losses on bad officiating or cheating by their opponents. Students who do well on tests usually view exams as valid indicators of knowledge, whereas students who perform poorly on exams may see them as arbitrary, unfair measures of knowledge. Teachers may take credit for the success of their students but blame lack of motivation, effort, or ability for student failures.

The self-serving bias allows us to maintain our self-esteem by blaming others or unforeseen circumstances as causes of bad decisions or poor performance. You can easily see how the self-serving bias can lead to harsh judgments of others and a distorted perception of self. We take credit for our good behavior and find scapegoats for our poor behavior.

Our tendency to emphasize our accomplishments and downplay or deflect our shortcomings and failures is normal. We accentuate the positive and diminish the power of the negative. Nevertheless, this is self-serving (Hamachek, 1992).

Unless we are aware of this tendency and consciously take steps to combat this bias, it can lead to a failure to see our own shortcomings and to address them effectively.

Relationships run into trouble when one or both parties refuse to take personal responsibility for human weaknesses. Blaming others for every wrong can provoke "fights between friends, breakups between spouses, and, on a larger scale, wars between nations" (Hamachek, 1992, p. 38). One study (Sedikides et al., 1998) found that men are more likely than women to exhibit the self-serving bias. In addition, the closer we feel to our partner, the less likely we are to exhibit the self-serving bias. The more remote we feel from our partner, the more likely we are to manifest the self-serving bias. This means that the self-serving bias can become an important contributor to the demise of a troubled relationship, but it is not a factor in healthy relationships.

Self-Disclosure

We reveal our self-concept and self-esteem to others through self-disclosure. **Self-disclosure is the process of purposely revealing to others information about ourselves that they otherwise would not know.** Self-disclosure is not accidental. You may demonstrate without meaning to that you're clumsy at sports, but this is not self-disclosure. If you tell a friend that you are afraid to give public speeches, however, and it is news to your friend, that is self-disclosure.

Constructive Goals for Self-Disclosure   There are many possible goals for self-disclosing to others. The primary constructive goals are:

1. *Developing relationships with others.* Self-disclosure encourages disclosure from others. This reciprocal sharing of information about self allows you to connect with others. The more you limit your self-disclosure to another person, the more you remain a stranger to that person. If you know little about someone, you have little that connects you to that person. Self-disclosure is critical to the development of close personal relationships.

Whether you and another person perceive each other as strangers, acquaintances, friends, or intimate partners depends largely on the breadth and depth of self-disclosure that takes place between the two of you (Altman & Taylor, 1973). *Breadth* refers to the range of subjects discussed. There may be several topics that you don't discuss with an acquaintance, but almost any topic is open for discussion with loved ones. *Depth* refers to how personal you become when discussing a particular subject. The more personal, the greater is the depth. Intimate relationships usually have both breadth and depth, whereas impersonal, casual relationships usually have little of either. Breadth and depth of self-disclosure are critical factors in connecting with others.

2. *Gaining self-knowledge.* Sharing information about yourself with others helps you gain perspective. If you disclose to another person that you lack self-confidence, that person may point out several instances where you appeared very self-confident in front of others. That may cause you to revise your perception of self in this regard.

3. *Correcting misperceptions.* Others may have misperceptions about you. They may perceive you to be unfriendly, for example. Revealing to them that you are

shy, and explaining that engaging in conversation has always been challenging and anxiety-producing for you, can open them to a different perception of you, one that is more accurate.

4. *Eliciting reassurance.* When we have doubts about our body image, communication abilities, or other capabilities, disclosing these doubts often produces reassurance from others. Students frequently come to me with doubts about their public speaking abilities. I reassure them that they are fully capable of mastering the fundamentals of speaking in front of an audience. It is helpful to hear from others that we are capable.

5. *Creating impressions.* We usually want others to like who we are. That's difficult to do if the other person knows little about you—your likes and dislikes, passions, goals, fears, and concerns. Self-disclosure is part of the process of creating favorable impressions with others. We let others know what makes us tick.

Counterproductive Goals for Self-Disclosure Two principal goals for self-disclosure are Me-oriented, not We-oriented, and they encourage incompetent communication. They are:

1. *Manipulation.* Trying to maneuver another person to provide some service or to perform some behavior that benefits one person but leaves the other person more vulnerable to hurt is a poor reason to self-disclose. It is ethically questionable because it is usually deceptive. Research clearly shows that self-disclosure by one person induces self-disclosure by another (Derlaga & Chaikin, 1975). Pretending to reveal important personal information about oneself merely to coax knowledge from another person that can be used against him or her is inappropriate. It may provide a competitive advantage—"So, Tom doesn't like confrontation; how interesting"—but it is dishonest and abusive.

2. *Catharsis.* Spur-of-the-moment purging of personal information to "get it off your chest" or to relieve guilt is a poor reason to self-disclose. This is especially true if it is likely to damage the relationship you have with another person. Getting it off your chest may put it on the other person's chest.

Guidelines for Appropriate Self-Disclosure Several characteristics act as guidelines for appropriate self-disclosure. They are:

1. *Trust.* Self-disclosure involves risk. When you reveal yourself to another person, you risk being hurt or damaged by that person. Trusting another person to honor your feelings and to refrain from divulging the disclosure to anyone unless given permission says "I value our relationship, and I trust that you will not hurt me."

2. *Reciprocity.* Reciprocal, or mutual, self-disclosure demonstrates that trust and risk-taking are shared. If one person discloses but the other person does not, you should be wary of further disclosures until reasons for the one-way self-disclosure become apparent. Perhaps the other person is merely reticent and needs encouragement. One-way self-disclosure leaves you vulnerable and the other person protected. That asymmetry can spell trouble. Therapy, of course, is one exception. Counselors need to hear about you; they don't need to self-disclose in return.

3. *Cultural appropriateness.* Not all cultures value self-disclosure. Compared to North Americans, Japanese students disclose very little about their personal lives. During initial interactions, North American students will discuss gossip, politics, marriage, life goals, friends, and after-graduation plans, topics that Japanese students will not discuss (Nishida, 1991). Japanese students discuss universities, ages, and club activities more than North American students during initial conversations. Both North American and Japanese students discuss more neutral topics such as the weather, recent movies, music, and college life. Appropriate self-disclosure in one culture may not be appropriate in another culture.

4. *Situational appropriateness.* Public settings and private information are a poor fit. A public speech before a large audience is an awkward, uncomfortable setting for self-disclosure, as several recent political campaigns have demonstrated. The classroom also doesn't usually lend itself well to intimate self-disclosure.

A colleague of mine told of a surprising incident in her public speaking class that illustrates the importance of situational appropriateness. Students were assigned a 4-minute speech in which they were to describe to the class some event that had altered their lives in an important way. My colleague expected to hear speeches about trips taken abroad, geographic relocations, the college experience, and so forth. She did hear this—and more. A female student in her thirties began her speech by informing the class that she had never achieved sexual fulfillment in her life until the previous weekend. She then proceeded to explain to her astonished classmates what it was like to experience her first orgasm. Such revelations might be appropriate in a professional counselor-client relationship whose purpose is to explore intimate issues in a comfortable setting. Such intimate self-disclosure might even be appropriate with certain close friends, but not in front of relative strangers in a classroom where the main purpose is to hone public speaking skills. She needed to consider her audience and the obvious embarrassment she caused her listeners.

5. *Incremental disclosure.* Overly zealous self-disclosure in which, for instance, you blurt out your whole life story in one sitting may overwhelm your listener and send him or her running to the nearest exit. Test the waters. Gradually disclose personal information to another person and see whether it is reciprocated. There is no urgency required. Let the other person savor the revelations you've shared. A person usually needs to get to know someone before a proper perspective can be given to intimate information about self. "I've always hated guys like you" or "Women make me nervous" probably aren't very good openers. Once you get to know the person, these disclosures may seem funny. Initially, they might end the conversation and the relationship.

Most conversations concentrate on commonplace topics. Self-disclosure is important, especially during initial stages of a relationship, but it isn't the principal focus of people's lives. There is only so much to disclose, then your partner has heard it all. Even couples in intimate relationships spend relatively little time divulging personal information to each other (Duck, 1991).

6. *Desire for intimacy or closeness.* When both parties are similarly inclined, self-disclosure can produce connection between you and others.

7. *Likelihood of constructive outcome.* Developing a stronger, more robust relationship makes it worth the risk.

Perception of Others

In one study, Kuiper and Rogers (1979) found that "how we summarize information about other people is bound up with our own view of self" (p. 514). This means that we use our self-concept as a reference point when we formulate perceptions of others. In this section you will learn more about how we perceive others and how this influences our human relationships.

Impressions of Others

Consider this description of a man named Phil:

(A) Phil stands at the counter of the hardware store waiting to be helped. The store is crowded. Phil mutters to himself while he waits. When a clerk waits on him, Phil explains that a wall socket he purchased a few days ago is defective. The clerk asks to see a receipt. Phil explains that he lost the receipt but points to the price tag with the store's name clearly marked on it. The clerk is hesitant to give Phil a refund. Phil asks to see a manager. After a short discussion with the manager, Phil receives his refund. On the way out of the store, Phil spots a young woman he knows from a class he is taking at the local community college. He turns and walks away from her, leaving the store.

(B) Phil is due to meet a friend for lunch. He hurries down the street and arrives at a small cafe where his friend is sitting at a table sipping a drink. Phil greets his friend. They converse for a while before Phil looks at the menu. A waiter comes to take Phil's order. Phil gives his order then continues his conversation with his friend. After lunch, Phil walks for a few blocks until he runs into an acquaintance from work. He talks to her for a few minutes, then continues on his way up the street.

What is your impression of Phil? On a scale from 1 (unfriendly) to 10 (very friendly), how would you rate Phil? Now read these two paragraphs about Phil to a friend, but read paragraph A *after* you read paragraph B. How does your friend rate Phil on friendliness? Is this different from your rating? Typically, the first paragraph we read has more influence on our impression of Phil than the second. In a classic study by Luchins (1957), only 18% of the study participants who read a two-paragraph story similar to the one above labeled the person in the story as "friendly" when the "unfriendly" paragraph appeared first, but 78% labeled the person in the story "friendly" when the "friendly" paragraph appeared first. This is called the **primacy effect,** or the tendency to perceive information presented first as more important than later information. The primacy effect accounts for the power of first impressions.

A first impression can encourage further transactions with others when it is positive, and it can prevent any further contact with a person when the impression is negative. Add to the primacy effect our strong tendency to weigh negative information more heavily than positive information, which is called **negativity bias,** and you can see how perceptions of others can become quite distorted. Anderson (1981) found a negativity bias when he asked participants to rate a person. The person described as "kind" received a highly positive rating. The person described as "dishonest" received a very poor rating, but the person described as both

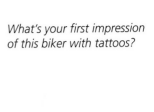
What's your first impression of this biker with tattoos?

"kind" and "dishonest" also received a fairly unfavorable rating. In other words, a positive and a negative quality are not equivalent. The negative quality is given more weight than the positive quality.

Webster (1964) found the negativity bias to be particularly strong during job interviews. In fact, negative information, especially if it is received early in the interview, is likely to lead to a candidate's rejection even when the total quantity of information about the candidate is overwhelmingly positive. In a hypercompetitive job market where differences in quality between candidates can be hard to discern, one poorly chosen phrase or inappropriate remark during an interview can negate a dozen very positive letters of recommendation.

We expect good people to be *consistently good* and capable people to be *consistently capable*. We expect bad people, however, to be good *sometimes* and incapable people to be capable *sometimes* (Matlin, 1992). Even a mass murderer could conceivably love his mother and treat animals with kindness. Even a fairly bad teacher can sometimes inspire a student.

If I described a person to you as "outgoing, casual, fun-loving, articulate, and manipulative," would you want to be friends with that person? Would the single negative quality cause you to pause despite the four very positive qualities? Conversely, if I described a person as "abrasive, rude, domineering, closed-minded,

A homeless family begging on the street invites the fundamental attribution error. We may attribute poor character as the cause of the family's plight, not bad luck or difficult circumstances.

and fun-loving," would the one positive quality even make a dent in the negative impression created by the first four qualities? Would you even want to meet such a person?

Sometimes the negative information should outweigh the positive. A heart surgeon who has a great sense of humor and a warm personality but is an alcoholic shouldn't inspire confidence as you're about to go under the knife. A potential date who is attractive, personable, articulate, and intelligent but occasionally loses his self-control and abuses women is a bad prospect. Not all qualities of a person are created equal. Some negative characteristics supersede even a host of positive traits.

When we formulate perceptions of others, initial information and negative information influence us more than later information and positive information. Sometimes this is appropriate. Most often it is not.

Attribution Error

We attribute or assign causes to people's behavior. According to attribution theory, each of us tries to make sense of our own and others' behavior. Two primary causes of behavior are the *situation,* or environment, and the *disposition,* or traits, of the person. Why are people on welfare? Is it due to racism and lack of opportunity (situation), or are welfare recipients lazy and shiftless (disposition)? Research shows that we have a strong tendency to commit the **fundamental attribution error,** that is, to overestimate dispositional and underestimate situational causes of other people's behavior (Kassin, 1998).

Even when we know a person is required to communicate in a certain way, we still tend to assign dispositional causes rather than situational ones to that behavior (Jones, 1979). In one study (Napolitan & Goethals, 1979) students conversed

Box 2-4   Sharper Focus

Attributions and Relationships

Marriage partners are inclined to attribute relationship problems to personal traits rather than to situational forces (Kelley, 1979, 1984). For instance, a wife might complain that her husband does not help out sufficiently with the housework, leaves his clothes on the floor to be picked up by his partner, and doesn't listen or pay attention to her. The tendency is for the wife to claim that her husband is lazy, sloppy, and uncaring, which are all dispositional causes. The husband, however, is likely to assign situational causes. He will claim that his behavior is caused by stress at work, exhaustion, or other factors beyond his control. If his wife is unmoved by such explanations, the husband is likely to attribute her anger and frustration to "moodiness" or "irritability," also dispositional causes.

Attributional patterns of communication can indicate whether couples have a happy or unhappy relationship (Fletcher & Fincham, 1991). Individuals in happy relationships, for instance, typically explain the nice behaviors of their partners as dispositional traits: "She did the grocery shopping after work because she is a caring, giving person." Negative behaviors are explained in situational terms: "He snapped at me because he's under a great deal of stress."

Individuals in unhappy relationships typically exhibit the reverse attributional pattern. Positive behavior is explained in situational terms: "She picked up my clothes at the laundry because she had nothing better to do with her time." Negative behaviors are explained in dispositional terms: "He was irritable with me because he is a very impatient person."

Attributional communication patterns do not necessarily produce happy or unhappy relationships. Such patterns may be a reflection of individuals blissfully pleased with their partners or of couples already in deep trouble. Nevertheless, diminishing positive behaviors by attributing situational causes to them and personalizing negative behaviors by attributing character flaws to them can create a spiral of unhappiness difficult to escape. Conversely, diminishing negative acts by attributing situational causes to them and personalizing positive acts by attributing strength of character to them can reinforce a sense of happiness in a relationship.

with a confederate of the experimenter who was either friendly or unfriendly. Even when the students knew that the confederate had been told to communicate in a friendly manner, they still perceived the confederate as "truly friendly." Knowing that the confederate was told to communicate in an unfriendly manner did not elicit a situational attribution from student participants. They perceived the confederate who acted unfriendly as "truly unfriendly."

Remember the self-serving bias, which leads us to believe our successes are dispositionally caused and our failures are situationally caused? Notice how kind we are to ourselves when speaking of individual failure but how harsh we are toward others (Box 2-4). Our tendency is to attribute dispositional causes to the behavior of others ("They're just lazy and unmotivated.") but to attribute situational causes to our own behavior ("I couldn't help going on unemployment; my company down-sized.").

Stereotyping

Which professional sport is women's favorite? Figure skating? Gymnastics? Baseball? Ice hockey? Basketball? Would you believe professional football? What percentage of National Football League fans are women? 10%? 15%? 20%? Would you believe 43%? That's what NFL Properties, the marketing and licensing arm of the National Football League determined (Killion, 1999). Seem difficult to believe? Sara Levinson, president of NFL Properties notes, "We had some disbelievers.

When there's a stereotype out there, it's hard to remove it" (as cited in Killion, 1999, p. A22).

Stereotypes are preconceived perceptions of others. Stereotypes group individuals according to categories such as ethnic origin, socioeconomic status, gender, sexual orientation, religious affiliation, and even body type and attribute common traits to all individuals in that group. For example, a Gallup poll (Lewin, 1996) conducted in 1995 surveyed 1,000 adults in 22 countries. It found that women were consistently described as more "talkative," "emotional," and "affectionate" than men. In the same poll, men were consistently perceived as more "aggressive," "courageous," and "ambitious" than women. Some stereotypes are positive ("Artists are creative, interesting people"), and some are negative ("College professors are stuffy and arrogant").

Stereotypes distort our perceptions of others in three ways (Hamachek, 1992; Wade & Tavris, 1990). First, stereotypes overgeneralize by underestimating the differences between individuals in a group other than the group to which we belong. Acclaimed African American poet Maya Angelou tells a story about a White friend of hers who mentioned a Black woman they both had met some time ago. Maya Angelou couldn't remember who this woman was, so she asked, "What color is she?" Her White friend responded, "I already told you she is Black." Ms. Angelou replied, "Yes, but what color of black?" (as cited in Matlin, 1992). No shades of difference are perceived when we stereotype. All Black people are perceived to be the same color.

Quattrone and Jones (1980) found that people tend to generalize about all members of a group based on the behavior of a single member. A loud, abrasive individual from the United States traveling abroad creates an impression that all people in the United States deserve the tag "ugly Americans." One rude French person might stereotype all French people as rude in the minds of some people. We don't perceive individual members of our own group, however, as necessarily indicative of the entire group, just members of outside groups.

Second, stereotypes distort our perceptions of others by creating a selective memory bias. **Selective memory bias** occurs when we tend to remember information that supports our stereotypes but forget information that contradicts them. In one study (Snyder & Uranowitz, 1978), student participants read a fictitious biography of a woman that included stereotypical behaviors for both lesbians and heterosexuals. Those who had been led to believe the woman was a lesbian remembered that she had never had a steady boyfriend in high school, but most of them forgot that she had dated several men in college. Those who had been led to believe that the woman was heterosexual, however, remembered that the woman had developed a steady relationship with a man in college but usually forgot that this relationship was more a friendship than a romance. Our stereotypes produce a selective memory bias and, in turn, our memory bias nurtures and hardens our stereotypes of others.

Third, stereotypes can magnify differences between groups while exaggerating commonalities within a group. This can create intergroup rivalry. Stereotypes emphasize what is different about others who are not in our group, not what we have in common. We exaggerate how odd, dangerous, or unlike us others are. In this way, stereotypes erect walls between people rather than building bridges.

Fourth, negative stereotypes can influence our perceptions of self and produce poor performance. Jacobs (1999a) summarizes several studies on "stereotype

Box 2-5 Sharper Focus

Stereotyping Asian Students

Based on their academic record, one of every three Asian public high school graduates in California is eligible for admission to the University of California (UC) system of higher education, the most competitive in the state. Only one in eight White students is similarly eligible (Lubman, 1998a). The stereotype of the academically excellent Asian student is largely true, but even with seemingly positive stereotyping, problems exist. The stereotype applies to Asian students in general, but many Asian students do not fit the stereotype. Some Asian students complain that they cannot get academic help as easily as other students because of the stereotype, despite the fact that almost half the remedial math students at the University of California, Riverside are Asian (Lubman, 1998b).

The studious Asian student stereotype has also produced ugly bigotry from non-Asian students at many UC campuses. Asians comprise about 10% of California's population but more than a third of the UC undergraduate population. The Irvine campus has 58% Asian enrollment (Lubman, 1998a). The ability of Asian students to compete effectively in a highly competitive educational system has produced a backlash. As Stephen Nakashima, a Japanese-American UC regent, explains, "Every Asian that's accepted means another person gets left out" (as cited in Lubman, 1998a, p. A21). As a result of this competitiveness, Asian students have been the target of vicious anti-Asian phone calls, e-mails, and graffiti. Ombudsman Ron Wilson, who handles student complaints at the Irvine campus, notes that an increasing number of non-Asian students use "tough competition with Asian students" as a reason to drop a class. He also notes that non-Asian parents complain that their children receive lower grades because there are "too many Asians" in the classes (as cited in Lubman, 1998a).

Asian students have become scapegoats, but the real culprit may be hypercompetitiveness. The more competitive the educational system becomes, the more stereotypes will feed the backlash against Asian students who are perceived as rivals standing in the way of non-Asian students' achievement of academic goals.

The stereotype of the studious Asian may be mostly accurate, but it allows for no individual differences.

vulnerability." Asian American women posted high scores on a standardized math test when reminded of their ethnicity before taking the test, but they scored much lower when reminded of their gender identity. When told that Asian students typically do better than Whites on a test, White students bombed the test. Female students scored as well as male students on a rigorous math exam when told beforehand that the exam didn't measure gender differences, but they scored far lower if made to think gender differences would be measured. Subtle reminders of stereotypes can have a negative effect on performance.

Stereotyping isn't always bad. Positive stereotypes of others—such as most Hispanics are good-hearted or hard-working people—can lead to cooperative transactions. Stereotypes are not necessarily completely incorrect either (Lee et al., 1995). Sometimes they are mostly true and accurate, such as college professors are avid readers. Nevertheless, stereotypes create cookie-cutter images of sameness that discount individual differences within a group (Box 2-5).

Stereotypes also tend to be simplistic. One characteristic can shape a global perception of those stereotyped. The fact that most college professors read a lot doesn't allow us to generalize that all professors are intellectual snobs. As Wade and Tavris (1990) note, a "grain of truth" contained in a stereotype shouldn't be assumed to be "the whole seashore."

Strategies for Communication Competence

In this final section you will learn about competent communication strategies that overlap more than one perceptual problem or issue. These strategies will help you connect the discussion of perception of both self and others to an interrelated whole.

Monitor Perceptual Biases

Self-serving bias and attribution errors need to be carefully monitored. If you see yourself rationalizing your mistakes and taking credit for successes that may be more luck and good fortune than personal achievement, recognize your self-serving bias. Practice humility by taking more overt responsibility for all your actions. Openly communicate to others that the responsibility is yours and that the blame does not belong elsewhere.

Resist attributing dispositional causes to the negative behaviors of others and situational causes to the positive behaviors of others. Practice the reverse. Try explaining the communication behaviors of your partner that irritate or anger you with a situational attribution. Explain behaviors that please you with a dispositional attribution, and see what happens. In other words, be experimental. Test new ways of communicating with others and see what results. If the results are constructive, continue. If the results are not constructive, modify your communication.

Avoid Snap Judgments

The primacy effect characteristic of first impressions can be countered effectively by reminding yourself to avoid snap judgments. Luchins (1957) found that simply telling participants to avoid snap judgments about others countered the primacy effect and produced a recency effect. **Recency effect** is the tendency to evaluate others on the basis of the most recent information or evidence available (Rathus, 1990). Giving more weight to recent information can keep perceptions of others current. In this way individuals do not become prisoners of their own history, trapped by the perceptual sets of others that may be timeworn and no longer accurate. People change. Let your perceptions of them change.

Manage Impressions

It is not enough to know that perceptual biases occur frequently in the human communication arena. Take an active approach, not a reactive one. Try to prevent perceptual biases before they occur. Create the impression you wish others to perceive. Of the many aspects of self, consider which you want to emphasize in a given situation. In a job interview, would you display your articulateness, friendliness, sense of humor, and dynamism, or would you display your irritability, cynicism, sarcasm, and interpersonal remoteness? These all may be aspects of your self-concept, but you can choose to display some aspects in a given situation and keep other aspects of self private.

This is not meant to encourage phoniness or dishonesty, only communication flexibility. When you are interviewed for a job, you make choices regarding which aspects of your self-image you wish to display. You put forward your best self to create a positive impression. This is not dishonest. It is adapting to the expectations of your audience. Communication is situational. We don't show the same self to strangers as we do to intimate partners—at least we don't if we know what's good for us.

If an interviewer expects a well-dressed, articulate interviewee, you need to dress and act the part. Communication flexibility is central to communication competence. The negativity bias is difficult enough to overcome. Showing some of your negative behaviors in an interview for the sake of honesty merely nurtures the negativity bias, and that is self-defeating.

Practice Empathy

You can counter attributional errors by practicing empathy. *Empathy* is "thinking and feeling what you perceive another to be thinking and feeling" (Howell, 1982, p. 108). Empathy is built on sensitivity to others, a necessary quality of a competent communicator.

Empathy has three dimensions (Stiff et al., 1988). The first is *perspective taking*. Here you try to see as others see, perceive as they perceive. You try on the viewpoint of another to gain understanding of their perspective. You don't have to accept the viewpoint of another to be empathic, just understand it. A second dimension is *emotional understanding*. You participate in the feelings of others, experiencing their joy, anxiety, frustration, irritation, and so forth. The last dimension of empathy is *concern for others*. You care what happens to them.

One study (Regan & Totten, 1975) found that attributional errors were countered by empathy. When college students were instructed to list their impressions of individuals either shown in a videotape or described in a short story, those who were instructed to empathize with the person as deeply as possible and attempt to picture how that person was feeling were prone to attribute situational causes to behavior. Participants given no instructions to be empathic were inclined to attribute dispositional causes to behavior. Not all behavior is situationally caused, of course, but the fundamental attribution error predisposes us to assign dispositional causes to the behavior of others almost to the complete exclusion of situational causes. Empathy can provide attributional balance.

Check Perceptions

Perhaps the most obvious yet most often ignored method for dealing with perceptual biases and distortions is **perception checking.** That is, we should not assume our perceptions of others are accurate without checking to see whether this is so. We should determine whether our perceptions—influenced by gender, culture, sensory limitations, and sets—are accurate.

Assuming another person is angry, for example, can lead to misunderstanding. Don't assume your perception is the "immaculate perception." Statements such as "You're so irritable" and "I know you're bored, but try to look interested" may assume facts not in evidence.

An effective perception check usually has three steps:

1. A behavior description
2. An interpretation of the behavior
3. A request for verification of the interpretation

Consider this example: "I noticed that you left the room before I was finished speaking (behavior description). You seemed offended by what I said (interpretation). Were you offended (request for verification)?" All three steps are present in this perception check. Sometimes an effective perception check is more abbreviated: "You looked very angry. Were you?" Here, the behavior description is implied along with the interpretation and the verification request follows.

Perception checking is a cooperative communication strategy. The goal is mutual understanding, a We-orientation. If you assume your perceptions are accurate without checking with the other person, you may elicit a defensive, competitive response.

Summary

Perception is the process of selecting, organizing, and interpreting data from our senses. The human perceptual process is biased by gender. Our self-concept and self-esteem are protected by the self-serving bias. Our perception of others is biased by the primacy effect, negativity bias, attribution error, and stereotyping. Our perception of self and others is a fundamental starting point of human communication. We reveal who we are to others by self-disclosing. To be a competent communicator, monitor your perceptual biases, avoid snap judgments, manage the impressions you make with others, practice empathy, and check your perceptions with others.

Suggested Readings

Cytowic, R. (1993). *The man who tasted shapes.* New York: Warner Books. This is a highly recommended account of clinical cases of synesthesia. Cytowic speculates on the meaning of such remarkable case studies.

Sacks, O. (1990). *The man who mistook his wife for a hat and other clinical tales.* New York: Harper Perennial. Sacks provides some early interesting clinical cases of individuals with bizarre perceptual experiences.

Sacks, O. (1995). *An anthropologist on Mars: Seven paradoxical tales.* New York: Knopf. Sacks was depicted by Robin Williams in the popular movie *The Awakening.* Here he provides a fascinating account of seven unusual individuals whose perception of the world is wildly different from the norm.

Tannen, D. (1990). *You just don't understand: Women and men in conversation.* New York: Ballantine. Begin with this book if you want to explore gender differences in communication. This is far superior to John Gray's Mars-Venus series of books.

Watzlavich, P. (1984). *The invented reality: How do we know what we believe we know?* New York: W. W. Norton. This is a mind-bending book on perception and reality.

Chapter 3

Intercultural Communication

The moon is a physical object visible to any person who has normal sight. Although the light energy from the moon stimulates each observer's optic nerve in similar fashion, the perception of the moon drawn from such sensory stimulation can be noticeably different from culture to culture. Americans often perceive a man in the moon, American Indians typically see a rabbit, Chinese perceive a lady fleeing her husband, and Samoans see a woman weaving (Samovar & Porter, 1995). We all sense the same object with similar pairs of eyes, but the culture we live in helps shape our perception.

Perceptual differences between cultures can affect communication enormously. The hypercompetitive U.S. culture encourages verbal combat. We are expected to defend our rights even if it means open confrontation with others. Our television talk shows often assume the character of verbal food fights where individuals fling insults at each other, and occasionally the insults erupt into physical violence. In politics, attacking your opponent for even minor human failings has become commonplace. Americans—generally referring to those individuals who share and are influenced by mainstream U.S. culture—can be blunt, critical, aggressive, abrasive, and argumentative. This is often the way we are viewed by other cultures (Samovar & Porter, 1995).

Imagine how American directness and in-your-face interpersonal communication is perceived by cultures that value harmony and accord between people. A Chinese proverb states, "The first man to raise his voice loses the argument." Chinese culture promotes "a conflict-free and group-oriented system of human relationships" (Chen, 1993, p. 6). Filipinos see bluntness and frankness as uncivilized. In a meeting, they will often agree outwardly, even if they have objections, in order to preserve smooth interpersonal relations and show respect for the feelings of others (Samovar & Porter, 1995). The Japanese are similarly inclined. This can be very frustrating to Americans who expect that everyone will speak openly and straightforwardly and who tend to view public agreement, but private disagreement, as phoney or manipulative.

Even silence is perceived differently from culture to culture. Speaking is highly valued in the United States. Oral communication skills are considered essential to success in the business world. Silence, conversely, is not prized. Quiet individuals do not become leaders in groups (Bormann, 1990). Americans interpret silence in mostly negative ways, as indicating sorrow, criticism, obligation, regret, or embarrassment (Wayne, 1974).

Other cultures do not place as much value on speaking ability as does U.S. culture. Instead they value silence. Inagaki (1985) surveyed 3,600 Japanese regarding their attitude toward speaking. He found that 82% agreed with the saying, "Out of the mouth comes all evil" (p. 6). Of 504 Japanese proverbs analyzed, such as "A flower does not speak" and "The mouth is to eat with not to speak with," 320, or 63%, were found to express negative values regarding speech (Katayama, 1982). Japanese, Chinese, and Koreans typically are more comfortable with long pauses or silence during business negotiations than are most American businesspeople (Samovar & Porter, 1995). Chinese negotiators usually do not like to engage in small talk (Hellweg et al., 1994).

Communication in the classroom exhibits these differences in the perceived value of speech in the United States and other cultures. Class participation is often encouraged, even required, as part of the grade in U.S. schools. Japanese students, however, initiate and maintain fewer conversations and are less apt to talk in class

The different values and expectations of appropriateness each person brings to a transaction can pose significant challenges to intercultural communication.

discussions (Ishii et al., 1984). One study found that in 76% of the small groups studied the member who talked the least during discussions was Asian (Kirchmeyer & Cohen, 1992). Students whose culture places little value on speaking are at a substantial disadvantage in U.S. classrooms where open and frequent participation is often expected. When you've been taught to value silence, speaking up is difficult to do, especially in a public forum.

There are many perceptual and behavioral differences between cultures. The principal purpose of this chapter is to show how culture shapes and influences our perception and communication. There are three primary objectives:

1. to show the underlying value differences that distinguish one culture from another,
2. to examine some of the common intercultural miscommunication that results from these value differences, and
3. to explain some ways to communicate competently across cultures.

Before beginning this discussion, let's define culture. Lustig and Koester (1999) define **culture** as "a learned set of shared interpretations about beliefs, values, and norms, which affect the behaviors of a relatively large group of people" (p. 30). Culture is not a genetically inherited trait of human beings. Culture is learned. The shared interpretations are the product of sharing meaning with others, namely, communicating. Anthropologist Edward Hall (1959) long ago observed that communication and culture are intertwined. Our communication reflects our culture, and our culture influences our communication. In this chapter you will learn more about the myriad ways that culture affects the communication behaviors of "a relatively large group of people."

Intercultural communication is important in our society because the United States has become increasingly multicultural. Two thirds of all immigrants in the world migrate to the United States (Ryan, 1991). There are almost 300 different ethnic groups in the United States (Klopf, 1998). In many schools, more than a hundred different languages are spoken by students. "Minority majorities," populations of non-Whites that outnumber Whites (European Americans), already exist in large cities such as Atlanta, Baltimore, Birmingham, Chicago, Cleveland, Dallas, Houston, Los Angeles, Memphis, New York, San Francisco, and Washington, D.C. (U.S. Bureau of the Census, 1998). The U.S. Census Bureau (Holmes, 1997) predicts that within 50 years about half of the U.S. population will be non-White, with Latinos, African Americans, and Asian Americans composing almost half.

Where once Americans could mostly avoid contact with other cultures merely by staying within the borders of their states, this is no longer possible. Individuals with different cultural backgrounds carry their culture with them; they don't discard it while living in the United States. This means that we all are exposed to diverse cultures without stepping outside the boundaries of our cities and counties. Almost 60% of students in one survey said that they had dated someone from a different culture (Martin & Nakayama, 1997). Understanding how culture plays an increasingly important part in our communication with others is imperative if we are to meet the challenge of a rapidly changing society and world.

Cultural Value Differences

Suppose a man and his wife, mother, and child are in a small boat that capsizes at sea. The man is the only person who can swim. He can save only one of the nonswimmers. Which one should he save? When Rubenstein (1975) presented this hypothetical situation to student participants, 60 of 100 American college freshmen favored saving the wife, and 40 chose the child. *None* chose the mother. *All* 100 of the Arab student participants, however, chose the mother. What was the reason for choosing the mother? You can replace your wife and you can replace your child, but you can never replace your mother. The dramatically different responses from American and Arab students show basic cultural values in operation. Values are the core of cultures (Hofstede, 1991). Differences in values produce differences in choices and communication.

Hofstede (1991) has derived a number of core value dimensions from his research. These value dimensions help explain why intercultural communication is such a daunting challenge. Cultures can perceive the world in dramatically different ways, making communication between cultures difficult and frustrating, yet interesting and rewarding.

One note of caution before Hofstede's value dimensions are introduced. Hofstede identifies *cultural* values; these values may not always reflect *individual* values. It would be a mistake to assume that every individual blindly conforms to his or her culture's values. There will be individual differences. Nevertheless, until we get to know someone from another culture, the best we can do is make guesses regarding their values and preferred communication patterns. Hofstede's value dimensions research allows us to make "educated" guesses about individuals based on their probable conformity to their culture's general, deep-seated values. (For a critique of Hofstede's study, see Box 3-4 later in this chapter.)

Individualism-Collectivism Dimension

All cultures vary in the emphasis they place on individualism and collectivism. The **individualism-collectivism dimension** is thought by most scholars to be, by far, the most important of all value dimensions that distinguishes one culture from another (Griffin, 1994; Hui & Triandis, 1986).

Individualist cultures have an "I" consciousness. Individuals see themselves as loosely linked to each other and largely independent of group identification (Triandis, 1995). They are chiefly motivated by their own preferences, needs, and goals. Personal achievement and initiative are stressed (Samovar & Porter, 1995). The self assumes special importance in an individualist culture. Emphasis is placed on self-help, self-sufficiency, self-actualization, and personal growth. Relationships are mostly viewed as interpersonal, not intergroup. People communicate as individuals and pay little heed to an individual's group memberships. Competition, not cooperation, is encouraged. Decision making is based on what is best for the individual, even if this sacrifices the group welfare. The saying "The squeaky wheel gets the grease" reflects the individualist perception. Words such as "independence," "self," "privacy," and "rights" permeate cultural conversations.

Collectivist cultures have a "we" consciousness. Individuals see themselves as being closely linked to one or more groups and are primarily motivated by the norms and duties imposed by these groups (Triandis, 1995). Relationships are seen as mostly intergroup, not interpersonal. People communicate with each other as members of groups, and they take notice of a person's place in the hierarchy of a group. In collectivist cultures, commitment to valued groups (family, organization) is paramount. Cooperation within valued groups is emphasized, although in- groups can be highly competitive with out-groups. Individuals often downplay personal goals in favor of advancing goals of a valued group (Samovar & Porter, 1995). The Chinese proverb "No need to know the person, only the family" and the African adages "The child has no owner" and "It takes a village to raise a child" express the collectivist perception. Words such as "loyalty," "responsibility," and "community" permeate collectivist cultural conversations.

A simple comparison illustrates the vast differences between individualist and collectivist cultures. In the United States, upon meeting a person for the first time we may ask whether we may address that person by his or her first name. Rarely, if ever, is this request denied in informal situations. In Indonesia, however, many people do not employ personal names during interactions but instead use *teknonyms* (Geertz, 1983). These teknonyms refer to birth order within a family (equivalent to, say, "first son of the Tong family"). The reference is to an individual's place in the family.

No culture is entirely individualist or collectivist. All cultures are a mix of individualism and collectivism, but one or the other tends to predominate in each culture (Gudykunst, 1991). In a worldwide study of 50 countries and 3 geographic regions (Hofstede, 1991), the United States ranked number one in individualism, followed by other Western countries such as Australia, Great Britain, Canada, Netherlands, and New Zealand. Eastern and Latin American countries ranked high on collectivism. Guatemala was the most collectivist, followed by Ecuador, Panama, and Venezuela, with Pakistan, Taiwan, Thailand, and Singapore following close behind (Figure 3-1). About 70% of the world's population lives in collectivist cultures (Triandis, 1990).

A poll of 131 businesspeople, scholars, government officials, and professionals in eight East Asian countries and the United States shows vast differences between individualist and collectivist cultural choices (as cited in Simons & Zielenziger,

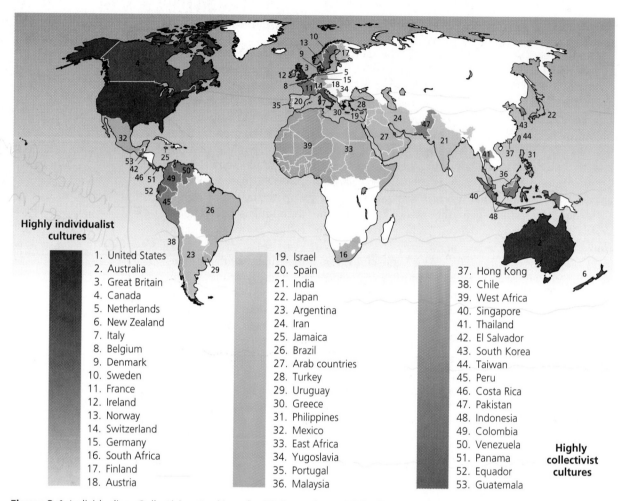

Figure 3-1 Individualism-Collectivism Rankings for 50 Countries and 3 Regions (Source: Hofstede, 1991)

Highly individualist cultures

1. United States
2. Australia
3. Great Britain
4. Canada
5. Netherlands
6. New Zealand
7. Italy
8. Belgium
9. Denmark
10. Sweden
11. France
12. Ireland
13. Norway
14. Switzerland
15. Germany
16. South Africa
17. Finland
18. Austria

19. Israel
20. Spain
21. India
22. Japan
23. Argentina
24. Iran
25. Jamaica
26. Brazil
27. Arab countries
28. Turkey
29. Uruguay
30. Greece
31. Philippines
32. Mexico
33. East Africa
34. Yugoslavia
35. Portugal
36. Malaysia

37. Hong Kong
38. Chile
39. West Africa
40. Singapore
41. Thailand
42. El Salvador
43. South Korea
44. Taiwan
45. Peru
46. Costa Rica
47. Pakistan
48. Indonesia
49. Colombia
50. Venezuela
51. Panama
52. Equador
53. Guatemala

Highly collectivist cultures

1996, p. A22). Respondents were asked the question, "Which of the following are critically important to your people?" The results were as follows:

	Asians	**Americans**
1. An orderly society	70%	11%
2. Personal freedom	32%	82%
3. Individual rights	29%	73%

Clearly, people from individualist and collectivist cultures perceive the world in markedly different ways (Box 3-1).

Differences in emphasis on individualism and collectivism influence communication. Individualist cultures expect a person to initiate a job search and engage in personal promotion. Useful social skills in an individualist culture include getting to know people quickly, engaging easily in conversation on a wide variety of subjects, being interesting enough to make an impression on others, and employing public speaking skills in meetings (Brislin, 1993). You're largely on your own in social interactions, and dating, flirting, and small talk play an important part in self-promotion. In fact, receiving help from friends or family can

An individualist culture such as the United States (above right) typically has a hetero-geneous population, unlike a collectivist culture such as Guatemala (left) that typi-cally has a homogeneous population.

make you appear somewhat desperate and ineffectual, such as getting set up with a blind date. Selection of a mate is considered a personal choice. Parental approval is desirable but not necessary, and marriage will occur even in the face of parental disapproval. During conflict, individuals tend to be direct, competitive, and more concerned with protecting their own self-esteem than worrying about the self-esteem of others (Ting-Toomey et al., 1991).

Collectivist cultures do not require the same social skills as individualist cultures. Self-promotion is discouraged because it can incite envy, jealousy, and friction within groups, and self-promotion is thought to divert energies away from the welfare of the group. In exchange for loyalty to the group and contributions to the group's effective-ness, members of collectivist cultures receive help from influential members of the group or organization in finding jobs and making social contacts (Brislin, 1993). Mate selection is often arranged by parents since family approval is important.

Hall (1981) was the first to identify a specific difference in communication styles between individualist and collectivist cultures. Individualist cultures typically use a low-context style and collectivist cultures use a high-context style (Griffin, 1994). A **low-context style** of communication has a message-*content* orientation. A **high-context style** has a message-*context* orientation. Hall and Hall (1987) explain:

Box 3-1   Focus on Controversy

Culture and Competition

In a hypercompetitive society such as the United States, it is easy for us to assume that competition is a natural part of being human. It is not until we see another culture responding to competition in a dramatically different way from our own that we understand the powerful role culture plays in our view of competition. Here is a story that makes this point powerfully.

> A newly trained teacher named Mary went to teach at a Navajo Indian reservation. Every day, she would ask five of the young Navajo students to go to the chalkboard and complete a simple math problem from their homework. They would stand there, silently, unwilling to complete the task. Mary couldn't figure it out. Nothing she had studied in her educational curriculum helped, and she certainly hadn't seen anything like it in her student-teaching days back in Phoenix.
>
> What am I doing wrong? Could I have chosen five students who can't do the problem? Mary would wonder. No, it couldn't be that. Finally, she asked the students what was wrong. And in their answer, she learned a surprising lesson from her young Indian pupils about self-image and a sense of self-worth.
>
> It seemed that the students respected each other's individuality and knew that not all of them were capable of doing the problems. . . . They believed no one would win if any students were shown up or embarrassed at the chalkboard. So they refused to compete with each other in public.

> Once she understood, Mary changed the system so that she could check each child's math problem individually, but not at any child's expense in front of classmates. They all wanted to learn—but not at someone else's expense. (Canfield et al., 1997, pp. 175–176)

There is plentiful evidence demonstrating that American hypercompetitiveness is primarily a product of an individualist value system, not a biological imperative common to all humans (Chatman & Barsade, 1995). Several studies show marked differences in competitiveness and cooperativeness of subjects, depending on their cultural roots. One such study (Cox et al., 1991) found that groups composed of individuals from collectivist cultural traditions (Asian, African, and Hispanic Americans) displayed far more cooperative behavior than groups composed of subjects from an individualist cultural tradition (Anglo Americans).

Even more compelling evidence comes from two separate studies (Parks & Vu, 1994) that compared people from cultures that vary widely on the individualism-collectivism dimension, Americans (extremely individualist) and Vietnamese (extremely collectivist). The first study showed that the Vietnamese "cooperated at an extraordinarily high rate." The Americans were inclined to be competitive. In the second study, Vietnamese subjects exhibited high rates of cooperation even when faced with competitive strategies from other subjects.

"In low-context communication, the listener knows very little and must be told practically everything. In high-context communication, the listener is already 'contexted' and does not need to be given much background information" (p. 183).

The chief difference between the two styles is in verbal expression. A low-context communication style is verbally precise, direct, and explicit. There is little assumption that others will be able to discern what you mean without precise verbal explanation. Self-expression and speaking ability are highly valued. Points of view are openly expressed and persuasion is an accepted goal of speech (Chen & Starosta, 1998B). Using a computer provides a technological example of low-context communication. Nothing can be left out of an e-mail or Internet address. Every space, period, number, and letter must be exact or the computer will exhibit how truly dumb it can be. Instructions given to computers must be precise and explicit; close doesn't count. Low-context human communication is similarly precise and explicit. "Say what you mean," "Tell me what you want," and "What's your point?" are statements that reflect a low-context communication style in individualist cultures.

In collectivist cultures, context is paramount, not the explicit message. A high-context communication style uses indirect verbal expression. You are expected to "read between the lines." Significant information must be derived from contextual

(*continued*)

Americans showed far less cooperation and more competitiveness. The authors of these studies conclude: "The difference between the extremely individualistic and extremely collectivistic cultures was very large and consistent with cultural norms" (p. 712).

Co-cultures can exhibit a similar relationship between degrees of individualism or collectivism and competitiveness. A **co-culture** is a group of people who live in a dominant culture yet remain connected to another cultural heritage that may be quite different from the dominant culture. African Americans are a co-culture. In a study of women conducted by Mariah Nelson (1998) and reported in *Embracing Victory*, African American women are the group most likely to support the statement that "friends should not compete with each other." Ruth L. Hall, psychology professor at the College of New Jersey, explains that many African American women are hesitant to compete with friends because they have been raised with the co-cultural value of cooperation and collectivism (as cited in Nelson, 1998). African American women are thus pulled in two directions—the competitive direction by a dominant individualist culture and a cooperative direction by a co-cultural collectivist value system.

The collectivist value is exhibited during Kwanzaa, a weeklong African American celebration that starts on December 26. There are seven guiding principles of Kwanzaa, and none of them include competitiveness. Three of them emphasize cooperativeness: umoja (unity), ujima (collective work and responsibility), and ujamaa (cooperative economics).

Cultural diversity makes enhancing cooperation an urgent goal. It is far too easy for us to perceive cultural differences and to make those differences an excuse to be enemies. We live in a "global village," where cultures rub against each other every day, but as Hall (1981) observes, "It is impossible to cooperate . . . unless we know each other's ways of thinking" (p. 3). As an individualist nation, the United States will find it challenging to become more cooperative. Nevertheless, as you will see in Chapter 8, cooperation can be incorporated into our culture to a far greater extent than is currently occurring.

Questions for Thought

1. Is competition in the classroom always a negative experience? Do some children thrive in a competitive environment? How might competitive and cooperative classrooms differ in teaching and learning styles?
2. Can you imagine a culture entirely free from competition? Would that be a desirable society? Could you avoid mass conformity in such a culture?

cues, such as the relationship, situation, setting, and time. Harmony is highly regarded in collectivist cultures, and verbal messages tend to be vague so no offense will be caused. Silence can mean disagreement without apparent embarrassment or loss of face to either party. High-context speakers tend to talk around a point and avoid saying "no" outright to preserve harmony (Chen & Starosta, 1998B). High-context communication conceals intentions and points of view, and low-context communication reveals them.

When cultural populations are quite similar, there is less need to be verbally explicit because there is historical understanding of the rules, roles, norms, and customary practices of the culture. Thus, a high-context, implicit communication style is appropriate in collectivist cultures because they tend to have more homogeneous (similar) populations (Hofstede, 1991; Samovar & Porter, 1995). Individualist cultures tend to have more heterogeneous (dissimilar) populations. With culturally diverse populations comes uncertainty. The rules, roles, norms, and customary practices are not immediately known by individuals from co-cultural backgrounds. There is a compelling need to be verbally explicit in individualist cultures to prevent misunderstanding and miscommunication. Thus, a low-context, explicit communication style is appropriate in individualist cultures.

Power-Distance Dimension

In the United States power imbalances are often the catalyst for aggressive behavior. The perceptions of power imbalances in some cultures, however, are strikingly different from those in the United States. Cultures vary widely in their attitudes concerning the appropriateness of power imbalances (Figure 3-2). Hofstede (1991) calls these variations in the acceptability of unequal distribution of power in relationships, institutions, and organizations the **power-distance dimension** (hereafter referred to as PD).

Countries that are classified as low-PD (relatively weak emphasis on maintaining power differences), such as the United States, Great Britain, Sweden, Denmark, Austria, Israel, and New Zealand, are guided by norms and institutional regulations that minimize power distinctions. Challenging authority, flattening organizational hierarchies to reduce status differences between management and employees, and using power legitimately are subscribed to by low-PD cultures. Low-PD cultures do not advocate eliminating power disparities entirely, and in a country such as the United States power differences obviously exist. The emphasis

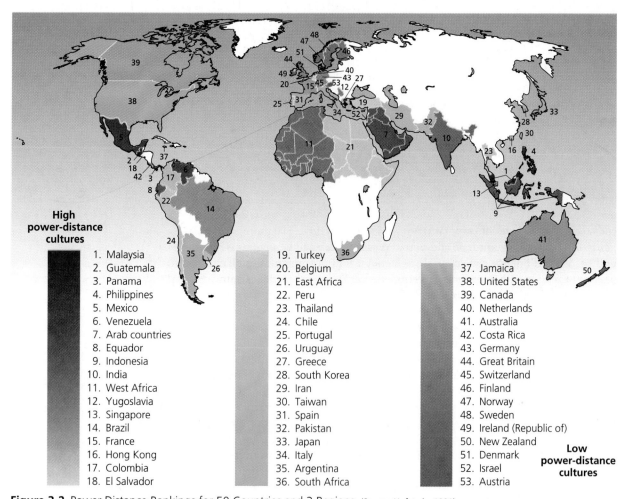

Figure 3-2 Power-Distance Rankings for 50 Countries and 3 Regions (Source: Hofstede, 1991)

on maintaining hierarchical boundaries between the relatively powerful and the powerless, however, are deemphasized in low-PD cultures.

Communication in low-PD cultures reflects the minimization of power disparities. Workers may disagree with their supervisors; in fact, disagreement may be encouraged by some bosses. Socializing outside the work environment and communication on a first-name basis between workers and bosses is not unusual (Brislin, 1993). Students can question and disagree with their teachers. Some professors even encourage students to address them by their first names.

When I taught at Western Washington University in Bellingham, Washington, one of the hottest issues was a proposal to establish a pub on campus. Three quarters of the students favored the proposal. The most common argument used to support the proposal was that students and professors would have an informal place to meet, relax, sip a brew, and discuss philosophy, politics, or the state of the world. The pub would diminish power disparities between professors and students. Not surprisingly, the administration was not enthusiastic about the proposed pub—but for mostly legal and liability reasons, not any desire to maintain power disparities. The pub was never established.

Cultures classified as high-PD (relatively strong emphasis on maintaining power differences), such as Malaysia, Guatemala, Philippines, Mexico, India, Singapore, and Hong Kong, are guided by norms and institutional regulations that accept, even cultivate, power distinctions. The actions of authorities are rarely challenged, the powerful are thought to have a legitimate right to use their power, and organizational and social hierarchies are encouraged (Lustig & Koester, 1993).

Communication in high-PD cultures reflects the desire to maintain power disparities. Children raised in high-PD cultures are expected to obey their parents

This arranged marriage between two young adults from India highlights the power-distance dimension of cultures. A high power-distance country such as India values the right of parents to arrange their children's marriages. A low power-distance country such as the United States accords no such right to parents.

Box 3-2   Sharper Focus

Teaching South Koreans to Smile

"Whiskey, whiskey, whiskey" they chant, much as we say "cheese" when a photograph is being shot of us. Bank tellers and accountants are learning to smile. This is part of the training at the Korean Air Service Academy, a school in Seoul, South Korea, that specializes in making Korean businesses more globally effective by teaching "international manners" (Jelinek, 1998). Smiling does not come easily to these employees. Years of authoritarian military governments programmed Korean citizens to show deference to authorities. The Confucian value of respecting elders and superiors also contributes to the difficulty of learning how to smile.

South Korea is an interesting example of a culture that has a high-PD history but is gradually moving toward becoming a moderate-PD culture. Smiling seems like such a simple nonverbal expression of warmth and friendliness. Most Americans find little difficulty smiling. South Koreans, however, must overcome years of social training that predispose them to reserved, formal communication, especially with high-status individuals. Smiling communicates informality and equal stature. A simple smile can exhibit a fundamental value difference between cultures.

without question. Students do not question nor disagree with their teachers. Workers normally do not feel comfortable disagreeing with their bosses, and friendships and socializing between bosses and employees are rare.

The reactions to power imbalances are likely to reflect where a culture falls on the power-distance dimension. One study (Bond et al., 1985) compared people's reactions to insults in a high-PD (Hong Kong) and a low-PD culture (United States). Subjects from Hong Kong were less upset than those from the United States when they were insulted, as long as the initiator of the insult was a high-status person. Brislin (1993) explains: "When people accept status distinctions as normal, they accept the fact that the powerful are different than the less powerful. The powerful can engage in behaviors that the less powerful cannot, in this case insult people and have the insult accepted as part of their rights" (p. 255).

Differences in power-distance do not mean that high-PD cultures never experience conflict and aggression arising from power imbalances. Members of low-PD cultures, however, are more likely to respond with frustration, outrage, and hostility to power imbalances than members of high-PD cultures. This occurs because low-PD cultures value power balance even though the experience of everyday life in such cultures may reflect a somewhat different reality. In a low-PD culture, the struggle to achieve the ideal of balanced power is more compelling, and the denial of power is likely to be perceived as more unjust, even intolerable, than in a high-PD culture where power balance is viewed differently (Box 3-2).

There is a strong correlation between the individualism-collectivism and the power-distance dimensions (Hofstede, 1991). High-PD cultures are likely to be collectivist, and low-PD cultures are likely to be individualist. Duane Alwin, a sociologist at the University of Michigan, studied parental values in the United States. Increasingly, parents in the United States encourage their children to become independent and autonomous (individualist). Alwin's study found that parents placed the highest value on "thinking for oneself" as the quality that will best prepare children for life. Questioning authority (low-PD) also emerged as an important parental value. As Alwin notes, "People are willing to question authority, to not necessarily believe that the parental generation is right or the church

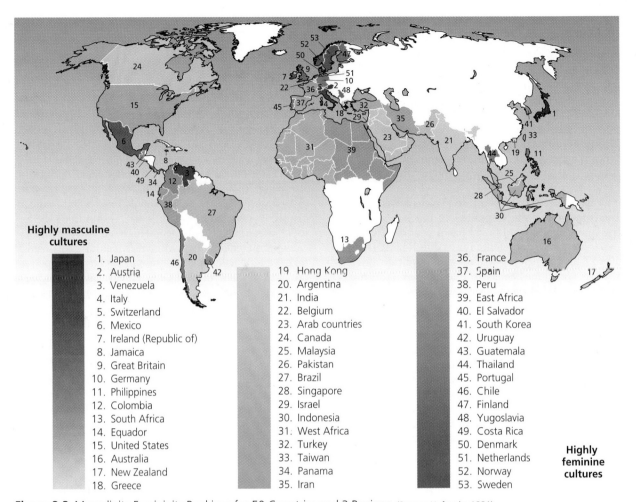

Figure 3-3 Masculinity-Femininity Rankings for 50 Countries and 3 Regions (Source: Hofstede, 1991)

Highly masculine cultures

1. Japan
2. Austria
3. Venezuela
4. Italy
5. Switzerland
6. Mexico
7. Ireland (Republic of)
8. Jamaica
9. Great Britain
10. Germany
11. Philippines
12. Colombia
13. South Africa
14. Equador
15. United States
16. Australia
17. New Zealand
18. Greece

19. Hong Kong
20. Argentina
21. India
22. Belgium
23. Arab countries
24. Canada
25. Malaysia
26. Pakistan
27. Brazil
28. Singapore
29. Israel
30. Indonesia
31. West Africa
32. Turkey
33. Taiwan
34. Panama
35. Iran

36. France
37. Spain
38. Peru
39. East Africa
40. El Salvador
41. South Korea
42. Uruguay
43. Guatemala
44. Thailand
45. Portugal
46. Chile
47. Finland
48. Yugoslavia
49. Costa Rica
50. Denmark
51. Netherlands
52. Norway
53. Sweden

Highly feminine cultures

is right or some institutional authority is right" (as cited in Frerking, 1995). This exhibits an individualistic, low-PD value system.

Masculinity-Femininity Dimension

Hofstede (1991) discovered that cultures differ along a masculine-feminine dimension. Masculine cultures exhibit stereotypic masculine traits such as male dominance, ambitiousness, assertiveness, competitiveness, and drive for achievement. Feminine cultures exhibit stereotypic feminine traits such as affection, nurturance, sensitivity, compassion, and emotional expressiveness. In Tannen's (1990) terms, a masculine culture has a strong need for status and a feminine culture has a strong need for connection. Cultures ranking high on masculinity include Japan, Austria, Venezuela, Italy, Switzerland, and Mexico. Cultures ranking high on femininity include Sweden, Norway, Netherlands, Denmark, Costa Rica, Finland, and Chile. The United States ranks relatively high on masculinity (Figure 3-3).

Box 3-3   Sharper Focus

The Falsetto Voice of Japanese Women

"The Voice is as fawning as her demeanor, as sweet as syrup, and as high as a dog whistle. Any higher, and it would shatter the crystal on the seventh floor" (Kristof, 1995). "The Voice" described by *New York Times* reporter Nicholas Kristof refers to the falsetto pitch used by Japanese women in formal settings, on the phone, or when interacting with business customers. (The falsetto is usually abandoned in normal conversation with family and friends.)

This unnaturally high-pitched voice historically has been viewed as a sign of politeness, much as a person in the United States would raise his or her voice at the end of a sentence to sound tentative or questioning (Kristof, 1995). This corresponds to a masculine culture's stereotype for "feminine" behavior, and Japan is at the top of Hofstede's (1991) list of masculine cultures.

Females in a masculine culture are expected to be deferential, polite, and nonaggressive—to conform to rigid gender stereotypes. "The Voice" shows such traits. Julie Saito, a reporter at *Asahi Shimbun*, explains, "A lower voice sounds too bullying, too aggressive, too manly. . . . A high voice sounds more cute, more like a girlish image of women" (as cited in Kristof, 1995). Hideki Kasuya, professor of speech science at Utsunomiya University, did studies of TV announcers in the United States and Japan. He discovered that female announcers in the United States speak in a markedly lower pitch than female announcers from Japan (Kristof, 1995).

Not all Japanese women accept speaking in falsetto as appropriate. Mari Shimakura, a teenager in Tokyo, expresses the changing viewpoint about the female falsetto voice, "When girls speak in really high voices, I just want to kick them in the head. It's totally fake and really annoying. It gives me a headache. Mom tells me I speak in too low a voice, and that I should raise it. But I can't change it" (as cited in Kristof, 1995). This attitude seems to be spreading, despite the feminine stereotypes historically prominent in Japan. More recent studies by Kasuya reveal that female Japanese announcers have dropped the pitch of their voices significantly. Similarly, studies of taped announcements on subway platforms and recordings of female singers from the past and present reveal a lowering of the female pitch (Kristof, 1995).

Cultures that score high on masculinity do not necessarily communicate rigid gender stereotypes in the same ways. The United States is a fairly masculine culture, yet use of the female falsetto voice in formal situations would startle most of us. What "The Voice" demonstrates is that cultures that are similar on the masculinity-femininity dimension can communicate this similarity in surprisingly varied ways.

In masculine cultures men typically communicate in ways that will enhance their esteem (e.g., speak often, control the floor, interrupt). Women in masculine cultures typically communicate in ways that will enhance relationships (e.g., express support, encourage, listen well). Women are expected to "act feminine" (Box 3-3). Gender roles are rigid. In feminine cultures, however, gender roles are less rigid, equality between the sexes is more typical, and individual achievement and competitiveness are deemphasized for both men and women. It is important to note here, however, that the rankings of cultures on the masculinity-femininity dimension are relative, not absolute. A high ranking on femininity doesn't mean that a culture treats women as well as men. It simply means that feminine cultures have less rigid gender roles, with their distinctly different behaviors for males and females, and more gender overlapping of behaviors than masculine cultures. As the 1993 United Nations Human Development Report concludes, "No country treats its women as well as it treats its men" (as cited in Wright, 1993).

Intercultural communication between members of masculine and feminine cultures poses challenges similar to the difficulties men and women in the domi-

Box 3-4   Focus on Controversy

Critique of Hofstede's Cultural Dimensions

Although Hofstede's (1980, 1991) monumental study of cultural value differences provides useful insights into underlying causes of intercultural communication difficulties and challenges, Hofstede's work is not without its critics. The first criticism is that although the data from Hofstede's original study are impressive, the dimensions he identifies from these data have not all received the same level of support from additional studies. The individualism-collectivism dimension has received the greatest support and has been validated in numerous studies (see especially Kim et al., 1994; Triandis, 1995). The power-distance dimension has been studied far less than individualism-collectivism, but some additional studies support this dimension as well (Bochner & Hesketh, 1994; Merritt, 1998). The masculinity-femininity dimension has received limited additional support beyond Hofstede's original study (Hofstede, 1996; Leung et al., 1990). Hofstede (1980, 1991) identifies a fourth dimension, uncertainty avoidance, in his original study. This dimension has not been discussed here, however, because several studies have been unable to validate it (Merritt, 1998; Schwartz, 1995; Smith et al., 1996), making the dimension suspect.

A second criticism of Hofstede's cultural dimensions is that his original research was conducted in the 1960s and 1970s. His data and the rankings of cultures on each dimension derived from his data may no longer be accurate. This would be an important criticism if it weren't for the fact that deep-seated cultural values are highly resistant to change, even over long periods of time (Samovar & Porter, 1995). There may be minor changes in rankings on each of his dimensions, but there is little reason to believe that general descriptions of cultures (e.g., individualist, high-PD) are any less valid now than when the data were gathered.

A third criticism of Hofstede's dimensions is that they were derived from data extracted from a detailed questionnaire with a Western bias. This criticism does not invalidate the three dimensions already discussed, but it does raise the question of whether other dimensions are missing from Hofstede's research. Hofstede (1991) accepts this criticism as valid, arguing that another more Eastern dimension, called Confucian dynamism, has some support. The degree of research support for this dimension is still slight, however, so it will not be explained here.

Questions for Thought

1. Can you think of additional value dimensions that distinguish cultures not included in Hofstede's work?
2. Why do you think deep-seated cultural values are highly resistant to change? Can you imagine American culture becoming collectivist, high power-distance, and feminine?

nant U.S. culture have communicating with each other. The potential for misunderstandings and miscommunication are enormous.

Remembering all the details on value dimensions that distinguish cultures can seem daunting. When trying to condense all this material on cultural value differences, concentrate less on the details and more on three primary points.

First, recognize that individualism-collectivism is clearly "the crucial dimension of cultural variability" (Griffin, 1994, p. 401). Be particularly familiar with this dimension because it has the greatest support in cross-cultural research.

Second, remember that individualism-collectivism and power-distance are strongly correlated. This means that individualist cultures also tend to be low-PD cultures and collectivist cultures tend to be high-PD cultures. If you know where a culture falls on one value dimension, you know where it will probably fall on the other dimension as well.

Third, the masculinity-femininity dimension is similar to Tannen's (1990) status-connection model of gender communication already discussed. Masculine cultures typically expect men to be concerned with status, women to be concerned with connection, and to see communication patterns that conform to these expectations. Feminine cultures expect a less rigid distinction in gender behaviors and more overlapping of status and connection for both men and women.

Intercultural Miscommunication

Cultures can vary dramatically in how their members perceive the world. With differences in core values come numerous opportunities for miscommunication between members of differing cultures. In this section, you will learn more about basic intercultural miscommunication.

Ethnocentrism

Imagine that you are invited to a friend's house for dinner. Your friend's family believes dinner is a ritual that allows family members to put aside diversions and distractions of the day. The focus should be on the family and what each person did that day—exciting things, happy experiences, problems, troubling issues, and the like.

The family begins by saying grace before eating, thanking God for the bounty. Each person seated at the table formally requests that food be passed to him or her. They also say "thank you" after the food is passed. No one reaches across the table and grabs anything. That is considered rude. Conversation is encouraged. Silence is noticed and discouraged. No one leaves the table without first asking "to be excused." When dinner is over, everyone busses their dishes and pitches in on cleanup.

Now suppose that your family does everything differently. Dinner is rarely eaten at the dinner table. It is usually consumed in front of the TV. When dinner is eaten together at the table, everyone grabs for the food as quickly as they can. No one asks for anything. No one thanks anyone for passing food. No grace is said. When dinner is over, the women take care of the dishes, and the men go about their business of relaxation or television watching.

Here we have two distinctly different ways of carrying out commonplace activities. Markedly different communication patterns result from these differing perceptions. Imagine telling your friend's family that the way they conduct dinner is all wrong and that it should be done the way your family does it. Picture the reaction. Imagine if your friend did the same to you. Can you picture your annoyance, even anger? Can you picture how inappropriate imposing your way on others when in their home would seem to you? What effect would this likely have on your friendship?

As silly and inappropriate as this insistence that your friend's family change its dinner rituals to accommodate your preferences may seem, this is fundamentally what ethnocentrism is about. The term *ethnocentrism* is derived from two Greek words: *ethnos,* meaning nation, and *kentron,* meaning center (Klopf, 1998). **Ethnocentrism** literally means "Our nation is the center of all things." Ethnocentrism is the common view that one's own culture is central to perceptions of the world and that all other cultures are judged in reference to it. The degree of difference between your own and other cultures determines ratings on

Ethnocentrism exists in all cultures. Typically, people exhibit ethnocentric preferences—in this case a culturally valued mode of dress—even when visiting or living in a different culture.

a superiority-inferiority scale. Those cultures found to be different from your own are judged inferior. The bigger the difference, the greater the perceived inferiority.

All cultures, to greater or lesser extent, are ethnocentric. This ethnocentric bias is often shocking, even brutal in its judgment of other cultures. Names of various tribes and groups sometimes reflect this bias. Kiowa means "real or principal people." Laplander means "human being." Jews are the "chosen people," gentiles are everyone else. Historically, among Christians "gentile" meant heathen or pagan. Greeks and Romans referred to outsiders as "barbarians" (Klopf, 1998). Yoshitake (1977) claims the following was a Chinese stereotypic, ethnocentric view of Japanese people:

> A Japanese man is an irrational, brutal, temperamental, and war-loving person, who lives with his hypocritical wife in a miserably small house in a hierarchical, submission-oriented and feudalistic society, communicating with his fellow men in an inadequate language, . . . all the while being unconsciously under the influence of the dominantly superior Chinese culture and civilization. (p. 23)

Immigrants to the United States are referred to as "aliens," legal or otherwise. Common definitions of alien include "strange," "unnatural," "repugnant," "outsider," and, of course, "visitor from another galaxy."

Ethnocentrism is a learned belief in the superiority of one's own culture. It is difficult to resist the temptation to devalue another culture simply because we are comfortable with how things are done in our own culture. Experiencing another culture's customs, practices, and beliefs that are different from what we are accustomed to may seem weird and wrong. Consider differences in teaching and learning in schools (Samovar & Porter, 1995). In Russia, China, Japan, Korea, Vietnam, and Cambodia, learning is passive. Teachers read to their students. Students are mostly silent unless called on to answer questions or recite. Rote memorization is common. In Mexico, students are more active, talking and learning through group work. In Germany, southern Italy, and the West Indies, students rise in unison when the teacher enters the classroom. In an Israeli kibbutz, students wander around the classroom, talk to each other, sharpen pencils, or get a drink without formal permission. They talk during lessons, even hum to themselves while working on an assignment. American classrooms are a mix of many of these practices, and they are less formal and more active places of learning than in most other cultures.

So which cultural communication practices are correct? Every culture believes the way it operates is preferable, elsewise the practices would change (unless enforced by an authoritarian regime). Ethnocentrism is judgment on a global scale.

Cultural (and communication) sensitivity moves us from a narrow view of the world to a broader worldview. This broadening worldview is expressed in the philosophy of cultural relativism. **Cultural relativism** views cultures as merely different, not deficient. A cultural relativistic attitude strives to understand these differences, not judge them, so intercultural cooperation can flourish. Cultural relativism is We-oriented. Ethnocentrism is Me-oriented. Achieving a cultural relativistic attitude takes empathy. You have to put yourself in the place of others who view the world differently.

Cultural relativism, however, does not mean that any form of cultural difference should be accepted. There are universal human rights. Sexism, racism, homophobia, and all the "isms" that breed "ethnic cleansings" and genocidal wars deserve no defense. Customs, practices, and communication behaviors that do not dehumanize people, however, should not be rejected as inferior simply because they are different from our own cultural ways of operating. Ethnocentrism spawns misperception, misunderstanding, and miscommunication.

Misattribution

Attribution, or the causes assigned to people's behavior, was discussed in Chapter 2. The self-serving bias assigns dispositional causes to our successes and situational causes to our failures. Attribution error occurs when we are prone to assign dispositional causes to the bad behavior of others but situational causes to their good behavior, when the reverse is more likely true.

Similar attributional problems occur during intercultural communication. What is appropriate and expected communication in your own culture may be perceived as rude, arrogant, or uncivilized by individuals from other cultures. This is called **misattribution,** or "an attribution about the reason for an event given by a foreigner which differs from that typically given by a member of the host culture" (Smith & Bond, 1994).

Misattributions aren't always negative. An individual from the United States might take a job teaching English to Japanese students. These students will likely show great courtesy, attentiveness, and respect to the teacher. The teacher, in turn, may attribute such positive treatment to the perception by students that he or she is a gifted and knowledgeable instructor. This may be a positive misattribution. Japanese students typically show respect, attentiveness, and courtesy to teachers regardless of their talent and instructional capabilities.

Intercultural communication is fraught with uncertainty and anxiety. When communicating with individuals from distinctly different cultures, we search for causes of each other's behavior, especially if the behavior is unexpected or seems odd by our culture's standards. We do this to reduce the uncertainty in intercultural encounters. Unfortunately, we often do not sufficiently understand the rules, norms, customs, and common practices of other cultures, so our attributions are made based on what makes sense and is expected in our culture. Individuals are too late for appointments or too early, too talkative or too quiet, express their anger too openly or hide their anger too much, stand too close or too far apart when conversing, look too directly at the other person or look down or away too often. Each of these behaviors can receive a positive or negative attribution. The principal factor influencing the attribution is the culture of the observer. For instance, looking down when conversing with another person could be interpreted as a sign of a weak, easily intimidated person (negative dispositional attribution) in American culture. The same behavior, however, when viewed by a member of an Asian culture, might be interpreted as an indication of a respectful, polite person (positive dispositional attribution). Conversely, looking directly at a speaker will likely be interpreted as a sign of a confident person in the United States but an indicator of a rude, impolite person in Asian cultures.

Attributions in individualist and collectivist cultures are likely to be markedly different, making misattribution commonplace. Individualist cultures typically are sensitive to characteristics of a person (dispositional causes) that explain behavior. Collectivist cultures are typically sensitive to the context (situational causes). A conversation between two people, one from an individualist and the other from a collectivist culture, invites misattribution and the friction that accompanies it (Box 3-5).

Interpersonal Miscommunication

Lustig and Koester (1999) provide a prime example of interpersonal miscommunication that can easily occur between members of distinctly different cultures:

> Brian Holtz is a U.S. businessperson assigned by his company to manage its office in Thailand. Mr. Thani, a valued assistant manager in the Bangkok office, has recently been arriving late for work. Holtz has to decide what to do about this problem. After carefully thinking about his options, he decides there are four possible strategies:
>
> 1. Go privately to Mr. Thani, ask him why he has been arriving late, and tell him that he needs to come to work on time.
> 2. Ignore the problem.
> 3. Publicly reprimand Mr. Thani the next time he is late.
> 4. In a private discussion, suggest that he is seeking Mr. Thani's assistance in dealing with employees in the company who regularly arrive late for work, and solicit his suggestions about what should be done. (pp. 67–68)

If you were Holtz, what choice would you make? Which one is likely to be both appropriate and effective? The first choice is a typical American solution. It is a low-context communication style (direct), and it fits a masculine culture that values assertiveness from men. It would probably be effective in curbing Mr. Thani's tardiness. In Thai culture, however, an individual does not directly criticize another person. This causes a loss of face and threatens harmony (collectivist value). The first choice would be very inappropriate, even embarrassing.

Box 3-5 Sharper Focus

Intercultural Misattribution

Triandis (1975) presents a dialogue between an American supervisor and a Greek subordinate to show the problem of misattributions during intercultural communication. The Greek employee, coming from a relatively moderate power-distance culture, expects to be told what to do. Since Greece is a collectivist culture with a high-context communication style, he also assumes that his supervisor will interpret his behavior as he would himself.

His American supervisor, however, coming from a low power-distance, individualist culture, expects participation, initiative, and responsibility from an employee. He also expects a direct, explicit communication style. In this conversation the clash of cultures can be seen readily by the misattributions that emerge due to cultural value differences.

Message	Attribution
AMERICAN: "How long will it take you to finish this report?	AMERICAN: I asked him to participate.
	GREEK: His behavior makes no sense. He is the boss. Why doesn't he tell me?
GREEK: I do not know. How long should it take?	AMERICAN: He refuses to take responsibility.
	GREEK: I asked him for an order.
AMERICAN: You are in the best position to analyze time requirements.	AMERICAN: I press him to take responsibility for his actions.
	GREEK: What nonsense! I better give him an answer.
GREEK: 10 days.	AMERICAN: He lacks the ability to estimate time; this estimate is totally inadequate.
AMERICAN: Take 15. It is agreed you will do it in 15 days?	AMERICAN: I offer a contract.
	GREEK: These are my orders, 15 days.

(In fact the report needed 30 days of regular work. So the Greek worked day and night, but at the end of the 15th day, he still needed one more day's work.)

AMERICAN: Where is my report?	AMERICAN: I am making sure he fulfills his contract.
	GREEK: He is asking for the report.
GREEK: It will be ready tomorrow.	(Both attribute that it is not ready.)
AMERICAN: But we agreed that it would be ready today.	AMERICAN: I must teach him to fulfill a contract.
	GREEK: The stupid, incompetent boss! Not only did he give me wrong orders, but he does not appreciate that I did a 30-day job in 16 days.

(The Greek hands in his resignation. The American is surprised.)

GREEK: I can't work for such a man.

The second choice, ignoring the problem, would be appropriate but ineffective since Mr. Thani would likely continue arriving late to work. Mr. Holtz would view this as intolerable. Ignoring a problem is not direct and assertive.

The third choice, public reprimand, would be neither appropriate nor effective. Mr. Thani, a valuable employee, would likely resign in shame. Thai culture is strongly feminine, and tenderness and compassion are highly prized. Public rebuke is neither tender nor compassionate. It is aggressive and domineering.

Thus, the first three options, if chosen, would be examples of miscommunication. Such communication would likely aggravate the problem. The fourth choice, a problem-solving approach, is preferred because it is likely to be both appropriate and effective (Lustig & Koester, 1999). Mr. Thani can receive the message indirectly that he must arrive at work on time without losing "face." Mr. Holtz can comment to Mr. Thani that he needs his help solving a problem. "Tardiness has recently increased in the office." No specific person is identified. "I would be very pleased if you would help solve this problem." Mr. Thani can recognize that his tardiness is a problem without any public acknowledgment or humiliation. He can "solve" the problem by changing his own behavior in the context of assisting his boss.

Ethnocentrism and misattributions that flow from deep-seated cultural value differences provide abundant opportunities for interpersonal miscommunication between individuals from diverse cultures. Frequent interaction between supervisors and subordinates in work situations may be highly appreciated by members of some cultures but resented by others. In Japan, it is typically perceived as caring, but in the United States it is often perceived as micromanaging or "spying" on workers to evaluate their performance. Close supervision of teenagers by parents is usually perceived by teens as showing love in collectivist cultures but as interference in individualist cultures (Triandis, 1995).

Confusion and conflict spring from such contradictory perceptions. Appropriate communication could address these opposing perceptions effectively, except we tend to be wedded to communication styles that intensify conflict. Similar to the difficulties men and women have communicating with each other in American culture, individuals from diverse cultural backgrounds will find that their typical communication styles often clash. As Tannen (1979) notes, "in seeking to clarify, each speaker continues to use the very strategy which confused the other in the first place" (p. 5). Individuals using low-context styles try to clarify issues and misunderstandings by being increasingly direct and explicit. Individuals using high-context styles, however, continue to be vague and indirect, as is their habit. This further frustrates both parties as the clash of poorly matched communication styles continues and misattributions abound.

The warm, friendly, say-whatever-you-feel communication style familiar to Americans that typifies an individualist, low power-distance culture can produce awkward confusion when it clashes with communication styles more typical of collectivist cultures. Brislin (1993) cites an apt example of poorly matched communication styles:

> [I]f a young man from an Asian culture interacts with an American woman who employs the warm and exuberant style . . . the man may attribute the style to a romantic interest in him, personally. For example, assume that an American woman helps an Asian male on a class assignment. The Asian (following norms in his culture) offers a small gift to show his appreciation. The American woman responds, "I just love it! It's great! How thoughtful of you!" The Asian may conclude that the comment about "loving it" extends to him, personally. (p. 225)

Confusion over romantic intentions can be embarrassing, and potentially nasty. Toning down her response would, of course, be the simple solution to this clash of communication styles. The woman would have to know there was a stylistic clash in the first place, however, as would the man if he were to draw a different interpretation of her response. This again underlines the importance of knowledge in the communication competence model.

Intercultural Communication Competence

Later chapters will delve into specific ways intercultural communication competence can be enhanced. In this section, you will learn more about two general ways to develop appropriate and effective communication: mindfulness and convergence.

Become Mindful

Cultural values are so deep-seated, and communication that flows from these values is so automatic, we often take no notice. We see differences in the content of messages and the outcomes, but we often fail to see the communication process that separates members of diverse cultures.

One general way to take notice is to be mindful. **Mindfulness** is paying attention to our behavior (Langer, 1989). We recognize our ethnocentrism and our tendency to stereotype and misattribute behavior.

We exhibit mindfulness in three ways. First, we make more careful distinctions. We aren't as prone to stereotype. We look for a wider variety of attributions for unfamiliar or unexpected behavior than we might at first. Second, we are open to new information, especially that which focuses on the process, not the content, of communication. It is easy to identify disagreements over the content of messages—"You've asked for more office space, but we have none to spare." The disagreement on content of messages is usually so apparent that we often fail to examine the communication process that is essential to resolving differences. When individuals from diverse cultures communicate, a content-only focus can trigger ethnocentrism and misattributions. Third, mindfulness is exhibited when we recognize different perspectives. This is the essence of empathy, and it is critical to competent intercultural communication. Members of differing cultures perceive the world from their own cultural perspectives, and each person believes his or her perspective is reasonable and comfortable. When we lock into our own cultural perspective, we respond in an unthinking, "mindless" way to cultural differences.

Mindless communication is a universe away from competent communication. Remember, part of sensitivity is recognizing signals that can alert us to potential difficulties or possible solutions to problems. You have to extend your antenna. Mindfulness raises your antenna.

Promote Convergence

DeVito (1990) offers an apt example of the difficulties we face when trying to determine what is appropriate communication in an intercultural event:

> An American college student, while having a dinner party with a group of foreigners, learns that her favorite cousin has just died. She bites her lip, pulls herself up, and politely excuses herself from the group. The interpretation given to this behavior will vary with the culture of the observer. The Italian student thinks, "How insincere; she doesn't even cry." The Russian student thinks, "How unfriendly; she didn't care enough to share her grief with her friends." The fellow American student thinks, "How brave; she wanted to bear her burden by herself." (p. 218)

Here we see divergent interpretations of a single event. **Divergence** refers to differences that separate people. The American college student is either insincere, unfriendly, or brave, depending on your cultural perspective. Ethnocentrism nourishes divergence. It makes difference a reason to dislike, hate, avoid, or feel contempt for individuals from other cultures.

Communication is at the core of divergence. When we communicate with individuals from other cultures, we immediately notice differences in language, rate of speech, tone of voice, markedly "odd" sounding accents even when English is the common language, unusual customs for greeting people such as bowing, embracing, kissing on the cheek, and a host of other verbal and nonverbal practices. All of these accentuate divergence. We seem so terribly separate from those who speak and behave differently from us. The contrast may magnify the differences beyond what they actually are.

Divergence widens the gap between cultures. Convergence closes the gap. **Convergence** refers to similarities that connect us to others. Convergence doesn't erase, nor attempt to change, core differences between cultures. Convergence is different from assimilation. **Assimilation** is the absorption of one group's culture into the dominant culture. The original idea of the United States as a "melting pot" encouraged immigrants to give up any customs and practices different from those of Americans; to blend, not to stand apart. Recently, the idea of assimilation has been criticized as a way of eradicating cultures and destroying the unique heritages of diverse peoples.

The Reverend Jesse Jackson has suggested the family quilt as a more appropriate metaphor. The quilt is composed of unique squares of material stitched together to form a whole. The unique squares of material in the quilt represent multicultural differences. Convergence is the stitching that binds unique people from diverse cultures. Convergence merely accentuates similarities that already exist and calls for minor adjustments in our communication to link people. Convergence says, "Celebrate our differences, but find commonalities that allow us to connect."

Initial encounters with individuals from very different cultures will likely accentuate divergence. Differences leap out at us because these differences create uncertainty and anxiety. Once the initial divergence comes into focus, however, a mindful communicator looks for ways to create convergence.

There are several ways to create convergence in intercultural transactions. First, adjust your style of speaking. Minor adjustments can promote convergence. For example, more closely align your speaking rate, pitch, vocal intensity, frequency of pauses and silences with those of the other person. If an individual from another culture seems bothered by the typically rapid speaking rate of "majority" Americans, slow down your speech. Likewise, individuals from cultures that are accustomed to slower speech patterns can increase their speaking rate slightly. If your vocal intensity seems to overwhelm your listener, tone it down. Such minor adjustments can help create convergence. This is similar to advice offered to public speakers—adjust your speaking style to your audience so listeners can identify with you.

The issue of speaking style can be controversial. Historically, relatively powerless groups (African Americans, Latinos) have been expected by the mainstream U.S. culture to shift their style of speaking to the mainstream speech style (Hecht et al., 1993). Asian Americans and Latinos have been expected to learn English so they might converge better with the U.S. American culture. People take their language and speaking style very seriously, however. Minor adjustments in speaking style may be more immediately practical than significant adjustments that are likely to be more controversial and political. Controversial adjustments may promote divergence between cultural groups that resent accommodating individuals and groups from the mainstream culture. Nevertheless, convergence requires effort from all parties, not just members of the mainstream culture, or individuals from co-cultures. Expecting one-sided adjustments in communication, even minor ones, creates a competitive power struggle that promotes divergence. You may have to take the first step, however, to encourage others to do the same.

Second, work together; cooperate to find common ground. Interest in sports, religion, politics, history, and the like may offer an opportunity to find commonalities. You are not trying to change people's interests; rather, you are attempting to share interests.

Third, reduce uncertainty. Ask questions, explore, and be inquisitive. Avoid judgments by adopting a cultural relativity attitude. Try approaching your conversation with individuals from other cultures as you would a research project. You are hoping to find out as much as you can before drawing any conclusions, and they, in turn, might do likewise. Paradoxically, exploring different customs and cultural values can be a fascinating and connecting source of convergence. We may find a mutual interest in our differences.

Summary

Intercultural communication is a fact of life. Where once intercultural communication could mostly be avoided by never leaving the borders of our state, this is no longer possible. The United States is thoroughly multicultural. With cultural diversity comes new challenges. We tend to misunderstand individuals from other cultures and co-cultures because deep-seated cultural values differ. The main value dimensions identified by Hofstede are individualism-collectivism, power-distance, and masculinity-femininity. Cultures vary widely on these dimensions. These value differences and the communication patterns and styles that emerge from them can result in ethnocentrism, or the attitude that your own culture is the measure of all things and cultures that differ from your own culture are deficient. This ethnocentric attitude can produce misattributions and miscommunication. Finding ways to create convergence and to deemphasize divergence can help produce competent intercultural communication.

Suggested Readings

Derber, C. (1996). *The wilding of America: How greed and violence are eroding our nation's character.* New York: St. Martin's Press. Derber critiques the excessive individualism of U.S. culture.

Hall, E. (1981). *Beyond culture.* New York: Doubleday. This is an excellent discussion of the role culture plays in our lives, by a recognized authority on the subject.

Hughes, R. (1993). *Culture of complaint: A passionate look into the ailing heart of America.* New York: Warner Books. An Australian who has lived in the United States for more than two decades offers a cultural criticism of U.S. life that is witty and provocative.

Wolfe, T. (1987). *The bonfire of the vanities.* New York: Bantam. Wolfe is a Pulitzer Prize–winning author who has written a powerful novel that exposes the many difficulties of multiculturalism in the United States.

Chapter 4

Language: Sharing Meaning With Words

On December 18, 1996, the Oakland, California school board voted unanimously to recognize "Ebonics" (Black English) as the "primary language" of many students in the school district and to use Ebonics as a bridge to learning standard English. Initially misunderstood, mostly because the board proposal was poorly worded, the Ebonics issue ignited an explosive national controversy. It seemed that everybody had an opinion on the board's action. Most of the arguments centered on whether Ebonics—a term Robert Williams coined in 1973 combining "ebony" and "phonics"—is a language, a dialect, or merely street slang spoken by some African Americans. Even Congress stepped into the fray. The Senate Appropriations Committee held hearings on the Oakland school board's decision to recognize Ebonics, fearing that federal funds might be used to teach Ebonics instead of standard English.

The Ebonics controversy reminds us that language is not merely a neutral vehicle of communication. Tell us the language we speak is inferior to other languages and see how exercised we become. Print voters' pamphlets in a language other than English and observe the animated disagreement it sparks. Try to pass legislation recognizing English as the "official" language of our nation and watch the fireworks explode. The specific language we speak identifies us as part of a nation, a region, an ethnic community, or a group. Almost no one takes his or her language lightly.

Without language there would be no science, history, literature, ethics, philosophy, technology or much of anything that characterizes humans as intelligent and cultured. We can learn and communicate without language, but not at a very advanced or complex level. Language facilitates learning. As psycholinguist Roger Brown (1970) explains, language "makes life experience cumulative. . . . Everyone can know much more than he or she could possibly learn by direct experience" (p. 212). Our knowledge advances because we can communicate with others. Language, both written and spoken, makes this possible.

Our capacity for language usage, however, does not automatically produce competent communication. Our use of language is frequently inefficient, clumsy, even inept and dangerous. The primary purpose of this chapter is to explain and illustrate how language influences our thoughts, perception, and behavior. This chapter has four objectives:

1. to describe the basic anatomy of language,
2. to identify in what specific ways language influences thought, perception, and human behavior,
3. to identify common problems of language misuse and malpractice, and
4. to discuss how to communicate competently with language.

The Anatomy of Language

Knowing how to use language competently begins with an understanding of what language is and how it works. In this section you will learn about the basic anatomy of language.

Definition of Language

Language is a structured system of symbols that communicates meaning. **Symbols,** in the form of words, are arbitrary representations of objects, events, ideas, and relations that can produce ambiguous meaning. Symbols, therefore, have three primary characteristics: arbitrariness, representativeness, and ambiguity.

Arbitrariness   Arbitrariness means that language symbols have no natural connection to **referents**—that is, that to which the symbol makes reference. We choose what to call objects, events, ideas, and relationships. A "house" could have been called a "brickstack." The English language has a word for work that piles up while we are on vacation, "backlog," but it has no word for work that accumulates before we leave on that same vacation. So invent a word, say, "forthlog." Natural law doesn't forbid such invention.

Frontiersman Davy Crockett is credited as the first person to use the word "blizzard" (Bryson, 1990): Shakespeare invented more than 1700 words (Bryson, 1990): "Barefaced," "critical," "leapfrog," "monumental," "excellent," summit," "obscene," "countless," and "submerged" are just a few of his creations. These words still remain useful because speakers of English incorporated them into their language by the common agreement of usage. "Internet," "computer," "floppy disk," "fax," "e-mail," and "zip drive" are all invented terms necessitated by technological creations in this century.

The word you choose to call something initially is arbitrary, an invention, but once that designation has been made, there must be common agreement (conventionality) to use that word for that referent with some consistency. Thus, *word origin is arbitrary, but word usage is conventional.* Not all of Shakespeare's creations were accepted by English speakers. "Barky," "brisky," "conflux," "vastidity," and "tortive" were some of his words that failed because speakers of English declined to use them. If we each used a personal language without common agreement, without shared understanding and usage, we would not understand one another (Box 4-1).

Representativeness   Words are symbols because they represent an object, event, idea, or relationships without being the referent itself. Korzybski (1958) provides a useful analogy to clarify this point. A word is to a referent as a map is to a territory. A map of San Francisco is obviously not the city of San Francisco, only a representation of it. You would be viewed as more than just a little odd if you spread a map of San Francisco in front of your car, then drove your car onto the map and happily pronounced your arrival in "the city by the bay." Similarly, the word "sandwich" certainly won't take the edge off anyone's hunger.

Words are arbitrary representations of referents. If words were natural representations of referents and not simply maps representing territories, "white" would not be printed in black type, nor would the word "big" contain fewer letters than the word "small." "Invisible" would be impossible to read, "oral" could not be written, and "wide" could not be narrower than any other word.

The English language is replete with examples of words that do not correspond to any literal translation (Lederer, 1990). There is no butter in "buttermilk," no egg in "eggplant," no grape in "grapefruit," no pine or apple in "pineapple," and no pea in "peanut." "Gooseberries" have no relation to waterfowl. A "nonstop flight" doesn't condemn you to circle the globe endlessly from 30,000 feet. None of these words are meant to be taken literally, as if their meaning must correspond to their literal referents. The word meanings are arbitrary, even if sometimes odd and confusing.

Box 4-1 Sharper Focus

Boontling

Word origin is arbitrary, but word usage is conventional. This important statement about language is illustrated by the fascinating creation of an artificial language called "boontling" (Bryson, 1990), concocted by local residents of Boonville, California around the turn of the century. Some Boonville locals, apparently with time on their hands, decided for the purpose of amusement to create a language only they could understand. They made up an extensive vocabulary based mostly on their Scots-Irish heritage, the language of the local Pomo Indians, and their own mental dexterity. Eventually, the language mushroomed to 1,360 words (Tomb, 1999).

Before too long, almost everyone in Boonville was "harpin' boont" (speaking boontling). Here is just a sample of the colorful vocabulary of boontling: "zeese" (coffee), "charlie brown" (pie), "shoveltooth" (doctor), "trashlifter" (heavy rain), "loglifter" (deluge), "billy ryan" (goatee), "floyd hutsell" (kerosene lantern), "madge" (prostitute), "smalch" (small change), "burlapping" (sexual intercourse), and "otting" (diligent work).

Some words were created based on local experience. For instance, "charlie brown" referred to pie because a local resident by that name ate his pie before the rest of his meal. "Shoveltooth" was created because a doctor in the town had protruding teeth. "Burlapping" became a euphemism for the sex act because of a story about a young man and woman who were discovered in passionate entanglement on a stack of old gunnysacks at the back of the general store.

There are still speakers of boontling, but most have "piked to the dusties" (died). What we learn from boontling is that what we choose to call something initially is arbitrary. Boontling did not have to make reference to any local experience, nor to the specific events that served as a basis for some of the vocabulary. The choice of words and the meanings for those words was arbitrary. Once a word has been created, however, it must be shared with others as boontling was, and speakers must agree to use the word with the designated meaning for communication to take place.

Onomatopoetic words may seem to be naturally connected to their referents since they are words that imitate sounds, yet even these words have an arbitrary representational quality when compared cross-culturally. In American English a rooster makes a "cock-a-doodle-doo" sound, yet in Japanese it goes *"kokeko ko"* and in French *"cocoricooo."* We say "splash," but the French say *"plouf."* We say "bang," but the Germans say *"paff."* We say "ring," but Turks say "can" (pronounced chan). American English has a dog making a "woof woof" or "bow wow" sound, but in Finnish a dog goes "hau hau." A pig goes "oink oink" in the United States, but *"boo boo"* in Japan. Crying in Japan is "eeeen," but "boo hoo" in the United States, and a sneeze in Japanese is *"hakushun"* (silent u), but "aachoo" in American English. The map is not the territory. There is no natural connection between words and referents because words are merely arbitrary representations of referents.

Ambiguity Black comedian and social critic Dick Gregory sat down at a lunch counter in a Mississippi town during the days of racial segregation. The waitress informed him, "We don't serve colored people." "That's fine," Gregory replied. "I don't eat colored people. I'd like a piece of chicken" (as cited in Pinker, 1994, p. 115). Words can have very ambiguous, multiple meanings. The 500 most frequently used words in the English language have more than 14,000 meanings. The word "set" seems simple enough until you look it up in a dictionary and discover that it has 58 meanings as a noun, 126 as a verb, and 10 as a participial adjective (Bryson, 1990). It has such variety of meaning that the *Oxford English Dictionary* takes 60,000 words—the length of a romance novel—to discuss them all.

Rhymes with Orange, © 1998 by Hilary B. Price. Reprinted with special permission of King Features Syndicate.

Legendary comedian Groucho Marx was notorious for his quips that played on the ambiguity of spoken language. Here are just a few:

> Outside of a dog, a book is a man's best friend. Inside of a dog, it's too dark to read.

> Time flies like an arrow. Fruit flies like a banana.

> Last night I shot an elephant in my pajamas. How he got in my pajamas I'll never know.

> I write by ear. I tried writing with the typewriter, but I found it too unwieldy.

Some English words even have contradictory meanings, seriously stretching our ambiguity tolerance. "Sanction" can mean either "permit" or "forbid." "Cleave" can mean either "cut in half" or "stick together." "Fast" might denote "move quickly" or "stick firmly." "Winding up" a watch starts it, but "winding up" a meeting finishes it. A "blunt" instrument is dull, but a "blunt" remark is sharp and pointed.

Some words and phrases seem contradictory but aren't. "Could care less" and "couldn't care less" mean the same thing. "Ravel" and "unravel," "habitable" and "inhabitable," "iterate" and "reiterate," "flammable" and "inflammable," and "fat chance" and "slim chance" seem like opposites, but these pairs of words mean the same thing.

The ambiguity of words requires us to interpret the meaning from the specific context in which the words are used. Some actual newspaper headlines illustrate the need for this interpretive process:

> *Include Your Children When Baking Cookies*
> *Iraqi Head Seeks Arms*
> *Prostitutes Appeal to Pope*
> *Panda Mating Fails; Veterinarian Takes Over*
> *Local High School Dropouts Cut in Half*
> *Kids Make Nutritious Snacks* (as cited in "Last Year's Best," 1997).

With ambiguity and the need for interpretation comes the potential for confusion and misunderstanding when we communicate with others. This problem will be explored later in this chapter.

The three characteristics of symbols are arbitrariness, representativeness, and ambiguity. Symbols are the raw materials of language. Symbols alone, however, do not constitute language.

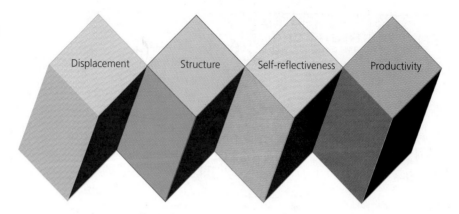

Displacement   Structure   Self-reflectiveness   Productivity

Essential Characteristics of Language

According to linguists, a language must have four characteristics. These are: structure, displacement, productivity, and self-reflexiveness (Figure 4-1).

Structure Language is a *structured system of symbols;* meaning is produced by adhering to certain linguistic rules that create structure. The basic units of every spoken language are sounds, or **phonemes.** (The basic units of sign language are gestures.) Phonemes consist of vowels, consonants, and blends of both. "Cat," for instance, has three phonemes: the "c" consonant (actually a "k" sound), the vowel sound of "a," followed by the "t" consonant sound. Phonemes have no meaning until they are combined in a proper order according to phonological rules. Such a combination produces a **morpheme,** or the smallest unit of meaning in a spoken language. Words, prefixes, and suffixes are morphemes. "Quack" is a word and a morpheme. Add an "s," however, and you have two morphemes: *quack* and *s* that pluralizes. "Dropcloth" is one word but two morphemes: *drop* and *cloth.* "Rewind" has two morphemes: *re* and *wind.*

Sometimes the mere sounds of a word, the arrangement of phonemes into morphemes, can be a source of controversy. In January 1999, David Howard, a member of Washington, D.C. Mayor Anthony Williams' staff, resigned as a result of a public outcry against Howard for using the word "niggardly" in a press conference ("Misunderstood Word," 1999). Mayor Williams, an African American, stated that "Mr. Howard's resignation was prompted by reports that he made an inappropriate racial comment" (p. A2). Niggardly, however, means "miserly" or "stingy" with money. Its first recorded use in English was in the year 1530, and it probably has a Norwegian or Scandinavian origin ("What Dictionaries Say," 1999). It has no historical association with racism. It merely sounds similar to a common racist epithet. As Mayor Williams admitted, "He (Howard) didn't say anything that was in itself racist" (p. A2). Nevertheless, Howard, a white man, resigned his position as a public advocate for the Mayor's office. After a 3-week outcry from around the nation protesting his treatment, Williams reconsidered his acceptance of the resignation and offered to reinstate Howard. Howard asked instead to be placed in a different city government job.

Phonemes cannot be combined meaningfully into morphemes if they do not exist in the specific language. "Quack" is a meaningful English word. "Kqcau" is not, even though it uses the same five letters. English is composed of only certain

Koko is the most famous, and controversial, example of an animal using sign language. Francine Patterson, Koko's trainer, claims Koko has command of almost 1,000 signs.

combinations of sounds, not just any sounds one can make. It does not have words beginning with "kqc" sounds.

Words, even meaningful ones, cannot be strung together randomly and still communicate meaning. Every language has a **grammar**, a set of linguistic rules that specify how sound, structure, and meaning interrelate. **Syntax** is that part of grammar that specifies how words are combined to form meaningful sentences. "Uncle Joe is a heavy man" is a meaningful sentence, but "Man Joe uncle heavy a is" does not conform to English syntactical rules governing noun-verb-object order and placement of adjectives and articles and is therefore gibberish.

Displacement   Language gives us the ability to communicate about "the not here and the not now." We can describe for others what our trip to Hawaii was like 5 years ago, or we can discuss our class schedule for next term. We can communicate about events that have never taken place or may never take place. We can describe worlds of some distant future that likely will never come to pass. No other form of communication has this potential and capability.

Productivity   Language allows us to communicate our thoughts in remarkably creative ways. With the exception of clichés or passages you've committed to memory, every sentence of more than a few words that you write or speak is unique, never having been stated exactly that way before, nor ever likely to be stated that way again. The number of different sentences with a limit of 20 words that an individual could produce in the English language alone is 10 to the 20th power, or one hundred million trillion sentences. It would take approximately a hundred trillion years to speak every possible sentence up to 20 words long if you never took a break and never repeated a sentence (Pinker, 1994).

Box 4-2   Focus on Controversy

Signing Simians: The Debate Over Animals' Linguistic Skills

The first notable results in the effort to teach language to animals were obtained by psychologists Allen and Beatrice Gardner, who claimed that a chimp named Washoe, using hand signs to compensate for lack of speech, showed language capabilities (Gardner & Gardner, 1969). Francine Patterson (1978) created the most attention, however, with a gorilla named Koko. Patterson claimed that Koko had become close to proficient in American Sign Language. Popular books, magazines, and television programs touted these simian antics with semantics. The public was fascinated.

A more sober examination of research results on language capabilities of apes dampened initial enthusiasm, however. Researchers have made several conclusions. First, apes have not been taught American Sign Language. As Pinker (1994) explains, "This preposterous claim is based on the myth that ASL is a crude system of pantomimes and gestures rather than a full language with complex phonology, morphology, and syntax. In fact the apes had not learned *any* true ASL signs" (p. 337). The only deaf signer on the team training Washoe concluded: "I just wasn't seeing any signs. The hearing people were logging every movement the chimp made as a sign. . . . When the chimp scratched itself, they'd record it as the sign for scratch" (Neisser, 1983, pp. 214 , 216).

Second, the vocabulary of even the most capable apes, even if you grant the authenticity of the signs credited to them, doesn't compare to the average lexicon of a young child. A 3-year-old understands more than 1,000 words; a 6-year-old between 8,000 and 14,000 words (Gerow, 1996). The signing simians, even after years of training, know comparatively few signs, a few hundred at most. Francine Patterson claims that Koko, after 25 years of training, knows over 800 signs, but no verification of this claim has been undertaken.

Third, the signing simians exhibit virtually no ability to construct grammatically coherent sentence structure (Pinker, 1994). "Give orange me give eat orange me eat orange give me eat orange give me you" (as cited in Brown, 1986), signed by an ape, is a word salad not a syntactically accurate sentence. Stringing phrases together doesn't constitute language.

Fourth, none of the signing simians has demonstrated self-reflexiveness. Chimps and gorillas don't use signs to discuss their use of signs. No chimp or gorilla has questioned the efficiency of certain signs allegedly taught to the apes. No suggestion from the apes has been made concerning how to improve the sign language training.

Recently, a pygmy chimp named Kanzi, by pointing to symbols on a board, has shown abilities that surpass those of other chimps (Savage-Rumbaugh & Lewin, 1994). Kanzi's linguistic abilities, however, only approach that of the average $2\frac{1}{2}$-year-old child (Plotnik, 1996). Dr. Herbert Terrace, a Columbia University psychologist, claims that Kanzi is merely "going through a bag of tricks in order to get things. If a child did exactly what the best chimpanzee did, the child would be thought of as disturbed" (as cited in Johnson, 1995). Regardless, chimps and gorillas may have mastered at least a rudimentary language capability, and that is certainly worth noting.

The point in comparing animal linguistic abilities with human language capabilities is not to ridicule our ape cousins, despite Mark Twain's comment that "our Heavenly Father invented man because he was disappointed in the monkey." Humans would have a tough time learning the shrieks and hoots that constitute signal communication of apes. Linguist Noam Chomsky argues that "attempting to teach linguistic skills to animals is irrational—like trying to teach people to flap their arms and fly. Humans can fly about 30 feet—that's what they do in the Olympics. Is that flying? The question is totally meaningless" (as cited in Johnson, 1995). Chomsky continues:

> If higher apes were incapable of anything beyond the trivialities that have been shown in these experiments, they would have been extinct millions of years ago. If you want to find out about an organism you study what it's good at. If you want to study humans you study language. If you want to study pigeons you study their homing instinct. Every biologist knows this (as cited in Johnson, 1995).

Language is the unique ability of our species. It is what we are "good at." As philosopher Suzanne Langer (1951) observes: "Language is, without a doubt, the most momentous and at the same time the most mysterious product of the human mind. Between the clearest animal call of love or warning or anger, and a man's [woman's] least, trivial word, there lies a whole day of Creation—or in a modern phrase, a whole chapter of evolution" (p. 94). Learning about language is learning in part about what it is to be human. Language is the window to our minds.

Questions for Thought

1. Do you agree with Chomsky that linguistic research with apes is trivial and pointless?
2. Would you continue the research on ape linguistic abilities?
3. Would you broaden language research to include other species such as dolphins?

Every language has a **lexicon,** the total vocabulary of a language. This lexicon gives you the capability to express your thoughts and feelings with infinite variety. The *Oxford English Dictionary* records more than 600,000 words. Technical and scientific terms, which sprout up like mushrooms in loamy soil, add more than a million words to the lexicon. Since the 1960s, English has acquired about 65,000 new words (Davidson, 1996).

For a speech instructor, it is frustrating to hear student speeches and conversation in which words such as "like," "absolutely," "totally," and "rad" (and new variants sure to be added) appear to be the extent of the creative experiment with language. With a language so rich in vocabulary, limiting our verbal expression by the repetitive use of favorite words and phrases misses the opportunity for unique, creative expression of thoughts and feelings. When you have Shakespeare as the measure of human language potential, why settle for so much less?

Self-Reflexiveness   We use words to refer to objects, events, and relationships, but we also use words about words. This is the **self-reflexiveness** of language. A discussion of Ebonics is an example of self-reflexiveness. This chapter is self-reflexiveness in action. I am using language to explain language and to identify ways to improve our use of this human communication capability.

The Abstracting Process

The abstracting process is a source of several significant problems of language usage. These problems will be discussed later in this chapter. Understanding the abstraction process, however, must come first.

All words are symbols, but all words do not reflect the same level of abstraction. **Abstracting** is the process of selective perception in which we leave out characteristics associated with objects, events, and ideas and focus on certain perceived common characteristics. The hundreds of makes and models of automobiles produced in this century are all classified as cars, even though they differ from each other in size, shape, quality, and price. We classify them as cars on the basis of the characteristics they have in common (engines, tires, steering wheels, seats) and their similar functions, and we ignore all the differences between each make and model.

The abstracting process consists of several levels: sense experience, description, inference, and judgment. Each will be discussed briefly.

Sense Experience   Figure 4-2 illustrates the abstracting process. The parabola represents the world we live in, the territory (a reference to Korzybski's map-territory analogy). The first level of abstracting occurs nonverbally when our sensory receptors are stimulated. As discussed in Chapter 2, our **sense experience** with the physical world is inherently selective. We are limited by the acuity of our senses and the neuronal wiring of our brains. In our day-to-day existence we do not perceive molecules, atoms, electrons, neutrons, protons, and quarks. Most of what composes our physical world is, in fact, not sensed.

The sense experience stage of the abstracting process is the level at which we live our lives. Without language, our experiences would remain essentially private ones. With language, however, we are able to share our perceptions of the world with others.

Figure 4-2 The Abstracting
Process

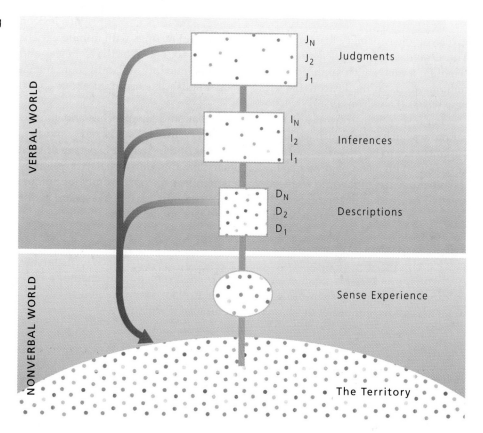

Description   The second level of the abstracting process is a description of our sense experience. **Descriptions** are verbal reports that sketch what we perceive from our senses. They are verbal maps for territories. These verbal maps—labels, classifications, and schemas—are representations of reality, not reality itself. Whenever we describe reality, we distort it. We leave important parts out, and we impose our own perceptual biases on the world around us. Our description of the world is an approximation of the world as we perceive it, not an exact duplicate. Something is always lost in the translation because we are describing what is in our heads, not reality itself.

When our descriptions go from "I am in a committed, long-term relationship with Fran" to "I am in a committed relationship" and finally to "I am living with someone," we have become increasingly abstract. The more general your description, the more details you leave out, the more abstract you are. The potential for confusion and misunderstanding increases as we become more abstract in our use of language.

Inferences   The third level of the abstracting process is the inferential stage. **Inferences** are statements about the unknown based on the known. They are guesses, educated or otherwise. Some inferences are more educated than others because their probability of accuracy is higher. You can infer that a neighbor is not home (the unknown) because newspapers have accumulated on the front porch, the mailbox is crammed, and repeated phone calls connect with a message machine (the known). This is a relatively safe inference, probably true, but it is an inference and not a fact. Your neighbor may be sick in bed, unable to attend to the newspapers, mail, and phone calls.

Inferring from the same information that your neighbor is away on vacation is not as solid as the first inference, because a greater range of possibilities exists to explain the newspapers, mail, and unanswered phone calls. Your neighbor may be away on business, visiting relatives, attending a funeral, searching for a new house, or hiding from the law. This second inference, however, illustrates how you can stack one inference on another, becoming ever more abstract in the process. If your neighbor is away from home, maybe she is on vacation. If she is on vacation, maybe she will be gone for several more days or even weeks, and so on, one inference stacked atop another and another.

Making inferences is unavoidable. The human thinking process is inferential. You'd drive yourself mad if you tried never to infer. In fact, trying not to infer is trying not to think, a dubious undertaking for any college student. Nevertheless, inferences are guesses, and guesses can be inaccurate, even dangerous, as you shall see later in this chapter.

Judgments   The fourth level of abstraction is making judgments. **Judgments are subjective evaluations of objects, events, or ideas.** "My partner is a caring, sensitive, loving person" is a judgment. This statement expresses a highly positive opinion. It appears to be a description, but it is a value judgment, a personal subjective evaluation, not a factual report (Box 4-3).

Judgments, like inferences and descriptions, can be stacked one on top of another in ever-increasing abstraction. For example, you may observe your neighbor spanking his son. Since you are opposed to corporal punishment, you conclude that the father is mean and uncaring. Since he is mean and uncaring, he is probably a bad parent. Because he is a bad parent, maybe he doesn't deserve to raise his son. Perhaps his son should be taken from him? One judgment can lead to a chain of judgments.

Compare the three levels of verbal abstraction in the following statements:

1. The woman sitting behind the desk is frowning.
2. The woman sitting behind the desk is angry.
3. The woman sitting behind the desk is unkind.

All three statements begin the same way, yet the first is descriptive, the second is inferential, and the third is judgmental. To see frowning is a simple observation. To perceive anger is an interpretive process because the woman may look, even act, angry but may be troubled, frightened, or concerned instead. "Unkind" is a judgment that expresses a subjective value of the observer.

The Power of Language

Language has the power to shape the way we think about and perceive people, events, and objects. The power of language is a complex issue. In this section you will learn some of the ways language shapes thought, perception, and behavior.

Box 4-3 Sharper Focus

Judgments and Language Varieties

The Ebonics debate mentioned earlier in this chapter illustrates the stigma that is sometimes attached to language usage. The dominant language of a culture inevitably becomes standardized. **Standardization** means that a language has certain formal rules of "correct" grammar and pronunciation. Judgments of how well or poorly we use the language are gauged by our degree of conformity to these prescriptive rules.

Linguists view grammar and pronunciation from a descriptive, not a prescriptive (judgmental), viewpoint. Linguists identify rules that indicate how a language *is* spoken, not how it *should be* spoken. Linguistically, there is no such thing as an inferior language (Pinker, 1994). "The social acceptability of a particular language variety is totally unrelated to its adequacy as a communication code" (Wolfram & Fasold, 1974, p. 7). In fact, many prescriptive rules of standardized English make little sense. "They are bits of folklore that originated for screwball reasons several hundred years ago and have perpetuated themselves ever since" (Pinker, 1994, p. 373).

We have Robert Lowth, an 18th-century clergyman, to thank for several of our most notable prescriptive rules (Bryson, 1990). Never end a sentence a preposition *with*. The "logic" behind this rule, that preposition means *pre-position*, as in coming before something, is purely arbitrary. Then there is the ban on double negatives. Two negatives make a positive in algebra; it must be so in language as well. Thus, "I ain't got no beer" becomes

"I do indeed have beer," an interpretation wholly removed from human communication as it actually occurs. Finally, there is the like-as distinction. "Telling it like it is" violates the rule. The "correct" form is "telling it as it is." Nevertheless, as far back as the 16th century some people used "like" and some used "as." It wasn't until the middle of the 19th century that "as" became a mark of a "superior person."

It makes good sense for members of a society to learn the standard form of their language in order to communicate efficiently and effectively. Job applications and interviews, for example, require standard English. If you don't know standard English, you will be unable to compete effectively in those arenas where it is expected. Nevertheless, standardization should not provide a basis for diminishing and ridiculing other languages and dialects. Ebonics is not a "poor" version of standard English; it is an English dialect. Some of the grammar rules of Ebonics are different from, not inferior to, standard English. For instance, in Ebonics "He sick" means "He is sick today," but "He be sick" describes a continuing or permanent condition. Standard English allows only the less descriptive, "He is sick."

Different does not mean deficient. Language should be a flexible tool of communication. One style of speaking does not fit all contexts. Knowing when standard English is appropriate and when it is not required separates the ordinary from the proficient communicator.

The Sapir-Whorf Hypothesis

A controversial idea articulated by anthropologist Edward Sapir (see Mandelbaum, 1949), and later popularized and expanded by his student Benjamin Whorf (1956), ignited a debate about what role language plays in shaping thought, perception, and behavior. The **Sapir-Whorf hypothesis** claims that language molds habits of thought and perception and that different languages steer speakers toward different perceptions of reality.

Whorf was not always clear about the degree to which he believed language determines thought. In some of his writings he appeared to believe language imprisons our thinking: we cannot think certain thoughts or perceive in certain ways if our language is not structured to allow us to do so (*linguistic determinism*). Mostly he claimed that the language spoken in a culture powerfully influences thought in ways different from other languages in different cultures (*linguistic relativity*).

Differences in grammar and vocabulary are the chief forms of support for the Sapir-Whorf hypothesis. In his studies of Hopi culture, Whorf claimed that Hopi language had no grammatical time tenses of past, present, and future (a claim that Pinker [1994] vigorously disputes), and thus, the Hopi do not emphasize history, dating, calendars, clocks, and the passage of time. Other grammatical differences between languages have been noted. For instance, speakers of English say "the red wine" (article, adjective, noun), but speakers of French say *"le vin rouge"* (article, noun, adjective: "the wine red"). These and many other differences in the grammatical structures of human languages reflect differences in cultures. They do not, however, prove that such differences in language *cause* differences in thought, perception, and behavior.

Cultures also vary widely in the number of words they have in their respective languages for certain objects and events. Thus, an elaborate vocabulary, so goes the argument, allows speakers of the language to see shades of difference that others who speak a language with a more restricted vocabulary cannot see. The Masai of Africa, for example, have 17 terms for cattle. The Hanunoo of the Philippines distinguish 92 kinds of rice. Trobriand Islanders have dozens of terms for yams. Italian has more than 500 terms for different types of pasta. Arabic has more than 6,000 words for what most of us think is simply your basic ill tempered camel, its parts, and equipment, and American English has an extensive color vocabulary for house paint.

These are interesting differences in languages, but an elaborate vocabulary for an object merely reflects the degree of importance given to this object by a culture. As Dale (1972) explains, "Differences in language prove only that languages differ" (p. 207).

Nevertheless, the availability of a lexicon can serve as an aid to the recognition of objects, events, and ideas that might go unnoticed, and it can enhance our memory of these as well (this is sometimes referred to as the "weak version" of the Sapir-Whorf hypothesis). There have been many studies where colors are more unhesitatingly named, recognized, and remembered when a language has readily available terms for them. Colors that have no such convenient labels are not so easily named, recognized, and remembered (Lantz & Stefflre, 1964).

The Way Language Influences Thought

The fact that only the weak version of the Sapir-Whorf hypothesis is supported by evidence should not lead you to conclude that language has little power. It is not the differences between languages that are so powerful but rather the way language is commonly used.

The Language-Thought Relationship If **thinking** is defined as the "manipulation of mental representations to reach a conclusion, [which includes] mental imagery, concepts, problem solving, and decision making" (Matlin, 1992, p. 697), then thinking is significantly influenced by language. Language influences thought, not in the sense that our ability to think is unavoidably imprisoned by the language we speak but in the sense that when we use language we tend to shape the conclusions we are likely to draw about people, objects, events, and ideas. If we act on those conclusions, language shapes behavior as well as thought.

Consider a study by Langer and Abelson (1974) in which well-trained psychologists and psychiatrists were asked to view a videotaped interview. When the interview was labeled a "job application," they rated the interviewee on the tape as reasonably well adjusted. Psychiatrists and psychologists who viewed exactly the same videotape but were told in advance that they would be viewing a "psychiatric interview" rated the interviewee as more than moderately disturbed. The perceptual set created by the labels dramatically shaped the viewpoint and professional opinion of the psychiatrists and psychologists. If you go for a job interview and two of your letters of recommendation say that you are a "difficult person," can you really believe that such a label will not influence the way the interviewers think about and perceive you? If you don't get the job because of the label "difficult person," are not people making conclusions based on a language label and acting on that label to your detriment?

We can think without language (infants do), but that does not mean language has little or no influence on thought. What kind of thinking occurs when no language is available? Helen Keller, blind, deaf, and unable to speak, experienced a world of chaos and meaninglessness when she had no language to communicate with others. In her book, *Teacher*, Keller (1955) describes the meaninglessness that enveloped her before she learned "finger talk" (an adapted sign language) from her teacher, Anne Sullivan. Referring to herself in the third person as "Phantom," Keller explains: "Phantom did not seek a solution for her chaos because she knew not what it was. . . . All she touched was a blur without wonder or anticipation, curiosity or conscience. . . . For her there was no beauty, no symmetry, no proportion. It was all want, undirected want" (p. 42).

Language is not thought, but language is interconnected with thought. Without language our world is a very different place. When Helen Keller learned finger talk from Anne Sullivan, "the nothingness vanished" (p. 42), not immediately, but gradually over time. Her world became meaningful where before it had been meaningless.

The Defining Power of Language   We use language to define ourselves or other people, events, relationships, feelings, and thoughts. Teachers define students (e.g., smart), physicians define patients (e.g., hypochondriac), bosses define employees (e.g., dependable worker), parents define children (e.g., incorrigible). The power of language to define is not inconsequential. The language we use to define our relationships can affect the quality and success of those relationships with others (Duck, 1994a; Spencer, 1994). When negative labels are used consistently, the relationship deteriorates (Cloven & Roloff, 1991).

The very act of labeling our relationships has vast interpersonal consequences. Relationships that are defined as heterosexual, homosexual, or bisexual can create an in-group versus out-group competitive mentality. "You're one of us" if you define your relationships the way we define ours, but "you're one of them" if you define your relationships differently. We place great stock in labels that define who we are in relation to others.

The Framing Power of Language   Two Irish Catholic priests, Father O'Hara and Father Kelly, disagreed with each other regarding whether smoking and prayer were compatible behaviors. Unable to resolve their differences, they wrote to the Pope to settle the issue. Both priests were triumphant when they received their answers. They were puzzled, however, that the Pope agreed with both of them. Finally, Father O'Hara said to Father Kelly, "What question did you ask the Pope to answer?" Father Kelly responded, "I asked the Pope if it was permissible to pray while smoking. The Pope said that praying should always be encouraged no matter what you are doing." Father O'Hara chuckled, then said, "Well, I asked the Pope whether it is permissible to smoke while praying, and the Pope said that praying is a serious act and shouldn't be trivialized by smoking." The way each priest framed the question determined the answer that he received.

When we use language to shape meaning for others, we are **framing.** Much like a photographer who frames a picture to communicate his or her point of view, so too does language frame problems, events, people, and ideas. Fairhurst and Sarr (1996) state that "frames determine whether people notice problems, how they understand and remember problems, and how they evaluate and act upon them" (p. 4). In other words, language, by its framing power, influences our thoughts and actions.

If you frame an issue to be decided by a group as a contest to be won, the focus of the group will likely be on defeating those viewed as competitors. If the issue is framed as a challenge that requires pooling resources and working together with other groups, the focus will likely be on how best to develop cooperation among groups. "Defeating an opponent" and "working together" are two distinctly different frames for decision making.

In one study (Loftus & Palmer, 1974) participants were asked to estimate the speed of cars involved in an accident, but each individual heard just one of five versions of the question: "About how fast were the cars going when they (smashed, collided, bumped, hit, contacted) each other?" The average estimates for the five variations were: smashed, 40.4 mph; collided, 39.3 mph; bumped, 38.1 mph; hit, 34.0 mph; and contacted, 31.8 mph. Conclusions about the speed of the cars were strongly influenced by a simple change in the intensity of the verb used in the question, even though everyone viewed the same car accident.

Even subtle alterations in language framing can significantly influence the conclusions reached. In one study (Loftus & Zanni, 1975) participants were shown a film of an automobile accident. They were then asked one of two questions: "Did you see *the* broken headlight?" or "Did you see *a* broken headlight?" No broken headlight was shown in the accident filmed, yet participants were far more likely to report that there was a broken headlight when asked about "*the* headlight" instead of "*a* headlight." This very slight change in choice of words biased the perception of participants and influenced the conclusion they reached even when it contradicted what they saw.

Surely you have noticed the effect the simple word *but* can have on a compliment. Suppose a parent compliments a child as follows: "You did a nice job cleaning your bedroom, *but* there is one other thing you can do." Tacking on "but" seems to erase the compliment. Notice what happens, however, when the parent reframes the compliment this way: "You did a nice job cleaning your bedroom, *and* there is one other thing you can do." This second version seems more helpful than critical.

Language and thought are not the same, but language does affect thought, perception, and behavior in significant ways. Labels that we choose can influence our perception and ways of thinking about people, events, and ideas (Box 4-4). Language has the power to define and frame the way we look at our world.

Box 4-4 Focus on Controversy

The Native American Name Frame

In 1995 the state of Minnesota enacted a law ordering counties to rename any natural geographic place with "squaw" in its name. Most of the places with the offending word (Squaw Pond, Squaw Lake, Squaw Creek) were so designated in the 19th century when Whites commonly referred to Native American women as squaws. Originally a corruption by the French of the Algonquin word for "woman," Native American linguists claim that it soon became an obscenity describing female genitals (Schmitt, 1996).

Every county in Minnesota met the legal deadline and replaced the offending word with a suitable alternative—except Lake County in the northern part of the state. "The term 'squaw' is in common use throughout North America, far beyond its Algonquin origin," argued Sharon Hahn, head of the Lake County Board of Commissioners (as cited in Schmitt, 1996). Claiming that it would cost tens of thousands of dollars to replace maps and signs, county officials offered to rename Squaw Creek and Squaw Bay, Politically Correct Creek and Politically Correct Bay.

Glen Yakel, geographic name keeper of the Minnesota Department of Natural Resources, saw it differently. "They're trying to bill this as political correctness, but it's a matter of civility" (Schmitt, 1996). According to the United States Geological Survey's Board on Geographic Names, there are over a thousand geographical places in the United States whose names include the word squaw, including a former site of the winter Olympics, Squaw Valley, California.

Changing the name of a place to eliminate an offending term is not a new idea. In 1967 the Board on Geographic Names ordered 143 places with "Nigger" in their name (this is difficult to believe) to replace the term with "Negro" and 26 places with "Jap" to replace that with "Japanese."

In Utah the battle is over the term "Redskin" used on personalized license plates. Attorney Brian Barnard, on behalf of two Native Americans, Michael McBride and Jay Brummett, filed a formal complaint with the Utah Tax Commission, demanding that personalized plates bearing the word *Redskin* be revoked and removed from use in Utah. Brummett claimed that the word *Redskin* is

the "N-word" applied to Native Americans. Attorney Barnard (1994), noting the relationship between Redskin and the National Football League's Washington Redskins, framed his argument this way, "Could you cheer for the Denver Darkies? Would you paint your face and go to a football stadium in freezing weather to scream for the Spokane Spics? Could you support the Kansas City Kikes? Would you watch the World Series as the Georgia Crackers took on the Nashville Niggers" (p. A9)?

Barnard's complaint was rejected in a split vote of the commission. Speaking for the majority, commissioners Val Oveson and Alice Shearer concluded, "In light of the fact that the term 'Redskin' is used pervasively throughout our society in reference to sports teams, it is the opinion of commissioners Oveson and Shearer that the term 'Redskin' is not 'offensive' and does not express 'contempt, ridicule or superiority'" (p. A9).

Notice in each case how the antagonists framed their positions. In the first case, the debate was framed between political correctness and civility and sensitivity. In the second case, the debate was framed between ethnic slurs and pervasiveness of usage. How would you have decided in each of these cases? Are you persuaded by the pervasiveness or political correctness arguments?

Language is a powerful shaper of thoughts, perceptions, and behavior. Do we have an obligation to respond sensitively to those who are offended by the labels we use? Clearly, some individuals can be inordinately offended by seemingly harmless terms. Nevertheless, the cases cited here may not be so harmless.

Questions for Thought

1. Can other ethnic groups make a similar case against offensive terms used to describe them?
2. One element of the communication competence model is sensitivity. Does sensitivity mean that we must recognize that labels might cause offense? Should we continue to use objectionable terms for groups if asked to stop?
3. Where do we draw the line? When does sensitivity become hypersensitivity? How do we decide?

Competent Language Use: Problems and Solutions

The anatomy and power of language have been discussed so you can understand how language misuse and malpractice occur. In this section, each language problem will be explained, followed by an explanation of solutions for each.

Signal Reactions to Words

An Ohio woman whose name was withheld, filed a criminal complaint in April 1993 against William Gray, a 42-year-old male. What made Gray's crime unusual was that the woman suffered from a psychological condition that caused her to faint at the mere mention of the word *sex*. The complainant charged that Gray found out about her condition and said the word *sex* to her in the lobby of her apartment building. She fainted and allegedly Gray had sexual contact with her. During the preliminary hearing, the woman fainted twice when the word *sex* was used. "She was sitting in a chair and immediately fell out," said Raul Tellez, the defendant's attorney. "Then the prosecutor spelled out the word sex and she fell out again" ("Mere Mention," 1996). This woman had a pronounced signal reaction to a word.

A **signal reaction** is an automatic, unreflective response to a symbol. Although you undoubtedly do not share this woman's unusual affliction, you probably respond signally to words more than you are aware. Responding unthinkingly and ritualistically to pledges, oaths, slogans, ritualized greetings, chants, and buzz words in politics and advertising are a few examples of signal reactions to words. Racist, sexist, homophobic epithets, and verbal obscenity can trigger violent, even tragic, signal reactions.

The political arena is saturated with signal reactions to words. The term *liberal* has become poison. "Feminazis," "welfare queens," "right wingers," "bureaucrats," "socialists," and similar labels are used to discredit opponents during rhetorical fistfights that pass for political debates.

GOPAC, a conservative Republican political action group headed by Newt Gingrich, published a booklet in 1990 entitled "Language: A Key Mechanism of Control." The booklet listed 133 words that candidates could use to slander their opponents and enhance their own images with voters. A candidate could refer to his or her opponent as a "sick, pathetic, incompetent, liberal traitor whose self-serving permissive attitude promotes a unionized bureaucracy and an anti-flag, anti-family, anti-child, anti-jobs ideology." A candidate's self-assessment might describe him or her as a "humane, confident, caring, hard-working reformer who has a moral vision of peace, freedom, and liberty that we can all build through a crusade for prosperity and truth" (as cited in Lutz, 1996, p. 54).

This bushel basket of buzzwords is meant to incite a signal reaction of hatred for an opponent and affection for the speaker. No thought need enter the minds of voters. This is what George Orwell (1949) called "duckspeak," which is "noise uttered in unconsciousness, like the quacking of a duck" (p. 48). Whether it comes from the mouths of conservatives, Republicans, liberals, Democrats, Libertarians, or the politically apathetic, mindless quacking to provoke signal reactions is insensitive and unethical communication.

Reacting signally to words is not always inappropriate, however. If I see a brick falling off a roof and speeding toward your head, I'll shout, "Look out!" If you ponder what I have said instead of reacting reflexively and covering your head, you'll have a very unpleasant experience with the brick. Nevertheless, signal reactions to words are usually inappropriate.

Here are some suggestions for dealing competently with signal reactions:

1. *Recognize signal reactions.* Signal reactions are reflex reactions that short-circuit a thoughtful use of language. Be mindful of the pervasiveness of signal reactions and how easy it is to react to words with a hair-trigger response.

Monitor your communication and the communication of others for signal reactions to words.

2. *Delay your response.* Competent language usage calls for a symbol reaction. **Symbol reactions** are delayed, reflective responses to language, and they are the responsibility of both parties communicating. The person who speaks has a responsibility to avoid words that are likely to provoke signal reactions. The listener has a responsibility to resist reacting signally even when provoked to do so by words chosen by the speaker. A symbol reaction does not mean that your language must be dull and lifeless or without emotion. Humans are not robots. Language can inspire and motivate action, but it should not short-circuit thought. If we engage our minds thoughtfully when words with emotional connotations are used, we can choose to be moved or we can choose to resist. The key is delaying the response and thinking about language, not just reacting to it. Choose to be the master of your language, not its slave.

3. *Ask clarifying questions.* One easy way to produce a symbol reaction is to get into the habit of asking the question, "What do you mean?" If someone says to you "You're a racist," you can respond signally by denying it outright and counterattacking, or you can ask "What do you mean by racist?" This gives you time to collect your thoughts and requires a more thoughtful response from the person making the statement. Refuse to become embroiled in an ugly name-calling contest. If the person refuses to engage in thoughtful dialogue, consider ending the conversation.

Problems of Meaning

Language has two principal types of meaning, denotation and connotation. **Denotation** is the objective meaning of symbols shared by members of a speech community. Dictionary definitions are examples of denotative meanings. **Connotation** is the volatile, private, subjective meaning of symbols. Connotations have *evaluation* (e.g., good–bad), *potency* (e.g., strong–weak), and *activity* (e.g., active–passive) dimensions (Osgood et al., 1957). Connotation is private meaning, so it changes from individual to individual, sometimes only in barely perceptible shades of difference and sometimes in dramatic ways.

To compare denotation to connotation, consider the term *married*. The denotative meaning found in any dictionary is "living together as husband and wife" (although the recent advocacy of gay marriage may amend this definition). The denotative meaning is straightforward, descriptive, objective, and sucked dry of any hint of emotion. If you fear commitment, however, the denotative meaning barely registers in your mind. Your connotative meaning might be "negative, wrong, unacceptable" (evaluation) or "frightening prospect and highly constraining" (potency) that will "keep you doing your partner's bidding" (activity). Another person who embraces commitment may have a different connotation for married, such as "positive, right, and good" (evaluation), which invites feelings of "warmth, intense affection, and great joy" (potency) and is perceived as "constantly challenging and exciting" (activity).

Problems of Denotation   Problems associated with denotative meaning complicate the communication process. Denotation is shared meaning, but we sometimes assume meaning is shared when it is not. Consider the cross-cultural difficulties Britons and Americans have understanding the English language. Our "private school" is Britain's "public school." "Boot" to us is a type of shoe, but to the British it is the trunk of a car. A British "vest" is an American "undershirt." Their "jumper" is our "sweater," and our "jumper" is their "pinafore dress." Clear? Remarking at the dinner table "I couldn't eat anything more; *I'm stuffed*" will invite an awkward silence in England. To be stuffed is to be impregnated. A Briton asking for a rubber in our drug store would be sent to the condom display, not to the school supplies section for an eraser. More than 4,000 English words shared by Americans and Britons have distinctly different meanings in their respective countries. It is little wonder that George Bernard Shaw reputedly remarked, "Great Britain and America are two countries separated by the same language." We cannot assume meaning is shared just because the words are in English and we all speak the language.

The problem of translating from one language into another poses substantial problems of denotation. Without the shared experience of a culture, shared meaning is superficial at best. Bryson (1990) cites several examples of translation problems at the denotative level. When President Jimmy Carter visited Poland in 1977, he wanted to tell the Polish people, "I wish to learn your opinions and understand your desires for the future." His Polish interpreter, however, translated this message as "I desire the Poles carnally." A Chinese restaurant in Santa Cruz, California includes an item on its menu called "rolling lettuce chicken salad," which is chicken rolled in lettuce. A well-known Mexican restaurant in Tucson includes a note on its menu: "The manager has personally passed all the water served here." A Parisian-style dress shop in Los Angeles displays a sign: "Dresses for street walking."

When a Japanese says *Kangae sasete kudasai* ("Let me think about it") or *Zensho shimasu* ("I will do my best"), he or she has actually said "no" in a polite way. This high-context, ambiguous use of language is characteristic of a collectivist culture. U.S. business executives and at least one president of the United States have misconstrued such statements as an understanding or agreement that did not exist. That is understandable because U.S. culture is low-context. Americans take a statement such as "I will do my best" as an explicit commitment to do exactly that.

Problems of Connotation   During the 1968 presidential campaign, a television commercial for Richard Nixon depicted U.S. soldiers fighting and dying in the jungles of Vietnam. Visible on the helmet of one of the soldiers in the last scene was the scrawled word "love." The voiceover for this scene was Nixon's: "I pledge to you: we will have an honorable end to the war in Vietnam." Much to the surprise of Nixon and his advisers, this political commercial drew a chorus of protest, especially from the Midwest. There was fierce objection to the word "love" written on the soldier's helmet. Love wasn't the sort of thing a soldier should be writing on his helmet, the offended viewers indicated. It connoted "radical protest against the war" and "lack of patriotism." The soldier with the offensive word on his helmet was deleted from the commercial for future showings. Shortly after, the agency that produced the commercial received a letter from the mother of the soldier who provoked the outrage. She wrote how thrilled she had been to see her son in a Nixon commercial and thanked the agency for a job well-done. She signed her letter, Mrs. William *Love*.

Connotations are often presumed to be shared meaning, but they are personal, private meanings acquired from each person's unique associations with the word. They can be a source of significant misunderstanding and strife. The terms "negro," "Black," and "African American" all have the same denotative meaning, yet the connotations for these terms vary from individual to individual. Recently, a student asked that I refer to his ethnicity as African American, not Black American. He felt that African American showed more respect. I honored his request. I have had other Black students, however, insist on Black American for exactly the same reason. Showing respect can be difficult when the connotative meaning associated with a label can trigger divergent preferences (Box 4-5).

Here are some suggestions for dealing competently with problems of meaning:

1. *Recognize that connotations are private, not shared, meaning.* You cannot expect others to appreciate fully the way you react to a word.

2. *Employ the same strategies you would use for signal reactions.* Connotation is the principal source of signal reactions.

3. *Clarify denotative meaning.* Don't by-pass. **By-passing** is making an assumption that all parties share the same meaning for a word without determining that this is true. "What does that word mean?" implies that meaning resides in the word, not in the person using the word. A more appropriate question to ask when there is an inkling that confusion exists is "What do you mean when you use that term?" This will determine whether the meaning is shared (denotative) or private (connotative).

Mislabeling

Eight individuals, none with any psychiatric problems, gained admission to 12 psychiatric hospitals in 1972. This was the initial step of an experiment conducted by psychologist David Rosenhan (1973). These pseudopatients gained admittance by complaining to the admissions staff at each hospital that they heard voices that said "empty," "hollow," and "thud." Once admitted, none of the pseudopatients complained of symptoms and, because they all were anxious to leave the hospital, they were very cooperative. The pseudopatients remained in the hospitals from 7 to 52 days (average was 19 days) before being released with the diagnosis "schizophrenia in remission." Ironically, 35 of the hospital patients recognized that the pseudopatients were sane, but no staff member questioned the diagnosis. This is a dramatic example of mislabeling.

Mislabeling is applying a verbal map to an incorrect territory. Word usage is conventional. When words have definitions (denotations) commonly agreed to by a speech community, speakers can't just use the terms unconventionally without causing confusion or harm. Nobody wants to be labeled mentally ill if they are of sound mind. If common usage of the term *organic* means food that is free of pesticides and grown without chemical fertilizers, then you don't want to buy vegetables labeled organic that have pesticide and chemical residues.

Accurate labeling is serious business. Justifiable homicide is far different from premeditated murder. Our system of jurisprudence goes to great lengths to apply these labels accurately according to legal definitions. Dr. Hiroshi Shimizu, while Director of the Speech and Hearing Clinic at Johns Hopkins Hospital, estimated

Box 4-5   Focus on Controversy

Verbal Obscenity

A friend of mine had a 4-year-old daughter named Janie at the time he told me this story. Janie was playing with a neighbor boy about the same age when the boy did something to Janie that made her angry. She yelled at him, "I'm going to shit on your head." Janie's mom heard this and sternly admonished her daughter, "Janie, we don't talk like that." Janie promptly turned to the boy and said, "I'm going to shit on your arm."

Is the offending word Janie used obscene? The perception of obscenity is a subjective evaluation, not a mere description derived from the nature of words or even what they mean. By common agreement we make a judgment that certain words are offensive and obscene. Janie obviously did not understand her mother's objection to a specific word, only to a specific act. This is understandable as the word "feces," which has the same denotative meaning and is freely used in doctor-patient conversation, is neither offensive nor obscene, underlining the subjective nature of the judgment. Janie's offensive term is used often in probably half the movies made in the United States, yet it was banned from motion pictures until the mid-1960s. Although in wide use as early as the 15th century, it was not even perceived as obscene until the early 19th century when Victorian values ruled (Bryson, 1990).

The subjective perception of certain words as obscene can also be demonstrated by considering words that were banned from motion pictures and newspapers until the second half of the 20th century: "virgin," "slut," "tart," "sex," "virtuous," and "bum" (Rothwell, 1982). The 1966 Oscar-winning film *Who's Afraid of Virginia Woolf?* started the demise of language taboos in movies.

Should we ban certain words as obscene? Tennis star Andre Agassi was forced to default a match at the Sybase Open in San Jose, California, in February 1999 when, on three occasions during the match, he used obscenities. Using obscenities on the court is a violation of the professional tennis players' code. Michigan has a law that dates back to 1897 that prohibits cursing or using vulgar or insulting language if women and children may hear the offensive terms. In 1998 Timothy Boomer fell out of his canoe into the Rifle River, about 130 miles from Detroit. A sheriff's deputy claimed that Boomer unleashed a 3-minute tirade of obscenities. A mother and her two children were within earshot. Boomer was given a ticket.

We know that words can hurt. Verbal obscenity was a contributing factor that provoked a "police riot" at the 1968 Democratic National Convention that resulted in widespread beatings of protestors. Verbal obscenity also was instrumental in inciting the killing of four students at Kent State University during a demonstration in 1970 (Rothwell, 1982). Terms that are perceived to be obscene can ignite strong passions. If, however, we banned the use of all words likely to incite violence or strong passions, our language would become bland indeed.

Ultimately, whether to ban words as obscene is a judgment we make as a society, not a description of the nature of words. It isn't the denotative meaning than seems to cause the fuss. Words with the identical referents as obscene terms are judged harmless. It is connotations that trigger the negative judgment. To widely varying degrees, obscene terms provoke the evaluation, potency, and activity dimensions of connotations. It is the association each of us has with the offending words that produces either the judgment "filth" or the question "What's all the fuss about?"

Questions for Thought

1. Can you think of words that have recently become less offensive? Why do you think this has happened?
2. Are there constructive reasons to ban certain words? Which words would you ban? Why? Should children be forbidden to use them?
3. Do you think the list of verbal obscenities will continue to shrink, maybe even disappear altogether, or will new words always be added to the list to replace old obscenities? Explain.

that as many as one third of the 5,000 institutionalized individuals in Maryland labeled "retarded," "brain damaged," or "schizophrenic" instead were probably deaf ("Children Labeled," 1978).

Here are some suggestions for dealing competently with mislabeling:

1. *Define your terms operationally.* This is a crucial communication skill. An **operational definition** pins a verbal map to a specific territory. It indicates what to do or observe to bring the word into your experience. When you ask speakers

The Harvard School of Public Health operationally defines binge drinking as "consuming five or more drinks at one sitting for men, and four or more drinks for women."

to "be specific" or to "provide an example," you are asking them to operationalize their language.

Operational definitions say, "For our purposes an *'A' student* is anyone who scores 90% or above in the class" or *"Severe anxiety* occurs when a person cannot eat, think clearly, remember details, or sleep at night because of stress." The Harvard School of Public Health operationally defines "binge drinking," a problem that affects almost half of the college students in the United States, as "consuming five or more drinks at one sitting for men, and four or more drinks for women" (Kalb & McCormick, 1998). The operational definition of "having sex" or "sexual relations" was at the heart of one of the two articles of impeachment against Bill Clinton. He claimed to the American people and in sworn testimony before a grand jury that he did not have "sexual relations with that woman—Miss Lewinsky." Independent Counsel Kenneth Starr charged Clinton with perjury for this "deception." Clinton, however, operationalized "sexual relations" as sexual intercourse. Fifty-nine percent of a sample of college students in a study by the Kinsey Institute agreed with this operational definition (Brown, 1999). Apparently, so did Monica Lewinsky. The Linda Tripp telephone tapes record Lewinsky claiming, "I never even came close to sleeping with him. We didn't have sex. . . . We fooled around. . . . Having sex is having intercourse" (as cited in "Ex-Pal's Tapes," 1998).

Operational definitions may provide some surprises. A poll of Virginia mental health and legal professionals showed that 20% of those surveyed felt frequent hugging of a 10-year-old was child abuse that justified intervention by state authorities. Over half felt that a parent giving a child a brief good-night kiss on the lips was sexual abuse (as cited in Pendergrast, 1995). Labeling someone a child abuser creates images of horrific treatment of children. Knowing that the term may be defined much more loosely by some can prevent serious misjudgments of people.

2. *Determine whether definitional agreement exists.* The essence of accurate labeling is conventionality (common agreement). For some teenagers, not being asked out for a date on Friday night is a crisis. Parents hardly ever define crisis so broadly. Similarly, you have probably seen this plaque in offices around the country: "Your crisis because of poor planning is not my emergency." What constitutes a crisis may not be shared. If definitional agreement does not exist, it will be tough for others to appreciate your perspective. Less emotive labels may need to be substituted ("All right, I'm experiencing a big disappointment, not a crisis") or a compromise on definitions may need to be negotiated.

3. *Apply labels accurately once the referent for the label has common agreement.* Don't apply a label more broadly than the definition stipulates. It is inappropriate to label a child a slow learner when the problem is that he or she can't see the chalkboard. Use labels according to conventional definitions, not in a random fashion. Labels can stigmatize people. Labeling elderly people senile simply because they have slowed down mentally and physically is inappropriate. Senility is not conventionally defined as merely slowing down.

False Dichotomies

Advice columnist Ann Landers once asked her female readers to answer the question: "Would you be content to be held close and treated tenderly and forget about 'the act'?" Landers received more than 90,000 responses; 72% of these said that they would prefer hugs rather than sexual intercourse. Radio and television talk shows translated these results into a debate on why men are such jerks to women. Many experts claimed the Landers' survey obviously showed that women were starved for affection from their insensitive lovers, willing to forgo sexual consummation for tender caresses from their partners. How would you have responded to the question Ann Landers posed?

If you noticed that Landers presented only two choices as mutually exclusive alternatives when a third choice exists, congratulations, you didn't fall victim to a false dichotomy. A **false dichotomy** is an either-or choice stated in the language of opposing possibilities when clearly more than two opposing possibilities exist. Describing people, objects, or events as moral or immoral, good or bad, rich or poor, corrupt or honest, intelligent or stupid locks us into a mindset of narrow vision and shows the power of language to shape perception and behavior. Shades of gray, not black or white, are usually more accurate options. How many hairs do you have to lose to become bald? If a few hairs grow back, are you no longer bald?

When does a hill become a mountain? When does failure become success? When does a girl become a woman or a boy a man?

If a thousand people were chosen at random and plotted on a graph according to height, weight, age, health, and intelligence, most of these people would bunch in the middle (e.g., average height, weight, etc.) and only a few would fit the extremes (e.g., very tall or extremely short). This result is called a bell-shaped curve, or a normal distribution. *False dichotomies focus our thinking and perception on the extremes while ignoring the vast middle.* Would the "men are jerks" debate have been fueled if the majority of women had chosen a third option, "both hugs and intercourse"?

False dichotomies are presented to us regularly. Is your relationship a success or a failure? Are your teachers good or bad? Do you like or dislike your neighbors? Who are your friends, and who are your foes? Are you a rich student or a poor student? Do you not, however, have *degrees* of success and failure, likes and dislikes, and so forth? Why view the world so narrowly that only two extreme, opposing choices are available?

In some instances only two opposing choices are available. It is difficult to be sort of pregnant or almost a virgin. The win-lose dichotomy created by hyper-competitiveness leaves no room for alternatives in between. You can't be sort of a winner in the hypercompetitive model. It's all or nothing. The cooperative model, however, allows for multiple successes of varying degrees of achievement because you don't have to defeat everyone else to achieve your goal. Success is measured not by defeating others but by achieving goals. The vast majority of dichotomies are false because the either-or choice implies that all possibilities are included in just two opposing options. Clearly this is not the case in most instances.

Here are some suggestions for dealing competently with false dichotomies:

1. *Be suspicious of absolutes.* Few phenomena have only two opposite choices and no others.

2. *Become pluralistic.* Look for multiple alternatives. If asked to respond "yes or no," answer "maybe" and see what happens. When asked whether you are "a conservative or a liberal," respond, "Are those my only two choices?" (You should also ask for an operational definition of both terms.) If asked "Is this moral or immoral?" answer "yes!"—a response that should give pause. Cause others to think about their language usage by refusing to be a party to their false dichotomies.

Dead-Level Abstracting

Wendell Johnson (1946) coined the term **dead-level abstracting** to refer to the practice of freezing on one level of abstraction. The most common form of dead-level abstracting occurs when we speak in generalities and use vague, ill-defined language. When Ross Perot ran for president in 1996, he talked about the importance of "re-engineering" the Social Security, Medicare, and tax systems in the United States. How would he do this? "We'll computer-simulate, test, optimize, and debug," he explained (as cited in Bailey, 1996). This was not a concrete proposal; it was a word salad of high-level abstractions.

James Herriot (1973), a veterinarian in Yorkshire, England, and author of several autobiographical books about his experiences treating various animals in his rural community, relates an amusing instance of conversation buried in dead-level abstracting:

"This is Bob Fryer."

"Good morning, Herriot here."

"Now then, one of me sows is bad."

"Oh, right, what's the trouble?"

A throaty chuckle. "Ah, that's what ah want YOU to tell ME!"

"Oh I see. . . ."

"That's perfectly true, Mr. Fryer. Well, why have you rung me?"

"Damn, I've told ye—to find out what the trouble is."

"Yes, I understand that, but I'd like some detail. What do you mean when you say she's bad?"

"Well, she's just a bit off it."

"Quite, but could you tell me a little more?"

A pause. "She's dowly, like."

"Anything else?"

"No . . . no . . . she's a right poorly pig, though."

I spent a few moments in thought. . . "What are her symptoms?"

"Symptoms? Well, she's just off color, like."

"Yes, but what is she doing?"

"She's doin' nowt. That's what bothers me."

"Let's see." I scratched my head. "Is she very ill?"

"I reckon she's in bad fettle."

"But would you say it was an urgent matter?"

Another long pause. "Well, she's nobbut middlin'. She's not framin' at all."

"Yes . . . yes . . . and how long has she been like this?"

"Oh, for a bit."

"But how long exactly?"

"For a good bit."

"But Mr Fryer, I want to know when she started these symptoms. How long has she been affected?"

"Oh . . . ever since we got 'er."

"Ah, and when was that?"

"Well, she came wi' the others . . ." (pp. 261–262).

Welcome to conversation hell. The pig's owner seems incapable of providing a specific, detailed account, and Herriot is prevented from learning the nature of the animal's illness.

"Define your terms" is a common phrase expressing a desire for greater message clarity, a request for specifics. Yet standard definitions for abstract terms are often just synonyms that remain highly abstract. Look up the word *joyful* in a dictionary and you will likely find it defined as "happy." Look up *happy* and sure enough it's defined as "joyful." If the first term is vague, the synonym is also vague. Consult a dictionary for a definition of *naughty* and it will say "disobedient or guilty of misbehavior." Ask a child to define naughty, however, and you'll likely get a more specific, concrete definition, such as, "It's when you punch your little brother in the face and make him cry."

When politicians use terms such as "civil rights," "democratic ideals," "permissiveness," "governmental intrusion," and "national security," you should insist that they define these vague abstractions with specific details, not mere synonyms that are similarly vague.

The person who persistently uses specific, detailed language—never attaching his or her messages to a more abstract concept, idea, principle, or point—is also dead-level abstracting. This is freezing your language at the lower abstraction levels. Trivia is dead-level abstraction. Factoids are facts isolated from a context, idea, principle, or concept. A list of the names of all the U.S. presidents doesn't say anything important about their role in U.S. history. You can memorize the list without knowing what they did, why they were important, and what is worth knowing about each of them.

Here are some suggestions for dealing competently with dead-level abstracting:

1. *Use language flexibly.* Competent language usage results from a constant interplay among the various levels of abstraction. Political leaders, for instance, should communicate both abstract goals (educational opportunity) and concrete specifics (Head Start programs). Use language flexibly. Don't freeze on vague abstractions or trivial specifics.

2. *Avoid by-passing.* By-passing easily occurs when words become very abstract. We often assume that freedom, justice, honor, and words of this sort have identical meanings for everyone. They don't. Two presidential elections (in 1992 and 1996) became embroiled in a competitive campaign over "family values." All contestants passionately advocated restoration of family values. Almost no one bothered to define what they meant by this vague term.

3. *Operationally define vague terms.* Einstein's conception of relativity is very abstract, yet notice how the great physicist tries to operationalize it for the layperson: "When you sit with a nice girl for two hours you think it's only a minute. But when you sit on a hot stove for a minute, you think it's two hours. That's relativity." When a couple sees a counselor to work out relationship problems, a good therapist will ask for frequent operational definitions. If the husband says, "My wife and I are having a problem," the therapist will ask, "What specific problem are you having?" If the husband responds, "We fight about money all the time," the therapist might ask, "Give me an example of a recent fight you had concerning money." *You don't have to agree with the operational definition for it to be useful.* You might define "insensitive" (or "sexual relations") one way and another person might define it differently. Operational definitions allow both parties to know what is meant specifically. Then you can proceed from there.

Inferential Errors

A story is told about two women from the United States (a grandmother and her granddaughter), a Romanian officer, and a Nazi officer seated together in a train compartment. As the train passes through a dark tunnel, the sound of a loud kiss and a vigorous slap shatters the silence. When the train emerges from the tunnel, no words are spoken but a noticeable welt forming on the face of the Nazi officer is observed by all. The grandmother muses to herself, "What a fine granddaughter I have raised. I have no need to worry. She can handle herself admirably." The granddaughter thinks to herself, "Grandmother packs a powerful wallop for a woman of her years. She sure is spunky." The Nazi officer, none too pleased by the course of events, ruminates to himself, "How clever is this Romanian. He steals a kiss and gets me slapped in the process." The Romanian chuckles to himself, "I am indeed clever. I kissed my hand and slapped a Nazi."

This story illustrates **inferential errors**—the assumption that inferences are factual descriptions of reality instead of interpretations made by individuals. The facts reported are that the four characters in the story heard what sounded like a kiss followed by a slap. The Nazi officer had a welt on his face. Any conclusions drawn from these facts is an inference (a conclusion about the unknown based on the known). It was completely dark in the tunnel, and inferences were made that the sounds heard were that of a kiss and a slap. These are reliable inferences because we've all heard the sound of a kiss and a slap many times, but still inferences, not descriptions of fact. The visible welt on the face of the Nazi officer is further evidence of the reliability of the slap inference. A less reliable inference, however, was made by each person regarding who kissed and slapped whom. Only the Romanian knows the truth.

The seriousness of inferential errors is demonstrated by a true story. In New York City, a woman who spoke only Spanish entered a tavern to get change for a telephone call. Nobody in the bar understood Spanish. The woman became excited. The police were called. When police officers arrived, the woman became terrified. She was taken into custody by the police, placed in a hospital for observation, and held for 5 days. On the fifth day a social worker was sent to her tenement apartment. The social worker found two babies who had died from thirst. The woman had been pleading with police and hospital workers to check her babies. Everyone inferred that she was hysterical and needed mental treatment. No one bothered to get someone who spoke Spanish to translate her pleas.

Professors infer that students who look alert, even nod their heads, understand concepts communicated to them when they may be woefully confused or wrong. You don't have to check every inference you make, but you should check important ones, especially if the quantity and quality of information on which the inference is based are limited or questionable. You should not act on rumor and gossip, except perhaps to put a halt to both, because they are unreliable inferences and have the potential to destroy relationships with others.

Words That Confuse and Conceal

Language can promote clear thinking, or it can confuse and conceal. Sometimes the confusion is unintentional, and occasionally concealment is warranted. Nevertheless, using words to confuse or conceal can be troublesome. Jargon, euphemism, and gobbledygook can make effective communication difficult.

Jargon is an efficient verbal shorthand for those who understand it. To those who do not understand it, however, jargon is gibberish.

Jargon Every profession, trade, or group has its specialized language, called **jargon.** Law, medicine, education, government, business, theology, and other professions all have their own jargon.

Jargon is not inherently a poor use of language. One study (Bross et al., 1972) found that medical jargon allowed surgeons to communicate important factual information briefly and clearly. Jargon is a kind of verbal shorthand. When lawyers use terms such as "prima facie case" and "habeus corpus," they communicate to other attorneys and officers of the court very specific information without tedious, verbose explanation.

Jargon, however, can pose problems for those who do not understand the verbal shorthand. Can you guess what this mountain of scholarly jargonese might refer to: "The cognitive-affective state characterized by intrusive and obsessive fantasizing concerning reciprocity of amorant feelings by the object of the amorance?" Did you guess *love*?

When doctors use terms such as bilateral perorbital hemotoma (black eye), tinnitus (ear ringing), agrypnia (sleeplessness), cephalalgia (headache), and emesis (vomiting), they communicate very specific conditions to medical staff, but they more than likely mystify patients. The message is concealed when it should be revealed to those who most need to know.

During the antitrust trial of Microsoft, a witness gave this answer to an attorney's question: "They would be the user32.dll, U-S-E-R 32.dll; gdi32.dll; kernel32.dll, K-E-R-N-E-L 32.dll; often vgadrv.dll, shdocvw.dll, shell32.dll, advapi32.dll, comctl32.dll, C-O-M-C-T-L 32.dll" (as cited in "The Perils," 1998). Presumably, some of the participants in the courtroom "drama" understood this technospeak, but to most laypeople it probably sounded closer to Klingon than any language they speak (Box 4-6). Imagine the difficulties the judge and attorneys had deciphering the technical code used by witnesses from the software industry?

Box 4-6 Sharper Focus

Jargon of the Computer World

Jargon does not have to be highly technical and dull. Sometimes it can be playful, even amusing. From the high-tech computerland of Silicon Valley come these late 1990s examples:

Batmobiling—putting up emotional shields as in "She started talking marriage and he started batmobiling."
Blowing Your Buffer—losing your train of thought
Carbon Community—the physical world as opposed to the virtual world

Percussive Maintenance—whacking a computer to get it working
Prairie Dogging—when workers who toil in cubicles pop up to look when something grabs their attention
Square-Headed Girlfriend/Boyfriend—your computer
Umfriend—your intimate partner, as in, "This is Sally, my . . . um . . . friend

Competent use of jargon has two guidelines:

1. Reduce or eliminate the use of jargon when conversing with someone unfamiliar with the jargon.

2. If jargon is necessary, operationalize terms unfamiliar to the receiver.

Euphemism Businesses and corporations don't lay off workers anymore; they engage in "force management programs," "repositioning," "schedule adjustments," "duplication reduction," or they give employees a "career-change opportunity." These are euphemisms. **Euphemism** is derived from the Greek, meaning "to speak well of." It substitutes "kinder, gentler" terms for words that hurt, cause offense, or create problems for us. Euphemism is a form of linguistic novocaine that numbs us to unpleasant or offensive realities.

Most languages have euphemisms, but English has the most by far, especially for obscenities and profanities (Bryson, 1990). This should come as no surprise once you learn a little British history. A British Act of Parliament in 1623 outlawed swearing. In 1649 British law cracked down on offensive language in earnest. Children caught swearing at their parents could receive the death penalty. Consequently, English has a vast lexicon of euphemisms for obscenities and profanities that endure even today. Cripes, dang, darn, drat, frick, fricken, gadzooks, goll darn, golly, gosh, gracious, gee whiz, shoot, shucks, and so on are just a few of the euphemisms for common profanities and obscenities, mostly inherited from the British.

Not all euphemisms qualify as language misuse and malpractice. Using "passed away" instead of "dead" is unlikely to cause harm to anyone, and it may cushion an ugly reality for grieving relatives and friends. Nevertheless, euphemisms can create mischief. When the Pentagon refers to an invasion of a Caribbean island as a "pre-dawn vertical insertion," citizens are left in the dark regarding what action was taken. When the nuclear power industry refers to out-of-control nuclear reactors simply going on "power excursions" or experiencing "rapid oxidation" (a major fire), the public is left in a fog. When "unplanned hypercriticality" (approaching a meltdown of the reactor core) can result in "spontaneous energetic disassembly" (a catastrophic explosion), the potential danger is hidden from us. When our government calls killing enemy soldiers "servicing the target," which results in "decommissioned aggressor quantum" (dead bodies), who can guess what's really occurring? When doctors refer to "therapeutic misadventures" (operations that kill patients), we have a clear case of language misuse and malpractice.

Here are two suggestions for dealing competently with euphemisms:

1. *Use Euphemisms Cautiously and Wisely.* This is a judgment call. Substituting euphemisms for profanities and obscenities should cause few, if any, problems. Using euphemisms to confuse, however, can be more problematic. Normally your communication goal should be clarity, not confusion. Confusing with language isn't always evil, but you wouldn't want to make it standard practice.

2. *Expunge Dangerous Euphemisms.* Euphemisms that simply lie to us in order to hide ugly, dangerous truths should be eliminated from our communication in all but the rarest instances.

Gobbledygook Texas Congressman Maury Maverick coined the term "gobbledygook" a number of years ago to refer to the word salads contained in government reports. "Gobbledygook" is incomprehensible language used to confuse. It is inflated babble. When Werner Erhard, founder of the controversial self-help group therapy EST, was asked why he offers EST training when he admitted "nobody needs it," he responded, "I do it because I do it, because that's what I do" (as cited in Gardner, 1981, p. 304). When Senator Edward Kennedy was about to declare his candidacy for president in 1980, he was asked by CBS correspondent Roger Mudd what he would do differently from President Jimmy Carter. His exact response was: "Well, it's um, you know you have to come to grips with the different issues that, ah, that, ah, we're facing—I mean we can, we have to deal with each of the various questions that we're talking about whether it's a question of the economy, whether it's in the area of energy" (as cited in Harwood, 1982, p. 42). No discernable, intelligible meaning is communicated by this jumble of words that purports to communicate a message.

The solution to gobbledygook is simple. Don't use it. If you find others using it, call them on it. Challenge them to make sense.

Summary

Language is not a neutral vehicle of communication. It can powerfully influence our thoughts, perceptions, and behaviors. Language comes naturally to humans, and it is an integral part of our communication process. Language has the power to define, to frame how we perceive events and other people, to incite signal reactions, and to confuse and distort our perceptions and thoughts. Recognizing signal reactions, false dichotomies, dead-level abstractions, problems of connotations and denotations, mislabeling, inferential errors, and words used to confuse and conceal are the first steps in using language competently. Practicing skills such as symbol reactions, operational definitions, and pluralism are the next steps.

Suggested Readings

Bryson, B. (1990). *The mother tongue: English and how it got that way.* New York: Avon. Bryson provides an excellent history of the English language with its many peculiarities.

Bryson, B. (1994). *Made in America: An informal history of the English language in the United States*. New York: Avon. This is a unique view of U.S. history from the perspective of the English language. It is very entertaining.

Orwell, G. (1949). *Nineteen eighty four*. New York: New American Library. This is the classic novel that explores the role language plays in furthering repression.

Pinker, S. (1994). *The language instinct: How the mind creates language*. New York: Harper Perennial. Few academics have the writing skills of Steven Pinker. This book is a superb treatment of linguistics written for a lay audience. It is loaded with interesting information and written with wit and enthusiasm for the subject.

Chapter 5

Nonverbal Communication: Sharing Meaning Without Words

On September 27, 1996, Roberto Alomar, all-star second baseman for the Baltimore Orioles, spat in the face of Umpire John Hirschbeck over a disputed call. The umpires' association threatened to strike over the incident. As Richard Lapchick, director of the Center for the Study of Sport in Society at Northeastern University explains, "There are very few things you could do that would be more obnoxious than spitting in someone's face. It's one of the ultimate signs of disrespect" (as cited in Seipel, 1997). It was a sign of disrespect copied by Denver Broncos linebacker Bill Romanowski a year later when he spit in the face of San Francisco Forty-Niners wide receiver J. J. Stokes and was fined $7,500 for the insult.

When heavyweight boxer Mike Tyson bit off a chunk of Evander Holyfield's ear in the third round of their championship fight, Tyson was disqualified. He received a fine and had his boxing license revoked for a year as punishment for his act. Some commentators wondered why the biting incident provoked such a howl of protest. After all, the point of boxing is to beat your opponent into bloody submission. If your opponent is rendered unconscious in the process, so much the better. It's called a knockout, and the boxer wins accolades for the achievement. Suddenly, the sight of a bloody, disfigured ear sent shock waves through the boxing world. Newspaper headlines reveled in the controversy: "Sucker munch," "Lobe blow for boxing," and "Tyson tastes defeat." Why was ear-biting worse than pounding an opponent into a pulp? Some argued that the biting incident symbolized a sport out of control. Biting is "unmanly" and "unsportsmanlike" conduct that violates the arcane rules of boxing.

Virtually every session of Congress includes a battle to pass a constitutional amendment to protect the American flag from desecration. Consistently three quarters of the American population support the proposed amendment. There have been numerous protests aimed at banning the Confederate flag from parades and public buildings because of its symbolic connection to racism. The Nazi swastika remains a vile symbol of a depraved tyrant and his goose-stepping mass murderers. Imagine the reaction when Nazi swastikas were spray-painted on Jewish graves in Lyon, France, in 1992.

All of these examples show the power and importance of nonverbal communication. Spitting, biting, waving flags, or painting swastikas are not inconsequential acts. They provoke deeply felt reactions. Despite the significance of language to human discourse, nonverbal communication also plays an important role in sharing meaning with others.

The principal purpose of this chapter is to explain the role nonverbal communication plays in the arena of human communication. There are four objectives:

1. to distinguish nonverbal from verbal communication,
2. to establish the significance of nonverbal communication in our transactions with others,
3. to discuss the types of nonverbal codes that have an impact on our communication with others, and
4. to suggest ways to communicate competently with nonverbal codes.

Verbal and Nonverbal Communication Compared

Communication is a lot more than just words. "Actions speak louder than words" is a cultural cliché. **Nonverbal communication** is sharing meaning with others nonlinguistically. Let me explain this definition in more depth by drawing distinctions between nonverbal and verbal communication.

Nonlinguistic Versus Linguistic

The previous chapter identified four essential characteristics of language: structure, displacement, productivity, and self-reflexiveness. Nonverbal communication doesn't possess the four essential linguistic characteristics (Hickson & Stacks, 1989). (Sign language is not nonverbal communication because it possesses all four characteristics of language.) Nonverbal communication is not structured for meaning. It possesses no explicit set of rules, grammar, or syntax. Nonverbal communication does not exhibit displacement because it communicates only about the here and now. Nonverbal communication can show only minimal productivity. For example, new gestures for insults, affection, solidarity with others, and the like are created from time to time, but such nonverbal productivity is rare and insignificant. Finally, nonverbal communication is not self-reflexive. We don't use facial expressions, for example, to communicate about facial expressions. Usually, language is used to explain nonverbal behavior.

Number of Channels

Verbal communication is single-channeled, but nonverbal communication is multi-channeled. You can express enthusiasm verbally by saying, "I can't wait to get started on our project," or you can say, "Wow! Hold me back, I'm ready to burst with excitement." The statements change, but the channel is the same.

The same enthusiasm can be expressed nonverbally through multiple channels: jumping up and down, flailing gestures, wide eyes, smiles, expressive tone of voice, rapid utterances, hugs, screams, to name just a few possibilities. The multi-channel nature of nonverbal communication can add impact and believability to a message. It isn't difficult to lie with words, for instance, but it is extremely difficult to lie convincingly in a dozen nonverbal channels. If the nonverbal channels reveal inconsistent messages, credibility is questioned.

When you say "I'm telling the truth," but your nonverbal communication says "no you aren't," we tend to believe the nonverbal message. Because nonverbal communication is more spontaneous, is physiologically based, and has to be consistent in more than one channel, it seems more believable and genuine.

The adult pattern of relying on nonverbal messages when verbal and non-verbal messages conflict is not typical of children. Infants begin life depending solely on nonverbal communication. Once language develops, however, children rely primarily on verbal communication (Burgoon, 1985). Verbal comments are taken literally by young children. Sarcasm, which is indicated by tone of voice and facial expressions, belies the verbal message. One study found that children only gradually learn to understand sarcastic messages. A mere 14% of kindergartners understood a teacher's sarcasm, but this gradually increased to 39% of 3rd-graders, 52% of 9th-graders, and 66% of 12th-graders (Andersen et al., 1985).

Box 5-1   Focus on Controversy

Deciphering Nonverbal Courtship Cues

David Givens (1983), in his once-popular book *Love Signals*, offered this advice to men courting women:

Men might try the following signals: Face to face with a woman, speak slowly. Tilt your head to one side and nod as she makes her points, to show you're listening. Lean forward, align your shoulders with hers, hold your face tipped down slightly toward the floor . . . and gaze upward into her eyes from under your eyebrows. Look for three seconds at a time, then drop your gaze to the table for three seconds before meeting her eyes again. Don't turn your head away to the side; keep it still as you listen. (pp. 207–208)

Givens claims that this courtship-by-the-numbers is powerful. He offers abundant specific advice on how to manipulate people into liking and falling in love with you by both accurately reading and displaying precise nonverbal cues.

As I write this, I'm looking at an advertisement I received in the mail from *Men's Health* magazine. "Inside: 10 female flirting signals that secretly say 'I want you!'" says the envelope, urging me to investigate further. On the inside (I opened the envelope with purely academic interest) I'm told "how to know what a woman's body language is really telling you." Simply by purchasing this book I can discover the "seven secrets of seduction" and signals of "mating magic."

The mistake both Givens and *Men's Health* make—aside from the questionable ethics implicit in manipulating others for personal benefit—is that their advice is based on a false premise. Both assume that nonverbal communication can be decoded with precise accuracy simply by carefully and knowledgeably observing the signals transmitted by others. This is not the case.

Mass market publications continue to offer such advice on courtship behavior and mating rituals. "How to use body signals a woman can't resist" trumpets the *National Enquirer*. These "irresistible signals" include copying the woman's gestures, flexing muscles, touching her arm as you talk, eyeing her body up and down, moving into her "privacy bubble," preening, and physically guiding her into a private place. This nonverbal communication may work with some women, but in more cases than not such behavior will likely produce some very unpleasant, possibly even legal, repercussions.

Questions for Thought

1. Should we ever try to use nonverbal cues to convince others to like us? Why or why not?
2. Is there any truth in the *National Enquirer* list of "irresistible signals" that "women can't resist"? How do you think a woman would likely respond to such nonverbal communication? Why?

Degree of Ambiguity

Nonverbal communication is at least as ambiguous as language, probably more so. This point was made abundantly clear by rock musician Frank Zappa when he appeared on a television talk show hosted by an obnoxious individual named Joe Pine. This incident occurred in the 1960s, when a person's physical appearance, especially hair length for men, symbolized nonconformity, rebelliousness, and antiwar sentiments. The most distinctive aspect of the show was Pine's shabby treatment of his guests, whom he tried to make look foolish. Pine had an amputated leg, but this was unremarkable until Zappa appeared on the show. When Zappa, sporting shoulder-length hair, was introduced to the audience, the following exchange took place:

PINE: I guess your long hair makes you a girl.

ZAPPA: I guess your wooden leg makes you a table (as cited in Cialdini, 1993a, p. 224).

Zappa's laser-quick ad lib exposed the absurdity of treating a nonverbal cue (e.g., hair length) as if only a single meaning could be attached. Meaning isn't embedded in the nonverbal **cue** (anything that triggers meaning). Hair length has

Box 5-2   Sharper Focus

The Nanny Trial

In 1997 Louise Woodward, a British teenager who was employed as a nanny by an American couple living in Newton, Massachusetts, was found guilty of manslaughter for the death of an infant under her care. Jonathon Raban (1997), also British and living in America, had an interesting take on this highly controversial trial. Regarding the truthfulness of Woodward's testimony claiming that the infant's death was an accident, Raban says, "My English eyes saw one thing; my American-resident eyes saw something else altogether" (p. 55).

Raban's "English eyes" observed a Louise Woodward with "shoulders hunched submissively forward, eyes lowered, voice a humble whisper. Ms. Woodward made a good impression as an English church mouse. Her posture announced that she knew her place; that she

acknowledged the superior authority of the court; that she was a nobody." He concluded, "I thought she was telling the truth" (p. 55).

Raban's "American-resident eyes" saw something quite different. "My second pair of eyes saw Ms. Woodward as sullen, masked, affectless, dissembling. Her evasive body language clearly bespoke the fact that she was keeping something of major importance hidden from the court." He concluded, "I thought she was telling lies" (p. 55).

Raban's dual-culture perspective of this widely publicized event emphasizes the ambiguity that results from having to interpret nonverbal cues. Different cultures may interpret the same nonverbal cues in strikingly different ways.

---

no meaning apart from those who observe it anymore than a wooden leg has an inherent meaning. We have to interpret nonverbal cues. With interpretation comes ambiguity (Box 5-1).

Can you "read a person like a book," as is so often asserted in the popular media? Consider the fact that even "experts" in lie detection do poorly when trying to determine truth-tellers from liars. This is primarily because, as Ekman (1992) explains, "There is no sign of deceit itself—no gesture, facial expression, or muscle twitch that in and of itself means that a person is lying" (p. 80).

In one study, 509 participants composed of polygraphers, psychiatrists, court judges, police detectives, and Secret Service agents were asked to detect deception. All of these people worked in professions where deception is a common occurrence and an important issue. Nevertheless, only the Secret Service agents did better than chance (i.e., guessing) detecting deception from nonverbal cues (Goleman, 1991). In another study, highly educated, well-trained child abuse experts, confident that their intuition and experience would enable them to discern true from false allegations, actually performed *worse* than chance. They concluded that the children who gave *the greatest amount of misinformation* were most credible (Horner et al., 1993).

If the experts have trouble accurately reading nonverbal communication, how do the rest of us do? Despite a tendency toward overconfidence, most of us don't do all that well. Women, however, tend to be more accurate decoders of nonverbal messages than men, and middle-aged people tend to be better at reading nonverbal communication than younger individuals (Rosenthal, 1979). Knowing the individual well markedly aids the accurate perception of nonverbal cues.

The ambiguity of nonverbal communication is a source of significant misunderstanding between cultures (Box 5-2). In the United States the "thumbs-up" gesture means "all right!" or agreement. In Sardinia and Northern Greece, however, it means the disdainful "up yours!" Upraised palm with fingers moving back and forth signals "come here" in the United States, but in Italy, China, and Columbia it means "good-bye" (Jandt, 1995).

Figure 5-1 Characteristics of Nonverbal Language

| Ambiguous | Multichanneled | Continuous | Unintentional |

Some nonverbal cues have universally shared meaning. Smiles and laughter signal pleasure and enjoyment the world over. A fist is a sign of anger and aggression virtually everywhere. Nevertheless, cultures have different display rules that govern when and where such nonverbal cues can appear. Boisterous laughter, for instance, is less acceptable in Japan than in the United States.

Accurate perception of ambiguous nonverbal cues will likely improve the more intimately familiar we are with the context in which nonverbal communication occurs. Couples in happy relationships, for example, tend to sit closer together than unhappy couples. When we feel psychologically distant from another person, we often create a physical distance as well. When individuals in relationships argue, it is not unusual for them to leave the room when the argument goes badly. Nevertheless, assuming distance between partners in a relationship always communicates tension or strife is too simplistic. Some couples rarely touch each other in public or private. Other couples touch each other frequently. You have to allow for individual preferences and personalities. Couples that touch rarely may be as happy or even happier than couples that touch often. You can best determine this by knowing the couples well. Simple observation of strangers will produce dubious results.

Discrete Versus Continuous

Verbal communication has discrete beginnings and endings. We begin sentences when we start talking, and we end them when we stop talking. Nonverbal communication, however, has no discrete beginning and end. We continuously send messages for others to perceive, even when we may wish not to do so.

Consider facial expressions, for example. Try not to display any facial expressions at all while another person looks at you. It can't be done. Even a blank stare is a facial expression that communicates a message. Others may perceive your blank stare to mean that you're introspective and are thinking deeply or that you don't want to be bothered by anyone or that you're inattentive, sullen, or disdainful.

Nonverbal communication is frequently unintentional. We blush, blink our eyes rapidly, and shuffle our feet without necessarily intending to do so. We are sharing meaning with others without necessarily wanting to share. As you stand

What emotion is exhibited in this photo? Turn the page to find out.

before an audience giving a speech, you may want desperately to hide your nervousness. Nevertheless, your knees may be knocking, your voice may be quavering, and perspiration may be forming on your brow. The nonverbal message that you are experiencing speech anxiety leaks out.

Keeping our thoughts hidden from others is relatively easy if verbal communication is the focus. Just don't say anything. Nonverbally, however, hiding our thoughts is far more challenging because nonverbal cues can continuously leak information about our thoughts (Figure 5-1).

Significance of Nonverbal Communication

Some experts claim that nonverbal communication is more important than verbal communication. Estimates vary from claims that 93% of the meaning or impact of a message is communicated nonverbally (Mehrabian, 1981) to claims that 65% of the social meaning of a conversation or interaction is communicated nonverbally (Birdwhistell, 1970; Philpot, 1983). The exact percentage is unimportant, and somewhat dubious, but clearly nonverbal communication often has a greater impact on receivers than does verbal communication. This is a remarkable

Oksana Baiul has just heard the announcement that she has won the 1996 Olympic figure skating gold medal. Did you guess joy was the emotion expressed? Nonverbal communication can be ambiguous.

conclusion considering the power of language to shape thought, perception, and behavior.

Verbal and nonverbal communication are interconnected. We don't speak without embellishing the words with gestures, facial expressions, tone of voice, eye contact, and so forth. A more complete way of appreciating the significance of nonverbal communication is to explore the many ways nonverbal codes interact with verbal codes. In this section you will note several ways verbal and nonverbal codes interconnect (Ekman & Friesen, 1969).

 ### Repetition

We say "Yes," then nod our head. We give verbal directions, then point in the appropriate direction. We profess our love for a person, then hug them. We curse at another driver, then shake our fist for emphasis. All of these nonverbal cues repeat the verbal message. This repetition diminishes ambiguity and enhances accuracy of message perception. *Consistency of verbal and nonverbal communication increases the clarity and credibility of the message.*

 ### Accentuation

When we use vocal emphasis such as "*Please* don't touch anything in the store," this accents the message. It adds emphasis where it is desired. "Don't you *ever* say that word" accents the unqualified nature of the verbal message. Pounding your fist on a table as you express your anger nonverbally repeats the message but also accents the depth of your emotion. Accenting enhances the power and seriousness of verbal messages.

Substitution

Sometimes nonverbal cues substitute for verbal messages. A yawn can substitute for the verbal "I'm bored" or "I'm tired." A wave can substitute for a "good-bye." An "uh-hum" can serve as a replacement for "I understand." Shaking your head "no" doesn't require a verbalized "no." We signal interest in courting another person without actually having to express this message in words. Eye contact, smiling, forward leans, room-encompassing glances, close distance, frequent nodding, and hair smoothing are just some of the nonverbal flirting cues (Muehlenhard et al., 1986). A later stage of courtship, sexual initiation, is usually accepted nonverbally but rejected verbally (Metts et al., 1992).

Regulation

Conversation is regulated by nonverbal cues. Turn taking is signaled by long pauses at the end of sentences and eye contact in the direction of the person expected to speak next, especially if the conversation occurs in a group. Interruptions may be prevented by speeding up the rate of speech, raising one's voice over the attempted interruption, or holding up one's hand to signal unwillingness to relinquish the floor. A teacher can recognize a student's desire to speak by pointing to the person. This means "Your turn."

Contradiction

"Sure, I love you," when said with eyes cast sideways and flat vocal tone doesn't exactly inspire believability. Sometimes we contradict verbal messages with nonverbal cues. These are **mixed messages,** inconsistencies between verbal and nonverbal messages. The words say one thing, but gestures, facial expressions, eye contact, posture, tone of voice, and physical proximity leak contradictory information. Leathers (1979) found that mixed messages had a highly disruptive impact on problem-solving groups. Mixed messages produced tension and anxiety, and group members found it difficult to respond to mixed messages in socially appropriate ways (Leathers, 1986).

Types of Nonverbal Communication

The definition and significance of nonverbal communication has been discussed. The main types of nonverbal communication used during transactions with others will now be explored.

Physical Appearance

He got his first tattoo—a rosary with a cross, etched on the back of his right hand—when he was 11 years old. At 13 he had Chinese characters that translate to "trust no man" tattooed on his left shoulder. At 16 an ornate cross that memorialized his dead older brother was added to his right hand. All of these tattoos were rites of passage into gang life in Watsonville, California for Mando (no last

Box 5-3   Focus on Controversy

Is Beauty Really Skin Deep?

Are there any universal standards of physical attractiveness, or does culture and individual taste determine what is attractive and therefore desirable? Certainly culture has an influence. Ubangi women insert wooden disks into their mouths to stretch their lips up to 10 inches in diameter. Some cultures prefer plump over skinny, whereas other cultures prefer the opposite. The "ideal" voluptuous female figure of the 1950s is considered fat by today's American beauty standards. There are also individual differences in what is considered physically attractive. Some women find the male body builder physique extremely attractive, and other women think it is repulsive.

Some universal standards of attractiveness, within a broad range of possibilities, seem to define physical attractiveness in all cultures. For example, a healthy look is preferable to a sickly appearance the world over. There is no evidence that rotting teeth, open skin sores, acne, or head lice are perceived as attractive in any culture. Small wonder that Americans spend so much time and money fussing over facial flaws and blemishes. Any one of these problems can have a significant effect on one's self-esteem.

Second, symmetry seems to be a universal attractiveness characteristic (Springen, 1997). Diverse cultures favor bilateral symmetry—that is, the right and left sides should match. Lopsided features of the face (one eye slightly lower than the other, a crooked mouth or nose, ears uneven) are perceived to be less attractive than more symmetrical features.

Third, the waist-to-hip ratio in women was found to be a more important characteristic than facial features, height, body weight and other physical attributes (Singh, 1993). The lower the waist-to-hip ratio—the smaller the waist is compared to the hips—the greater the perception of attractiveness. This is true whether those judging the female shape were 8 or 80 years old, or from different cultures and backgrounds (Springen, 1997). The "ideal" shape was a .70 waist-to-hip ratio (the waist is 70% the size of the hips). The range of perceived attractiveness, however, ranged rather broadly from .60 to .80.

Despite the marked change in preferred weight of women reflected in the Rubenesque female of the Renaissance era to the current waif-like body types, the waist-to-hip ratio preference still applies. Singh (1993) found that *Playboy* centerfolds and Miss America winners from 1923 to 1990 stayed within the narrow waist-to-hip ratio of .68 to .72 even though height and total weight varied significantly. Despite the "thin is in" images presented in the mass media, the size of the female body doesn't seem to be an essential characteristic of physical attractiveness. The shape matters more.

name given). "I had found a way of life," he explains simply (as cited in Barnett, 1996). After his brother's death, however, he began questioning his way of life and looking for alternatives. When he searched for a job, though, he found that potential employers would eye his gang tattoos and say, "Sorry, we don't have any openings."

Mando is only one of over 2,000 youths in Santa Cruz County who want to remove their gang-related tattoos and make a fresh start. The county's Youth Resource Bank began a tattoo removal program to help these youths find employment and turn their lives around. Mando was 18 when he had his tattoos removed. Other counties in California, Illinois, and Arizona have started similar tattoo removal programs. Santa Clara County Superior Court Judge LaDoris Cordell states, "It's certainly an excellent thing to do. From my talking to kids it's a liberating experience to be rid of the mark on them because these kids get stereotyped very quickly, even if they decided to cut their gang affiliation" (as cited in Garcia, 1996).

Physical appearance, from adornments we put on our bodies to physical features we accentuate or camouflage, is of no small concern to us. Morris (1985) claims: "Nothing fascinates us quite as much as the human body. Whether we

(*continued*)

Some research suggests that relatively broad shoulders and narrow waist and hips is an attractive physique for men (the wedge shape). Thus far, however, no ratio similar to the waist-to-hip ratio in women has been documented for male attractiveness.

Finally, an average looking face is considered more attractive than a face with extreme features (Langlois et al., 1994). Exotic noses, tiny lips, and so forth are less attractive as a rule than average noses, lips, and eyes.

Despite these universal standards of physical attractiveness, other nonphysical attributes influence perceptions of physical attractiveness. Women, for instance, rated men as more physically and sexually attractive if they were considerate of others and showed sensitivity (Jensen-Campbell et al., 1995). Chalk up another advantage for the competent communicator. The We-orientation can alter perceptions of physical attractiveness. Beauty can be more than skin deep.

Physical attractiveness is clearly a human bias that affects communication. In a hypercompetitive society, attractiveness too often is skin deep because every attribute that seems to accord a person even a slight advantage when competing for jobs, friends, partners, and lovers becomes exaggerated in importance. We're looking for an edge. If attractiveness is perceived to be an important competitive attribute when vying for a promotion, trying to impress a date, or winning an award, we are encouraged to communicate attractiveness with our bodies. When competitiveness is deemphasized and cooperation is enhanced, physical characteristics that provide a competitive advantage become less important. Those characteristics that help the group (e.g., knowledge, skills, ability to work with others) or enhance a relationship (e.g., loving, caring, regard for partner, sense of humor) become central concerns. Physical attractiveness will always play a part in human transactions, but it becomes less important as we get to know a person at a deeper level through communicating with them.

Questions for Thought

1. Do you agree that we are overly concerned with physical attractiveness in the United States? Why or why not?
2. Should we accept our looks and body shape as they are, or should we try to enhance them to be attractive to others? Why or why not?
3. Do you think the universal standards of beauty identified here make much difference in your perception of the attractiveness of others? Explain.

realize it or not, we are all obsessed with physical appearances. Even when we are engaged in a lively conversation and seem to be engrossed in purely verbal communication, we remain ardent body watchers" (p. 7).

Physical Attractiveness   Perceptions of physical attractiveness occupy considerable attention in American culture. The American obsession with physical appearance is dramatically evident in the increasing popularity of cosmetic surgery. Every year almost 400,000 surgeries are performed to make people look younger, more attractive, and more vigorous (Kato, 1996, p. C8). The link between physical attractiveness and hypercompetitiveness in our society is revealed by some of those who opt for cosmetic surgery.

Michele Kelly, who owns a public relations firm, explains why she had plastic surgery performed: "I'm in a competitive job market, dealing with people in their 20s and 30s. I just wanted to look the best I can" (as cited in Kato, 1996, p. C8). Dr. Alan Gaynor, a San Francisco cosmetic surgeon, states, "More than ever, our boom in business as cosmetic surgeons is driven by the local economy. . . . They (clients) see it (surgery) as something they want to do to look competitive as they search for new work" (as cited in Kato, 1996, p. C8).

Yale psychologist Alan Feingold and his research assistant Ronald Mazzella found that the number of women in the United States who are unhappy with their body image has increased steadily since 1970. Feingold explains: "In the workplace, women face heightened pressure to be attractive, which makes them more vulnerable to poor body image" (as cited in Billie & Chatterjee, 1998, p. 22). They have to compete for acceptance, promotions, pay raises, and responsibilities, and appearance matters. Thomas Shanks, director of the Center for Applied Ethics at Santa Clara University, laments this surgery-to-compete trend. "It's a sad commentary on our society that people feel they can only compete if they look good. Has our value system eroded to the point where we've determined that youth and attractiveness are more important than integrity or responsibility" (as cited in Kato, 1996, p. C8)?

Those who opt for plastic surgery typically experience a boost in self-esteem and body image. Communication behavior also changes. "Typically the change in communicative behavior after plastic surgery seems to manifest itself in a drastic reduction in inhibitions and in an openness, candor, and trusting type of behavior which is the ideal sought by so many authorities in interpersonal communication" (Leathers, 1976, p. 107).

Physical attractiveness is an important nonverbal cue because first impressions rely so heavily on the most obvious cues. When we know little or nothing about a person, we formulate impressions based on the little information we have, and how attractive a person looks is a nonverbal cue that we see immediately when first meeting a person (Box 5-3).

Physical attractiveness provides certain advantages. Attractive individuals are perceived to be "more sociable, dominant, sexually warm, mentally healthy, intelligent and socially skilled than physically unattractive people" (Feingold, 1992, p. 304). The attractiveness bias begins early (see Knapp, 1980). Preschoolers liked attractive children most, but unattractive children least. Unattractive children were blamed more for naughty behavior. Teachers are not immune to the attractiveness bias (Ritts et al., 1992). Attractive students receive more favorable judgment from teachers than do less attractive students. They are perceived to be friendlier, more intelligent, and more popular than their less attractive peers. Physical attractiveness is also a highly significant aspect of courtship and marriage. Numerous studies show that mate selection is heavily influenced by physical attractiveness (Knapp, 1980).

The news on good looks is not all positive, however. Attractive individuals may be perceived as vain and self-centered, especially if their good looks seem to occupy too much of their attention (e.g., primping, posing, etc.). Narcissism—the love of one's own image—isn't usually thought to be attractive. Attractiveness was also found to be detrimental to female managers who tended to receive less favorable evaluations than less attractive employees (Heilman & Stopeck, 1985).

Clothing Physical appearance can be enhanced or diminished in a variety of ways. Clothing expresses a person's identity. "It is impossible to wear clothes without transmitting social signals. Every costume tells a story, often a very subtle one, about its wearer" (Morris, 1977, p. 213). One study of dress in an international airport reported Tongans wearing ceremonial gowns, Sikhs in white turbans, Africans in white dashikis, Hasidic Jews in blue yarmulkes, next to Californians in running shorts and halter tops (McDaniel & Andersen, 1995). The variety of clothing choices is astonishing.

Clothing matters. Dress communicates social position, economic status, level of sophistication, social background, educational level, even moral character (Thourlby, 1978). Just observe the reactions to dress codes. School uniforms have become increasingly popular in elementary and high schools around the nation—not popular with students but with administrators and parents. Parents and school boards opt for uniforms to combat gang violence at schools provoked by gang colors and attire and to instill a stronger focus on school work, not wardrobe. Strict dress codes often substitute for actual uniforms in many schools. Again, students object to the restriction on their "freedom of expression" and the conformity that rigid dress codes require.

Ironically, as dress codes become more restrictive in schools, they are becoming looser in work environments almost everywhere in the United States. The business suit for men and the power suit for women are losing their popularity. Casual attire—jeans, athletic shoes, shirts/blouses—is the dress of choice. One survey of 505 personnel managers in a wide range of businesses shows that 9 out of 10 companies nationwide let inside office staffers dress casually all or part of their work week ("The Dress-Down," 1996). Casual dress has become a serious issue in job negotiations. The new dress-down policies help businesses attract top talent, say the managers surveyed. There's a simple reason for this—people prefer comfort to discomfort.

Even casual attire, however, has rules of appropriateness. *Clothing choices communicate messages* (Gottschalk, 1996). Casual dress at work does not include tight-fitting clothes (too provocative), cutoffs and bare midriffs (too sloppy and unkempt looking), tank tops (too recreational looking), sleeveless muscle shirts (too self-absorbed looking), nor running shorts, sweatpants, and sweatbands (gym attire). Clothes should be neat, clean, unwrinkled, loose fitting, and undamaged (no rips or holes). Casual dress doesn't mean unprofessional looking.

Appropriate dress is an issue for teachers. One study (Morris et al., 1996) found that formal professional attire receives the highest instructor competence ratings from students, with casual professional dress a close second. Casual dress, however, produced the highest sociability ratings (e.g., sociable, cheerful, good-natured) from students. Interesting presentation of material was also associated with casual instructor dress. Casual professional dress seems to make instructors more approachable and more interesting from the student vantage point.

Hair   Another significant element of physical appearance is hair. Hair style expresses self-concept. Hair styling is big business. A "bad hair day" can be cause for alarm. Losing your hair can send a person into therapy.

Hair has enormous communicative potential. Philip Dau, a fifth-grader at Woodland School in Menlo Park, California, was suspended from school for a week in 1996 because his hair was too short. "The kid's head was shaved, OK? And that's just not appropriate," asserted school director Lynne Nelson (as cited in Clendenin, 1996).

The short-cropped hairstyle became a national issue in 1994 when Shannon Faulkner attempted to be the first woman to enter The Citadel, a military college in South Carolina. The issue concerned whether or not she should receive the same

Box 5-4   Sharper Focus

When a Woman Loses Her Hair

Hair is intricately connected to self-concept and self-esteem. The billions of dollars spent each year on hair transplants, hair restoration products, and wigs is testament to how deeply men, in particular, cherish their hair follicles.

When a man's mane wanes, we know this is cause for panic, but what happens to a woman who loses her hair? Martha Chiarappa began losing her hair when she was 33 years old. Her baldness was caused by a condition called alopecia areata. Devastated by the news of her affliction, she watched helplessly as her hair fell out in clumps over a period of weeks. She began wearing a bandanna all day, even to bed. She was petrified to show her husband and her two daughters what she looked like without hair. She cried a lot. One day, when she was wiping tears from her eyes, she saw clumps of lashes on her fingertips. More were scattered on her cheeks. She knew that all of her hair was falling out—eyelashes, eyebrows,—all of it. Martha began wearing a wig. When she finally got the courage to show her husband and children what she looked like without hair, they

were very loving and supportive. One of her daughters joked, "You're lucky, Mom. Your hair always looks good!"

Martha's wig, however, was problematic. "I couldn't go anywhere without worrying about my wig staying put; when shopping, I'd push the cart with one hand and keep the other free, just in case. In restaurants, I'd sit by the wall to avoid waiters who might knock it off as they rushed by" (as cited in Chiarappa, 1996, p. 36).

Martha began a support group for alopecia sufferers. Eventually, she found an Australian wig maker who fashioned a custom-fitting wig for her. "The day my hairpiece arrived is right up there with my wedding day and the births of my daughters. . . . I looked in the mirror and saw myself again. Not only that, I could be myself again" (p. 40). Her self-esteem was boosted enormously. She became a distributor for the Australian wig maker. More than 15 years later, her hair still has not grown back. As she puts it, "I'm good for a couple of cries a year. But most of the time, I'm just too busy to worry about my hair" (p. 40).

"knob" haircut all the male cadets receive on entering the school. The doorknob shaped haircut has a communicative purpose. "The whole point is the subjugation of the individual to the interests of the group," explained Dawes Cooke, attorney for the school. "Many cadets have described that haircut as the most humiliating moment of their lives" (as cited in Goodman, 1996). "Shave Shannon" bumper stickers emerged all over South Carolina. The issue went to court. The same judge that forced the college to accept Shannon Faulkner ruled: "The Citadel is perfectly at liberty to treat the hair on her head the same way it treats the hair of every other cadet" (as cited in Goodman, 1996). This decision was not well-received by women's groups. They argued that Shannon Faulkner was being targeted for harassment because she dared to enter an all-male bastion of power. The buzz cut hairstyle is far more humiliating, they claimed, on a woman than on a man (Box 5-4). The military hairstyle is a rule made by men with no female input or influence.

Facial Communication

Your eyes and face are the most immediate cues we use to form first impressions. In this section you will see how your eyes and face can have an impact on communication with others.

Eyes   Boston College neuropsychology professor Joe Tecce claims stress can be measured by how often someone blinks. Tecce examined the 1996 presidential and vice-presidential debates and found some interesting results. The normal blink rate of someone speaking on television, according to Tecce, is between 31 and 50 blinks per minute. Republican presidential contender Bob Dole averaged 147 blinks per minute. His highest blink rate was 163—nearly 3 blinks per second—when asked the question, "Is the country better off than it was four years ago." President Clinton, who averaged a mere 43 blinks per minute in the 1992 presidential debates with George Bush and Ross Perot, averaged a surprising 99 in the 1996 debate. Clinton spiked to 117 blinks when asked about increases in teenage drug use. Vice-presidential candidates were apparently less stressed. Gore registered a mere 42 and Jack Kemp averaged a sleepy 31. According to Tecce, the faster blinker has lost every presidential election since 1980 ("In the Blink," 1996).

The Tecce blink-rate-equals-stress-level hypothesis is interesting and may have validity, but generalizing from a single channel nonverbal code requires caution. The blink rate of Jack Kemp was exceedingly low, yet anyone observing Kemp during the debate would have noticed the sheen of perspiration on his face and his stiff posture, as well as several verbal miscues. Perspiration, rigid posture, and verbal mistakes suggest stress and nervousness. Nonverbal communication is multichanneled. Thus, one nonverbal cue may suggest relaxed demeanor while another nonverbal cue contradicts this observation. Concluding that Kemp was relaxed from blink rate alone is a shakey claim.

Eye contact is an important aspect of nonverbal communication. Eye contact regulates conversational turn taking, communicates involvement and interest, manifests warmth, and establishes connection with others. It can also command attention, be flirtatious, or look cold and intimidating (Andersen, 1999).

Interpersonal communication is quite dependent on eye contact, especially in the United States. Eye contact invites conversation. Lack of eye contact is usually perceived to be rude or inattentive. One study (Burgoon et al., 1985) found that individuals interviewing for a job were less successful when they averted eye contact than those who maintained eye contact with the interviewer. As you will see in later chapters, eye contact is a critical element of effective public speaking.

Cultures differ regarding the appropriateness of direct eye contact (Samovar & Porter, 1995). In Korea "direct eye contact among unequals connotes competition, constituting an inappropriate form of behavior" (p. 323). Indonesians, Chinese, Japanese, and many Latin Americans will show deference to others by lowering their eyes. This is a sign of respect. It is also easy for Americans to misread this nonverbal cue and assume that Asians and Latin Americans lack self-confidence and can be easily manipulated.

Co-cultures within the United States also show different preferences regarding eye contact. Hopi dislike direct eye contact. Navajos have a creation myth that tells the story of a "terrible monster called He-Who-Kills-With-His-Eyes." This story teaches Navajo children that "a stare is literally an evil eye and implies a sexual and aggressive assault" ("Understanding Culture," 1974).

Our eyes are highly communicative whether we want them to be or not. Pupil dilation (i.e., pupils open) offers a subtle but significant cue that communicates arousal or attraction. Experienced gem buyers wear sunglasses to hide pupil dilation that would reveal how much they want to buy a particular gem. In an amazing study (Hess & Goodwin, 1974), students were shown two photos of a mother holding her baby. The photos were identical in all respects, except one photo was

Box 5-5 Sharper Focus

The Girl With No Smile

Seven-year-old Chelsea Thomas underwent facial surgery on December 16, 1995, to correct her perpetually grumpy facial expression. Chelsea suffered from an unusual condition called Moebius syndrome. She couldn't smile because the nerves that trigger the facial muscles that control smiling were missing. Chelsea's mother described how the inability to smile affected her daughter: "It's been hard for her because people think she's unfriendly or ignoring them or bored. . . . Kids stare at her. Adults are pretty understanding, but she has a worse time with kids" ("Girl Undergoes," 1995).

Surgery grafted leg muscles and nerves from her leg to her facial muscles used for chewing. Chelsea now has a smile, but imagine what it would be like to be unable to smile when we feel joy or perceive humor. Imagine how others would respond to you if you always seemed to be frowning and you had no way of changing the sour expression on your face. Think of what that would do to your self-esteem and to your ability to communicate with others.

retouched to show constricted pupils and the other retouched to show dilated pupils. The students were asked, "Which mother loves her baby more?" Every student chose the mother with the dilated pupils. Most student participants gave reasons other than the dilated pupils, even though pupil dilation was the only difference between the two photos. "She's holding her baby closer," "She has a warmer smile," or "Her face is more pleasant" were some of the explanations offered.

Not surprisingly, heterosexual men display more pupil dilation when viewing photos of women, and gay men display greater pupil dilation when viewing photos of other men (Hess et al., 1965). Pupil dilation is subconsciously perceived during interpersonal interactions and actually may increase the observer's attraction for the person with dilated pupils (Andersen et al., 1980). Candlelight dinners, moonlight walks, and conversations by firelight produce wider pupils due to the soft light. This is probably part of the reason such experiences increase romantic attraction (Andersen, 1999).

Facial Expressions "The face is your personal billboard," says Dane Archer. "It never gets totally hidden" (as cited in Townsend, 1996). There has been extensive research on facial expressions. Several conclusions can be drawn from this research.

First, the face signals specific emotional states: a smile signals happiness and a frown signals sadness. Research on facial expressions in 20 Western cultures and 11 nonliterate and isolated cultures shows that members of all of these cultures recognized the same basic emotions from photographs of specific facial expressions. These universal emotions identified by all cultures from specific facial expressions are fear, anger, surprise, contempt, disgust, happiness, and sadness (Ekman, 1994; Matsumoto, 1994).

Second, members of diverse cultures recognize the same emotions from specific facial expressions, but they don't necessarily perceive the same intensity of emotion (e.g., from annoyance to rage) communicated by facial expressions. One study asked members in 10 different cultures to rate the intensity of the perceived emotions exhibited by facial expressions. Significant differences were found. Non-Asian cultures rated the emotions as more intense than did Asian cultures (Ekman et al., 1987).

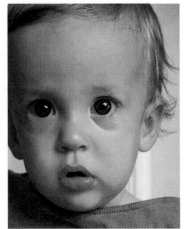

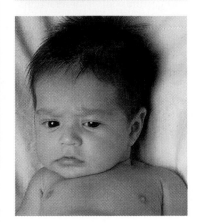

Universal facial expressions of emotions are exhibited naturally by infants. They don't have to be taught expressions for (from left to right) happiness, sadness, disgust, fear, anger, and surprise.

Third, there are also differences in display rules for facial expressions. **Display rules** are culture-specific prescriptions that dictate the appropriateness of facial expressions of emotions (Ekman, 1993). Japanese would be more likely than Americans to suppress negative emotions (e.g., anger, contempt) if the emotion occurs during a private conversation and the target of the emotion is an in-group member. If, however, the target of the negative emotion were a rival group or individual, Japanese would be more likely than Americans to display the emotion. Showing contempt or anger toward one of your own group members creates disharmony and may hurt the group. Showing anger or contempt to a competitive rival, however, may create in-group cohesion (Matsumoto, 1990).

Facial expression is an enormously complicated communication cue. A single emotion such as anger can be exhibited in 60 different facial expressions depending on the intensity of the anger and the different types of anger expressed (indignation, vengeance, resentment). Facial expressions influence our self-esteem and color the reactions others have toward us (Box 5-5). Facial expressions usually occur when we interact with others, not when we are alone. Smiling, for instance,

Box 5-6 Sharper Focus

Cultural Diversity and Gestural Confusion

The thumb inserted between the index and middle fingers is an old American gesture commonly used playfully with children that typically means, "I've got your nose!" This same gesture is a nonverbal invitation to have sex in Germany, Holland, and Denmark, but in Portugal and Brazil it wishes a person good luck or protection. Tapping your temple with the index finger of one hand is a gesture meaning "He is smart" in the United States, but it means "He is stupid" in Europe. In some contexts it can mean the opposite in both places.

Shared gestures don't always produce shared meaning, especially across cultures. One large study of 40 different cultures isolated 20 common hand gestures, all

of which had different meanings in each culture (Morris et al., 1979). Pointing to objects with the index finger in parts of Central Africa is deemed vulgar and crude. Friendship is symbolized in Jordan by touching index fingers side by side. Flamboyant gestures are discouraged in Germany. As Ruch (1989) explains, "Hands should be used with calculated dignity. They should never serve as lively instruments to emphasize points in conversation. The entire game plan is to appear calm under pressure" (p. 191). African Americans, however, prefer an expressive gestural communication and display greater variation of body movements during interactions than do White Americans.

is primarily transactional. Smiling occurs with much greater frequency and to a greater degree in the presence of other highly involved individuals than it does when a person is alone (Andersen, 1999). This is true of most facial expressions.

Gestural Communication

Gestures come naturally to us. Many gestures are unconscious manifestations of inner feelings. Individuals who talk on the telephone usually gesture while they are talking even though the person on the other end cannot see the gestures. When we communicate with others, we often are a wiggling, fidgeting, finger-tapping, hand-waving, toe tapping, arm-flailing body in motion (Box 5-6).

There are three main categories of gestures: manipulators, illustrators, and emblems (Ekman, 1992). **Manipulators** are gestures made by one part of the body, usually the hands, rubbing, picking, squeezing, cleaning, or grooming another part of the body. They have no specific meaning, although people observing such manipulators may perceive nervousness, discomfort, or deceit from such gestures. Manipulators, however, also occur when a person is relaxed and feeling energized and when no deceit is occurring. Nevertheless, studies show that people will mistakenly judge deceitfulness when a person exhibits many manipulators (Ekman, 1992). The important point is not to jump to conclusions concerning what manipulators mean.

Illustrators are gestures that help explain what a person says to another person. They have no independent meaning of their own. Telling a person to go to the left, then pointing in the appropriate direction, is an example of an illustrator. Describing how to "zig-zag," while drawing the movement in the air, is another example. Many of the unconscious gestures we make that emphasize what we are saying are illustrators.

Emblems are gestures that have precise meanings separate from verbal communication. Nodding your head up and down signals "yes" in the United States. Moving your head side to side signals "no." There are fewer than 60 emblems used in the United States. Israel, however, uses more than 250 (Ekman, 1992). As cultures mix and countries become multicultural, misunderstanding can occur when a specific emblem has different meanings in two cultures. For instance, nodding your head up and down in Turkey means "no." Shaking your head from side to side doesn't mean "no" to a Turk; it means "I don't understand."

No emblems are unique to the United States. The French, however, have a unique gesture for "He's drunk." The gesture is a fist placed around the nose and twisted. Germans have a unique "good luck" emblem. The emblem consists of two fists with the thumbs inside pounding an imaginary table (Ekman et al., 1984).

Many common emblems, especially obscene or vulgar ones, have spread to other cultures around the world. The extended middle finger is recognized almost everywhere as an obscene gesture and is used widely beyond the borders of the United States. Some Latin American cultures add to the gesture by extending the middle finger while raising the arm abruptly and grabbing the arm with the other hand.

The competent communicator needs to be mindful of the vast potential for misunderstanding inherent in the gestural code. Very few gestures are emblems with precise meanings in all contexts. Most gestures are far more ambiguous and require sophisticated interpretation tied specifically to the context in which they occur. Folding your arms across your chest may mean that you are closing yourself off to others in a defensive gesture, or it may simply be a comfortable way for you to rest your arms. Be cautious when interpreting the meaning of gestures. When you do interpret the meaning of gestures, match them with other nonverbal codes and look for consistency of meaning.

Touch Communication

There are approximately 5 million touch receptors in our skin, about 3,000 in a single fingertip, all sending messages through our spinal cord to our brain. Skin is the largest organ in the human body, covering about 19 square feet on the average-sized human (Colt, 1997). Touching skin is an enormously powerful and important communication code as you will see in this section.

Significance of Touch   American playwright Tennessee Williams testified to the power of touch when he wrote, "Devils can be driven out of the heart by the touch of a hand on a hand, or a mouth on a mouth." Premature babies studied at Miami's Touch Research Institute show the remarkable benefits of touch to human well-being. With just three 10-minute gentle massages each day, premature babies will be more alert, responsive, and active than infants of the same size and condition who are not massaged. Premature infants who are massaged will tolerate noise, sleep more soundly, gain weight 47% faster, and leave the hospital an average of 6 days sooner than premature babies who are not massaged (Colt, 1997). With 430,000 premature babies born in the United States each year, the 6-day earlier departure from the hospital would translate into a $4 billion annual savings if gentle baby massage were practiced in all hospitals.

Voluminous research on infant and child development reveals that touch is not only beneficial but even critical for life itself. Infants in orphanages who do not receive much, if any, touch from other humans are usually maladjusted, quiet, and show difficulty learning and maturing normally (Andersen, 1999). During Romania's strife in the early 1990s, thousands of infants were warehoused in

The situation influences the appropriateness of touch communication.

orphanages, virtually alone in their cribs for 2 years. They were found to be severely impaired by the lack of physical contact, and some even died.

Touch has an impact on emotional health and well-being. Massage is a stress reducer. Approximately 25 million Americans visit massage therapists each year (Colt, 1997). A growing number of businesses and institutions offer massage in the workplace. Volunteer therapists gave massages to exhausted rescue workers, traumatized survivors, and medical pathologists to help them cope with the bombing of a federal building in Oklahoma City in 1996 (Colt, 1997).

Touch is essential to the expression of love, warmth, intimacy, and concern for others. Misuse of touch can repel, frighten, or anger others. Touch communicates power. Sexual harassment is often an issue of inappropriate, unwanted touch communication. Those with greater power typically feel less constraint in touching those with lesser power than vice versa. Touch can also be quite influential. When teachers touched students on the arm in the beginning and at the end of a conference, there was a 25% increase in positive evaluations of the teacher-student conference compared to the no-touch condition (Steward & Lupfer, 1987). Waitresses receive bigger tips, on average, when they touch patrons subtly (Crusco & Wetzel, 1984). Psychologists gain greater compliance from their clients when they touch them appropriately (Patterson et al., 1986). Even shoppers purchase more merchandise when they are unobtrusively touched (Smith et al., 1982).

Despite the clear benefits of touch communication, Americans are "touchy about touch." Psychologist Tiffany Field, director of the Touch Research Institute, worries that Americans are becoming touch-phobic (as cited in Colt, 1997). The growing concern about sexual harassment and child abuse has created a "touching is taboo" atmosphere. The National Education Association, the voice of 2 million teachers in the United States, advocates the slogan: "Teach, don't touch."

Compared with other cultures, Americans are a "nontactile society." Field found that French parents and children touch each other three times as often as American parents and children, a pattern that doesn't vary with age. Field compared French and American teenagers in Paris and Miami McDonald's restaurants. French adolescents engaged in significantly more casual touch (leaning on a friend, putting an arm around another person's shoulder) than American teens. Field also concludes that "French parents and teachers alike are more physically affectionate and the kids are less aggressive" (as cited in Colt, 1997, p. 62). The French, however, are not the "touchiest" culture. One study found that Italian and Greek dyads (pairs) touched more than French, English, and Dutch dyads (Remland et al., 1995).

Types of Touch   There are several types of touching. Knowing which type of touch is appropriate for which context is a vital concern to the competent communicator. Heslin (1974) identified five types of touching based on their function, usage, and intensity.

The *functional-professional touch* is the least intense form of touching. The touch is instrumental communication that takes place between doctors and patients, coaches and athletes, and the like. Lately, teacher-student touch communication is limited to this type, if engaged in at all. Functional-professional touching is businesslike and limited to the requirements of the situation. A nurse helping a patient sit up in bed or a football coach demonstrating the "bump-and-run" are examples.

The *social-polite touch* occurs during initial introductions, business relationships, and formal occasions. The handshake is the standard form of social-polite touch in American culture. Many European cultures greet strangers with a hug and a perfunctory kiss on each cheek.

The *friendship-warmth touch* is the most ambiguous type of touch and leads to the most misunderstandings between people. The amount of touch has to be negotiated when showing friendship and warmth toward others. Too little touch may communicate unfriendliness, indifference, and coldness. Too much touch that seems too intimate communicates sexual interest when such interest may not be wanted. Friendly touches, especially those taking place in private, can mistakenly be perceived as sexual, especially by males (Andersen, 1999).

The *love and intimacy touch* is reserved only for a very few, special individuals— close friends, family members, spouses, and lovers. This is not sexual touch, although it may blend with sexual touch. Tenderly holding a friend's hand, softly touching the cheek of a spouse, or hugging are examples of this type of touch.

The *sexual touch* is the most personal, intimate touch, and the most restricted. Mutual consent is the most important consideration to the competent communicator. Engaging in this type of touch when it is unwanted will produce serious repercussions.

Appropriateness of touch largely depends on understanding which type of touch is acceptable and desirable in which situation. Types of touch help define relationships between people. If one person initiates a friendship touch but the other person recoils because no real friendship has been established, clearly this type of touch was inappropriate. Both parties must define their relationship similarly or problems will occur. Ignoring the social-polite touch during introductions can provoke a negative response from the party shown such indifference and disrespect. Choosing to engage in too much or too little touch communication in a particular situation can send a powerful message.

Touch Taboos   A manual published by the University of California at San Francisco instructs nurses not to touch Cambodians on the head. That is where they believe their soul resides. Greeting a Muslim by shaking his or her left hand is an insult because the left hand is reserved for toilet functions. In Korea, young people are forbidden to touch the shoulders of their elders. Kim (1992) notes: "Southeast Asians do not ordinarily touch during a conversation, especially one between opposite sexes, because many Asian cultures adhere to norms that forbid displays of affection and intimacy" (p. 321).

According to research conducted in the United States by Jones (1994), about 15% of all touches on a daily basis are unwanted and rejected. Jones identifies forms of taboo touching in the United States. The competent communicator manifests sensitivity by recognizing these forbidden forms of touch and adopting more appropriate communication behavior. These taboos of touch are:

1. *Strangers are the "untouchables."* Nonfunctional touch is usually perceived as too intimate and personal. Inevitable jostling and bumping take place in crowded elevators, buses, stores, and the like. The American norm is to apologize when we bump or otherwise touch a stranger. Sexual touch by a stranger is highly inappropriate, even cause for arrest.

2. *Harmful touches should be avoided.* Children have to learn early that hurting someone by hitting, biting, scratching, or otherwise damaging someone is forbidden. Even if the person who inflicts the hurt is a spouse or partner and the hurt is accidental, the recipient of the painful touch will cry out in protest.

3. *Avoid startling touches.* Sneaking up on a person and tapping them on the shoulder when they think they are alone will likely startle them and produce a strong negative response. There is no equivalent immediate countermove a person can use. You can't startle the person who tapped you on the shoulder. Even though the startling touch is sometimes done playfully, most people resent being startled.

4. *Avoid the interruption touch.* Touches should not interfere with principal activities. Throwing your arms around your partner and hugging him or her tightly while your partner desperately tries to mix ingredients for dinner interrupts the primary activity. It will likely produce rejection of the touch. Trying to kiss your partner on the lips when he or she is trying to watch an engrossing movie will also likely produce rejection.

5. *Don't move others.* This is especially important advice when dealing with strangers. Ushering people from one place to another without warning or permission is usually seen as an aggressive act. Warning people that they need to move and offering a quick explanation, however, can nullify the negative reaction to being moved by someone. "Excuse me, I need to get through" or "Watch out, this coffee is very hot" followed by a touch gently moving a person out of the way will not likely produce the response that touch alone will produce.

6. *Avoid "rub-it-in" touches.* Don't intensify a negative remark with a touch. A husband pinching the thigh of his wife and remarking that "That's pretty fattening," as she orders a dessert, inappropriately rubs in the nasty dig. A woman who tells her male partner to "walk your mother to her car" while slapping his arm intensifies the rebuke.

Dealing with those who violate touch taboos is fairly straightforward (Jones, 1994). Determining how accidental or purposeful the violation is will guide you in your response. Unintentional lapses of touch protocol are easily forgiven. Intentional violations usually require a stronger response.

Here are some suggestions for dealing competently with touch violations:

1. *Begin by assuming the violation is accidental.* Your nonverbal rejection—pulling away, frowning, and so forth—may be all that's required to convey the message that the touch is unwanted and inappropriate.

2. *Use descriptive statements to identify your reaction and the behavior that ignited it.* "I don't like to be moved out of the way like that. It seems aggressive, so please don't do it" is an example.

3. *Use intense nonverbal cues when faced with a purposeful violator.* Hard core touch violators are fond of putting the person who is upset on the defensive with statements such as "Don't be so touchy" or "Lighten up, I didn't mean anything by it." No need to engage in a tit-for-tat verbal competition. A prolonged glower, a disgusted look held for a bit longer than usual, or a penetrating stare without comment can make the violator very uncomfortable and communicate the appropriate message.

4. *Repeat offenders require strong nonverbal signs of rejection plus a direct, firm command.* "Don't ever touch me that way again" or "Don't ever grab my shoulder" are examples.

5. *A brief apology should follow your own touch violation.* If you inadvertently violate a touch taboo, simply apologize. "Oh, I'm sorry. I didn't mean to bump you."

Space Communication

Space communicates in very powerful and significant ways. In this section, the many ways space impacts our relationships with others will be explored.

Distance   Anthropologist Edward Hall (1969) has identified four types of spatial relationships based on distances between individuals conversing. These four types are intimate, personal, social, and public distances. The actual distances in each

Type	Distance	Usage of Nonverbal Cues	Overlapping Nonverbal Cues
Table 5-1 Four Types of Spatial Relationships and Their Characteristics in Mainstream U.S. Culture			
Intimate	0–18 in.	Loving; showing tenderness	Limited eye contact; touch; smell
Personal	18 in. – 4 ft	Conversing with intimates, friends	Eye contact; some touching; gestures
Social	4 ft–12 ft	Business talk; social conversing	Formal vocal tone; gestures; eye contact
Public	12 ft or more	Lectures; speeches	Eye contact; gestures; vocal tones

category vary according to culture. The distances, their usages, and overlapping nonverbal cues for each distance for the mainstream culture of the United States are shown in Table 5-1.

The distance zones identified by Hall are averages. Individual preferences vary within a culture. Typically, strangers stepping into an intimate zone will produce great discomfort, even hostility. This is usually perceived as an aggressive act. An intimate partner, however, avoiding the intimate zone signals a distancing in the relationship. Counselors look for such cues to signal trouble or disagreement between relationship partners even when couples verbally insist that a problem doesn't exist. We signal that we are "far apart" in negotiations by moving away literally from our adversaries in the bargaining process.

Sometimes we are forced into intimate zones with strangers. A crowded elevator is an example. Being forced to rub elbows with individuals we've never met before is uncomfortable. Usually, when the intimacy zone is violated through nobody's fault, we try to establish a psychic distance from others. That is why occupants of crowded elevators often stare at the numbers indicating what floor is coming up next. This act distances us mentally from strangers and allows us to cope with an uncomfortable situation.

The personal space of short people is more often violated than that of tall people. In one study (Caplan & Goldman, 1981), short males (5 ft 5 in.) had their personal space invaded more than twice as often (69% to 31%) as tall males (6 ft 2 in.). Males also claim a larger personal spatial bubble around themselves than do women (Mercer & Benjamin, 1980).

In a multicultural country such as the United States, opportunities for misunderstanding associated with spatial zones are plentiful. Comfortable social distance for an Arab may violate personal or even intimate zones of Americans. Arabs typically move very close when conversing. Part of the reason for this is that Arabs perceive a person's smell to be an extension of the person and, thus, important. Hall (1969) describes the importance of smells to Arabs during conversation:

Not only is it [smell] one of the distance-setting mechanisms, but it is a vital part of the complex system of behavior. Arabs consistently breathe on people when they talk. However, this habit is more than a matter of different manners. To the Arab good smells are pleasing and a way of being involved with each other. To smell one's friends is desirable, for to deny him your breath is to act ashamed. Americans, on the other hand, trained as they are not to breathe in people's faces, automatically communicate shame in trying to be polite. (p. 149)

Not recognizing the cultural differences associated with distance can make an individual seem pushy and aggressive or distant and stand-offish.

Territoriality   Twenty-nine-year-old Rene Andrews pulled onto I-71 near Cincinnati, Ohio one fateful day in July 1997. Apparently upset by the way Andrews pulled into her lane, 24-year-old Tracie Alfieri attempted to pass Andrews on the right shoulder of the freeway, then passed on the left, cut in front of Andrews, and slammed on the brakes. Andrews swerved and crashed into a stopped tractor-trailer rig. Andrews died in this accident. Alfieri suffered multiple injuries, and her 6-month-old fetus died. Alfieri was charged with and convicted of aggravated vehicular homicide and was sentenced to 18 months in prison.

Road rage is territoriality taken to an extreme. Intruders in "their car" trespass into "our lane" as we're driving "our car." Just as we feel morally righteous defending our homes from intruders, so also do we defend our strip of blacktop as if we owned it. A once-popular bumper sticker read, "As a Matter of Fact, I Do Own the Road."

Road rage is manifested by a blend of nonverbal cues. The most common manifestations are obscene gestures, blocking other vehicles with one's car, aggressive tailgating, headlight flashing, repetitive honking, and sometimes flashing a gun and even gunfire.

Road rage is an increasing problem in the United States. Ricardo Martinez, head of the National Highway Traffic Safety Administration, attributes 28,000 highway deaths each year to road rage (Wald, 1997). He claims that an increase in a "me first philosophy" is a primary cause of road rage.

A hypercompetitive, individualistic culture such as that found in the United States is very concerned about who owns what. Private property is defended in law. The Fourth Amendment to the U.S. Constitution supports "the right of the people to be secure in their persons, houses, papers, and effects."

We stake out our territory in a variety of ways (Box 5-7). A coat laid over the back of a chair signals temporary possession of that specific seat. Resting a lunch tray on a table in a cafeteria signals "That's my eating area." When office space is limited, we erect partitions that make our environment look like a rabbit warren. Sometimes mere habit creates territoriality. Students who sit in the same chair every class period quickly assume the chair is theirs. Dare to sit in "my chair" and see what happens.

Environment   Winston Churchill once said, "We shape our buildings, then our buildings shape us." The design of our environment shapes communication. Airports and fast-food restaurants design brightly lit buildings with uncomfortable plastic furniture to hurry people along and limit communication transactions. Such spaces are not meant for loitering, intimate communication, nor relaxation. The environment communicates "Do your business and leave."

Box 5-7   Focus on Controversy

Gated Communities

There are approximately 20,000 gated communities in the United States (D. Diamond, 1997). One poll showed that 65% of respondents would like to live in a gated community ("The Gate Debate," 1997). Gated communities come in many varieties. Some are housing projects that require using a keypad code to open a metal gate blocking access to the community. Other gated communities have erected much more elaborate barriers to entrance. Gates may be accompanied by fences surrounding the community, armed guards, security patrols, and tire-piercing devices that are triggered by improper entrance. The Hidden Valley community in Santa Clarita, California (a gated neighborhood of 400 homes) discourages intruders with a military-style antiterrorist device that launches a 3-foot metal cylinder from ground level into the bottom of any car trying to sneak past the gate. This device disables and seriously damages the intruder's car.

Protection of personal property and security against crimes of violence are the primary motivators for gating a community. Proponents claim they feel safer and that gated neighborhoods promote a sense of community where everybody knows everybody else. Opponents see it differently. Edward Blakely, dean of the School of Urban Planning and Development at the University of Southern California, warns, "Gated communities will accelerate the economic and social fragmentation of the nation" (as cited in D. Diamond, 1997, p. 4).

The desire to be safe in person and property cannot be taken lightly. Do gated communities afford real security or merely the illusion of safety? Ed Cross, member of the San Antonio planning commission and a real estate broker, claims, "People are living with a false sense of security. It's [gated community] a marketing gimmick; it's a fad" (as cited in D. Diamond, 1997, p. 5). Blakely and Mary Gail Snyder (1997), authors of *Fortress America*, note that crime rates typically drop in the first year or two after a neighborhood becomes gated, but thereafter crime rates rise to levels equivalent to outside areas. In 1984 the 4,800 residents of Sudden Valley, a gated community in Bellingham, Washington, voted to tear down their five gates. Most residents felt that the gates enticed burglars instead of deterring them. When the gates were removed, crime rates went down (D. Diamond, 1997).

Regardless of who's right in this debate, gated communities manifest an adversarial, competitive territoriality. They signal to the outside world "Keep Out!" Gated communities segregate in-groups and out-groups. Dividing America into thousands of enclaves homogenizes neighborhoods and very likely promotes divisiveness and conflict between groups. We see ourselves as adversaries competing for space. Out-group members resent the restraint on their freedom of travel.

Typically, gated communities are affordable only to the well-off or the rich. A poor family's gated community consists of a locked apartment building. Finding common ground between ethnic groups and socioeconomic classes, developing opportunities for cooperation, working together as teams to make decisions and to solve personal and societal problems are probably more difficult when we wall ourselves in against those who look and act differently from us. As Blakely puts it, "The nation's dream was equality and mutual assistance and the melting pot. . . . Take that away and we're just people who live on a piece of territory" (as cited in D. Diamond, 1997, p. 5).

Questions for Thought

1. Do you like the idea of gated communities? Would you like to live in a gated community?
2. If gated communities truly provided security, would that make them a good idea?
3. Can you think of alternatives to gated communities that might produce the benefits proponents claim occur without closing off communication with groups who can't afford to live in such neighborhoods?

Recently jails and prisons have been designed with communication in mind. The traditional prison environment provides little privacy and personal space, separates prisoners from guards, and restricts inmates' mingling. The Federal Bureau of Prisons began building prisons with a different design to encourage direct supervision of inmates. Prisons were built with open areas for inmate interactions. Guards mingle directly with prisoners, developing ongoing relationships with the inmates and spotting trouble before it explodes. There are no enclosed booths for officers. Inmates have small rooms, not cells with bars. Inmates control the lights in their rooms. There are more televisions available to reduce conflicts over which programs to watch. Furniture is "soft" (cushy and comfortable) not institutional "hard" (plastic and resistant), and floors are carpeted. These new prisons, despite their innovativeness, actually cost less to build than traditional jails.

Violent incidents are reduced 30% to 90% in the new prisons compared to traditional prisons. Inmate rape is virtually nonexistent, and vandalism and graffiti drop precipitously. Guards, hesitant at first, feel safer, and tension between inmates is reduced (Wener et al., 1987). Direct-supervision jails are still perceived to be prisons by the inmates, but the communication outcomes are dramatically different from traditional jails.

Voice Communication

Our voice is second only to our face in communicating our emotions. Our voice communicates information about our age, sex, socioeconomic status, ethnicity, and regional background. Vocal cues, or paralanguage, are usually divided into three classifications (Samovar & Porter, 1995): *vocal characterizers* (laughing, yelling, moaning, crying, whining, belching, yawning), *vocal qualifiers* (volume, tone, pitch, resonance, rhythm, rate), and *vocal segregates* ("uh-hum," "uh," "mm-hmm," "oooh," "shh"). A whispering soft voice may indicate speech anxiety when it occurs in front of a large audience. A flat, monotone voice can induce sleep in listeners. Speaking at hyperspeed may communicate nervousness and excitement. Typically, listeners prefer a speaking rate that approximates their own speech pattern (Buller & Aune, 1992).

There are cultural differences regarding vocal communication. Arabs speak very loudly because it connotes strength and sincerity. Israelis view high volume as a sign of strong beliefs on an issue. Germans assume a "commanding tone that projects authority and self-confidence" (Ruch, 1989, p. 191). People from Thailand, Japan, and the Philippines tend to speak very softly, almost in a whisper. This communicates good manners and education. Laughing signals joy in Japan, but laughing often camouflages displeasure, anger, embarrassment, and sorrow (Samovar & Porter, 1995).

Communicating Competently With Nonverbal Codes

Knowledge of the myriad ways nonverbal codes influence our communication with others is the first step toward competent nonverbal communication. As indicated repeatedly throughout this chapter, appropriateness and effectiveness of nonverbal communication are key parts of the competence equation. Suggestions have been offered already on how you might improve your understanding and skill in nonverbal communication. This section will tie together common threads linking all the nonverbal codes to communication competence.

Monitor Nonverbal Communication

Knowledge is not useful if it isn't applied. Use your knowledge of nonverbal codes to monitor your own communication and the communication of others. Observe nonverbal communication in action. Become sensitive to the subleties of these codes. Try experimenting. Maintain eye contact during interviews or in conversations with others. Observe how this effects the outcome of the communication. Try appropriate touching to see if it produces greater closeness and more positive responses from others. If you tend toward a monotone voice, enliven it on purpose. If your facial expressions tend to be constrained, try to communicate your emotions with more dramatic facial expressions.

Resist Jumping to Conclusions

By now you should be aware that nonverbal communication can be highly ambiguous. Don't make the mistake that others have made. Don't assume that you can "read a person like a book," especially if you don't know that person well. Knowing the person well reduces the ambiguity of nonverbal cues. Nonverbal cues suggest certain messages, but you must consider them in their appropriate context. The easiest way to determine if you have interpreted nonverbal cues correctly is to ask. Check your perceptions with others. "I noticed you tapping your fingers and tugging at your ear. Are you nervous or upset about something?" is a quick way to determine if your nonverbal read is accurate.

Observe Multiple Nonverbal Codes

Relying on a single nonverbal code will often produce a false perception. Blinking rate may suggest relaxed demeanor, but observe other nonverbal cues as well (e.g., posture, gestures). Silence may indicate disagreement, but do other nonverbal codes contradict this assessment? Be careful not to make a broad generalization based on a single nonverbal cue. Look for nonverbal clusters to determine more accurately what is being communicated.

Recognize Cultural Differences

The vast differences in cultural use of nonverbal codes have been stressed repeatedly. When you communicate with individuals from another culture or co-culture in the United States, recognize the nonverbal communication differences. If you come across a nonverbal cue that puzzles you, don't assume anything. Observe members of other cultures to determine what is appropriate behavior. If you still feel doubtful about your interpretation, check your perception by asking someone who would know.

Strive for Consistency

Try to match verbal and nonverbal communication. Mixed messages confuse those who communicate with us. Exhibiting nonverbal behavior that contradicts what we are saying will produce a negative reaction from others.

Get in Sync With Others

Fast talkers need to slow down when they are conversing with slow talkers. Getting "out of sync" with another person means that you aren't matching their nonverbal communication. "Dress for success" means adopting a style of clothing and attire that matches what other people wear within a specific context. Yelling when they are talking softly, gesturing when the other person is using almost no gestures, touching when the other person does not return the touching, slouching in a chair with feet propped on a coffee table when other people are sitting straight in their chairs with feet firmly planted on the ground can produce awkward, counterproductive communication. Try practicing more synchronous communication. Match more closely what other people do and see what happens. This doesn't require blind conformity. Pick your spots when synchrony is most important and when you desire productive outcomes. Knowledge regarding when matching is critical and when it doesn't much matter to you puts you in charge.

Summary

Nonverbal communication affects our communication with others in powerful ways, yet nonverbal communication is often ambiguous and difficult to read. Assuming that an accurate perception of others can be determined from a single nonverbal cue is always a doubtful undertaking. There are numerous types of nonverbal communication, each with its own guidelines for competent communication. Consider multiple nonverbal cues, not merely a single cue, and consider the entire context before drawing any conclusions concerning nonverbal communication.

Suggested Readings

Ekman, P. (1992). *Telling lies: Clues to deceit in the marketplace, politics, and marriage.* New York: W. W. Norton. This is a fine treatment of nonverbal communication that focuses on deceit.

Hall, E. (1959). *The silent language.* New York: Doubleday. This book popularized the subject of nonverbal communication. It is far superior to most mass market books on the subject.

Montagu, A. (1986). *Touching: The human significance of the skin.* New York: Harper & Row. This is the classic work on touch communication by an internationally renowned anthropologist.

Listening to Others

We have speech contests, but no listening contests. We give awards to great speakers, but not to great listeners. A list of the 100 greatest speakers of all time doesn't seem ludicrous, but a list of the 100 greatest listeners of all time seems odd at best. Until recently, listening has been an underappreciated part of communication in our hypercompetitive society. Speaking, not listening, earns us power and status. The necessity to train people to be effective listeners has gained recognition in a variety of arenas. Twenty-five years ago, finding a college course on listening would have been a challenge. Today, many colleges offer a course on listening. Colleges that do not offer a listening course often offer a listening unit in a speech course.

Abundant research testifies to the importance of competent listening. Listening consumes more time of college students than any other communication activity. College students devote 53% of their communication time to listening, on average, but only 14% to writing, 16% to speaking, and 17% to reading (Barker et al., 1981). Poor listening in college produces poor academic performance. Sleeping or daydreaming your way through classes thwarts the learning process.

In the workplace, we spend an equivalent amount of time listening. The average worker spends 55% of his or her time at work listening, 23% speaking, slightly more than 13% reading, and a little more than 8% writing (U.S. Department of Labor, 1991). Numerous studies identify listening as the most important communication skill necessary to obtain a job and earn a promotion (Wolvin & Coakley, 1996). Poor listening at work can be extremely costly. Corporate consultant Lyman Steil (1980) explains: "With more than 100 million workers in this country, a simple $10 mistake by each of them, as a result of poor listening, would add up to a cost of a billion dollars. And most people make numerous listening mistakes every week" (p. 65).

Interpersonally, listening is extremely important. When college students listened to taped conversations, the person who talked substantially more than he or she listened was the least liked (as cited in Wolvin & Coakley, 1996). In another study, adults answered that listening was the most important communication skill in family and social situations (Wolvin, 1984).

Listening is a vitally important communication activity, but most of us receive little training in listening. We all have extensive experience listening to others. Experience alone, however, may be a very poor teacher. Without proper training, experience may simply reinforce bad habits. As Mortimer Adler (1983) observes, "How utterly amazing is the general assumption that the ability to listen well is a natural gift for which no training is required" (p. 5).

Perhaps this assumption is the product of inflated self-appraisals (see Chapter 2). One study (Brownell, 1990) asked 144 managers in a business environment to rate their listening effectiveness. None of the managers rated themselves as "very poor" or even "poor" listeners. A surprising 94%, however, rated themselves as "good" or "very good" listeners. These flattering self-appraisals didn't jibe with the perceptions of employees, many of whom claimed that their supervisors' listening skills were in vast need of improvement.

Experience without training produces many lousy listeners. Elgin (1989) observes that some individuals have had "nonlistening habits for so long that they are almost incapable of listening—if they had a listening gland, it would be atrophied from disuse" (p. 90). Shere Hite's (1987) report on 4,500 self-selected female respondents, most of whom were unhappy with their male partners, revealed that poor listening is a key element in unhappy relationships. When asked, "What does your partner do that makes you the maddest?", 77% of the respondents answered, "He doesn't listen." Speech professor Wayne Cameron (as cited in Adler & Towne, 1999) confirmed the worst fear of college instructors delivering a lecture to a room full of students. A gun was fired (not their worst fear) at random intervals during a lecture. Students immediately recorded their thoughts at that moment. Only 20% were mildly attentive to the lecture, and a mere 12% were actively listening. The rest were pursuing erotic thoughts (20%), reminiscing (20%), or worrying, day-dreaming, thinking about lunch or religion (8%).

Listening is important. We don't do it very well, and we receive scant instruction regarding how to improve our listening. The principal purpose of this chapter is to provide instruction concerning effective listening. There are four objectives:

1. to define and explain the listening process,
2. to discuss several general listening problems,
3. to explore different kinds of listening and problems unique to each kind, and
4. to identify specific ways you can become a competent listener.

The general thrust of this chapter can be summed up in the slogan of the Sperry Corporation (now part of UNISYS): "Nothing new ever entered the mind through an open mouth."

The Listening Process

The International Listening Association adopted an official definition of listening. With slight modification, it defines **listening** as "the process of receiving, constructing [and reconstructing] meaning from, and responding to spoken and/or nonverbal messages" (Emmert, 1996, p. 2). This definition implicitly highlights listening as a dynamic, active process, not a passive activity. In the next several sections you will learn more about this process by looking at three primary elements of listening: comprehending, retaining, and responding.

Comprehending

Constructing meaning from the messages of others is, in reality, more a process of *re*construction. The speaker constructs the original message. A competent listener reconstructs that message to match the original as closely as possible. This reconstruction process requires comprehension, or understanding, of the message received. Shared meaning comes from understanding messages.

The first challenge facing the listener operates at the most basic level, namely, accurately discriminating speech sounds. This may seem ludicrously simple, but it isn't. For years, in hundreds of speech classes, my colleagues and I have played a tape I obtained from Dr. John Lilly at a conference in Portland, Oregon. The tape repeats a single word with no variation (the word was recorded once, then re-recorded hundreds of times from a loop). In every instance, within a 10-minute period, students record 50 to 75 words and phrases, frequently in several languages. Most believe there is more than one word on the tape. Ninety to 100% of the students can't give the correct word on the tape. Many give an incorrect word

Box 6-1   Sharper Focus

Mondegreens

Many of us have difficulty deciphering song lyrics, famous quotations, and aphorisms. Sometimes we mishear the phonemes and construct odd phrases and sentences. These mishearings are called **mondegreens.** (The obscure term *mondegreens* was coined by Sylvia Wright in an article in *Atlantic* in 1954. She had misheard the line in a folk song "and laid him on the green" as "and Lady Mondegreen.") We try to make sense out of a seeming jumble of phonemes. Gavin Edwards (1995) compiled a list of commonly misheard song lyrics. Here are a few samples:

Mondegreen: "Excuse me while I kiss this guy."
Correct lyric: "Excuse me while I kiss the sky." (Jimi Hendrix)

Mondegreen: "The girl with colitis goes by."
Correct lyric: "The girl with kaleidoscope eyes." (The Beatles)

Mondegreen: "I wanna be a dork."
Correct lyric: "I wanna be adored." (The Stone Roses)

Mondegreen: "Life in the Vaseline"
Correct lyric: "Life in the fast lane." (The Eagles)

Mondegreen: "And donuts make my brown eyes blue."
Correct lyric: "And don't it make my brown eyes blue." (Crystal Gayle)

Mondegreen: "I'll never leave your pizza burning."
Correct lyric: "I'll never be your beast of burden." (The Rolling Stones)

Mondegreen: "The ants are my friends, they're blowing in the wind; the ants are blowing in the wind."
Correct lyric: "The answer my friend, is blowing in the wind; the answer is blowing in the wind." (Bob Dylan)

Pinker (1994) offers this mondegreen:

Mondegreen: "He is trampling out the vintage where the grapes are wrapped and stored."
Correct lyric: "He is trampling out the vintage where the grapes of wrath are stored." (The Battle Hymn of the Republic)

and insist that it is the correct word. In his lecture at the conference, Lilly noted that he played the tape at a meeting of the American Association of Linguists, attended by almost 300 linguists who spoke 22 different languages. He tortured the linguists by playing the tape for 25 minutes (students grow restless after a few minutes). The linguists "heard" 2,730 different words in 22 languages (Box 6-1).

Discriminating speech sounds and interpreting meaning from phonemes is more difficult than you might expect. Hearing speech sounds and listening are not the same thing. **Hearing** is the physiological activity of registering soundwaves as they hit the eardrum. The particular sounds have no meaning until we construct meaning for them. We derive phonemes from sounds and translate the phonemes into morphemes. Morphemes are translated into words, which, in turn, are translated into phrases and sentences. We hear the sentences and interpret their meaning. This process of interpretation is very complex; it involves perception (Chapter 2), language (Chapter 4), and nonverbal cues (Chapter 5).

Retaining

Memory is essential to the listening process. This may seem obvious once you ponder what it is that you do when you listen to a lecture in a college course. If you listen to the lecture and retain none of the information, of what value was it to you? All of those multiple-choice exams would truly become multiple-guess tests. You can't construct meaning from nothing. The information we retain when

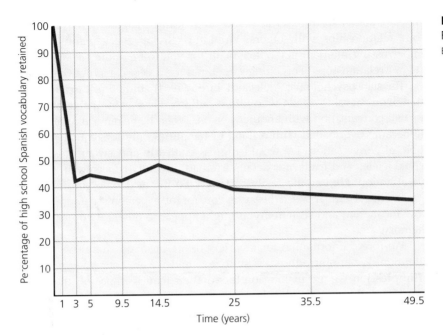

Figure 6-1 Long-Term Forgetting Curve (Source: Bahrick, 1984)

engaged in the listening process is the raw material from which meaning is constructed.

Naturally, our minds do not retain every morsel of information as we listen to someone. In fact, Hunt (1982) notes that by the time college students receive their diplomas, they have forgotten, on average, almost 80% of what they learned. Part of the reason this occurs may be a result of cramming information into short-term memory, only to have it forgotten before it moves into long-term memory. Wurman (1989) calls this cramming process *information bulimia.* We binge on information to pass an exam, then purge it from our minds once the exam is over.

One study (Bahrick, 1984) found that the forgetting curve (the rate at which we no longer retain information in our memory) drops rapidly initially but levels out and remains almost constant for many years thereafter. Students who took Spanish in high school or college, for instance, had forgotten 3 years later much of the vocabulary they had learned. After 3 years, however, forgetting leveled off and retention of vocabulary showed only slight diminishment after 50 years (Figure 6-1). Those students who took the most Spanish in school and learned it well remembered best. Even those students who hadn't used Spanish for years still retained a significant vocabulary if they learned it well initially.

We can also enhance retention of information by using the information immediately. "Use it or lose it," as they say in the memory business. If you immediately apply what you have learned in college to your life's profession or to your relationships, your retention will improve markedly and last longer. The forgetting curve will be far less pronounced.

Retention is important, but remembering everything you hear would be a curse. Imagine what it would be like forgetting nothing. Every telephone number, e-mail address, advertising jingle, slogan, song lyric, irritating noise, angry moment, embarrassing episode, and painful event would be available to clutter up your ability to think clearly and analytically. Imagine how this would affect your relationships with others. Wouldn't reliving every painful memory and embarrassing moment make it difficult for you to be optimistic and constructive in your relationships? Forgetting sometimes has a very constructive effect.

Russian psychologist Aleksandr Luria (1968) studied a Russian named Soloman Shereshevskii, a man who forgot nothing. He was incapable of conducting a normal conversation with another person. When he began a simple conversation, he became overloaded with a flood of memories only tangentially related to the topic of conversation. He would digress endlessly and swamp his listener with trivial asides and irrelevant details. He had difficulty concentrating and focusing his attention. He became easily scattered. So the next time you forget a fact for a test or feel embarrassed because you forgot a person's name, just remember how incoherent and scattered you might appear to others if you had an infallible memory.

We forget information for a variety of reasons. Sometimes we just don't pay attention. We are introduced to strangers, and we are concerned with what kind of impression we are making on them. Their names glance off the edges of our memory and promptly skip irretrievably into space. We are forced to say, "I'm sorry, but I've forgotten your name." We also forget because we don't properly organize the information we hear. We don't attach the information to any meaningful concept, idea, event, or phenomenon. The numbers 1865, 1945, and 1953 don't mean much unless you realize that they are the ending dates of three significant American wars. You can remember the dates more easily knowing that. Forgetting also results from lack of motivation to listen carefully and remember. Imagine if your professor stated at the start of a lecture, "You don't need to know this for the test." Would you pack up your notebook, put away your pen, and hunker down in your seat with no concern about your attention drifting or your eyelids slamming shut?

We forget a great deal for many reasons. A perfect memory would be a curse, but what we do remember is vital to our ability to listen and comprehend what another person communicates to us. Linguist Herbert Clark (as cited in Hunt, 1982) explains: "We bring to bear an enormous amount of knowledge to even the simplest utterances, in order to comprehend them" (p. 119).

Consider a simple statement used by Rumelhart (as cited in Hunt, 1982): "Mary heard the ice-cream truck coming down the street. She remembered her birthday money, and ran into the house." What can you infer from these sentences? Do you infer that Mary is a little girl, that she wants ice cream, that she is running into her house to get money so she can buy a Sidewalk Sunday or Eskimo Pie? Such inferences seem obvious perhaps, but look again at the two sentences. Where did your inferences come from? Nowhere is there any reference to Mary being a little girl or getting money to buy specific kinds of ice cream. You filled that in based on your previous experiences stored in your memory. Without those memories, such inferences would not be possible. Your inferences may be wrong, but you will draw some based on what you remember.

Notice how your interpretation changes when the sentences are slightly altered to: "Mary heard the police car coming down the street. She remembered her gun, and ran into the house." An entirely new set of remembered experiences allows you to draw different inferences about what is happening, and what will likely happen. Is Mary still a little girl? Is she running from the law? Does she plan to defend herself with a gun? You make such inferences because you have experience with police cars, sirens, and guns (indirectly if not directly). Memories of different experiences would produce different inferences.

Whenever we listen, we depend on our memories to fill in the blanks. Speakers presume knowledge of their audiences. If you had no common experiences with others, you couldn't communicate even rudimentary messages effectively. Retention of information is an integral part of the listening process.

Responding

Responding is a third essential element of listening (Purdy & Borisoff, 1997). Listening is a transactional process between speaker and audience. Effective listening depends on both participants in the transaction. Speakers look for responses from listeners to determine whether a message is being processed or ignored. Without a response from the listener, we have no way of knowing whether listening actually occurs. We determine the quality and type of listening from the responses of listeners. These responses can be both verbal and nonverbal. As listeners, we indicate confusion by frowning or by asking a question for clarification. If listeners are staring out a window, doing a face plant onto the desktop, doodling, talking to the person next to them, or reading the sports page when you are talking, then listening to you probably isn't a top priority.

One study (Lewis & Reinsch, 1988) revealed that responsiveness is a key determinant of effective listening. Analyzing 195 incidents in medical and banking environments, researchers determined that listeners' attentiveness to the speaker was critical. Verbally, listeners exhibited attentiveness by answering questions and sharing ideas. Nonverbally, listeners exhibited attentiveness by maintaining eye contact and using facial expressions that showed interest (e.g., smiles, raised eyebrows). Another study (Brownell, 1990) found that the quality of listening varies by degrees depending on how much or how little a person exhibits these characteristics: sensitivity, understanding, recall, objectivity, attention, concentration, sharing information, and giving feedback.

Specific Listening Problems

In the previous section, general behaviors that indicate ineffective listening were listed. In this section you will learn some more specific behaviors that are equated with poor listening.

Shift Response

Charles Derber (1979) conducted an extensive study of **conversational narcissism.** (Narcissus was a Greek mythological character who fell in love with his own reflection in a spring.) Conversational narcissism is the tendency of listeners "to turn the topics of ordinary conversations to themselves without showing sustained interest in others' topics" (p. 5). Conversational narcissists are self-absorbed. Consequently, they are ineffective listeners. They are perceived by others to be socially unattractive and inept communicators (Vangelisti et al., 1990).

Derber tape-recorded and transcribed 100 dinner conversations among 320 friends and acquaintances conducted in restaurants, dining halls, and homes. The predominant pattern found in these conversations was the strong inclination to employ the attention-*getting* initiative, called the shift response, as opposed to the attention-*giving* initiative, called the support response (see also Vangelisti et al., 1990). The **shift response** is a competitive vying for attention and focus on self by shifting topics. It is Me-oriented. The **support response** is a cooperative effort to focus attention on the other person. It is We-oriented. You can see the difference between the two responses in these two conversations:

BORIS: I'm feeling pretty depressed.

NATASHA: Oh, I felt really depressed last week when I flunked a math exam. (Shift response)

BORIS: I'm feeling really depressed.

NATASHA: Why are you feeling depressed? (Support response)

As you can see from these examples, the shift response sets the stage for a competitive battle for attention. One person's shift response will likely be countered with the other person's shift response, as in this example:

BORIS: I love listening to jazz.

NATASHA: I hate jazz, but I love country. Don't you think country is more truly native to the U.S.? (Shift response)

BORIS: I think country is cornball. All those silly lyrics like "My baby left me high and dry and now I have altitude sickness and skin like a prune" are for Gomers. Have you ever listened to jazz, I mean really listened to it? (Shift response)

NATASHA: No, and I don't plan to. Let me play some country tunes for you. You'll like them if you put aside your prejudice. (Shift response)

In this conversation, the two individuals compete for attention. Each attempts to make his or her topic the focus of the conversation. Neither party ever gets an opportunity to explore a topic he or she introduced.

Three types of support responses encourage the speaker to explore the topic initiated. They are the *background acknowledgment* (e.g., "Uh huh," "really," "yah"), the *supportive assertion* (e.g., "That's great," "I didn't think of that," "You must have considered this carefully"), and the *supportive question* (e.g., "How is jazz different from blues?" "Why do you hate math?").

Conversational narcissists favor the shift response and rarely, if ever, use the support response. Men more often than women are conversational narcissists (Derber, 1979). The shift response may be necessary in some conversations where individuals drift from the main task. The shift response becomes a listening problem, however, when it becomes a patterned response. The competent communicator primarily uses the support response, not the shift response.

Competitive Interrupting

Interrupting is closely related to the shift response. Interrupting can be used to shift attention to oneself and away from the other person talking. One study found that interrupting was the second most frequent indicator of conversational narcissism, behind the shift response (Vangelisti, et al., 1990). The difference between

Interpersonal arguments often produce competitive interrupting.

interrupting and the shift response, however, is that the shift response usually observes the "one-speaker-at-a-time" rule. **Interrupting** occurs when one person stops speaking when another person starts speaking (Tannen, 1994). Those who interrupt don't wait their turn. They step into the conversation when so moved. Also, the shift response changes topics. An interrupter may break into the conversation and make a point directly relevant to the topic.

Interrupting can be competitive, just like the shift response. Interrupting is competitive when we interrupt others to seize the floor and dominate the conversation. Competitive interrupting can create reciprocal interrupting where both parties battle each other for conversational control.

Interrupting also can be used for a variety of reasons that are noncompetitive. Expressing support ("She's right"), showing enthusiasm for the speaker's point ("Great idea"), stopping the speaker to ask for clarification of a point ("Hold on! I'm lost. Could you give me an example to clarify that point?"), warning of danger ("Stop! You're going to tip over the computer"), or giving a group a break from a talkaholic's nonstop monologue all are noncompetitive forms of interrupting. Most interruptions are noncompetitive (James & Clarke, 1993).

Listening problems occur with competitive interrupting but only rarely with noncompetitive interrupting. In competitive interrupting, the focus is Me-oriented narcissism. The interrupter is not concerned with listening to the speaker. The agenda of the interrupter is to break into the conversation and make his or her own point. Competitive interrupting creates winners and losers in ordinary conversation. Fighting for the floor, trying to dominate the conversation, and hogging the stage by cutting off other speakers in midsentence, creates rivalry, hostility, and, in some instances, reticence to continue with the conversation.

Do men interrupt more than women? Actually, they do not (Canary et al., 1997; James & Clarke, 1993). There is some evidence, however, that men and

Glazing over is a common listening problem.

women interrupt for different reasons (Mulac et al., 1988; Stewart et al., 1996). Men are more frequent competitive interrupters and women are more frequent supportive interrupters. Nevertheless, a critical review of the research indicates that the differences in interrupting patterns between men and women are small (Canary et al., 1997). Typically, men and women mirror the interrupting patterns of their partners in conversation. If one person interrupts to seize the floor, the other person may interrupt to seize it back. If one person interrupts supportively, others may be encouraged to do likewise.

Glazing Over

The third most common behavior of the conversational narcissist is what researchers call glazing over (Vangelisti et al., 1990). When listeners glaze over, they exhibit no interest in the speaker or what the speaker is saying. Listening is an active process. You have to be committed to listening.

The average listener can think at a rate of about 500 words per minute, but the normal speaking rate is about 150 words per minute (Wolvin & Coakley, 1996). This leaves plenty of opportunity for daydreaming and glazing over. Listeners may benefit from a faster speaking rate. Studies have shown that there is no significant loss of message comprehension when the speaking rate increases to 275 words per minute (Orr, 1968). A lethargic speaking rate may put listeners to sleep. Picking up the pace may counteract glazing over by listeners. If the pace is slow, the listener should try to put the differential between the rate of speaking and thinking to good use. Think about the speaker's message. Apply the message to your life experience.

Box 6-2 Sharper Focus

Focused Attention

To make the point that we do not remember unless our attention is focused, answer the following questions:

1. On which side of the Apple icon for Macintosh computers is the bite located, left or right?
2. How many sides on a stop sign?
3. In which hand does the Statue of Liberty hold her torch?
4. On which side of their uniforms do police officers wear their badges (to them, not to you)?
5. When you look at a dime, which way does Franklin Roosevelt face?
6. How many geometric shapes are in the CBS "eye" logo?
7. Is the top stripe on an American flag red or white?
8. What is in the center of the backside of a one dollar bill?
9. Every number key on the main portion of a standard computer keyboard has a symbol on it as well. What symbol is on the 5 key?
10. What is the lowest number on a standard FM radio?
11. Which of the following can be found on all current U.S. coins?
    a. "United States of America"
    b. "E Pluribus Unum"
    c. "In God We Trust"
    d. "Liberty"
12. When you rewind a videotape, does the tape fill up the left or right side of the cassette?

The correct answers (don't sneak a peak until you've answered all the questions) for these 12 questions are: 1. right side, 2. eight sides, 3. right hand, 4. left, 5. faces left, 6. two geometric shapes: a circle twice and a football shape, 7. red, 8. ONE, 9. %, 10. 88, 11. all of them, 12., left side.

How did you do? It is not unusual to answer many of these questions incorrectly. What you don't pay attention to because it isn't meaningful to you isn't remembered. A coin collector would answer correctly the Franklin Roosevelt question because coin collectors spend a great deal of time examining coins for minute details. It is part of their business. Most of us, however, pay little attention to the details on coins aside from recognizing what coin it is. Even this can be attended to rather casually, as many people discovered when they used Susan B. Anthony silver dollars as quarters, necessitating the withdrawal of the silver dollars from circulation.

Pseudolistening

Hearing and listening are different. Hearing is the brain's recognition of certain sounds. You can hear without effort and attention. Listening requires attention. We have to be committed to listening for it to be effective. A pseudolistener is someone who pretends to listen.

Individuals pretend to listen for many reasons. Often we engage in pseudolistening to keep from making a partner upset with us. We don't really want to put any energy into listening to what he or she has to say, but we don't want to be accused of not listening because that could start a quarrel. So we nod our heads, say "Uh-huh" and "really" to indicate listening, when all the time our minds are out in the Andromeda galaxy floating far away from the topic of conversation.

Students can be skillful pseudolisteners. Pretending to listen to a boring lecture, nodding your head when the professor asks the class "Does everyone understand what I just explained?", and focusing eye contact on the professor can fake listening. The listening process requires effort. Effective listening necessitates *focused* attention. *We do not remember what has not received our focused attention* (Box 6-2).

We remember what is important to us because it receives our attention. Pseudolisteners' attention is unfocused and drifts away. They remember none or next to none of the details of a conversation. Queried later, they look blankly at their inquiring partner, or they launch an offensive (e.g., "You never told me that"). Pseudolistening can be maddeningly frustrating for speakers.

Ambushing

When we ambush, we listen with a bias. That bias is to attack what the speaker says. We're looking for weaknesses and ignoring strengths. This is focused attention with prejudice. Ambushers may distort what a speaker says to gain an advantage. Ambushing is competitive and Me-oriented.

Some of the most obvious examples of ambushing occur in the political arena. Individuals running for political office are coached to ambush their opponents. It's called "going negative." The listener is looking to tear down his or her opponent. Journalists also can be ambushers. They're drawn to the mistakes made by public officials and celebrities (Tannen, 1998). They're listening to frame a story as a scandal, a blooper, or an egregious error.

Ambushing is not a problem of comprehension, although comprehension may be sacrificed when a person looks only for the negative. Ambushing is also not primarily a problem of retention. The listener is focused and attending. What is remembered, however, is very selective and not always representative. Ambushing is primarily a problem of responding. The listener responds with a rebuttal or refutation of the speaker. This twists the listening process into a wholly negative experience.

Content-Only Response

Content-only response focuses on the content of a message, but it ignores the emotional side of communication. A content-only response comprehends the literal meaning of messages from others but doesn't recognize the feelings that ride piggyback. Consider this example:

BETTINA: I can't believe we're so far in debt.

JEREMY: I've been in worse trouble.

BETTINA: Look at these visa bills, and the mastercard is maxed out too.

JEREMY: Actually, we haven't hit the limit on the mastercard yet. We have another $800 to go.

BETTINA: That's small comfort. What if we lose our house because we can't pay the mortgage?

JEREMY: We could use the mastercard to buy food and pay some bills up to the $800 that's still short of the limit. Then we could use our paychecks to cover the mortgage next month.

Nowhere does Jeremy, the content-only responder, ever acknowledge Bettina's fears and concerns (e.g., "I understand your fear. I'm feeling very anxious too about our pile of debt."). Every response only increases her fears that they are in debt up to their eyebrows and that they may lose their home. Content-only responding ignores feelings.

Competent Informational Listening

Informational listening is listening for comprehension of a speaker's message. Your goal is to understand what the speaker has said. When listening to others, it is usually better to be sure that you comprehend the speaker's message before you critically evaluate it. Too often we are prone to judge another person's ideas without fully understanding what the person actually said and believes. Accurate comprehension is more difficult than it may appear to be.

Confirmation Bias

Several years ago I was watching *Nightline* on TV, and the issue being debated was compulsive suing. The first person questioned by Ted Koppel was a representative of the insurance industry. He told a story of a man who was seriously injured when an automobile went out of control and crashed into the phone booth he was occupying. The injured man sued the phone company for millions of dollars, and won. The insurance man asserted that this was a classic case of a frivolous lawsuit. Obviously, the injured man sued the "deep pocket," the party with the cash, not the person responsible for the injury, namely, the driver of the automobile. As I listened, I began nodding my head in agreement and feeling annoyed at the verdict. Koppel, however, turned to the lawyer who represented the injured man and asked for his response. The lawyer presented a different set of facts. The phone company, according to the lawyer, had been notified on numerous occasions that the phone booth involved in the accident had a door that would jam and trap occupants inside the booth. When the automobile spun out of control, the man inside saw the car coming toward him, tried desperately to exit the phone booth, but could not because the door jammed. The man inside was crushed by the automobile and permanently paralyzed. The phone company was held liable for negligence. Now I felt irritated with myself for not withholding my judgment until I had heard both sides of the issue.

This case is an example of confirmation bias. **Confirmation bias** is the psychological tendency to look for and listen to information that supports our beliefs and

Luann reprinted by permission of United Features Syndicate, Inc.

Box 6-3   Focus on Controversy

Confirmation Bias in Child Abuse Cases

Every year there are approximately 125, 000 *substantiated* cases of sexual abuse of children in the United States (Bruck et al., 1998). No one should attempt to diminish the seriousness of this problem, nor the desirability of significantly reducing this reprehensible treatment of children. In an effort to identify and punish child abusers, however, clear instances of confirmation bias have created a new controversy. Are some people being falsely accused of child abuse? There are notable instances of false accusations (Bruck et al., 1998; Ofshe & Watters, 1994; Loftus & Ketcham, 1994; Pendergrast, 1995).

The accuracy of accusations of child abuse is a significant interpersonal issue because even the accusation of child abuse has a shattering effect on families. Children often refuse to have any contact with an accused parent, and parents are often bewildered by the accusations. Lives are destroyed. People are even sent to prison for acts that never occurred (Pendergrast, 1995).

Confirmation bias plays an important part in cases of false accusations by children—and by adults who "remember" years later previously "repressed memories" of abuse during childhood. Poorly trained therapists, attorneys, parents, teachers, and police can, and have, induced false memories of child abuse (Bruck et al., 1998; Loftus & Ketcham, 1994; Ofshe and Watters, 1994). All of these individuals typically interview children extensively about possible sexual abuse when suspicion arises. They are understandably eager to discover actual child abuse and gather evidence to prosecute the perpetrators and help the victims. In their zeal to find the truth, those who interview children may inadvertently plant false memories in a child's mind (Bruck et al., 1998). They can do this by selectively encouraging statements that confirm suspicions of abuse (e.g., vigorous head nodding, smiling, or making statements such as "Good! Tell me more") and discouraging denials of abuse (e.g., shaking head, scowling, or making stern statements, such as "Come on, you know something happened. Tell me."). Asking erroneously suggestive questions (Bruck et al., 1998) that assume without corroboration that abuse occurred also can plant false memories (e.g., "When Jimmy was bad to you, did he act this way more than once?").

Interviewers of possible victims of sexual abuse often listen only to answers from children and adults that confirm their worst fear that abuse occurred. They are often predisposed to "hunt for abuse" (Ofshe & Watters, 1994). Typically, interviewers do not ask questions that might *disconfirm* the allegations of abuse. Questions that might produce another explanation for the allegations often are not asked (e.g., "Did anyone tell you that this happened to you?" "Did you see it happen?" "Did you remember this happening to you before you were told by someone that it happened?").

Denials of abuse, even emphatic ones, may be ignored. Denials may even provoke more energetic efforts to

---

values and to ignore or distort information that contradicts our beliefs and values. As I listened to the first interview, I became incensed that someone would sue the phone company when clearly the person responsible for the injury was the driver of the car. This version of events supported my belief that Americans are suit-happy. When I heard the facts presented by the lawyer for the victim, however, I felt dumb for not having waited to hear the entire story.

Confirmation bias is a common problem (Gilovich, 1997). It is especially common in small groups (Schittekatte & Van Hiel, 1996). Group members have a strong tendency to "show interest in facts and opinions that support their initially preferred policy and take up time in their meetings to discuss them, but they tend to ignore facts and opinions that do not support their initially preferred policy" (Janis, 1982, p. 10). This confirmation bias often produces poor, sometimes disastrous, decisions (Box 6-3).

As listeners, we have to be constantly vigilant, ready to counter confirmation bias. We need to adopt the habit of waiting to draw a conclusion until we have heard dissenting viewpoints, then weigh the evidence before making a decision.

(*continued*)

ferret out abuse by those trying to "get the goods" on a possible abuser (Ofshe & Watters, 1994). As several researchers explain, interviewers may "attempt to gather only confirmatory evidence and . . . may fail to gather any evidence that could potentially disconfirm their hypotheses" (Bruck et al., 1998, p. 140). This is biased informational listening, not an objective, dispassionate attempt to comprehend the truth. These interviewers are listening only to information that confirms their belief or suspicion.

Employing competent informational listening skills is not always a matter of counteracting relatively benign instances of confusion or misunderstandings between people. Sometimes, competent informational listening can affect people's lives in terribly serious ways. Child abuse affects all of us directly or indirectly. Pendergrast (1995) estimates that there are approximately 1 million claims of "recovered memories" of child abuse by adults each year. The legitimacy of recovered memories of child abuse, however, has been seriously questioned (Loftus & Ketcham, 1994; Ofshe & Watters, 1994; Pendergrast, 1995). More than 15,000 families have contacted the False Memory Syndrome Foundation to seek help, but this is probably a small fraction of the families faced with false accusations of abuse. Some experts estimate that as many as 35% of accusations of sexual abuse turn out to be false (as cited in Bruck et al., 1998).

We all want to protect children from the scourge of child abuse, and we don't want to discourage children from revealing real abuse. Refusing to accept a child's accusation of abuse because the idea is too horrible to contemplate would use confirmation bias to protect abusers. Covering our ears to an ugly revelation perpetuates child abuse. Given the seriousness of the crime, however, we also do not want to make false accusations that needlessly destroy families. Effective informational listening can help guard against "making monsters" out of innocent people. Effective informational listening by those who initially suspect abuse (e.g., parents, teachers) and by those who later investigate allegations is vital. We need to hear all relevant evidence to weigh it properly. Informational listening free from confirmation bias can help us all feel confident that those who are prosecuted, found guilty of child abuse, and punished, truly received what they deserve.

Questions for Thought

1. Does the fact that child abuse is a highly charged emotional issue contribute to confirmation bias in such cases? Explain.
2. Is it possible to maintain objectivity and be "dispassionate" when listening to a possible victim of child abuse? If not, how can we combat confirmation bias in such cases?

The Vividness Effect

In April 1999, 18-year-old Eric Harris and 17-year-old Dylan Klebold walked into Columbine High School in Littleton, Colorado and began a 4-hour massacre of their fellow students. Armed with shotguns, semiautomatic handguns, a semiautomatic rifle, and 30 homemade pipe bombs, they eventually killed 12 students and a teacher. The siege ended when they killed themselves. The story was international news. Every newspaper and television station covered the story extensively for days. This horrific incident resurrected a national debate on gun control. New legislation restricting gun ownership was passed by the U.S. Senate one month after the Columbine shootings. The vividness of this single incident led many to believe that school children are in imminent peril across the country. A *Newsweek* poll of 757 randomly selected adults, taken just 2 days after the school massacre, found that 63% of the respondents thought a shooting incident at their children's school was very or somewhat likely ("Anatomy of a Massacre," 1999). Is a shooting at school a likely event? So it would seem from the vividness of the reporting and the sensational nature of the crime.

The news each night fills the airwaves with graphic stories of murder and mayhem. It's enough to make you want to hide in your home. Yet the Columbine High School incident, as tragic and inexplicable as it was, occurred at a time when violent crime was plunging in the United States by about a third since 1993 (Glassman, 1998). There are millions of high school children in the United States attending 20,000 secondary schools. In the 5 years prior to the Columbine High School shootings, there were six similar incidences in schools (Glassman, 1998). *Six!* That's six too many, but it is not cause for national breast-beating about our violent youth. Only 10% of schools register even one serious violent crime, on average, in a year. A high school senior is 200 times more likely to be admitted to Harvard University as to be killed at school (Adler & Springen, 1999). Juvenile murder rates also declined by almost a third in years prior to the Columbine shootings (Glassman, 1998).

This is an example of the **vividness effect.** When graphic, outrageous, shocking, controversial, and dramatic events distort our perceptions of the facts, we listen to the dramatic example and conclude that we have problems wholly out of proportion to the facts. The vividness effect seriously distorts informational listening because the shocking example can negate a mountain of contradictory evidence. How many times have you avoided a class based solely on the claim of another student that the professor was "incredibly boring" or "sexist" or "terribly unfair"? Perhaps the student told a startling tale of poor behavior from the teacher. You might reply, "Wow! I hadn't heard that. Thanks. I'll make sure not to take his class."

A sample of one is hardly conclusive evidence upon which to base such choices, yet we do make such choices. Listening to information from a single source with a vivid tale to tell—possibly a biased one at that—is generally poor listening practice. If you seek out other students' opinions of the same professor, you might be surprised to discover that many may actually have very positive things to say, completely countering the single student with the negative opinion. There are exceptions, however, where you may need to take seriously a vivid tale, even if told by only one person. If you hear that someone is dangerous and potentially violent, even if it proves to be erroneous, it deserves to be listened to seriously until proven wrong. In general, be on guard for the vividness effect. Don't jump to conclusions based on a single dramatic example. Seek more information, ask questions, and research the issue before making a conclusion.

Competent Critical Listening

Listening involves more than accurately understanding the messages of others. Comprehension is an important first step in the listening process. Once we understand the message, however, we need to evaluate it. All opinions are not created equal. People used to think that the earth was flat, that pus helped wounds heal, that bloodletting cured diseases, and that drilling a large hole in an afflicted person's skull cured mental illness by letting evil spirits escape. A book published in 1902 entitled *The Cottage Physician*, written by a group of "the best physicians and surgeons of modern practice," offers some unusual advice. It claims that cataracts can be cured by generous doses of laxatives, tetanus can be treated effectively by "pouring cold water on the head from a considerable height," and

Figure 6-2 Skepticism Continuum

difficulty urinating can be relieved by marshmallow enemas (as cited in Weingarten, 1994).

We hear a dizzying variety of claims every day. We hear that most of us are raised in dysfunctional families, that 96% of Americans experience codependency, that psychics can make accurate predictions about our love lives, and that extraterrestrial beings have abducted some of our citizens and performed sexual experiments on them. (Incidentally, Goodfellow Rebecca Ingrams Pearson, a London firm, offers an insurance policy for two extraterrestrial occurrences: abduction and alien impregnation. Cost: $155 a year ["Insurance Policies," 1996]). How do we separate the likely facts from the almost certain fantasies and nonsense? Critical listeners examine the merits of **claims,** defined here as generalizations that remain to be proven.

In this section you will learn about skepticism, probability, and the criteria for analyzing and evaluating claims. As listeners, we need to know the difference between prime rib and baloney.

Skepticism

Critical listening begins with skepticism. Skepticism, unlike the media's version of it, is not simply finding fault with the claims of others. **Skepticism** is a process of examining claims, evaluating evidence and reasoning, and drawing conclusions based on probabilities. Skepticism falls between the two extremes of true belief and cynicism (Figure 6-2).

True believers willingly accept claims by authorities or valued sources *without question.* They exhibit confirmation bias. They actively seek evidence (even if weak) that supports already accepted beliefs, and they ignore or distort contradictory evidence. *True believers are belief-driven, not evidence-driven.* They refuse to change their point of view no matter how much evidence refutes the claim.

Thirty-nine members of the Heaven's Gate cybergroup committed mass suicide in March 1997, blindly following the dictates of their leader, Marshall Applewhite. Members were not interested in having their beliefs challenged by evidence that contradicted those beliefs. Their minds were locked shut (Gardner, 1997). They believed the Hale-Bopp comet was a sign that extraterrestrial spaceships were coming to pick them up after death to transport them to a higher plane of reality. No amount of evidence contradicting their beliefs could penetrate their minds. These were not unintelligent people. Some of them were highly educated computer whizzes. That's what makes true belief scary. Intelligent, highly educated individuals can close their minds to facts and evidence just like anyone else. You have to choose to unlock your mind and consider the facts and evidence.

Cynics have a negative attitude. H. L. Mencken once described a cynic as a person who "smells flowers and looks around for a coffin." Cynics are fault-finders.

Both cynics and true believers have their minds on automatic pilot, never changing their direction. Cynics, however, act as if there is software in their heads that programs them to tear down and ridicule others. Cynicism was a concern of astronomer Carl Sagan's (1995) before he died. Although he did not use the term *cynicism*, he warned against belittling others when disagreeing with the ways they think. This is an important point. You don't make critical listeners by cynically mocking others. *Evaluate claims, not people.* Be hard on the claim, soft on the people making the claim. During a lifetime, each of us is likely to feel embarrassed at least once, probably several times, by the realization that we believed in something or someone that immediately should have struck us as silly.

Skeptics operate in the middle of the two extremes of true belief and cynicism. Skeptics approach each claim they listen to with a willingness to be shown the truth of the claim, neither blindly accepting, nor sneering at, the beliefs of others. *Skeptics are evidence-driven, not belief-driven.* If a used car salesperson told you that "This honey of a car has never had a problem," wouldn't you want to see evidence to support such a claim? A skeptic doesn't ridicule the salesperson for making the claim. Skeptics simply expect something more than a salesperson's say-so (e.g., maintenance records, engine tests, a mechanic's report). Evidence and reasoning guide skeptics' decision making.

Having drawn distinctions between true belief, cynicism, and skepticism, please understand that true belief, as used here, does not simply mean "strong belief." Skepticism also does not mean "no belief." As Ruggeiro (1988) notes, "It is not the embracing of an idea that causes problems—it is the refusal to relax that embrace when good sense dictates doing so." *The key distinction between a true believer and a skeptic is not the strength of the belief but the process used to arrive at and maintain a belief.* True believers use confirmation bias and assertions of authority figures as primary avenues to belief formation and perpetuation. A true believer is an individual whose mind has slammed shut. Skeptics show a willingness to change beliefs, even strongly held ones. If a belief cannot withstand mounting evidence, they don't ignore or distort the evidence (confirmation bias). They change the belief and all related claims. Skeptics do not change beliefs lightly or without a struggle, but they do not cling obstinately to erroneous beliefs.

So, how should a skeptic confront a true believer without belittling or showing contempt? Consider this dialogue:

TRUE BELIEVER: You should join my group.

SKEPTIC: Please correct me if I'm misinformed, but aren't you pressured to sell all of your possessions and give the proceeds to the group?

TRUE BELIEVER: Yes, that shows true commitment.

SKEPTIC: Doesn't it bother you that the leader of your group uses those proceeds to buy expensive cars and live a lavish lifestyle, while group members are required to wear inexpensive robes and live frugally?

TRUE BELIEVER: We believe our leader is the exalted one and should have, as you put it, "a lavish lifestyle." We are merely his servants.

SKEPTIC: It seems contradictory to me to teach commitment and to attack materialism but expect only you to make sacrifices while your leader lives very comfortably without visible sacrifice.

TRUE BELIEVER: That simply shows how little you understand us and our leader.

SKEPTIC: Perhaps, but I'm trying to understand. Are you ever allowed to doubt the teachings of your leader?

TRUE BELIEVER: No! Doubt leads to confusion and weak commitment.

SKEPTIC: Well, this is where we really disagree, because I have serious reservations about a group that requires me to accept without question what a group leader teaches.

Throughout this dialogue, respect is shown to the true believer even though differences in belief are obvious and strong. You can disagree, even strongly, with a true believer without being disagreeable. Skepticism is a process for belief construction and validation. There can be reasonable disagreement even among skeptics. Show others respect when discussing beliefs, because few people take their beliefs lightly.

Probability

Skepticism rests on probabilities of truth. Whenever we make a truth claim (e.g., "Single women in their forties have a worse chance of getting married than being kidnapped by a terrorist," "Men self-disclose less often than women," "Students who like their teachers give instructors higher evaluations"), we should first determine the degree of likelihood that the claim is true. Note the differences between these examples:

> *Possibility:* You could receive an "A" grade in a class even though you flunked all the tests and assignments and rarely came to class.
>
> *Plausibility:* There is at least one other galaxy in the universe with life forms similar to us.
>
> *Probability:* Leaping out of an airplane without a parachute from 3,000 feet will result in death.
>
> *Certainty:* All of us will die.

Each claim rests on the *likelihood* that it is true. The first is highly unlikely, but not certain. Thus, it is possible. A student could get an "A" grade in a class despite flunking everything assigned. A clerical error by the instructor or a computer glitch could produce such a result, but don't bet your educational future on such an unlikely event occurring.

The second claim is more likely because, instead of just blind luck or random chance, it can be supported by a rational argument. It is plausible that another galaxy has life forms similar to us. Astronomers tell us that there are approximately 100 billion galaxies, each with about 100 billion stars. With numbers that enormous, it doesn't defy logic to expect that life exists elsewhere. Nevertheless, this claim is not very probable without evidence, and we have no credible evidence of life in other parts of the universe (despite accounts of UFO sightings). We merely have intriguing speculation.

The third claim is a step up from a plausible argument. Not only is the claim plausible (i.e., people usually injure themselves falling from only an 8-foot ladder), it is very likely to be true. Plentiful evidence shows that when people jump out of planes and their parachutes fail to open the results are almost always tragic. The human body isn't made to withstand such a fall. Nevertheless, although highly probable, the claim is not certain. We've all read about cases where people have survived such free falls.

Box 6-4   Focus on Controversy

Skepticism and Open-Mindedness

In April 1993 the Roper Organization polled 992 adults and 506 high school students ("Poll," 1993). Thirty-four percent of the adults and 37% of the high school students thought it was "possible that the Holocaust did not happen." Thirty-seven percent of the adults and almost half of the high school students did not know that the Holocaust was Hitler's systematic effort to exterminate the Jews, the disabled, gays, gypsies, and other humans who did not qualify as members of the "Master Race" during World War II. A *Washington Post* poll surveyed 1,000 Americans in July 1994 (Fisher, 1994). If results were generalized to the entire U.S. population, about 20 million citizens think it is "possible" no one has ever landed and walked on the moon.

Why do so many people believe that two of the most thoroughly documented events of the 20th century might not have happened? The answer might lie in a misunderstanding of what it means to be open-minded. During one period in my life, I explored myriad alternative medicines and therapies, partly out of curiosity and partly from a need to help a sick friend. I explored herbal remedies, homeopathy, polarity therapy, radiasthesia, dowsing, psychic healing, crystal healing, and faith healing, among others. One consistent pattern emerged from my personal exploration. Whenever I expressed doubt about the validity of these alternative approaches to disease and afflictions, believers in the therapies and remedies denounced me as "closed-minded." At first I was bothered that others perceived me as closed-minded. It seemed that to be open-minded to my detracters meant I had to accept without question what they wanted me to believe. My academic training in speech and debate, however, kept emerging. "Show me convincing evidence supporting your position," I said,

"not just testimonials and opinions from biased sources eager to sell a product."

The polls on the Holocaust and the moon landing asked respondents if it was "possible" that neither event occurred. Perhaps respondents wanted to appear open-minded by allowing for the possibility that these two events did not happen. Similarly, on talk shows individuals who claim the Holocaust never happened "debate" Jews who survived the death camps. Talk show hosts justify this spectacle as an open-minded exchange of two opposing sides. Student editors run ads from Holocaust deniers in college newspapers (Lipstadt, 1993). The editor of the *Georgetown Record* justified the appearance of such an ad by claiming that "there are two sides to every issue and both have a place on the pages of any open-minded paper's editorial page" (as cited in Lipstadt, 1993).

Remaining open to obviously false claims, however, is not the sign of an open-minded person. As Lipstadt (1993) explains, "One can believe that Elvis Presley is alive and well and living in Moscow. However sincere one's conviction, that does not make it a legitimate opinion or 'other side' of a debate" (p. xiii, xvi).

The more a claim bumps against well-established knowledge and facts, the less plausible becomes the claim (Adler, 1998). It is possible, for example, that recurrent stories of alien abductions are true. Such accounts, however, must withstand the "vast evidence of the established physical laws that would have to be violated or strained" (Adler, 1998). Testimonials of alien abductions, even from sincere individuals, are unconvincing when weighed against certain facts. Visits by aliens require speed-of-light space travel—a monumentally implausible occurrence (Paulos, 1988). Credible alternative

For a claim to be certain there can be no exceptions—ever. Our mortality seems certain. Nevertheless, there are few claims that are even arguably absolute. Consequently, *a skeptic initially views claims of certainty as dubious.*

Truth claims vary in likelihood from possible to certain (Freeley, 1996) (Figure 6-3). As we make claims of increasing likelihood, our burden of proof also increases. **Burden of proof** is the obligation of the claimant to support any claim he or she has made with evidence and reasoning. Thus, if you claim plausibility, you must meet that standard of proof. If you claim probability, you must meet that higher standard of proof for us to have confidence in your claim. If you claim certainty, you have accepted an enormous burden of proof. Only a single exception disproves your claim of certainty. Even a few exceptions, however, do not disprove a probability because you claim

(continued)

psychological explanations for accounts of alien abductions explain the testimonials and do not require rewriting the laws of physics (Adler, 1998).

We do not have the time, energy, and resources to listen equally to every opinion and claim. Those claims that have been studied and found deficient must be discarded unless truly impressive proof is produced to warrant a rehearing. Current knowledge of historical facts and scientific evidence contradicts claims that the earth is flat, that bloodletting cures disease, that drilling holes in a person's head cures mental illness, and that the Holocaust and the moon landing did not occur. A true believer of such things would hang on to such viewpoints despite the evidence. A skeptic would not.

Adler (1998) notes, "What truly marks an open-minded person is the willingness to follow where evidence leads. If the evidence against alien abductions and many other supernatural and paranormal speculations is overwhelming, then an open-minded person must reject them" (p. 44). Conversely, a closed-minded person is someone who refuses to examine his or her beliefs when there is compelling evidence that contradicts the validity of those beliefs. Clinging steadfastly to unwarranted beliefs can make you feel secure, and discarding beliefs that cannot withstand a preponderance of proof can be unsettling, even anxiety-producing. Human knowledge and progress do not advance, however, by holding onto beliefs based more on wishful thinking than critical thinking.

There are, of course, customs and common practices that cannot be proven or disproven by any evidence. Many differences exist between cultures in what is valued and in how individuals communicate (Chapter 3). Ethnocentrism is prejudice that elevates one's own culture while diminishing another culture because values and behaviors differ. Cultural preferences regarding the "right" and "wrong" way to address a person of status, greet a stranger, show respect for others' feelings, express emotions, or conduct oneself during courtship cannot be proven or disproven by evidence. These are untestable differences based on deep-seated cultural values that make human diversity interesting and challenging. Open-mindedness in this context requires a willingness to understand differences and to recognize that difference doesn't necessarily mean deficient. Closed-mindedness in this context would be ethnocentrism. A closed-minded person devalues the customs and practices of another culture simply because they are different and fall outside his or her comfort zone. When traveling abroad, a closed-minded person judges how "advanced" or "primitive" a culture is based on how closely customs and common practices parallel his or her own culture.

Questions for Thought

1. Can you think of other claims besides Holocaust and moon landing denials and alien abductions that have been justified by appeals to open-mindedness? Creationism? Channeling? Astrology? Explain your answer.
2. Can you have too much skepticism and become closed-minded? Explain.
3. Should we give an open-minded hearing to claims that women are the inferior sex and men make poor parents?
4. How should an open-minded person deal with cultural practices that dehumanize, such as female circumcision?

Figure 6-3 Probability Continuum

Possible   Plausible   Probable   Certain

high likelihood, not certainty. *Whoever makes a claim has the burden to prove it* (Box 6-4).

Sometimes speakers try to shift the burden to listeners by challenging them to "prove that it is not true." When you listen to speakers make a claim, remember that the claim is theirs to prove. It is not yours to disprove until they have met their burden of proof.

This anti-gay protester at the funeral of murdered gay college student Matthew Shepard expresses his point of view. Open-mindedness doesn't mean we have to listen to hateful bigotry.

Burden of proof increases as our claims move toward certainty. Consequently, claims of probability that meet the burden of proof should be taken more seriously than those that merely meet the less burdensome plausibility or possibility standards. For instance, let's say that a stranger asks you to walk blindfolded across a busy freeway. Would you do it? Not unless you're out of your mind. What if you saw another person do it successfully before you were asked? Would you do it then? One successful case shows that it is possible to walk blindfolded across a busy freeway and not collide with a speeding car that could distribute your bodily parts across several counties. Nevertheless, you would be a fool to try it, because possible doesn't mean likely, and one successful case is a weak standard of proof. The stranger meets his burden of proof by showing that it can be done, but he doesn't show with one case that it is *likely* others can also be successful. You should also weigh likelihood against the consequences of failure. In this instance, that could be serious injury or death.

Criteria for Evaluating Reasoning and Evidence

Critical listeners are skeptical listeners. Skepticism rests on probabilities of truth. The more probable the claim, the more valuable it is to listeners as a basis for decision making, provided that the claimant meets his or her burden of proof. Proof is composed of reasoning and evidence. Thus, we determine if the burden of proof has been met by evaluating the reasoning and the evidence. There are several criteria, or standards, to use in such evaluations. In this section you will learn about the most important criteria and the **fallacies,** or errors in evidence and reasoning, that fall short of these criteria.

Credibility   Can we believe the evidence others use to support their claims? Is this evidence trustworthy and reliable? Credibility is a key criterion for evaluating evidence as you listen to others make claims. Several fallacies significantly diminish the credibility of evidence presented.

Questionable Statistic   Some statistics cannot be accurate, but that doesn't prevent individuals and groups from manufacturing a statistic or making an attempt to count something. The skeptic must ask, "How could you compile such a statistic accurately?" Consider the example of the number of homeless people in the United States. Every report on homelessness in this country tries to quantify the extent of the problem. As Crossen (1994) notes, however, estimates of the homeless have varied from 230,000 to 3 million, not exactly a precise count. There is simply no way to count the number of homeless with any precision because the homeless "are transient, wary of authority and sometimes mentally ill or addicted to drugs" (p. 137). If our homeless shelters are overwhelmed by greater demand than supply of beds and food, we know there is a problem to be addressed. Even if we only fill those shelters to half or three-quarters capacity, we still have a problem. There are better ways to make a case for aid to the homeless than manufacturing inflated and unreliable statistical estimates of the problem.

Biased Source   Special interest groups or individuals who stand to gain money, prestige, power, or influence if they advocate a certain position on an issue are biased sources of information. You should consider their claims as dubious. Look for a source that has no personal stake in the outcome of a dispute or disagreement, a source that seeks the truth, not personal glory or benefit. Consider these examples (Crossen, 1994). Chocolate may actually prevent tooth decay, reported a newsletter from the Princeton Dental Resource Center. M&M/Mars—makers of chocolate snack foods—finances the center. Quaker Oats sponsored studies that reported reductions in cholesterol from oat bran. Manufacturers added oat bran to more than 300 of their products even though the reduction in cholesterol claimed was a paltry 3%. Nacho chips sprinkled with oat bran were proclaimed to be health food. Advertisers announced that oat bran had been added to toothpaste, licorice, and beer.

Bald men are three times more likely to suffer a heart attack than men not follicly challenged, claimed a study sponsored by Upjohn Company, maker of Minoxidil, a hair restoration product. Drug companies do their own studies and almost always seem to find that their new drug outperforms older competitors (Crossen, 1994). Bias seriously diminishes the credibility of a source.

Expert Quoted Out of Field of Expertise   Iben Browning, the chief scientist for Summa Medical Corporation, has a doctorate in physiology and a bachelor's degree in physics and math. He predicted a major earthquake for December 3 and 4, 1990, along the New Madrid Fault in the Midwest. Schools in several states dismissed students for these two days as a result of Browning's prediction. Browning had some scientific expertise, but not in the area of earthquake prediction. In fact, earthquake experts around the country denounced Browning's predictions. No earthquake, large or small, occurred on the dates Browning predicted. Browning was not a credible source on earthquakes. Quoting experts outside their field of expertise is inappropriate.

Relevance   Information used to support claims must relate directly to those claims. Several fallacies fail the relevance test.

Irrelevant Statistic   Frank Lautenberg, a U.S. senator from New Jersey, claimed, "In 1996, 41 percent of some 42,000 deaths due to traffic crashes were alcohol-related" (as cited in Mulshine, 1998). Does this mean that drunk drivers caused almost half of these 42,000 deaths? Lautenberg used this statistic to support legislation to lower the national standard for drunk driving from a blood alcohol level of .10 to .08. The statistic, however, is deceptive. Most of the deaths that were "alcohol-related" did not involve drunk driving. According to the National Traffic Safety Administration, 19%, not 41%, of fatalities involved a drunk driver (Mulshine, 1998). The 41% figure includes sober drivers but drunk pedestrians. It also includes any driver who had an alcohol level above .0l. A driver who had a few swallows of wine and was involved in a car crash where someone died would be included in the "alcohol-related" death statistic. The 41% figure is mostly irrelevant to the claim of drunk driving fatalities.

Ad Hominem   Elbert Hubbard once said, "If you can't answer a man's argument, all is not lost. You can still call him vile names." The ad hominem fallacy is a personal attack on the messenger to avoid the message. It is a diversionary tactic. "There's an article in the student newspaper charging student government with misuse of student funds. Why should we listen to anything that rag prints." This is an ad hominem fallacy because it doesn't directly respond to the claims made in the newspaper article; it merely disparages the newspaper. What if the paper is correct? Shouldn't the charges be considered?

Not all personal attacks are ad hominem fallacies. If a claim raises the issue of a person's credibility, character, or trustworthiness, the attack is not irrelevant to the claim made.

Ad Populum   A 1997 national survey of college freshmen conducted by UCLA found that 56.4% opposed "affirmative action in college admissions" (as cited in Lubman, 1998c). Arguing that affirmative action related to college admissions should be abolished because a majority of incoming freshmen believe it should be abolished is an example of the ad populum (or popular opinion) fallacy. You should not judge a claim simply on the basis of how many people feel a certain way. A finding such as the one in the UCLA survey should cause concern among supporters of affirmative action and motivate campus-wide discussions on the issue. It should not determine whether affirmative action is unfair or ineffective and should be abolished. Majorities can be and often are wrong in their judgments, a point Republicans kept making while they pushed impeachment of Bill Clinton in 1999 in the face of his 73% public approval rating.

Sufficiency   The person who makes a claim has the burden to prove that claim. This means that sufficient evidence and reasoning must be used to support a claim. Sufficiency is a judgment. There is no precise formula for determining sufficiency. Generally, strong, plentiful evidence and solid reasoning meet the sufficiency criterion. Several fallacies clearly exhibit insufficiency.

Inadequate Sample   Almost every day we read in the newspaper or hear on radio or television about some new study that "proves" coffee is dangerous, certain pesticides sprayed on vegetables are harmful, power lines cause cancer, or massive doses of vitamin C prevent colds. What's a person to believe? A single study proves very little and is insufficient to draw any general conclusion. In science, studies are replicated before results are given credence because mistakes can be made that may distort the results. The greater the number of studies that show similar or identical results, the more sufficient the proof. More than 40,000 studies show that cigarettes are a serious health hazard ("Advertising Is Hazardous," 1986). Now that's sufficient proof.

Some polls report results from a very small sample of people. In general, the margin of error in polls goes up as the number of people chosen randomly goes down. A poll of 1,000 people typically has a margin of error of about plus or minus 3%. This means that if the poll says that 65% of respondents approve of the job the president is doing, the actual result, if every adult American were surveyed, would be between 62% and 68%. No poll is perfect, but increasing the sample size improves the chances that the poll is accurate. The national survey of 250,000 freshmen students conducted at UCLA in 1997 had a margin of error of .6% (Lubman, 1998c).

Self-Selected Sample　Any poll or survey that depends on respondents selecting themselves to participate will provide results that are insufficient to generalize beyond the sample. A **random sample** is a portion of the population chosen in such a manner that every member of the entire population has an equal chance of being selected. A **self-selected sample** attracts the most committed, aroused, or motivated individuals to fill out surveys on their own and answer polling questions. Printing a survey in a magazine and collecting those that have been returned is an example of a self-selected sample. Calling an 800-number to answer a question about politics or social issues is another example of a self-selected sample.

Shere Hite (1987) mailed 100,000 surveys to gather data for *Women and Love*. Her survey included 127 essay questions. Only 4,500 were completed and returned. Her most startling result was that a whopping 98% of the women who responded were dissatisfied with their relationships with men. Several national polls at the time completely contradicted this finding (Gallup & Gallup, 1989). Those women who filled out the survey had to be very motivated, probably by anger toward the men in their lives, to spend time answering 127 essay questions. Hite's results tell us about women who are dissatisfied with the men in their lives, but her findings cannot be generalized to all women because her sample was self-selected, not random.

Testimonials　Praising a product that you have used is called a **testimonial.** Testimonials are not sufficient proof for a claim. One person can make a mistake and believe psychic, bare-handed surgery cured an ailment. A hundred such testimonials on psychic surgery don't make the claim any stronger because a hundred people can also be wrong. Testimonials are persuasive, that's why advertisers use them, but they are lousy proof for a claim. For every 10 people who claim a product was effective, there might be 1,000 who found the product worthless. Testimonials are confirmation bias in action. Advertisers use only the supportive testimonials. Resting your claim on testimonials is fallacious and insufficient proof.

Correlation Mistaken for Causation　A consistent relationship between two variables is called a **correlation.** A variable is anything that can change. Suppose a strong relationship was found between two variables, amount of exercise and degree of health, for example. Increased exercise and improved health seem related. Increase exercise and health improves. Can you conclude from this that increased exercise causes improved health? No! *Correlation does not prove causation.* Increased exercise *may* cause improved health in adults, but there may be more to it. Adults who increase their exercise may also stop smoking, reduce fat intake, or reduce their stress at work at the same time. So was it the exercise, cessation of smoking, diet changes, stress reduction, or all of them combined that caused the improved health? Correlations suggest *possible* causation and may be worthy of further study, but correlations alone are insufficient reason to claim *probable* causation. Stephan Jay Gould (1981) notes that "the vast majority of correlations in our world are, without doubt, noncausal" (p. 242).

Out of a sample of 100 college students, what if you found that 45 had eaten breakfast then dumped their girlfriend or boyfriend the same day, but none of the 55 individuals who had skipped breakfast dumped their girlfriend or boyfriend? Here's a perfect correlation (no exceptions). Incidence of breakfast eating is perfectly related to frequency of girlfriend/boyfriend dumping in a given population. Eat breakfast—dump girlfriend/boyfriend. Don't eat breakfast—keep girlfriend/boyfriend. Would you conclude that this perfect correlation was sufficient proof that eating breakfast causes a person to dump his or her girlfriend or boyfriend?

All of us have a strong inclination to leap from correlation to causation. We don't see the insufficiency of such proof. "The invalid assumption that correlation implies cause is probably among the two or three most serious and common errors of human reasoning" (Gould, 1981, p. 242).

False Analogy   A claim based on an analogy alleges that two things that resemble each other in certain ways also resemble each other in further ways as well. Thus, both things should be treated in similar ways. Consider this analogy: "In Turkey, farmers grow poppies as a cash crop. In the United States, farmers grow corn and soybeans for cash crops. Why outlaw poppies in the United States when we don't outlaw corn and soybeans?" Sound reasonable to you? Analogies become insufficient proof and fallacious logic when significant points of difference exist despite some superficial similarities between the two things being compared. These kinds of analogies are false. Poppies, corn, and soybeans are all cash crops, but that doesn't warrant similar treatment. This is a superficial similarity. Poppies are outlawed in the United States because they are a source of heroin, a dangerous drug. Corn and soybeans are grown in the United States to feed the world, not to produce narcotics. Poppies are not an indispensable crop. Corn and soybeans are indispensable crops. The world can do just fine without poppies, but millions would likely starve without corn and soybeans.

A. J. Jacobs wrote a book entitled *The Two Kings* in which he compared Elvis Presley with Jesus Christ (a more absurd analogy would be difficult to find). Jacobs points out that Jesus was a carpenter, and Elvis majored in woodshop in school. Jesus was arrested for defying the Romans, and Elvis was arrested for beating up a gas-station attendant ("Book News," 1994). Let's assume that you see the glaring differences between "the two kings." Arguing that Elvis deserves to be accorded similar notoriety and respect as Jesus based on a tortured analogy is stretching a point.

Sufficiency of proof is directly tied to the degree of your truth claim. As already noted, claims alleging possibility require less proof than claims alleging plausibility or probability. Claims of certainty allow no exceptions. Even one exception is sufficient to disprove a claim of certainty. *An extraordinary claim requires extraordinary proof* (Abell, 1981). A few UFO sightings are grossly insufficient to amend our laws of physics and accept alien visitation.

Competent Empathic Listening

Informational listening and critical listening achieve important goals for the competent communicator. Informational listening expands our knowledge and understanding of our world. Critical listening helps us sort through bad ideas to discover good ideas that will solve problems and help us make quality decisions that improve our lives. There are times, however, where the point of conversation is to establish a relationship with another person or to help them through an emotional event. These situations require empathic listening, or what some people refer to as therapeutic, or helpful, listening. Empathic listening requires us to take the perspective of the other person, to listen for what that person needs.

Response Styles

Rogers and Roethlisberger (1952) conducted a series of studies on **response styles.** Five styles emerged from their research. They are, in the order of their frequency of use: evaluation, interpretation, support, probing, and understanding. These five styles are the types of initial responses we make when another person comes to us with a problem, reveals a frustrating event, or is experiencing an emotional crisis. In this next section, these five styles, plus the advising response, will be examined in the context of empathic listening (Figure 6-4).

Evaluative Response   A friend comes to you, obviously upset, and says, "I hate my job. I've got to find something different to do." You respond, "You haven't given the job much of a try. Perhaps you'd like it better if you put more effort into it." This is an evaluative response. It makes a judgment about the person's conduct. It assumes a standard of evaluation has or has not been met. As you read the evaluative response, perhaps you said to yourself, "I wouldn't respond that way." Perhaps not, but the most frequent response people make in situations like the one just presented is to evaluate (Rogers & Roethlisberger, 1952).

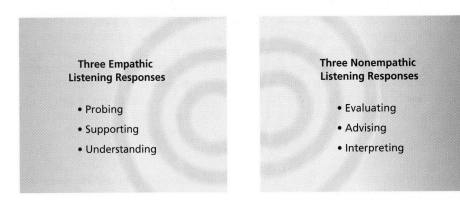

Three Empathic Listening Responses

- Probing
- Supporting
- Understanding

Three Nonempathic Listening Responses

- Evaluating
- Advising
- Interpreting

Figure 6-4 Listening Responses

A hypercompetitive, individualistic culture such as ours promotes the evaluative response. Competition focuses us on discerning weaknesses in our adversaries. Even when we are conversing with a friend, there is a tendency to focus on weaknesses. Competitors don't try to bolster their opponents. Adversaries try to diminish each other to win. Evaluating a friend who comes to you with a problem is nonempathic. It disconfirms the person. Your friend will feel worse, not better, and he or she will likely be defensive when evaluated.

Evaluation is the least effective response when we need to be empathic. Harold Kushner, author of *When Bad Things Happen to Good People* (1981), makes this point:

> It is hard to know what to say to a person who has been struck by tragedy, but it is easier to know what not to say. Anything critical of the mourner ("don't take it so hard," "try to hold back your tears, you're upsetting people") is wrong. Anything which tries to minimize the mourner's pain ("it's probably for the best," "it could be a lot worse," "she's better off now") is likely to be misguided and unappreciated. (p. 89)

When you're suffering, the last thing you need is criticism and judgment.

Advising Response   "My roommate drives me crazy. She has so many odd quirks." How would you respond to this? If you would respond in this fashion, "Why don't you change roommates?" you are offering advice. The advising response is also a common initial reaction to those who make a complaint or reveal a problem.

Men more than women tend to offer advice when others come to them with a problem or complaint (Tannen, 1990; Wood, 1994). Giving advice under these circumstances does two things (Wood, 1994). First, it fails to acknowledge the other person's feelings. Second, it communicates superiority of the person giving the advice. Giving advice presumes that the person with the problem hasn't figured out the solution, so the listener offers advice. Take the perspective of the other person before giving advice. Does the person seem interested in receiving advice from you? Is that what he or she is seeking? Have you considered your advice carefully, or is it merely a glib response made without thoughtful examination?

Interpreting Response   When we interpret we express what we think is the underlying meaning of a situation presented to us. A friend says to you, "I don't understand why he says such embarrassing things to me in front of my family." You respond, "Perhaps he is just uncomfortable around your parents and doesn't really know quite what to say, so he says silly things that embarrass you because he's socially clumsy." This is an interpreting response. You are clarifying the meaning of the situation for the other person. Interpreting responses are what we pay counselors, psychiatrists, and therapists to do for us when we can't make sense of our relationships, feelings, conflicts, and traumas. The interpreting response is useful in some situations, but, like advising, it tends to ignore the feelings of the person. It also places the listener in a superior position. One can "play guru" too often if the interpreting response becomes frequent.

Supporting Response   A supporting response acknowledges the feelings of the speaker and tries to boost the person's confidence. When nervous about starting a new job, you might offer reassurance (e.g., "First day on the job can be a little nerve-racking, but you have the skills to do the job really well.").

When a person is suffering the loss of a loved one, he or she needs empathy. In our struggle to help someone shoulder his or her burden, we may choose the wrong response. One survey (Davidowitz & Myricm, 1984) found that bereaved individuals considered 80% of the responses made to them during mourning to be *un*helpful. Almost half of the responses were advice (e.g., "You need to get out more," "You have to accept his death and move on with your life"), but they were hardly ever perceived as helpful to the bereaved. Acknowledging and validating the feelings of the bereaved was the most helpful response (e.g., "I can see how much you miss him. He was a warm and sensitive person.").

Probing Response   The probing response seeks more information from others by asking questions. Several types of questions qualify as a probing response (Purdy & Borisoff, 1997). There is the clarifying question (e.g., "Can you give me an example of what you mean when you say that she is insensitive?"). There is the exploratory question that urges the speaker to examine possibilities posed by a problem or situation (e.g., "Can you think of some ways to defuse her anger?" "Can you think of any alternative besides resigning from your position?"). There is also the encouraging question that inquires about choices made and implies agreement at the same time (e.g., "You didn't have any other choice did you? Who could blame you for sticking to your principles?"). Probing responses show interest in the speaker by seeking more information from and being attentive to the plight of the other person.

Understanding Response   The understanding response requires a listener to check his or her perceptions for comprehension of the speaker's message or to paraphrase the message to check accuracy. Perception checking was discussed in Chapter 2. **Paraphrasing** "is a concise response to the speaker which states the essence of the other's content in the listener's words" (Bolton, 1979, p. 51). Paraphrasing is not a long-winded parroting of a person's message. Paraphrasing is concise and to the point. For example:

JOSEPH: My roommate hums to himself while he studies. He hums stupid, irritating little tunes that stick in my head like annoying ads on TV. I'm trying to study, and I can't concentrate with his humming. I have a major exam in chemistry class tomorrow, and I'm worried that old hum-till-you're-dumb will screw up my chances of acing the exam.

TOM: You're worried about your chemistry exam, and your roommate's humming is a distraction.

JOSEPH: Yah! Got any suggestions what I should do about him?

Paraphrasing helps a listener understand the essence of a speaker's message. Paraphrasing, however, should be used only occasionally during a conversation. Look for the significant points in a conversation and then paraphrase. Details and elaborations of important points usually don't require paraphrasing.

Now that you have read about these response styles, test yourself by identifying the listening response in Box 6-5.

Response Styles and Empathic Listening

Empathic listening is composed of probing, supporting, and understanding responses. All three put the focus on the speaker and are therefore confirming

Box 6-5   Sharper Focus

Distinguishing Listening Responses

Read the following situation, then identify which type of response it is. Mark **A** for advising, **E** for evaluation, **I** for interpreting, **P** for probing, **S** for supporting, and **U** for understanding.

My boss is a total jerk. She's always giving me these huge projects to do, then yelling at me for not getting my other work done. She never has anything nice to say to anyone, and she actually times us when we take breaks to make sure we don't take longer than we're allowed. I feel like quitting.

_____ Aren't you being a little unfair? She can't be that bad.

_____ What have you tried so far to deal with your boss?

_____ Your situation is a classic power struggle.

_____ I think you should quit and find a job more to your liking.

_____ You feel overworked and underappreciated.

_____ I know you'll make the right decision whatever it is.

Which response do you think would be the best? Second best?

Answers: E, P, I, A, U, S.

responses (enhance the person's self-esteem and confidence). Hamachek (1982) explains:

> An understanding response is a way of letting a person know that you're listening to both the content of what's being said and the feeling accompanying it; a probing response lets a person know that you want to know more and, on a deeper level, that he or she is worth knowing more about; a supportive response is a way of saying that you care and that you hope things will get better. (p. 214)

When building a relationship and connecting with a person are the principal goals of your communication, probing, supporting, and understanding responses establish trust, deepen the connections between you and another person, and keep communication open.

Evaluating, advising, and interpreting responses tend to be disconfirming (they diminish the person and reduce confidence). They are nonempathic responses from the speaker's perspective (Hamachek, 1982). Should you therefore avoid such responses? Empathy is not always the type of listening that is competent in a given situation, so the answer is "no." Therapists interpret meaning for clients. Interpreting is an important listening response when we are confused and want clarity. Advising others can be constructive and helpful, especially if a person seeks our advice. Evaluating a person's self-destructive behavior may save that person's life.

Three variables influence the appropriateness and effectiveness of evaluating, advising, and interpreting responses. The first variable is frequency. *Frequency* refers to how often you use disconfirming responses. Occasional evaluation, interpretation, or advice, especially in a strong relationship, will rarely cause more than a ripple of disturbance. Frequent use of such disconfirming responses, however, can swamp even resilient relationships.

A second variable is timing. *Timing* refers to when you evaluate, interpret, or advise. "This is politics, pure and simple. You've handled them wrong. Stand up to these creeps." This statement begins with interpreting, follows with evaluating, and closes with advising—the triple crown of disconfirmation. Making such a statement early in a relationship when the two parties hardly know each other would likely be received negatively. Making the same statement much later in a relationship when the two parties are familiar with each other's style and trust each other might be received in a more neutral, even positive, way. Additionally, evaluating, interpreting, or advising responses used when a person is feeling fragile and in need of support will likely disconnect speaker and listener. Such responses can make a person feel inferior and diminished.

Finally, evaluating, advising, and interpreting responses are more appropriate and likely to be more effective when the speaker solicits them. *Solicitation* refers to whether you are asked to evaluate, interpret, or advise the speaker. A person may simply want to be heard by you, not told what to do. He or she may reject unsolicited advice, even resent it. "I already thought of that. It won't work" is a typical rejoinder to unsolicited advice. If individuals request such advice, however, they will more likely perceive it to be helpful. Individuals who seek help from a therapist implicitly request an interpreting response. People rarely request evaluation, but if they do, it is more likely to be accepted than if a critique is unsolicited.

Summary

Listening is the most frequent type of communication any of us does on a daily basis. Listening is first and foremost an active process. You cannot comprehend information, retain it, or respond appropriately to what you hear from others without focused attention. Listening requires effort. Competent communicators avoid shift responses, competitive interruptions, glazing over, pseudolistening, ambushing, defensiveness, and content-only responses. The competent communicator recognizes when informational, critical, and empathic types of listening are appropriate and effective. Be an informational listener when the principal focus of the communication is learning or retaining information. Be a critical listener when you need to decide solutions to problems or make decisions that have consequences for yourself and others. Be an empathic listener when you are trying to build or maintain a relationship with another person and that person comes to you with a problem or crisis.

Suggested Readings

Hoffer, E. (1951). *The true believer.* New York: Harper & Row. This work still remains the classic book on fanatical thinking.

Kohn, A. (1990). *The brighter side of human nature: Altruism and empathy in everyday life.* New York: Basic Books. If you plan to research the topic of empathy, start with this book. Kohn presents the research on empathy clearly and effectively.

Lipstadt, D. (1993). *Denying the Holocaust: The growing assault on truth and memory.* New York: Penguin. The author expertly answers the Holocaust deniers and shows the dangers of true belief. She also provides a nice history lesson in the process.

Tannen, D. (1998). *The argument culture: Moving from debate to dialogue.* New York: Ballantine. Tannen offers an interesting and insightful treatment of how U.S. culture predisposes people to attack rather than listen effectively to others.

Interpersonal Communication

Part Two

Chapter 7

Power: The Inescapable Interpersonal Dynamic

Henry Adams said, "Power is poison." Lord Acton reputedly observed that "power tends to corrupt, and absolute power corrupts absolutely." Karl Marx asserted that political power is "the organized power of one class to oppress another." Even a pope joined in the power bashing. Pope Pius XI claimed that power is "unbridled ambition for domination." We are accustomed to thinking of power in illegitimate or unpleasant terms. We speak of power struggles, power plays, seizures of power, and we talk about those who are high powered, power hungry, even power mad.

Most people are simply uncomfortable with the very idea of power. In a hypercompetitive society such as the United States, power mostly seems aimed at domination of others in a win-lose contest for superiority. With this single power-as-dominance view, many people find explicit references to power to be in bad taste and better left unstated (Kipnis, 1976). "So who has the most power in your relationship?" will likely produce an awkward silence and a reluctance to answer. When some do attempt an answer, it is typically halting and hesitant (Hocker & Wilmot, 1995). Naomi Wolf (1994) claims that women in particular have "great ambivalence about claiming power. Often women's fears are legitimate: They come from seeing power used harmfully" (p. 235).

Some individuals find the idea of power so unsavory that they innocently assert that power plays no part in their relationships with others. Rollo May (1972) terms this denial of one's own power "pseudoinnocence," where people "make a virtue of powerlessness, weakness, and helplessness" (p. 49). When we feel relatively powerless, despair can easily result. When we feel helpless to change things, we become indifferent, which perpetuates a bad situation. Powerlessness creates apathy, shrivels our desire to perform at work, strains personal relationships, creates interpersonal disconnection, erodes self-esteem, and makes us ineffectual in most or all of our dealings with others (Lee, 1997). Feelings of powerlessness strangle our spirit and stifle our motivation to improve our lives and the lives of those we love. It can lead to self-destructive behavior or aggression toward others.

The primary purpose of this chapter is to establish power as an inescapable, significant variable in all interpersonal relationships that can have constructive or destructive effects on transactions with others. There are five objectives:

1. to explain the significance of power in the human communication arena,
2. to define what power is and is not and to explain the differences between types of power,
3. to examine problems associated with an imbalance of power,
4. to describe the primary indicators and sources of power, and
5. to discuss how to transact power competently in interpersonal relationships.

Significance of Power

Power is inescapable in human transactions. "There is power in a word or a gesture. There is power when women and men live together, work together, talk together, or are simply in each other's company. There is power in a smile, a caress, and there is power in sex. . . . There is power in how we choose to resolve our conflicts, and how we negotiate the most intimate aspects of our lives" (Kalbfleisch

& Cody, 1995, p. xiii). Relationships between parents and children, doctors and nurses, teachers and students, judges and lawyers, supervisors and employees, or coaches and athletes are hierarchical and fundamentally power-oriented. Parents, doctors, teachers, judges, supervisors, and coaches have the power to tell others what to do.

Even in less hierarchical relationships power is ever-present. As noted in Chapter 1, every message has two basic dimensions: content and relationship. The content of a message communicates information regarding events and objects. The relationship dimension communicates information regarding the power distribution between individuals. Power is constantly being negotiated during conversations with others.

Consider this dialogue and the comments interjected in parentheses that indicate the power dynamics in the conversation:

> Jennifer continues washing the dishes. Geoff seems not to notice. "I'm tired of dealing with my mother's demands on me," begins Jennifer (*control is an issue*).
>
> Geoff responds, "Don't let her make you feel guilty for not spending every holiday with her and your father" (*advising as a parent to a child*).
>
> "I'm not letting her make me feel guilty (*asserting control*). I just get emotionally exhausted having to explain over and over again why we aren't coming to her house on Christmas."
>
> Geoff picks up a towel and begins to dry some dishes. "Tell her just once why we won't be coming for the holidays, then refuse to talk about it any further. Stand up to her" (*encouraging assertion of power*).
>
> Jennifer scrubs a plate a bit more vigorously than necessary (*exhibiting tension when implicitly accused of being weak*). "It isn't a question of standing up to my mother (*rejecting Geoff's characterization of weakness*). You make it sound like I'm putty in her hands."
>
> "Well, maybe not putty; more like sculpting clay," he says with a chuckle (*reasserting weakness by Jennifer*).
>
> "You're one to talk. You haven't stood up to your father in years. Why don't you practice what you preach?" (*moves to the offensive in battle to win the argument; asserts weakness by Geoff*).
>
> Geoff moves next to Jennifer, looking down at her with an unpleasant expression on his face (*dominance posture*). "That's hitting below the belt."
>
> "Now you know how it feels to receive such flip advice," Jennifer retorts (*continues with powerful offensive*).

Power is central to this conversation. It is the subtext; the meaning beyond the words. Each person is struggling to define the main issue of contentiousness in an interpersonal tug-of-war for dominance.

You can't achieve your individual goals, resolve conflicts, or communicate competently in relationships without exercising power in some form. Don't use power in Machiavellian, self-centered ways, however. Such Me-oriented communication is hypercompetitive and destructive. Hocker and Wilmot (1995) explain that "one does not have the option of not using power. We only have options about whether our use of power will be destructive or productive for ourselves and our relationships" (p. 74).

Definition of Power

Power is the ability to influence the attainment of goals sought by yourself or others. This is a general definition. In this section, you will learn more about what power is and is not.

The Nature of Power

Power does not reside in the individual. *Power is relational.* The power you exercise is dependent on the relationships you have with others. Teachers normally have more power than students, but this isn't so if students have little respect for the teacher and refuse to pay attention to the teacher's requests or dictates. In some instances, bad student evaluations can invite dismissal of an instructor; good evaluations may produce promotion. Power is not a characteristic of any individual. Power is determined by our transactions with others.

Power is not dichotomous. We often identify individuals as powerful *or* powerless. This is not an accurate assessment of power distribution in a relationship. No one is all-powerful or completely powerless, not even an infant, as many weary parents can attest when they have tried to attend to their crying baby's needs in the middle of the night. If each person has some degree of power in a relationship, the appropriate question is not the dichotomous "Is Person A powerful or powerless?" The apt question is "How much power does Person A have in comparison with Person B?"

Forms of Power

There are three forms of power: dominance, prevention, and empowerment (Hollander & Offerman, 1990). **Dominance** is the exercise of *power over* others. Dominance is a competitive, win-lose form of power. It results from dichotomous, either-or thinking. You're perceived to be either a winner or a loser in a power struggle.

Prevention is *power from* the influence of others. Prevention is the flip side of dominance. When someone tries to dominate you, you may try to prevent the dominance. The willingness to say "no" can be formidable, even in the face of dominating attempts. Prevention power is competitive. Dominators and preventers engage in power struggles to become winners and to avoid becoming losers.

Empowerment is *power to* accomplish your own goals or help others attain theirs. Empowerment is power used positively and constructively. It is a cooperative form of power. You do not have to defeat anyone to achieve personal or group goals. Empowered individuals feel capable, effective, and useful—not because they beat someone but because they performed well. You become empowered by successfully accomplishing an important task that you chose to do. That accomplishment has an impact on you and on others (Thomas & Velthouse, 1990; Frymier and Shulman, 1996).

The three forms of power—dominance, prevention, and empowerment—are considerably different from each other. Those who try to dominate see power as an *active effort* to advance personal goals at the expense of others. Power is a **zero-sum contest.** This means that for every increment of power I gain you lose an

Table 7-1 The Three Forms of Power

Type	Definition	Description
Dominance	Power over; competitive, hierarchical	Active: zero-sum
Prevention	Power from; competitive, hierarchical	Reactive: zero-sum
Empowerment	Power to; cooperative, egalitarian	Proactive: multisum

equivalent amount of power. My gain is your loss; we both can't be winners. From this perspective the power pie can't be enlarged, so the battle is for the biggest possible slice.

Those who seek to prevent domination by others see power as *reactive*. Prevention power is competitive. Individuals who attempt to prevent domination react to the power initiatives of others by fighting back. Preventive power is self-protective. You're trying to keep the slice of the power pie that you have, not enlarge your portion.

Those who seek to empower themselves and others see the power pie as expandable. When the power pie is expanded, there is more for everyone. Thus, no zero-sum competitive game need take place. Empowerment is *proactive*. Individuals take positive actions to assist themselves and others in attaining goals cooperatively (Table 7-1).

If you have a negative view of power, you are more than likely responding to the dominance form of power and its companion, prevention. It would be naive, however, to argue that we can replace dominance with empowerment in all, or even in most, cases. If individuals in a relationship are satisfied with an unequal power distribution, empowerment may not be necessary. Dominance is the primary form of power in a hypercompetitive society, and it will likely remain so. Establishing a better balance between competition and cooperation, however, requires greater emphasis on empowerment.

Power Imbalance

Dominance is a competitive form of power. When power is unequally distributed and dominance becomes the focus, power struggles often ensue (Hocker & Wilmot, 1995). In this section, you will learn about the five effects of dominance: physical violence, psychological abuse, spirals of mutual abuse, sexual harassment, and commonplace difficulties in ordinary transactions. With the exception of the last effect, all are part of what some researchers have called the "dark side of interpersonal communication" (Cupach & Spitzberg, 1994).

It is common practice in most human communication textbooks to ignore the dark side of relationships, or at most make only passing mention of it. The desire to present relationships in a sunny, "positive" framework is understandable. Ignoring the dark side because it is unpleasant, however, makes communication textbooks seem sadly unrelated to the all too frequent experience of readers as they live their often complicated lives. As two communication experts observe, "To fully understand how people effectively function requires us to consider how individuals cope with social interaction that is difficult, problematic, challenging, distressing, and disruptive" (Cupach & Spitzberg, 1994, p. vii). As another puts it, the "dark side is integral to the experience of relationships, not separate from it" (Duck, 1994b, p. 6). Few problems in life, especially significant difficulties, are solved by ignoring them. If verbal and physical violence, abuse, and harassment were infrequent, insignificant occurrences, ignoring them here would be appropriate and welcomed. As you will see in the next few sections, however, these problems occur frequently in relationships, and they are significant. We ignore them at our own peril.

Ultimately, this examination of the more unpleasant side of personal relationships has a very positive goal. This analysis is intended to help you recognize the sometimes subtle encroachment of the dark side into relationships, to provide insight into how to prevent the dark side from intruding into your life, and to identify effective ways to manage the more disagreeable aspects of relationships as they emerge. A competent communicator can handle commonplace difficulties that occur as well as the truly difficult and unpleasant challenges.

Physical Violence

On February 11, 1990, Terry Shapiro shot her husband, Abe, five times while he slept. Terry had been repeatedly abused by her husband for 3 years. Abe Shapiro totally dominated his wife. Santa Clara police Sergeant Ross Horton described it this way: "In twenty-seven years of police work, I've never seen a woman beaten that badly, and I worked sexual assault for several years" (as cited in Gathright, 1990).

How extensive is spousal or partner abuse? Finding accurate statistics on this problem is difficult. Studies and surveys use different definitions of abuse, ask different questions, and survey different populations. A woman in the United States is beaten by her husband or boyfriend every 18 seconds, 15 seconds, 10 seconds, 7.4 seconds, or 5 seconds, depending on which source you consult (see Shevlin, 1994). Anywhere from 200,000 to 6 million women are victims of violent abuse by their partners every year (see Sommers, 1994). Estimates of the proportion of women who will be assaulted by an intimate partner during adulthood range from 21% to 34% (Browne, 1993). These statistics don't include abuse in gay and lesbian relationships. What little research has been done on these populations, however, reveals that partner abuse in gay and lesbian relationships is roughly equivalent to that found among heterosexual couples (Renzetti, 1991). Similar patterns of relationship violence are also found in many other cultures (Walker, 1999).

Relationship violence is a serious problem no matter which statistics are used. Physical violence against a partner or family member clearly violates the We-orientation of communication competence. Sensitivity to others and commitment to making a relationship a healthy, constructive experience for everyone involved is violated by relationship violence. Ethically, respect must be shown to one's partner. Physical violence shows gross disrespect. Some studies show that individuals who resort to physical violence in relationships exhibit deficiencies in communication knowledge and skills (Infante et al., 1992). Difficulties in making claims and arguing those claims effectively in the midst of conflict are significant contributors to relationship violence (Infante et al., 1989; Infante et al., 1990).

Adolescent homelessness is often the result of physical or sexual mistreatment by more powerful adult parents.

An imbalance of power, either actual, perceived, or desired is a central element in relationship violence. Violence is more prevalent in relationships where power is unequally distributed than in relationships where the power distribution is relatively equal (Lloyd & Emery, 1993; Coleman & Straus, 1986). An extensive study of family violence concludes:

> The greater the inequality, the more one person makes all the decisions and has all the power, the greater the risk of violence. Power, power confrontations, and perceived threats to domination, in fact, are underlying issues in almost all acts of family violence. (Gelles & Straus, 1988, p. 82)

The study goes on to conclude that "egalitarian marriages [equal distribution of power] have the lowest risk of intimate violence" (p. 112).

The perception that one member is entitled to a superior position in a relationship, even though that person may not in fact be accorded such deference, also provokes violence (Baumeister et al., 1996). Again, the dominance perspective is central. Power imbalance is desired. A husband who beats his wife to show her "who's boss" feels entitled to dominate his spouse. He views his wife as his possession. Male spousal abusers typically hold traditional views of male dominance in marriage. They believe they are the patriarchs of the family, and any perceived threat to that lofty position invites a violent response. Nevertheless, wife beaters often lack status and power (Peterson, 1991). Their wives may have higher status employment and make more money, which threatens the abusers' perceived entitlement to dominate their wives.

A study of partner abuse in lesbian relationships found a similar result (Renzetti, 1991). Abusers want to be the decision makers in the relationship, but they are dependent on their partners for money and resources. Thus, the lesbian abuser wants high status, feels dependent, resents the dependency, and becomes violent to signify her power.

Violence that results from a desire to control others can produce a chain reaction of abuse. As Gelles and Straus (1988) explain:

> It is not unusual to find a pattern of violence in a home where the husband hits his wife, the wife in turn uses violence toward her children, the older children use violence on the younger children, and the youngest child takes out his or her frustration on the family pet. One explanation for this pattern is that at each level the most powerful person is seeking to control the next least powerful person. (p. 35)

Physical aggression (i.e., pushing, shoving, and slapping) against children was reported by 62% of parents in one study (Straus & Gelles, 1990). Eleven percent of parents reported using severe aggression (i.e., kicking, beating, and using a weapon) against their children. Two thirds of teenagers physically attack a sister or brother at least once a year, and in more than one third of these cases the assault is severe (Straus & Gelles, 1990).

Verbal and Nonverbal Abuse

Power struggles in relationships that take on a dominance-prevention quality do not always end in violence. In fact, more likely than not, no fists will fly, nor any pots and pans. Partners will simply abuse each other verbally and nonverbally by tearing apart each other's self-esteem and self-worth. Communicating contempt for one's partner has a corrosive effect on a relationship (Gottman, 1994a, 1994b).

Contempt is intended to insult and emotionally abuse a person. A 36-year-old female trucking company executive describes men in power positions as "a bunch of shallow, bald, middle-aged men with character disorders. They don't have the emotional capacity it takes to qualify as human beings. One good thing about these white, male, almost extinct mammals is that they are growing old. We get to watch them die" (as cited in Gates, 1993, p. 49). Now that's contempt! When couples argue as adversaries trying to win a verbal exchange, contempt can easily become a verbal weapon, both for the dominant partner trying to exert control and for the weaker partner trying to equalize the power distribution.

There are four ways to communicate contempt (Gottman, 1994a, 1994b). First, *contempt can be communicated by verbal insults and name-calling.* Bastard, bitch, moron, jerk, imbecile, fathead, and even cruder, more vicious insults are targeted at tearing apart the self-concept and self-worth of one's partner.

Second, *hostile humor communicates contempt.* Camouflaged as "only a joke," hostile humor, if you're the target, aims to make others laugh at your expense. "Marsha's so sweet I fear getting diabetes just being around her," and "Harry's a very passionate lover—of himself," ridicule the person shown contempt. Sensitivity, a key ingredient of competent communication, is nowhere to be seen, and hostile humor shows disrespect for the abused individual.

Third, *mockery communicates contempt.* You mock someone by imitating them derisively. A man says to his partner, "I really do love you," and his partner responds with a contorted facial expression and fake, exaggerated voice, "You really do love me." Mockery is meant to make fun of a person. It assaults that person's sincerity.

Fourth, *certain body movements communicate contempt.* Sneering, rolling your eyes, curling your upper lip, and using obscene gestures are all signs of contempt for one's partner. When a person leaves the room while a partner or coworker is speaking to him or her, this nonverbally communicates contempt.

Spirals of Mutual Abuse

The competitive, dominance approach to power produces spirals of mutual abuse, both in physical violence and in psychological abuse. The stereotype we have of the batterer is that of a man beating a defenseless woman incapable of retaliation. Violence in gay relationships, however, occurs about as often and with as much intensity as violence in heterosexual relationships (Renzetti, 1991).

Almost a dozen studies (see Gelles & Straus, 1988) reveal that men are targets of spousal or partner violence about as often as are women, a finding that startles many and has produced white-hot debate among partisan groups. John Archer, a psychologist at the University of Central Lancashire in Great Britain, reviewed tens of thousands of interviews of men and women in Canada, Great Britain, the United States, and New Zealand. Archer found that women resorted to physical violence during an argument as often as men (see "Women Can Be Violent," 1998). Younger women, and women dating a partner rather than married to or living with a partner, were most prone to use violence. Studies also show little difference between men and women regarding threats of violence (Figure 7-1). One study of college students (Marshall, 1994) found that 77% of males and 76% of females had made threats of violence to their partners, and 72% of males and 79% of females had received threats of violence from their partners.

Two critical points of difference must be considered when comparing threats of violence and frequency and levels of actual violence of males and females in relationships (Gelles & Straus, 1988). First, men are usually physically stronger and can do more serious injury to women than vice versa. Thus, threats of violence are more menacing for women than men in most cases. Almost 10 times as many women as men are treated in emergency rooms at hospitals for injuries inflicted by spouses or partners (Lardner, 1997). Second, nearly three quarters of the violence committed by women against their partners is *in self-defense* (Gelles & Straus, 1988). One example of a 44-year-old woman who told how she defends herself against her husband's beatings illustrates the self-defensive nature of most female violence:

> When he hits me, I retaliate. Maybe I don't have the same strength as he does, but I know how to hold my own. I could get hurt, but I am going to go down trying. You know, it's not like there is anyone else here who is going to help me. So . . . I hit back . . . I pick something up and I hit him. (p. 90)

Here is a case of dominance and prevention power colliding. Violence begets violence.

A mutual abuse spiral easily occurs when dominance produces aggression between partners. The expression of domestic abuse usually begins with contempt, manifested both verbally and nonverbally. When a man assaults his female partner, her

Threats of Violence

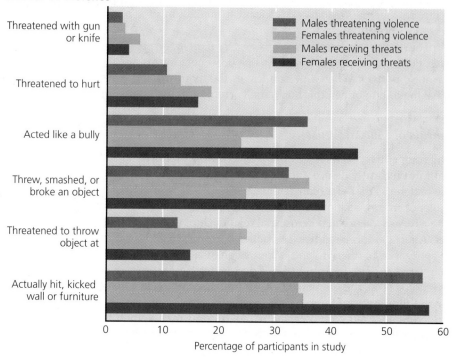

Acts of Violence

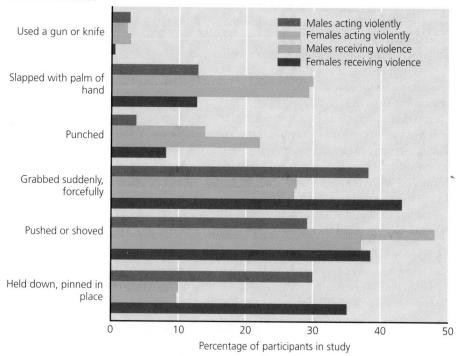

Figure 7-1 Percentage of Males or Females Who Threatened or Carried Out Acts of Violence (Data Source: Vitanza, 1991, and Vitanza and Marshall, 1993)

most common response, besides crying, is yelling at and cursing her abuser (Gelles & Straus, 1988).

As previously noted, three quarters of female violence against men is self-defensive, but this means that in one quarter of the instances women strike the first blow. Fewer than 15% of men hit back when struck by their partners (Gelles & Straus, 1988). The most common first response of men is to yell at and curse their partners. About 5% of men cry as their first response to being hit by their partners. Men, however, jump from verbal contempt to physical aggression more easily than do women (Campbell, 1993).

Women take much longer to graduate from verbal abuse to physical violence, and when they do, their response is different from men. The most frequent form of violence by men in relationships consists of pushing, shoving, and grabbing their female partners. When women reach the boiling point, however, they not only push, shove, and grab, but they also slap, kick, bite, gouge, and hit (Campbell, 1993). They lash out in all directions. Campbell (1993) comments on what this communicates to men:

> This behavior [lashing out in all directions] appears to men to be truly senseless, because it does not achieve the "obvious" instrumental goal of dominating another person. But women's thoughts at such moments are likely to be along the lines of, "Get away from me. Leave me alone. I cannot stand to be on the same planet as you right now." (p. 74)

Thus, *women's aggression in relationships is usually preventive, whereas men's aggression is typically dominating.* Why? The principal reason is that men are socialized to value status and independence (Tannen, 1990). Relationships, however, require intimacy and interdependence in order to thrive. Abusive men cannot rid themselves of the nagging idea that interdependence makes them weak and vulnerable and that this weakness and vulnerability could be used against them by their partners. Aggression reclaims control in the relationship (Campbell, 1993). Aggression, both verbal and physical, puts the male abuser in a competitive arena. Here he has the decided advantage because of superior physical strength and because the struggle for dominance that inevitably ensues when partners become antagonists is a contest familiar to men who have been socialized to compete for status (Campbell, 1993).

Sexual Harassment

Mike Hughes, a journalist, was eating breakfast at Bette's Ocean View Diner in Berkeley, California one fall morning in 1991 while reading an article in *Playboy* magazine on freedom of the press. His waitress, Barbara (only name given), was highly offended and, with the assistance of the restaurant's manager, insisted that Hughes put away the magazine or leave. Hughes left. This incident was reported in the press. Demonstrators conducted a "read-in" in front of the diner to dramatize their opposition to censorship. Counter-demonstrators also showed in equal numbers to protest "pornography in the workplace." As Barbara explained, "I think pornography is offensive, and I feel pornography in my workplace is sexual harassment" (as cited in Hentoff, 1992, p. 14).

Sexual harassment is an explosive issue. Part of its explosiveness comes from serious disagreements, illustrated by the Bette's Diner conflict, regarding what constitutes sexual harassment. One study asked female faculty and graduate

Notice the multiple nonverbal cues—all of which signal sexual harassment.

students whether they had experienced 31 situations legally defined as sexual harassment. Almost 90% of the study participants had experienced at least some of these. Yet only 5.6% of the faculty and 2.8% of the graduate students surveyed answered "yes" to the question that directly asked them if they had been sexually harassed (Brooks & Perot, 1991). The distinction between harassing communication and communication that is natural between friends or romantic partners at work is not always clear (Witteman, 1993). Complimentary comments and gestures, nonsexual touching, and staring can be viewed either way. What is flirtation to one person may be harassment to another.

The law defines two principal types of sexual harassment: quid pro quo (you give something to get something) and hostile environment (Witteman, 1993). **Quid pro quo harassment** occurs when the more powerful person requires sexual favors from the less powerful individual in exchange for keeping a job, getting a high grade in a class, landing an employment promotion, and the like. **Hostile environment harassment** is not quite so obviously an abuse of power. The Supreme Court in 1986 endorsed the hostile work environment interpretation of sexual harassment. According to the Court's decision, employees have a right to work in an environment free from discriminatory insult, ridicule, or intimidation (Paetzold & O'Leary-Kelly, 1993). Recently, colleges and universities have expanded this ruling to include hostile learning environment to protect students.

The *Playboy* incident at Bette's Diner demonstrates the problem of interpreting what constitutes a hostile environment. Sexist language, sexual jokes, pictures of spouses in skimpy bathing suits at the beach, and pin-up pictures of either sex are banned in most workplaces. Complicating the issue further, consensual romantic relationships have been deemed sexual harassment at some colleges and places of employment. The perception that such romantic relationships bestow benefits on fellow workers or classmates not justly earned is perceived as a hostile environment issue by some individuals. San Francisco State University in 1998 created a firestorm of controversy when it proposed to ban all romantic relationships between students and faculty, even if a student wasn't in the professor's class or under his or her supervision. Most students interviewed on campus felt that this violated their rights as adults to choose a romantic partner.

The hostile environment form of sexual harassment has some validity. A District of Columbia court awarded Elizabeth Reese $250,000 for damages incurred while she worked for the architectural design firm, Swanke, Hayden, and Connell. Reese's male supervisor repeatedly made lewd comments to her, incessantly asked about her sex life, encouraged her to prostitute herself for the firm, then told fellow workers that she had.

Power imbalances are at the heart of most sexual harassment. Quid pro quo harassment is a clear instance of dominance, usually by more powerful males against less powerful females. Dealing with this kind of sexual harassment is extremely difficult because the harasser has legitimate authority and can punish the victim for openly complaining. Laws forbidding such behavior, policies that explicitly punish such harassment, and enforcement of laws and policies are all helpful in combatting quid pro quo harassment. Firm, unequivocal rejection of such harassment by the target of an unwanted sexual advance is also an important communication approach. "Do not *ever* make sexual remarks to me" is an unequivocal rejection of the harassment.

Hostile environment sexual harassment typically flows from power imbalances as well. It is particularly prevalent where women try to compete in traditionally male occupations. Smith Barney, a Wall Street brokerage firm with 400 offices nationwide, established a pattern of hostile environment sexual harassment that led to a class action lawsuit by 25 female stockbrokers. Male employees gawked at the women's breasts and made lewd and suggestive remarks. Senior male managers in the Garden City, New York office maintained a basement room dubbed the "Boom-Boom Room," where female employees were confronted with unwanted sexual advances, groping, and kissing on the lips. Women at work were sent condoms and food shaped in the form of penises. Plaintiffs claimed that their complaints to superiors were ignored. In some cases, women were punished with menial tasks and public humiliations for complaining. Pamela Martens, one of the plaintiffs, noted, "It's like they have a manual in their heads as to how to crush women" (as cited in Jackson, 1997). Even though the harassment often came from fellow brokers of equal position and power, most of the Smith Barney brokers were men. This put female brokers at a decided disadvantage when trying to combat the hostile "men's club" environment created by male brokers.

Combatting hostile environment sexual harassment is difficult. Most often a dominance-prevention dynamic occurs. Sometimes the hostile environment is the product of incompetent communication, not ugly intentions (Bingham, 1991). A firm, clearly defined policy staunchly supported by those in power positions goes a long way toward diminishing this type of sexual harassment. With such a policy, those who are harassed can more safely and confidently reject poor treatment. Communication strategies of assertiveness, threat of formal complaint, or deflection of sexual remarks by diverting discussion to neutral topics can be successful when hostile environment harassment is clearly not tolerated in the workplace or educational environment (Bingham, 1991).

Commonplace Difficulties

Power imbalances don't always lead to verbal or physical abuse and harassment. Many, perhaps most, instances of power imbalance never graduate to the dark side of interpersonal relationships. They remain part of the lighter side of personal difficulties experienced with others.

Consider the remote control wars. Invented for Zenith Corporation by Dr. Robert Adler, the remote control made its debut on June 8, 1956. The Consumer Electronics Manufacturers Association estimates that there are about 400 million remote controls in use, and guess who typically controls that use? According to a study conducted by sociologist Alexis Walker, president of the National Council on Family Relations, men are the predominant channel surfers, much to the displeasure of most women (as cited in McCall, 1996). Numerous studies have found similar results (Bellamy & Walker, 1996). One woman in Walker's study expressed her frustration this way: "He just flips through the channels. It drives me crazy because he just goes through, and goes through, and goes through" (as cited in McCall, 1996 p. D1). Walker herself recalls, "My parents bought a second TV set because my mother said to me, 'I will not watch TV with your father any more because of the way he uses that remote control'" (p. D1). Women told Walker that they videotaped their preferred shows to view at a later time so they could still be with their male partners while they watched sports.

When the issue of who is in charge of the remote control is confronted directly, a man may give control to his partner but then insist that she turn quickly to another channel to check on a sports score. The woman is still doing his bidding even though he is not actually pressing the buttons on the remote control.

Walker concludes that the balance of power at home, as reflected in the battle over the remote control, is still tilted in men's favor no matter how equal a couple sees their relationship. Men, however, are mostly unaware that they are in charge of the remote control. "I guess I don't think about it, I just switch the channel," said one man in the study (as cited in McCall, 1996, p. D6). "Power dynamics among couples are rarely conscious," explains professor Stephen Marks of the University of Texas at Austin. "He gets to watch it the way he wants to watch it, whether she's there or not. She has to watch by herself or the way he watches it. To put it in the most simple way, it's not fair" (p. D6).

Power imbalances are apparent in a wide variety of daily occurrences. At work, the shift from work to personal talk is usually initiated by the most powerful person (Tannen, 1994). If the office manager takes a break and begins telling stories and chatting, everyone else in the office sees fit to follow suit. Taking breaks and chatting, however, can be perceived as goofing off unless sanctioned by a more powerful person. Such power imbalance can make employees wary, even resentful, of the "double standard."

Doctor-patient relationships are rarely equal. Patients wait for doctors, sometimes for unreasonably long periods of time, not vice versa. My doctor developed a reputation for mistreating his patients by making them wait for up to an hour and a half. I witnessed several instances where patients became so angered by the delay that they stormed out of his office, enraged by his apparent lack of concern. On one occasion, after a tedious delay, I felt compelled to leave before seeing him, whereupon he raced out into the parking lot, chased me down, and cajoled me into returning for immediate treatment. The less powerful do have options.

Doctors usually wear white coats as symbols of their authority. Patients wear casual clothes, humiliating hospital gowns with a breezy backside, and sometimes no clothes at all, which can be embarrassing. Patients refer to the physician by title, such as "Dr. Schmidt," not "Harry." The physician, however, often addresses the patient by his or her first name. This pattern is not always displayed, however, when the doctor is female. Some male patients may inappropriately try to upset the power imbalance by referring to female physicians informally (e.g., "Hi Kate") or even by making lewd or suggestive remarks (Tannen, 1994). Such references are insulting, and they make the female doctor's task of caring for the patient exceedingly difficult.

The formal-informal means of address in unequal power situations is reflected in most work environments. Bosses often refer to assistants by their first names but may be addressed by subordinates as "Mr. Burns" or "Ms. Simpson." Perceptions of inequality in a relationship are reinforced when the manner of addressing a person is not parallel. If both parties address each other formally, equality is indicated. If they both address each other informally, equality is also indicated. If one uses formal address, however, but the other uses informal address, inequality is apparent. This distancing produced by nonparallel forms of address may be necessary in certain circumstances (e.g., few would think it appropriate to address the President of the United States by his first name since that would show disrespect for his position). In most situations, however, nonparallel forms of address display status differences where none need exist, at least in a low power-distance culture such as the United States.

Apologies for mishaps or misdeeds are expected from the less powerful, reminding them of their subservient position. Children are expected to apologize to parents for cracking up the car, but parents do not normally apologize to their kids for a similar mishap, even though the children may be seriously inconvenienced by the car being out of commission. The more powerful person may resist mightily offering any apology for fear that it will undermine his or her authority. Nevertheless, apologizing can cement relationships between unequal individuals. Parents apologizing for mishaps or mistreatment of their children is appropriate and will likely gain respect from kids rather than subvert authority.

Compliments are more typically offered by the more powerful person in a working environment (Tannen, 1994). The failure of bosses to compliment adequately those who have worked diligently and performed admirably is a serious omission that will likely create resentment or even hostility. Subordinates, however, may fear looking like they are trying to "suck up" to the boss if they are too free with compliments.

Giving criticism is dicier for a less powerful person because the more powerful individual could strike back in ways not available to the subordinate. Bosses can fire employees, but employees rarely get a boss fired no matter how frustrating their behavior.

An imbalance in power alters the way we communicate with others. Sometimes it produces violence and psychological abuse that can easily spiral out of control. An imbalance in power also creates an environment that is ripe for sexual harassment. Dominance, even when no violence nor harassment occur, still often produces friction, anger, wariness, awkwardness, strife, frustration, and an assortment of other difficulties in a wide variety of relationships. A central concern to any competent communicator must be how to balance the power more appropriately in relationships where power imbalances are counterproductive. This central concern will be explored in the next three sections.

Indicators of Power

An imbalance of power in a relationship can produce verbal and physical abuse and encourage sexual harassment and many lesser difficulties. The quick answer to these problems is just balance the power. Easier said than done, especially when some individuals would rather maintain their dominance in relationships and groups. The place to begin correcting destructive power imbalances is knowing how to assess the relative power each partner has in a relationship. No precise measurement of relative power can be ascertained because relationships are dynamic, fluid transactions. Nevertheless, a rough estimate can be determined from considering general as well as verbal and nonverbal indicators of power.

General Indicators

There are several general indicators of power. First, those who can define others have power in relationships and groups. Teachers define students (e.g., smart, slow learner), physicians define patients (e.g., healthy, hypochondriac, addict), psychiatrists define clients (e.g., paranoid schizophrenic, psychotic), parents define children (e.g., incorrigible, obedient), and bosses define employees (e.g., hard worker, sluggard).

Definitional prerogative as an indicator of power can be seen from our attitudes about rape, not of women, but of men. The rape of women in the United States is an outrage recognized by government, social service agencies, and most Americans. The rape of men, however, is largely ignored, even made the subject of television sitcom humor. Rape of both women and men is a brutal crime of dominance. There is strong reason to believe that the number of rapes of males by other males (mostly in prison) is equal to or greater than the number of rapes of women by men (see Farrell, 1993). The important point here isn't whether women or men suffer the most from this violent crime. Suffering shouldn't be framed as a competition. The central point is that because most men who are raped are "criminals," the rape of men is virtually ignored, a point dramatically depicted in the movie *The Shawshank Redemption.*

Most of the men raped in prison have not been incarcerated for committing violent crimes. Prisoners, however, have no power to define rape inside the prison as either a crime or at least a serious problem to be solved. Prisoners are dependent on others who do have power to make such a definition (e.g., judges, lawmakers). Imagine the sense of powerlessness a man would feel if he were sent to prison for possessing drugs, whereupon he is repeatedly raped, and no one does anything about it nor seems to care that it happened. Those who define, control.

Second, whose decisions are followed is another general indicator of power. Employees follow the directives of supervisors, not vice versa. Children obey parents. Wouldn't it be odd to see parents obeying children (e.g., "Dad! Go do the dishes now, and no back talk.")?

Third, the **principle of least interest** indicates that the person who cares less about continuing a relationship has more power (Waller & Hill, 1951). The person with the greater interest and investment in maintaining the relationship can be held hostage by his or her partner's lack of interest, forced to try resurrecting an intimacy that only one partner cares much to rejuvenate. The partner with the lesser interest is in the dominant position because of the implied or stated threat to terminate the relationship. The only person controlled by a threat to end a relationship is a partner who cares about maintaining the relationship.

Verbal Indicators

Power is indicated by the way we speak. Tavris (1992) poses an interesting question, then answers it:

> What would happen to your language if you played a subordinate role in society? You would learn to persuade and influence, rather than assert and demand. . . . You would learn to placate the powerful and soothe ruffled feathers. You would cultivate communication, cooperation, attention to news and feelings about others . . . the characteristics of such a language develop primarily from a power imbalance. . . . They develop whenever there is a status inequity, as can be seen in the languages of working-class Cockneys conversing with employers, blacks conversing with whites, or prisoners conversing with guards. (p. 298)

The speech of a less powerful person is often flooded with self-doubt, approval seeking, overqualification, hesitancy, and personal diminishment. Examples of speech patterns commonly viewed as relatively powerless in U.S. culture include (Mulac & Bradac, 1995):

Hedges: "*Perhaps* the best way to decide is . . ."; "I'm a *little* worried that this *might* not work."

Hesitations: "Well, *uhm,* the central point is . . ."; "*Gosh, uh,* shouldn't we, *uhm,* act now?"

Tag question: "Dinner will be served at 6 o'clock, *okay*?"; "This section of the report seems irrelevant, *doesn't it*?"

Disclaimers: "*You may disagree with me,* but . . ."; "*This idea is probably very silly,* but . . ."

Excessive politeness: "I'm *extremely sorry* to interrupt your conversation, but . . ."; "*Yes sir/Ma'am* . . ."

Powerless speech suggests uncertainty, indecisiveness, lack of confidence, vacillation, and deference to authority. It advertises a person's subordinate status. Powerful speech, by contrast, is generally direct, fluent, declarative, commanding, and prone to interrupt or overlap the speech of others. It advertises superior status (Box 7-1).

Powerful forms of speech are not always appropriate. Abusive and obscene language sounds powerful because it is shocking, but it will likely offend others. Sometimes deferential language is a sign of respect and not merely powerless speech. Even tag questions can sometimes be used powerfully. If your boss says "You'll see that this is done, won't you?", this may be more a directive than a request. If so, the tag question is authoritative, not weak. Competent communicators understand that in some contexts it is important to use language that acknowledges another person's power.

Box 7-1 Sharper Focus

Gender, Culture, and Powerful/Powerless Language

Verbal indicators of power in U.S. culture show several clear gender differences. Men are typically more verbose, more inclined to give long-winded verbal presentations, and more talkative in mixed-sex groups than women (James & Drakich, 1993). Talkativeness is associated with leadership. Men are more verbally aggressive than women (Nicotera & Rancer, 1994), meaning that men are more inclined to attack the self-concepts of others (dominance). Men are also more argumentative than women (Stewart et al., 1996), meaning that men are more likely to advocate controversial positions or to challenge the positions on issues taken by others. Women are inclined to view verbal aggressiveness and argumentativeness as strategies of dominance and control, a hostile, competitive act (Nicotera & Rancer, 1994). Since men are more likely to seek status and women are more likely to seek connection in conversations (Tannen, 1990), these gender differences in verbal indicators of power are not surprising.

The issue of powerless versus powerful speech takes on more complexity when culture is added to the mix. What is viewed as powerful speech is culture-specific. Japanese, for example, and most Asian cultures would view our version of powerful speech as immature because it indicates insensitivity to others and is likely to make agreement more difficult (Wetzel, 1988). Collec-tivist Asian cultures desire harmony; the group is more important than the individual. In Western societies, verbal obscenity and swearing are perceived as powerful language. Individualistic Western cultures place high value on personal uniqueness. Verbal obscenity marks you as an individual willing to flout cultural values that discourage verbal obscenity. Neither Japanese men nor women use such language except in rare instances (De Klerk, 1991), but it is increasingly common among Americans.

When cultures clash over significant issues, these different views of powerful and powerless speech can pose serious problems. When negotiating teams from Japan and the United States meet, misunderstandings easily arise (Hellweg et al., 1994). The language of Japanese negotiators is rife with indirect phrases typical of a high-context communication style. Japanese negotiators use expressions such as "I think," "perhaps," "probably," and "maybe" with great frequency because they strive to preserve harmony and cause no offense that would result in loss of face for anyone (Samovar & Porter, 1995). This indirect language is viewed as powerless by American negotiators more accustomed to the direct, explicit, "powerful" language of a low-context communication style.

Nonverbal Indicators

In 1996 Manchester, England became the first major British city to replace the traditional conical-shaped helmets worn by the police with more practical, American-style caps. Brian Mackenzie, president of the Police Superintendents Association, opposed the change. The helmet, he asserted, "provides stature, height, authority and protection" (as cited in "Hats Off," 1996).

Clothing is a strong indicator of power. Uniforms clearly indicate power and authority. The "power suit" indicates stature and status associated with financial success and position in an organization. Tattered clothing scrounged from the trash communicates powerlessness associated with poverty.

Touch is another important nonverbal power indicator. The more powerful person can usually touch the less powerful person more frequently and with fewer restrictions than vice versa (Henley, 1995). Sexual harassment laws recognize this difference and try to protect subordinates from tactile abuse.

Eye contact indicates a power difference. Staring is done more freely by the more powerful person. Less powerful individuals must monitor their eye contact more energetically. A boss can show lack of attentiveness or interest by looking away from a subordinate, but a subordinate doing the same to his or her boss may invite a reprimand. Submissiveness is typically manifested both in the animal and people worlds by lowering one's eyes and looking down.

Space is a clear nonverbal indicator of power. The more powerful usually have more of it. Those who dream of winning the lottery imagine buying a large house, not a cramped studio apartment. The master bedroom in a house is reserved for the more powerful parents, and the children are given smaller bedrooms. The higher up in the corporate hierarchy you travel the bigger is your office space. Reserved parking spaces, part of the "parking wars" on college campuses across the United States, clearly designate power differences. Reserved faculty parking spaces often are closer to classroom and office buildings. Student parking spaces often are located somewhere in the next time zone.

In the spring term of 1999 a skirmish erupted over parking at Cabrillo College. Some faculty members were upset that students were "stealing" faculty parking spaces and that violators were not being ticketed sufficiently. The campus e-mail system was inundated for weeks by a debate on this controversy. Gated parking lots, entered only by inserting a special plastic card into a device that would raise and lower a gate, was one proposal circulated. One tongue-in-cheek proposal suggested that the college dig a moat around faculty lots and toss in some crocodiles to keep out student violators. Space and power are clearly connected.

Much more could be added here, but the point seems clear. You can ascertain the relative distribution of power among individuals by observing both verbal and nonverbal indicators and noticing a few general communication patterns.

Power Resources

Power is the ability to influence the attainment of goals sought by you or others. Power is inherent in all human relationships, and it is negotiated through communication transactions. Power resources are an important part of these transactions. A **power resource** is anything that enables individuals to achieve their goals, assists others to achieve their goals, or interferes with the goal attainment of others.

The range of power resources is broad. In this section the primary resources from which power is most extensively derived will be discussed. In the next section the role these resources play in transacting power will be explored.

Information

We live in the Age of Information, where information is power. Not all information, however, becomes a power resource. Information has power potential when it is not easily or readily available. Lawyers can charge eye-popping fees because they have information about the law that clients must have. Information that is restricted and scarce can be a powerful resource.

Studies of censorship demonstrate conclusively that restricting information increases both its perceived value and its credibility (see Cialdini, 1993). When judges order jurors to disregard the testimony of a witness, jurors give greater credibility and value to the testimony than if no attempt to restrict the information had been made (Broeder, 1959).

Scarcity also makes information seem more valuable and useful (Cialdini, 1993). In this era of information overload, where massive quantities of information are easily located on computer databases, scarcity of information is the exception, not the rule. Thus, when information is scarce, whatever is available seems terribly important. Secrets become intensely interesting because the information is scarce. We want to know and you're the only source, so your stature is at least momentarily enhanced.

In the 1980s J. Z. Knight, a controversial woman who portrayed herself as a celestial "channeler" in contact with a 35,000-year-old Cro-Magnon prophet named Ramtha, ran a School of Enlightenment in rural Washington (Conway & Siegelman, 1995). The main attraction for Ramtha devotees was to hear the "wisdom" of this prophet as he spoke to small gatherings of fascinated followers. Ramtha "spoke" in a guttural voice through Knight, who appeared to be in a trance. Ramtha didn't speak to just anybody. He spoke only to those who joined Knight's enlightenment school (and presumably paid the hefty entrance fee).

It's not every day that you get an opportunity to hear from a 35,000-year-old guru from another spirit dimension. The scarcity of such elder prophets makes what Ramtha had to say more inviting. What Ramtha said, among other things, was that every orgasm brings you nearer to death (the same could be said, of course, for every breath you take). When you die, do not seek the light because "light beings" are waiting and they will suck experience from your spirit and leave you to reincarnate with no memory of your last life. Instead, Ramtha entreatied, seek the darkness, the void.

If a 35-year-old guy named Fred provided the same information as Ramtha, do you think anyone would pay much attention? Many did pay attention, however, when it was viewed as scarce, restricted information from Ramtha, a supposed prophet who communicated only through Knight (Conway & Siegelman, 1995). Knight made it seem that the information was scarce and restricted because only a select few would be privy to the experience of hearing Ramtha. Anybody, presumably, could hear Fred.

Information can be a positive power resource. Teachers are accorded stature because they have information that is valuable for students to learn. Sharing this information can empower students. Ministers, priests, and religious leaders have information that brings them respect and prestige, but the information when shared is spiritually empowering for laypersons. The information teachers and ministers share is a power resource because it is restricted to students and laypersons, not by censorship or legal stricture but by the limited background and experience of those desiring the information. Teachers and ministers can translate the information so it is understandable. Information from teachers and religious leaders is also restricted by the limited time a person has to study the information without having someone edit and condense it to a manageable form.

Expertise

There is an old story told about an expert who was called in to fix a brand new diesel locomotive that wouldn't start. The railroad that owned the diesel engine requested an itemized billing once the expert had successfully finished his labor. His bill was for $1,500. He broke the bill into two items: $15 for swinging a hammer and $1,485 for knowing the right spot to hit and how to hit it. We pay big money to experts for knowing what to do and how to do it.

Information and expertise are closely related, but a person can have critical information without being an expert. You might possess a valuable technical report without being able to decipher any of the information. Expertise is more than just having information. An expert knows how to use the information wisely and skillfully.

We have a love-hate relationship with experts. We often require their skills and advice but seem to resent them for simply occupying positions of power or for making a buck off their expertise. Lawyers are a good example of this; jokes deriding lawyers have become commonplace (e.g., What do you have when you bury six lawyers up to their necks in sand? Not enough sand).

No individual nor group could ever hope to function effectively without at some time requiring the services of experts. Families require financial advisers, roofers, carpenters, exterminators, counselors, physicians, hair stylists, mechanics, and those who repair our appliances, phones, computers, broken pipes, and broken hearts. Expertise can be a very positive power resource.

Expertise functions as a power resource under two conditions. First, the person is perceived to have the requisite skills, abilities, knowledge, and background to function as a real expert. Normally, real expertise includes appropriate education and training, intelligence, experience, and demonstrated mastery of relevant information. In some cases, however, it doesn't take much to be designated an expert. In a study by Channel Marketing Corporation ("PC Buyers," 1996), 55% of customers in computer stores made purchases based almost entirely on the expertise of sales clerks who may or may not have known what they were talking about.

A gender bias often affects the perception of who qualifies as a "real expert." Both men and women do not usually think of women as experts (Propp, 1995). Women find that they have to assert their expertise more persistently than men to be perceived as credible. Once an individual of either sex is accepted as an expert, however, people are strongly influenced by the expert to accept recommendations that even contradict their own points of view (Foschi et al., 1985). This can be empowering for both the expert who is listened to and those who benefit and learn from the expert advice.

A second condition for individuals to be perceived as experts is that they be considered trustworthy. People everywhere are more influenced by experts who stand to gain nothing personally than they are by those who would gain personally by lying or distorting information (McGuinnies & Ward, 1980).

In the summer of 1992 the *National Law Journal* and LEXIS, a database service, conducted the most comprehensive national poll of jurors ever undertaken. Of the nearly 800 individuals who had recently sat on a jury, 95% said that they were impressed by expert testimony during a trial and 70% felt that expert testimony influences the outcome of a trial. Nevertheless, 51% of the jurors said that they didn't necessarily trust the testimony of police officers, and 70% of African American jurors felt police testimony was suspect ("Jurors' Views," 1993).

Legitimate Authority

Participants were told to deliver increasingly painful electric shocks to an innocent victim whose "crime" was merely making a mistake on a word association test. The purpose of these series of studies (Milgram, 1974) was to determine whether subjects would blindly obey a legitimate authority even when that authority ordered them to harm an innocent victim. No one, neither the experimenters, groups of psychiatrists, college students, nor middle-class adults, thought any of the participants would deliver the maximum shock of 450 volts. Nevertheless, two thirds of the participants in some of the studies obeyed the experimenter and delivered the maximum shock to the victim, who in some cases screamed in agony. No shocks were actually delivered, but the experiments were made to seem real, and none of the participants suspected trickery.

In all, 18 variations of these obedience to authority studies were conducted. More than 1,000 participants from all ages and walks of life took part. Other researchers replicated these studies in the United States and abroad, gaining as high as 85% compliance (Milgram, 1974). It didn't matter if the innocent victim complained of a heart condition or demanded to be freed from the experiment, most participants obeyed the orders of the legitimate authority.

In one of the more dramatic replications, participants were told to shock a cute fluffy puppy dog (Sheridan & King, 1972). Although the victims in the previous studies appeared to be, but weren't actually, shocked, the puppy did receive shocks (at reduced levels). Despite the disbelief commonly exhibited by my students that anyone would continue to shock an adorable puppy held captive in a box whose floor was an electrified grid, the results of the experiment duplicated previous studies. Three quarters of the subjects, all college students, were obedient to the end (54% of the men and 100% of the women).

Participants in the study delivered electric shocks not because they were evil or sadistic but because they couldn't resist legitimate authority (Milgram, 1974). The experimenter was the legitimate authority. He insisted that participants continue to deliver increasing levels of electric shock to the victims. Those who are perceived to have a right to direct others' behavior because of their position, title, role, experience, or knowledge are typically considered **legitimate authorities.**

The strength of legitimate authority can be seen outside the experimental laboratory. David Cline, a driver education instructor at Northern High School in Durham, North Carolina, resigned from his teaching post in October 1997. While acting as a driving instructor, he ordered a teenage student driver to chase a car that cut them off. When they caught up to the offender, Cline jumped out of the car and punched Jon David Macklin in the nose. Macklin took off. Cline ordered the student driver to chase after him again, which the student did. A police officer pulled them over for speeding. The student broke traffic laws and endangered several people on the orders of a legitimate authority—her driver education instructor.

No individual possesses legitimate authority. This is conferred by others. Participants in the Milgram studies could have perceived the orders of the experimenter as illegitimate and refused to obey. Parents exercise legitimate authority over their children by virtue of their caregiver role. This is usually a positive use of power because most parents want what is best for their children. They typically use their legitimate authority to guide, protect, and teach their children. Parental authority, however, inevitably erodes when children become adults. "I'm not your little child anymore; you can't order me around" is an assertion of maturity and a signal that parental authority has lost some of its legitimacy.

Even if granted authority by virtue of a formal title, position, or role, the authority must be perceived to be legitimate to function as a power resource.

Baby-sitters sometimes face this predicament. Parents put them in charge of their children, but the perception by children that the sitter is not a "real parent" can undermine this power resource.

The competent communicator must adopt the skeptical view and distinguish between appropriate and inappropriate use of authority. Blindly refusing to obey police officers, teachers, parents, judges, and bosses is as dangerous as blindly obeying authority. Ethical criteria—respect, honesty, fairness, and choice—provide the means for determining when we should comply with and when we should defy authority. In the Milgram studies, the victims were pleading with participants to stop shocking them. The victims were given no choice, and the delivery of seemingly painful electric shocks showed little respect and sensitivity toward the innocent victims of the experiment.

Rewards and Punishments

Distributing rewards and punishments can be an important source of power. Salaries, bonuses, work schedules, perks, hirings, and firings are typical job-related rewards and punishments. Money, freedom, privacy, and car keys are a few of the rewards and punishments found in family situations. Grades, letters of recommendation, and social approval or disapproval are rewards and punishments available to teachers when dealing with students.

The power potential of punishment depends on the degree of certainty that the punishment will be administered. Idle threats have little influence on behavior. Parents who threaten spankings or denial of privileges—but never follow through—soon realize that their children have learned to ignore such impotent bluster. Punishment is a source of power if it can be, and likely will be, exercised.

Punishing as a power source, however, is delicate business. Punishing can be used positively to change behavior from antisocial to prosocial. Punishing, however, is coercive and reinforces dominance. Consequently, it easily triggers psychological backlash. Individuals on the receiving end of punishment typically rebel. Those who punish create interpersonal distance between themselves and those punished. We don't normally like our tormenters. Punishment also indicates what not to do, but it doesn't indicate what to do.

Reward as a power resource tends to induce rewarding behavior. If you disseminate rewards, you become more attractive in the eyes of those rewarded. This, of course, depends on whether the rewards are structured as a cooperative or competitive system. Rewards, especially when used to bribe a person to behave in a certain way, can be used as a strategy of dominance. "Do what I say and I'll buy you a car" seeks submissiveness from the person rewarded.

Personal Qualities

We all know individuals who exert some influence over us, not because of any of the power resources already discussed but because of personal qualities they seem to possess in abundance that we find attractive. Mother Theresa, the Pope, several U.S. presidents, some sports figures, political leaders, teachers, and parents exhibit these personal qualities that draw people to them and make them positive role models. This constellation of personal attributes that people find attractive is often referred to as **charisma.**

Can you explain how the Pope utilizes information, expertise, legitimate authority, punishment and rewards, and personal qualities to maintain his power as head of the Catholic Church and as a worldwide figure of renown?

Good looks, an attractive personality, dynamism, persuasive skills, warmth, and charm are some of the personal qualities that make an individual charismatic. There is no precise formula for determining charisma. What is attractive to you may be unattractive to others. Your friends may be flabbergasted by your choice for a date. Cult leaders Charles Manson, Marshall Applewhite, and David Koresh seem like lunatics to many, but others followed them unhesitatingly. Who can adequately explain the grief exhibited by Elvis worshippers on the 20th anniversary of his death in 1997? Many of the grief-stricken weren't born until after Elvis died. The cult of celebrity and personality can be a very powerful resource.

None of the five resources—information, expertise, legitimate authority, punishments and rewards, and personal qualities—have inherent power. Power resources are not properties of individuals. A person does not possess power but is granted power by others. Your relationship partner, a group, or an organization must endorse the resource for it to be influential. Charisma means little in a job interview if a hiring committee prefers diligence, expertise, and efficiency. Charisma might look like flash without follow-through. A reward that nobody wants will influence no one. Information that is irrelevant to the needs of individuals or groups has no power potential. When Richard Nixon faced impeachment because of the Watergate scandal, he had to resign because the American people no longer endorsed the legitimacy of his presidency. Bill Clinton, however, weathered the impeachment storm because a significant majority of the American public opposed his removal from office. Power is transactional.

Transacting Power Competently

In the first part of this section, the dominance-prevention power transaction, which is competitive in nature, will be explored. In the second part of this section, you will learn how to empower individuals and groups in cooperative, positive transactions of shared power.

Dominance-Prevention Transactions

Three primary communication strategies are used by the less powerful to prevent domination by others. These three strategies are: forming coalitions, defying more powerful individuals, and resisting more powerful persons. As these strategies are discussed, keep in mind that the win-lose, dominance power perspective provokes these prevention power plays.

Coalition Formation Individuals form temporary alliances, called **coalitions,** to increase their power relative to others. Coalitions occur in group situations when there are disputes. Coalitions have been formed when group members jointly use their combined power to control a decision and to take action. One study (Grusky et al., 1995) found that arguments and disagreements in families lead to coalitions about 30% of the time. Many arguments are settled directly between the individuals involved, but individuals sometimes engage in power struggles. Coalitions can balance the power in a group when the relatively powerless form a coalition and increase their strength. Coalitions can create power imbalances when the more powerful group members move to consolidate their strength by banding together against the weaker members.

In most families the father is considered the most powerful person, followed by the mother, then the oldest child, followed by the younger siblings (Grusky et al., 1995). Parental coalitions are the predominate coalition in a four-person family, and they are virtually unopposable. Such coalitions maintain the family structure and support the status differences between parents and children. The next most frequent coalition is between a parent and an older child. Children-only coalitions are the least frequent and are almost always unsuccessful (Grusky et al., 1995).

Coalitions may be useful in the political arena, but they can be destructive in family situations (Rosenthal, 1997). Coalitions create a "them versus us" competitive mentality. Parental coalitions are sometimes necessary to present a united front when a dispute with children arises. Parent-child coalitions, however, can disrupt the family structure. Parental stability is the most vital part of family stability. Asking children to choose sides in a dispute between parents can rip a family apart, especially if the issue is significant and the dispute is recurrent. It is usually more constructive and effective when parents work out their differences without seeking allies among their children.

Defiance Low-power persons sometimes overtly defy higher power persons. **Defiance** is unambiguous, purposeful noncompliance. It is a refusal to give in to those with greater power. Defiance is the prevention form of power. Those who defy stand against those who attempt to dominate.

Defiance can be contagious. A defiant child can embolden siblings to defy parents unless the parents take effective action. A single worker who defiantly walks off the job may encourage a wildcat strike. Those in authority are anxious to halt defiance before it spreads.

Relatively powerful people typically use four communication strategies to quell defiance (Leavitt, 1964). First, the more powerful person or the entire group will try to *reason* with the defiant individual. (This doesn't mean that the reasons will necessarily be good ones.) Arguments will be used to convince the defiant person to get back in line and comply. Second, *seduction* is used. Seduction can be a psychological ploy to make the defiant person feel guilty, uncomfortable, or ineffectual. "Your refusal to comply will accomplish nothing" or "Why are you wasting everybody's time with such childish defiance?" are examples of the seduction strategy. Bribing the defiant person with offers of promotions, monetary incentives, and perquisites is another seduction tactic. Third, *coercion* is used to extinguish defiance. Threats, ridicule, and contempt are used to force compliance. "Do what I tell you or you're fired" is an example of coercion. Fourth, *isolation*, both physical and psychological, is used to quell defiance. If expelling the defiant person from the group is not possible, the troublemaker can be isolated physically by relocating his or her office to a distant corner of the building, for example, or by clearly discouraging friendship or even social contact with the offender.

A son or daughter who insists on marrying or being intimate with a person of a different race, religion, or sexual orientation from that of the son or daughter's parents might produce all four strategies. "It'll never work. You're too different. This is not the way you were raised" (reason) may be the first response. "You'll kill your poor father. You know his heart is weak" (seduction) may follow to make the defiant son or daughter feel guilty or uncomfortable with the planned relationship. "We'll cut you off entirely. You can't afford to finish college without our help" (coercion) may result if the first two strategies are unsuccessful. "If you marry him/her, you're no son/daughter of ours. Your presence will never grace our doorstep again" (isolation) may be the final effort to produce capitulation.

Defiant individuals hoping to counter dominance from others often fight these four strategies, and occasionally they convert an entire group to their point of view. If a person cannot be expelled from the relationship or group (e.g., family member), remaining unalterably and confidently defiant provides the best chance of successfully countering pressure to comply (Gebhardt & Meyers, 1995). Parents in the previous example may eventually accept the relationship, especially if it appears that the relationship will be long term, because the alternative (isolation from their son or daughter) is too painful. When a group has the power to expel a person, however, remaining unalterably defiant will likely prove to be an impotent choice. Remaining uncompromisingly defiant until the group is about fed up, then switching to a more compromising position, is an option likely to produce better results (Wolf, 1979).

Remaining uncompromisingly defiant risks straining friendships and jeopardizing relationships with partners, relatives, and coworkers (Box 7-2). Any time individuals are defiant, they run the risk of alienating those who disagree with them, and sometimes even those who agree. Defiance is a highly competitive communication behavior. It will make a person a loser far more often than a winner simply because the very nature of defiance is disagreeable to those who want compliance, and they usually are the majority. In most cases, consider defiance an option of last resort.

Box 7-2   Sharper Focus

Henry Boisvert Versus FMC Corporation

Henry Boisvert was an engineer who worked on the Bradley Fighting Vehicle, a controversial 25-ton military weapon that is part tank and part troop carrier. In the early 1980s, Boisvert began warning his superiors at FMC Corporation, a military contracting company in San Jose, California, that there were serious flaws in the Bradley (Mintz, 1998). Boisvert was concerned about safety problems, including its tendency to sink in water despite being advertised to the U.S. Army as an amphibious vehicle. Boisvert's efforts to include safety problems in testing reports were snubbed by FMC.

When Boisvert finally went public with his accusations that FMC had defrauded the federal government of billions of dollars for a military weapon that was unsafe and ineffective, his life became a nightmare. In 1986 he was fired from FMC (coercion). FMC labeled Boisvert a flake and a troublemaker, denying all of his accusations. Almost all of his friends, most of whom had worked at FMC, deserted him (isolation). He was unable to find work. He sent out 8,000 resumes, had 5 interviews, but received zero job offers, even for low-level positions. Concerned that his phone was tapped and that FMC was responsible for burglarizing his lawyer's office, Boisvert constantly worried about his safety. Unable to find work, he went broke and exhausted his retirement fund.

For 12 years he fought FMC in court. Finally, in April 1998, a U.S. district court jury decided unanimously that Boisvert was right and awarded him millions of dollars in damages and fined FMC over $350 million, most of it to go to the federal government as repayment for the fraud. An Army veteran, Boisvert explained after the verdict, "I wanted a jury to make them pay the government back. I promise I'll give most of the money away. I'll set up trusts to help society. The bottom line was to save troops' lives. I was just hoping nobody got killed" (as cited in Mintz, 1998, p. A9).

Whistleblowers like Boisvert, who alert the public and government of fraud and criminal activity by businesses and corporations, face nasty consequences for their defiance of company orders to keep quiet. On December 10, 1993, CNN reported that 88% of whistleblowers suffer personal reprisals for their defiance. On March 6, 1989, CBS News reported that partly because of pressures to keep quiet about abuses 17% of whistleblowers studied lost their homes, 15% divorced, and 10% attempted suicide. Knowing full well that coercion and isolation are two favorite strategies used to discredit and combat the defiant, it takes courage and resilience to defy those in positions of power.

Resistance   Defiance is *overt* noncompliance. **Resistance** is *covert* noncompliance. It is often duplicitous and manipulative. Resisters are subtle saboteurs. The sabotage is ambiguous. Truly successful resistance leaves people wondering if resistance even occurred.

Resistance, like defiance, is usually the choice of the less powerful. Resistance has an advantage over defiance. It is often safer to use indirect means of noncompliance than direct confrontation when faced with a more powerful person or group. *Those who are defiant dig in their heels and openly cause trouble, but those who resist merely drag their feet.*

There are several resistance strategies. Resistance strategies are sometimes referred to as passive aggression.

Strategic Stupidity   This is the playing stupid strategy. When children don't want to do what their parents tell them to, they sometimes act stupid when they know better. "But mom, I don't know how to fold the laundry" may simply be an effort to frustrate the parent who may give up in disgust and fold the laundry rather than show the child for the 'bizillionth' time what should be plainly obvious.

Strategic stupidity works exceedingly well when the low-power person claims stupidity, is forced to attempt the task anyway, then performs it ineptly. In one study of 555 married adults ("Home Chores," 1993), 14% of the men admitted purposely botching house chores to get out of doing them again. The poor performance becomes "proof" that the stupidity was real. The passive aggressor can assert, "I told you I didn't know how to do laundry."

Loss of Motor Function This resistance strategy is an effective companion to strategic stupidity. The resister doesn't act stupid, just incredibly clumsy, often resulting in costly damage. There is a mixed message here of resistance on one hand but apparent effort on the other. "I tried really hard not to let dishes slip out of my hands; I'm sorry I broke two plates" may be an honest apology from your housemate for accidental behavior. If it becomes repetitive, however, it may be an effort to avoid doing dishes.

The Misunderstanding Mirage This is the "I thought you meant" or the "I could have sworn you said" strategy. The resistance is expressed "behind a cloak of great sincerity" (Bach & Goldberg, 1972, p. 110). Students sometimes excuse late assignments by using this strategy. "You said it was due Wednesday, not today, didn't you?" they'll say hopefully. The implied message is that since this is a simple misunderstanding, penalizing the student for a late paper would be unfair.

Selective Amnesia Have you ever noticed that some people are particularly forgetful about those things that they clearly do not want to do? This temporary amnesia is highly selective when used as a resistance strategy. Selective amnesiacs rarely forget what is most important to them. No outward signs of resistance are manifested. Resisters agree to perform the task—but conveniently let it slip their minds.

In a sophisticated version of this strategy the individual remembers all but one or two important items. A person shops for groceries and purchases all but two key items. Hey, no one's perfect. He or she remembered almost everything. The dinner menu, however, will have to be altered because the main course wasn't purchased.

Tactical Tardiness When you really don't want to attend a meeting, a class, a lecture, or a party, you can show contempt by arriving late. Tactical tardiness irritates and frustrates those who value the event. It can hold an entire group hostage while everyone waits for the arrival of the person who is late. Consistently arriving late for class is disruptive, especially if the resister requests an update on material missed.

Tactical tardiness may be used on occasion by high-power persons to reinforce their dominance and self-importance. Celebrities often arrive late to functions. They may hope to underscore their prestige by making fans wait for them.

Purposeful Procrastination Most people put off doing what they dislike. There is nothing purposeful about this. Purposeful procrastinators, however, pretend that they will pursue a task "soon." While promising imminent results, they deliberately refuse to commit to a specific time or date for task completion. They delay completion of tasks on purpose. Trying to pin down a purposeful procrastinator is like trying to pin Jell-O to a wall—it won't stick. If those waiting for the task to be completed express exasperation, they appear to be nagging or fussing. Parents who try to get their kids to clean their rooms are often faced with this maddening strategy. When parents grow weary of monitoring their childrens' room-cleaning progress, they may give up in disgust and perform the task themselves or leave the room chaotic. This makes the resistance successful.

All six of these resistance strategies result from power imbalances. It is difficult to know for sure when such strategies are being used. A single occurrence of forgetfulness or tardiness doesn't indicate resistance necessarily, although resistance may be occurring. If the behavior becomes repetitive, it is safe to conclude that resistance strategies are being used.

Resistance strategies are underhanded, deceitful, and dishonest. This doesn't make for terribly competent communication. In extreme cases, resistance strategies may be the only feasible option available to prevent evil. In most instances, however, there are better ways to prevent dominance, as you will see later in this text. There are two principal ways for competent communicators to discourage resistance strategies, especially when the resistance is unjustified:

1. *Confront the strategy directly.* Use first-person singular language to describe the resistance strategy (see Chapter 2). Discuss why the strategy has been used, and work cooperatively with the resister to find an equitable solution so resistance strategies are not employed.
2. *Thwart the enabling process.* We become enablers when we allow ourselves to become ensnared in the resister's net of duplicity. When we continue to wait for the tactically tardy, we encourage the behavior. If we perform the tasks for those who use loss of motor function or strategic stupidity, we reward their resistance and guarantee that such strategies will persist.

   You thwart the enabling process by refusing to encourage the resistance. If staff members "forget" important items when shopping for office supplies, send them back for the items. Encourage them to make a list and check off items as they shop. If a person is persistently late for meetings, continue without them and do not interrupt the meeting to fill them in on missed information. Encourage them to be punctual. Continued tardiness may necessitate punishment or expulsion from the group. Refrain from rescuing those who use strategic stupidity or loss of motor function. Compensation for damage caused by such resistance strategies should be the responsibility of the resister.

Despite the negative aspects of resistance strategies, the primary focus should not be on how to combat resistance. Instead, focus on how to reduce power imbalances and dominance-submissiveness transactions that foster a desire to resist.

Empowering Self and Others

Empowerment is a constructive form of power. Individuals become empowered by learning to communicate competently. Acquiring communication knowledge and developing a broad range of communication skills can give us confidence that we can adapt our communication appropriately whatever the context. We are empowered by this knowledge and these skills because more options are available to us. In this section several ways to empower people will be explained.

Developing Assertiveness The terms *assertive* and *aggressive* are often confused. *Assertiveness* is "the ability to communicate the full range of your thoughts and emotions with confidence and skill" (Adler, 1977, p. 6). Those who confuse assertiveness with aggressiveness tend to ignore the last part of this definition. Assertiveness isn't merely imposing your thoughts and emotions on others. Assertiveness requires confident and especially skillful expression of thoughts and emotions. Assertiveness falls between the extremes of aggressiveness and passivity and is distinctly different from both of them. Aggressiveness puts one's own needs first, whereas passivity underemphasizes one's needs (Lulofs, 1994). *Assertiveness considers both your needs and the needs of others.*

Although assertiveness can be employed to defy others, it is primarily an empowering skill. We are most often assertive, not to defy anyone but to assure that our needs, rights, and responsibilities are not ignored or to make a relationship or group more effective. Assertive individuals seek to enhance their significance in the eyes of others, not alienate anyone. When passive, reticent individuals learn assertiveness, they become more productive contributors in groups. When aggressive individuals learn to be assertive, they are more likely to receive a fair hearing than if they try to bulldoze through disagreement that stands in their way.

Assertiveness may even save lives. The National Transportation and Safety Board recommended assertiveness training for cockpit crews. Several airline crashes were partially linked to lack of assertiveness by flight crew members who recognized pilot errors but were reluctant to correct the more powerful captain (Foushee, 1984).

Assertiveness involves four key steps (Bower & Bower, 1976):

1. *Describe* your needs, rights, and desires or the basis of your conflict with others. Use first-person singular language.
2. *Express* how you think and feel. "It upsets me when my ideas are ignored" is an example.
3. *Specify* the behavior or objective you are seeking. "I want to be included in future decision making" specifies the objective.
4. Identify *consequences.* The emphasis should be on the positive, not the negative, consequences. "I like working here, and I will continue for as long as I'm treated fairly" is better than "If you continue to treat me unfairly, I'll be forced to quit."

It is important to note that assertiveness doesn't mean being impolite to others. Competent communicators show respect to others. You can remain firm and direct and still be unwaveringly polite and respectful.

Assertiveness isn't always appropriate. Asian cultures typically do not value the low-context directness that characterizes assertive communication. Standing up for yourself and speaking your mind are seen as disruptive and provocative acts likely to create disharmony. Women in highly masculine cultures (e.g., Japan, Venezuela, Italy) may also find that assertiveness poses problems for them because only men are expected to be assertive. Even in an individualist culture like the United States where a low-context communication style is encouraged, overly persistent assertiveness can result in less favorable evaluations from supervisors, lower salaries, greater job tension, and greater personal stress than less-vigorous assertion of one's needs and desires (Schmidt & Kipnis, 1987). Assertiveness by battered wives can be potentially hazardous, even fatal (O'Leary et al., 1985). The

Speaking skills can be very empowering.

competent communicator analyzes the context to determine the appropriate use of assertiveness.

Increasing Personal Power Resources   Individuals can empower themselves in numerous ways by developing their power resources. Women who have been homemakers may significantly empower themselves by returning to college, earning a degree, and finding employment. The additional income benefits the entire family. A wife and mother becomes a "professional" with all the prestige and status that is accorded such a position. Her self-esteem may be bolstered by her sense of independence, resulting from a college education and employment in her field of study.

Husbands who assume a greater portion of the domestic chores and child rearing may increase their value in the family. They do not have to depend on the expertise of their partners to perform domestic activities competently. The stereotype of the bungling husband and father burning the dinner and falling prey to the antics of his children when his wife leaves the domestic responsibilities in his hands while she is away doesn't have to be the reality. Men can empower themselves to handle domestic responsibilities and tasks with dexterity. They don't have to become the passive victims of their own self-imposed ineptitude.

Developing expertise can be empowering. Learning computer skills can make you a valuable asset in a group or organization. Developing public speaking and interpersonal skills is empowering. Such skills open up new horizons, new capabilities and options. Becoming informed on topics, especially if the information is specialized, can make you a valuable group member. The more we develop our personal power resources, the more empowered and significant we can become.

Mentoring and Networking   Mentors are knowledgeable individuals who have achieved some success in their profession or jobs and who assist individuals trying to get started in a line of work. Mentors can provide information to the novice that can prevent mistakes by trial and error. Mentoring seems to be especially empowering for women in their rise to upper echelons of organizations (Noe, 1988). One study showed that women who have mentors move up the organization ladder much faster than women without mentors. Women also receive more promotions faster when they are assisted by mentors (as cited in Kleiman, 1991). Mentors are essential for women trying to advance to the highest levels of corporate leadership.

Networking is another form of empowerment. Individuals with similar backgrounds, skills, and goals come together on a fairly regular basis and share information that will assist members in pursuing goals. Networks also provide emotional support for members, especially women's networks.

Leadership and Empowerment   Leaders can take actions that empower individuals and groups. Encouraging meaningful participation in decision making, providing opportunities to perform complex and challenging tasks, giving greater responsibility, and providing opportunities to expand knowledge and expertise all empower individuals in groups and organizations (Burpitt & Bigoness, 1997). Teams evaluated as most innovative actively sought out, learned, and applied new knowledge and skills. Becoming a competent communicator is empowering.

Summary

Power is the ability to influence the attainment of goals sought by yourself or others. Power is inherent in all human relationships. There are three forms of power: dominance, prevention, and empowerment. Power imbalances produce several consequences: physical violence, psychological abuse, spirals of mutual abuse, sexual harassment, and commonplace difficulties. Power imbalances also produce anger, frustration, wariness, and resentment in common everyday situations. Information, expertise, legitimate authority, rewards and punishments, and personal qualities are the primary power resources. Coalition formation, defiance, and resistance strategies are the chief ways dominance is combatted by the less powerful. Although dominance and prevention forms of power can produce "the dark side" of interpersonal relationships, empowerment is a very positive form of power. Becoming empowered is an important step in becoming a competent communicator. Empowerment is a win-win cooperative approach to interpersonal relationships.

Suggested Readings

Farrell, W. (1993). *The myth of male power: Why men are the disposable sex.* New York: Simon & Schuster. This is a highly provocative polemic on the myth of the patriarchal society and the abuse of men written by a former board member of the National Organization for Women. I guarantee that this book will spark debate.

Hoff-Sommers, C. (1993). *Who stole feminism? How women have betrayed women.* New York: Simon & Schuster. This is an extremely controversial attack on "gender feminists." It challenges the notion that men are the enemy of women and that power must be seized from men to benefit women.

Wolf, N. (1994). *Fire with fire: The new female power and how to use it.* New York: Fawcett Columbine. Wolf, a self-proclaimed feminist, has written a nicely balanced treatment of power and how it relates to women.

Chapter 8

Making Relationships Work

As we enter the new millennium, personal relationships seem to be ever more fragile. Divorce rates dropped slightly during the 1990s but remain high. The unprecedented surge of women entering the workforce, acquiring college degrees, assuming an increasing percentage of management positions, and entering prestigious professions has afforded women a greater opportunity to leave unhappy relationships than at any time in history (Coontz, 1997). Gay and lesbian relationships are even less durable than heterosexual marriages (Huston & Schwartz, 1995). Making relationships work in the long term, always a daunting prospect, seems more challenging than ever.

It may seem pleasant to envision a return to the "good old days" of the 1950s, depicted in television shows such as *Father Knows Best, Leave It to Beaver,* and *Ozzie and Harriet.* These shows presented an idealized picture of happy, intact families with manageable problems. Divorce was hardly ever mentioned, and single-parent families were a rarity. A Knight-Ridder poll (Thomma, 1996) found that 38% of respondents picked the decade of the 1950s as the best time for children to grow up (highest of any decade).

Yearning for the good old days, however, diverts attention from a deeper truth. The 1950s were good only for a small portion of our society. This "best decade" saw widespread racism, sexism, and homophobia. More than 27% of America's children lived in poverty, and almost half of African American families were impoverished (Coontz, 1997). The lower divorce rate of the 1950s doesn't necessarily mean that couples were happier than couples are today. Alcoholism, child abuse, and partner abuse were significant social problems that were mostly hidden from public view and largely ignored by social agencies. Leaving a bad relationship was not as acceptable in the 1950s as it is today.

One study (Wallerstein & Blakeslee, 1995) of present-day happily married couples found that only 5 of 100 spouses "wanted a marriage like their parents." The husbands "rejected the role models provided by their fathers," and the wives said "they could never be happy living as their mothers did" (p. 15). It is unlikely that women's and men's expectations of marriage and work will ever revert to the rigid gender roles of the past. This means that making relationships work now requires different answers from those offered in the past.

Sustaining relationships has never been more challenging, and there is no magic formula for making them work. The way we communicate with our partners, friends, family members, and coworkers is central to the degree of relationship success we enjoy. We know more about what makes relationships successful than at any previous time in our history. The primary purpose of this chapter is to discuss what makes relationships at home, at work, at school, and at play successful, and what destroys them. There are five objectives:

1. to identify the predictable stages of development through which relationships evolve,
2. to explain dialectics inherent in relationships,
3. to address difficulties associated with intercultural relationships,
4. to discuss how to construct cooperation in relationships, and
5. to explore ways to sustain relationships.

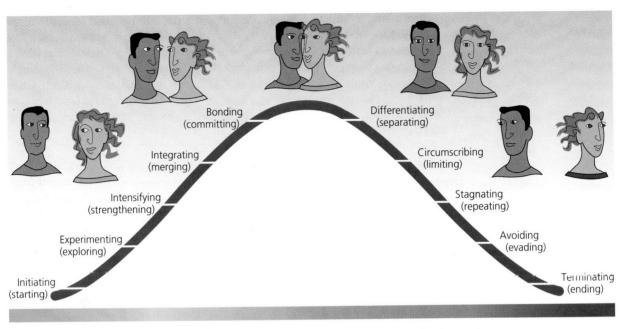

Figure 8-1 Stages of Relationship Development

Stages of Relationship Development

Understanding what makes relationships succeed or fail begins with a focus on stages of relationship development. Knapp and Vangelisti (1992) provide five stages of "coming together" and five stages of "coming apart" (Figure 8-1). Particular patterns of communication occur in each stage, allowing us to identify whether a relationship is progressing or deteriorating. Movement through the stages may be rapid, especially the early stages, or it may be slow when one partner wants to move forward or backward but the other partner resists. Let's look at each of these stages of relationship development.

Coming Together Stages

Spouses, gay partners, siblings, tennis pals, and coworkers all travel down the same road of relationship development. Spouses and partners just travel farther down the road.

Initiating (Starting)   Communication with others begins with a first step. Someone has to initiate contact. The commonplace greeting "Hi, how are you?" followed by the usual "I'm fine, how are you" is rarely meant to be taken literally. Rather, it is a kind of ritual greeting whose main purpose is to open contact with another person. In fact, a literal interpretation and response would be disconcerting, even shocking. "My life actually sucks, but thanks for asking" would likely not encourage further contact if you did not know the person well.

During the initiating stage, we are surveying the interpersonal terrain. We try to put our best foot forward, appearing friendly, open, and approachable. The somewhat awkward initial communication that occurs on your first day at a new job as introductions are made typifies this stage of relationships. There is simple acknowledgment of another's existence. This stage is particularly difficult when divorced individuals, each with children, marry. Introducing children who are strangers to each other with the intent of "being a family" can produce strained, even hostile, initial communication.

Experimenting (Exploring)   The experimenting stage is where we audition for the part of acquaintance, which may be a stepping stone to friendship. We experiment by engaging in small talk to discover areas of commonality: "What's your major?" "Can you believe how awful the weather has been?" "Have you worked at this job long?" We're casually probing, searching for ways to connect with others. All of us have superficial contacts with hundreds of people that never develop to any extent. Most of our transactions, especially at work, do not progress beyond the experimenting stage of development. They are fleeting contacts with no future. Think of the many students you have come in contact with in high school and college, but now you hardly remember their names. At work you may get to know only a handful of coworkers well; the rest fade into the background.

Intensifying (Strengthening)   The intensifying stage is where relationships develop into close friendships. Romance may blossom, and nonverbal indicators of intimacy, such as touching, hugging, and kissing, may be explored. Expressions of commitment begin: "I'm sure glad I met you." "It's great being around you." We introduce our friend to family members, other friends, and coworkers. Conversations in the experimenting stage usually stick to safe, impersonal topics. Conversations during the intensifying stage, however, move to riskier, more personal subjects (sexual experience, political attitudes). The desire to please your friend increases. Jealousy can show its ugly tentacles and is sometimes used to test the sincerity and commitment of a partner or friend. You become publicly identified as friends or as a romantic couple.

Integrating (Merging)   The integrating stage fuses a relationship. Individuals seem to merge into a clearly distinct couple. Social circles of friends mix. Nonverbal markers of intimacy are displayed, such as rings, pictures, pins, or clothing belonging to the other person. Self-disclosure is more revealing and potentially risky. Life goals and aspirations are shared. A sexual relationship often occurs at this stage. Partners may begin living together, indicating that the couple has clearly moved beyond the "just friends" stage.

Bonding (Committing)   The public ritual stage that institutionalizes the relationship is called bonding. We are communicating to the world that we have a committed relationship. There is a public contract, of which marriage is the most obvious example. Gay couples do not have this option in most states. Nevertheless, any public announcement, ceremony, or proclamation that the relationship is considered exclusive and binding moves the couple into the bonding stage.

Coming Apart Stages

"Happily ever after" is a great finish to a fairy tale, but relationships often don't move in just one direction—from friendly to intimate to happy to blissful. Relationships can move forward (coming together) or backward (coming apart), and the outcome is not inevitable. Couples who were once happy but become dissatisfied don't necessarily end their relationship. Friendships that fell apart may reignite. Coworkers who worked well together, then became adversaries, may become friendly again. The direction of a relationship can be turned around. Nevertheless, some family relationships, friendships, marriages, and work relationships do dissolve. Let's look briefly at the stages of relationship deterioration.

Differentiating (Separating)   The first stage of disengagement is differentiating. Differences, not similarities, between partners, friends, relatives, or coworkers emerge.

HOMER: I thought you liked pizza?

MARGE: I just pretended to like it because I wanted to please you.

What were thought to be similarities are discovered to be differences. The pretense of being alike in most things erodes.

The orientation becomes more "Me" than "We." Assertions of individuality become more frequent. Conflict occurs, although differentiating can occur without conflict. Differentiating is an expected stage in parent-adolescent relationships. Teenagers often begin to assert their individuality by stridently communicating that they are *not* like their parents.

Circumscribing (Limiting)   When we establish limits and restrictions on communication with our partner, friend, relative, or coworker, we are circumscribing. Both the breadth and the depth of our communication become constrained. Fewer topics are perceived to be safe to discuss for fear of igniting a conflict, and topics that are addressed are discussed superficially. Communication interactions become less frequent. We circumscribe with friends because of differences in values, interests, and points of view. Formerly close friendships may become no more than acquaintanceships. "I thought I knew him well, but now I almost feel like we're strangers when we get together" is a statement that typifies the shift in closeness.

Stagnating (Repeating)   Stagnating relationships experience the treadmill effect. Many miles are covered, but no destination is reached. Stagnating relationships aren't growing or progressing. Partners, friends, coworkers, or relatives are caught in a repetitive cycle, and they may find it difficult to break the cycle and step off the treadmill.

Friendships become dull and predictable. Adult children never seem to resolve troublesome issues with their parents. Coworkers argue about the same issues with the same results. The feeling is, "nothing changes." Communication becomes even more restricted, narrow, hesitant, and awkward than in the circumscribing stage. "We should talk about our relationship" is likely to provoke dread of yet another conflict with an unhappy outcome. In work situations you often don't get to choose your coworkers. Your relationship with a coworker or a boss may have little chance of improvement, yet you don't have the option of terminating the working relationship. In such cases, you have to make the best of a bad situation. You may jump to the next stage in such instances.

Avoiding (Evading)   In the avoiding stage, partners, friends, relatives, or coworkers simply keep a distance from each other, hoping not to interact. Separation, not connection, is desired. If physical separation is not possible, people act as if the other person does not exist. Roommates in college sometimes adopt this communication pattern when their relationship disintegrates. Unable to move out of a shared dorm room or apartment, roommates may stay away from their common abode as much as possible. When present, each may act as if the other is invisible. Awkward silences may increase the tension.

Terminating (Ending)   Some relationships terminate before they ever get started. You greet a person, perceive no chemistry between you, and shuffle off in search of more promising prospects. Other relationships may take years, even decades, to terminate. This is the final pulling apart stage. The relationship is over—done, finished, ceased, dead, kaput.

In romantic partnerships, friendships, even family relationships, termination is normally chosen by one or both parties involved. In relationships with coworkers, however, termination may be chosen by outsiders. A boss may fire a coworker, or you may be transferred to a location hundreds or thousands of miles away. Even productive relationships at work may end because of the intervention of outsiders.

Although there is a tendency to view the coming together stages of relationships as good and the coming apart stages as bad, this is not necessarily true. Some relationships may be destructive to one or both parties and should not progress. Terminating abusive relationships is positive, not negative. Childhood friends may drift apart in adulthood; people change. Sometimes relationship participants have to step back before they can step forward. I know an individual who avoided communicating with his parents for 2 years while he repaired his personal life. Parental interference merely added stress and made his situation even more difficult. He has since resumed his relationship with his parents, and it is better than it ever was. Stages of relationships merely describe what is, not necessarily what should be.

Relationship Dialectics

Relationships are often messy. As we move through the stages and become increasingly intimate, the relationship will rarely follow the profile for textbook-perfect communication. Most romantic partners talk to each other on average for a mere hour a day, rarely self-disclose, often fight, even become violent verbally and sometimes physically, are less polite to each other than they are to strangers, and are more concerned with task accomplishment than with sharing intimacies (Baxter & Montgomery, 1996). We typically don't measure up to the ideal because

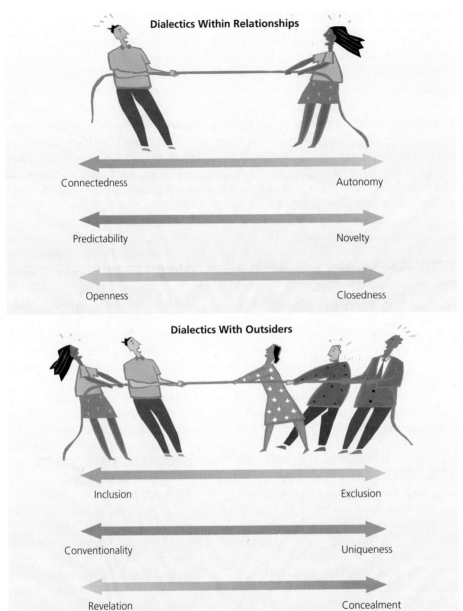

Figure 8-2 Relationship Dialectics

romantic partnerships, close friendships, family relationships, even work relationships face difficult contradictions every day. Communication theorists historically have tended to gloss over the contradictions inherent in relationships (Baxter & Montgomery, 1996).

In this section you will learn about the contradictory impulses, or **dialectics,** that push and pull us in conflicting directions in our relationships with others (Figure 8-2). Communication strategies for dealing with these relational dialectics will also be discussed.

Dialectics Within Relationships

We experience impulses that push and pull us in opposite directions simultaneously within our relationships with others. There are three such dialectics common to most relationships: connection-autonomy, predictability-novelty, and openness-closedness.

Connection-Autonomy   The desire to come together with another person (connection) yet remain apart, independent, and in control of one's own life (autonomy), is one dialectic faced in all relationships. We want to connect with our partner, friends, parents, or siblings, but we simultaneously want to exercise some control and independence, some autonomy, over our lives. We want to be an "us" without losing our individuality within a relationship with others.

Adult children, for example, want to be connected to their parents in a loving relationship, but they usually rebel when parents interfere in their lives too much or make them feel as though they are still children to be supervised. As a relationship moves increasingly toward intimacy, the **connection-autonomy** dialectic becomes a central tension of the relationship. Intimacy means connecting with another person emotionally, intellectually, and physically. Intimacy requires greater We-ness than Me-ness, but intimacy doesn't require complete loss of self. Increasing levels of intimacy move us progressively toward greater connection with another person and away from autonomy. This can produce some anxious moments for individuals who become commitment phobic from fear of losing control of their lives.

Excessive emphasis on connection usually leads a person to feel smothered by his or her partner, parent, or personal friend, to feel entrapped and controlled by others, to have no life of his or her own. Excessive emphasis on autonomy, however, leads to complaints of insufficient time spent together, lack of commitment, and loss of affection (Baxter, 1994). Too much emphasis on either connection or autonomy can push a relationship into one of the stages of coming apart.

Workplace friendships pose an interesting challenge because the connection-autonomy dialectic emerges as a result of proximity. Working in the same office can provide many opportunities for people to connect and solidify a friendship. At the same time, however, daily contact with a friend at work may provide insufficient autonomy or separation and excessive connection (Bridge & Baxter, 1992). Romantic partners who also work together may find the connection-autonomy dialectic particularly troublesome. Opportunities for autonomy become fewer when you see your partner both at home and at work.

Predictability-Novelty   Relationships require a fair degree of stability and constancy to survive, that is, some predictability. Families are a primary stabilizing force in most people's lives. Families provide an anchor in a sea of change. When marriages dissolve, it is not unusual for one or both partners in the breakup to seek comfort, even guidance, from parents. Some may even seek temporary refuge with parents until life's tempests can be faced.

Predictability can be comforting because you know what to expect. There are no unpleasant surprises. Predictability is stabilizing. When teenagers prepare a lavish meal for their parents and expect them to arrive home at 5:30 p.m., having them show up at a novel time, say 7:30 p.m., is the last thing they

Life in front of the television set can make a relationship overly predictable and boring, inviting a need for greater novelty. Novelty if not taken to an extreme can prevent a relationship from becoming stale and too predictable.

want. Predictability, however, does not produce pleasant surprises either, and this can induce boredom, possibly leading to the stagnating stage of a relationship. Teenagers, in particular, often come to see their families as suffocatingly predictable and unexciting. Spending a summer vacation with parents and siblings loses its allure during adolescence and may become unendurable when early adulthood hits. The **predictability-novelty dialectic** that flows from desiring both stability and change is a central concern in relationships.

The early stages of relationships—initiating, experimenting, intensifying—are inherently novel. Everything seems new and different, and that can be exciting. Interacting with a new college roommate can be an interesting and challenging enterprise. Dating someone for the first time can be exciting because both individuals are exploring and discovering. A new romance brings change, and change can be thrilling and energizing. At some point, however, dating partners will often wish to settle into a long-lasting partnership to provide some predictability because of the comfort and stability it produces.

As relationships become long term, the desire for novelty increases. Predictability, like an old shoe, can be pleasant but dull. To keep the spark in a relationship and avoid monotony, couples need to find ways to stimulate interest in each other. Similarly, friendships can grow stale without novelty: "We always sit around and gossip. Let's do something different for a change." We can become bored with our friends if activities and conversations with them become repetitive and predictable. Coworkers can seem tedious because you see them in the same situations doing mostly the same things, day in and day out. This can increase your desire to find new employment, with new coworkers, to counteract the tedium of predictability.

Openness-Closedness   U.S. culture encourages openness and discourages closedness. We view an open mind and an open society with admiration. We usually view a closed mind and a closed society with disdain. Open expression of feelings and self-disclosure are necessary for bonding and intimacy to occur in a

Box 8-1 Focus on Controversy

Is Honesty Always the Best Policy?

You are gay. You are celebrating Christmas with your parents and siblings, and you want to bring your partner to the festivities. Your father is intensely homophobic. He is also recovering from a heart attack. Do you pretend that your partner is just a friend, or do you reveal the true nature of your relationship (revelation-concealment)?

Your spouse asks you whether you've ever had an affair. You have, but it ended 2 years ago. There is little chance that the affair would ever be discovered unless you tell your spouse. Your spouse would be devastated to know you had cheated, even though you have no intention of ever being unfaithful again. Would you answer honestly (openness-closedness)?

Your close friend at work feels insecure about her body image. She asks whether you think she is fat and unattractive. She is very overweight and poorly groomed. Would you be honest (openness-closedness)?

You feel smothered by your partner. You have little time alone. When you plan outings with friends, your partner invites him- or herself along. Do you tell your partner you need time alone or with friends, knowing that your partner will feel excluded (connection-autonomy)?

Dialectical forces pose a challenge to the oft-stated claim that honesty is always the best policy in relationships. The desire to be open, to reveal, and to connect with others pushes us toward honesty with our partners, friends, family, and coworkers. Nevertheless, circumstances can pull us toward closedness, concealment, and autonomy. Pulled in this direction, we are inclined to lie

to protect ourselves and others. The issue of lying brings into focus a principle dilemma we all face in relationships. Honesty is an important ethical guideline for the competent communicator and the cornerstone of trust, but relationship dialectics complicate the tidy, but simplistic, advice: "Just be honest."

Lying is widespread in the United States. One survey cited by NBC News on August 24, 1998, reported that 93% of employees "lie habitually" at work. A study by DePaulo and colleagues (1996) found that 147 study participants told more than 1,500 lies in a 1-week period. Half the subjects were undergraduate students and half were members of the general public. Undergraduates lied in 1 of every 3 interactions they had with others. Nonstudent participants lied in 1 of every 5 interactions. Students lied to 38% of the people they interacted with; nonstudents lied to 30%.

Lying is pervasive, but not because honesty is no longer valued. In fact, when asked to choose among telling a hurtful truth, telling a face-saving lie, or equivocating, only 6% chose lying, about 4% chose the truth, and over 90% opted for **equivocation.** We equivocate when our language permits more than one plausible meaning. For instance, when asked "Do you like the dinner?", you might respond that "It is most unusual." The questioner can interpret the answer as either approval or disapproval. Equivocation spares the feelings of the questioner and avoids the brutal truth that dinner is headed for the dog dish at the first opportunity.

Even outright lies rarely are told to cause psychological damage to another ("so he'd look like a fool"). Fewer

relationship. Some privacy, however, is also necessary if a relationship is to survive. The **openness-closedness dialectic** is an important dilemma that every relationship faces. How much self-disclosure and openness, candor or honesty, with your friends, family members, or romantic partner is enough, and how much is too much (Box 8-1)? Indiscriminate self-disclosure strains most relationships and is incompetent communication. No effort is made to determine the appropriateness of the self-disclosure or to show appreciation for the audience. Telling your partner or friend personal information that he or she is not prepared to hear can doom the relationship. Excessive closedness, however, makes you a silent partner. Friendship and intimacy don't flourish when you share little with another person about who you are.

The openness-closedness dialectic takes an interesting twist when friendships are established at work (Bridge & Baxter, 1992). Close friends are expected to be open with each other. Organizational rules, however, may require confidentiality in certain circumstances, such as worker hirings, employee evaluations, and top-secret projects. In such instances, friends are pulled in opposing directions.

(*continued*)

than 1% of lies told by college students and slightly more than 2% of lies told by nonstudent adults are of this damaging variety (DePaulo & Kasby, 1998).

Honesty is an important ethical standard for the competent communicator, but honesty can clash with sensitivity toward others. We don't always lie for self-centered reasons (to gain an advantage or manipulate others), and most of our fabrications are minor fibs, or "white lies," not whoppers. About a third of our lies (DePaulo et al., 1996) are told for altruistic reasons, such as to spare the feelings of a friend. When a friend or partner asks, "Am I fat?", you may lie by responding, "You're not fat. You look fine." The lie is meant to bolster your friend or partner's self-esteem.

Complete honesty can sound very good in the abstract, but total honesty can be hurtful and destructive, as amusingly illustrated by the Jim Carrey movie *Liar, Liar*. Psychology professor Bella DePaulo explains: "I can go as far as saying it would be a disaster if everyone tried to tell the truth all the time. If you tell the whole truth, you start alienating people. You'd have to go back and apologize because you've made a mess of your interpersonal relationships" (as cited in "Lying Is Part," 1996).

So, when is it appropriate to tell the truth, and when is lying acceptable? No absolute answer can be given. Several guidelines can assist you, however, in deciding whether to tell the truth or lie. First, *honesty should be the norm, and lying should be the exception*. Communication with others would be chaotic if we could never trust what others say to us. Relationships must have a foundation of honesty even if an occasional lie for

altruistic reasons seems warranted. Second, *those who ask for honest answers must be prepared to accept the truth*. If not, then they probably shouldn't ask the question. If you can't accept a "Yes, you're fat" answer, don't solicit an honest response. Don't set yourself up to be hurt. Third, *try to determine what the questioner is seeking*. This requires sensitivity—picking up signals from the person. If it is clear that the person is seeking support and encouragement, not absolute honesty, then a small lie may be appropriate. Fourth, *weigh the likely consequences of an honest response versus a lie*. Lying to a friend or spouse about his or her weight may encourage the person to continue an unhealthy lifestyle. An honest response may sting initially, but it may also motivate change.

Bok (1978) summarizes the issue well when she explains: "To say that white lies should be kept at a minimum is not to endorse the telling of truths to all comers. Silence and discretion, respect for the privacy and for the feelings of others must naturally govern what is spoken" (p. 76). Honesty isn't *always* the best policy, but it *usually* is the best policy.

Questions for Thought

1. How would you have answered the questions posed in the four situations described at the beginning of this box? Explain your answers.
2. Do you agree that honesty is *usually* the best policy? Why or why not?
3. What would occur in your own relationships if dishonesty were the norm?

"Go ahead and tell me who they plan to hire. I won't tell anyone" encourages openness based on friendship but collides with the ethical requirement to remain closed about confidential hiring details. If confidential information is spilled to a network of friends, your job security may become an issue if a supervisor gets wind of the infraction. This could severely strain friendships. Similarly, if a friend at work told you that he or she had mismanaged a project or misused funds, imagine the dilemma you would face if your boss asked you to tell what you know about such events.

Dialectics With Outsiders

The dialectical tugs-of-war that push and pull us in opposite directions occur not only within relationships but also with outsiders (Box 8-2). Anyone who is not directly involved in a specific relationship is considered an outsider. In a parent-child relationship, everyone who is neither the parent nor the child is an outsider. In a marriage, anyone outside of the marriage is an outsider, even a

Box 8-2   Sharper Focus

Stages and Dialectics: The Meg Ryan-Dennis Quaid Relationship

Meg Ryan and Dennis Quaid met in 1987 on the set of the movie *Innerspace*. During the initiation stage of their relationship, Ryan was very guarded because Quaid had a wild, party image, and both Ryan and Quaid already had romantic partners. Their interactions were professional and friendly, but not romantic. As Dennis explains, "We went out to dinner as friends. I really liked her and was convinced that she didn't like me" (as cited in Natale, 1994, p. 153).

They stepped into the experimental stage of their relationship a year later when they worked on the movie thriller *D.O.A.* Both were now unattached. Dennis was interested. She was less enthusiastic at first. "He wasn't what I was expecting in life, you know, this wild guy from Texas. I kept thinking to myself, 'No, not him, please, not him'" (as cited in Black, 1993). During the filming of *D.O.A.* Meg and Dennis went to a local establishment. Dennis relates what happened, "For some reason, I just put my arms around her, and it was like a thunderbolt. Both of us felt, 'This is it. We're gonna be together,' without saying a word" (as cited in Nash, 1998, p. 97). They had quickly jumped to the intensification stage of their relationship. Meg notes, "He courted me relentlessly" (as cited in Schneider, 1993, p. 69). The couple vacationed together in Bora Bora after the *D.O.A.* production wrapped, where they entered the integrating stage.

Meg and Dennis were rapidly moving through the coming together stages of their relationship, on the verge of moving to the bonding stage, when they suddenly stepped into the first stages of coming apart. Dennis, whose behavior had sometimes been erratic during their courtship, had a hell-raising night at a Los Angeles club in 1990. Meg and Dennis had a huge fight about it, and the next morning Dennis revealed that he was hooked on cocaine and alcohol. "I was really angry and then amazed by how brave he was to tell me," says Meg (as cited in Sessums, 1995, p. 110). They had entered the differentiating stage where differences, not similarities between partners, take focus. "I had to come to terms with the fact that I had a really black-and-white attitude about judging alcoholics and drug addicts," Meg explains. "It was hard as hell, but it was a really good thing in the end. It was a time when both of us grew a lot" (as cited in Natale, 1994, p. 152). Dennis asked for time away from their relationship (circumscribing stage) to enter a drug rehab program. Meg stood by Dennis, and on Valentine's Day in 1992 they were married.

Their relationship during all its various stages exhibits several dialectics. The connection-autonomy dialectic is clearly present. Meg admits that her desire for autonomy (independence) was an impediment to her initiating a relationship with Dennis. "I was independent to a fault. Self-sufficient and very defensive. It's not a great thing in terms of letting people in. . . . I wanted to take care of my own needs and not let anyone else take care of me" (as cited in Natale, 1994, p. 152). Dennis was also independent when he began his relationship with Meg. Surviving the drug addiction crisis brought them closer together. Having a child further connected them as

---

parent of either one of the spouses. We experience three dialectics with outsiders: inclusion-seclusion, conventionality-uniqueness, and revelation-concealment.

Inclusion-Seclusion   In a relationship with another person, we are pulled in two directions when outsiders enter the picture. This is called the **inclusion-seclusion dialectic.** We may want our partner to spend time with outsiders (inclusion), yet we may also want time alone together to nurture our relationship. Including a larger network of friends and family can provide emotional support and encouragement that is highly supportive of the relationship. Too much involvement of outsiders, however, can provide few moments for relationship partners to connect. Thus, we may be torn between larger "family responsibilities" imposed by parents, in-laws, relatives, and friends, such as spending holidays together, and a desire to be alone with our partner without stress from outsiders.

The desire for seclusion marks the relationship as special. Going camping with a friend with no one else invited says, "I want to spend time with just

(*continued*)

a couple. Meg gave birth to Jack in 1992. As Dennis puts it, "I don't have time to dwell on what I now consider to be petty issues because I've got, 'Dad-dee, Dad-dee, Dad-dee' always going on. That prevents me from being so self-absorbed" (as cited in Mills, 1996, p. 162). They are a family unit, not separate individuals. The pressure of their independent acting careers remains, however, which takes them away from home, sometimes for extended periods, and can be disconnecting.

The predictability-novelty dialectic is also apparent in their relationship. The fact that Meg stood by Dennis during his fight with drug addiction means that he can predictably depend on her in the future to be there for him. "It's great to have that kind of support" says Dennis, "and I think I bring a certain stability to her life. Basically we make each other laugh. We are really good friends and help each other get through things" (as cited in Hoban, 1998, p. 42). At the same time, there is an awareness that relationships can become stale if not refreshed by novelty. Meg explains: "You've got to make it new all the time. I've found it much better if you suddenly get away from the routine. . . . We all get in a way of doing things, organizing our days—working mothers do have to be organized—but you have to break out and be silly at times. . . . What brings people down is the same thing. It's dull and downbeat (as cited in "Something About Meg," 1998). Meg and Dennis participate in "mystery weekends"; one of them plans a romantic getaway, and the other comes along for the surprise.

The openness-closedness dialectic was exhibited in the crisis Meg and Dennis faced over drug addiction. Dennis hid his cocaine habit from Meg, fearing what it would do to their developing relationship. His erratic behavior, however, forced him to be open with her about his problem. Wanting to hide our frailties, yet knowing that secrets can erode intimacy, is a continuing tug-of-war in relationships.

Meg and Dennis also confront dialectics with outsiders. The inclusion-seclusion dialectic is manifested by their need to seek refuge on their ranch in Montana while still remaining available to the public to maintain their celebrity status. "It's nice to be alone there," says Meg about their ranch (as cited in "Meg Ryan," 1993). The conventionality-uniqueness dialectic emerges in a somewhat different way than for most couples. Meg and Dennis are celebrities, and Hollywood marriages are known for their short shelf life. They are married and raising a son (conventionality), but they have a unique relationship because they are a merger of two internationally recognized actors. Their relationship operates to a certain extent in a fishbowl for all to observe. The issue of how much of their personal life to reveal to the public and how much to conceal, how inclusive to be with outsiders and how secluded from others, are never-ending dialectics. Whether Meg Ryan and Dennis Quaid stay together or eventually terminate their relationship ultimately will depend on how well they can manage dialectics as new challenges and pressures emerge.

you." At the same time, friends and romantic partners may also desire inclusion and want relatives and friends to accept their relationship. Not including a partner in an invitation for a family get-together when their relationship is known would be insulting and hurtful. Failure of others to accept a romantic partner or friend is a common source of intense, even bitter, conflict in the larger family network.

Conventionality-Uniqueness   When we have relationships with others, we usually want to "fit in" and conform to certain family and societal expectations. Such conventionality just makes life less difficult generally. We're not bumping against how others believe we should act. Yet, by conforming to familial and societal expectations, our relationships may lose their sense of uniqueness, their special quality. They may begin to look like everyone else's relationships. We are torn between wanting our relationships to be the same, yet different. This is called the **conventionality-uniqueness dialectic.**

Consider marriage, for example. The conventional institution of marriage has not lost its appeal for most people despite high divorce rates. Very few adults will live out their entire lives never having been married. Although the number of single parents in the United States in the late 1990s was more than 12 million (Coontz, 1997), single parenthood tends to be a temporary state. About three quarters of divorced parents remarry (Gottman, 1994a). Even cohabiting couples (unmarried partners living intimately together) are still relatively unconventional today. For every 100 married couples there are only 8 cohabiting couples (Vobejda, 1998). A significant portion of cohabiting couples will eventually get married. The increased interest in marriage among gay and lesbian couples also illustrates the desire for some conventionality in relationships. Among gays, 85% view legal gay marriage as "very" or "somewhat important" (Leland & Miller, 1998). At the same time, couples typically want outsiders to view their relationship as unique. Talk of a "soul mate" and the "love of my life" expresses a desire to have a special relationship with a special "irreplaceable" person.

Revelation-Concealment   Both intimate relationships and friendships face this dilemma: How much do we reveal to outsiders about the relationship, and how much do we keep private? Revealing too much breaks the confidentiality that intimacy requires, but revealing too little denies the couple an important source of support and legitimation.

The **revelation-concealment dialectic** is a particular dilemma for gays and lesbians. The military's "don't ask, don't tell" policy creates pressure to conceal same-sex relationships from outsiders. The military discharged 1,145 men and women in 1998 for violating this policy (Myers, 1999). Gay and lesbian teachers also reveal their same-sex relationships at their own peril in most states. Few states have antidiscrimination laws to protect gay and lesbian teachers from being fired or pressured out of their teaching jobs once their sexual preference becomes public knowledge (Irvine, 1998).

The revelation-concealment contradiction also is present in office romances. Office romances are a frequent occurrence. According to Dillard and Miller (1988), one third of subjects surveyed admitted having an office romance and two thirds had observed one. A more recent survey of 1,007 randomly selected adults, commissioned by the romance novel publisher Harlequin (as cited in Jackson, 1999), found that almost 40% of employees admitted dating a coworker, and 39% of these romances, according to the American Management Association, result in marriage or long-term committed relationships ("We Met," 1999). Despite their frequency, and contrary to most couples' desire to announce their romance to friends and coworkers, office romances are often concealed from fellow workers and bosses (Eng, 1999). Fear of violating workplace policies, gossip, general disapproval, and concern that accusations of sexual leverage to attain promotion will be levied, encourage romantic couples in the workplace to hide their relationships (Witteman, 1993).

Dialectical Strategies

How can you, as a competent communicator, manage relationship dialectics? What can be done about these ever-present opposing impulses? Baxter and Montgomery (1996) argue that dialogue between partners in a relationship is at the center of dialectical management. They maintain that *communication that discourages dialogue is "interactionally incompetent"* (p. 201).

If a husband has more power than his wife, he does not have to understand her point of view, or even listen to her position in a conflict. He can achieve greater autonomy, for instance, by simply telling his wife that he plans to spend more time with his male friends. Announcing choices, however, is a monologue, not a dialogue. Dialogue is a conversation, not an announcement. It is a cooperative effort to find mutual solutions to problems. For dialogue to take place, both parties need to listen empathically to each other. As the strategies for managing relationship dialectics are presented, keep in mind that none are likely to be effective without open and honest dialogue.

Selecting (Choosing)   Giving attention to one contradictory impulse while the other is ignored is called **selecting.** One chooses to concentrate on one of the two contradictory impulses. Constant attention to novelty leaves no time for establishing predictability in a relationship. Without some predictability, most people feel insecure in a relationship. One form of novelty, after all, could be that your partner decides you're too dull and he or she needs a different partner. Novelty can be exciting, but it doesn't provide predictability and security in relationships.

Likewise, focusing attention on autonomy leaves no room for connection. Intimacy suffers. Partners who spend most of their time pursuing career goals, hobbies, and personal interests separate from one another leave little or no time for developing intimacy. They become strangers living together. Friends who rarely see each other can become disconnected and distant. Coworkers who insist on being around you all the time at work can seem cloying and suffocating. When a coworker tries too hard to connect with you, it can induce a screaming desire to be alone.

Selecting is the least satisfying method for managing relational dialectics because one need is sacrificed for its opposite (Baxter, 1990). Addressing both impulses in a dialectic is usually preferable to addressing one need at the expense of the other.

Neutralizing (Balancing)   Striking a balance between opposing dialectical impulses by partially satisfying both impulses is called **neutralizing.** Partners negotiate some personal autonomy, for instance, but not as much as desired. Consider the case of Mark and Sandy. Mark wants to spend time with his male friends at least twice a week. Sandy wants him home to help take care of the kids. She agrees to "guys night out" once a week. She, in turn, takes a "gals night out" with her female friends. Both partners would like to have more personal independence, but they compromise on at least some independent time away from their partner and children. Neutralization doesn't fully satisfy any of the conflicting needs in a relationship, but it may be satisfactory given the circumstances. After all, children require parenting. It is unlikely that any parent will have as much independent time as he or she might like.

Segmenting (Categorizing)   When partners divide certain parts of their relationship into segments, or categories, they are **segmenting.** In dealing with the openness-closedness dialectic, for instance, partners may designate certain subjects as "off limits" for sharing with each other to reduce the possibility of hurting each other's feelings or provoking jealousy. For instance, previous boyfriends or girl-friends may be segmented as a taboo topic. How each partner spends money from his or her own bank account may also be categorized as off limits. With coworkers, confidential information may be one area that is off limits. Office gossip about personnel files and hiring interviews can create dicey, even illegal, situations. Openness, however, would be encouraged in all areas other than those designated as removed from discussion.

Couples might also segment novelty and predictability in similar fashion. The weekends might be set aside for novel activities (trying a new sport, traveling to a new destination), whereas the weekdays might follow a predictable routine. Similarly, couples might set aside certain holidays to visit parents and relatives (inclusion) but keep certain special occasions, such as birthdays or New Year's, just for themselves (seclusion).

Segmenting is potentially one of the most effective means of managing relational dialectics because both partners' needs are being addressed for the sake of the relationship (Baxter & Montgomery, 1996). Unlike neutralizing, where compromises have to be made and needs are only partially met, segmenting attempts to satisfy fully the needs of both individuals in the relationship by a joint effort.

Reframing (Redefining) Sometimes we can take a seeming contradiction be-tween two impulses and look at it from a different frame of reference. This change in perspective is called **reframing.** Time for yourself (autonomy), for example, might be explained as connection because personal time may rejuvenate the bond between partners and lessen interpersonal friction. Predictability in a relationship might be presented as necessary to appreciate novelty when it occurs. A couple might view their relationship as unique because it has survived for an entire year, a new record for both partners, even though outsiders might view this as unspectacular and ordinary.

Reframing is a very sophisticated strategy for dealing with relational dialec-tics. It takes practice to create a new perspective on dialectical needs, but refram-ing has the potential to be very effective in addressing relational dialectics.

Effectively managing relational dialectics can be a complex process. Two points should be emphasized. First, *dialectics are not dichotomies.* In a relationship, you should not have to choose between openness *or* closedness, connection *or* autonomy, predictability *or* novelty. These should not be *either-or* choices, but rather *both-and* choices (Baxter & Montgomery, 1996). Relationships need both openness *and* closedness, connection *and* autonomy, predictability *and* novelty, and so forth. Recognizing when one need requires more attention than its opposite shows sensitivity. Addressing the need effectively requires dialogue between partners.

Second, *approaching relational dialectics as a competition is self-defeating.* If one partner "wins" greater autonomy at the expense of the other partner's need for connection, then both lose because the relationship is diminished. Approaching relational dialectics as a competition is usually ineffective. None of the strategies for dealing with relational dialectics is likely to be successful without cooperative dialogue between partners.

Culture and Relationships

Relationship dialectics don't disappear when members of different cultures mix. Dialectics can pose even more significant challenges for intercultural relationships than for individuals from the same culture. Individualist, low power-distance cultures such as the United States, for example, emphasize autonomy, openness, uniqueness, and novelty. Individual freedom is valued, and status differences are deemphasized. Collectivist, high power-distance cultures such as Singapore value harmony as a way of nurturing relationships. Conformity and group well-being are highly valued. Connection (within relationships), closedness (with outsiders), conventionality (following the rules), and predictability (stability) further harmony. In a collectivist culture autonomy, openness, uniqueness, and novelty are likely to upset cultural harmony.

Given the sometimes enormous perceptual differences, how do individuals from distinctly different cultures develop friendships and romantic relationships? Not easily!

Cross-Cultural Friendships

The initial stages of a developing friendship between individuals from different cultures must address three problems (Martin & Nakayama, 1997). First, the differences in values, perceptions, and communication style can be troublesome. These are deep-seated, not superficial, differences (Chapter 3). Second, anxiety is a common experience in the initial stages of any friendship, but intercultural friendships are likely to induce greater anxiety. We experience greater fear of making mistakes and causing offense when we are unfamiliar with the norms and rules of another culture. Third, overcoming stereotypes about a different culture and resisting the impulse to be ethnocentric can be difficult.

A study of American and Japanese students who were friends revealed some interesting ways to nurture cross-cultural friendships (Sudweeks et al., 1990). First, some similarities that transcend the cultural differences must be discovered, whether it is sports, hobbies, lifestyle, or political attitudes. Bridges must be constructed from common experience. Second, making time for the relationship is critical. It takes more time to develop a friendship with a member of another culture because we are typically drawn to others who are like us, not to those who are unlike us. Third, sharing the same group of friends can be very important. A shared group of friends can lend support to an intercultural relationship. Finally, capitalizing on key turning points in a developing friendship is vital. **Turning points** are key moments that move the relationship forward, such as sharing an interest, disclosing a personal secret, requesting a favor, or lending your car. Reluctance to respond positively to such a turning point can end the relationship.

Ultimately, cross-cultural friendships require more "care and feeding" (Pogrebin, 1987) than do friendships between similar individuals. More explaining and

Cross-cultural relationships present unusual challenges for couples. Consensus, learning about and adopting aspects of each other's culture, is an effective strategy for meeting intercultural relationship challenges.

understanding must take place. Pogrebin (as cited in Gudykunst & Kim, 1992) notes, "Mutual respect, acceptance, tolerance for the faux pas and the occasional closed door, open discussion and patient mutual education, all this gives crossing friendships—when they work at all—a special kind of depth" (p. 318).

Intercultural Romantic Relationships

Romantic relationships can be even stickier than friendships. Once the difficulties of developing a friendship have been overcome, additional problems can develop when romance flowers. Families may raise a stink about cross-cultural friendships, and romance may intensify this opposition (Kouri & Lasswell, 1993). Opposition from one's family isn't necessarily based on prejudice, although surely bigotry sometimes plays a part. Concerns about child rearing styles, religious differences, politics, gender roles, power issues, place of residence, and rituals and ceremonies may also increase opposition.

Romano (1988) identifies four strategies that are used in intercultural marriages. *Submission* is the most common strategy. One partner abandons his or her

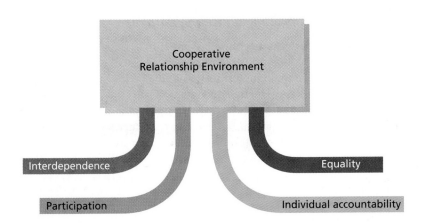

Figure 8-3 Cooperative Relationship Environment

culture and submits to the partner's culture, adopting the religion, value system, politics, and so forth. This is rarely effective because individuals find it enormously difficult to erase their core cultural values and background. A second strategy, *compromise*, means giving up only part of one's cultural beliefs, values, and habits. This is also very difficult in most situations. Asking one partner to forgo Christmas decorations and celebration while the other partner is asked not to observe the Muslim holy month Ramadan isn't likely to be a smooth compromise. A third strategy, *obliteration*, is sometimes used. Obliteration occurs when both partners attempt to erase their respective cultures from the relationship. This is difficult to accomplish, and it means avoiding basic support groups such as family and friends. Finally, there is consensus, which seems to work best. *Consensus* is based on negotiation and cooperation. Learning the partner's language, studying the religion, and learning about the cuisine erect bridges between partners. Consensus is built by emphasizing similarities and commonalities in relationships and by deemphasizing differences. Consensus is difficult even among culturally similar individuals. It is doubly difficult between culturally dissimilar individuals who plan to marry.

Establishing a Cooperative Environment

Dialogue is necessary to the management of relational dialectics, especially in cross-cultural relationships. *The foundation of dialogue is cooperation.* A competitive approach to dialogue short-circuits the dialogue. When partners try to win the argument triggered by dialectical friction, such as a disagreement regarding what information about the relationship should be kept private, dialogue quickly becomes dueling monologues. Neither party listens effectively, and issues are difficult, sometimes impossible, to resolve. Thus, a necessary requirement for constructive dialogue is establishing a cooperative interpersonal environment. Creating a cooperative interpersonal environment requires the skillful use of certain patterns of communication and the avoidance of others. A cooperative interpersonal environment also depends on defusing defensiveness and establishing interdependence, equality, individual accountability, and meaningful participation (Figure 8-3).

Emphasizing Cooperative Communication Patterns

Some communication patterns encourage competitive, defensive responses, and others promote cooperative, supportive responses. Defensive communication patterns disrupt constructive dialogue on relational dialectics; supportive communication patterns encourage constructive dialogue.

Defensive communication patterns provoke defensive responses. A **defensive response** is a reaction to a perceived attack on our self-concept, self-esteem, or self-identity. A defensive response is self-protective. Defensive communication patterns seriously threaten the well-being of relationships at home, at work, and at play (Gottman, 1994a, 1994b).

In an 8-year study of groups, Jack Gibb (1961) identified specific communication patterns that provoke defensive, competitive responses, and corresponding supportive communication patterns that promote cooperative responses. See whether you recognize your own communication style in any of these patterns.

Evaluation Versus Description   A friend of mine was in his townhouse when the Loma Prieta earthquake hit central California in 1989. Objects flew across the rooms, kitchen cabinets emptied onto the counters and floor, and glass shattered throughout his home. When those tumultuous 15 seconds of nature's nervous breakdown subsided, the timid little voice of my friend's 5-year-old daughter came from the back room: "Daddy, it wasn't my fault." We are quick to defend ourselves if we even think an evaluation might be offered.

Evaluations are value judgments made about individuals and their performance. Statements of praise, recognition, admiration, or flattery are positive evaluations; criticism, contempt, and blame are negative evaluations. We are ever wary of negative evaluations, and for good reason. Negative evaluations produce a defensive environment that foments destructive conflict. A study of 108 managers and white-collar workers found that criticism, especially criticism handled ineptly, produced more conflict in the workplace than mistrust, personality clashes, power struggles, or pay (Baron, 1990). In a study at Rensselaer Polytechnic Institute, harsh criticism demoralized participants, reduced their work effort, and prompted participants to refuse to cooperate on future projects with the criticizers (Baron, 1988).

Negative evaluations have even been linked to stereotyping. College students were asked to rate managers after the managers had evaluated the students' responses to a survey on interpersonal skills. When female or African American male managers gave good reviews of the students' answers, they got as high a rating as the white male managers. When the evaluations of the students' answers were strongly negative, however, the students rated the female and African American managers far more harshly than they did white males. Why? When individuals are evaluated negatively, ugly stereotypes rise to the surface. Psychologist Ziva Kunda, co-author of the study, notes, "As black people and women gain in power, they'll more often find themselves having to deliver bad news, and will be seen more through the lens of negative stereotypes" (as cited in "Female Boss," 1997, p. 24).

There are two cooperative communication alternatives to negative evaluations. First, accentuate the positive. Gottman (1994a , 1994b; Gottman & Silver, 1999), in his 20-year study of 2,000 married couples, was 94% accurate when predicting which couples would stay together or split up. The key element in making accurate predictions was the "magic ratio" (5 to 1) of positive to negative communication. Relationships of most kinds are sustained by plentiful praise, recognition, flattery, and signs of admiration. They are jeopardized by even moderate amounts of criticism, contempt, and blame.

Occasional negativity between individuals is not necessarily damaging, however, especially if the criticism is mild. In fact, some negative criticism may provoke needed change. Infrequent negativity will not corrode a relationship if it is counteracted with abundant positivity (Gottman, 1994b). Unfortunately, most people are inclined to criticize and blame others more readily than to praise them. A study of the 1,000 largest companies in the United States found that lack of recognition and praise was the number one reason employees left their companies. Robert Half, who conducted the study, concluded, "Praising accomplishments provides psychological rewards that are critical to satisfaction" (as cited in "Praise thy employees," 1994).

Of all the suggestions made in this chapter regarding how to make relationships work at home, at work, and at play, *accentuating the positive is the most crucial.* If you are puzzled about where to begin improving your relationships with others, begin by establishing at least a 5 to 1 ratio of positive to negative communication with your partner, friends, relatives, and coworkers. Once you have accomplished that goal, you can turn to other suggestions for improving your relationships.

Description is a second communication alternative to evaluative communication patterns. A *description* is a first-person report of how we feel, what behaviors we observe, or what we perceive to be true in specific situations. Three primary steps can help you become more descriptive:

1. *Use "first-person singular" statements* (Narcisco & Burkett, 1975). Begin by identifying your feelings; use the "I" form and then describe behavior linked to the feeling. "I feel alone and unconnected to you when I share my concerns with you and receive no response" is an example of a descriptive, first-person singular statement. Unlike an "I" statement, a "you" statement places the focus on the other person. "You make me feel stupid and uninformed" is an accusation that assigns blame and is likely to provoke a denial or a counterattack.

2. *Make your descriptions specific, not vague.* "I feel sort of weird when you act inappropriately around my boss" is an inexact description. "Sort of weird" and "inappropriately" require more specific description. "I feel awkward and embarrassed when you tell jokes to my boss that ridicule gays and women" makes the description much more concrete.

3. *Eliminate editorial comments from descriptive statements.* "I get annoyed when you waste my time by talking about silly side issues" uses the first-person singular form without the supportive intent or phrasing. "Waste time" and "silly side issues" are editorial, opinionated language. Instead, say, "I get annoyed when you introduce side issues." Then provide specific examples of side issues.

Textbook-perfect first-person singular statements produce no supportive response, of course, if the tone of voice used is sarcastic or condescending, eye contact is threatening or leering, facial expressions and body language are contemptuous or intimidating, and gestures are abusive. Place the spotlight on your own feelings and on the specific behaviors you find objectionable without sending mixed messages composed of verbal descriptions and nonverbal evaluations.

Control Versus Problem Orientation   "He who agrees against his will, is of the same opinion still" observed the English poet Samuel Butler. Most people dislike being controlled by others. **Control** is communication that seeks to regulate or direct a person's behavior. Control is the dominance form of power in action, and it is likely to provoke a defensive reaction in the form of resistance.

Control can easily lead to a contest of wills. Brehm (1972) developed his theory of psychological reactance to explain most people's resistance to efforts aimed at controlling their behavior. **Psychological reactance** means that the more someone tries to control our behavior and restrict our choices, the more we are inclined to resist such efforts, especially if we feel entitled to choose. If the pressure to restrict becomes intense, we may be strongly attracted to that which is prohibited. This phenomenon is well known to parents. As advice columnist Ann Landers (1995) observed: "There are three ways to make sure something gets done: Do it yourself, hire someone to do it, or forbid your kids to do it" (p. D5).

When parents oppose romantic relationships, such as a teenage daughter dating an older boy, it often intensifies feelings of romantic love (Driscoll et al., 1972). Parents step into the psychological reactance quicksand when they insist that their children obey them. Nevertheless, parents have a responsibility to protect children from foolish or dangerous behavior. All controlling communication can't be eliminated, but it should be kept to a minimum and used only when other choices are not practical.

We prevent defensiveness from occurring when we collaborate on a problem and seek solutions cooperatively. The focus is on the problem and how to solve it, not on how best to control other people's behavior. Parents and children can work together, brainstorming possible solutions to troublesome conflicts. This takes the focus away from controlling children's behavior and places the emphasis on solving the problem.

The same communication approach also works well in the work setting. One study (McNutt, 1997) of strategic decision making at 356 U.S. companies found that 58% of the plans were turned down when the executives overseeing the plans tried to impose their ideas on colleagues. Psychological reactance was triggered. When executives sought participation and counsel from colleagues, however, 96% of the plans were adopted. Merely asking individuals for input and seeking suggestions for solving problems from all parties affected invites a cooperative communication environment.

Strategy Versus Spontaneity   Imagine that you have just met an interesting person at a party. This person seems very open, honest, and attentive. You are complimented by the attention this person pays you. Then imagine that you hear later from a friend that this same person was using you to gain favor with your older sibling. You were a pawn in a chess game. How would you feel to be used in such a callous and deceptive way?

A strategy is a conscious maneuver to achieve a goal. **Strategic communication** is manipulative, an attempt by one person to maneuver another toward the manipulator's goal. Most people resent manipulation, especially if it is based on deception. Even knowing that someone will attempt to manipulate us can make us defensive. This is the difficulty phone solicitors face. Calling during the dinner hour to ask people to buy products, donate to charities, or buy tickets to help worthy causes immediately creates a defensive atmosphere. Popular services are now available to screen telemarketers so they cannot solicit purchases from you over the phone.

Gibb (1961) suggests spontaneity as the answer to strategic communication. Spontaneity is communication by impulse. The term *spontaneity* suggests off-the-top-of-your-head, ill-conceived communication. Knowledgeable, skillful communication used appropriately and effectively requires careful thought and consideration, not impulsiveness. A better term is assertiveness, a skill discussed in Chapter 7. Impulsive communication is often aggressive. Assertiveness requires thought, skill, and concern for others. Assertive communication says "No games are being played. This is how I feel and this is what I need from you."

Neutrality Versus Empathy   The Fatherhood Project at the Families and Work Institute in New York concludes that "it is presence, not absence, that often lies at the heart of troubled families. It is common for family members to be in the same room and be oblivious to each other's thoughts and feelings" (as cited in Coontz, 1997, p. 160). This **neutrality,** or indifference toward others, is a sign of a disintegrating family. It also encourages further family deterioration and conflict. Harvard psychologist Samuel Osherson notes, "Sometimes a father or mother can be in the same room as a child, but emotionally already have walked out the door" (as cited in Coontz, 1997, p. 160).

Such indifference can produce defensiveness. A father's indifference to his children attacks their self-esteem. The lowest self-esteem among teenagers occurs in two-parent families in which the father shows little interest in his children (Clark & Barber, 1994). Children often grow resentful of an indifferent or absent parent. This resentment can turn into outright hostility, making future reconciliation between parent and child difficult. "Why didn't you care enough to stay?" "You didn't care about your own child. Why should I care about you?" shows defensiveness that grows from a parent's indifference.

Pseudolistening or not listening at all also exhibits indifference, whether it occurs in the home, school, or work environment. Students want their professors to hear what they have to say. Romantic partners want to be listened to, not ignored. Employees feel snubbed when fellow workers or supervisors pay no attention to them when they speak.

You counter indifference with empathy. Empathy is built on sensitivity to others, a quality of the competent communicator. Parents who are indifferent to their children might try putting themselves in their children's shoes. What would it have been like if their parents had shown no interest in them? Would they have felt abandoned, worthless, or hostile? Can they empathize with their children's anger and disappointment? What does it mean to a child when a father refuses to pay child support? What message does that send to the child?

Box 8-3   Sharper Focus

Male Superiority Attitudes

Historically, the superiority attitude has been communicated by men to the disadvantage of women. Consider a few examples of the sexist superiority attitude of some of the world's great thinkers and authors (as cited in Starr, 1991), and see if, even now, they don't provoke a defensive reaction.

Philosopher Aristotle (384–322 B.C.) made this not so brilliant comment:

The male is by nature superior, and the female inferior; and the one rules, and the other is ruled. The lower sort are by nature slaves, and it is better for them as for all inferiors that they should be under the rule of a master.

St. John Chrysostom (347–407) added this gem:

What else is a woman but a foe to friendship, a cosmic punishment, a necessary evil, a natural temptation, a desirable calamity, a domestic peril, a delectable detriment, a deadly fascination, a painted ill.

Poet Alexander Pope (1688–1744) adds this:

Most women have no characters at all.

French philosopher Jean-Jacques Rousseau (1712–1778) offered this:

Dependence is a state natural to women, and girls realize that they are made for obedience.

Poet Alfred Lord Tennyson (1809–1892) contributes this:

God made the woman for the use of man.

Russian author Leo Tolstoy (1828–1910) opines:

Clearly all disasters, or an enormous proportion of them, are due to the dissoluteness of women.

Think and feel as the child might think and feel. Take the child's perspective. That's empathy.

Rosenfeld (1983) found that when an instructor exhibited empathic behaviors, students liked the class and the teacher. These empathic behaviors included showing interest in the problems students face, exhibiting a perception of subject matter as students see it, and making students feel that the instructor understands students.

Superiority Versus Equality   Treat anyone as an inferior and there is likely to be a defensive reaction. The history of the women's movement, the battle for civil rights, and the fight for the rights of the disabled all reveal that labeling and treating people as inferior will produce a strong defensive reaction (Box 8-3). In fact, the dispute over substituting the term "differently abled" for "disabled" spotlights the defensiveness caused when some individuals are perceived as being less able than others.

The superiority attitude invites defensiveness because it communicates a competitive, dominance viewpoint. It says, "You're less than I am. You're a loser. Stay in your place." Few like to be viewed as inferior in anyone's eyes. Rosenfeld (1983) found that behaviors of instructors in disliked classes communicate an air of superiority. "My teacher makes me feel we are not intelligent" was one of the primary complaints by students in disliked classes. "My teacher treats us as equals with him/her" was a common response from students who liked their classes.

Were you ever treated with disdain by a supervisor at work? Were you ever made to feel you deserved to be abused? If so, how did it make you feel? Some bosses have a superiority complex and communicate it loudly and clearly to all. It doesn't make for harmonious working relationships.

Whatever the differences in our abilities, talents, and intellect, treating people with respect and politeness, as equals on a human level, is supportive and encourages harmony and cooperation. Treating people like gum on the bottom of your shoe will invite defensiveness, even retaliation.

Certainty Versus Provisionalism   Few things in this world are certain—death, taxes, and that buttered toast will always fall buttered side down. Because most things are not certain, there is room for discussion and disagreement. When someone makes absolute, unqualified statements of certainty, however, he or she closes off discussion and disagreement. Defensiveness is often the result.

Dogmatism, a common form of the certainty communication pattern, is a "belief in the self-evident truth of one's opinion. The dogma, or declaration of truth, warrants no debate in the mind of the dogmatist" (Rothwell, 1998, p. 128). A dogmatic person shows closed-mindedness, rigid thinking, and an unwillingness to consider alternative ideas. Spell the word dogma backward and you get *am-god*, an easy way to remember what a dogmatist is. Dogmatists act god-like in the certainty of their own opinions.

In one study (Leathers, 1970) typical dogmatic statements were introduced into conversations. The five statements used were:

1. That's a ridiculous statement. I disagree.
2. Are you serious in taking such an absurd position?
3. You are wrong. Dead wrong!
4. I don't understand why I ever agreed with you.
5. That's downright foolish.

Study participants reacted to these dogmatic statements with heightened tension (rubbing their hands together nervously and squirming in their seats). These statements also provoked opinionated statements from other individuals.

Provisionalism is an effective substitute for dogmatism. **Provisionalism** means we qualify our statements, avoiding absolutes. Problems and issues are approached as questions to be investigated. Options not yet explored are viewed as possibilities worthy of discussion. "Let's discuss it," "That's an interesting idea," or "I hadn't thought of that" exhibit provisional communication. We look for under what conditions and to what extent a statement is true, not is it absolutely true or false.

These six defensive (competitive) and supportive (cooperative) communication patterns can produce tit-for-tat responses—like begets like. If you disparage others, they will likely denigrate you. One famous interaction occurred between Lady Astor, the first female member of the British Parliament, and Winston Churchill. Exasperated by Churchill's opposition to several of the causes she espoused, Lady Astor bitingly stated, "Winston, if I were married to you, I'd put poison in your coffee." Churchill shot back, "And if you were my wife, I'd drink it." Verbal attack spawns verbal attack. We often get from others what we give.

Perhaps you are thinking this discussion of defensive and supportive communication patterns appears useful in the abstract but not very useful when you are in the middle of a heated argument with your partner, friend, coworker, or boss.

Several points are germaine to this issue of applicability to real-life situations. First, supportive communication is primarily preventive in nature. The more you learn to use supportive communication patterns, the less likely heated arguments will unfold. Defensive patterns provoke anger and aggression. Supportive patterns can dampen anger and aggression and create connection. Second, don't attempt to learn all six supportive patterns simultaneously. Pick the one that seems best suited to your current circumstances, and practice it first. You want to learn supportive patterns so well that they become virtually automatic. When one pattern is learned, go on to another. When a heated argument does surface, your new skills may help to turn down the heat. Instead of escalating the battle with defensive communication, your supportive responses may turn the conflict into a problem to be solved together.

Defusing Defensiveness

Supportive communication patterns can prevent defensiveness from occurring, but what if your partner, relative, friend, or coworker becomes highly defensive despite your best efforts to create a cooperative environment? You're trying to resolve a difference of viewpoint, for example, but the other person becomes defensive the moment the subject is introduced. What do you do?

There are several ways to short-circuit defensiveness exhibited by others. First, *refuse to be drawn into a defensive spiral.* This means that you must speak and listen nondefensively, even if your partner, friend, relative, or coworker exhibits defensive communication patterns. This takes discipline and patience. You have control over your communication. Try using that control to create a constructive dialogue, not a malignant spiral of defensiveness.

Second, *focus on the problem, not the other person.* Unless the problem is the other person, stick to the agenda for discussion. Refuse to be drawn down side avenues during your dialogue. For example:

SHASHA: We need to go out more. We don't do anything exciting.

MIKE: Do you have to tap your fingers on the table all the time? It drives me nuts.
    Maybe we'd go out more if you didn't irritate me so much.

When serious issues get detoured by irrelevant remarks about the person, not the problem, defensiveness is encouraged. Mike's response diverts attention from the issue raised and centers the discussion on irritating mannerisms. That shifts the agenda. Shasha could respond to the criticism of her finger tapping this way: "We can talk about my finger tapping another time. Let's discuss going out more often, and let's do it without insulting each other." Insist on staying focused and constructive.

Third, *be an empathic listener.* Give probing, understanding, and supportive responses (Chapter 6). Try to view the other person's defensiveness from his or her perspective. Strive for understanding, not retaliation.

Building Interdependence

Cooperation in human relationships is enhanced by building interdependence. **Interdependence** means that all parties rely on each other to achieve goals (Box 8-4). Interdependence can be established by creating a mutually desirable goal that can

Box 8-4   Sharper Focus

The Hensel Twins

Britty drinks milk while Abby, who hates milk, gulps orange juice. The Hensel twins are nourishing each other through their mingled bloodstream. Brittany and Abby Hensel are conjoined twins—the result of a single egg that failed to divide completely into identical twins. They share a single torso and two legs, but they each have a separate heart and stomach. Their two spines join at the pelvis, but below the waist they have the organs of separate people. If Abby is tickled on the right side, Britty does not feel the sensation, and vice versa, yet the two little girls manage to move as one person.

The Hensel twins are an extraordinary example of interdependence at work. Each child has a distinct personality. Britty loves animals; Abby enjoys drawing. Abby tends to be the leader; Britty is more thoughtful and quicker academically. Abby likes to eat; Britty thinks food is boring. Brittany wants to be a pilot, and Abby aspires to be a dentist. Each is an independent thinker, but they work interdependently in an admirable example of collaborative behavior and decision making. They have to, because if they can't agree on even simple things, such as which direction they want to travel, they can't move. When putting on their sneakers, Abby consults Britty: "I think I should make a double knot, don't you?" Britty nods and helps tie the lace. When one girl misbehaves, both are sent to their room. As their kindergarten teacher, Connie Stahlke, observes, "They could give a speech on cooperation" (as cited in Miller, 1996, p. 51).

Cooperation is an essential part of their lives. They have grasped the concept more quickly and thoroughly than their peers. When several of their classmates got into an argument, Abby and Britty led a class discussion on how to get along and work together. As their teacher notes, "They've definitely had to do *that* their entire lives" (as cited in Miller, 1996, p. 56). Their mother, Patty Hensel, observes, "If they had to be put together, I think they were put together perfectly" (p. 56).

The Hensel twins serve as excellent role models for how to cooperate through interdependence. They have to be interdependent and work together. They have no choice. We have a choice, but if we approached more communication situations as if we didn't, we would probably find ways to cooperate more often.

The Hensel twins are cooperation in action.

only be achieved by the effort of everyone involved, and by an interdependent division of labor and resources. This story of Fred Beasley, a rookie fullback drafted by the San Francisco 49ers in 1998, and his family illustrates both forms of interdependence.

When Fred was 12 years old, his father died suddenly, leaving a wife and nine children to live on a meager Social Security income. The family survived the crisis by working together. The interdependent goal was for the family to survive intact, and the means used to accomplish this interdependent goal were sharing labor and resources interdependently. Alma Beasley, Fred's mom, worked cleaning houses. All of the kids found odd jobs. Whatever was earned was pooled to meet family, not individual, needs. Four boys slept in a single room. Dresser drawers were divided among the children, and household chores were everybody's responsibility. As Alma Beasley explains, "It was tough on all of us. . . . I just did the best I could. I think we all pulled together" (as cited in Judge, 1998). Fred says this about his mom, "She almost took food out of her mouth to give to us. She did what a mother has to. She raised nine kids on her own. . . . There is no way to pay her back for what she did. I just want to give her love, help her out financially and give her the things she always wanted." Fred's mom displays her obvious pride in her son, "I thank God all the time for the way he turned out. He turned out to be a great young man."

Promoting Equality

Equality doesn't mean treating everyone as though there were no differences in degrees of talent, skill, ability and the like. Equality means giving everyone the same opportunity to succeed and expecting that they each will shoulder their fair share of responsibility.

Equality can be structured into relationships in two ways. First, labor and responsibilities could be shared equally whenever possible. This, of course, must be negotiated between the parties involved using supportive communication patterns. The failure by some men to share household and child care chores and responsibilities equally, for instance, is a primary cause of relationship conflict (Coontz, 1997). One study comparing six different living situations found that men do far less housework than their female partners, and married men do the least housework (Adelmann, 1995).

Lesbian couples typically negotiate domestic chores in a more equal way than do heterosexual couples or gay male partners (Huston & Schwartz, 1995). Lesbians are more inclined to communicate cooperatively when making decisions about division of household labor. Gay men, however, follow the pattern of heterosexual males. The man with the greater income usually exercises greater dominance. With greater power comes the privilege of avoiding domestic chores (Huston & Schwartz, 1995).

When coworkers do not accept their fair share of labor and responsibility on a team project, the inequality can produce friction. When friends do not share equally in the planning and workload for a ski trip, for example, hard feelings and hostility can result. Cooperative communication is unlikely in such an atmosphere. Bickering will likely ensue. An equal sharing of labor and responsibilities can create harmony.

A second way to structure equality is to distribute rewards, if any, among everyone involved in achieving a mutually desirable goal. Most pay raises in the workplace are distributed equally to avoid the nasty communication fostered by competitive merit pay (only the best receive the reward) and equity pay (those who did the most get the most) schemes (Schuster, 1984). Merit pay and equity pay typically pit worker against worker in a battle for limited resources. The final report of the Merit Pay Task Force of the California State University Academic Senate (Charnofsky et al., 1998) notes that of the 3,000 studies of merit pay, only 100 (3%) claim any positive outcomes. The report concluded that most merit pay systems fail to motivate workers to improve performance, and they often produce hostile and divisive communication among employees and supervisors.

Establishing equality can occur only if it is a key agenda item during any negotiation between individuals. Roommates, housemates, married couples, family members, and coworkers must agree that equality is essential in their relationships.

Some people believe an equal distribution of rewards encourages unequal labor on the part of all but the most committed individuals. Admittedly, there are those who would take advantage of a reward system of equal distribution if there is no individual accountability—the topic addressed in the next section.

Establishing Individual Accountability

Individual accountability provides consequences for performance, ensuring that everyone honors his or her agreements and commitments in relationships and groups. If there is no individual accountability for lackluster performance, then some will hitchhike on the effort of others. Working with others is not truly cooperative if some individuals let others do most or all of the work.

You can establish individual accountability by negotiating *minimum standards of performance* with every individual affected. Spouses, roommates, and living together partners, for example, have to agree on what constitutes a fair division of labor and the level of quality expected when the tasks are performed. All parties should embrace the minimum standards. Those who fail to honor the agreement once it has been accepted by all parties are held accountable by confronting their lack of commitment to the agreement. Picking up the slack of those who fail to honor a division of labor agreement by performing their tasks for them merely encourages persistent loafing.

Individual accountability is often more straightforward in work situations than it is in personal relationships. In the workplace, pay sometimes can be withheld for inadequate performance. Work teams can set specific standards, such as no more than two absences from meetings, arrival on time for all work sessions, and so forth. Persistent slackers can ultimately be booted out of the group or, in some cases, fired from a job, often with little personal consequence to team members.

Accountability is more difficult in close relationships because connection is desired. (Love and affection can be withheld from a loafing partner, but that uses emotional blackmail as a weapon.) Accountability, however, is certainly necessary and achievable even in close relationships. The chief way to hold partners, friends, and family members accountable is to confront them when they have failed to abide by agreements and commitments.

A system of individual accountability does not institute a competitive structure into human transactions. Cooperation, working together, is the goal, not working against others to claim a victory. Minimum standards set a level that all can reach, and they allow everyone to share the results equally (e.g., a clean house). The emphasis is placed on raising everyone to at least a minimum level of performance and effort, not on looking for a way to designate who did best, second best, or worst. *Minimum standards establish a floor below which no one should sink, not a ceiling that only a very few can reach.*

Developing Meaningful Participation

Few people in our culture like others to make decisions that affect their lives without any participation in the decision making from those affected. If the father in a family decides to accept a promotion and move everyone from the west coast to the east coast without even consulting with family members and seeking their feedback, he should not be surprised when his spouse and children do not nominate him for Husband or Father of the Year awards.

Participative decision making is essential to cooperation in human relationships in our culture, and it cannot occur without dialogue. When everyone has a say in the decision, communication is the primary vehicle by which choices are explored and decided. A review of 47 studies showed that meaningful participation in decision making worked well in organizations (Miller & Monge, 1986). Worker productivity and job satisfaction were enhanced.

For participation to be meaningful, several conditions must be met:

1. *Participation must have a significant effect on the outcome.* Asking for input after the decision has been made doesn't encourage cooperation. Rubber-stamping is not meaningful participation.
2. *All affected parties should be involved in the decisions,* although some may have more weight than others (e.g., parents more than children).
3. *Decisions made by participants should be consequential.* Asking for participation only when the decisions are trivial will not promote cooperation.
4. *Messages communicated from all parties must be given serious consideration.* If your input is always ignored, soon you will decide that participation is a charade.

Summary

As we begin the new millennium, relationships are more challenging than ever. Every relationship travels through specific stages. Keeping a relationship from moving into the coming apart stages is a principal concern. Each relationship is challenged by dialectics, or contradictory impulses, pushing and pulling each partner in two directions simultaneously. Intercultural relationships are even more challenging. Individuals from collectivist cultures have a We-emphasis, but persons from individualist cultures have a Me-emphasis. This fundamental distinction in cultural values can put a strain on an intercultural relationship. A key step in meeting the increasing challenges of sustaining relationships is to establish a cooperative environment. Establishing supportive communication patterns is a critical part of making relationships work. Building interdependence, equality, individual accountability, and meaningful participation in decision making are additional ways to develop a cooperative environment for productive relationships.

Suggested Readings

Gottman, J. (1994). *Why marriages succeed and fail: And how you can make yours last.* New York: Simon & Schuster. Psychologist John Gottman summarizes results of 20 years of research on marriage. This is a very readable work that is loaded with insights.

Gottman, J., & Silver, N. (1999). *The seven principles for making marriage work.* New York: Crown. This is a nontechnical presentation of conclusions drawn from years of research on what makes marriages work and what makes them fail.

Chapter 9

Interpersonal Conflict Management

Experience tells us that conflict is often an unpleasant, even nasty, business. Look up the word *conflict* in a thesaurus, and you find synonyms such as "discord," "disagreement," "struggle," "strife," "clash," "fight," "hostility," "disharmony," "adversity," "dissonance," and "opposition." You will have to look long and hard to find any positive meaning ascribed to conflict.

Research on marital conflict certainly doesn't paint a very happy picture. The more couples engage in conflict, the more they become verbally aggressive, and verbal aggression often provokes physical violence (Cahn & Lloyd, 1996). Conflict episodes often become more intense and ugly as conflict becomes more frequent. Marital conflict is also associated with a wide range of problems for children, including depression, weak academic performance, poor social skills, and discipline difficulties (Hetherington et al., 1998). These results are likely to be more serious as the frequency of conflict increases. Children of intact (nondivorced) families with frequent conflict, for example, have greater problems with psychological adjustment and self-esteem than do children living in both low-conflict divorced and nondivorced families (Amato & Loomis, 1995).

Conflict is an unavoidable fact of life. One study found that college students engage in conflicts, on average, seven times per week (Benoit & Benoit, 1987). Another study reported two substantial arguments per week between adolescents and parents, and three additional conflicts between siblings (Montemayor, 1986). In the same study, a quarter of the parents complained about conflicts with their teenagers, and a fifth of the adolescents claimed that they had "many serious" conflicts with their parents.

In the workplace, escalating conflict is a serious problem. The United States has the highest incidence of homicide at work of any industrialized nation, averaging more than 1,000 murders per year ("Survey," 1998). According to a 1998 Justice Department report, almost 2 million people each year are victims of violence in the workplace (Lardner, 1998). "Workplace bullying" is rapidly increasing. Workplace bullying occurs when supervisors shout at subordinates and coworkers, criticize employees, and demoralize competent workers by taking away their responsibilities when work isn't performed exactly as ordered by bullying supervisors ("Survey," 1998).

Despite the frequency and negative potential of conflict, however, the principal theme of this chapter is that conflict can be a constructive force in relationships at home, at work, and at play *if managed competently*. Conflict can appear ugly and destructive to us when it is frequent and we lack the skills necessary to manage it constructively. Conflict, however, can be a signal that change needs to occur for a relationship to remain vital. It also can help partners recognize boundaries in their relationships (Lulofs, 1994). Conflict can also produce creative problem solving in the workplace by raising tension, which may encourage an energetic search for innovative answers. Reducing the severity of conflict episodes by learning conflict management techniques is a key to constructive conflict (Canary et al., 1995). Consequently, the main purpose of this chapter is to show you ways to manage conflict constructively so relationships can remain vibrant. There are three objectives related to this purpose:

1. to define conflict in both its constructive and destructive forms,
2. to describe the primary communication styles available for managing conflict, drawing distinctions between them, and
3. to discuss ways to manage conflict competently.

Definition of Conflict

Ways to manage conflict competently begins with clear definitions of terms. In this section conflict in its general form is defined. Then its destructive and constructive aspects are explained.

General Definition

Janice Lightner is a student in Professor Leticia Winthrop's Human Communication intensive 4-week summer course. Professor Winthrop has a strict policy on attendance. Five absences result in an automatic "F" for the course. Janice has to fly from Eugene, Oregon to Toronto, Canada to attend the funeral of her grandfather. She must be absent from class for an entire week. The class meets every day of the week, so Janice will miss five classes. She approaches Professor Winthrop and asks her for an exemption from the attendance policy, explaining the unforeseen circumstances of her grandfather's sudden death. She promises to make up the work and miss no other classes. Professor Winthrop expresses regret but tells Janice that she will not pass the course if she misses a week of class. Janice becomes upset and tells Professor Winthrop that her attendance policy is unreasonable and unfair. Professor Winthrop defends the policy as essential for her students to learn difficult class material. They part feeling angry.

Conflict is the expressed struggle of interconnected parties who perceive incompatible goals and interference from one or more parties in attaining those goals (Folger et al., 1993; Hocker & Wilmot, 1995). The Professor Winthrop-Janice Lightner situation illustrates each element of this definition.

First, conflict is an *expressed struggle* between two or more parties. If Janice had accepted Professor Winthrop's attendance policy without confronting her about it, no conflict would have existed. Even if Janice had been angry about the policy, for a conflict to exist Janice had to indicate her unhappiness to Professor Winthrop in some fashion. The expression of the struggle could be obvious, such as Janice talking directly to Professor Winthrop. The expression could also be very subtle, even exclusively nonverbal, such as cold stares or slouching posture by Janice during class.

Second, conflict involves *interconnected parties.* The behavior of one party must have consequences for the other party. Professor Winthrop and Janice are interconnected. Janice faces a dilemma because of Professor Winthrop's attendance policy. Professor Winthrop affects the choice Janice must make. Does she miss her grandfather's funeral so she can pass her class, or does she attend her grandfather's funeral and flunk the class? Janice affects Professor Winthrop because Janice is a disgruntled student challenging her attendance policy. Professor Winthrop may question whether her policy is too harsh or unfair.

Third, *perceived incompatible goals* must be present for conflict to occur. The goals of Professor Winthrop and Janice seem to be incompatible. Professor Winthrop's goal is to have students attend class regularly so they can learn difficult material. Janice's goal is to attend the funeral without failing the class. Professor Winthrop's attendance policy and Janice's desire to attend her grandfather's funeral clash directly.

Finally, *perceived interference from parties* who pursue incompatible goals is necessary for conflict to occur. For two people to have a conflict, either one or both must interfere with the other's goal attainment. Professor Winthrop clearly interfered with Janice's goal to attend her grandfather's funeral without affecting her class grade. If Janice attends the funeral, she thwarts Professor Winthrop's goal. Janice will fall seriously behind in the class.

Perception plays an important role in conflict. Goals may not be incompatible, and goal attainment may not be interfered with by anyone. Nevertheless, if you act as if your goals are incompatible with your partner's goals and as if your partner is trying to interfere with your goal achievement, conflict will occur until perceptions are clarified and accepted.

Destructive Conflict

To most people, conflict always seems to be destructive. Conflict can make us angry, fearful, frustrated, and upset. These are feelings we don't usually like to experience, especially if the feelings are intense and frequent. Our communication, however, determines to what degree conflict will be destructive or constructive.

Destructive conflict is characterized by escalation, retaliation, domination, competition, cross-complaining, and inflexibility (Hocker & Wilmot, 1995; Lulofs, 1994). When conflict is destructive, it spirals out of control. Participants lose sight of the initial goals. Hurting the other party becomes a primary focus. Complaints by one party are countered by complaints from the other party in a competitive one-upsmanship contest. This cross-complaining is "the most dysfunctional thing that people in conflict do" (Lulofs, 1994, p. 132) because it escalates conflict. The ability to prevent the escalation of a conflict distinguishes the competent from the incompetent communicator.

Donohue and Kolt (1992) argue that the key to recognition of destructive conflict is the ability to say to oneself in the middle of a conflict, *"Gee, I'm getting stupid"* (p. 24). When you begin to lose sight of why you're battling with someone and you become petty, even infantile, in your tactics to win an argument, you're getting stupid. When you can no longer think clearly because conflict triggers emotional reactions that clog the brain's ability to reason, then you are moving into destructive conflict territory. Gottman (1994b) calls this **flooding.** Men are far more likely to experience flooding than women.

Gottman (1994b) defines flooding this way:

> When people start to be flooded, they feel unfairly attacked, misunderstood, wronged, or righteously indignant. If you are being flooded, you may feel that things have gotten too emotional, that you just want to stop, you need to calm down, or you want to run away. Or you may want to strike back and get even. . . . The body of someone who feels flooded is a confused jumble of signals. It may be hard to breathe. People who are flooded inadvertently hold their breath. Muscles tense up and stay tensed. The heart beats faster and it may seem to beat harder. The flooded person longs for some escape and relief. (p. 112)

The movie *War of the Roses* depicts escalation of conflict and "getting stupid" in uncomfortable detail. A couple, played by Michael Douglas and Kathleen Turner, in the midst of divorcing savage each other and completely lose sight of any useful goals. They simply want to hurt each other. Each tries to dominate the other. Each character meets abuse with retaliation that ratchets to a higher level of stupidity. Their communication is completely inflexible and uncompromising. They destroy their house and each other in the process. One study (Ting-Toomey,

1983) found a *War of the Roses* pattern among couples dissatisfied with their marriages. Dissatisfied couples in this study often engaged in 10 turns of attack-and-defend communication. The dissatisfied couples didn't seem able to halt the escalation of the conflict, thus putting further strain on an already tattered relationship. This is a conflict pattern that sometimes spirals out of control.

Constructive Conflict

Conflict is sometimes constructive, not destructive. **Constructive conflict** is characterized by a We-orientation, cooperation, and flexibility (Hocker & Wilmot, 1995; Lulofs, 1994). The focus is on achieving a solution that is mutually satisfactory to all parties in the conflict. Participants work together flexibly to deal effectively with their conflicts by controlling and de-escalating them.

Dialectics in relationships, especially close relationships, inevitably produce conflict. Dialogue is the chief means used to address this conflict effectively. Destructive conflict shuts off dialogue, whereas constructive conflict embraces it. Tannen (1998) explains: "In dialogue, there is opposition, yes, but no head-on collision. Smashing heads does not open minds. . . . Even cooperation, after all, is not the absence of conflict but a means of managing conflict" (p. 26).

Constructive conflict doesn't mean we have to feel all warm and fuzzy as we work out our differences with others. Constructive conflict can be contentious, frustrating, and difficult. It is constructive, however, because the communication is competent; that is, it is knowledgeable, skillful, sensitive, committed, and ethical.

The distinctions between destructive and constructive conflict are perhaps most apparent during and after divorce, especially when children make contact between estranged parents unavoidable. Cooperative, mutually supportive coparenting is the most advantageous communication pattern in such situations for both parents and children (Hetherington et al., 1998). Such coparenting techniques reduce the frequency and severity of conflicts. Children adapt more effectively to their parents' divorce and accept remarriages more readily. Unfortunately, only about one quarter of divorced parents manage such conflicts constructively. An equal number maintain bitter, destructive conflicts with partners and children. The remaining estranged parents adopt a more indifferent, parallel coparenting approach marked by infrequent contact (Maccoby & Mnookin, 1992).

When divorced parents express contempt for each other in front of children, insist that children choose sides in a conflict, use children as leverage in a power struggle with a former spouse, or ridicule their ex-spouse's new partner, they are engaged in destructive conflict. When divorced couples encourage children to have contact with both parents, focus on supportive communication patterns, and maintain respect for former spouses and their new partners even while they themselves disagree on important issues, they are engaged in constructive conflict (Box 9-1).

We cement our relationships when we reconcile our conflicts cooperatively and supportively (Gottman, 1994b). When we try to impose our will on others in a competitive test of power and control, we propel ourselves toward the relationship graveyard where the pathetic remains of a once happy relationship are buried for eternity. In the next two sections ways to manage conflict cooperatively are addressed.

Box 9-1   Focus on Controversy

The Culture of Conflict

Our culture values debate and the exchange of opposing arguments on issues of controversy and conflict. There is a difference, however, between *making an argument* and *having an argument*. Making an argument—building a logical case supported by high-quality evidence—can be quite constructive. Having an argument typically refers to engaging in a fight—expressing aggression toward others. Tannen (1998) maintains that our culture has become an "argument culture," not a culture that values argumentation. In an argument culture, the atmosphere is warlike. We see it often on daily talk shows where conflicts are provoked, even staged, and ugliness is the norm. Shouting, interrupting, and verbally or physically assaulting those who disagree replaces serious discussion of issues.

Tannen claims that our argument culture promotes adversarial approaches to conflict. Despite the voluminous evidence that competitive, adversarial approaches to managing conflict are ineffective, disputes too often are litigated, not mediated. The courts are clogged with neighbor suing neighbor and strangers suing each other. According to the National Center for State Courts, approximately 15 million civil suits are filed each year in the United States. There is approximately one lawyer for every 50 people in this country. Compare that to Japan, a collectivist culture that values harmony and conflict avoidance, where there is approximately one lawyer for every 10,000 people (Berko et al., 1997). We are a litigious society.

Even children are getting into the act. Fourth-grader Ryan Rose hired attorney Monte Walton to fight for better food at his elementary school in Alcoa, Tennessee. "Me and my friends got mad because there was not anything to eat" ("Fourth Grader," 1999). Fed up with week-old leftovers, cold food, and lack of "good stuff," 10-year-old Ryan hired Walton, paying him a $1 fee. Ryan's mom worked for Walton as a paralegal, so Walton took the case. Walton proposed adding hamburgers to the menu. The case was settled out of court.

Politics has become a battleground of incivility and nastiness. Republican Senator John McCain of Arizona noted, "When it gets nasty these days, it really gets nasty" (as cited in Dewar, 1997). President Clinton, no stranger to personal attacks from his opponents, called it the "politics of personal destruction" during his presidential campaigns and his impeachment.

Democratic Senator Patrick Leahy of Vermont claimed, "Advice and consent has become harass and maim" (as cited in Dewar, 1997). In such an atmosphere, criticizing and expressing contempt are mistaken for critical thinking. Cynicism, not skepticism, reigns supreme.

This cynicism has become so serious that Congressmen Ray LaHood and Tom Sawyer put together the 1999 Bipartisan Congressional Retreat. This was a gathering of members of Congress whose purpose was to diminish "the toxic level of discourse in politics" and to halt efforts by both major political parties to "demonize the opposition" ("Give Congress," 1999).

We are a culture immersed in conflict. This fact, in and of itself, is not a stunning revelation. How we approach conflict in this culture, however, is significant. Tannen (1998) presents a wealth of evidence supporting her claim that we live in an argument culture—we engage in destructive conflict. Tannen notes that our culture tends to devalue cooperative conflict management approaches even though they work better than more competitive, aggressive strategies. "It's as if we value a fight for its own sake, not for its effectiveness in resolving disputes" (p. 23).

Honest, open, energetic, lively debate on issues is constructive, but such debate cannot occur in an atmosphere of personal attack, viciousness, and win-at-all-cost tactics. The answer lies not in eliminating debate but in conducting debates as true exchanges of differing points of view. Venting aggression toward "enemies" is not constructive. Parties in conflict would be more successful if they tried harder to mediate, not litigate, disputes.

Questions for Thought

1. Do you agree that we live in an argument culture? Explain.
2. In your view, is an argument culture truly destructive?
3. What steps, if any, should we take to combat the argument culture?
4. Why do you think so many people are drawn to argument? What is the appeal of talk shows that encourage and incite ugly arguments?

Styles of Conflict Management

Communication styles of conflict management have been the focus of much research. A **communication style of conflict management** is a typical way a person addresses conflict. There are five communication styles: collaborating, accommodating, compromising, avoiding, and competing (Blake & Mouton, 1964; Kilmann & Thomas, 1977).

Collaborating (Cooperating)

Working together to maximize the attainment of goals for all parties in a conflict is called **collaborating.** This is a cooperative style of conflict management. It is We-not Me-oriented. The collaborating style has three key components: confrontation, integration, and smoothing.

Confrontation The overt recognition of conflict and the direct effort to find creative ways to satisfy all parties in the conflict is called **confrontation.** It is an assertive strategy that is the opposite of avoidance. Confrontation brings the conflict out into the open for careful examination and discussion. Although mass media often use the term "confrontation" in a negative sense (e.g., "There was a violent confrontation between police and demonstrators"), this is not the meaning that applies here. Confrontation as a collaborating strategy should utilize all the elements of supportive communication already discussed (i.e., describe, problem solve, empathize, be honest, treat others as equals, and qualify your statements).

Confrontation, however, can be used excessively. Some conflicts are too trivial to warrant confrontation. Sometimes the timing is wrong. Individuals wake up irritable and need time to gather their thoughts. Confronting them before they've had their morning coffee or when they are late for a meeting at work will probably escalate a conflict. Confrontation is best attempted at a time when people are able to work on problems. Additionally, confrontation should be used judiciously, for important issues. Incessant confrontation can become annoying and counter-productive. "Can't you just let some things slide?" will be the likely response to excessive use of confrontation.

Integration A collaborative strategy that meets the goals of all parties in the conflict is called **integration.** Two integrative tactics are expanding the pie and bridging.

Expanding the pie refers to finding creative ways to increase resources, typically money. Scarce resources often cause conflict (power struggles). These conflicts can easily degenerate into competitive clashes where adversaries struggle to divide a woefully inadequate budget. *Bridging* considers the goals of all parties in the conflict and offers a new option that satisfies the interests of everyone involved.

A family I knew employed both strategies to resolve a conflict. The parents wanted to travel to Europe on vacation. The children wanted to camp in Yellowstone National Park as they usually did each summer. Initially, the parents tried to convince their children that they would enjoy a trip to Europe. The children countered that the trip would be too expensive so why even consider it. The parents agreed that the trip would be expensive, but they claimed that going to Yellowstone and camping had become boringly repetitive since they had done that for the last five summers.

After a lengthy discussion, it became apparent that the children's primary interest was not going to Yellowstone as much as it was camping together as a family. The parents admitted that their primary interest was to expose their children to different cultural experiences and thus expand their horizons. Discussions revealed that the parents didn't mind camping through Europe. That sounded exciting and certainly less expensive than staying in hotels. The children became excited when it was suggested that the family could travel by ship to Europe and come home by plane. The ocean voyage sounded particularly appealing. This meant, however, that the cost of the vacation would be a problem. Further discussions led to the suggestion by the oldest child that everyone in the family could find extra jobs and earn additional money that they could pool for the trip. Everyone agreed, and for 6 months the family worked toward their goal to raise enough money to make the trip feasible. They were ultimately successful, traveled to Europe by ship, camped for a month in four countries, and returned by plane with memories of many adventures.

This family used both expanding the pie and bridging as integrative methods for resolving their conflict. Initially, it appeared that there was a conflict of two mutually exclusive interests (i.e., camping in Yellowstone versus traveling to Europe). After confronting the problem directly, it became apparent that no real conflict of interest existed. The interests of all family members (i.e., camping and new cultural experiences) could be met with a little creative problem solving. They expanded the pie by pooling extra resources, and they bridged by creating a trip that satisfied all family members' real interests.

Smoothing   The act of calming the agitated feelings of others during a conflict episode is called **smoothing.** When tempers flair and anger turns to screaming or tears, no collaborating is possible. Address inflamed emotions. Here is an example:

JENNIFER: (Trying to hold back tears) It totally fries me that you never called to tell me where you were. I was a wreck all night wondering if you'd been in a terrible accident. How can you be so insensitive?

TIM: I'm really sorry. I didn't mean to worry you. I can understand why you're upset with me.

Smoothing addresses the emotional side of conflict. Smoothing can make integrative solutions possible by defusing emotionally volatile situations.

Research on collaborating as a conflict management style is consistently positive (Hocker & Wilmot, 1995). Collaborating produces better decisions than other styles, and participants typically are more satisfied with the decisions, the process, and the interpersonal relations developed during conflict management.

Accommodating (Yielding)

When we surrender to the needs and desires of others during a conflict, we are using the **accommodating** style. This is a nonassertive style of conflict management. It may appear that accommodating is We-oriented because the accommodater yields to others "for the sake of the relationship or group." This may be true in some cases, but yielding to others to maintain harmony can easily build resentment that one's own needs have been sacrificed. This can lead to a martyr complex and ultimately to bitterness and complaint.

Accommodating is most often the style of the less powerful. Less powerful individuals are expected to accommodate more often and to a greater degree than more powerful individuals (Lulofs, 1994). Employees are expected to yield to the requests or demands of their supervisors. Your boss is less likely to feel a need to accommodate your wishes. One mistake made by more powerful individuals, however, is failing to appreciate the value of accommodating even when yielding isn't required. When a person is clearly wrong about an issue or point of contention, it makes sense to yield on it. This yielding demonstrates reasonableness and enhances the relationship with the other person. Yielding also makes sense if the issue is more important to the other person. This flexibility is an aspect of constructive conflict management. The roles may be reversed in the future, and it may be appropriate for the other party to yield. Accommodating by others is more likely when there is a history of mutual flexibility.

Accommodating can be a constructive and necessary style of conflict management. A less powerful person may need to yield to a more powerful person to keep a job, maintain a relationship, or avoid nasty consequences. Yielding can sometimes maintain harmony in a relationship. Nevertheless, being too accommodating can make you someone else's doormat.

Compromising

When we give up something to get something we are **compromising.** The compromising style of conflict management occurs most often between parties of relatively equal power. More powerful individuals do not usually consider compromising as necessary. They can dominate, and they often choose to do so.

Compromising emphasizes workable, but not optimal, decisions and solutions. Some have referred to compromising as a lose-lose style of conflict management because trade-offs and exchanges are required to reach agreement. Only some of the goals and needs are met in a compromise. Gain is counterbalanced by loss. As one anonymous wag put it, compromise is "a deal in which two people get what neither of them wanted." Pruitt and Rubin (1986) express this negative point of view when they argue that compromising arises "from two sources—either lazy problem-solving involving a half-hearted attempt to satisfy the two parties' interests, or simply yielding by both parties" (p. 29).

Despite these negative views, compromising may be the only feasible goal in a conflict of interest where parties have relatively equal power. Half a loaf is better than starvation, so goes the thinking. Compromising can be a useful strategy when an integrative decision is not feasible, when issues are not critical, when essential values are not undermined, and when such a settlement is only temporary until a better solution can be found and negotiated.

Avoiding (Withdrawing)

When we sidestep or turn our back on conflict, we are **avoiding.** The avoiding style is exhibited in many ways (Lulofs, 1994). We avoid conflict when we ignore it or deny it exists, even though it does. When we shift topics so we don't have to address a conflict, we avoid. We may crack jokes to deflect a focus on disagreeable issues. We may quibble about the meaning of a word used by another who is probing uncomfortably about a subject of some dispute, or we may simply not respond to a question.

A particularly powerful form of avoiding is called stonewalling (Gottman, 1994b). **Stonewalling** is exhibited by stony silence, monosyllabic mutterings (e.g., "Yah," "Nope," "Hmmm"), refusal to discuss problems, or physical removal when one partner is complaining, disagreeing, or attacking the other partner. Consider this example:

JUANITA: We need to talk about your reluctance to pick up after yourself. I'm
    frustrated every time I see your dirty clothes strewn across our bedroom.

ROBERTO: There's nothing to talk about. Get used to it.

JUANITA: There's plenty to talk about!

ROBERTO: No there isn't. (He leaves the room.)

Stonewallers often justify their withdrawal from conflict by claiming that they are merely trying to remain under control and not make the contentiousness worse by responding. Stonewalling can be extremely frustrating to those faced with the withdrawal. Stonewalling can also communicate disapproval, conceit, self-righteousness, and cold indifference, a defensive communication pattern.

Avoiding is a frequently used conflict style. One study (Sillars et al., 1982) reports that students use avoiding in more than half of their conflicts. Another study (Larson, 1989) found that managers often avoid giving negative feedback to employees because they find it to be the most unpleasant and difficult task they have to perform. They are reluctant to stir up a conflict. Men more than women tend to withdraw from conflict, partly because men are more likely to experience flooding (Gottman & Carrere, 1994). As a result, men stonewall in the hope that they can prevent flooding. Gottman's (1994b) research found that about 85% of stonewallers are men.

These flights from fights are not often constructive. How can we heal a relationship when one party refuses to confront problems? Avoiding increases the frequency of marital disagreements because spouses repetitively revisit issues that don't get resolved (McGonagle et al., 1993). Managers who avoid critiquing employees' poor work performance typically become increasingly annoyed by the continued bad performance. When the annoyance rises to extremely high levels, they give feedback that is usually biting, sarcastic, harsh, threatening, and personal (Baron, 1988). This merely intensifies anger by both parties.

Couples that brag to others that they "never fight" may be avoiding underlying discord for the sake of appearances. Frequency of conflict alone does not indicate how healthy a relationship is, or is not (Gottman, 1994b). In fact, avoiding is a strategy often used by abused partners to keep from provoking violence from their abusers (Gelles & Straus, 1988). This avoidance creates a **chilling effect** wherein a partner low in power avoids discussing issues with his or her abusive partner that might trigger aggression (Roloff & Cloven, 1990).

Avoiding is not always an inappropriate and ineffective style of conflict management. We can avoid trivial issues without damage to our relationships. Avoiding "hot button" issues that trigger intense disagreements and hurt may also be appropriate. Reminding a partner of an affair confronted long ago dredges up

Power-forcing is sometimes an unavoidable conflict style, but it should be a last resort and used only when other styles have failed.

anger and hurt feelings with no constructive outcome likely. The fact of the affair cannot be changed. Repeatedly reliving damaging events keeps partners prisoners of their history. If your choice is to stay in the relationship, then don't pick the scab. Let the wound heal. If unresolved anger persists, consider resolving it with a third party.

Competing (Power-Forcing)

When we approach conflict as a win-lose contest, we are competing. The **competing**, or power-forcing, style of conflict management flows from the dominance perspective on power. The competing style is exhibited in a variety of ways: by threats, criticism, contempt, hostile remarks and jokes, sarcasm, ridicule, intimidation, fault-finding and blaming, and denials of responsibility (Hocker & Wilmot, 1995). All of these behaviors upset the ratio of positive to negative communication. As discussed in Chapter 8, at least a 5 to 1 ratio of positive to negative communication between partners is necessary to sustain a relationship (Gottman, 1994b). The competing style of conflict management emphasizes the negative. The competing style is aggressive, not assertive. It is a Me-oriented style that is focused on winning a dispute at other's expense.

The essence of the competing style is pressuring others to change their behavior to your advantage. The more we try to force others to do our bidding, however, the more we ignite psychological reactance. Simply put, *the competing style has the greatest potential for destructive conflict because it can easily escalate a conflict even beyond stupidity and pointlessness.* Incidents of road rage that end as shoot-outs on our nation's highways exemplify how the competing style can escalate mild conflicts into pointless tragedies.

The chief flaw of the competing style is that the focus is on victory for oneself, not on a mutually satisfactory decision for all parties involved. The competing style attempts to create or to expand power imbalances in relationships. The deficiencies of competition were outlined in Chapter 1. The competing style suffers from many of these same deficiencies.

[handwritten margin note: aggression always produces more aggression. —only use when don't care about relationship & issue's all that matters]

257

Managing Conflict Competently

In this section how to competently transact conflict is addressed. Topics include appropriate and effective use of conflict styles, anger management, forgiveness, and the connection between culture and conflict.

Conflict Styles in Action

In my small group communication classes, at least one group every semester approaches me about problems they are having with a group member. Typically, the group member is unreliable, fails to show for group meetings, and hasn't shared the group workload on class projects. Consistently, their first question to me is "Can we kick Josh, Jamie, Janine, or whomever out of the group?" When I ask if they have confronted this person and expressed the group's concerns and feelings, virtually every time they admit that they have yet to confront their slacker. They avoid the problem because it makes them uncomfortable to confront, but when the problem keeps getting worse, they choose power-forcing, the least effective style. This is not surprising in a hypercompetitive society.

Research shows clearly that the collaborating style is the most constructive and effective means of managing conflict. The competing style is the least effective, and the avoiding style is only slightly better than the competing style (Canary & Spitzberg, 1987). One study by Markman (as cited in Edwards, 1995) of 135 married couples, 21 of whom later divorced, showed that escalating conflicts into ugly verbal battles (competing) and refusing to face conflicts directly (avoiding) predicted divorce in almost every instance.

Collaborating depends on dialogue. Dialogue is central to the management of conflict provoked by dialectics in relationships (Baxter & Montgomery, 1996). Competing and avoiding both stifle dialogue. Competing sets up a power relationship that discourages dialogue. If you can force your point of view on others, you don't have to engage in dialogue. You can demand compliance. Those with the power disadvantage also have little motivation to engage in dialogue. Expressing dissenting viewpoints might invite retaliation from the more powerful individual. Avoiding dialogue and controversial viewpoints becomes an act of self-protection in a competitive, power-imbalanced situation.

Despite the clear advantages of the collaborating over the competing style, research shows that typically we use the least effective and appropriate style when trying to manage conflict. One study compared the collaborative and competing styles in 52 conflict cases (Phillips & Cheston, 1979). Participants used the competing style twice as often as the collaborating style. In half of the cases, competing produced bad outcomes. In all cases where participants used collaborating, the outcomes were good. Another study (Gayle, 1991) showed that only 5% of supervisors, middle managers, top managers, and administrators actually used the collaborating style in specific conflict situations. Instead, 41% of this same group selected competing, and 26% chose avoiding. This was true of both male and female supervisors and managers.

A key to appropriate and effective use of conflict management styles is more than how often you use a style. Timing is important. If you begin using a competing style, the likely result will be anger, hostility, and retaliation. Realizing that the competing style isn't working well, you may decide to try the collaborating

Box 9-2   Sharper Focus

Crisis and the Competing Style

The competing style should be a style of last resort unless a crisis or an emergency requires quick action where time-consuming styles such as collaborating and compromising are impractical. Greg Clark, a former Stanford University football player experienced a crisis that mandated the immediate use of the competing, power-forcing style of conflict management. When he was 20 years old, he was doing Mormon missionary work in Illinois. He befriended a young woman attending Illinois State University. When the woman didn't attend church one Sunday, Clark became anxious. His friend had been having trouble with an ex-boyfriend. Clark went to her apartment where he was casually confronted by the ex-boyfriend who told him that the woman had gone to church. Clark noticed what looked like blood on the ex-boyfriend's shirt. Clark then heard the muffled scream from inside the apartment, "Help me! Please call the police!" (as cited in Judge, 1997). The ex-boyfriend yelled at the woman to shut up, then ordered Clark to leave. Clark leapt into action. "I punched him, knocked him down and jumped on top of him. I never felt that strong before. We wrestled around, and he fell into the railing of the deck on the walkway." He subdued the ex-boyfriend, called police, and rescued his friend. The ex-boyfriend had tied up the woman with a phone cord, gagged her, and was drowning her in the bathtub when Clark arrived. He saved his friend from certain death. Power-forcing is sometimes appropriate as a first reaction in emergency situations.

style. Good luck! Once you have competed, it is much more difficult to cooperate. Suspicion and mistrust will permeate your transactions. It is far better to begin with the collaborating style. If collaborating does not work, you may have to use other styles to manage the conflict. If the issue is not very important, accommodating or avoiding might work. You could use compromising as an interim style until you find a more integrative solution. Ultimately, you may have to use the competing style.

The students in my small group communication course must first confront group members who are not producing and try to resolve the conflict cooperatively. If these efforts are unsuccessful, I do allow the students to inform their slacker that he or she will be booted out of the group unless these behaviors change. Competing is the style of last resort, but you may have to use it when all other styles fail or are inappropriate (Box 9-2). Employees who are frequently tardy or absent, do not complete required work on time, and manifest a negative attitude may have to be fired if no other style changes their behavior. Divorce is often a power-forcing style, especially when one partner wants out of the relationship and the other does not. Nevertheless, divorce may be the last-resort solution to years of bitter conflict. It isn't pretty, but it may be necessary in some circumstances.

Communication Styles and Partner Abuse

The problem of partner abuse has been addressed (Chapter 7), but the relationship between partner abuse and communication styles of conflict management has not. A person's style of handling conflict can be an important indicator of potential abuse early in a relationship. Spotting potential abuse early can prevent abuse from emerging.

If a partner's chief style of resolving conflict is competing (power-forcing), you should take this as a warning sign of possible future abuse. In particular, controlling behaviors, such as wanting to know who you were with when you weren't with your partner, trying to specify which friends you should associate with, and attempting to dictate with whom you can socialize, are troublesome power-forcing behaviors. Even if your partner presents these controlling behaviors as requests rather than demands at first, be concerned. Yielding to such requests or demands won't end disagreement, and it may feed the abuser's desire to control you.

Psychologically abusive communication such as contemptuous remarks, ridicule, and humiliating comments are dominance strategies aimed at keeping a partner "in line." Verbal threats of physical violence when resistance is offered, of course, are even more serious power-forcing behaviors. Verbal aggression often leads to physical aggression (Infante et al., 1992). Verbal aggression in relationships either precedes or accompanies physical violence in 99% of abuse cases (Straus & Sweet, 1992). Psychological abuse as an intimidating conflict strategy is dangerous and cause for alarm.

Accommodating is normally an ineffective conflict style to use when signals of possible abuse first appear. Yielding to power-forcing demands may be necessary in the immediate situation if one's partner is showing signs of losing self-control. Nevertheless, accommodating the demands of a partner out of fear for one's safety places the potential abuser in charge of his or her partner's life.

Compromising usually doesn't satisfy a potential abuser. Abusers, especially outright batterers, want total control and obedience (Jacobson & Gottman, 1998). There should be no compromise on the goal of eradicating verbal and physical aggression. Do not try to defend or rationalize "a little bit of abuse."

Avoiding is the most common style used by women to deal with physical abuse from their partners (Gelles & Straus, 1988). It reduces the frequency of physical violence in relationships by avoiding "hot buttons" that trigger violence in a partner. This style, however, is difficult to recommend except in the most dire situations where avoiding might be a temporary expedient necessary for self-protection. As a long-term style, it is woefully deficient. It reinforces power imbalances and puts the abuser in charge of the victim's life.

Confrontation is most effective for dealing with potential or actual abuse in relationships. As Gelles and Straus (1988) explain: "Delaying until the violence escalates is too late. A firm, emphatic, and rational approach appears to be the most effective personal strategy a woman can use to prevent future violence" (p. 159). They suggest *confronting the very first incident* of even minor violence and stating without equivocation that such behavior will not be tolerated and must never occur again.

In the Vitanza and Marshall (1993) study of college students, almost a third of college women admitted slapping their partners, and almost a fifth admitted slapping a partner in the face. As a freshman in college, I dated a woman who, when angry at me, would slap me in the face. The first time it happened, I avoided discussing it, mostly because I was embarrassed. When it happened a second time, months later, I still did not confront her. Finally, when it happened a third time, I confronted her. I described how it made me feel when she slapped me. I explained to her that when she slapped me my first reaction was to slap her back, but that might injure her physically. I further explained that I hated the feeling of wanting to strike her in retaliation. Finally, I said to her, "I cannot and will not hit you when you slap me, but you put me in an embarrassing and unfair position. You can hit me, but I can't hit back. What am I supposed to do?" She responded by saying that she had never considered her actions from my perspective. She promised never to slap me again, and during a long relationship, she never did. It is vital that even relatively minor acts of aggression be confronted before they escalate into tragic abuse. I should have confronted my partner sooner than I did.

If physical or psychological abuse continues after you confront it, you should seriously consider ending the relationship. Abuse that is excused, rationalized, or ignored almost always recurs and grows worse (Jacobson & Gottman, 1998). The best way to handle it is assertively, directly, and unequivocally at the outset. Partners can stop their abuse, but it is infinitely more difficult to stop abuse once it has become standard practice.

Once again, the evidence is clear. Cooperation has distinct advantages over competition. Collaborating instead of power-forcing has greater potential for constructive management of conflict. Start with collaborating and work hard to make it work. Only when all else has failed should competing, or power-forcing, be seriously considered.

Anger Management

"She slurps when she eats soup—it makes me crazy." "He drives like a maniac. I hate it." "She squirrels money away like we're poor. We make plenty of money, but you'd never know it from the way she hoards it." "He never cooks a meal. He acts like I'm his personal chef and waitress all in one." The issues that create conflict are virtually infinite in number. Marriage counselor David Mace notes, "Marriage and family living generate in normal people more anger than those people experience in any other social situation in which they habitually find themselves" (as cited in Tavris, 1989, p. 221). Conflict over serious issues or silly ones is a natural part of marriages and all close personal relationships. Anger is a frequent companion of such conflicts.

Learning to manage anger is an important step in managing conflicts competently. Ahrons (1994) notes that the chief difference between divorced parents who were effective coparents to their children and those who were ineffective "was that the more cooperative group managed their anger better" (p. 145).

Constructive and Destructive Anger   Two conditions determine how destructive or constructive anger is (Adler & Towne, 1999). The first condition is the *intensity*, or relative strength, of the anger. Anger can vary in intensity from mild irritation to rage. Mild, even moderate, anger can be constructive. It can signal the existence of a problem, and it can motivate necessary change. Rage, however, is destructive. Temper tantrums and screaming fits are never endearing. In relationships, rage frightens partners and children. In the workplace, rage is never appropriate because it "shows you've lost control—not to mention that it's tough to be articulate if you're having a conniption" (Black, 1990a, 1990b). Ranting and raving make you look like a lunatic. When used to get your way on an issue, rage is a power-forcing style of conflict management that will likely produce an equivalent counter-response. Rage times rage equals rage squared.

Duration, or how long something lasts, is the second condition that determines to what degree anger is constructive or destructive. The length of an anger episode can vary from short-lived to prolonged. Quick flashes of temper may hardly cause notice by others. Even fairly intense expressions of anger, if short-lived, can make

Road rage produced four wrecked cars and three dead people in this Washington, D.C., crash.

the point powerfully that you are upset. If your anger goes on for too long, however, you and anyone listening will lose sight of the issue that caused the anger. Protracted anger episodes can make conflict management extremely difficult. When expressions of anger are highly intense and long-lasting, the combination can be extremely combustible.

There is a popular notion that venting one's anger is constructive and that suppressing anger is unhealthy. The popular notion is wrong. *Venting anger, or "blowing off steam," usually increases one's anger* (Baron, 1990; Tavris, 1989). Replaying our anger about past events, especially if the anger is unresolved, simply rehearses it. When we tell friends of past "injustices," blood pressure rises, heart beat increases, and the face flushes. You are experiencing the anger all over again. This doesn't put the anger to rest. It awakens it, pops it out of bed, and starts it doing jumping jacks.

Anger and Attribution   In a study by Zillmann (1993), a confederate of the experimenter acted as a rude assistant who insulted participants riding an exercise bike. When provided a chance to retaliate by giving the rude assistant a bad evaluation that they thought would adversely affect his effort to get a job, all of the angry participants did so with enthusiasm. In another version of the experiment, however, another confederate tells the rude assistant, just before the participants have a chance to retaliate, that he has a phone call down the hall. The rude assistant makes a snide comment to the new confederate and leaves. The new confederate takes the snide comment well, explaining to the participants that the rude assistant is under a great deal of pressure, worried as he is about his upcoming graduate oral exam. The participants' anger is defused in this instance, and they choose not to retaliate. Instead, they express compassion for the rude assistant.

Anger and the desire to lash out at others are choices. Imagine, for instance, that you are stopped at an intersection in your car and another car "steals" your right-of-way by moving into the intersection before you. Do you get angry? Do you make an obscene gesture? Do you shout at the driver? Now imagine what your reaction would be if you saw that it was your best friend driving the car. Would your reaction be the same? Probably not. We can be righteously indignant, or we can choose to be calm, even amused, by the same stimulus.

Anger can be a thoughtful choice unless our anger reaches the level of rage (Zillmann, 1993). Rage floods our thought process: we can't think straight, and we "get stupid." Attributing meanings, causes, or outcomes to conflict events shapes the way we think about and respond to disagreements and perceived poor treatment. Attribution can influence enormously whether we get stupid or we get smart on potentially volatile issues (Baron, 1990).

Intent and blame are two common forms of attribution that ignite anger (McKay et al., 1989). Trying to ascertain the motivation of another person is mind reading. Unless a person tells us, we must guess what motivated them. Behaviors from others that we perceive to be intentional, not accidental, easily trigger our anger. Deliberately shoving someone is perceived to be more worthy of anger and hostility than accidentally tripping and shoving a person while trying to regain your own balance. Blaming someone for negative behavior is the companion of intent. If the behavior of others is intentional and negative, it "deserves" reproach. We can justifiably blame them for unfortunate outcomes. If their behavior is not intentional, we can still blame them for the outcome, but it doesn't seem as justified to be angry with them. How we think about potential conflict-producing events influences our emotional response.

Managing Your Own Anger   There are several ways to defuse and de-escalate anger, both your own and others' (Figure 9-1). Try these suggestions for managing your own anger:

1. *Reframe self-talk.* Thoughts trigger anger. Reframing the way we think about events can deflate our anger before it has a chance to escalate (Baron, 1990). Very often we have no way of knowing whether the act of another person was intentional or not. Instead of assuming it was intentional, assume it was unintentional. "He probably didn't see me." "She looked stressed out." "Her day isn't going too well." This kind of self-talk reframes events as unintentional, even haphazard—not intentional.

2. *Speak and listen nondefensively.* Criticism, contempt, and cross-complaining ignite angry passions (Baron, 1990). Refuse to become defensive. Reframe criticism as a problem or challenge. Use supportive communication.

3. *Deliberately calm yourself.* Exercise some discipline, and refuse to vent your anger. You will feel your heartbeat increasing when your anger starts to rise. This is a signal that your anger is escalating. Check your pulse if you are uncertain whether you are feeling overwhelmed. A pulse rate that climbs 10% higher than your normal resting pulse rate is cause for concern (Gottman, 1994b). If your normal resting pulse is 80 beats per minute, be concerned if it increases to 88. If your pulse reaches 100, you are in the throes of flooding (Gottman, 1994b).

Figure 9-1 Managing Anger

Managing Your Own Anger
- Reframe self-talk
- Speak and listen nondefensively
- Deliberately calm yourself
- Find distractions

Managing Others' Anger
- Be asymmetrical
- Validate the other person
- Probe
- Assume a problem orientation
- Refuse to be abused
- Disengage

When you feel the adrenaline surge, deliberately take slow, deep breaths and concentrate on reducing your heartbeat. Count to 10 before responding. A cooling-off period may be necessary in serious cases. A cooling-off period works well to calm a person's anger (Goleman, 1995). Typically, it takes 20 minutes to recover from an adrenaline surge. Take the 20 minutes away from the person or situation that triggers your anger. Go for a walk, shoot a basketball, kiss a frog, or do whatever diverts your attention and moves you out of the situation. Return to discuss your anger with others only when you are certain that flooding has subsided. Then express your anger to others in a calm, descriptive manner (first-person singular language).

4. *Find distractions.* Don't rehearse your anger. Revisiting past injustices won't change your history. You can't get beyond old issues if you keep replaying them in your mind. Distract yourself when old hurts resurface. Read the newspaper, watch television, or make plans for a family outing. Just get your mind off your anger for a little while. When angry thoughts rush into your mind, distract yourself.

Don't attempt to learn all four of these suggestions at once. Pick one and work on learning it until it becomes virtually automatic. Then you can attempt a second suggestion, and so forth.

Managing the Anger of Others You can defuse and de-escalate the anger of others so you can confront issues constructively. It is usually best to address the person's anger first, then deal with the substance of the dispute that triggers the anger (Donohue & Kolt, 1992). Dialogue cannot take place when tempers are white hot. Try these suggestions to defuse another person's anger and restore a climate conducive to dialogue:

1. *Be asymmetrical.* When a person is exhibiting anger, particularly if it turns to rage, it is critical that you not strike back in kind. Resist reacting signally to words of criticism. Be asymmetrical; that is, you do the opposite. Counteract rage with

absolute calm. Stay composed (Black, 1990a, 1990b). Hostage negotiators are trained to defuse highly volatile individuals by remaining absolutely calm through-out the negotiations and employing the smoothing technique to quiet the enraged person. Matching a person's rage with rage can produce ugly, violent outcomes.

2. *Validate the other person.* Validation is a form of the smoothing technique of collaborating. Let the person know that his or her point of view and anger has some validity, even though you may not agree with him or her. Validation is par-ticularly vital for men to use because men tend to respond to a woman's emotional upset by becoming hyperrational (Gottman, 1994b). Offering advice or trying to solve a problem while a person is extremely upset invalidates that person's feelings by ignoring them.

You can validate another person in several ways. You can take responsibility for the other person's anger. "I upset you didn't I?" acknowledges your role in provoking anger. You can apologize. "I'm sorry. You're right to be angry" can be a very powerful validation of the other person. Don't apologize, of course, unless you really bear some responsibility. Sometimes a compliment can defuse another person's anger: "I actually think you handled my abrasiveness and moodiness rather well." Finally, actively listening to the other person and acknowledging what the person has said can be very validating. "I know it upsets you when I play my music too loudly while you're trying to study" makes the other person feel that he or she has been heard, even if conflict still exists.

3. *Probe.* Seek more information from the other person so you can understand his or her anger (McKay et al., 1989). When you ask a question of the angry person, it forces the person to shift from emotional outburst to rational response. Simply asking, "Can we sit down and discuss this calmly so I can understand your point of view?" can momentarily defuse another person's anger. If your partner angrily criticizes you, "You're a jerk of epic proportions; a reigning king of the principality of jerkdom. You are the essence of jerkness, the embodiment of all that is jerky," listen, then probe. "Wow! How about giving me some examples so I can understand why you think I'm such a jerk" probes for specific information necessary to resolve the conflict.

4. *Assume a problem orientation.* This is a supportive communication pattern. This step should occur once you have calmed the angry person by the previous steps. Approach the emotional display as a problem to be solved, not a reason to retaliate. The question "What would you like to see occur?" invites problem solving.

5. *Refuse to be abused.* Even if you are wrong, feel guilty, or deserve another person's anger, do not permit yourself to be verbally battered (McKay et al., 1989). Abusive assaults are unproductive no matter who is at fault in a conflict. "I cannot discuss this with you if you insist on being abusive. I can see that you're upset, but name-calling won't lead to a solution" sets a ground rule on how anger can be expressed.

6. *Disengage.* This is the final step when all else fails to calm a person's anger. This step is particularly important if the person continues to be abusive and en-raged. Simply and firmly state, "This meeting is over. I'm leaving. We'll discuss this another time."

Keeping track of all six of these steps, especially when faced with an enraged person, is too much to expect. Concentrate on one or two steps until you have

Box 9-3   Sharper Focus

Bill Gates Goes Ballistic

Bill Gates is enraged. "His eyes are bulging and his oversized glasses are askew. His face is flushed and spit is flying from his mouth. . . . He's in a small, crowded conference room at the Microsoft campus with 20 young Microsofties gathered around an oblong table. Most look at their chairman with outright fear, if they look at him at all. The sour smell of sweaty terror fills the room" (Moody, 1996, p. 12). Gates continues his tirade, flooded with anger; seemingly incapable of rational resolution of the problem. The anxious programmers seated around the table try to reason with him, but to no avail. None seems able to calm down their boss—except a diminutive, soft-spoken Chinese American woman. She maintains eye contact with Gates as everyone else in the room looks away. Twice she short-circuits his outburst by addressing him in a calm, even voice. Gates is momentarily calmed by the woman's first attempt before revving up

again. Her second attempt makes him pause. He listens to her, thoughtfully considers what she has said, then says, "Okay, this looks good. Go ahead." Crisis past, the meeting adjourns.

What this woman said to Gates was only slightly different from what several people in the room had been trying to say throughout his tirade. What she said, however, was not nearly as important as how she communicated it. She responded asymmetrically to Gates' angry eruption. Gates was flooded and "acting stupid"; she was calm and able to think straight. Her tranquil demeanor broke through and quelled the outburst. It signaled that the intense anger was unnecessary. Blazing anger was extinguished by asymmetrical calm. Exercising self-control when faced with someone out of control can be very empowering.

---

learned them so well that they become a habit. Being asymmetrical is the crucial step, with validation a close second. The remaining steps can be learned gradually. Being asymmetrical provides the greatest chance that the other person's anger will be defused and that you will remain safe in the process (Box 9-3).

Anger is a central element in conflict. The constructive management of conflict can occur only when you keep anger under control. This does not mean squelching anger. A person can feel angry for excellent reasons. Anger acts as a signal that changes need to occur. Anger should not, however, be used as a weapon to abuse others. We need to learn ways to cope with and express anger constructively, not be devoured by it.

Typically it is best to express your anger directly to the person with whom you are upset, not to innocent bystanders (Tavris, 1989). Coming home and chewing out your roommate because your boss at work angered you is inappropriate. Express your anger when you have calmed yourself and can confront the person in a descriptive manner. Expressing anger is most satisfying when the behavior that caused the anger changes. Gaining behavioral change from others happens more often when both parties engage in constructive dialogue, taking the problem-solving approach to communication. Expressing anger is also most satisfying when there is no retaliation from the target of your anger. Power-forcing, competing styles of expressing anger are likely to provoke retaliation. Collaborating, assertive styles of expressing anger are more likely to avoid retaliation and produce just solutions.

Transforming Competing Into Collaborating

Conflicts are transactional. What one party does affects the other party in a conflict. Defensive communication from one person can ignite defensive communication from another. Supportive communication from one person encourages supportive communication from others. It takes two to compete, and it takes two to cooperate. The big question is "What do I do when I want to cooperate but the other person wants to compete?" In a hypercompetitive society, chances are good that you will have to address this problem more often than not. Knowing that collaborating works far better than competing in most conflict situations doesn't automatically mean that others will share your informed viewpoint.

Here are some suggestions for how you might transform a competitor into a collaborator:

1. *Always be "unconditionally constructive"* (Fisher & Brown, 1988). Refuse to be abused, but also refuse to be abusive. Don't return contempt with contempt, intimidation with intimidation. If others become abusive, remain civil. If they confuse issues to hide their weak position, clarify. If they try to intimidate you, don't bully back. Attempt to persuade them of the merits of your viewpoint. If they lie, neither trust nor deceive them. Remain vigilantly trustworthy at all times. If they don't actively listen to you, encourage them to listen carefully. Always listen actively and empathically to them. Meet defensive communication with supportive communication. This is not a guide to sainthood, although you probably deserve some small award for remaining composed when dealing with certain individuals. Remaining unconditionally constructive serves your own interests. As Fisher and Brown (1988) explain: "If you are acting in ways that injure your own competence, there is no reason for me to do the same. Two heads are better than one, but one is better than none" (p. 202).

2. *Ask problem-solving questions* (Ury, 1993). Your goal is to move the other party from a power-forcing, controlling communication pattern to a problem-solving, collaborative pattern. One way to do this is to engage the other person in joint problem solving. Encourage joint effort to find an integrative solution. Ask "Why?" "Why not?" and "What if?" questions. "Why is it a problem for you that I don't talk much when I come home from work?" "Why not do it as I suggested? Can you see some problems?" "What if you let me do extra credit? What would happen?" You should not ask these questions, of course, as if you are cross-examining a terrorist on the witness stand.

3. *Confront the process* (Ury, 1993). Confronting the process can encourage collaborating. Don't attack; be assertive. Simply make an observation about the process. "Have you noticed that every time I try to explain my point of view you interrupt me before I can finish my thought? Perhaps we can both agree to listen to each other without comment for 1 minute. What do you think?" If the other party gets nasty and belligerent, don't return fire. Address the process. "Do we really want to get nasty with each other? I don't see any good coming of it, do you?" This forces the other party to justify the nastiness; not an easy thing to do. Notice that the phrasing uses "we" to express inclusiveness. This removes the appearance of accusation. Sitting next to the person to discuss a family budget or credit card debt instead of across from each other also nonverbally shows inclusiveness not exclusiveness.

4. *Ask for advice* (Ury, 1993). "What would you do if you were in my position?" This requires some empathy—taking the perspective of the other person. "What do you suggest we do to satisfy both of our needs?" Again, the focus is on mutually solving problems and moving away from power-forcing strategies. To paraphrase

Ury (1993), you're trying to bring others to their senses, not bring them to their knees.

Of these four suggestions, remaining unconditionally constructive is crucial. It is the close companion of an asymmetrical response to anger. Don't try to learn all four steps at once. Concentrate on remaining unconditionally constructive first until it becomes second nature to you. Then gradually use and refine the other three suggestions, one at a time.

Forgiveness

One of the most starkly horrifying images of the Vietnam War is Associated Press photographer Nick Ut's picture of 9-year-old Phan Thi Kim Phuc running naked from her village, screaming in pain from a napalm attack that scorched 75% of her body with third-degree burns. Ut snapped the photo, then rushed the anguished little girl to a hospital, saving her life. Her two younger brothers died in the same napalm attack.

Kim Phuc spent 14 months in a Vietnamese hospital recovering from her terrible burns. When her wounds were washed and dressed, she lost consciousness from the excruciating pain. Even today, almost three decades later, the pain of those disfiguring wounds remains. "They are like a knife. They feel like they are cutting me" (as cited in Schultz, 1998).

In 1996 Kim Phuc brought a message of forgiveness to a Veteran's Day gathering at the Vietnam War Memorial in Washington, D.C. Addressing the crowd, she said, "Even if I could talk face to face to the pilot who dropped the bombs, I could tell him we could not change history. We should try to do good things for the present and the future to promote peace" (as cited in Schultz, 1998). One veteran of the war, John Huelsenbeck, present at the ceremony said, "It's important to us that she's here, part of the healing process. We were just kids doing our job. For her to forgive us personally means something" (as cited in Sciolino, 1996, p. A14). Kim Phuc exhibited Mark Twain's conception of forgiveness—"The fragrance the violet sheds on the heel that has crushed it."

Forgiveness plays an important role in resolving conflict and dealing with anger. Although not widely researched, some studies show that forgiveness seems to promote marital adjustment (Woodman, 1991) and to reduce hostile anger (Williams & Williams, 1993). "Forgiveness is the final stage of conflict and is the one thing that is most likely to prevent repetitive, destructive cycles of conflict" (Lulofs, 1994, p. 288).

What Is Forgiveness? In Neil Simon's play *California Suite,* a woman catches her husband committing adultery and says to him, "I forgive you. And now I'm going to go out and spend all your money." Great line, but this isn't forgiveness. **Forgiveness** is "letting go of feelings of revenge and desires to retaliate" (Lulofs, 1994, p. 276). The focus of forgiveness is on healing wounds, not inflicting them on others.

Forgiveness is not simply forgetting what happened. How could Kim Phuc ever forget what happened to her? The painful scars covering her body remind her every day. Yet she forgave her attackers. Forgiveness is not excusing the behavior. When we forgive, we remove the desire to mimic the behavior we hate.

Kim Phuc (center) as a child runs screaming down a Vietnamese road after suffering severe burns from napalm. As an adult, she meets John Plummer, an American officer who coordinated the bombing attack, for the first time since the war. He gives a heartfelt apology, and she forgives him.

Forgiveness is also not tolerating reprehensible behavior. Kim Phuc clearly showed that she did not tolerate bombing innocent children in villages. The best indicator that you have forgiven someone for bad behavior is honestly wishing that person well when you think of them (Smedes, 1984).

Forgiveness, of course, is the opposite of the popular bumper sticker, "Don't get mad—get even." Forgiveness doesn't come easily. The more hurtful the behavior, the more difficult it is to forgive. When a friend ridicules your style of dress or taste in music in front of others, it can hurt and make you angry, but you usually can forgive the insult easily. In fact, as Smedes (1984) explains, "It is wise not to turn all hurts into crises of forgiving. . . . We put everyone we love on guard when we turn personal misdemeanors into major felonies" (p. 15). Stealing your boyfriend or girlfriend from you, however, makes forgiving a bit more difficult.

Revenge may be our first impulse in response to transgressions, but seeking revenge doesn't resolve conflict. A movie such as *The First Wives Club* depicts revenge as a normal, even constructive, response to the hurtful actions of others.

This makes good entertainment, depending, of course, on your taste in movies. In the real world, however, revenge stimulates anger and perpetuates and escalates conflict.

The Process of Forgiveness So how does forgiveness occur? Forgiveness is a process that occurs in stages. Smedes (1984) offers a four-stage model: We hurt, we hate, we heal, and we come together. Hurting and hating are natural results of the painful actions of others. Dwelling on the hating stage, however, paralyzes us. Hate is like a parasite drawing our life's energy from us, making us too weak to move forward. Our lives can become consumed by hatred for those who have inflicted pain on us. The only way to break free from the grip of hatred is to forgive. Forgiveness starts the healing process.

Perhaps you're thinking, "Easy for you to say, but there are just some things that can't be forgiven." Remember that forgiveness doesn't mean acceptance or tolerance of bad behavior by others. It doesn't mean you shouldn't get angry when you are mistreated. It also doesn't mean that you necessarily return to a relationship. Wishing a person well and no longer desiring revenge and retaliation won't necessarily mean that a relationship is salvageable. Think, though, what the alternative is to forgiving. Holding onto hatred and seeking revenge does nothing constructive to enhance your life. Hatred and desire for revenge are physically and psychologically damaging (Lulofs, 1994).

Mary Nell Verrett is the sister of James Byrd Jr., a 49-year-old African American who was beaten and dragged to death behind a pickup truck in Jasper, Texas on June 7, 1998. Despite her terrible loss, Verrett eloquently testifies to the futility and danger of hating: "Our family has no use for destructive hate . . . it tears away at you. You become sick. You become a victim all over again. It can keep you from sleeping, eating, and thinking straight. It can keep you from going forward" (as cited in "Message of Hope," 1998, pp. 9–10). If Mary Nell Verrett can forgive what racist White men did to her beloved brother, and Kim Phuc can forgive the transgressors who inflicted unspeakable pain and suffering on her, surely we can forgive those who hurt us.

Forgiveness is a transactional process. Although some individuals can readily forgive others, it is extremely difficult for others to forgive. In such cases, what the transgressor does to encourage forgiveness can help. Individuals who have inflicted pain on us can take two steps to initiate the forgiveness process. First, they can openly and sincerely accept guilt for what they have done. "What I did to you was wrong and totally unprovoked" expresses guilt. Second, transgressors can apologize. "I'm very sorry for hurting you" is a short apology. An apology is a particularly important step that encourages forgiveness (McCullough et al., 1997). Elaborate, sincere apologies work best when the transgression is serious (Weiner et al., 1991).

The forgiveness process was manifested in a Santa Cruz County, California, courtroom at the sentencing of Bryce Kurek, an 18-year-old found guilty of drunken driving that killed three of his friends and paralyzed a fourth. Stricken by the horror of what he had foolishly and irresponsibly done, while weeping he issued this apology to the court and to the parents of his dead and injured friends: "I just want to say I'm so sorry for what I did. I just apologize with all of my heart and soul. It's all I can give you when I took so much from you. I can't imagine how it must feel to lose your child. I want to be punished, your honor, for what I've done. I know whatever I do it'll never bring them back, but it might ease the pain of the parents" (as cited in Gammon & Clark, 1997, p. A4).

The apology was elaborate and sincere, and he accepted guilt by asking the judge to punish him. It did not excuse his behavior, and no one will forget what happened. All of the victims' parents lost their only children in the fiery crash. Nevertheless, Laurie Maze, mother of one of the victims, said after the judge passed sentence, "We never had revenge for him. We just wanted justice served. I hope he learns and matures and accepts the full responsibility of his actions" (p. A1). Veta Jackson-Smith, also a victim's mother, actually pleaded with the court for mercy: "I want something good to come out of this instead of all this bitterness. It's enough of a sentence that he knows until the day he dies that he killed his friends" (p. A4). Judge Robert Yonts sentenced Bryce Kurek to 8 years in prison.

Others can start the forgiveness process, but ultimately we have to forgive in our hearts. As the victim, we can forgive by reframing the event. We recast the behavior that hurt us into an uncharacteristic departure from the norm. The hurtful act doesn't have to become a defining moment in our relationship with the other person. A friend can hurt us and still remain a friend. We can also reframe the event by attributing situational causes for the act. "He stole my money because he lives in desperate circumstances, not because he is evil" reframes the event for forgiveness. The parents in the Bryce Kurek tragedy might have reframed the event as, "He was a kid who did a dumb, irresponsible act brought on by alcohol abuse, but before this event he was a good person and he probably still is."

The final stage of the forgiveness process is the coming together part. This step can continue the healing and nudge us toward closure so we can move on with our lives. Coming together occurs when the victim openly communicates forgiveness to the transgressor. "I forgive you. I have no desire for revenge" expresses forgiveness. A hug or some expression of affection, if possible, is also helpful in bringing parties together. In cases of serious transgressions, the transgressor may have to demonstrate his or her commitment to make amends (Tavris, 1989). Forgiveness doesn't mean that trust springs back immediately. If the transgressor, for instance, agrees to clean the house every week for 3 months without being asked, this might serve as an outward sign that regaining trust is important. This indicates that commitment to the relationship is firm.

Personal injury inflicted on us by others becomes a part of who we are, but it does not have to be the whole of who we are (Lulofs, 1994). Expressing forgiveness, and acting in ways that show forgiveness, can heal.

Culture and Conflict

The value differences between cultures discussed extensively in Chapter 3 highlight the potential for intercultural conflict. Misinterpretation of a person's intentions and behavior is common when value differences are pronounced. The ways individuals from different cultures manage conflict can pose significant problems as we become a more multicultural society (Box 9-4).

Individualist and collectivist values markedly influence the communication styles of conflict management that are preferred when conflict erupts. Consider differences between Chinese and Americans. Chinese culture, far more collectivist

Box 9-4 Sharper Focus

Managing Cultural Conflicts

Two Japanese students, Norrie Kobayashi and Kentaro Ebiko, were raised in Japan but had lived in the United States for 3 years and had been dating each other for 7 months when they were interviewed. As you read this brief excerpt from their interview, notice how they attest to the influence on conflict management of the cultural value of collectivism, with its high-context (indirect, ambiguous) communication style.

QUESTION: According to researchers, there are considerable differences between the way conflicts are dealt with in the United States and Japan. Do you agree?

KENTARO: Definitely. In the U.S.A. being direct and expressive is very important. In Japan, just the opposite is true. You almost never talk about conflicts there, at least not openly.

QUESTION: If people don't talk about conflicts, how do they resolve them?

KENTARO: Sometimes they don't. In Japan the tradition is not to show your emotions. Outside appearances are very important. If you're upset, you still act as if everything is okay. So there are lots of times when you might be disappointed or angry with somebody and they would never know it.

QUESTION: Do conflicts ever get expressed?

KENTARO: They aren't discussed openly, assertively very often. But in Japan a lot more is communicated nonverbally. If you guess that the other person is unhappy from the way they act, you might try to change to please them. But even then you wouldn't necessarily talk about the conflict directly.

QUESTION: Norie, does Kentaro hide his feelings very well?

NORIE: No! He's more American than I am in this way. . . .

QUESTION: It sounds like you're less comfortable facing conflicts than Kentaro?

NORIE: That's right. I think it's partly my Japanese upbringing and partly just my personality but I don't like to confront people. For example, I was having a hard time studying and sleeping because one of my housemates would wash clothes late at night. I wanted her to stop, but I would never have talked to her directly. I asked my housemother to take care of the problem. Asking a third party is very common in Japan.

Source: Chen and Starosta, 1998b, pp. 151–152.

than American culture, emphasizes harmony as a goal. "The Chinese consider harmony as the universal path which we all should pursue. Only when harmony is reached and prevails throughout heaven and earth can all things be nourished and flourish" (Chen & Starosta, 1998a, p. 6). A conflict-free interpersonal relationship, therefore, is the ultimate goal (Chen & Starosta, 1998a).

The Chinese philosophy of harmonious relationships translates into a strong desire to avoid a conflict with a friend or member of an in-group (e.g., family). When conflicts are unavoidable, there is a preference for accommodating, not confronting, the dispute, so harmony is maintained (Chen & Starosta, 1998a). Handling a dispute ineptly can bring shame, a loss of face, not just on the individual but also on the individual's entire family. Thus, one must avoid stirring up trouble for fear of bringing shame on the family (Yu, 1997).

Conflicts with individuals from an out-group, however, are often handled quite differently among Chinese than are conflicts within the group. Although not the initial choice, competing is not an uncommon way to approach conflict with outsiders, especially if the interests of the opposing parties are highly incompatible. Vicious quarrels, even physical fights, are not uncommon in such circumstances (Chen & Starosta, 1998a; Yu, 1997).

Imagine the difficulty that would occur when an American and a Chinese try to resolve a conflict. Americans favor direct, competing or compromising styles of conflict management. These styles clash with the avoiding and accommodating styles initially favored by Chinese. Consider a slightly different intercultural conflict with similar difficulties. Tannen (1998) cites an example of a Japanese woman married to a Frenchman. The French love to argue, in fact, they may change topics at the dinner table until they find one that ignites a disagreement. For the first 2 years of marriage, this Japanese woman spent a great deal of time in tears. She tried accommodating her husband and avoided arguing with him. This seemed to frustrate him. He would try to find something to start an argument. Finally, she couldn't take it any more, and she began yelling at him. Her husband was thrilled. To him, starting an argument with his wife showed that he valued her intelligence and that he was interested in her. Enthusiastic debate between partners was considered a sign of a solid relationship.

Many Middle Eastern and Mediterranean cultures favor a forceful, aggressive, argumentative style of communication typical of power-forcing (Samovar & Porter, 1995). Native Americans in the United States find assertiveness too direct and aggressive displays of anger distasteful (Moghaddam et al., 1993).

The key to effective intercultural conflict management is flexibility. If you find yourself in a situation or relationship that calls for intercultural conflict management, try broadening your approach to conflict. Learn to use all conflict styles well, not just those you are most comfortable with or used to using. Change to a different style when a conflict style seems to clash with another person's cultural values. If you know that someone comes from a collectivist culture, don't abandon collaborating, but be prepared to seek accommodation wherever possible. In any case, recognize that competing is as ineffective and troublesome to use interculturally as it is to use intraculturally. When you make mistakes, and you will, be prepared to apologize. Seek forgiveness for embarrassing or shaming the other person. Elaborate apologies work best when the insult or embarrassment seems to be great. Above all, try to empathize with people whose cultural values and standards are different from your own. Consider their perspective and respect their right to disagree. Find ways to build bridges between culturally diverse individuals, not tear them down.

Summary

Most people view conflict with some dread. Conflict, however, can be constructive as well as destructive. Our communication determines the difference. Destructive conflict is typified by escalating spirals of conflict that can easily turn ugly. Constructive conflict is characterized by controlling or de-escalating conflict by using a We-orientation, cooperation, and flexibility in applying communication styles of conflict management. There are five communication styles of conflict management. They are collaborating, accommodating, compromising, avoiding, and competing. Collaborating has the greatest potential for appropriately and effectively managing conflict; competing has the least potential. Learning to control our anger and to manage the anger of others is an important part of dealing with conflict effectively. The final stage of conflict is forgiveness. Forgiveness is letting go of the desire for revenge and retaliation. Intercultural conflicts can be extremely difficult to manage because members of individualist and collectivist cultures differ dramatically in how they view conflict and how best to manage it.

Suggested Readings

Fisher, R., & Brown, S. (1988). *Getting together: Building a relationship that gets to yes.* Boston: Houghton Mifflin. This is an extension of *Getting to Yes* in which collaborative principles of negotiation are applied to interpersonal relationships.

Fisher, R., & Ury, W. (1981). *Getting to yes: Negotiating agreement without giving in.* New York: Penguin. This is the bible of collaborative negotiation. Fisher and Ury have made a strong case for cooperative approaches to negotiation.

Stone, D., Patton, B., & Heen, S. (1999). *Difficult conversations: How to discuss what matters most.* New York: Viking. This is a very good treatment of how to keep conflict constructive.

Tavris, C. (1989). *Anger: The misunderstood emotion.* New York: Simon & Schuster. Tavris debunks many myths about anger and how to express it constructively.

Ury, W. (1993). *Getting past no: Negotiating your way from confrontation to cooperation.* New York: Bantam. Ury provides many creative ways to transform a competitive negotiation into a more cooperative one.

Group Communication

Chapter 10

The Anatomy of Small Groups

"A camel is a horse designed by a committee." Countless individuals have passed along this cynical witticism as a sage observation about groups. Similarly, J. B. Hughes comments, "If Moses had been a committee, the Israelites would still be in Egypt." Richard Harkness offers this: "What is a committee? A group of the unwilling, picked from the unfit, to do the unnecessary." Then there is this anonymous contribution: "Trying to solve a problem through group discussion is like trying to clear up a traffic jam by honking your horn."

Groups clearly suffer from bad public relations. It seems that almost everyone has a negative opinion about working in groups. Sorensen (1981) coined the term **"grouphate"** to describe this negative view. The most interesting finding from her research, however, was that individuals who received the most instruction in communicating competently in groups had the most positive view of groups. Instruction in communicating competently in groups directly influences our perception of the group experience. As is true of so many things in life, if you do not have the knowledge and skills necessary to perform effectively and appropriately, the value you ascribe to the experience is low, and your enjoyment is diminished.

There are good reasons to feel negatively about groups. Often, they seem to be an impediment to decision making and problem solving, not an aid. Probably everyone, however, can point to one, two, or a few very positive experiences with groups. The experience may have been with a sports team, a study group at school, a family activity, a project team at work, or a social gathering of friends. The most successful teams are composed of individuals who love working in groups (Goleman, 1998). A basic question to ask is why some group experiences are unpleasant and others a joy. Finding answers to this question is important because there is no escaping the group experience—regardless of how you feel about groups now.

Primary groups such as family and friends provide us with warmth, affection, support, and a sense of belonging. **Social groups** such as fraternities and sororities, athletic teams, and hobby or special interest groups share a common purpose or pursue common goals. **Service groups** such as PTAs, Kiwanis and Lions clubs, Habitat for Humanity, and many campus clubs help others. **Self-help/support groups** empower individuals to deal with addictive behavior, physical or mental illness, or make life transitions. There is a self-help group for almost every medical disorder identified by the World Health Organization (Balgopal et al., 1992). In California alone there are approximately 4,000 self-help/support groups, and in the United States about 7.6 million people participate in such groups (Lieberman & Snowden, 1993). "The self-help and support group phenomenon reminds us of the importance of groups in meeting human needs" (Kurtz, 1997, p. xiii).

"Most of the important decisions that affect your work life are made by groups" (Tropman, 1988, p. 7). Work teams have become increasingly popular in organizations across the United States. **Work teams** are self-managed groups that work on specific tasks or projects within an organization. Nearly half of all U.S. employees will participate in work teams as we enter the 21st century (Freeman, 1996).

Study groups are an outgrowth of cooperative learning strategies. **Study groups** are an increasingly popular way to learn academic course material by sharing knowledge and understanding with other students. A Harvard University study found that college students learn more "when they do at least some of their studying in small groups rather than logging long, solitary hours of study" (Fiske, 1990, p. A1).

This is not an exhaustive list of groups, but the point is clear. There is no escaping groups, so we had best learn how to make them a positive experience.

A positive group experience begins with knowledge of how groups function. The primary purpose of this chapter is to learn the nature of small groups. There are three primary objectives:

1. to explore the advantages and disadvantages of communicating in groups,
2. to analyze the structure of small groups, and
3. to learn communication strategies that can improve the small group experience.

First, let's define what a group is. A **group** is composed of three or more individuals, interacting for the achievement of some common purpose(s), who influence and are influenced by one another. Two people qualify as a couple or dyad, not a group. Communication between two people is typically viewed as an interpersonal transaction, not a group transaction. Also, a group is not merely any aggregation of people, such as 10 strangers standing in line waiting to buy tickets to a rock concert. These strangers are not standing in line to achieve a common purpose, such as helping each other buy tickets. The same is true for a crowd in a shopping mall or a collection of people waiting to board a plane. In both cases the presence of other individuals is irrelevant to the achievement of a common purpose, which is buying clothes or traveling from point A to point B. To qualify as a group, three or more people must succeed or fail *as a unit* in a quest to achieve a common purpose. The essence of a group, therefore, is a We- not Me-orientation. As Zander (1982) notes, "A body of people is not a group if the members are primarily interested in individual accomplishment" (p. 2). Any of these examples, of course, could qualify as a group if circumstances required united action to achieve a mutual goal.

The focus here is on *small groups,* but trying to draw a meaningful line between small and large groups is problematic. Communication theorists typically set the upper limit on small groups at between 12 (the size of most juries) and 25 individuals. Some teams, however, can be composed of 30 or more members and still be viewed as small by corporate standards. There is no absolute number, however, that clearly demarcates small from large groups. It seems more appropriate to define groups in terms of process, not number of individuals. Groups are small as long as each individual in the group can recognize and interact with every other group member. Recognition means knowing who is in the group and remembering something about their specific behavior when the group met.

Pros and Cons of Groups

It is easy to be cynical about groups, but groups have significant benefits as well as disadvantages. Both advantages and disadvantages of groups are addressed in this section.

Group Size

With groups, size matters. All small groups are not created equal. A group composed of 3 members doesn't function the way a group of 10 does. As the size of the group increases, complexity of group transactions and decision making increase enormously. The possible number of interpersonal relationships between group members grows exponentially as group size increases. Bostrom (1970) provides these calculations:

Group Size	Number of Possible Relationships
3	9
4	28
5	75
6	186
7	441
8	1,056

A triad, or three-member group, has nine possible interpersonal relationships, as shown in Figure 10-1.

The relationship member A has with member B may not be the same as the relationship member B has with A. Member A may see the relationship with member B as close; B may see it as just a work relationship, no more. Different perceptions of relationships increase the complexity of transactions between group members. Individual members also can have very different relationships with two or more other members (see 7, 8, and 9 in Figure 10-1). Adding even one member to a group is not an inconsequential event. As newscaster Jane Pauley once observed on the *Today Show*, "Somehow three children are many more than two."

Several disadvantages emerge as groups increase in size and complexity. First, the number of nonparticipants in group discussions increases when groups grow much beyond six members. Reticent members may be intimidated by the prospect of speaking to a group, especially a large one. Second, larger groups easily become factionalized. Members of like mind may splinter into smaller factions, or subgroups, to withstand the pressure from other members to conform to the majority opinion on an issue. Third, larger groups may take much more time to make decisions than smaller groups. With more members, there are potentially more voices to be heard on issues being discussed. Finally, even scheduling a meeting at a time when all members are available can be a daunting task when groups grow large. Schedule conflicts are inevitable with groups of 10 or more.

Smaller groups avoid the disadvantages of larger groups. They are less complex and factionalized and more efficient than larger groups. Small groups, however, can be too small to be effective. Too few members may provide too few resources to make decisions and solve problems effectively. A larger group of, perhaps, seven can provide more input and has a potentially greater knowledge pool to assist in decision making. Also, complex, politically charged issues may require much larger groups (10 or more) just to give a voice to all interested factions.

So what is the ideal group size? Offering a precise number would be arbitrary and debatable. Instead, *the smallest size capable of fulfilling the purposes of the group should be considered optimum.* Each group experience is unique. The key point is to keep groups relatively small to reap the greatest advantages. As groups grow in size, complexity and potential difficulties increase.

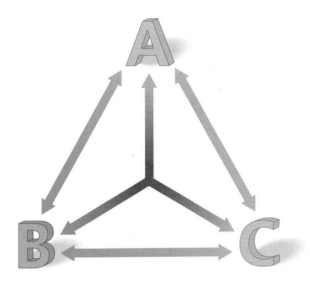

Figure 10-1 Number of Possible Relationships in a Group of Three

1. A to B   2. B to A

3. A to C   4. C to A

5. B to C   6. C to B

7. A to B and C   8. B to A and C

9. C to A and B

Support From Groups

Support and self-help groups have become a national phenomenon. The diversity of such groups is astonishing. Alcoholics Anonymous, the original self-help group, has been imitated by groups such as Depressives Anonymous, Gamblers Anonymous, Cocaine Anonymous, Batterers Anonymous, Impotents Anonymous, Prostitutes Anonymous, Families Anonymous, Parents Anonymous, and Overeaters Anonymous. There are groups for most addictive behaviors, physical or mental illnesses, life transitions (e.g., Recently Divorced Catholics), and friends and relatives of those with a problem (e.g., Adult Children of Alcoholics). Support groups range from the conventional to the bizarre.

Some of the more unusual support groups include Hot Flashes (for menopausal women), Good Tidings (for women who continually fall in love with priests), Crossroads (for male transvestites), and Compulsive Shoppers. An unnamed support group was organized in 1993 by a hypnotherapist to assist the poor unfortunates who have been abducted by extraterrestrials (the ultimate illegal aliens) and lived to tell about it. Even distraught rock fans, grief-ridden at the news of a recently departed rock star can find a support group, such as the group that formed after the Grateful Dead's Jerry Garcia died in 1995.

Most support and self-help groups are small, and even the larger organizations such as Alcoholics Anonymous operate from local chapters whose group meetings typically include 8 to 12 members (Kurtz, 1997). Research on support groups reveals that they give emotional support to members, impart information, share experiences, convey a sense of belonging, and teach coping methods to deal with problems common to the group (Kurtz, 1997). In a word, support groups *empower* members. This is a significant advantage of groups.

The attraction to support groups is more than sharing a common bond brought about by similar problems. It is also the desire to learn how to solve difficult problems and to cope with life's tribulations by receiving support, comfort, and advice from fellow sufferers.

Synergy

Synergy is the product of cooperation within a group. The end product of efforts by group members working cooperatively isn't necessarily just the sum of those individual efforts. Sometimes the whole is greater than the sum of its parts. **Synergy** (syn = together + ergon = work) occurs when the work of group members yields a greater total effect than the sum of the individual members' efforts could have produced. When this joint action of group members produces performance that exceeds expectations based on perceived abilities and skills of individual members, synergy has occurred (Salazar, 1995). Synergy is like combining cancer-fighting drugs to produce far greater effects than taking the drugs separately could produce. This is the basis of chemotherapy.

A study of military tank crews showed results that far exceeded what was predicted based on the individual abilities of crew members (Tziner & Eden, 1985). As Chairman of the Joint Chiefs of Staff, Colin Powell applauded the benefits of synergy as a military strategy in times of war ("New Pentagon," 1991).

An NBC News at Sunrise report on June 23, 1998, reported an apt example of synergy. A Little League team in Tucson, Arizona, called the Diamondbacks, was composed of players no other teams wanted because they were considered misfits that were not good enough to play. These misfits compiled a perfect record of 18−0 to win the league championship. The group effort far exceeded expectations of success based on the individual abilities of the players.

How does synergy happen? It occurs primarily through teamwork based on cooperation and the We-orientation. Individuals work together, unselfishly, in a coordinated effort to achieve a common goal. Rafael Aguayo (1990) draws from his own experience as a Little League soccer coach to explain how synergy occurs. Aguayo emphasized having fun, improving skill levels, and teamwork. He deemphasized winning. Before each game he told his players that scoring goals and winning weren't important. Playing hard, improving skills, and acting like a team were important. After a game, he would ask his players, "Who scored that first goal?" At first, the player who scored the first goal would raise a hand. "No!" Aguayo would cry. "We all scored that goal. Every person on a team is responsible for scoring a goal." Then he repeated his question, "Now, who scored that goal?" All the players on the team raised their hands. Aguayo never singled out any player as better than any other. Instead, he gave *every* team member a "best player" trophy at the end of the season. Each player got to be captain at least once. What were the results of this experiment in cooperation, teamwork, and a We- not Me-orientation? Synergy was the result. In the 4 years Aguayo coached Little League soccer, his team lost only a single game.

Even in a larger competitive environment, cooperation can thrive. Aguayo's coaching philosophy echoed that of legendary college basketball coach, John Wooden. "Many people are surprised to learn that in 27 years at UCLA, I never once talked about winning. . . . I always taught players that the main ingredient of stardom is the rest of the team" (as cited in Aguayo, 1990, p. 99). Wooden's teams never had a losing season. In his final 12 years of coaching at UCLA, his teams won 10 national championships, 7 in a row (both current records). His teams hold the world record for the longest winning streak in any major sport—88 games without a loss. Groups don't have to be a hateful experience. Sometimes groups can surpass our wildest expectations. The synergy produced through teamwork can make the group experience joyful.

Groups don't always produce synergy, however. Sometimes groups produce results that are beyond bad. This is called negative synergy. **Negative synergy** is the product of joint action of group members that produces a result worse than that expected based on perceived individual abilities and skills of members (Salazar, 1995). The whole is not greater than the sum of its parts in this case. Instead, the whole is less than the sum of its parts. Negative synergy is like mixing alcohol and tranquilizers, which can cause accidental death. The mixture is far worse than the sum of the effects produced when taking each separately.

I give cooperative exams in my classes. Group members work on the exam together and turn in a single answer sheet. An individual accountability test, which sets a minimum standard of performance to earn the group grade, follows the group exam. Most groups score much higher than the average of individual test scores (synergy) and often higher than any member of the group scores on the individual test. Occasionally, however, negative synergy occurs. On one exam all the groups but one scored in the 80s or 90s. One group of six, however, scored 50. Their group score was actually *lower* than the average of their individual scores. The group performed worse than any group member. I had listened to their discussion during the test, and I heard members talk the group into choosing incorrect answers. The group was capable of scoring much higher on the test, but lack of motivation, poor communication in the group, lackluster preparation, and conflict diminished their result.

Synergy won't magically occur simply because individuals form a group. A single expert on a technical topic can provide better advice than a group of uninformed members. If you have a legal question, go see a good lawyer. Seeking legal advice from a group of friends who know next to nothing about the law is inviting disaster. Nevertheless, groups can often produce exceptional results because they can share the labor required to research even technical or complex subjects, they can pool knowledge and share information, and they can correct errors more readily because there are more heads devoted to spotting mistakes and misjudgments (Rothwell, 1998). As the Japanese proverb says, "None of us is as smart as all of us."

Social Loafing

Social loafing is one of the most common complaints about working in groups. Members do not share the same level of commitment to the group and the task. Those who are fully committed, even inspired, to work in the group, become demoralized and frustrated by the apathy and disinterest shown by one or more group members. **Social loafing** is the tendency of individuals to reduce their work effort when they join groups. Social loafers "goof off" when tasks need to be accomplished. They miss some meetings and show up late to others. They fail to complete tasks important to overall group performance. Social loafers exhibit scant effort because of weak motivation, disinterest in the group, or poor attitude. Social loafing is not the same as shyness. Shy individuals may have a strong motivation to work in the group but are reticent to participate in discussions because of communication anxiety or fear of disapproval. Shy members may attend all meetings and never be tardy.

Social loafing is a serious disadvantage of working in groups. Social loafing increases with group size. One study (Latane et al., 1979) asked participants to clap and cheer "as loud as you can." These efforts were measured as individuals, dyads (two partners), and four- or six-person groups. Dyads performed at 71% of each person's individual capacity, four-person groups at 51%, and six-person groups at only 40%. Social loafing occurs because individual group members often do not see the connection between their personal effort and the outcomes desired by the group (Karau & Williams, 1993).

Social loafing occurs in a broad range of groups working on a variety of tasks. Males and females of all ages and from many different cultures may be social loafers. Social loafing is more common in an individualist culture such as that of the United States than it is in collectivist cultures such as those of Singapore, China, Thailand, Pakistan, and Indonesia (Early, 1989; Gabreyna, 1985). People in individualist cultures are not as heavily influenced as those in collectivist cultures by what the group might think of a person's effort. Individual group members may establish their "uniqueness" by showing how uninvolved they can be, even in the face of group pressure to perform. In collectivist cultures, however, pleasing the group, maintaining group harmony, and submerging individual accomplishment for the sake of the group encourage strong group commitment and discourage loafing. The collectivist attitude is "don't let the group down." Lackluster performance by loafers could bring loss of face.

So what steps can be taken to address this common problem? How can you diminish or eliminate the disadvantage of social loafing associated with group work? Motivation is the root of this problem. There are no magic formulas, no simple list of dos and don'ts, that will motivate loafers.

Before discussing what might motivate loafers, let's be very clear regarding what doesn't motivate others. Exhortations from motivated group members usually have no lasting effect on loafers. This is analogous to hiring a "motivational speaker" to lecture employees in the workplace. Kohn (1993) sums up the failure of this approach: "At best, the result is a temporary sense of being re-energized, much like the effect of eating a doughnut. When the sugar high wears off, very little of value is left in the system" (p. 187). Cheerleading doesn't address a loafer's lack of interest in the group and its tasks. It assumes that every member can be inspired, even if the group task is tedious.

Performance evaluation also is unlikely to jump-start a loafer, especially if it is tied to some kind of reward system (Aguayo, 1990; Kohn, 1993). Grading a group member's effort, aside from the obvious difficulties of determining objective criteria for such an evaluation, creates a defensive atmosphere. This is especially true when the appraisal results in a reward or punishment. In the workplace, performance evaluations are often tied to wages and other forms of compensation. Exceptional work earns a bonus. Poor appraisal of a worker typically results in no pay increase or even a pay reduction. Consultant Peter Scholtes (1990) says, "Using performance appraisal of any kind as a basis for reward is a flat out catastrophic mistake" (p. 46). The likely result of such schemes is demotivation of workers given mediocre or poor appraisals for lackluster performance.

Any step that creates a competitive, defensive environment is unlikely to motivate social loafers (Kohn, 1993). Kohn (1993) offers "the three C's of motivation" that encourage cooperation, not competition. The three C's are collaboration, content, and choice. These are aspects of teamwork, a subject to be discussed in detail in Chapter 11.

Collaboration is the cooperative style of conflict management. It is also synonymous with teamwork. Developing teamwork and cooperation can motivate loafers because they no longer see themselves as individuals separate from the group. They identify with the group. Groups that achieve success and receive rewards for such success typically have little problem with loafers. This is especially so when each group member perceives that his or her individual effort is necessary for the group to succeed (Karau & Williams, 1993). If a group member's individual performance can be identified separately from the group's, social loafing also decreases (Karau & Williams, 1993). When a group member has been given a specific task to perform and he or she does not complete the task because of weak effort, the entire group notices. Not wanting to let the team down can be a powerful motivator.

Content refers to the group task. What work are group members asked to perform? "Idleness, indifference and irresponsibility are healthy responses to absurd work," claims Frederick Herzberg (as cited in Kohn, 1993, p. 189). Few group members will be motivated to work on tasks that hold no interest for them. Granted, not all tasks can be motivating. Some tasks have to be performed even though they are dreary, tedious jobs. Nevertheless, busy work and paper chasing should be kept to a minimum so the totality of a group's work is viewed as involving and interesting. Group members need to see the value of performing a task before they are likely to take responsibility for meeting their individual obligations to the group effort. Social loafing decreases when group members see work as meaningful (Karau & Williams, 1993).

Choice is a nice complement to content. One way of making group projects and tasks challenging and interesting to group members is to allow as much choice as possible. Try letting group members choose which part of a project they would most like to tackle. Arbitrarily imposing task assignments on group members will quickly produce loafing, even grumbling. Let group members participate in decision making. That's what encourages teamwork and cooperation. Group tasks become meaningful when members have a say in what is done and how it is accomplished.

Kohn's three C's provide general principles for motivating group members and discouraging social loafing. Teamwork is the overall solution.

Meetings

The major difference between meetings and funerals is that "most funerals have a definite purpose. Also, nothing is ever really buried in a meeting." So claims humorist Dave Barry (1991, p. 311). Having to attend meetings is perceived by many to be a serious disadvantage of group work. Grouphate is nourished by the prevalent belief that group meetings are mostly a waste of time. Studies have found that about a third of the time spent in meetings is wasted, costing billions of dollars to organizations and businesses (Green & Lazarus, 1990; Lazar, 1991). Business consultant Mitchell Nash (as cited in Dressler, 1995) identifies six common complaints made about group meetings: (1) the meeting has an unclear purpose, (2) participants are unprepared, (3) key individuals are absent or tardy, (4) discussion drifts into irrelevant conversation, (5) some group members dominate discussion, and (6) decisions made at meetings often are not implemented.

Meetings don't have to be time-wasters. Whoever chairs a meeting can take steps that will make the meeting productive and efficient. Here are some suggestions:

1. Don't call a meeting unless no other good alternative exists. If immediate action is required, group participation is essential, group members are prepared to discuss relevant issues, and main players can be present, then hold a meeting. If objectives can be met without a meeting, don't meet. One of life's little pleasures is the surprise notification, "Meeting has been cancelled."

2. Identify the specific purpose of the meeting. Notify each group member of where the meeting will be held and when and how long it will likely last. Let participants know if they should bring certain materials or resources to the meeting. Encourage each member to be prepared to discuss important issues. Typically, only about a quarter of group members are prepared most of the time for meetings (Green & Lazarus, 1990).

3. Prepare a clear agenda that lists the topics of discussion in the order that they will be addressed. Include a time allotment for discussion of each issue (Box 10-1). Provide accurate, concise information on issues discussed.

4. Above all, keep the discussion on track. Don't allow drift. Aimless discussion sucks the life out of meetings. Also, do not allow any member to hog the stage. Encourage participation from all members.

5. Start the meeting on time and be guided by the "what's done is done" rule (Tropman, 1996). Do not interrupt the flow of the meeting by bringing latecomers up to speed except to indicate which item on the agenda is under discussion. Latecomers can be filled in briefly after the meeting or during a break if necessary.

Box 10-1   Sharper Focus

A Sample Agenda for Group Meetings

Meeting of the Student Senate
November 15, 1999
Boardroom
2:00–4:00 p.m.

Purpose: Biweekly meeting

  I. Call meeting to order

 II. Approval of the minutes of last meeting (5 minutes)

III. Additions to the agenda (2 minutes)

 IV. Committee reports
    A. Student clubs committee (5 minutes)
    B. Student transportation committee (5 minutes)
    C. Student activities committee (5 minutes)

  V. Officers' reports

    A. Treasurer's report (3 minutes)
    B. President's report (10 minutes)

 VI. Old business (previously discussed but unresolved)
    A. Campus security problems (15 minutes)
    B. Cost of textbooks (10 minutes)
    C. Parking garage proposal (10 minutes)
    D. Student credit card proposal (5 minutes)

VII. New business
    A. Hate speech on campus (15 minutes)
    B. Expanding the bookstore (10 minutes)
    C. Open access computer use (10 minutes)
    D. Student elections (5 minutes)

VIII. Agenda building for next meeting (5 minutes)

 IX. Adjournment

Instructors don't restart classes each time a student comes in late. Nothing would get accomplished. Concerts aren't stopped in midstream to accommodate those who amble in late. Movies aren't rewound and begun again when latecomers appear 20 minutes into the movie. Punctuality discourages late arrival, especially when the meeting moves forward and isn't derailed by tardiness.

6. Do not discuss an issue longer than the time allotted unless the group decides to extend the time. This prevents talkaholics from pointlessly extending the meeting well beyond expectations. Three out of four meetings don't end on time (Green & Lazarus, 1990). Meetings that end ahead of time are cause for celebration; those that end late are cause for exasperation.

7. Take a few minutes at the end of the meeting to determine if all objectives were accomplished. Two thirds of meetings fail to accomplish stated objectives (Green & Lazarus, 1990). Schedule time in the next meeting to consider any unresolved issues.

8. Distribute minutes of the meeting to all participants as soon as possible. The minutes should indicate what was discussed, who said what, what action was taken, and what remains to be discussed and decided.

The meeting monster can be slain and grouphate quelled if these simple steps are followed to keep meetings efficient and productive.

The advantages of working in groups are many. Groups can pool knowledge and information, correct errors often missed by an individual working alone, accomplish broad-range tasks by sharing the load among members, and, above all, empower group members and produce synergy. The main disadvantages of groups—factionalism, scheduling conflicts, negative synergy, social loafing, and wasting time in meetings—are correctable. The group experience can be unpleasant if we allow it to be, but it does not have to be that way.

The Structure of Small Groups

Every group has a discernable structure. In this section you will learn about group structure, which is composed of the relationship between task and social dimensions, norms, and roles.

Task and Social Dimensions

Every group has two primary interconnected dimensions. The **task dimension** is the work performed by the group and its impact on the group. The **social dimension** consists of relationships between group members and the impact these relationships have on the group.

Interconnectedness of Productivity and Cohesiveness   Walter V. Clarke Associates, a consulting firm, conducted a study of more than 700 professional athletes, NFL draft choices, and college players. They found that skill at performing tasks is not enough to be successful in groups (as cited in Goleman, 1998). Gifted athletes who haven't mastered how to work cooperatively with group members can create havoc. Athletes who listened poorly, wouldn't take directions, and came late to meetings were rated by their coaches as being less motivated, harder to coach, less talented, and less likely to be leaders. Although technical, task-oriented skills are important, a study by the U.S. Department of Labor Employment and Training Administration (Carnevale, 1996) showed that the critical skills are all socially oriented—oral communication, interpersonal communication, and teamwork abilities (see also Goleman, 1998).

The goal of the task dimension is **productivity.** The extent of a group's productivity is determined by the degree to which it accomplishes its work efficiently and effectively. The goal of the social dimension is *cohesiveness.* The extent of a group's cohesiveness depends on the degree to which members identify with the group and wish to remain in the group (Langfred, 1998).

One national survey (Silva, 1982) found that the cohesiveness of sports teams was the number one concern of coaches. Why?—because cohesiveness and productivity (performance) are interconnected; one affects the other (Cohen & Bailey, 1997). High cohesiveness alone doesn't guarantee group success, but it seems to be a necessary condition for successful task accomplishment. When groups lack cohesiveness, their productivity typically suffers. Small groups of exceedingly talented individuals will not accomplish tasks well if interpersonal relations among members are immersed in disharmony, anger, resentments, hostilities, and rivalries (Goleman, 1995). Low cohesiveness almost always dooms a group to poor performance and low productivity. Members who do not like each other and wish they weren't a part of the group will typically exhibit feeble effort and poor performance. Competitiveness among group members, especially when combined with time pressure to accomplish tasks, diminishes cohesiveness (Klein, 1996).

Group members can be so cohesive, however, that they become too concerned with maintaining harmony. When disagreement is avoided because members fear disrupting group cohesiveness, error correction may be sacrificed. This is one aspect of groupthink, a problem for later discussion.

Finding the proper balance between productivity and cohesiveness is a persistent dialectical struggle in all groups. Too much focus on productivity can strain interpersonal relationships within a group. Too much focus on cohesiveness can lead to anemic effort on the task. Strong cohesiveness combined with a strong group work ethic is an effective combination (Langfred, 1998). Both task and social dimensions should be addressed, not one at the expense of the other.

Dealing With Difficult Group Members In one of my small group classes, a group of six women was formed to work on a class project. Their communication was warm, friendly, and harmonious. They appeared enthusiastic about working together. They brainstormed a long list of ideas for their project and settled on one option within a short period of time. The following class period, a male student needed to join a group because he had missed the previous class. He joined the all-women group because other groups in the class were already somewhat larger. This new group member single-handedly transformed a harmonious, task-effective group into a frustrating group experience for everyone. This particular individual enjoyed telling sexist jokes, making derogatory remarks to the other members, and fighting any suggestions that were not his own. He proudly (and loudly) proclaimed to the entire class that he was the "leader of a chicks group." He also told his astonished group members that he "hoped PMS wouldn't be a problem" when they worked on their project.

The women were stunned. After class, they all approached me and requested that this disruptive individual be assigned to another group. I turned down their request, not wanting to pass the problem to another group. When I asked what steps they had taken to deal with their difficult group member, they confessed that none had yet been taken. This is not unusual. When faced with a difficult group member, ridding the group of the troublemaker is a common first response. As previously discussed, however, the power-forcing conflict style should be used as a last resort, not a first option.

The pervasiveness of troublesome group members is significant. A 1991 survey of U.S. employers conducted by the Harris Education Research Council found that 40% of employees do not work cooperatively with fellow employees (as cited in Goleman, 1998). Their communication patterns are defensive, not supportive. They are not team players but Me-oriented individualists. They diminish the group performance by disrupting social relationships. Difficult group members can destroy group cohesiveness.

So what should you do about difficult members? You can take several steps (Rothwell, 1998). First, *make certain a cooperative atmosphere has been created by the group.* Are communication patterns supportive or defensive? Is meaningful participation encouraged? Are all group members treated with respect? Is there an interdependence of goals and division of labor and resources? Troublesome group members can be a cancer that threatens the health of a group. Problems associated with troublemakers will spread if the group climate is competitive and defensive.

Second, *don't encourage disruptive behavior.* Laughing nervously at a disrupter's offensive "jokes" encourages the antisocial behavior. All six women laughed nervously at the disrupter's sexist jokes and remarks. He became convinced that the women actually appreciated his humor. He had no antenna to pick up fairly obvious signals from his group members that they were offended and embarrassed by his behavior. When a feedback form was filled out weeks later by all group members, his self-assessment showed that he believed the female group members thought he was funny and liked his humor. He was flabbergasted when all six women wrote on their feedback form that his humor was offensive and disruptive.

Don't allow the disrupter to dominate conversations, interrupt other members, or in any way intimidate the group. Giving the troublemaker a soapbox only encourages the bad behavior. Simply ask the disrupter to wait his or her turn, respect other members, and listen.

Third, *confront the difficult person directly* (see Chapter 9). If the entire group is upset with the disrupter, the group should confront the troublemaker. Follow the guidelines for supportive communication when confronting a difficult member.

Fourth, if all else fails, *remove the disrupter from the group.* In one study (Larson & LaFasto, 1989) of 75 diverse teams, a very clear message emerged: "There is no longer any room on teams for people who cannot work collaboratively" (p. 71). Ruth Rothstein, who at the time of the study was CEO of Mt. Sinai Hospital in Chicago, summarized this point of view:

> One person who doesn't work well with others can set the team off into oblivion. One person like this can ruin a team. When that happens, you give feedback to [confront] that individual and help them make the necessary changes. But if they can't adapt, then you have an obligation to remove them from the team. Otherwise, the rest of the team can become pretty resentful. (p. 71)

If the troublesome group member cannot be removed for some reason, keep interactions with this person to a minimum. *No matter what, be unconditionally constructive.* Do not reciprocate the bad behavior of the disrupter. Model constructive communication. If you must remain in a group with a difficult member, imitating the disrupter's troublesome behavior will not improve the situation.

So how did the six women in my class manage their disruptive member? None of them would confront him directly, despite my prompting. All of them, however, remained unconditionally constructive. They eventually stopped laughing nervously at his "jokes," and they refused to be bullied by him. Since there were six of them and only one of him, they managed to silence him on several occasions by ignoring his disruption and focusing on the task, thereby giving him no soapbox and no appreciative audience. They all performed wonderfully during their group presentation to the class. He, on the other hand, embarrassed himself by performing ineptly. Sometimes the most you can hope for is containment, not transformation, of the disrupter.

Norms

Andrew Martinez, better known as "the naked guy," gained national attention in the early 1990s for attending classes at the University of California, Berkeley nude. He walked across campus wearing no clothes and sat during class sans attire. Some students objected to his lack of clothing, charging that it was sexual harassment because it created a "hostile environment" for women. Other students, both male and female, countered that Martinez accosted no one, made no lewd gestures, minded his own business, and seemed like a gentle soul trying to make a point. When Martinez appeared before the Berkeley City Council wearing only a smile, however, he inspired passage of a nudity ordinance. Other instances of nudity in Berkeley soon followed. A group of people paraded down Telegraph Avenue wearing only mud smeared on their bodies. Only one case was prosecuted

Every social situation has norms for attire and conduct as this theatre crowd and rock concert gathering illustrate.

under the ordinance. Nina Shilling and her friend Debbie Moore, members of the X-plicit Players theatre troupe, were arrested for performing nude. The women claimed a First Amendment right of free speech, had a jury trial, and were acquitted (Koury, 1998).

Every group, large or small, has norms that guide behavior. **Norms** are rules that indicate what group members have to do (obligation), should do (preference), or cannot do (prohibition) if they want to accomplish specific goals. Norms regulate group behavior. The Berkeley nudity ordinance attempted to regulate public exposure to nudity, with little success. Other locales, however, have had no such difficulty prosecuting violations of similar ordinances. Why the difference? Norms are not absolute. Group members don't necessarily agree that a norm is appropriate.

In this section small group norms are discussed, including types of norms, their purpose and source, and conformity to norms.

Types of Norms   There are two types of norms: explicit and implicit. Explicit norms specifically identify acceptable and unacceptable behavior. Explicit norms are typical of a low-context communication style. You want group members to know unambiguously what behavior is expected, preferred, and prohibited, so you tell members explicitly. No smoking signs posted around campus and in public buildings indicate an explicit norm. Laws of society and by-laws of a group are explicit norms. When your instructor tells the class not to interrupt a student during discussions or to attend regularly and be on time, he or she is providing explicit norms.

In small groups, however, most norms are implicit. You learn implicit norms by observing patterns of behavior in the group: all group members sit in the same seats for every meeting, no one eats or drinks during meetings, all members dress neatly, everyone is polite, humor is never sarcastic or offensive, no one says anything derogatory about any other member. These patterns indicate implicit norms. There is no book of rules on how to behave in such meetings, yet members all act as if there were.

Implicit norms may become explicit on occasion, especially when there is a norm violation. Instructors rarely feel compelled to tell students at the beginning of a school term that loud talking during lectures is unacceptable. This is an implicit norm that is taken for granted. It is unlikely that you would find such a rule in the college catalogue, on the schedule of classes, or on a syllabus. If students have ignored this implicit rule, however, instructors may make the implicit norm explicit by pointedly telling the class that talking while a lecture is in progress should cease.

Purpose of Norms The primary purpose of norms is to achieve group goals. Shimanoff (1992) provides the example of Overeaters Anonymous to illustrate the goal-oriented nature of norms. Losing weight is the principal goal of Overeaters Anonymous groups. Norms help achieve this goal. Members are permitted to talk about food only in general terms (carbohydrates, proteins, and so forth) but not in terms of specific foods (such as candy bars, burgers, or ice cream). The norm is based on the assumption that references to specific foods will induce a craving for those foods and make losing weight more difficult. References to foods in general terms, presumably, will produce no such cravings. Apparently you won't hear the refrigerator calling your name when merely talking about carbohydrates, but mention Ben and Jerry's ice cream and there better be an unobstructed path to the Frigidaire or somebody's going to get trampled.

Conforming to Norms Group members tend to conform to group norms. **Conformity** is the inclination of group members to think and behave in ways that are consistent with group norms. In a study of bulimia (Crandall, 1988), conformity was found to be a primary element of this eating disorder. Bulimia is a problem in certain social groups such as cheerleader squads, dance troupes, sports teams (e.g., gymnastics), and sororities. Norms are established that promote this binge-and-purge behavior. Instead of seeing bulimia as a bizarre and abnormal practice, the groups studied by Crandall promoted bulimia as a reasonable method of weight control. Group norms even prescribed a preferred rate of binging and purging. Popularity within the groups depended on conforming to this standard. Even members who did not initially feel a desire to binge and purge buckled under group pressure and followed the crowd.

Members conform to group norms for two principal reasons. First, it makes group life easier and more orderly than nonconformity. Nonconformity typically triggers a negative response from the group such as social ostracism, personal attack, or expulsion from the group. Members "go along to get along" and to accomplish group goals. Social acceptance, support, and friendship are often the rewards for conformity. Second, conformity can keep lines of communication open. Sources of information are likely to be shared when we conform to group norms. Failure to conform, however, can lead to the severing of informational sources that may be critical to meeting personal goals within the group (Box 10-2).

Box 10-2   Focus on Controversy

Crying in the Workplace

Members of the Committee on Workplace Conditions are meeting to construct a proposal to present to management for improvement of job-related conditions. The discussion becomes heated and members' anger begins to show. One member begins speaking slowly to the group, chokes back tears, apologizes for this display of emotion, then succumbs to the intensity of the moment and cries openly. As this scene was described, did you see an image of a woman or a man crying? What if the crying group member had been a man? Would you make the same assessment of this person as you would if the member were a woman?

Women far more than men are inclined to tear up or openly cry in the workplace (Domagalski, 1998; Hoover-Dempsey et al., 1986). Crying at work is usually an expression of anger and frustration caused by perceived mistreatment. Domineering, uncivil behavior is the most common reason for tears in the office (Domagalski, 1998). In one study, women indicated that they could imagine themselves shedding tears in the workplace, but not yelling, arguing, or "telling someone off" (Hoover-Dempsey et al., 1986). Some of these women said they were ashamed when they cried, others were confused by it, but all of them felt badly about crying at work during and after the episode. Common perceptions of women who cry in the workplace, especially in male-dominated work environments, are "women are not tough enough" and "their crying is unprofessional" (Murphy & Zorn, 1996).

Men far more than women express their anger in the workplace with outbursts of yelling, venting, and rage (Domagalski, 1998). Although this is often not condoned, such outbursts may foster the image of a tough, unyielding individual capable of withstanding any pressure to change. Crying in the workplace, however, does a man no good. "Crying in the office may undermine a woman's credibility as a tough professional, but it can destroy a man's reputation on both personal and professional levels" (Murphy & Zorn, 1996, p. 217).

Crying at work is a violation of an implicit norm. As Kathryn Black unequivocally states (1990) in *Working Woman* magazine, "It's [crying] a response that doesn't belong in the office" (p. 88). A person is expected to act differently at work than at home. Crying can interrupt, even halt, a meeting at work. Shedding tears might be perceived as manipulative—trying to achieve a goal by making others feel uncomfortable (Hoover-Dempsey et al., 1986). Crying in front of coworkers or strangers, especially during group meetings, can leave everyone feeling helpless and uneasy. Group members are usually not prepared to deal with tears and often can't offer much comfort or assistance in a public forum. Crying at home, however, will not be branded as unprofessional behavior. An individual will also likely get greater support and comfort at home than at work when crying occurs. Men can cry at home usually without fear of being labeled "weak" or "too emotional." Norms at home and at work differ.

With an ever-increasing number of women entering the job market, the issue of how to deal with tears in the office and on the job becomes more relevant. Male supervisors report that the mere anticipation of a woman crying causes them great discomfort and induces them to soften criticism or withhold feedback (Murphy & Zorn, 1996). They are unaccustomed to dealing with this nonconformity. Crying is mostly a reflection of anger, as is yelling, slamming doors, and "chewing out" someone. All of these behaviors can be disruptive in the workplace. The advice provided in Chapter 9 on dealing with anger also applies to crying. Domineering, uncivil communication is the usual cause of crying at work. Eliminate or substantially reduce the cause of crying at work, and it will be a rare issue of concern. Competent communication reduces the need to cry, yell, or pound inanimate objects because we're treating people in a sensitive manner.

When crying does occur, all parties to the event can choose to ignore it and continue with the group discussion, take a brief break to allow the person shedding tears to regain composure and perhaps receive comfort and support from others in a more private venue, or acknowledge the tears (Black, 1990a, 1990b). The person who cries might say, "I am crying because I'm angry, but I want to continue discussing this issue until it is resolved." Acknowledging the tears while remaining firmly resolved to produce constructive outcomes may eventually lead to a relaxation of the restrictive norm against crying at work.

Questions for Thought

1. Do you agree with Black that crying is always inappropriate in the workplace? Explain your answer.
2. Can you think of any circumstances where crying at work might be constructive?
3. How should we deal with the stereotype that "real men don't cry" on the job?

Group conformity is strongest when cohesiveness is high, when members expect to be in the group for a long time, and when members perceive that they have somewhat lower status in the group. Groups have little leverage against members who are not committed to the group, don't plan on remaining in the group for long, or have high status that gives them "the right" to occasional nonconformity.

Roles

Roles and norms are interconnected. Small group **roles** are patterns of behavior that members are expected to exhibit. The expectation tied to a role is based on a group norm. We expect leaders to guide the group. If they don't, we usually view them as ineffective.

There are two general types of roles: formal and informal. **Formal roles** assign a position. Formal roles are a standard part of the structure of organizations. Titles such as "president," "chair," or "secretary" usually accompany formal roles. Formal roles do not emerge naturally from group transactions; they are assigned. Normally, an explicit description of expected behaviors corresponds to each formal role.

In small groups, roles are mostly informal. **Informal roles** identify functions, not positions. They usually emerge naturally from group transactions. The informal roles a group member plays are identified by observing patterns of communication. If a member often initiates group discussion, the member is playing the role of initiator-contributor. The group does not explicitly tell a member how to play an informal role. Groups do, however, indicate degrees of approval or disapproval when a member assumes an informal role.

Informal roles are generally divided into three types: task, maintenance, and disruptive roles (Benne & Sheats, 1948; Mudrack & Farrell, 1995). **Task roles** advance the attainment of group goals. The central communicative function of task roles is to extract the optimum productivity from the group. **Maintenance roles** address the social dimension of small groups. The central communicative function of maintenance roles is to gain and maintain group cohesiveness. **Disruptive roles** are Me-oriented. They serve individual needs at the expense of group needs and goals. Group members who play these roles often deserve the label "difficult group member." The central communicative function of disruptive roles is to focus attention on the individual. Competent communicators avoid disruptive roles. Table 10-1 identifies some common task, maintenance, and disruptive roles found in small groups (Benne & Sheats, 1948; Mudrack & Farrell, 1995; Rothwell, 1998). This list is not exhaustive.

Assuming appropriate task and maintenance roles during group discussion is a matter of timing. A devil's advocate is not needed during initial discussion. You do not want to kill potentially creative ideas by immediately challenging them. A harmonizer–tension reliever is needed when conflict emerges and threatens to derail the group discussion. It is irrelevant if there is no tension and disharmony. Disruptive roles embody incompetent communication. Deal with those who act out disruptive roles the way you would approach difficult group members.

Role playing is a fluid process. During a single meeting a group member may play several informal roles. Groups usually function better when members exhibit flexibility by playing several roles, depending on what is required to make the group effective. **Role fixation,** where a member plays a role rigidly with little or no inclination to try other roles, will decrease group effectiveness. The chosen role

Table 10-1 Sample of Informal Roles in Small Groups

Task Roles

1. *Information giver*—provides facts and opinions; offers relevant and significant information based on research, expertise, or personal experience.
2. *Information seeker*—asks for facts, opinions, suggestions, and ideas from group members.
3. *Initiator-contributor*—provides ideas; suggests actions and solutions to problems; offers direction for the group.
4. *Clarifier*—explains ideas; defines the group position on issues; summarizes proceedings of group meetings; raises questions about the direction of group discussion.
5. *Elaborator*—expands the ideas of other group members; helps the group visualize how an idea or solution would work if the group implemented it.
6. *Coordinator-director*—pulls together the ideas of others; promotes teamwork and cooperation; guides group discussion; breaks group into subgroups to work effectively on tasks; regulates group activity.
7. *Energizer*—tries to motivate group to be productive, a task cheerleader.
8. *Procedural technician*—performs routine tasks such as taking notes, photocopying, passing out relevant materials for discussion, finding a room to meet, and signaling when allotted time for discussion of an agenda item has expired.
9. *Devil's advocate*—gently challenges prevailing viewpoints in group to test and evaluate the strength of ideas, solutions, and decisions.

Maintenance Roles

1. *Supporter-encourager*—offers praise; bolsters the spirits and goodwill of the group; provides warmth and acceptance of others.
2. *Harmonizer-tension reliever*—maintains the peace; reduces tension with gentle humor; reconciles differences between group members.
3. *Gatekeeper*—controls the channels of communication, keeping the flow of information open or closed depending on the social climate of the group; encourages participation from all group members and open discussion.

Disruptive Roles

1. *Stagehog*—recognition seeker; monopolizes discussion and prevents others from expressing their points of view; wants the spotlight.
2. *Isolate*—withdraws from group; acts indifferent, aloof, and uninvolved; resists inclusion in group discussion.
3. *Fighter-controller*—tries to dominate group; competes mindlessly with group members; abuses those who disagree; picks quarrels, interrupts, and generally attempts to control group proceedings.
4. *Blocker*—expresses negative attitude; looks to tear down other members' ideas without substituting constructive alternatives; incessantly reintroduces dead issues.
5. *Zealot*—attempts to convert group members to a pet cause or viewpoint; delivers sermons on the state of the world; exhibits fanaticism; won't drop an idea that has been rejected or ignored by group.
6. *Clown*—interjects inappropriate humor during discussions and meetings; engages in horseplay; diverts attention from the group task with comic routines.

will be appropriate only some of the time, but irrelevant or inappropriate most of the time. Every group needs an energizer, but no group needs an energizer all of the time. Constant cheerleading grows tiresome. If that is the only role a member chooses to play, the member will be mostly an annoyance for the group.

Leadership

Gibb (1969) notes: "Almost every influential thinker from Confucius to Bertrand Russell has attempted some form of analysis of leadership" (p. 205). Scholars, philosophers, social scientists, communication theorists, even novelists have shown an interest in leadership. The first recorded use of the word "leadership" appeared in writings about political influence in the British Parliament more than 200 years ago. Egyptian hieroglyphics had a symbol for leader about 5,000 years ago. More than 7,500 scholarly books, articles, and papers have been written on leadership (Dorfman & Howell, 1997).

Leader is often thought to be the most important group role. Geier (1967) interviewed 80 U.S. students, males and females, who participated in 16 discussion groups. Seventy-eight of the students said that they would like to be the leader of their group. This is not an unexpected result in an individualist culture where status associated with the leader role provides an opportunity to enhance one's ranking in the social hierarchy. In this section you will learn more about the role of leader and the exercise of leadership.

Definition of Leadership

There are as many definitions of leadership as there are individuals attempting to define it. Most definitions share several components, however (Northouse, 1997; Rothwell, 1998). Leadership is primarily a social influence process. Leaders influence followers, but what kind of influence do leaders exercise? Is it the "ability to inflict pain" on followers, as one corporate executive claimed in a 1980 *Fortune* magazine article? Is this influence "power over other people," which "enables a man to do things, to get things, to accomplish feats that, by himself, are unattainable?" (Fiedler, 1970). Sidestepping the obvious sexism of Fiedler's view, his definition presents leadership as dominance of followers. This is the competitive viewpoint of leadership.

A different viewpoint, consistent with an earlier definition of communication, is that leadership is a transactional influence process. This means that the influence is a two-way process negotiated between leader and potential followers. The influence occurs with the "consent of the governed." Leaders influence followers, but followers also influence leaders, making demands on them to meet expectations and evaluating their performance in light of these expectations.

Leadership is also goal-oriented. The influence exercised by leaders has to have a purpose. That principal purpose is group goal achievement. This frames leadership as a We-oriented, not a Me-oriented role.

Finally, leadership is fundamentally a communication process. Leadership is exercised and influence is achieved through communication with group members. The communication competence of leaders, therefore, is an important part of leadership.

The main elements of leadership are that it is an influence process that is transactional, goal-oriented, and dependent on competent communication. A simple definition of leadership can be derived from these elements. **Leadership** is a transactional influence process whose principal purpose is group goal achievement produced by competent communication.

Leader Emergence

In formal groups and organizations, the role of leader is often assigned. In certain cases, it is a formally elected position. In some small groups the leader role is designated (chair of a committee), but in most small groups a leader emerges from group transactions. Emergence of a leader is an important event in the life of a small group. Geier (1967) studied 16 small groups for 4 months. In 5 of these groups a leader did not emerge, and none of these groups was successful in completing tasks and tending to social relationships. All of the groups in which leaders did emerge were successful.

Leader emergence is a process of elimination (Bormann, 1990). Small groups typically know what they don't want in a leader but are less certain about what they do want. The first to be eliminated from consideration for the leader role are quiet, uninformed, seemingly unintelligent, and unskilled members. Group members who express strong, unqualified assertions and those perceived to be poor listeners are also quickly eliminated as candidates for the role of leader (Bechler & Johnson, 1995). A second phase of this process of elimination rejects bossy, dictatorial members and individuals with irritating or disturbing communication styles.

If a leader hasn't emerged after these two phases, the group typically looks for a member who provides a solution to a serious problem or helps the group manage a crisis. Members who are perceived to be effective listeners also frequently emerge as leaders during this stage (Johnson & Bechler, 1998). A member may acquire a lieutenant, an advocate who promotes him or her for the leader role. This member will become the leader unless another member acquires a lieutenant. If there are competing lieutenants, a stalemate may ensue and no clear leader will emerge.

Groups expect more from leaders who emerge naturally from group transactions than they do from assigned leaders (Hackman & Johnson, 1996). Emergent leaders are held to a higher standard, and failure is tolerated less because the group has more invested in their chosen leader. How the leader performs reflects well or badly on the group. When an outsider (i.e., supervisor, executive) assigns a leader to a group, gaining credibility with group members may be the biggest hurdle for the leader (Box 10-3).

Effective Leadership

Emerging as leader of a group and exercising effective leadership may be distinctly different processes. Emergent leaders aren't always effective leaders. In this section you will learn about several perspectives on leadership effectiveness.

Traits Perspective   Do you have the "right stuff" to be an effective leader in small groups? That is the core question of the traits approach to leadership. This is the

Box 10-3 Focus on Controversy

Gender and Ethnicity: The Glass Ceiling and the Brick Wall

Group bias against women and ethnic minorities is still an issue in leader emergence. Groups tend to favor White men when selecting and evaluating leaders (Forsyth et al., 1997; Shackelford et al., 1996). This bias in choosing group leaders occurs despite impressive evidence that women and men exhibit equivalent leadership effectiveness (Eagly et al., 1995), and one study showed that African Americans (male and female) were perceived to have more leadership ability than Whites (Craig & Rand, 1998).

Although significant gains have been made in women's rise to positions of leadership in the workplace, much more still needs to be accomplished. The **glass ceiling,** an invisible barrier of subtle discrimination that excludes women from top leadership positions in corporate and professional America, remains. Although about 40% of all management positions in the United States are filled by women, fewer than 10% of senior management positions in U.S. government service are occupied by women. Only 5% of senior management positions at *Fortune* 1,000 companies are occupied by women (Jacobs, 1996). Once women do climb to the highest levels of corporate America, the pay disparity between male and female executives is stark. Female senior executives earn, on average, only 68 cents for every dollar paid to male senior executives ("Heat's On," 1999).

The situation for ethnic minorities is worse. In its final report the U.S. Labor Department's Glass Ceiling Commission noted that African, Asian, and Hispanic Americans fill only a measly 1% of the executive management positions at *Fortune* 500 companies ("Glass Ceiling Intact," 1994). The report also noted that ethnic minorities hold 28% of all federal jobs but hold only 8% of the top positions. Female ethnic minorities face the toughest time emerging as leaders because they face a double bias. Their predicament is closer to a "brick wall" than a glass ceiling (Smith, 1997).

Any approach to reducing gender and ethnic bias in leader emergence is best aimed at empowering all members in a group so each has a greater chance of being chosen group leader. A competitive power struggle for leadership is unlikely to prove successful for women and minorities who are often badly outnumbered at the outset.

Women and ethnic minorities can improve their chances of emerging as group leaders in several ways (Rothwell, 1998). First, their chances are improved by increasing the proportion of women and ethnic minorities in small groups (Shimanoff & Jenkins, 1996). This is known as the **Twenty Percent Rule** (Pettigrew & Martin, 1987). Discrimination decreases when at least 20% of group membership is composed of women or minorities. Flying solo is the most difficult position for women and

"leaders are born not made" perspective. The first systematic scientific investigations of leadership looked for a list of traits that distinguish leaders from followers. **Traits** are relatively enduring characteristics of a person that highlight differences between people. There are physical traits such as height, weight, physical shape, physique, and beauty or attractiveness. There are personality traits such as being outgoing or sociable. There are traits associated with inherent capabilities such as intelligence and quick-wittedness. There are traits associated with consistent behaviors such as integrity, trustworthiness, and confidence.

Hundreds of studies have generated separate lists of traits that identify leaders (see Northouse, 1997). Tall, attractive-looking individuals seem to have an advantage in becoming leaders. Charisma, a constellation of traits that a group finds attractive in a leader, is often thought to be an essential quality for an effective leader.

Several problems with the trait perspective, however, make it only marginally insightful. First, certain negative traits can predict who will not become leader, but positive traits don't permit accurate predictions regarding who is likely to emerge as leader and exhibit effective leadership. Tall, attractive individuals may have an advantage over short, unattractive individuals in a competition for leader emergence. Nevertheless, this doesn't explain why Bill Gates is the richest person in the

(*continued*)

minorities (Taps & Martin, 1990). Being the only woman or minority in a group can brand a person as a "token," thus diminishing his or her chance of emerging as leader. In some circumstances, increasing the representation of women and ethnic minorities may require a power-forcing style as a last resort to produce change, but at the outset it may be merely a matter of sensitizing the group to the need for greater diversity in group membership.

Second, encourage mingling and interaction among members before choosing a leader. Getting to know group members while working on a project puts the emphasis on individual performance instead of gender and ethnicity (Haslett, 1992).

Third, emphasize task-relevant communication during group discussions. Play task roles. This can be empowering. Task-oriented female group members are as likely to become small group leaders as are task-oriented male group members (Hawkins, 1995). This suggestion applies primarily to work groups. Support groups may prefer a more social-oriented leader.

Fourth, women and minorities improve their chances of emerging as leaders of small groups when they are among the first to speak in the group and when they speak often (Shimanoff & Jenkins, 1996). In the United States leaders are expected to speak often and to initiate conversation in groups. One study of all-male groups

(Kelsey, 1998) found that "token" White males (one White male, three Chinese males) were judged to be leaders in every instance, whereas "token" Chinese males (one Chinese male, three White males) were never seen as leaders. The key factor was not ethnicity, however, but degree of participation. Token White males spoke much more often and longer than did the majority Chinese males in every instance. Speaking first and often marks a person as leadership material in U.S. culture.

Fifth, honing communication skills and becoming a competent communicator will greatly improve an individual's chances of emerging as group leader (Hackman & Johnson, 1996). Communication is the core of leadership, and communication skills are empowering. The best communicators have the best chance of emerging as group leaders.

Questions for Thought

1. Have you experienced discrimination in small groups that prevented you from emerging as leader?
2. Will men easily accept greater representation of women and ethnic minorities in groups? Explain.
3. Can power struggles for leader emergence be avoided by the steps suggested, or do you think they will inevitably occur?

world and runs the powerful Microsoft corporation. Diminutive Barbara Boxer and Barbara Mikulski became United States Senators. Ross Perot, twice a serious candidate for President of the United States and a billionaire businessman is often described as "jug-eared" and "squeaky-voiced." Fellow Texan Molly Ivins (1992), a columnist, described Perot as "a seriously short guy who sounds like a Chihuahua" (p. 38). Who would have predicted on the basis of traits alone that Jesse "The Body" Ventura would become governor of Minnesota in the 1998 election? As one pundit described him, "He's a shaved-head, muscle-bound, ex-pro wrestler with the voice of a carnival barker" (Thomas, 1998, p. P3). Garrison Keillor, host of the public radio program "A Prairie Home Companion," gives an even less flattering description. Ventura is "this great big honking bullet-headed shovel-faced mutha who talks in a steroid growl and doesn't stop" (as cited in "Ventura," 1999, p. A2). Traits aren't very accurate predictors of leader emergence and effective leadership.

Second, traits may cancel each other. Physical attractiveness and sociability may be outweighed by lack of integrity. Intolerance may cancel charisma. How does one predict which traits will be most important with which group? Researchers can't even agree on which traits are universal attributes for all effective leaders (Northouse, 1997).

The trait perspective explains little about former pro wrestler Jesse Ventura's successful campaign for governor of Minnesota. Political pundits were stunned by his victory.

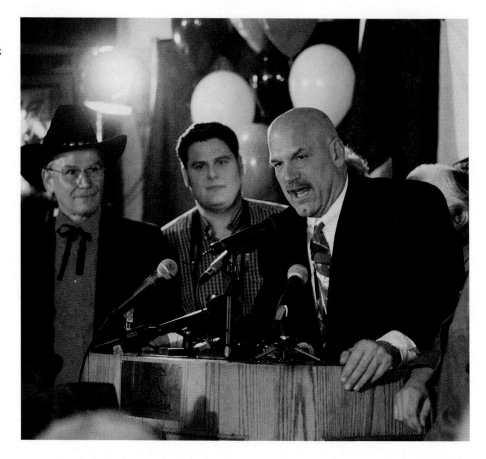

Third, certain traits may be necessary but not sufficient to emerge as an effective leader. Fiedler and House (1988) claim that "effective leaders tend to have a high need to influence others, achieve, and they tend to be bright, competent, and socially adept, rather than stupid, incompetent, and social disasters" (p. 87). Intelligence, social and verbal skills, integrity, sense of humor, confidence, or other traits may influence a group. Such traits, however, are not sufficient to be an effective leader. Why? The trait approach assumes that leadership is a person. It is not. *Leadership is a transactional process* (Hollander, 1985). A leader must have followers. Labeling the behavior of an individual "leadership" in the absence of followership "is no more leadership than the behavior of small boys marching in front of a parade, who continue to strut along Main Street after the procession has turned down a side street toward the fairgrounds" (Burns, 1978, p. 427).

If a person possesses requisite leadership traits, why doesn't he or she become an effective leader in all groups? Ross Perot and Steve Forbes tried to translate their leadership in business to the political arena. Both were unsuccessful presidential candidates. Traits that prove effective in one context may prove to be ineffective in other arenas. The trait perspective is too limited in scope to explain much about leadership effectiveness.

Styles Perspective   There are two principal leadership styles. The **directive style,** originally called *autocratic,* puts heavy emphasis on the task dimension with slight attention to the social dimension of groups. Member participation is not encouraged. Directive style exhibits an imbalance of power. Directive leaders assume that they have greater power than other group members. Such leaders tell members what to do, and they expect compliance. The **participative style,** originally called *democratic,* places emphasis on both the task and social dimensions of groups. Task accomplishment is important, but social relationships must also be maintained. Unlike the directive style, which uses the dominance form of power, the participative style is empowering. Group members are encouraged to participate meaningfully in discussions and decision making. Participative leaders work to improve the skills and abilities of all group members.

Initially, researchers thought the participative style would prove to be superior. Research results, however, have been mixed (Gastil, 1994). Both directive and participative leadership styles can be productive. Although the participative style fosters more member satisfaction than does the directive style (Van Oostrum & Rabbie, 1995), the difference is neither large nor uniform (Gastil, 1994). Some groups don't want their leaders to be participative. The military wouldn't function effectively if every soldier got to vote on the wisdom of a military action: "All those in favor of attacking the heavily armed enemy on the ridge signal by saying aye; those opposed, nay. Okay, the nays have it."

High power-distance cultures tend to expect and prefer the directive leadership style (Brislin, 1993). In such cultures, the participative style may not work as well as the directive style. The directive style also tends to be more effective when groups face stressful circumstances or time constraints, whereas the participative style is usually more effective in nonstressful situations (Rosenbaum & Rosenbaum, 1985). These research results indicate that effectiveness of leadership style depends on the situation.

Situational Perspective   No single style of leadership will be suitable for all situations. Thus, effective leadership is contingent on adapting the appropriate style for each situation. The Hersey and Blanchard situational leadership model is one of the most widely recognized approaches to leadership effectiveness (Hersey & Blanchard, 1988). Hersey and Blanchard have subdivided the directive and participative leadership styles into four types: telling, selling, participating, and delegating. As Figure 10-2 indicates, the telling style emphasizes task, the selling style emphasizes both task and relationships, the participating style emphasizes relationships, and the delegating style has little focus on either task or social dimensions of groups. The key situational variable that every leader must consider to determine which style is appropriate is the readiness level of followers. **Readiness** is composed of the ability of group members, their motivation, and their experience with relevant tasks. Lots of experience and strong motivation to accomplish a task aren't enough if a member's ability is poor. Likewise, substantial ability and experience don't compensate for weak motivation.

When the readiness level of followers is low, the telling and selling styles are most appropriate. As readiness levels increase, effective leaders choose the participative and delegating styles. When someone is hired for a job, for example, effective leaders begin diagnosing the readiness level of the employee. Readiness levels vary from R1 (unable, unwilling, and lacking confidence) to R4 (able, willing, and confident). Normally, a person at the R1 level would not be hired. Who would want someone of this caliber? Thus, the telling style would mostly be used

Figure 10-2 Situational Leadership Model *The Telling (S1), Selling (S2), Participating (S3), and Delegating (S4) leadership styles related to follower readiness.* (Source: Situational Leadership® is a registered trademark of the Center for Leadership Studies, Inc. Reprinted with permission. All rights reserved.)

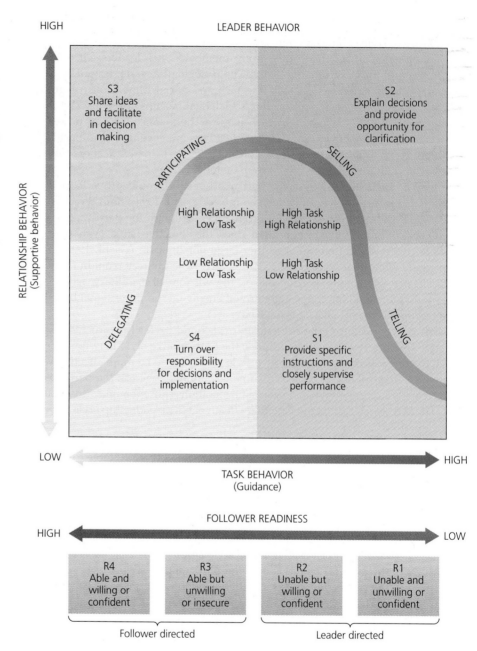

HIGH   LEADER BEHAVIOR

RELATIONSHIP BEHAVIOR (Supportive behavior)

S3
Share ideas and facilitate in decision making

S2
Explain decisions and provide opportunity for clarification

PARTICIPATING   SELLING

High Relationship Low Task

High Task High Relationship

Low Relationship Low Task

High Task Low Relationship

DELEGATING   TELLING

S4
Turn over responsibility for decisions and implementation

S1
Provide specific instructions and closely supervise performance

LOW   HIGH

TASK BEHAVIOR (Guidance)

FOLLOWER READINESS

HIGH   LOW

| R4 Able and willing or confident | R3 Able but unwilling or insecure | R2 Unable but willing or confident | R1 Unable and unwilling or confident |

Follower directed   Leader directed

with an employee whose readiness level falters because of stress, personal trauma, or technological advances beyond the employees' abilities. Using the telling style with an able worker would seem like micromanaging. The selling style requires interaction between leader and follower. This style would normally be used with a new employee as the supervisor and the employee begin to establish a relationship. With greater readiness comes a further shift in leadership style.

The participating style is appropriate for the worker who now knows the ropes and has sufficient readiness to offer suggestions and engage in decision making. Finally, when the readiness level is high, an effective leader steps out of the way and delegates responsibility and decision making to the worker.

The situational leadership perspective makes intuitive sense, although the research to support this perspective is somewhat skimpy (Northouse, 1997). One leadership style does not fit all situations. An effective leader matches the style with the readiness level of followers and the group as a whole. Newly formed groups require greater supervision and direction than experienced groups. Experienced, capable groups work best when leaders are "guides on the side." They offer relational support and encouragement but allow the group to perform its task without much interference. Leaders can become more directive (telling or selling) if groups or individual members slip in their readiness levels because of stressful events or personal difficulties. This means that leaders should be sensitive to signals from group members that readiness levels have diminished and a different style of leadership is required.

Communication Competence Perspective   Previous leadership perspectives offer useful insights about leadership effectiveness. Effective leadership, however, is ultimately a matter of communication competence. No set of traits, particular styles, or matching of styles with situational readiness will be effective without competent communicators. The most effective leaders are the most proficient communicators. As Hackman and Johnson (1996) conclude, "Extraordinary leadership is the product of extraordinary communication" (p. 81).

The We-orientation of the communication competence model is crucial for leadership effectiveness. Larson and LaFasto (1989) studied 75 highly diverse teams (e.g., mountain climbing, cardiac surgery, and professional football teams). Their conclusion was unequivocal: "The most effective leaders . . . were those who subjugated their ego needs in favor of the team's goal" (p. 128). Bennis and Nanus (1985) interviewed 90 successful leaders from a broad range of environments and concluded that "there was no trace of self-worship or cockiness" among these leaders (p. 57). Effective leaders try to empower group members, not stand out as dominant and deserving of adoration or blind obedience. Garfield (1986) interviewed more than 500 top leaders and concluded that they use three primary skills: delegating, stretching the abilities of team members, and encouraging thoughtful risk-taking. All three skills empower group members. As Larson and LaFasto (1989) concluded, "leaders create leaders" (p. 128).

Competent communication is critical to effective leadership because groups are affected enormously by the leader. *A leader sets the emotional tone of the group.* Top executives who fail as leaders exhibit insensitivity to others, are brutally critical, and are too demanding (Goleman, 1998).

As the young leader of the team that developed the Apple Macintosh computer in the early 1980s, Steve Jobs was less than sensitive to team members. He was noted for what was dubbed by team members "management by walking around." Jobs would appear without warning, walk around and look at members' work, then make caustic criticisms. His favorite critique was, "This sucks!" (Bennis & Biederman, 1997). Jobs' youth and immature leadership style prompted the joke, "What's the difference between Apple and the Boy Scouts?" Answer: "The Boy Scouts have adult supervision" (as cited in Bennis & Biederman, 1997, p. 81).

Box 10-4   Sharper Focus

"Chainsaw Al" Dunlap and Aaron Feuerstein: A Lesson in Opposites

He wrote a self-promoting book entitled *Mean Business*. He developed a reputation for cold-heartedness. As CNN financial correspondent Peter Viles observed in a December 8, 1998, report, "If one man symbolized the ruthless restructuring trend of the 1990s, it was Al Dunlap, known as the pit bull who would attack any cost, lay off any unit in order to protect shareholder value"(as cited in Fields, 1998). Dunlap's slash-and-burn approach to management earned him several unflattering labels including "Rambo in Pinstripes" and "Chainsaw Al."

Albert Dunlap is a notorious CEO whose standard approach to "turning around" a faltering company includes slashing costs by "downsizing," increasing stock values, and selling off the remaining carcass (Fields, 1998). In the process, thousands of workers lose their jobs. Dunlap slashed 18,000 jobs at Scott Paper Company and cut more than half of the 12,000 employees at Sunbeam. His 3-year, $70 million contract with Sunbeam prompted him to brag, "You can't overpay a great executive. . . . Don't you think I'm a bargain?" In his book, Dunlap has this to say about workers who lose their jobs from his downsizing strategy: "Those whose jobs will be eliminated in a restructuring should still consider the outcome philosophically, and have enough confidence in themselves to know they will have opportunities somewhere else. A company is not your high school or college alma mater. Don't get emotional about it" (Dunlap, 1997, p. 272). Those are the only consoling words from the multimillionaire CEO. "Don't get emotional" he tells displaced workers who must figure out how to support their families after their abrupt unemployment.

Once the darling of stockholders who were anxious to avoid a financial disaster, Dunlap was fired in June 1998, as CEO of Sunbeam, maker of appliances. His trademark downsizing strategy didn't work at Sunbeam (Sloan, 1998). Stock value initially shot up, then faltered. The company continued to lose money, and directors lost faith in Dunlap's methods. Remaining employees at Sunbeam reportedly cheered when they heard the news that Dunlap was fired.

Aaron Feuerstein is a boss of a completely different sort. Given the Lincoln Award for Ethics in Business in 1997, Feuerstein, the 70-year-old owner of a textile company, Malden Mills, in Lawrence, Massachusetts, saw his business gutted by a fire in 1995. His family, board of directors, and other executives advised him to collect the insurance money and forget about his mill. Feuerstein ignored their advice. He maintained his entire workforce of 2,400 employees on his payroll while the mill was rebuilt. It cost him $1.5 million per week. Demonstrating an extraordinary We-orientation, Feuerstein believed that if he closed his mill for good the city of Lawrence would die with it. "I wasn't going to be the guy to finish it off. We have a responsibility to our community. Keeping the mill open helps to keep the town alive" (as cited in Amparano, 1997, p. E3). Feuerstein chose not to downsize. His reward was loyalty and commitment from the workers whose jobs were saved. Before the fire, workers produced, on average, 130,000 yards of fabric each week. When the mill reopened, workers produced 200,000 yards of fabric per week. Ethical, compassionate leadership is good business.

When a leader expresses rage, shows disrespect for members, berates those who make mistakes, humiliates members in front of the group, and exhibits arrogance and pettiness, the entire group is tarnished by this incompetent communication (Goleman, 1998). Such emotional outbursts and insensitivity ripple throughout the group. Birgitta Wistrand calls it "emotional incontinence" (see Goleman, 1998). When leaders fail to control themselves emotionally, members become hesitant, anxious, fearful, angry, and depressed. Box 10-4 provides a comparison of two leaders, one who showed cold-heartedness, and another who exhibited extraordinary sensitivity and kind-heartedness.

Effective leaders create a supportive climate, encourage open communication, stimulate cooperation and a collaborative spirit, show empathy, and express optimism and a positive attitude (Goleman, 1998). "Going ballistic" is not an option for an effective leader. Effective leaders adapt to changing circumstances and a variety of styles and personalities.

Summary

Grouphate is a prevailing problem. Communication competence is central to our attitude about groups. Those who have little communication training typically find the group experience daunting and frustrating. Those who learn to communicate competently typically find the group experience far more positive.

Many benefits can be derived from working effectively in groups. Members can pool information and knowledge to produce better decisions. Groups can tackle broad-range, complex problems that would overwhelm a person working alone. Groups can empower members and produce synergy. The main disadvantages of groups—factionalism, scheduling conflicts, negative synergy, social loafing, and wasted time in meetings—are all correctable once there is an appreciation and understanding of how effective groups function.

The structure of small groups is composed primarily of norms and roles. Norms are rules that govern the behavior of group members. Roles are patterns of behavior that group members are expected to exhibit. The leader role is central to group structure. Playing the role of leader, however, does not equate with effective leadership. Effective leadership is not a person; it is a transactional process. Effective leadership requires competent communication. Leaders should be sensitive to the changing needs and situations within the group, assume the appropriate style for a given situation, and resist displays of competitive, defensive communication when dealing with group members.

Suggested Readings

Abramson, J. (1994). *We, the jury: The jury system and the ideal of democracy.* New York: Basic Books. This is the best single work on one of the most important small groups in our society—the jury.

Adams, Richard. (1972). *Watership Down.* New York: Avon. Adams has written an allegorical story about rabbits, but it is so much more than this. All the elements that constitute small groups are contained in this highly entertaining novel.

Burns, J. (1978). *Leadership.* New York: Harper & Row. This is an excellent general work on leadership in the political arena.

Singer, M. (1995). *Cults in our midst: The hidden menace in our everyday lives.* San Francisco: Jossey-Bass. Singer discusses small groups gone wrong.

Chapter 11

Teambuilding and Teamwork in Small Groups

On March 27, 1977, a Dutch KLM 747 aircraft (flight 4805) crashed into a Pan American 747 (flight 1736) shortly after takeoff at the Tenerife airport in the Canary Islands. Of the 614 passengers, 583 were killed in the crash, the worst commercial airline disaster in history. Numerous small mistakes accounted for the crash, but overall there was a serious lack of teamwork among crew members on the KLM flight. Weick (1990) observed that "the KLM crew acted less like a team than like three individuals acting in parallel" (p. 580).

Following a series of airline mishaps, the Federal Aviation Administration investigated Delta Airlines in 1987. The FAA's report stated, "There is no evidence that Delta's crews are (on the whole) either unprofessional or purposefully negligent. Rather, it was observed that crew members are frequently acting as individuals rather than as members of a smoothly functioning team" (as cited in Whitkin, 1987). According to Goleman (1995), 80% of airline crashes result from poor communication and lack of effective teamwork among crews. Technical proficiency of crews is insufficient to prevent disasters. Crew training now emphasizes teamwork and cooperation as an equally important aspect of crew effectiveness.

Developing effective teams is an important concern for all of us, not just to those who hop on an airplane and brave the sometimes not-so-friendly skies. Most of us have our first exposure to teams from our early participation in sports. Basketball, baseball, softball, football, ice hockey, field hockey, and soccer provide common experiences with teams for millions of girls and boys, women and men, every year. In addition, theatre productions in high school and college require team effort, as do fund-raising activities to support college clubs and service groups. Also, group projects in college classes are most successful when approached from a team perspective.

Perhaps our most important and long-term exposure to teams, however, occurs in the workplace. McCann and Margerison (1996) note, "Today's business environment is so complex and in such a continual state of change that success often depends on the outputs of teams or work groups rather than the efforts of a single person" (p. 50). A national survey of 750 top U.S. companies found that 71.4% of respondents listed "ability to work in teams" as an essential employment qualification (as cited in DuBois, 1992). The Center for Creative Leadership conducted a study of top U.S. and European executives whose careers went sour. They found that the *inability* to build and lead teams was the common reason for executive failure (Spencer & Spencer, 1993).

Every team is a group, but not every group is a team (Hackman & Johnson, 1996). There are three primary distinctions between small groups and teams. First, teams commonly exhibit a higher level of cooperation and cohesiveness than standard groups. Teams are inherently We-oriented. Each member develops skills "for the good of the team." A forward may have to switch to playing center to help his or her basketball team, even though this may mean scoring fewer individual points. Teams may function within a competitive, intergroup environment, but to be successful, they depend on intragroup cooperation. Second, teams normally consist of individuals with more diverse skills. Not everyone can be a goalie in soccer or a pitcher in baseball. A team requires complementary, not identical, skills. Third, teams usually have a stronger group identity. Teams see themselves as an identifiable unit with a common mission. Thus, Katzenbach and Smith (1993b) define a **team** as "a small number of people with complementary skills who are equally committed to a common purpose, goals, and working approach for which they hold themselves mutually accountable" (p. 45).

Boards of directors, standing committees, student and faculty senates, and similar groups are not usually teams. These groups often lack cohesiveness and cooperation, and group members may have similar rather than diverse skills. Members are asked to attend periodic meetings where discussion occurs and an occasional vote is taken, but members do not have to work together. In fact, contact with fellow members may never take place except indirectly and formally during meetings.

Some groups may pit members against each other, thwarting the possibility of teamwork. The House Judiciary Committee in 1998 sent four articles of impeachment against President Bill Clinton to the full House for a vote. Members of the Judiciary Committee voted along party lines—every Republican voted for impeachment, every Democrat voted against. This committee clearly was not a team. Members did not work together to accomplish a common goal, in fact, contradictory goals seemed to be pursued by the two political parties. There was little cooperation exhibited throughout the proceedings, and less cohesiveness. Committee members acted as adversaries, not team members.

Although some groups are not and will never become teams, most groups can profit from *acting more team-like*. The more team-like small groups become, the more likely they will function effectively. Teams embody a central theme of this text—that cooperation in human communication arenas has distinct advantages. These benefits of cooperation should be exploited far more than occurs at present. Thus, the principal purpose of this chapter is to explore teambuilding and teamwork in small groups to expand the application of cooperation. There are two objectives related to this purpose:

1. to explore ways to build teams, and
2. to explain how to develop teamwork in small groups.

Teambuilding

Teams share a common structure. Building a team means building that structure. In this section the specific structure necessary to build effective teams is explained.

Establishing Goals

Teambuilding begins with goal setting. A team needs a purpose, and goals provide that focus. Goals should be clear, challenging, and cooperative.

Clear Goals   An ancient Chinese proverb states, "If you don't know where you are going, then any road will take you there." Groups that have no particular focus drift aimlessly. They achieve little because little is planned. Without exception, every effectively functioning team studied by Larson and LaFasto (1989) had clear, identifiable goals, and members had a clear understanding of those goals. Vague goals such as "do our best" or "make improvements" provide no clear direction. "Complete the study of traffic congestion on campus by the end of the term" or "raise $100,000 in donations for a campus child care center within one year" are clear, specific goals. For a group to become a team, clearly focused goals are essential.

Romig (1996) found one department in an organization had developed 60 goals to achieve in a single year. This department accomplished none of its goals but threatened the future of the entire organization by losing huge sums of money flailing aimlessly in all directions. Too many goals can diffuse effort and scatter group members. A few clear goals are preferable. Each member should be able to recite from memory the primary goals of the team. This allows all team members to have a shared mission and a common vision. Goals for a team work best when they are clearly stated and limited in number.

Challenging Goals   Accomplishing the trivial motivates no one. Groups need challenging goals to spur interest among members. Challenging goals can stretch the limits of group members' physical or mental abilities. Problems never faced nor solved present a challenge. Finding solutions to problems when time is short and the need is urgent can also challenge a group. Groups are elevated to teams when they see their mission as important, meaningful, and beyond the ordinary.

The team that developed the original Macintosh computer had this elevated sense of purpose. Randy Wigginton, a team member, puts it this way: "We believed we were on a mission from God" (as cited in Bennis & Biederman, 1997, p. 83). Steve Jobs, the team leader, promised team members that they were going to build a computer that would "put a dent in the universe" (p. 80).

Cooperative Goals   In individualist cultures such as the United States, the cooperative aspects of teambuilding are a bit more challenging than in collectivist cultures such as those of Singapore, China, and Malaysia. Competitive goal structures abound in the United States. Developing cooperative goal structures can seem perplexing initially.

There are several elements that compose cooperative goals. First, cooperative goals require interdependent effort from group members. This is achieved by all members working together in a coordinated fashion.

Second, cooperative goals necessitate a We-orientation. A study at Cambridge University of 120 teams found that assembling highly intelligent team members didn't produce stellar results (Belbin, 1996). High-IQ members were intensely competitive. Instead of working together, they exercised their intellectual abilities by striving to impress each other with their brilliance. Each member's individual status became more important than any group goal. Teams composed of members with more ordinary intellectual abilities outshown the high-IQ teams. They exhibited a We-orientation by putting personal agendas aside for the sake of team goals. The result was synergy. The most common complaint registered in the Larson and LaFasto (1989) study of teams was that some team members were self-oriented, not team-oriented. Putting personal goals ahead of team goals weakens group resolve and diminishes cohesiveness. Teams need unified commitment from all members. "The essence of a team is common commitment. Without it, groups perform as individuals; with it they become a powerful unit of collective performance" (Katzenbach & Smith, 1993a). Those members who do not demonstrate sufficient commitment and effort necessitate the use of suggestions for dealing with social loafers and difficult group members (Chapter 10).

Box 11-1 Sharper Focus

The U.S. Women's Olympic Basketball Team

The crowd of 32,987 in Atlanta was on its feet cheering wildly as the final seconds ticked away. The women's basketball team from the United States had soundly defeated its long-time nemesis, Brazil, for the gold medal in the 1996 Olympic games. Brazil, a powerful team that had humbled previous U.S. teams in the 1991 Pan America games, the 1992 Olympics, and the 1994 world championships, was no match for the smooth teamwork of the U.S. women. The final score was 111–87. The U.S. total was the most points ever scored by a women's basketball team in the Olympics.

The U.S. women's success was achieved primarily by establishing cooperative goals from the outset. Sportswriter Ann Killion (1996) summed it up when she attributed the U.S. women's success to "setting [their] sights on a goal and working for it, [and] sacrificing one's self for the team" (p. D1). Tara VanDerveer, the U.S. women's basketball coach, explained her team's success this way: "There's a stereotype that women can't work together. What makes this special is that people had a team agenda. They weren't individuals. This team put the gold medal as their mission" (as cited in Killion, 1996, p. D3).

The road to the gold medal was long and difficult. The team traveled 100,000 miles during the year prior to the Olympic games to play international powerhouse teams such as China and Russia. Players endured intensive physical training. They participated in a team-building experiment in Colorado Springs. Players and coaches walked on parallel cables 30 feet above ground as the cables gradually split wider apart and participants were forced to rely on each other to keep from falling. As a result of a carefully constructed teambuilding effort, the women's team won all 52 preparation games, then scored wins in all 8 Olympic contests for a perfect 60–0 record.

The 1996 U.S. women's basketball team set a clear, focused, challenging goal for itself. Players wanted to win the Olympic gold medal. To achieve this overriding goal, they set cooperative goals such as putting the team above individual stardom and glory and committing themselves to a full year of training and preparation to achieve their mission. In the process, these capable women demonstrated that even in the intensely competitive arena of international sports, success requires substantial cooperation.

Third, goals established by team members, not imposed by outsiders or a team leader, usually gain greater commitment (Romig, 1996). Cooperative goals are the product of member participation. It is very difficult for members to get excited about goals foisted on them. If members have little say in determining team goals, they may have little interest in or commitment to those goals (Box 11-1).

Developing a Team Identity

James Carville, chief strategist for Bill Clinton's 1992 presidential campaign, knew how to create a team identity. Self-described as the "Ragin' Cajun" from Louisiana and odd looking—Republican political consultant Roger Ailes said he looked "like a fish who's swum too close to a nuclear reactor"—Carville ran the "War Room" team. The team name was Hillary Rodham Clinton's idea, and it gave the team an instant identification.

The War Room was the political nerve center of the Clinton campaign. Located in Little Rock, Arkansas, the team responded to every perceived threat, every attack from the Bush campaign, every stumble or miscue by Clinton with lightning speed. As Carville put it, "You create a campaign culture, and ours was based on speed" (as cited in Bennis & Biederman, 1997, p. 93).

The War Room team's identity combined speed with informality. The T-shirt was part of the War Roomers' uniform. Carville liked wearing one that read "Speech kills . . . Bush." He also wore ragged jeans with holes. There was a

The War Room political team, with team leader James Carville (center), was instrumental in the successful 1992 Clinton presidential campaign and shows what teamwork can accomplish.

constant air of immediacy and high drama. Team members ran to copy machines, they didn't walk. Carville promoted a 24-hour-a-day sense of urgency. Like him or hate him, and he does have vociferous detractors, Carville unquestionably built a remarkably effective team.

Group identity is an important part of building a team. There isn't a single way to do this. Often team identity is fostered by a uniform or style of dress common to team members. A team name is not essential, but it helps. An identifiable style of behaving, such as the War Room's focus on speed, also creates an identity, especially if the style is different from other groups. Offering awards and prizes for team accomplishments, creating rituals and ceremonies unique to the group, establishing a clearly identifiable space that belongs to the team, and sometimes creating an air of secrecy all contribute to team identity. Every team will create its own identity in its own way. Part of being an effective team, however, is building that identity early in the group's life.

Designating Clear Roles

Roles emerge informally in most small groups, but teams require greater structure than groups in general. Group members won't function as a team if they are uncertain of the roles they are supposed to play. A team of lawyers will divide the responsibilities among members. One lawyer may be the chief researcher (information giver). Another may write the legal briefs (clarifier-elaborator). A third may challenge the briefs to find flaws in the arguments (devil's advocate), and a fourth lawyer might direct the entire team (leader). In each case team members are given specific responsibilities befitting their talents, experience, and expertise. This assignment of roles is often made by the team leader, but in some cases team members will volunteer to play specific roles.

Poor role clarity can produce confusion, duplication of effort, and overall weak group performance. Team members need to demonstrate coordinated activity to be successful. Clear designation of roles can produce high performance. Dr. Don Wukasch, a respected open-heart surgeon, describes what happened when a hurricane hit the Texas Heart Institute while his surgical team was performing a heart operation:

> A hurricane again—the power went out, and the patient was on the heart-lung machine. When the power goes off, the heart-lung machine goes off. You have about a minute or two before the patient starts to die. I didn't know we had them, but there are hand cranks under each heart-lung machine. The team started cranking, and within 15 seconds we were going at normal. Here again, no panic, just a smooth operation. That's real professionalism. That's a high-performance team. (as cited in Larson & LaFasto, 1989, p. 54)

Each member of the surgical team played his or her part in the performance of a successful operation. No one tried to play all the roles. Every team member had a specific set of tasks to perform well, and all roles were coordinated. Clearly defining each team member's role is critical to team effectiveness.

Using the Standard Agenda

Decision making and problem solving without structure will usually waste enormous amounts of time and produce negligible results for teams (Romig, 1996). Without a structure for decision making, teams often leap to consideration of solutions before adequately discussing and exploring the causes of problems. This leads to ineffective decision making (Hirokawa, 1985). A set of steps, called the Standard Agenda, helps teams avoid this mistake (Figure 11-1). The six steps in the Standard Agenda are:

1. *Identify the goal(s).* Establish a clear, specific goal or goals. Let's say that your team has a project assigned in your group discussion class. Your instructor has told the class that each group must choose a project from a list of five options. The group's overall specific goal might be to choose an option that will earn the team an "A" grade. A secondary goal might be to work on a project that interests all group members.

2. *Analyze the problem.* When we analyze a problem we break it down into its constituent parts. We examine the nature of the problem. The group project assigned in class might produce an analysis of the pros and cons for the five options available. Team members might consider how much research will be required and what information is readily available for each option, how much time the group has to do the necessary research, how much background knowledge is necessary to do the project well, and how interested members are in each option.

3. *Establish criteria.* Criteria are standards for judgment, guidelines for determining effective decision making and problem solving. When I visited the National Gallery of Modern Art in Washington, D.C., I was immediately drawn to a huge painting. The entire canvas, which covered most of an interior wall, was

Figure 11-1 The Standard Agenda

The Standard Agenda

✔ Identify the goal

✔ Analyze the problem

✔ Establish criteria

✔ Generate solutions

✔ Evaluate solutions, make final decision

✔ Implement decision

painted off-white except for a solitary red dot about the size of a basketball in the lower right quadrant. Why was this painting chosen as special enough to hang in the National Gallery? I asked myself. Why would the National Gallery pay tens of thousands of dollars for such a painting? Could it be the reputation of the painter? Perhaps its attention-getting quality made it a worthy choice. I couldn't help thinking that I could duplicate this work. "If I can do it, it can't be great art" has always been my starting criterion for assessing the relative merit of art works. Knowing what criteria were used by art experts who chose this painting would have helped me understand why their decision made sense. I never found out what criteria were applied to this painting, and my appreciation of its merits remains minimal.

Without establishing criteria in advance of final decisions, it is very difficult to gauge whether group choices will likely prove to be effective. In the case of a class project, the instructor will normally provide the specific criteria for the groups. In other circumstances, the group should discuss criteria and choose three to five before proceeding with the next step. Criteria should answer the question "What standards should be met for the decision/solution to be a good one?" Some possible criteria for a group project in a class might be (1) stay within the prescribed time limits for the class presentations, (2) exhibit clear organization, (3) use at least one clear attention strategy and cite at least three credible sources of information during each group member's presentation, and (4) employ one visual aid per member's speech. The extent to which the group meets these criteria will determine whether members all earn an "A" on their project.

4. *Generate solutions.* When weighing the merits and demerits of each project option, don't assume that the objections to each option can't be solved. Let's suppose that the group is torn between two options: exploring a campus problem such as parking or researching an international problem such as rain forest

depletion. Initially, the parking problem might seem a less satisfactory choice. Finding credible sources and sufficient quality information in the limited time available for preparation might seem to be insurmountable impediments. If the group has a greater interest in the parking problem than in rain forest depletion, however, group members might brainstorm possible solutions to these impediments. Perhaps the group could conduct a campus survey to generate credible information where a lack of such information might be a problem. School officials and campus security could be interviewed.

5. *Evaluate solutions and make the final decision.* Before team members decide which option to choose for their project, the group should consider each option in terms of the criteria. Which option will best allow the group to achieve its goals? Will exploring a campus problem such as parking or an international problem such as rain forest depletion best permit the group to reach its goal of an "A" grade? Which option is most interesting to group members? The likelihood of satisfying the criteria will allow group members to make a reasonable decision. *It is particularly important during this step that group members consider both the positive and negative aspects of each choice.* Groups often become enamored with a solution without considering **Murphy's Law,** which is, anything that can go wrong likely will go wrong.

When Boeing Corporation builds an airplane, designers account for Murphy's Law in the plans. An airplane with four engines is designed to fly temporarily with but a single engine. Boeing doesn't expect three engines to malfunction during the same flight, but, just in case, it is better to err on the side of safety. Expect the unexpected and build it into your team decision.

The enormously successful Mars rover Sojourner, which explored the surface of Mars in 1997, was repeatedly tested for Murphy's Law (Shirley, 1997). Sojourner's task was to take pictures, measure the chemistry of rocks, and discover how difficult it is to drive in the Martian soil. The rover, which looked like a microwave oven on six wheels, had to cost no more than $25 million to build—an unheard of pittance for an interplanetary spacecraft. Sojourner had to weigh less than 22 pounds and survive in 150-degree-below-zero temperatures. These specifications for the rover were daunting, yet the rover was built within these restrictions. The rover operated at a peak power of 16 watts, but most of the time at a mere 8 watts, the equivalent of your ordinary bathroom nightlight. In an April Fool's issue *Road and Track* magazine compared the rover to high-performance automobiles. It estimated rover's top speed to be 0.0037 miles per hour. These severe limits caused many in the Pathfinder Mars project to doubt the ability of the rover to accomplish its mission.

An engineer named David Gruel was assigned the task of sabotaging the rover in any way he could imagine to test the probability of success for the mission. A model of the rover was tested in a "sandbox" that simulated the Mars surface. Gruel created difficult terrain for the rover to overcome. The Sojourner team, headed by Donna Shirley, successfully maneuvered Sojourner around every obstacle. By the time Sojourner actually landed on Mars, the team was confident the rover would be up to the task. Expected to operate for about a week, Sojourner lasted for almost 3 months and traveled more than 100 meters on the surface of Mars—ten times as far as thought possible—before failing batteries ended the mission (Shirley, 1997).

Team members prepare the Mars rover Sojourner for another test in the sandbox in anticipation of Murphy's Law.

6. *Implement the decision.* To implement the team's decision, the group divides labor among the members in a coordinated fashion. Each member must be given a clear role to perform that contributes to the eventual implementation of the team decision. One or two members might do interviews, another might write a survey, others might research the parking problem. All of these tasks are interdependent. Leave any out and successful implementation may be jeopardized. Merely talking about doing the project doesn't get it done. Deadlines for completion of each stage of the project should be set so all members know what is expected of them and when the product of their labor is due. Members should then discuss the results, condense the material into usable form, and organize the presentation of results to outsiders.

Some groups don't stick rigidly to the Standard Agenda. They may jump around some from step to step. Two points are critical, however. First, the problem should be explored thoroughly before any solutions or options are considered. Second, establish criteria before making any decisions.

7. Evaluate Success (on powerpoint)

Employing Decision-Making Rules

Choices have to be made at every step of the Standard Agenda. How those decisions will be made depend on rules of decision making. There are three chief decision-making rules for small groups: unanimity or consensus, majority rule, and minority rule. Each has its benefits and drawbacks.

Box 11-2   Sharper Focus

How to Achieve a Consensus

Achieving a consensus is a major challenge for any team. Here are several suggestions that can guide a team toward achieving consensus (Hall & Watson, 1970; Saint & Lawson, 1997):

1. Follow the Standard Agenda, and use suggestions for running productive meetings. Consensus requires structured deliberations, not aimless conversation.
2. Encourage supportive patterns of communication throughout discussions. Discourage defensive patterns that creep into discussions.
3. Identify the pros and cons of a decision under consideration. Write these on a chalkboard, large tablet, or transparency for all to see.
4. Discuss all concerns, and try to resolve those concerns to everyone's satisfaction. Look for alternatives if concerns remain.
5. Avoid arguing stubbornly for a position. Be prepared to give where possible. Look for ways to break an impasse.
6. Ask for a "stand aside." Standing aside means a team member still has a reservation about the decision but does not feel that it warrants continued opposition to the final decision.
7. Avoid conflict-suppressing methods such as coin flipping and swapping ("I'll vote for your proposal this time if you vote for mine next"). A straw vote to ascertain the general level of acceptance for a decision or proposal is useful, but the goal should be unanimity.
8. If consensus cannot be reached, seek a supermajority (at least two-thirds agreement). This at least captures the thrust of consensus decision making by requiring substantial, if not total, agreement.

Consensus Some groups operate under the unanimity rule. This is usually referred to as consensus decision making. **Consensus** is "a state of mutual agreement among members of a group where all legitimate concerns of individuals have been addressed to the satisfaction of the group" (Saint & Lawson, 1997, p. 21). Juries are one example of consensus groups. Criminal trials in most instances require all jurors to agree. All legitimate concerns of jurors must be addressed to achieve a consensus. If jurors ignore a legitimate concern, even a single dissenter can hang the jury and force a retrial or dismissal of charges.

Consensus requires unanimity, but it doesn't mean that every group member's *preferred* choice will be selected. Consensus is reached when all group members can support and live with the decision that is made. This means that group members interact cooperatively. Members exhibit give and take during discussions. Some team members may have to modify a preferred choice before every team member can climb aboard and sail with the decision. Conversely, giving in too easily will negate the value of the unanimity rule. Airing differences of opinion is constructive. It takes a team effort to achieve a consensus (Box 11-2).

There are several advantages to using the unanimity rule to structure decision making. First, consensus requires full discussion of issues, which improves the chances that quality decisions will be made. Every group member must be convinced before a decision becomes final. Minority opinions will have to be heard. Those who disagree can't be ignored because they can stymie the group. All points of view must be considered. Second, team members are likely to be committed to the final decision and will defend the decision when challenged by outsiders. A group decision that is less than unanimous can be undermined by dissenters. Third, consensus usually produces group satisfaction. Members typically are satisfied with the decision-making process and the outcome.

The unanimity rule has two chief drawbacks. First, consensus is very difficult to achieve; the process is time consuming and sometimes contentious. Members can become frustrated by the length of deliberations and perturbed with holdouts who resist siding with the majority. Second, consensus becomes increasingly unlikely as groups grow larger. Teams of 15 or 20 will find it difficult to achieve consensus on anything.

Consensus is not the only way teams make decisions. Consensus decision making is useful, however, when team policy, priorities, and goals are being considered (Romig, 1996). Consensus is most relevant for important team decisions. Many choices made by team members do not require consensus. The team does not need to reach a consensus on where research should be conducted to gather information. Presumably, the team member who plays the information seeker role will be knowledgeable about where to look. Members can provide suggestions, but insisting on a consensus in such situations micromanages team members and will likely build resentment. If consensus cannot be reached, other decision making rules can be used to break a deadlock.

Majority Rule   The most popular method of decision making in the United States is majority rule. The U.S. political system is dependent on it. Majority rule has important benefits. It is efficient and can provide rapid closure on relatively unimportant issues. In large groups, majority rule may be the only reasonable way to make a decision. Unlike consensus, majority rule won't produce a deadlock. Once a majority emerges, a decision can be made.

Majority rule also has significant disadvantages. First, majorities sometimes support preposterous positions. Racism, sexism, and homophobia have been supported by majorities at various times in the history of the United States. The majority in the South accepted slavery as a "peculiar institution" worth defending. Prior to 1920, the majority in the United States thought women should not be allowed to vote. A majority of the adult U.S. population supported the roundup of Japanese Americans and their internment in camps during the Second World War. Sometimes the "tyranny of the majority" can produce awful decisions.

Second, groups using majority rule may encourage a dominance power dynamic within the team. Those with the most power (the majority) can impose their will on the less powerful minority. This could easily lead to a competitive power struggle within the team, thereby eroding team identity and team spirit.

Third, majorities may be tempted to decide too quickly, before proper discussion and debate have taken place, squelching the chance of creating synergy. Groups can make reckless, ill-conceived decisions. Minority opinion can be ignored.

Typically, teams use majority rule only when consensus is impossible or when quick decisions about commonplace issues must be decided. A consensus decision regarding where the team should meet, when, and for how long is useful, but bogging down from lengthy discussions about such "housekeeping" tasks will quickly grow old. A simple majority vote may prove satisfactory to move the team along.

Minority Rule   Majorities don't always make decisions in small groups. Occasionally, a group will designate an expert to make the decision for the group. Sometimes a group merely advises a leader but doesn't actually make decisions. The leader can choose to listen to the advice or ignore it. On rare occasions a forceful faction can intimidate a group and assert its will on the majority.

Minority rule has serious disadvantages. First, a designated expert can ignore group input, or simply not seek it. Second, members may engage in power plays

THE FAR SIDE   By GARY LARSON

"Okay, Williams, we'll vote . . . how many here say
the heart has four chambers?"

to seek favor with the leader who makes the decision. Third, group members will likely have weak commitment to the final decision because they had little participation in the outcome.

Teams rarely use minority rule. Nevertheless, minority decision making may be warranted in some limited circumstances. Eisenhardt (1989) studied eight Silicon Valley microcomputer companies in California. These companies used the unanimity rule with minority rule as a backup when they considered discontinuous change decisions in the high-velocity computer industry. **Discontinuous change decisions** involve major changes that depart significantly from the direction the team is taking currently. In business, wanting to start a new product line, offer a new service, or move location are examples of discontinuous change decisions. These are unlike **continuous changes,** which are merely extensions of previous decisions (ordering a greater quantity of a product or staying open an hour longer on weekends).

Consensus with qualification is a two-step decision-making process. First, the team tries to reach a consensus on the discontinuous change. If consensus is reached, the decision is made. If consensus cannot be reached, a supervisor, manager, or expert makes the final decision, using input from all team members. Thus, consensus with qualification begins with the unanimity rule and ends with minority rule.

Employees engage in a team training exercise. Some training methods are highly controversial.

Training and Assessment

Assessments of individual team members' productivity and performance should not be tied to wages, salaries, and promotions or demotions. This will quickly fracture a team and destroy motivation. Nevertheless, overall team performance and productivity should be assessed, especially in light of any training members might receive.

Formal training of teams is an important part of teambuilding. A college course can provide such training for student groups, but in the workplace training is often imported from outside sources. Goleman (1998) notes, however, that despite millions of dollars spent on training each year, business and corporate training programs are rarely assessed for their effectiveness.

"The world of training seems prone to whims and infatuated with fads" (Goleman, 1998, p. 249). The 1960s and early 1970s saw the rise of "encounter groups" and "sensitivity training," wherein thousands of employees were "trained" by sometimes obnoxious individuals with dubious backgrounds. These training sessions encouraged (some would say intimidated) participants to vent raw emotions. No evidence emerged showing that this form of training helped workers perform better on the job, and some studies showed damaging effects for some participants (Galanter, 1989; Singer, 1995).

Many current training programs are little better. Nevertheless, it is increasingly likely that you will be required to participate in team training as a condition of your employment. Requiring employees to participate in training that has not been shown to be effective and could be damaging to the participant raises serious ethical issues that should concern you (Box 11-3).

Box 11-3   Focus on Controversy

Questionable Training, Dubious Ethics

Training on the job may involve far more than nuts-and-bolts information on the technical aspects of tasks you will be expected to perform. Approximately $150 million is spent each year by U.S. businesses on sometimes controversial team training programs (Singer, 1995). These training programs include a surprising conglomeration of fads and fanciful notions to incite worker motivation and build teams. According to the Equal Employment Opportunity Commission (EEOC), a federal oversight agency, team training programs include aura readings, biofeedback, faith healing, guided visualization, meditation, mysticism, therapeutic touch, yoga, and fire walking (lighting a fire under team members was never meant to be taken literally). The list of dubious training programs is long and controversial: Actualizations, Direct Centering, the Forum, Lifespring, MSIA/Insight Training Seminars, PSI World, Silva Mind Control, Sterling Management Systems, and Transformational Technologies are just a sample. Singer (1995) claims that "most of these programs do not provide the skills training they advertise" (p. 211). The skills training they do provide includes meditation, neurolinguistic programming, biofeedback, unusual relaxation techniques, visualization, trance inductions, and "attack therapy," which promotes suspension of critical listening and in some cases challenges employees' religious beliefs (Singer, 1995).

New fads and untested training programs spring up every year. Goleman's (1995) excellent best-selling book, *Emotional Intelligence*, stimulated the emergence of new training programs that purport to teach teambuilding by developing the emotional intelligence of workers. Goleman (1998) notes that these programs are "often only a repackaging or slight remodeling of a program they had offered before under another name" (p. 258).

Many training programs have come under fire. As Singer (1995) notes, "Besides making complaints to the EEOC, many employees have filed civil suits objecting to training program content or related pressures at the workplace. Some lost their jobs by objecting. Other employees have suffered psychological decompensation as a consequence of what occurred in the training programs" (p. 191).

Mandatory training programs, whose effectiveness is unproven and techniques questionable, may violate several ethical standards discussed in Chapter 1. Many of the training programs are deceptively packaged as workshops on job-related skills and teambuilding when they are actually confrontational, psychologically intense therapy groups (Singer, 1995). This violates the ethical standard of honesty. Team members should know what to expect before entering the program.

Some trainers are openly abusive to trainees (Singer, 1995). This violates the ethical standard of respect. No team member should have to endure abusive remarks from trainers as a requirement for continued employment.

Finally, the mandatory nature of many programs forces team members to endure training that seems pointless or offensive. Coercing members to participate in questionable training programs violates the ethical standard of choice. Aside from the ethical concern, forced training programs usually produce lackluster participation from team members, resentment instead of an enthusiastic desire to learn new skills, and even exit from the team (Goleman, 1998).

The best programs are not one-size-fits-all types of training where every team member, regardless of differences in individual skill level or motivation, is given identical instruction. Programs with proven records of effectiveness allow team members to choose for themselves from a menu of possible training experiences tailored to their individual needs (Goleman, 1998). This menu could include such work-related skills as empathic listening, anger management, creative decision-making techniques, or dealing with difficult team members.

Questions for Thought

1. Should a team member have an absolute right to refuse training if he or she views it as objectionable? Why or why not?
2. Should training programs ever be a requirement of employment? Explain.
3. What should be done with a team member who refuses to receive training because he or she views it as objectionable or pointless, even though the member is deficient in certain skills?

Before teams engage in training, members should seek evidence of program effectiveness that goes beyond "happy sheets" indicating how much participants have liked the training and what about it they liked most. As Goleman (1998) points out, liking doesn't equal learning. Popularity rating sheets favor slick, cleverly packaged programs that are fun and entertaining. Whether they produce better teams and teamwork is questionable. The best evidence of effectiveness of training programs is an objective pre- and post-training test that targets specific skill performance. Are the teams more productive after the training than before? Programs that cannot provide such data should be approached with caution. Training and assessment of team effectiveness are key components for structuring teambuilding. Done correctly, teams can flourish.

Teambuilding depends on proper structure. Establish clear, challenging, and cooperative goals; develop clear roles for each member; use the Standard Agenda to guide decision making; attempt to reach consensus whenever it is possible and practical; and train members to function as a team. Effective teambuilding, however, doesn't guarantee proficient teamwork.

Teamwork

Teamwork is the process of members exercising competent communication within the framework of teams. Teamwork operates within the structure erected by teambuilding. All the necessary structures for teambuilding may exist without teams working effectively. How members communicate within the team structure strongly influences the level of teamwork proficiency.

Competent communication is the essence of teamwork. Some of the key aspects of communication competence particularly relevant to teamwork already discussed are: establishing a cooperative environment, empowering team members, exercising a healthy skepticism without showing contempt for different viewpoints, using empathic listening, choosing the most effective conflict management style, employing situational and competent leadership, and managing anger effectively. Expanding on these discussions, this section explores three topics relevant to teamwork: conflict management in teams, creative problem solving, and defective teamwork (known as groupthink).

Conflict Management in Teams

Managing conflict in interpersonal relationships can be daunting. The challenge is considerably magnified when teams enter the picture. As the size of groups increase, complexity increases exponentially. The potential for conflict and the complexity involved in managing it effectively are markedly different for a team of 3 members than for a group of 10, 15, or more. Working out differences with a partner can be tough; working out differences with half a dozen or more team members can be mind-boggling.

One study (Rath and Strong Inc., 1989) of 22,600 employees of *Fortune* 500 companies found that subjects rated conflict management as the part of their work that provoked the most dissatisfaction. Team members can follow a number of steps to improve conflict management (Romig, 1996).

Pick the Appropriate Time   As a general rule, handling a conflict early prevents it from erupting into a more serious problem at a later time. Nevertheless, trying to manage a team conflict when members are hungry, tired, or severely stressed from deadline pressure can backfire (Romig, 1996). An ideal time may never emerge, but look for the best opportunity to deal with a conflict. This may mean postponing a confrontation for a day until members are more rested, less stressed, and have full stomachs.

Manage Feelings   Many of the best teams are those composed of members with very diverse skills and personalities (Shirley, 1997). This diversity, however, can be a mixed blessing. Diversity provides a deep reservoir of resources for the group, but with diversity sometimes comes friction and intense conflict. Personality clashes within teams are not uncommon. When disagreements erupt into angry exchanges between members, managing this anger effectively is a critical issue for the entire team. Emotionally charged debates characterized by angry outbursts and bad feelings can erode teamwork (Goleman, 1998). Team members all have to feel responsible for quelling angry outbursts during discussions and disagreements. This means following suggestions already presented for defusing anger and rage, such as remaining unconditionally constructive and asymmetrical, especially when strong disagreements emerge.

Create a Supportive Climate   Competition within a team destroys teamwork (Aguayo, 1990). Merit pay schemes, contests to determine who is the best team member, and comparison ranking of employees by grading their performance all encourage team members to work against others to gain an advantage and garner recognition. Create a supportive climate instead. Use supportive communication patterns (Chapter 8). Create a We- not Me-oriented climate. Basketball coach John Wooden said it well, "It's amazing how much can be accomplished if no one cares who gets the credit" (as cited in Aguayo, 1990, p. 100). Teamwork is cooperation in action.

Use Appropriate Styles of Conflict Management   The most appropriate conflict management style for teams is collaboration. Unlike some other types of groups, teams are set up for members to work together collaboratively. Some initial research suggests that the collaborative style of conflict management is used by team members more frequently than other conflict styles (Farmer & Roth, 1998). The interdependence of goals, clearly defined role structure, and team identity all encourage a cooperative approach to conflict management.

On occasion, however, teams may find other conflict styles useful or even necessary (Chapter 9). The point to remember is that conflict management is most successful when team members begin with styles that have a high probability of success, using lower probability styles as a last resort. This means beginning with collaboration, accommodating where possible, compromising only when no integrative decision emerges from creative problem-solving efforts, avoiding issues only when it would be counterproductive to confront them, and using the power-forcing, competitive style when no other style works and issues must be resolved.

A casual, looser work environment can promote creativity.

Creative Problem Solving

Four deer hunters hire the same float plane every hunting season, fly into northern Maine, and "bag" a deer apiece. This season is no different. The pilot of the plane looks at the four deer carcasses and informs the hunters that he can't fly all the men and deer in one trip. The hunters complain, the pilot resists; the hunters complain more strenuously, the pilot wavers; they finally load the plane. The pilot taxies the plane across the lake, guns the engine, picks up speed, and lifts off. A few minutes into the flight the plane crashes. The men crawl from the wreckage and one hunter asks, "Where are we?" The pilot looks around and answers, "Looks like we're about 100 yards from where we crashed last year."

Groups can get into ruts. Creative problem solving requires breaking free from thinking that is repetitive, ritualistic, and rigid. The rigid thinking that characterizes the hunters' problem solving is an impediment. They continue to repeat the same mistake because their thinking is stuck.

In this section ways to unstick a team's thinking so creative, original, and effective solutions to problems can be devised are explained. Creative problem solving is a vital aspect of teamwork. As Carnevale and Probst (1998) note, "Successful conflict resolution often requires that disputants develop novel alternatives, new perspectives, and a fresh outlook on the issues. Creative problem solving is often required in negotiation" (p. 1308). Solving problems is a primary purpose of teams, and doing it effectively requires creativity.

Promoting Team Creativity Several conditions can promote creative problem solving (Figure 11-2). First, establish a cooperative expectation. Competitive ex-

Figure 11-2 Conditions for Creative Problem Solving

pectations can freeze thinking (Carnevale & Probst, 1998). When group members anticipate an adversarial exchange, thinking often becomes rigid, and counterproductive power struggles can distract the team. "An individual who anticipates competition may use precious cognitive resources in the effort to beat the other negotiator rather than develop creative optimal solutions. Cognitive resources may be used to plan, strategize, and coerce rather than to problem solve and collaborate" (p. 1308). A cooperative expectation can unfreeze thinking. Team members have little reason to be combative, and the focus is on solving a problem together to everyone's satisfaction.

Second, creativity is promoted by challenges. As the adage says, "Necessity is the mother of invention." Trying to discover a solution to a previously insoluble problem can stir the creative juices. Attempting to do what others have not been able to accomplish can be a powerful motivator.

Third, creativity flourishes when there is a moratorium on judging ideas. Create an atmosphere where any idea, no matter how zany, can be offered without fear of ridicule. Ideas must be evaluated for their practicality and effectiveness, but instant assessments are creativity killers (Goleman, 1998). Team members should withhold critiques of ideas until there has been an opportunity to explore the solution and to tinker with it.

Fourth, relax deadlines as much as possible. Creativity can flourish under pressure, but relentless and unreasonable deadlines can panic a team. Panic doesn't usually spur creativity, but it can lead to a mental meltdown.

Fifth, a fun, friendly atmosphere usually promotes creativity best (Goleman, 1998). Fun relaxes team members and reduces concerns about power, status, and esteem. Having fun is the great equalizer among diverse individuals. Having fun means modifying some nonessential rules. Casual dress instead of more formal work attire may help signal a looser, friendlier, less power-conscious atmosphere.

Specific Methods Team creativity is enhanced by structured methods of problem solving (Romig, 1996). Edward DeBono (1992), author of several books on creativity, argues that unstructured creativity "is a dead end. It appears to be attractive at first, but you really can't go far. There are systematic structured approaches to creativity that I believe have more substance" (p. 37).

The first and most popular structured approach is brainstorming. **Brainstorming** is a creative problem-solving method characterized by encouragement of even zany ideas, freedom from initial evaluation of potential solutions, and energetic participation from all group members. The brainstorming method was originally introduced by Alex Osborn, an advertising executive, in 1939. Team members produce the best results when several rules are followed:

1. *All members should come prepared with initial ideas.* Most research that shows disappointing results from group brainstorming excludes this vital first step (Rothwell, 1998). Team members must be prepared adequately to brainstorm in the group. Provide necessary background information to all team members. Make certain the problem is clearly defined. Each member generates ideas prior to team interaction.

2. *Don't criticize any idea during the brainstorming process.* Idea slayers, such as "You can't be serious," "What a silly idea," "That'll never work," "We don't do it that way," and "That's crazy," will quickly defeat the purpose of brainstorming. This is especially true if the more powerful members make these criticisms of ideas offered by less powerful, hesitant members. An air of equality is important for productive brainstorming. If less powerful members concentrate on what more powerful members will think of them, they will be overly cautious about contributing ideas. Prohibiting instant evaluations of ideas can reduce initial reticence to participate fully in brainstorming sessions because all ideas are treated as equal during the brainstorming.

3. *Encourage freewheeling idea generation.* The more ideas the better. Even zany ideas may provoke a truly terrific solution to a problem by causing team members to think "outside the box." You want team members to expand their thinking, to think in new ways. This is where the fun atmosphere is important. A loose, relaxed, enjoyable brainstorming session encourages freewheeling idea generation, and it can minimize power distinctions between members. When team leaders are as zany and relaxed as other members, it momentarily equalizes power in the group. Team members see the leader as "one of them." This can be empowering for the more hesitant, cautious members.

4. *Don't clarify ideas during the idea generation phase.* That will slow down the process. Clarification can come later.

5. *Piggyback on the ideas of others.* Build on suggestions made by team members by modifying or slightly altering an idea.

6. *Record all ideas for future reference.* Don't edit any ideas during the initial phase of the brainstorming.

7. *Encourage participation from all team members.* Keep the brainstorming fun and fast-paced so all members will want to offer suggestions (Box 11-4).

Box 11-4   Sharper Focus

Brainstorming in Action

"Encourage Wild Ideas" reads the sign on the wall of each brainstorming room at IDEO Product Development in Silicon Valley, California. Brainstorming rooms are sanctuaries for creativity where product design teams composed of engineers, industrial designers, and behavioral psychologists hurl ideas back and forth in a frenzy of mental activity (O'Brien, 1995). IDEO brainstormed designs for the Macintosh Duo docking system for laptops, Levolor blinds, virtual reality headgear, AT&T's telephones and answering machines, and a host of other diverse products. One of its most notable and early accomplishments was the design for the Apple computer's original point-and-click mouse. Steve Jobs, Apple's driving force in its early days, went to Xerox first for the design. Xerox had a crude idea for a mouse, but it would have cost the consumer $1,200. This wasn't very practical for a computer that would cost only $1,000. Next, Jobs consulted Hewlett-Packard engineers, who claimed it would take 3 years to design a practical mouse, and it would cost the consumer $150. Jobs finally consulted David Kelley, owner and president of IDEO. Kelley assembled a team and in 3 weeks designed a workable mouse. "We made the outside from a Walgreen's butter dish. It cost $17 to make," explains Kelley (as cited in O'Brien, 1995, p. 14).

Brainstorming is a key element in designs concocted by IDEO. Faced with the problem of an electric car that is so quiet it would likely cause accidents because no one would hear it approaching, the brainstorming team at IDEO attacks the problem with relish. "How about tire treads that play music?" one team member offers. "Different tread patterns will play different tunes," offers another. "How about a little Eric Clapton?" another chimes in, and the ideas flow, one piggybacked on another.

Presented with the challenge to design a commuter coffee cup that allows pedaling a bicycle without spilling the drink, the brainstormers rapidly fire questions at the customer who requests the product. "Do you want to sip or suck the coffee as you ride?" "Sip," is the response. The brainstormers quickly draw designs of 15 contraptions, among them are a "camelback" that puts a container with a plastic hose in a backpack, a coffee cup with a temperature gauge attached to a helmet, and a "Sip-o-matic" with a suction valve. The Sip-o-matic is a hit with the customer. The brainstorming atmosphere is kept light-hearted and zany. No idea is too goofy during the idea generation phase of the brainstorming session, and all ideas are written on "writeable walls." Brainstormers repeatedly piggyback on the ideas of other team members, and all team members are totally engrossed, enjoying the challenge.

Nominal group technique is a second structured method of creative problem solving. **Nominal group technique** involves these steps:

1. Team members work alone to generate ideas.
2. The team is convened and ideas are shared in round robin fashion. All ideas are written on a chalkboard, tablet, or easel. Clarification of ideas is permitted, but evaluation is prohibited.
3. Each team member selects five favorite ideas from the list generated and ranks them from most to least favorite.
4. Team members' rankings are averaged, and the ideas with the highest averages are selected.

Brainstorming has a higher level of team member participation than nominal group technique, tends to be more exciting and fun, and is successful in generating both numerous and effective solutions to problems. The nominal group technique is more impersonal than brainstorming, tends to be less fun and involving, and does not capitalize on the benefits of group discussion. It does generate as many or more ideas, on average, as brainstorming, and it also produces quality solutions to problems.

A third method of creative problem solving is reframing. *Reframing* is the creative process of breaking rigid thinking by placing a problem in a different frame of reference. A service station proprietor put an out-of-order sign on a soda machine. Customers paid no attention to the sign, lost their money, then complained to the station owner. Frustrated and annoyed, the owner changed the sign. It now reads "$5" for a soda. No one made the mistake of putting money in the soda pop dispenser. The problem was reframed. Instead of wondering how to get customers to recognize that the machine was out of order, the owner changed the frame of reference to what would make customers not want to put money in the dispenser. Reframing opens up possible solutions hidden from our awareness by rigid thinking.

Levi Strauss, a huge manufacturer of jeans, faced a troublesome dilemma when it learned that two of its sewing contractors in Bangladesh were employing child laborers. Human rights activists pressured the company to take a stand against this abuse of children. They wanted Levi Strauss to insist that the contractors cease using underage children in the factories. The company investigated the situation, however, and discovered that no longer employing the children wasn't necessarily a good decision. The children would be impoverished if they lost their jobs, and some might even be driven into prostitution. This dilemma could have been viewed rigidly by Levi Strauss as a dichotomy, a choice between two opposites. Instead, the company reframed the problem by seeking a solution that neither fired the children from their jobs nor kept them working while they were underage. The company kept the children on the payroll while they attended school, then hired them again when they reached legal working age (Sherman & Lee, 1997). Reframing can produce creative solutions to seemingly intractable problems.

Reframing a team dispute from a competitive, adversarial contest of wills to a cooperative problem to be solved by mutual effort and goodwill can prevent conflict from becoming destructive. Winning a contest and solving a problem are distinctly different frames of reference.

When teams become stumped by narrow or rigid frames of reference, asking certain open-ended questions can help reframe the problem so new solutions might emerge. "What if . . . ?" is a very useful question. "What if we don't accept the inevitability of worker layoffs and downsizing?" "What if we tried working together instead of against each other?" "What if management is telling the truth about the budget?" All these questions encourage a different frame of reference and a different line of thinking. Additional reframing questions include:

Why must we accept what we've been told?
Why are these the only choices?
Could there be a different solution than the one we've discussed?
Can the problem be described in any other way?
Is there any way to make this disadvantage an advantage?

Brainstorming, nominal group technique, and reframing are three useful methods of creative problem solving. In some instances, methods can be combined, such as brainstorming ways to reframe a problem before brainstorming ideas to solve the problem.

Groupthink

How could the United States have been caught sleeping when the Japanese executed a sneak attack on Pearl Harbor resulting in the worst naval disaster in U.S. history? Why did John Kennedy and his cabinet advisers ever launch the Bay of Pigs invasion? After all, 1,400 Cuban exiles were facing a 200,000 strong Cuban army in a fruitless attempt to overthrow Fidel Castro. Kennedy lamented afterward, "How could I have been so stupid to let them go ahead?" (as cited in Janis, 1982, p. 16). Add to these disasters the escalation of the Vietnam War under Lyndon Johnson, the Nixon Watergate scandal, Jimmy Carter's failed mission to rescue hostages in Iran, the Iran-Contra scandal during the Ronald Reagan presidency, and the space shuttle *Challenger* disaster and you have a list of major fiascoes produced by teams. These are all examples of wretched teamwork.

Each of these events is an instance of "groupthink" (Janis, 1982; Mansfield, 1990). **Groupthink** is teamwork gone awry. It is a process of group members stressing cohesiveness and agreement instead of skepticism and optimum decision making. Too much emphasis is placed on members being "team players" and too little emphasis is placed on the group making quality decisions. Consensus seeking, cooperation, and cohesiveness are all part of teamwork, but these normally vital and constructive aspects of teamwork can produce terrible consequences when taken to an extreme.

Groupthink has several specific characteristics (Janis, 1982; Mohamed & Wiebe, 1996; Street, 1997). First, disagreement is discouraged during group discussions because it is viewed as disruptive to team cohesiveness. Second, there is a strong pressure to conform so there is at least the appearance of team unity. The team usually has a self-appointed "mindguard" whose task is to discourage ideas and viewpoints that might threaten team unity. Dissenters are pressured to be "team players." Third, the group lacks a structured decision-making process that encourages consideration of divergent options and opinions. Confirmation bias is prevalent. Lack of structured decision making combined with a high concern for maintaining team cohesiveness produces poor group decisions (Mullen et al., 1994). Fourth, there is an in-group–out-group team mentality. Everyone who is not a team member is considered part of the out-group. This in-group–out-group mentality gives rise to feelings that the team is morally superior to out-groups; outsiders are often negatively stereotyped or branded as evil. An offshoot of this in-group–out-group view of the world is a strong team identity that gives members a feeling of pride and prestige from belonging to the team (Street, 1997).

Janis (1989) offers four suggestions to prevent groupthink and to produce effective teamwork. First, the team could consult an impartial outsider with expertise on the problem discussed. This would reduce the danger from excessive cohesiveness leading to poor team decisions. This is sometimes why consultants are hired from outside an organization or group to give advice and counsel. Second, to reduce pressure on team members to conform, the team leader could withhold his or her point of view during early discussions. In this way, the appearance of dominance in power relationships between a more powerful team leader and less powerful members can be avoided, and members will be more inclined to express honest opinions.

John Kennedy, anxious to avoid committing another blunder after the Bay of Pigs fiasco, instituted leaderless group discussions with his advisory team. On occasion, especially during the early stages of team discussion where alternatives were brainstormed, Kennedy would leave the group. This proved to be especially effective during the 1962 Cuban Missile Crisis when the United States and the U.S.S.R. took the world to the brink of nuclear war over the U.S.S.R.'s secret installation of nuclear missiles in Cuba. Ted Sorenson, an Executive Committee member who worked on the crisis, noted, "One of the remarkable aspects of those meetings was a sense of complete equality. . . . I participated much more freely than I ever had . . . ; and the absence of the president encouraged everyone to speak his mind" (as cited in Janis, 1982, p. 144).

Third, the team could assign the devil's advocate role to a specific member. This can combat the excessive concurrence-seeking typical of groups that slide into groupthink. The devil's advocate would challenge any decision the group is likely to make to test the ideas. Fourth, the team can set up a "second chance" meeting where members can reconsider a preliminary decision. This allows teams to reflect on any proposal and avoid making impulsive decisions.

Summary

Teams are cooperative groups. Teambuilding provides the structure for teams: clear, challenging, and cooperative goals; clear roles; use of the Standard Agenda; consensus decision making whenever possible; and team training. Teamwork is competent communication in the context of teams. Teamwork often requires creative problem solving. There are three structured methods of creative problem solving: brainstorming, nominal group technique, and reframing. Finally, groupthink is poor teamwork in action. Groupthink occurs when team members place too much emphasis on cohesiveness and concurrence-seeking.

Suggested Readings

Goleman, D. (1998). *Working with emotional intelligence.* New York: Bantam. This is an excellent treatment of how to build teamwork in the workplace.
Larson, C., & LaFasto, M. (1989). *Teamwork: What must go right, what can go wrong.* Newbury Park, CA: Sage. This is still the best work on teamwork and teambuilding. It is highly readable.

Public Communication

Chapter 12

Preparing to Speak

Freedom of speech is the bedrock of a democratic society. Virtually every major and minor protest that occurs in our sometimes tumultuous society relies on public speaking to move the populace. The entire history of student protest in this country exhibits the power of public speaking. From the "Free Speech Movement" at Berkeley in 1964, through the Vietnam War era, and continuing with the battle on college campuses over racism, sexism, and "politically correct" speech, students have depended on public speaking to produce change. Ideas have to be framed, issues have to be crystallized, and arguments have to be made for change to occur. Public speaking is a powerful and essential method for accomplishing this.

It is difficult to identify a profession that does not rely on or benefit from competent public speaking. Teaching, law, religion, politics, public relations, marketing, and business are communication-oriented professions. They require substantial knowledge and skill in public speaking. Company recruiters and business consultants uniformly recommend that job seekers develop public speaking skills (Patterson, 1996).

Average citizens are frequently called upon to give speeches of support or dissent at public meetings on utility rate increases, school board issues, and city or county disputes. One survey found that 55% of adults had given a speech during the previous 2 years (Kendall, 1985). College courses in diverse disciplines increasingly require oral presentations as class assignments. Those students who have public speaking knowledge and skills enjoy an enormous advantage in college courses when presentations in front of the class are required.

Competent public speakers know how to present complex ideas clearly and persuasively, keep an audience's attention, make reasonable arguments, and support claims with valid proof. They also move people to listen, to contemplate, and to change their minds. This is an impressive array of knowledge and skills for anyone to possess, and its application is virtually boundless. When would a person not find such public speaking knowledge and skills useful?

The principal purpose of this chapter is to begin examining the public speaking process, in particular, the initial preparation for speaking to an audience. There are three objectives:

1. to analyze the causes of speech anxiety and suggest ways to control stage fright,
2. to discuss topic selection and development, and
3. to explain how to research your speech topic.

The communication competence model will guide us throughout the discussion of public speaking. Public speakers must make choices regarding the appropriateness and likely effectiveness of topics, attention strategies, style and delivery, evidence, and persuasive strategies. When you are giving a speech, you must be sensitive to the signals sent from an audience that indicate lack of interest, disagreement, confusion, enjoyment, support, and a host of additional reactions. This allows you to make adjustments during the speech, if necessary. A committed public speaker must expect to spend generous amounts of time and energy preparing to speak to an audience. Finally, ethics is always an important part of giving speeches. Effectiveness of a speech must be tempered by ethical concerns. What works may not always be honest, respectful, or fair.

Additionally, public speaking is primarily a cooperative, interdependent transaction between the speaker and his or her audience. A speaker needs to think

A speaker needs to work with an audience, not against it. Changing the collective mind of an audience is a cooperative effort. You may win the debater points but turn the audience against you, as this booing crowd demonstrates.

in terms of what will induce an audience to work with, not against, the speaker. When an audience turns against a speaker and exhibits a collective desire to engage in an adversarial contest of wills, the speaker is almost always the loser. Speakers who project an image of arrogance, superiority, and dogmatism—competitive communication patterns—usually turn an audience against them. An effective public speaker takes the perspective of the audience (empathy) and works with that perspective to frame issues and ideas that will resonate with listeners. As many experienced public speakers can attest, you can "win" all the debater points but lose the audience because listeners just don't like the attitude you project. As the process of public speaking unfolds in the next few chapters, keep uppermost in your mind that cooperation—working with an audience and building good will—is a key to public speaking success.

Speech Anxiety

Speech anxiety, or stage fright as it is sometimes called, "refers to those situations when an individual reports he or she is afraid to deliver a speech" (Ayres & Hopf, 1995). Speech anxiety is often discussed in a chapter on speech presentation. It is included in this chapter on speech preparation, however, for two reasons. First, when a speech assignment is given, the immediate concern for most individuals is speech anxiety. This concern can powerfully occupy one's mind and adversely affect the ability to prepare a speech. Second, managing speech anxiety effectively requires specific preparation for the potentially stressful event of giving a speech. If you wait until you actually give your speech before considering what steps need to be taken to manage your anxiety, it is usually too late. Simply put, you need a clear plan for managing your speech anxiety, and that plan is part of the preparation process.

Speech Anxiety as a Problem

As an undergraduate, I took a persuasion course that required several speeches. During one speech assignment, I observed a startling instance of speech anxiety. A young woman, bright and articulate outside of class, was terrified to give her speech. As if hoping for some cataclysmic natural disaster to strike and save her from the even worse fate of having to give her speech, she waited until all the other students had performed. Facing her audience from behind a podium, she opened her mouth and began to speak. All that came out was a breathy sound, but no words. She grabbed her throat, then swallowed hard and began again with the same result. At first, I believed she was merely gaining the audience's attention. I was curious to see how she would make this display relevant to her topic. Soon, however, I realized that I was witnessing a very unusual case of intense speech anxiety, so extreme that this terrified student actually lost her voice momentarily.

The professor quickly diagnosed the problem and gently told his anxious student to take her seat and see him after class. Remarkably, her voice returned as soon as she sat down. She met with the professor and discussed several ways to control her anxiety. In the next class period she gave her speech in full voice and received the enthusiastic applause of her classmates. In three decades of teaching public speaking, I have never witnessed a repeat occurrence of such extreme speech anxiety, but this example should provide you comfort. Even in the worst cases of speech anxiety there is an effective, relatively simple remedy.

Speech anxiety is a significant problem for most people. Motley (1995) found that about 85% of the population fears public speaking. Another study found that approximately 70% of the general population experiences moderately high to high speech anxiety (Richmond & McCroskey, 1989). My own surveys of college students in public speaking courses show that the vast majority, often everyone in class, experience at least some nervousness before giving a speech. Even college instructors must manage speech anxiety. One study revealed that 87% of psychology instructors experience speech anxiety when teaching (Gardner & Leak, 1994). Sixty-five percent of these same instructors rated their most severe case of speech anxiety between "definitely unpleasant" and "extreme."

Take any four individuals and odds are that two of the four have some butterflies in their stomach prior to a speech. The third individual has anxiety that is bothersome but not incapacitating. The fourth individual has anxiety so severe that he or she is almost paralyzed by fear of giving a speech. These individuals will avoid classes that require oral presentations, skip meetings, refuse job promotions, or even change jobs or occupations to escape public speaking. The fear of public speaking is one reason most colleges and universities make a public speaking course mandatory. If left as an option, the great majority of students would avoid this beneficial class because of fear (Box 12-1).

Symptoms of Speech Anxiety

We often fear what we do not understand. Understanding speech anxiety so you can learn to manage it begins with identification of common symptoms associated with speech anxiety and an explanation for why these symptoms occur.

Box 12-1   Sharper Focus

Stage Fright Among Great Speakers and Performers

Those who are unaccustomed to performing in front of the public usually experience anxiety. Those accustomed to public performance, however, also often experience stage fright. One survey (as cited in Hahner et al., 1997) revealed that 76% of experienced speakers have stage fright before performing. Biographies of famous speakers such as Demosthenes, Cicero, Abraham Lincoln, Henry Clay, Daniel Webster, and Winston Churchill reveal that these giants of history had such a strong desire to overcome their fear of public speaking that they took every opportunity to mount the speaker's platform. Actor Harrison Ford was so terrified to speak in front of an audience that he studied acting to overcome his fear. Singer Carly Simon, however, succumbed to her stage fright, refusing to perform in live concerts for 5 years until she finally took steps to manage her performance anxiety. Legendary Oscar-winning actor Laurence Olivier suffered such intense stage fright that he forbade cast members to look him in the eye while he was acting. Willard Scott, sometime weatherman and most of the time vaudeville act on NBC's *Today* show, experienced such intense stage fright that he hyperventilated on camera. Barbara Streisand, Madonna, Randy Travis, and Luciano Pavarotti are just a few performers who have admitted that they have stage fright before performing.

If you experience speech anxiety, don't feel alone. You're in good company. Even the professionals must learn to manage their fear of performing in public. I. A. R. Wylie, novelist and sometime lecturer, offers this observation about stage fright: "Now after many years of practice I am, I suppose, really a 'practiced speaker.' But I rarely rise to my feet without a throat constricted with terror and a furiously thumping heart. When, for some reason, I am cool and self-assured, the speech is always a failure" (as cited in Bradley, 1991, p. 36). Speechwriter Peggy Noonan (1998) notes that Ronald Reagan "was always nervous before he spoke. Good performers always are, because they're serious about what they're doing and want badly to do well" (p. 11). As Edward R. Murrow, acclaimed radio and television commentator, explains: "The best speakers know enough to be scared. . . . The only difference between the pros and the novices is that the pros have trained the butterflies to fly in formation" (as cited in Osborn & Osborn, 1997, p. 56).

Physiologist Walter Cannon labeled the physiological defense-alarm process triggered by stress the "fight or flight response." Physiologically, animals and humans are equipped with the same defense system for dealing with stress. The myriad physiological changes that are activated by a threat prepare both animals and humans to either fight the threat or flee the danger.

The fight or flight response produces a complex constellation of physiological symptoms (Figure 12-1). Some of the more pronounced symptoms are (Zimbardo, 1992):

Dilated pupils (to accommodate far vision)
Accelerated heart beat and increased blood pressure (increased oxygen supply)
Blood vessel constriction in skin, skeletal muscles, brain, and viscera (cut off blood supply to less necessary functions)
Increased perspiration (cooling)
Bronchial tubes dilate (increased oxygen supply)
Inhibited digestion (unnecessary energy drain)
Stimulated glucose release from the liver (energy supply)
Increased blood flow away from extremities and to large muscles (supply oxygen and glucose to major muscles used to fight)
Tightened neck and upper back muscles (preparation for fighting)
Stimulated adrenal gland activity (alertness, motion, and strength)

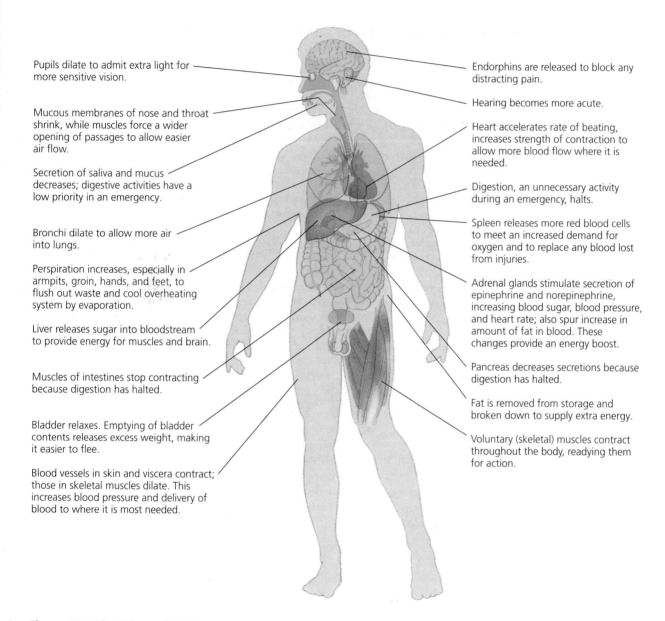

Pupils dilate to admit extra light for more sensitive vision.

Mucous membranes of nose and throat shrink, while muscles force a wider opening of passages to allow easier air flow.

Secretion of saliva and mucus decreases; digestive activities have a low priority in an emergency.

Bronchi dilate to allow more air into lungs.

Perspiration increases, especially in armpits, groin, hands, and feet, to flush out waste and cool overheating system by evaporation.

Liver releases sugar into bloodstream to provide energy for muscles and brain.

Muscles of intestines stop contracting because digestion has halted.

Bladder relaxes. Emptying of bladder contents releases excess weight, making it easier to flee.

Blood vessels in skin and viscera contract; those in skeletal muscles dilate. This increases blood pressure and delivery of blood to where it is most needed.

Endorphins are released to block any distracting pain.

Hearing becomes more acute.

Heart accelerates rate of beating, increases strength of contraction to allow more blood flow where it is needed.

Digestion, an unnecessary activity during an emergency, halts.

Spleen releases more red blood cells to meet an increased demand for oxygen and to replace any blood lost from injuries.

Adrenal glands stimulate secretion of epinephrine and norepinephrine, increasing blood sugar, blood pressure, and heart rate; also spur increase in amount of fat in blood. These changes provide an energy boost.

Pancreas decreases secretions because digestion has halted.

Fat is removed from storage and broken down to supply extra energy.

Voluntary (skeletal) muscles contract throughout the body, readying them for action.

Figure 12-1 The Fight-or-Flight Response

Spleen releases red blood corpuscles (aid in clotting a wound)
Bone marrow stimulated to produce white corpuscles (fight possible infection)

Some of the more prominent corresponding verbal and nonverbal symptoms of speech anxiety are:

Quivering, tense voice and weak projection (constricted throat muscles)
Frequent dysfluencies such as "uhms" and "ahs" (restricted blood flow to the brain causing confusion of thought)

Box 12-2   Sharper Focus

Odd But Frequent Symptoms of Speech Anxiety

Several physiological manifestations of speech anxiety occur often, and they may perplex you. Why do we suffer that fluttery feeling in the pit of our stomach known as butterflies? Why do goose bumps appear when we're anxious about making a speech? The expression "getting cold feet" refers to extreme reticence to perform certain actions, but why do individuals giving speeches often literally get cold feet?

Chemicals, notably adrenaline, secreted into the blood stream when fear is aroused in humans are responsible for butterflies. These chemical secretions shut down the digestive system, so our undigested food sits in our stomachs like globules of grease floating on top of dishwater. Digestion is relatively unimportant when compared to threats to the person's well being, so digestion is temporarily postponed until the threat subsides.

The pimply effect on your skin that erects the hairs on your arm is known as goose bumps. It is an evolutionary relic from our ancient ancestors who had furry bodies.

Erecting body hair increases insulation, thereby conserving body heat. In nonhuman mammals, erecting body hair is a means of defense against an opponent. A cornered cat, for instance, will erect its fur, making it appear much larger and therefore more menacing to an opponent.

Human body hair is too short to be of much use either to insulate or to appear formidable, so goose bumps serve no relevant purpose, especially to public speakers. Your goose bumps will not likely terrify anyone nor keep you warm, but they do remind us of an evolutionary connection to our ancient past.

Cold feet (and cold hands for that matter) are caused by what physiologists call peripheral vascular constriction. In plain English, blood vessels in our extremities (hands and feet) narrow, reducing the blood flow. During stress, blood flow shifts away from the periphery of the body and the digestive tract toward the large muscle groups in the torso and legs where it is needed most for fighting or fleeing.

Rigid, motionless posture (constricted muscles of legs and torso)
Flailing arms, tapping fingers, shaky hands, aimless pacing, side-to-side swaying (adrenaline surge)
Dry mouth, sometimes called "cotton mouth," that makes speaking difficult (digestive system shutdown)

These physiological symptoms make sense if you are about to grapple with a crazed grizzly or sprint from a rampaging bull, but they don't seem especially relevant to making a speech. Increased perspiration (cooling), respiration (oxygen), glucose (energy), and blood flow to major muscles (strength) would certainly help with the grappling and sprinting. Shutting down functions not immediately relevant to fighting or fleeing also makes sense. You do not need to waste energy digesting your burger and fries when dealing with a sudden danger. Digesting can be postponed until the threat is past (Box 12-2).

What, though, does the fight or flight response have to do with performing a speech in front of an audience? Neither fighting nor fleeing is considered an appropriate response to the stress of public speaking. The sight of a student wrestling with an instructor or bolting from the classroom when he or she is called to begin a speech would be startling. Granted, some of the physiological responses to threat are relevant to public speaking. If the speech is lengthy, the room hot and stuffy, and the occasion momentous, increased glucose, respiration, perspiration, and adrenaline will help you sustain yourself throughout such a challenging task. Adrenaline can also assist you in performing at a peak level. Clothes saturated with perspiration, increased red and white corpuscles, a quivering voice, dry mouth, shaky hands, rigid posture, nausea, and a pounding heart are unnecessary and often distracting when making a speech—unless a real threat to life and limb truly exists (an unlikely classroom occurrence).

Our physiological responses to a perceived threat are controlled by our autonomic nervous system. When a person experiences stress from whatever source, the autonomic nervous system reacts reflexively, initiating the fight or flight response. The process is like a light switch. You have two choices—on or off. You may prefer a dimmer switch that gives a proportional response to stress, but your body prepares for the worst-case scenario. After all, what begins as a seemingly harmless event may balloon into a life-or-death struggle. Best to play it safe, so goes the internal logic of your body's fight or flight response. Thus, your anxiety may feed on itself, even spiral out of control. You sweat profusely even when the room isn't hot, your heart races and your respiration increases even though you're standing still, and the meal in your stomach, undigested, feels like you swallowed a chunk of radial tire.

Causes of Dysfunctional Speech Anxiety

Dysfunctional speech anxiety occurs when the intensity of the fight or flight response prevents an individual from performing appropriately. **Functional speech anxiety** occurs when the fight or flight response is managed and stimulates an optimum presentation. The degree of anxiety and our ability to manage it, not anxiety itself, determines the difference. Speakers who experience low to moderate anxiety that is under control typically give better speeches than do speakers who experience little or no anxiety (Motley, 1995). Low to moderate anxiety means the speaker cares about the quality of the speech. Anxiety can energize a speaker and enhance performance. You will present a more dynamic, forceful presentation when energized than when you feel so comfortable that you become almost listless and unchallenged.

Causes of dysfunctional speech anxiety fall primarily into two categories: self-defeating thoughts and situational factors. Let's briefly examine each.

Self-Defeating Thoughts Some individuals see giving a speech as a challenging and exciting opportunity, whereas other individuals see it as an experience equivalent to swallowing a live snake. How you think about speaking to an audience will largely determine your level of stage fright.

There are three self-defeating ways of thinking about public speaking. First, some individuals predict *catastrophic failure*. I'm not referring to mild problems here such as a brief stutter or a momentary lapse of memory. I'm referring to a complete collapse. Those with irrational fears of catastrophic failure can experience heart rates that exceed 200 beats per minute (Motley, 1995). Thinking irrationally about a speech presentation wildly exaggerates potential problems. Those with irrational fears predict not just momentary memory lapses but a complete mental meltdown (e.g., "I know I'll forget my entire speech, and I'll just stand there like a goober."). They fear that audiences will not just think that their ideas are different or even wrong but instead will laugh and hoot them off the stage and view them as fools. Minor problems of organization are magnified into graphic episodes of total incoherence and nonstop babbling. Predictions of catastrophes are irrational. I personally have listened to more than 10,000 student speeches. I

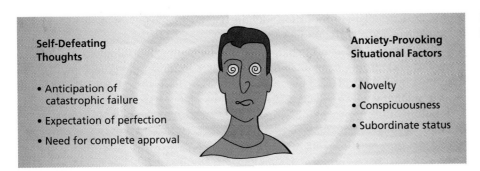

Figure 12-2 Factors in Speech Anxiety

have witnessed some unimpressive speeches, but not more than a handful of these speeches qualified as outright disasters, and the obvious cause in each case was total lack of preparation.

A second form of self-defeating thought is *perfectionist thinking.* Perfectionists anguish over every perceived flaw and overgeneralize the significance of even minor defects. For example:

> "I totally failed—I forgot to preview my main points."
> "My knees were shaking. The audience must have thought I was out of control."
> "I feel like an idiot. I mispronounced the name of one of the experts I quoted."

Flawless public speaking is a desirable goal, but why beat up on yourself when it doesn't happen? Even the most talented and experienced public speakers make occasional errors in otherwise riveting and eloquent speeches. Martin Luther King Jr. stumbled twice during his famous "I Have a Dream" speech. Who noticed? Ironically, the imperfections so noticeable to perfectionists usually go unnoticed by most people in the audience.

Believing we must acquire *complete approval* from an audience is a third form of self-defeating thought. Comedian Bill Cosby offers an interesting observation regarding complete approval: "I don't know the key to success, but the key to failure is trying to please everybody." All of us desire approval, especially from those whose opinion we value. It is irrational thinking, however, to accept nothing less than complete approval from an audience. You cannot please everyone, particularly if you take a stand on a controversial issue. Making complete approval from your audience a vital concern merely sets you up for inevitable failure. When you set standards for success at unreachable heights, you are bound to take a tumble.

Anxiety-Provoking Situations   Several anxiety-provoking situations are relevant to public speaking (Figure 12-2). First, the *novelty* of the speaking situation can easily make us tense. When we do not know exactly what to expect because the situation is new to us, we feel anxious. As you gain experience speaking in front of groups, the novelty wears off and anxiety diminishes.

A second anxiety-provoking situation is *conspicuousness.* I have polled more than 1,000 students in public speaking classes. When asked what causes their speech anxiety, a large proportion identify being "on stage" or "in the spotlight." Being conspicuous, or the center of attention, increases most people's anxiety. You feel as if you are under a microscope being meticulously examined. As the size of an audience grows, conspicuousness increases in most individuals' minds. The solution to anxiety provoked by conspicuousness is to develop confidence through experience that you can be successful in front of a large audience.

A third anxiety-provoking situation is *subordinate status*. When placed in a situation where some or all of your audience have higher relative status than you, tension can mount. Students appearing before boards of trustees for the college or speaking to the faculty senate can easily feel intimidated and nervous. Again, preparation and practice are vital means of dealing with this anxiety-provoking situation.

All of these causes of speech anxiety, both self-defeating thoughts and anxiety-provoking situations, can produce a spiraling effect that feeds on itself. We begin by viewing a speech as a performance. This, in turn, stimulates physiological arousal. We then interpret the physical symptoms as fear, which triggers irrational thoughts, which stimulates more intense physical symptoms, greater fear, followed by more irrational thoughts, and so forth (Motley, 1995). *The key to managing speech anxiety is to prevent the spiral of fear from ever occurring*.

Strategies for Managing Speech Anxiety

There is one surefire way to experience absolutely no anxiety prior to and during a speech. Simply don't care about the quality of your speech at all. You'll be very relaxed, but you'll also give a crummy speech. Your goal should not be to eliminate speech anxiety. Your goal should be to manage the anxiety that you do experience and use it to energize and stimulate peak accomplishment.

Many individuals have suggested strategies for managing speech anxiety; some are simple and others complex. Laurence Olivier sometimes swore at his audience backstage hoping to replace anxiety with anger. Willard Scott tried sticking a pin in his butt, hoping to startle away the stage fright. He also tried screaming off camera before giving weather reports on the *Today* show (not a very practical strategy for students in a classroom setting). Imagining members of your audience nude, clothed in their underwear, or in diapers are strategies offered so frequently by various people that they almost amount to folk wisdom. All of these suggestions have some merit, particularly if they work for you. They are unquestionably limited solutions, however, because they are diversionary tactics rather than strategies that directly address the primary causes of speech anxiety. In this section you will learn several ways to manage your speech anxiety.

Prepare and Practice Public speaking is a novel experience loaded with uncertainty for the inexperienced. Novices fear catastrophic failure because they don't know quite what to expect. Preparation and practice build self-confidence. As is true in almost anything you do, whether it is conversing with strangers at social gatherings or playing a musical instrument in front of a crowd, you tend to be less anxious when you are confident of your skills. You fear making a fool of yourself when you don't know what you're doing. You won't appear foolish if you have learned the requisite skills to present a speech effectively. You'll remove most of the novelty and uncertainty from the speaking experience when you are adequately prepared. So prepare your speech meticulously, and practice it before speaking in class to reduce your anxiety (Menzel & Carrell, 1994). Give it to friends. Give it to your dog. Practice it while taking a shower. Give it in your car on your way to class. Practice, practice, practice!

Speaking experience, of course, won't reduce anxiety if you stumble from one traumatic disaster to the next. Preparation is absolutely critical. If you make speech after speech, ill-prepared and untrained, don't expect your anxiety to diminish. Your dread of public speaking will become dysfunctional. "Practice makes perfect" if it is practice based on knowledge of effective public speaking for appropriate skill building. Without requisite knowledge, practice will make perfectly horrible because you will be rehearsing incompetent public speaking.

Read the chapters in this text on effective public speaking. Listen to the advice of your instructor as you prepare and present speeches. There is no substitute for preparation and practice. Both can significantly reduce your speech anxiety (Ayres & Hopf, 1995).

Gain Proper Perspective   Irrational, self-defeating thoughts are a primary cause of dysfunctional speech anxiety. How we think about our anxiety largely determines its level. One study (as cited in Motley, 1995) compared three groups of anxious speakers that were randomly divided. A metering device that monitored the heart rate of speakers as they made their presentations was attached to the podium in plain view of the speakers. High, normal, and low anxiety zones were clearly designated on the metering device for speakers to see as they spoke. A prepared speech was delivered by each speaker, and researchers monitored their actual heart rates. What the speakers didn't know was that researchers had rigged the heart monitor to give false readings to the speakers. Members of one group saw high heart rate readings on the monitor, members of a second group saw low heart rates on the monitor, and the third "control group" gave speeches while the monitor was turned off. The results were dramatic. Speakers who saw high heart rate readings did experience elevated heart rates. Speakers who saw low heart rate readings on the monitor experienced diminished heart rates. Control group speakers experienced varied heart rates. You can exaggerate your anxiety by concentrating on your symptoms and thinking your anxiety is severe.

There are three phases to speech anxiety symptoms (Motley, 1995). There is the *anticipation phase,* where your symptoms elevate just prior to giving your speech. The *confrontation phase* occurs when you face the audience and begin to speak. There is a tremendous surge of adrenalin, heart rate soars—sometimes to 180 beats per minute—perspiration increases, and so forth. The *adaptation phase* kicks in soon after the confrontation phase, within 60 seconds or less. Adaptation takes place even more swiftly for low-anxiety speakers, usually within 15 to 30 seconds. During this phase symptoms steadily diminish, reaching a comfortable level within a couple of minutes (Figure 12-3).

Knowing the phases of anxiety allows you to gain a proper perspective on your experience of speech anxiety. First, recognizing that your anxiety will diminish dramatically and quickly as you speak should provide some comfort. Second, if you learn to monitor your adaptation, you can accelerate the process. As you begin to notice your heart rate diminishing, say to yourself, "It's getting better already . . . and better . . . and better." Anxiety levels, even for the inexperienced, high-anxiety speaker, will diminish rapidly.

Figure 12-3 Heart Rate
Patterns of Typical High-
and Low-Anxiety Speakers

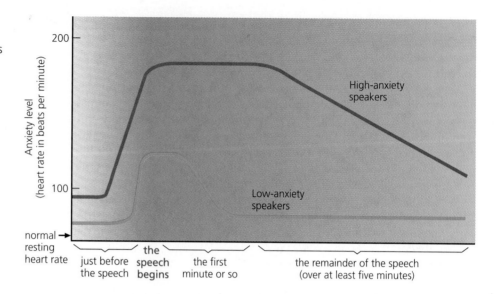

Another aspect of gaining proper perspective is learning to recognize the difference between rational and irrational speech anxiety. A colleague of mine, Darrell Beck, concocted a simple formula for determining the difference. The *severity* of the feared occurrence *times* the *probability* of the feared occurrence gives a rough approximation of how much anxiety is rational and when you have stepped over the line into irrational territory. Severity is approximated by imagining what would happen if catastrophic failure did occur. Would you fear for your life? Would you leave the country? Would you hide from friends and family, afraid to show your face? Would you drop out of college? None of these choices seems reasonable.

You gain perspective regarding the severity of your anxiety by deciding what's the worst that could befall you if disaster struck and you bombed the speech. You might drop the speech class, but even this is unlikely. Students are an understanding lot, and you'll have other opportunities in class to redeem yourself. Even a lousy speech doesn't warrant significant life changes. A few moments of disappointment, mild embarrassment, or discouragement because you received a mediocre grade is about as severe as it gets. Then, when you consider the probability of the "worst-case scenario" occurring, you should realize that there is not much to concern you. *High severity times low probability equals pointless anxiety.* Concentrate on the probable (low severity), not the merely possible (high severity).

Peggy Noonan (1998), a professional speechwriter, confesses that she had a phobia about public speaking that kept her from making her first speech until she was 40 years old. She learned to control her speech anxiety primarily by putting it in proper perspective. She explains it this way:

> (One) thing that has helped me is realizing that if I fail utterly, if I faint, babble or spew, if people walk out flinging the heavy linen napkins onto the big round tables in disgust . . . my life continues as good as it was. Better. Because fewer people will ask me to speak. So flopping would be good for me. The minute I remember this I don't flop. (p. 191)

Even individuals for whom English is a second language will benefit from gaining a proper perspective. Giving a speech in a second language can increase anxiety (McCroskey et al., 1985). There is an unrealistic expectation that English should be spoken perfectly. I have witnessed hundreds of speeches by non-native speakers of English. Never once have I observed an audience of college students be rude to that speaker because his or her English was not perfect. Normally, students admire a speaker who tries hard to give a good speech in a relatively unfamiliar language. They usually listen more intently as well. Working yourself into a lather over an impending speech simply lacks proper perspective.

Adopt a Noncompetitive Communication Orientation   Desiring complete approval, fretting over your conspicuousness onstage, and feeling intimidated by status differences with listeners all occur when you view public speaking as a performance. Reframe this performance orientation of the high-anxiety speaker. Replace it with a communication orientation. Motley (1995) makes the case for reframing this way: "I have never encountered an anxious speaker who did not have a performance orientation, or one whose anxiety was not substantially reduced when the communication orientation replaced it. Very simply, changing your overall approach to public speaking is the key to reducing and controlling the anxiety" (p. 49).

A performance orientation emphasizes the "do's" and "don'ts" of speaking. Anxious speakers have inflated concerns about saying "ah" or "uhm" too many times. They worry about gestures, vocal inflection, eye contact, posture, and a myriad of style and delivery problems. They worry that word choice won't be precise, so they memorize the speech or read from a manuscript. Memorization increases anxiety (you worry about forgetting parts of your speech), and reading creates an artificial speaking style. This all places the focus on impressing critics and scoring style points, not on the audience and your message.

Giving a speech isn't the Olympics, and you're usually not competing to score more points than someone else. Your audience won't hold up cards indicating your score immediately after you sit down. Granted, your speech instructor will likely give you a grade on your speech, but even here the performance orientation is counterproductive. No speech instructor expects silver-tongued oratory from novice speakers. Your instructor expects you to make mistakes, especially during your first few speeches. Speech classes are learning laboratories, not speech tournaments. Dump the performance orientation. It makes a speech into a contest. Most, perhaps all, of the speeches you will ever give will be evaluated on their own merits, not competitively in relation to someone else's speech. The competitive performance orientation feeds perfectionist thinking.

The irony is that you will perform better as a speaker if you move away from the competitive performance orientation (Motley, 1995). Your speaking style and delivery will seem more natural, less forced and stiff. When conversing with a friend or stranger, you rarely notice your delivery, gestures, posture, and so forth. You're intent on being clear and interesting, even having some fun. Approach your speech in the same way.

The **communication orientation** focuses on making your message clear and interesting to your listeners. The communication orientation is audience-centered, not self-centered. Focus on communicating with your listeners, not impressing them with your oratorical ability. What good is a speech that impresses an audience with its flamboyant style, powerful delivery, and weighty language if the audience is confused or uninterested in the subject? Be concerned first with substance and only secondarily with stylistic eloquence. As Motley (1995) counsels, "Make the message clear and interesting and leave the performance ego out of it" (p. 63).

The communication orientation works well to reduce anxiety because you connect with your listeners. The focus becomes your message, not your fear of speaking.

Does the communication orientation work? When compared to other methods of anxiety reduction and control, the communication orientation is the most successful (Motley, 1995). Simply concentrating on communicating with an audience, not impressing them, reduced anxiety levels of speakers from high to moderately low.

The first three methods for reducing and controlling your speech anxiety work so well that the remaining methods to be discussed will be given only brief treatment. These methods are your insurance policy—just in case you may need them.

Use Coping Strategies Coping statements shift the thought process from negative to positive. Negative, disaster thinking triggers high anxiety. You stumble at the outset of your speech and say to yourself "I knew I couldn't do this well" or "I've already ruined the introduction." Try making coping statements when problems arise. "I'm past the tough part," "I'll do better once I get rolling," and "The best part is still ahead" are examples of positive coping statements. Make self-talk productive, not destructive.

Use Positive Imaging (Visualization) Prepare for a speech presentation by countering negative thoughts of catastrophe with positive images of success. Some call this visualization. Create images in your head that picture you giving your speech fluently, clearly, and interestingly. Picture your audience responding in positive ways as you give your speech. Inexperienced speakers typically imagine what will go wrong during a speech. Exercise mental discipline and refuse to allow such thoughts to creep into your consciousness. Keep imagining speaking success, not failure.

Try Systematic Desensitization This method of managing anxiety is very effective. Its chief drawback, however, is that it is time-consuming. Systematic desensitization is a technique used to control anxiety, even phobias, triggered by a wide variety of stimuli (Ayres & Hopf, 1995). Fear of snakes or heights can be managed effectively using this method.

Systematic desensitization involves incremental exposure to increasingly threatening stimuli coupled with relaxation techniques. Applied to giving speeches, an individual would make a list of perhaps 10 steps in the speaking process, each likely to produce an increased anxiety response. Find yourself a comfortable, quiet place to sit. Read the first item on your list (e.g., your speech topic). When you experience anxiety, put the list aside and begin a relaxation exercise. Tense your muscles in your face and neck. Hold the tensed position for 10 seconds, then release. Now do the same with your hands, and so on until you've tensed and relaxed all the muscle groups in your body. Now breathe slowly and deeply as you say the word "relax" to yourself. Repeat this for 1 minute. Pick up the list and read the first item. If your anxiety remains pronounced, repeat the process. If your anxiety is minimal, move on to the second item (e.g., organizing your speech material) and repeat the tense-and-relax procedure. Work through your entire list of 10 items, stopping when you are able to read the final item (e.g., beginning the introduction of your speech) without appreciable anxiety. Use systematic desensitization several days in a row before your actual speech presentation. Your anxiety level should fall to lower levels.

Topic Choice and Analysis

A frequent concern of students that is a close second to speech anxiety is what topic to choose for their speech. In some instances you may be asked to give a speech on a particular subject because of your expertise (e.g., a nurse asked to give a speech on flu shots; a student volunteer for "Food Not Bombs" asked to speak on the local homeless problem). In a speech class, however, the choice, within broad limits, will likely be up to you. In this section you will learn how to choose a topic that is appropriate for you, your audience, and the occasion. In addition you will learn how to narrow your topic to a specific purpose statement.

Exploring Potential Topics

Choose a bad topic, and you are stuck with a bad speech. Choose a good topic, and the potential for a great speech looms large. How do you systematically explore potential topics for a speech? There are three primary ways: do a personal inventory, brainstorm ideas, and scan popular periodicals and newspapers.

Calvin and Hobbes

by Bill Watterson

Do a Personal Inventory   Begin your exploration of appropriate topics by looking within yourself. What interests you? Make a list of every topic you can think of that you find interesting. What are your hobbies (e.g., woodworking, whittling, model airplanes, doll collecting)? What sports do you play (e.g., tennis, racketball, softball, ice skating)? List any unusual events that have occurred in your life (e.g., caught in a tornado, observed a bank robbery). Have you done any volunteer work (e.g., Habitat for Humanity, United Way, American Cancer Society)? What form of entertainment interests you (e.g., romantic movies, rap music, dancing, rodeo, car shows)? Do you have any special skills (e.g., surfing, cooking, carpentry, sewing)? Have you traveled to any interesting places (e.g., London, Paris, Cairo, Moscow)? Have you met any exciting people (e.g., rock stars, political leaders, professional athletes, actors)? What's the worst thing that's ever happened to you (e.g., divorce, serious illness, car accident, death of a relative)? What's the best (e.g., met your romantic partner, won a scholarship, saved someone's life)? How do you spend your free time (e.g., reading novels, hiking, watching TV, playing video games, exploring the Internet)? This list contains many possible choices for a speech topic.

Brainstorm   Your personal inventory won't necessarily provide an immediate topic for your speech. You will probably need to brainstorm additional possibilities. Take your list of things that interest you, examine it, then choose five topics that seem most promising. Write down each topic on a separate list, and with each topic brainstorm new possibilities. For example, brainstorm "trip to London" by letting your mind free-associate any related topics, such as double decker buses, driving on the left, the Thames River, British accent, Parliament, Buckingham Palace, Princess Diana's death, royalty, Hyde Park, Soho, British money, and British rock groups. Each of these topics is rather general. Consider each one, and try to brainstorm a more specific topic. British money, for example, might lead to a comparison of British money to American currency. Driving on the left could lead to an interesting presentation on why the British drive on the left, yet we drive on the right. Parliament could trigger a comparison between the U.S. Congress and the British Parliament. If this approach does not generate excitement, try a third method—scanning.

Scan Magazines and Newspapers   There is no shortage of magazines and newspapers readily available to you for scanning potential speech topics. Pick up a copy of *Newsweek, Time, Consumer Reports, Life, Sports Illustrated, Psychology Today,*

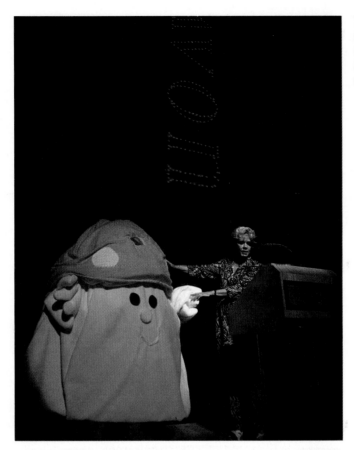

This speech on Avon products, and the accompanying unusual visual aid, would be appropriate in very few contexts.

Entertainment, Muscle Media 2000, or any popular magazine. Look at the table of contents, and leaf through the articles. Don't spend time reading the articles. You're scanning quickly just to get ideas. If you see a promising topic, write it down and note the magazine, the article, and the date. Do the same with newspapers. Your library will have local, national, and international newspapers that will be filled with hundreds of potential topics for speeches.

Analyzing Appropriateness of Topic Choice

Appropriateness and effectiveness are key elements of the communication competence model. Choosing a topic that is inappropriate for a particular audience virtually guarantees that your speech will be ineffective. Appropriateness is contextual. A speech topic that works in one instance may be an abysmal failure in another instance. There are three central elements to consider when analyzing the appropriateness of your topic choice: speaker, audience, and occasion.

Speaker Appropriateness   If a topic is chosen merely to fulfill an assignment but you find it uninteresting, even tedious, then it is not appropriate for you, the speaker. Choose a topic that interests or excites you. An appropriate topic for you can motivate your desire to research the topic and build a quality speech. An inappropriate topic for you will make researching and constructing your speech drudgery. If you're interested and excited about your topic, you can communicate that to your audience. It is a rare individual who can take a topic that he or she finds as dull as watching someone blink their eyes and successfully fake interest to an audience. If you think the subject is dull, what must your audience think?

Some topic choices are not suitable because of who you are. You and the topic may be a poor or awkward fit. A White person speaking of the "Black experience in America" is an awkward fit. Similarly, young people talking about "what it's like being old" sounds goofy. Men speaking about female menopause is also awkward. A flabby, out-of-shape individual speaking about the wonders of weight lifting doesn't work (unless it is meant to be a humorous speech). No matter how gifted you are as a speaker, some topics will sink your chances of presenting an effective speech. Choose a topic that suits your interests and fits who you are.

Audience Appropriateness   Public speaking is transactional. A speaker and his or her audience are interconnected and influence each other. *The appropriateness of a topic is largely audience centered.* Over the years, my colleagues have shared many horror stories about student speeches that were startlingly inappropriate. Almost every speech instructor has heard at least one speech by a male student on "how to score with the babes." One student gave a speech on "how to assassinate someone you hate." Another student gave a distasteful speech on "proper methods of inducing vomiting after a big meal." My colleagues and I have heard speeches on "spitting for distance," "effective nail biting techniques," "harassing the homeless," "opening a beer bottle with your teeth," "constructing a bong," "maintaining your 'pot' plants," and "shoplifting techniques that work." These topics are inappropriate because they are offensive, trivial, demeaning, or they encourage illegal, unethical behavior. Most of them are pointless, adolescent silliness.

There are other reasons why a topic might be inappropriate for an audience. An audience may find a topic choice difficult to relate to or appreciate. Giving a speech on how to surf to an audience living in Kansas is an awkward fit. A topic can also be too technical or complex. Students occasionally try to justify creationism and refute evolution when explaining the origins and development of the universe by referring to the second law of thermodynamics. Their explanation is almost always confusing to the audience because it requires an understanding of physics.

The increasingly multicultural makeup of audiences, especially student audiences, presents another source for inappropriate topic choice. Homogeneous audiences composed of highly similar individuals are rare these days. College campuses in particular are a heterogeneous conglomeration of diverse cultures. Even without intending to, a topic choice can be insulting to individuals from other cultures or co-cultures. Giving a speech on religion or politics should be approached cautiously lest insult be given to those with different cultural perspectives.

Occasion Appropriateness   When you're speaking at a particular event, topic choice must be appropriate to the occasion. A topic choice should meet the expectations of your audience concerning what is appropriate. A graduation ceremony invites topics such as "employment possibilites for the future," "skills for success," and "thinking in the future tense." A sermon at a Sunday religious service warrants a topic related to ethical or moral behavior. Don't choose a topic unrelated to the occasion. It won't fulfill audience expectations. Soliciting support for a political cause at a graduation ceremony or an awards banquet will get you booed off the stage. The occasion dictates the appropriateness of a topic choice.

Narrowing the Topic

Sometimes you are given a very broad topic on which to speak. Other times you find an interesting topic, but it is too broad and general for the time available to speak. Narrowing your topic to fit the audience and the occasion is a significant task for any speaker.

Stay Within the Time Limit   President Woodrow Wilson, a former college professor and the only U.S. president to earn a Ph.D., took his public speaking very seriously. A reporter interviewed him once regarding his speech preparation. "How long do you spend preparing a 10-minute speech?" Wilson was asked. Wilson replied, "About two weeks." "How long do you spend preparing an hour-long speech?" the reporter queried. "About a week," answered Wilson. Surprised, the reporter then asked Wilson how long he prepared for a 2-hour speech. Wilson replied, "I could do that now." Giving a long-winded speech takes less effort than narrowing the speech to fit neatly into a shorter time allotment.

Once you have settled on a general topic that is appropriate for you the speaker, the audience, and the occasion, begin narrowing the topic to fit your time limit. A 5-minute speech obviously requires much more narrowing than a 15-minute speech. You can't accomplish a great deal in only 5 minutes. Take the general topic and brainstorm more specific subtopics. For example, a general topic such as "the cost of a college education" is very broad and could easily require half an hour to explore in any depth. Break down this general topic into these more specific subtopics for a much shorter speech: problems with financial aid, how to get a scholarship, part-time student employment, the high cost of textbooks, room and board fees for campus living, college tuition, and college fees.

Don't choose a topic that is so broad and complex that you couldn't possibly do it justice in the time allotted. Heed Mark Twain's observation, "Few sinners are saved after the first 20 minutes of a sermon." Staying within your time limit is critical. Long-winded speeches, no matter how well constructed and delivered, won't be effective if the audience expects a short presentation (Box 12-3). If you are asked to address a luncheon meeting of a civic organization and you are scheduled for a 15-minute presentation, narrow your focus to fit that time limit. You'll be addressing a roomful of empty chairs if you go much beyond the time limit. People attending luncheon meetings often have only an hour for the entire meeting, of which your speech is but a small part.

Construct a Purpose Statement   Once you have narrowed a general topic into more specific subtopics, construct a purpose statement. A **purpose statement** is a concise, precise declarative statement phrased in simple, clear language that states both the general goal and the central idea of your speech.

The general goal contained in the purpose statement of your speech tells your audience why you're giving your speech (to inform, persuade, celebrate, memorialize, entertain, eulogize). The general goal will be given to you if your speech is a classroom assignment (e.g., give a persuasive speech). If you have no direction from others, you must decide what general goal is appropriate for the audience and occasion. Once you have determined the general goal, decide what will be your central idea (sometimes referred to as your thesis statement). The central idea contained in your purpose statement identifies exactly what you want the audience to understand, believe, feel, or do.

Box 12-3 Sharper Focus

The Never-Ending Speech

His speech was scheduled to last no more than 15 minutes. Bill Clinton, at the time a 41-year-old governor of Arkansas, had the political plum of the 1988 Democratic National Convention in Atlanta. A gifted speaker, his nominating speech for presidential candidate Michael Dukakis could have provided Clinton with invaluable publicity and national stature. Instead, it turned into a disaster. His speech lasted more than twice as long as his scheduled time allowed. With convention delegates growing restless in anticipation of the acceptance address by Dukakis, Clinton droned on despite increasing annoyance throughout the convention hall. Some delegates began chanting "Give him the hook" and "wrap it up." Jim Wright, the convention chair, at one point edged close to Clinton and admonished him to finish his address. Even the television networks switched from showing the speech to shots of delegates drawing their forefingers across their throats in a "cut" signal. CNN focused its camera on the red podium light glaring at Clinton to stop speaking. In desperation, convention officials turned off the TelePrompTer hoping to shut down the single-minded Clinton. Clinton received his most enthusiastic cheer when he said, "In closing . . ."

Massachusetts delegate William Bulger joked during the speech, "When this started I was a young man."

After the speech finally ended, a network executive taped a hand-lettered sign onto the front of an Atlanta phone book that read: "Transcript of Gov. Clinton's Speech." On the Johnny Carson show a few nights after his speaking disaster, Clinton joked, "It was not my finest hour, or even hour-and-a-half." Clinton was given his topic (i.e., nominate Dukakis), but he failed to narrow it sufficiently for the occasion, and it doomed an otherwise decent presentation.

As president, Bill Clinton still hasn't seemed to have learned from his disastrous 1988 speech. His 1999 State of the Union speech took 1 hour and 17 minutes to deliver—proving that he did not heed the words of an anonymous wit who observed that "the brain can absorb only what the seat can endure."

Clinton is capable of great eloquence in flourishes, but he can't sustain eloquence for more than an hour, nor can media-saturated audiences easily maintain their attention for his excessively lengthy speeches. After all, Abraham Lincoln's Gettysburg Address, considered one of the great American speeches, lasted about *two minutes*. Famed orator Edward Everett, who preceded Lincoln, gave a 2-hour-plus speech. He later wrote Lincoln: "I shall be glad if I could flatter myself that I came as near to the central idea of the occasion in two hours as you did in two minutes" (as cited in Noonan, 1998, p. 65).

TOPIC: Cost of a college education
NARROWED TOPIC: The high cost of textbooks
GENERAL GOAL: To inform
CENTRAL IDEA: The reasons textbooks are expensive.
PURPOSE STATEMENT: To discuss the three primary reasons textbooks are expensive.

Once you have constructed your purpose statement, test its appropriateness and likely effectiveness. Ask the following questions:

1. *Is your purpose statement concise and precise*? A long, wordy statement will confuse listeners or put them to sleep. You should be able to phrase an effective purpose statement in 15 words, or fewer. If your purpose statement is much beyond 15 words, rephrase it until it is more concise and precise.

2. *Is your purpose phrased as a declarative statement*? Phrasing a purpose statement as a question asks your listeners to provide the answers (e.g., "Why are textbooks so expensive?"). Make your purpose statement declarative (i.e., *declare* the direction of your speech), and begin with an infinitive phrase (i.e., to inform, to persuade, to celebrate, to teach, to demonstrate, to eulogize).

3. *Is your purpose statement free of figurative language*? Keep your purpose statement plain and direct. Figurative language is fine for the body of your speech, but

it can be confusing in a purpose statement. For example, "To tell you why text-books are the golden fleece of education" will likely leave some of your listeners scratching their heads and saying "huh?" to themselves.

4. *Is your purpose statement more than simply a topic*? "To inform my audience about the cost of textbooks" is a topic statement not a purpose statement. What about the cost of textbooks? Listeners are provided with no direction for your speech. Give them a direction. Tell them specifically what you seek to accomplish. "To discuss the feasibility of a private college bookstore as a way to lower textbook prices" is a purpose statement with a direction.

5. *Is your purpose statement practical*? Can your listeners accomplish what you ask them to do? "I want to teach you to be a top-notch computer programmer" will not happen in a single speech, even a lengthy one. "My purpose is to inform you about the many changes in the new tax code" is too technical and complex for a single speech to an audience of mostly uninformed taxpayers. Make your purpose statement practical: "I want to convince you that taking a computer programming course is worthwhile."

Now you know how to choose a topic, determine its appropriateness for the speaker (you), the audience, and the occasion, and how to construct a purpose statement that appropriately narrows your topic for the time allotted. The next step is researching your topic so you have something interesting and meaningful to say.

Researching Your Topic

Researching your topic should be a focused undertaking. Wandering aimlessly through a library or searching randomly on the Internet will waste time and accomplish little. In this section how to research a speech topic is explained.

Libraries and Librarians

The obvious place to begin your research is the college library. Every college library offers one or more tours of its facility. Take the tour. Even if you are already knowledgeable about using a library, the tour will familiarize you with where materials are located in a specific library.

Begin researching early. A frenzied attempt to research your speech topic the night before your presentation will jump-start your anxiety and prove to be a less than satisfactory experience. If you do not know quite where to begin, ask the librarian; there is no better single source of information on researching a speech topic. I have consulted the reference librarians at Cabrillo College on dozens of occasions while researching this textbook. They are the experts on information location. Use them. Do not expect the librarian to do your research for you, but he or she will guide you on your journey through the maze of information.

Library Catalogues

For decades the card catalogue was a standard starting point for most research. The card catalogue, listing all books contained in the library on 3×5 cards by author, title, or subject, is rapidly becoming a dinosaur. The old card catalogues have been computerized in almost all libraries in the United States.

The computer catalogue, like its predecessor, lists books according to author, title, and subject. An important distinguishing characteristic of the computer

Calvin and Hobbes

by Bill Watterson

catalogue is that you can do a keyword search. Type in "mountain climbing" and a list of titles will appear related to this subject. Computer catalogues will also indicate if the book is available or checked out, saving you time.

Periodicals

The research bible for many students is *The Reader's Guide to Periodical Literature.* This reference provides current listings for articles in more than 250 popular magazines in the United States (e.g., *Newsweek, Time, Consumer Reports, Ms., Popular Science, Rolling Stone, Business Week, Ebony*). Articles are listed by both author and subject. There is also a computer version of *The Reader's Guide.* It is entitled *Reader's Guide Abstracts.* This computer version is faster to use, and it includes a brief abstract, or summary, of the listed magazine articles.

There are many other periodical indexes. Some examples are: *InfoTrac Magazine Index* (magazines on current affairs, science, art, education), *Public Affairs Information Service* (journal articles and government documents), *Hispanic American Periodicals Index* (Hispanic American interests), *Index to Black Periodicals* (African American issues), *Women's Resources International* (women's issues), *ABI/Inform* (business and management journals), *ERIC* (education materials), *Social Sciences Index* (sociology, psychology, and so forth), *Psychological Abstracts* (psychology), and *ProQuest General Periodicals Ondisc* (general interest and scholarly periodicals). Check with your librarian to discover which of these are available at your college library.

Newspapers

Newspapers are one of the richest sources of information on current topics available. Your college library will undoubtedly subscribe to the local newspaper. The *New York Times Index* is a valuable resource. Database indexes for newspapers include *Newsbank Index,* the InfoTrac *National Newspaper Index,* and UMI's *Newspaper Abstracts.*

Reference Works

Encyclopedias are standard references used for researching a wide variety of topics. The most widely known encyclopedias are the *Encyclopaedia Britannica,*

Box 12-4 Sharper Focus

Cruising the Net Skeptically

"It used to be in the old days that people would say, 'I read it in a book,' as if that were enough to make it true," says Dr. Dean Edell, physician, highly regarded medical journalist, and talk show host. "It seems for many these days, 'I saw it on the Internet' is enough to convince" (as cited in Rezendes, 1998, p. A1). How do you separate the high-quality information from the hokum? Several easy steps should remind you of material covered in Chapter 6.

First, *consider the source.* Are you looking at medical information from the Mayo Clinic or from Frank the taxi driver who lives in Hoboken? An author's name without accompanying credentials is suspicious. Perhaps no source is identified for an article. In that case be doubly cautious. Check and see if sources are cited in the article, and make a quick check of some of them to see if they exist or are from credible sources.

Second, *try to determine if the source is biased.* No matter what the source, if the website uses a hard sell to peddle products, therapies, or ideas, be wary. Look for sites that have no vested interest, no products to peddle, and no axe to grind.

Third, *avoid chatrooms as a source of valid information.* As Dr. Edell explains, "People can represent themselves as just about anything. . . . It can be the beginning of rampant urban cyber-rumor. It's like a cocktail party. Don't believe everything you hear, and keep a healthy skepticism" (as cited in Rezendes, 1998, p. A5).

Colliers's Encyclopedia, World Book Encyclopedia, and *Encyclopedia Americana.* Many encyclopedias can be accessed by computer. Microsoft's *Encarta* is a popular CD-ROM encyclopedia.

Other useful general reference works are *Statistical Abstracts of the United States, World Almanac, Monthly Labor Review, FBI Uniform Crime Report, Vital Statistics of the United States, Facts on File, The Guinness Book of World Records,* and *Who's Who in America.*

References for government related information include: *Monthly Catalogue of United States Government Publications, Congressional Quarterly Weekly Report, The Congressional Record, The Congressional Digest,* and *The Congressional Index.*

Internet

The Internet has quickly become a popular source for research. Unfortunately, it is very difficult to separate information from *mis*information on the Internet. Unless you know the credentials of the author of an article or statement, the information lacks credibility. Remember, credibility means that the information is trustworthy, reliable, and unbiased (Chapter 6). The credentials of sources—who they are, their expertise, their degree of neutrality on an issue—allow us to judge the trustworthiness, reliability, and level of a source's bias. The Centers for Disease Control, a federal agency based in Atlanta, Georgia that tracks the spread of contagious illnesses, is a far more credible source of information on the spread of AIDS, tuberculosis, and flu viruses than someone on the Internet named Sally Reese whose credentials, if any, are unknown.

Be very cautious when using the Internet. Sources are often biased and unqualified (Box 12-4). I have had students quote the Internet as their source of information. That is tantamount to quoting your fax machine as your source of information. The Internet is an electronic medium of information transmission, not a credible source. A high percentage of what passes for credible information is worthless junk. Be selective when cruising the Net. Look for credentials to establish credibility.

Box 12-5   Focus on Controversy

The Plagiarism Problem

Joseph Biden, a U.S. senator from Delaware, was running for president of the United States in 1987. Biden, a gifted orator, was given a decent chance of securing the Democratic nomination. His candidacy went into the dumpster, however, when news accounts revealed that Biden had plagiarized his conclusion to a speech he gave at the Iowa State Fair. His conclusion was lifted almost verbatim from a speech by British Labor Party leader Neil Kinnock. Biden had even cribbed Kinnock's personal history. For example, Kinnock asked rhetorically, "Why am I the first Kinnock in a thousand generations to be able to get to university? Why is Glenys [his wife] the first woman in her family in a thousand generations to be able to get to university?" (as cited in Jamieson, 1988, p. 221). Biden's conclusion asked rhetorically, "Why is it that Joe Biden is the first in his family ever to go to a university? Why is it that my wife, who is sitting out there in the audience, is the first in her family to ever go to college?" (p. 222). Biden was not the first in his family to receive a college education (Jamieson, 1988).

Confronted with the charge of plagiarism, Biden claimed that the similarity between his speech and Kinnock's was merely coincidental. The news media, however, sensed a bigger story and discovered that Biden had also lifted passages from speeches by Hubert Humphrey and Robert Kennedy. Biden was further damaged by his admission that he had plagiarized when he was a law student at Syracuse University. Biden's presidential campaign came to a screeching halt, and he was never again a viable presidential candidate.

Some might pass off Biden's plagiarism as a lot of huffing and puffing about very little. Plagiarism, however, is unethical behavior. Speaking someone else's words without giving attribution is dishonest and disrespectful and, therefore, incompetent communication. How do we know who the real Joe Biden is if he speaks the words of another, even assuming someone else's personal history to sound eloquent?

Biden was guilty of selective plagiarism, or stealing portions of someone else's speech or writings. That is bad enough, but plagiarism becomes even more serious when entire speeches are stolen and presented as one's own. Some students attempt such blatant theft of another's words, usually because preparation of a speech has been left until there is too little time to construct a decent speech themselves. Prepare early and remove any temptation to plagiarize. Stealing someone's words is pilfering a part of that person's identity. That is never an inconsequential act.

Questions for Thought

1. Do you agree that Biden deserved to be denounced for his plagiarism and to fall out of the presidential race?
2. In Chapter 8, honesty was not always presented as the best policy. Does this mean that plagiarism is sometimes permissible? Explain.

Some credible research sites on the Internet are:

Government Sources
http://www.census.gov/ (U.S. Census Bureau stats)
http://www.ed.gov (education issues)
http://www.ecology.com/ (ecological issues)
http://www.naic.nasa.gov/fbi/ (FBI's information on law enforcement)

Health and Medicine Sources
http://www.healthcentral.com (Dr. Dean Edell)
http://www.cdc.gov/ (health and disease issues)
http://www.mayohealth.org (Mayo Clinic's Health Oasis)
http://www.ama-assn.org/consumer.htm (American Medical Association)
http://www.intelihealth.com (Johns Hopkins University)
http://www.nih.gov/ (National Institutes of Health)
http://www.quackwatch.com (health fraud issues)

General Information

http://www.trib.com/NEWS/apwire.html (Associated Press news)

http://www.nytimes.com (*New York Times*)

http://www.boston.com/globe (*The Boston Globe*)

http://www.phillynews.com (*The Philadelphia Inquirer*)

http://www.abcnews.com (ABC News)

http://www.cnn.com (CNN news, current events)

Education

http://www.cc.columbia.edu/acis/bartleby/bartlett/(great quotations)

http://www.apa.org (psychology)

http://www.public.asu.edu/corman/infosys (International Communication
Association)

Ethnic Issues

http://www.mit.edu/activities/aar/aar.html (Asian American special
interests)

http://www.aawc.com:80/aawc.html (African American special interests)

http://www.hanksville.phast.umass.edu/misc/NAresources.html (Native
American history, language, art, and so forth)

http://www.hisp.com/tesoros/index.html (Hispanic American special
interests)

Researching can be a time-consuming process. Learn about your library. Seek instruction in using the Internet efficiently and effectively.

Summary

Speech preparation begins with managing your speech anxiety. Virtually all novice speakers experience substantial anxiety. Your goal is not to eliminate anxiety but to control it and use it to energize your speaking. Self-defeating thoughts and anxiety-provoking situations trigger speech anxiety. There are many speech anxiety management methods available. The most effective methods include diligent preparation and practice, gaining proper perspective, and replacing the competitive performance orientation with the noncompetitive communication orientation. Speech preparation also includes topic choice and analysis. The effectiveness of your speech will depend in large measure on the appropriateness of your topic choice. A topic should be appropriate to you the speaker, your audience, and the occasion. Narrow your topic to fit the time allotted by constructing a purpose statement. Finally, speech preparation means thoroughly researching your topic. Research your topic early and become very familiar with your library and all of its materials.

Suggested Readings

Hentoff, N. (1992). *Free speech for me, but not for thee.* New York: Harper Perennial.
The importance of public speech is forcefully argued by Hentoff.

Jamieson, K. (1988). *Eloquence in an electronic age.* New York: Oxford University
Press. This is a wonderful treatment of the importance of the spoken word and
the new challenges offered by television.

Chapter 13

Developing a Speech

A well-known and high-priced speaker was invited to address the Cabrillo College faculty. She was articulate, poised, and dynamic. For 45 minutes she told stories and anecdotes that brought frequent laughter from her audience. As a speech presentation, it appeared that she had succeeded admirably. Faculty broke into groups following the speech to discuss the subjects the speaker had raised. Unlike the apparent positive response the speaker received during her speech, an avalanche of criticism followed. The chief complaint was that the speaker had entertained everyone but hadn't presented substantial material that warranted a generous speaker fee. The speech was so dissatisfying for most that the college was hesitant for several years afterwards to invite any outside speaker to address the faculty. This speech failed, not because it wasn't prepared well nor presented skillfully but because it was not developed effectively. Its content was poorly suited to the audience. A competent speech is far more than good style and delivery. Your thoughts have to resonate with an audience.

The primary purpose of this chapter is to explain the fundamental audience-centered process of developing a speech. There are four objectives:

1. to discuss the process of audience analysis,
2. to identify ways to gain and maintain the attention of your audience,
3. to discuss how to develop an introduction and conclusion to your speech, and
4. to explain how to organize and outline your speech.

Audience Analysis

Edmund Muskie, former United States senator from Maine, once remarked: "In Maine we have a saying that there's no point in speaking unless you can improve on silence." Improving on silence requires careful audience analysis. Almost 2,500 years ago Aristotle wrote: "Of the three elements in speechmaking—speaker, subject, and person addressed—it is the last one, the hearer, that determines the speech's end and object" (as cited in Cooper, 1960, p. 136). Meeting the expectations of your audience is a key element in competent public speaking. This is a cooperative effort between speaker and listeners. You are working with your listeners, not against them.

A speaker who berates his or her audience for some perceived wrongdoing invites angry responses from listeners. Teachers who lecture students on their inadequacies create a defensive, competitive communication climate. Making adversaries out of your audience rarely produces a positive result for a speaker. Think of audience analysis as the process of discovering ways to build bridges between yourself and listeners, to identify with their needs, hopes, dreams, interests, and concerns. In general, you develop a speech with the audience always in mind. In this section types of audiences and audience composition will be discussed.

Types of Audiences

Begin analyzing your audience by considering what type of audience will hear your speech. There are four general types of audiences: captive, committed, concerned, and casual. The **captive audience** assembles to hear you speak because they are compelled to, not because they expect entertainment or intellectual stimulation. A required speech class is an example of a captive audience. Formal ceremonies, luncheon gatherings of clubs and organizations, and most meetings conducted in places of business are other examples of captive audiences. Power, especially in its dominance form, can be an issue with captive audiences. Listeners may attend a speech only because those with greater power (supervisors, teachers) insist. This can easily trigger psychological reactance and establish a competitive, defensive environment where listeners initially view the speaker as an annoyance and cause for complaint.

A captive audience presents a special challenge to a speaker. Gaining and maintaining the interest of a captive audience, engaging listeners actively, is a primary consideration for the speaker. When listeners would just as soon be elsewhere, snaring their attention and keeping them listening to you is no small accomplishment.

The **committed audience** voluntarily assembles to hear a speaker because they want to invest time and energy listening to the speaker's thoughts and being inspired by his or her words. A committed audience usually agrees with the speaker's position already and is presumably interested since they voluntarily appeared to hear the speech. Listeners who gather for Sunday sermons, political rallies, and social protest demonstrations are all examples of committed audiences. Gaining and maintaining the interest and attention of a committed audience is not nearly as difficult as doing the same with a captive audience. Inspiring action, persuading, and empowering listeners to act decisively are primary considerations for a speaker addressing a committed audience, not stirring interest or seeking agreement. Committed listeners want to be inspired to act, and as the speaker, you want to "rally the troops," provide listeners with a "can do" attitude, and motivate change.

A **concerned audience** is one that gathers voluntarily to hear a speaker because listeners care about issues and ideas, and they want to learn from the speaker. A concerned audience is a motivated audience. Unlike a committed audience, however, listeners haven't attended the speech to show commitment to a particular cause or idea. Concerned listeners want to gather information and learn. Listeners who gather for book and poetry readings or lecture series are examples of concerned audiences. A primary consideration for a speaker addressing a concerned audience is to be informative by presenting new ideas and new information in a stimulating and attention-getting fashion. Concerned listeners may eventually become committed listeners.

A **casual audience** never anticipates being an audience in the first place. A casual audience is composed of individuals who are picked as listeners because they happen to be milling about or they're passing by and hear a speaker, stop out of curiosity or casual interest, and remain until bored or sated. Individuals wandering in front of the student union, sitting on the steps of a government building having lunch, or walking in a park on a sunny day might be a casual audience for a speaker. Street performers snare passersby to create an audience. A primary consideration for a speaker addressing a casual audience is to connect with listeners immediately and create curiosity and interest. Unlike a captive audience that feels compelled to act as listeners, members of a casual audience are free to leave at a moment's whim.

When I was in Bath, England in 1995 I happened upon a street performer, or busker, as they are called in England. The busker was entertaining his casual audience composed primarily of tourists and shoppers. He gathered an audience mostly with clever banter, corny jokes, audience interaction, and whimsical tricks. Curious about the gathering crowd and happy to be entertained after a long day of sightseeing and shopping, I joined the audience. Within minutes I was picked out of the crowd to "assist" the busker in performing one of his "daring" tricks. He billed the trick as an "underwater escape." My job was to tie the busker's hands tightly behind his back with a chain, put a bag over his head, and count to 30 while the performer "escaped" from his confinement while on his knees with his head submerged in a one-gallon bucket of water. Immediately following his successful "underwater escape" a reporter from the BBC television network pulled me aside and asked if I would agree to be interviewed for a BBC documentary on buskers in England. The reporter wanted the "American viewpoint" on busking. I agreed. I was a casual member of an audience who ended up on British television.

Each type of audience—captive, committed, concerned, or casual—presents its own challenge to a speaker. Each audience has its own expectations that a speaker must address to be successful.

Audience Composition

Your speech should be developed with your audience always in mind, so knowing something about your audience is critical. The appropriateness of your remarks and their effectiveness with a specific audience depend in large part on connecting with your listeners. Again, you are working cooperatively with your audience, not competitively against your listeners. Connection comes from framing your speech to resonate with listeners. This means shaping your material to address the expectations, interests, knowledge, needs, and experiences of audience members. You may have an opportunity to survey listeners and determine some of this important information about your audience. Students sometimes poll classmates about issues and problems before composing their speeches. Often, however, you must make educated guesses about an audience based on **demographics**—characteristics of an audience such as age, gender, culture and ethnicity, and group affiliations. Let's briefly consider each of these demographics.

Age   The average age of an audience can provide valuable information for a speaker. College instructors, for instance, must speak to the experience of college students, most of whom weren't even born before 1980. This means that most college students have no direct experience of the Vietnam War, Watergate, eight-track tapes, ditto machines, or manual typewriters, and only fleeting recollections of a time when wristwatches did nothing more than tell time, e-mail was only a futurist's fantasy, and automobiles could be repaired without computer technology. They've never known a time when space travel wasn't possible, color television didn't exist, computers wouldn't fit on a desktop, overnight mail wasn't available, ATMs weren't readily available even in foreign countries, and copy machines weren't readily accessible.

It is difficult for most college students to imagine a time not very long ago when indoor shopping malls were rare and transistor radios the size of a shirt pocket were the boom boxes. The primary age of your audience tells you quite a bit about the experiences they haven't had as well as the experiences they have

Gender and ethnicity are important elements in public speaking situations.

had. As a speaker, develop the content of your speech in such a way that it speaks to the experience of audience members. References to insider trading, mutual funds, problems of leadership in corporations, and planning retirement accounts don't speak directly to the experience of a young audience. Older audiences, however, may relate to detailed explanations on such topics.

Gender Gender differences in perception and behavior do exist, as discussed in Chapter 2. You need to be careful, however, not to assume too much from these differences. For instance, during political elections women in the United States tend to place greater emphasis on issues such as education, health care, and social justice, whereas men tend to emphasize economics and military security. Nevertheless, effective audience analysis means that you present your material in a way that interests all audience members.

Develop your speech from different perspectives to include all audience members. A speech on sexual harassment, for instance, could be linked to both men and women by discussing effects on victims (typically women, but sometimes men) and offering ways to avoid charges of sexual harassment (usually involving men). In addition, men can relate to the indignity and powerless feelings associated with sexual harassment indirectly by seeing what wives, girlfriends, or daughters experience when victimized. Men don't want to see the women they love or care about subjected to indignity and injustice.

In addition, sensitivity to an audience may require judicious attention to language when framing issues. Consistently referring to leaders as "he," "him," or "his," as in "A leader must inspire, and *he* must motivate *his* followers" excludes women. Similarly, referring to elementary school teachers as "she" or "her," as in

"A third grade teacher works hard and *she* spends long hours with *her* students" excludes men. Try to speak in more inclusive terms, using "him or her" or plural forms such as "doctors . . . they."

Ethnicity and Culture   Throughout this textbook the role of ethnicity and culture in communication transactions has been made apparent. Ethnicity and culture are no less important for the public speaker analyzing his or her audience. Sensitivity is a key component of communication competence. Be sensitive to your entire audience.

Students who fail to analyze the multicultural makeup of college audiences can create embarrassing speaking situations. Despite my efforts to encourage sensitivity to individuals from diverse cultures, I have witnessed several student speeches that ignited awkward, even hostile, moments in class. One Jewish student gave a speech on peace agreements in the Middle East. She referred to Palestinians as "terrorists and war mongers." This did not sit well with several Arab students in the class. Policies and issues can be questioned and debated without resorting to insults and sweeping generalizations. Take care not to offend a chunk of your audience if you hope to have receptive listeners.

Group Affiliations   The groups we belong to tell others a great deal about our values, beliefs, and points of view. Membership in the National Rifle Association usually indicates a strong belief in the right of gun ownership and a somewhat conservative political bent. Membership in the National Organization for Women usually indicates a strong belief in equal rights for women and a somewhat liberal political point of view. Membership in clubs, sororities, fraternities, national honorary societies, or educational groups provides information about your listeners. This information can be vital in shaping your speech, as you will see later in the discussion of informative and persuasive speaking.

Sensitivity to your audience's expectations, needs, values, interests, and beliefs is a necessary component of competent public speaking. Sensitivity means picking up clues about your listeners so you can successfully frame your speech. Picking up clues about your audience is part of the development process of speech construction.

Gaining and Maintaining Attention

A youth minister, Melvin Nurse, at the Livingway Christian Fellowship Church International in Jacksonville, Florida wanted to make his point emphatically that sin is like Russian roulette. To draw attention to this point during his sermon to 250 parents and youngsters, he placed a .357-caliber pistol to his temple and pulled the trigger. Nurse apparently expected that the blank cartridge in the pistol's chamber would cause him no harm. Unfortunately, in front of his wife and four daughters, the blank cartridge flew apart on impact and shattered Nurse's skull. He died making his point. His attempt to gain attention was successful but with a disastrous result (as cited in "Minister," 1998).

Gaining and maintaining the attention of your audience is a central task of any speaker, but it must be accomplished in a constructive manner. Your efforts to grab and hold the attention of your audience should enhance your presentation, not detract from it.

Both speakers and listeners have a responsibility to maintain attention.

Nature of Attention

Attention is a focused awareness on a stimulus at a given moment. Attention is not the same as listening, although it is related (Chapter 6). You can attend to a message without comprehending, retaining, or evaluating it, but without attention, no listening takes place. Attention is a necessary but not sufficient condition for listening.

Attention is inherently selective. Approximately 99% of all stimuli received by our brains is filtered out as irrelevant (McAleer, 1985). Gaining and maintaining attention is a process of directing a listener's awareness toward the stimulus you provide and steering them away from competing stimuli. Herein lies the challenge. How do you induce an audience to attend to your message and ignore all others? When competing stimuli (kinds of noise) are everywhere, how can any speaker effectively gain and maintain an audience's attention?

A speaker can gain the attention of listeners by appealing to specific characteristics of stimuli that draw attention. These include appeals to that which is novel, startling, vital, humorous, intense, or varied. Each of these characteristics will be explored in the next section, but it is important to note first that gaining and maintaining the attention of listeners is not the exclusive responsibility of the speaker. Communication is transactional. Listeners have a responsibility to make a concerted effort to pay attention to a speaker and not to be diverted by competing stimuli. Nevertheless, a great deal of the responsibility for dealing with selective attention rests with the speaker. You are failing as a public speaker if your listeners must force themselves to stay focused on your message. Don't make listening to you a struggle; make it a pleasure.

✴ *Attention Strategies*

Appealing to specific characteristics of stimuli can gain attention. When these appeals are planned in advance they become strategies.

Novel Appeal   Audiences are naturally drawn to the new and different. Novelty attracts attention. The commonplace can produce a coma-like stupor. Recognizing this means never beginning your speech with a snoozer, such as "My topic is . . ." or "Today I'd like to talk to you about. . . ." Stimulate interest in your subject before giving your purpose statement.

There are several ways to make novel appeals to stimulate attention. First, sprinkle your speech with unusual examples that illustrate important points. For instance, consider using real examples such as these pulled from a newspaper story:

> "The check is in the mail" used to be the standard ploy to ward off bill collectors. Not so anymore. Delinquent customers have adopted more original stalling tactics. Collection agencies have received excuses from the bizarre to the ridiculous. One woman claimed that she had run over her husband with a car, breaking both of his arms thereby making it impossible for him to write checks. Another woman living in Fargo, North Dakota, claimed that she slipped on her way to the post office, lost her checks in the snow, and was forced to wait until the spring thaw before retrieving them. A flower-shop owner insisted that she couldn't pay her bills until someone died and had a funeral. "Business should pick up soon," she said hopefully. Then there was the businessman who placed his own obituary in the local newspaper and promptly sent the clipping to his creditors. These are silly excuses for failing to pay one's bills, but mounting personal debt is no laughing matter.

Compare this opening to the more commonplace opening, "I want to talk to you about how to handle personal debt." The more novel opening invites attention. The commonplace opener encourages a nap.

A second way to make a novel appeal is to tell an unusual story. Newspapers are filled with novel stories that can be used to snare listeners' attention. For example:

> Supermarket customer Etharine Pettigrew was enraged that a woman named Vickie Lemons went through the express checkout line with more than 10 items. Despite the fact that Lemons had been motioned to enter the express line by the cashier, the violation apparently was more than Pettigrew could take. Pettigrew slashed off half of Lemons' nose with a pocket knife. Pettigrew was charged with second-degree reckless endangerment and Lemons had to undergo reconstructive surgery to repair her nose. Civility in America has been replaced by uncivilized, violent behavior and it is time to address this problem.

The example invites attention because it is unusual, yet it is presented as typical of a larger problem.

A third way to interject novelty into a speech is to use colorful phrasing or unusual wording. Notice how an ordinary expression of a point of view can be transformed by a cleverly phrased statement.

Ordinary: Lack of effort will get you fired.

Novel: If you aren't fired with enthusiasm, you'll be fired with enthusiasm. (Vince Lombardi)

Ordinary: Choosing the right word is important.

Novel: The difference between the right word and the almost right word is the difference between lightning and the lightning bug. (Mark Twain)

Novelty is a very effective attention strategy, but it can sometimes miss the mark. Using profanity in a church sermon is novel but hardly appropriate for the context.

Startling Appeal   Shake up your audience. Stun them out of their complacency. Surprise your listeners. A startling statement, fact, or statistic can do this effectively. Consider a few examples.

Startling Statements
1. Calories can kill you.
2. The United States is the obesity capital of the world.
3. America is a culture of murder.
4. "I've seen Mel Gibson naked. And not only did I see him in the raw, he also touched me. Impossible, you say. Not with virtual reality" (Maureen Wilson [1992, p. 119], a student at Northern State University in South Dakota).

Startling Facts/Statistics
1. "During the past two decades nearly half-a-million Americans have been murdered, and an additional 2.5 million have been wounded by gunfire—more casualties than the U.S. military has suffered in all the wars of the past 200 years" (Schlossler, 1997, p. 38).
2. "Every American—because of the amount of resources he or she consumes—does 20 to 100 times more damage to the planet than any one person in the Third World. If the American is rich, he or she causes 1,000 times more destruction" ("Scholar," 1990).

Startling statements, facts, and statistics can be unsettling. They are meant to alarm, shock, astonish, and frighten an audience into listening intently to what you have to say (Box 13-1).

The Vital Appeal   We attend to stimuli that are meaningful to us, and we ignore stimuli that are relatively meaningless to us (Chapter 6). Your principal challenge as a speaker is to make your message meaningful to your listeners so they will pay attention to your speech. Problems and issues that vitally affect our lives are meaningful to us. In this sense, audiences tend to be Me-oriented. Listeners heed warnings when a societal problem affects them personally. The AIDS epidemic was slow to seize the attention of the average American when it was erroneously thought to be a "gay disease." When the disease became rampant in the general population of heterosexual males and females, however, more people started to pay attention.

When attempting to grab the attention of your listeners, don't just make a general appeal, citing the seriousness of the problem for nameless, faceless citizens. Personalize the appeal to your listeners. Maria Ciach (1994), a student at West Chester University in Pennsylvania, established how vitally significant the problem of Hepatitis B is, and she personalized it to her student audience:

> The *Journal of the American Medical Association* reports that over 300,000 people between the ages of 18 and 39 will contract life-threatening cases of Hepatitis B each year. Even

Box 13-1 Sharper Focus

Inappropriate Use of the Startling Appeal

A Southern Illinois University speech student splashed gasoline on himself and ignited the explosive fuel as part of a demonstration speech. He was quickly sprayed with a fire extinguisher that was mounted on a wall in the hallway outside the classroom, and he was wrapped in a wet sheet the student had brought with him to class. Ricardo de la Pietra, a graduate student conducting the speech class, said that the student had asked permission to "do something special" but hadn't indicated exactly what (Berko, 1996). The student suffered first- and second-degree burns and was taken to a hospital.

Kate Logan, a graduating student at Long Trail School in Dorset, Vermont, stunned her audience of 200 faculty, friends, classmates, and parents when she shed all of her clothes during her speech at the graduation ceremony. Logan, 18, spoke of her "journey on a road less traveled" that inspired her individuality ("Naked," 1998). As she spoke, she tossed away her cap and white gown, exposing her naked body to the startled assembly. A spokesperson for the school had this response: "This incident was overwhelmingly inappropriate and is not reflective of our student body."

Simply startling your audience to gain attention, even to make a point, isn't always appropriate. Startling an audience should enhance your speech and your personal credibility with the audience, not detract and distract from these goals.

Every speech instructor remembers notable examples of student miscalculations when using a startling appeal to gain an audience's attention. For instance, one student punched himself so hard in the face that he momentarily staggered himself and produced a large bruise under his eye (the speech was on violence in America). Another confused student fired a real handgun (blanks) at his student audience. Classmates shrieked and scattered in all directions, fearing for their lives.

The competent public speaker exercises solid judgment when choosing to startle his or her listeners. The speaker's goal should not be to gain attention by being outrageous, irresponsible, or by exercising poor judgment. The competent public speaker considers the implied or stated rules of a speech context when choosing attention strategies. Gaining attention by performing illegal acts violates explicit rules of society established to protect people, sometimes from their own foolishness. An audience can turn on a speaker and become an adversary, not an ally, when angered or offended. Startle an audience, but make certain your attention strategy is appropriate.

---

more frightening, the American College Health Association reveals that Hepatitis B has now reached near-epidemic proportions in colleges and universities across the country. Every college student in America is in the highest risk group in the nation and thousands of us will die each year. (p. 111)

Make your topic a vital concern for all of your listeners. When speaking of breast cancer, personalize it not only to the women in the audience who are at risk but also to the men who have girlfriends, sisters, mothers, and possibly daughters concerned about this potential killer. Vital concerns that affect us personally focus our attention.

Humorous Appeal   Everyone enjoys a good laugh. Humor is a superior attention strategy when used adroitly. Humor is everywhere. It is on television, in books, newspapers, and magazines, and in your own personal experiences. Incorporating humorous anecdotes, quotations, and personal stories in your speech will help keep the audience attentive and on your side.

There are several guidelines, however, for using humor competently as an attention strategy. They are:

1. *Don't force humor.* If you aren't a particularly funny person and have never told a joke without omitting crucial details or flubbing the punch line, avoid

Humor is a very effective attention strategy.

humiliating yourself. Listening to a speaker stubbornly try to be funny without success can be an excruciatingly uncomfortable experience for all involved.

The inability to tell jokes, however, does not rule out humor as an attention strategy. Humorous quotations, funny stories you've heard from others, or amusing occurrences in your life can be included to amplify or clarify points. Just don't set them up as canned jokes. Avoid using a lead-in such as "I heard a really funny story" or "Let me tell you a hilarious experience I had." It isn't necessary to signal an audience that you plan to be funny. That simply sets you up for an embarrassing moment if the audience doesn't share your sense of humor.

2. *Use only relevant humor*. Humor should amuse listeners while illustrating a point in your speech. The humorous story, anecdote, quotation, or personal experience that makes a relevant point saves you from embarrassment if the audience doesn't laugh. You can act as if no humor was intended. You just wanted to illustrate your point. Here is an example of humor that doesn't make a relevant point:

> A middle-aged businessman, burned out from overwork, decides to take a year's leave of absence from his job to search for the meaning of life. He reads every philosophy book he can find, travels the world, takes college courses, and meditates. After nine months he still hasn't discovered the meaning of life. Then he hears about a guru living on a mountaintop in Nepal who supposedly has the answer. With renewed vigor he uses his final three months of leave and his remaining savings, and finds the guru. With great anticipation, the businessman begs the guru to tell him the meaning of life. "My son," the guru begins, "the meaning of life is—(pausing for dramatic effect)—a waterfall!" Stunned, the businessman berates the guru. "You mean I came all this way, exhausted my savings only to be told this gibberish that life is a waterfall?" The guru looked pained, and replied, "You mean it isn't?"
>
> This is my favorite story and I can see that it has put you in a looser mood. That's good because what I want to discuss with you today can make you tense. I want to discuss abuses of power by the IRS.

Making an audience laugh or loosen up isn't sufficient justification for using a humorous story, especially a lengthy one. Humor needs to be relevant to the main purpose of your speech.

Making humor relevant is not difficult. All you need to do is tie the humor directly to a main point, principal theme, or purpose statement. For example:

> Someone once said, "I want to die peacefully in my sleep like my grandfather. Not screaming in terror like his passengers." You've all experienced it—the nerve-wracking anxiety every time you see an old person behind the wheel of a car. Last month the National Transportation Agency reported that elderly drivers are the second most dangerous group of drivers, exceeded only by very young drivers. I want to convince you that greater restrictions on elderly drivers should be instituted to protect us all.

The humor is simple, direct, and it leads directly to the purpose statement.

3. *Use good taste*. Glib one-liners and slapstick do not mesh well with funeral services. Sexist, racist, and homophobic "jokes" exhibit poor taste. Offending an audience with ridicule or sarcasm may produce laughter, but it will win few allies. (A formal "roast," however, has as its purpose the sarcastic ridicule of a respected individual who agrees to be roasted.) Coarse vulgarities, obscenities, and sick jokes invite anger and hostility from many listeners. Humor that rests on stereotypes and putdowns may alienate vast sections of an audience, unless the humor is self-deprecating, making the speaker the target.

A speaker I heard recently cracked this "joke" to his mixed-sex audience: "What's the difference between a terrorist and a woman with PMS? You can negotiate with the terrorist." Watching the audience's reaction was instructive. Some laughed. Some started to laugh, then thought better of it. Others not only didn't laugh, they booed the speaker. The speaker seemed surprised by the mixed response and searched for a graceful recovery. He never found one.

Intensity   We are drawn to the intense. **Intensity** is concentrated stimuli. It is an extreme degree of emotion, thought, or activity. Relating a tragic event, a moving human interest story, or a specific instance of courage and determination plays on the intense feelings of your audience.

At the 1996 Democratic National Convention, Vice President Al Gore made the centerpiece of his speech a lengthy, detailed, emotional account of the final painful days of his sister's life as she died from lung cancer caused by years of smoking cigarettes. Although some listeners felt Gore's appeal to intensity was melodramatic and manipulative, others were moved to tears. Life can have its intense moments, and relating some of them can rivet an audience's attention as long as the appeal doesn't become excessive.

Intensity can be created in ways other than by powerful stories and examples. Several delivery techniques capitalize on intensity; these techniques will be discussed in Chapter 14.

Gaining and maintaining the attention of your audience is a critical challenge for any speaker. Attention doesn't just happen, you have to plan it carefully.

Introductions and Conclusions

The beginning and end of your speech can be as important as the body of your speech. Getting off to a good start alerts your audience to expect a quality presentation. Ending with a bang leaves a lasting impression on your listeners. In this section the requirements for effective introductions and conclusions will be addressed.

Requirements for Competent Introductions

There are four principal requirements for a competent introduction to a speech: gain attention, make a clear purpose statement, establish the significance of your topic, and preview your main points.

Gain Attention   In the previous section, general attention strategies were discussed that could be used throughout your entire speech. For the introduction to your speech, however, more specific suggestions can be offered. These are:

1. *Begin with a clever quotation.*

President John F. Kennedy, in a speech at a White House dinner honoring several Nobel Prize winners, said: "I think this is the most extraordinary collection of talent, of human knowledge, that has ever been gathered together at the White House with the possible exception of when Thomas Jefferson dined alone."

President Kennedy deftly complimented his esteemed honorees without becoming effusive in his praise. He demonstrated skill in giving compliments. Complimenting others is an important but often overlooked way to cement interpersonal relationships, build teamwork, and promote goodwill among coworkers and friends. Giving compliments unskillfully, however, can provoke embarrassment and awkwardness between people. Today I will discuss three effective techniques for giving compliments.

Note that the quotation relates specifically to the purpose statement.

2. *Ask a rhetorical question or questions.* A question asked by a speaker that the audience answers mentally, but not out loud, is called a **rhetorical question.** Imagine if one of your classmates began his or her speech this way:

> When you walk downtown and are approached by a street person begging for change, do you make a donation? When you pull off a freeway or interstate and see a person holding a cardboard sign reading "Money for food—just a little help, please," do you reach into your wallet or purse and help the less fortunate? When members of the Salvation Army stand in front of stores during Christmas shopping season ringing their bells and asking for donations, do you drop change into their pots? Have you ever wondered what happens to the money donated to the poor? Well, I plan to inform you where that money goes and on what it is spent.

Rhetorical questions involve the audience and invite interest in the subject. Rhetorical questions can personalize a topic. Make sure, however, that your rhetorical questions are meaningful and not merely a commonplace device to open a speech. "Have you ever wondered why feet smell?" is likely to produce a "not really" mental or even verbal response from the audience. The question seems trivial, not meaningful.

3. *Tell a relevant story.* Storytelling captivates the attention of audiences of all ages. We love to hear good stories, especially when they make a point relevant to the purpose statement. Tara Kubicka (1995), a student at Moorpark College, began her speech with this relevant story:

> Brian Clark was the kind of son that all parents dream of having, a star football player, junior class president, 3.8 GPA, and a devoted brother. Sounds too good to be true, right? Early one afternoon at football practice, Brian collapsed, and tests revealed that he had advanced leukemia and the only thing that would help him would be an immediate bone marrow transplant. Against all hope a match was found—Brian received his life-saving transplant. The story doesn't end there, however. You see the donor died 9 months later of complications stemming from AIDS-related pneumonia. Brian's donor had been infected with the HIV virus and now . . . so was Brian. (p. 9)

Tara went on to develop her case that postsurgical infections following transplantations are a serious problem.

4. *Refer to remarks introducing you to your audience.* In some cases, your planned introduction may need to be altered slightly following remarks made about you by the person introducing you to the audience. A simple, clean reference to those remarks is sufficient before launching into your prepared speech. Walter Mondale, former United States senator from Minnesota had a standard response when he was extravagantly introduced to an audience: "I don't deserve those kind words. But then I have arthritis and I don't deserve that either" (as cited in Noonan, 1998, p. 148). Former President Lyndon Johnson also had a standard line prepared if the introduction of him to an audience was effusive in its praise: "That was the kind of very generous introduction that my father would have appreciated, and my mother would have believed" (as cited in Noonan, 1998, p. 148). Following an underwhelming, bland introduction of him to his audience, Mondale would begin: "Of all the introductions I've received, that was the most recent."

5. *Begin with a simple visual aid.* Carrie Clarke (1995), a student at Southern Utah University, began her speech with a simple visual aid apparent from her introductory sentence:

> When I flip this coin, I have a 50–50 chance of getting heads. You have the same odds of getting a qualified physician in an emergency room. (p. 103)

She used a simple visual aid to draw in her audience and make her point.

Make a Clear Purpose Statement   Purpose statements were discussed in some detail in Chapter 12. The purpose statement provides the blueprint for your entire speech, guiding the audience as they listen to the points you make. Imagine a classmate giving this introduction to his or her speech, and notice the blending of the opening attention strategy and the purpose statement:

> Matthew Shepard, a gay 21-year-old University of Wyoming student, was lured away from a bar in October 1998 by two young males pretending to be gay. Shepard was then robbed, beaten senseless, and tied to a fence outside of Laramie, Wyoming and left for dead. He was found in a coma, and 5 days after his horrific assault Shepard died. This tragic instance of gay bashing aroused the entire nation. At his funeral, more than a thousand mourners showed up to pay their respects to "this gentle soul," as he was described by those who knew him. During the funeral, however, a dozen protesters stood across the street from the church holding signs that read, "No Tears for Queers" and "Get Back in Your Damn Closet." It was a tasteless and insensitive protest, and incidences like this one might make us inclined to support legislation that bans such hate speech. I hope to convince you, however, that outlawing hate speech will produce three significant disadvantages.

The opening example invites attention because it is intense, and it leads directly to a clear purpose statement.

Establish Topic Significance for the Audience   Audiences tend to be Me-oriented, not We-oriented. When told about a local, national, or international problem, listeners typically want to know "How does this affect me?" As a speaker, you must answer that question. During your introduction, establish the basis for why listeners should be concerned about the problem, information, or demonstration central to your purpose. If you are an avid golfer, surfer, card player, quilter, or woodworker, your audience will see your enthusiasm for your topic. Why should the audience be enthusiastic, though, if they haven't ever tried such activities or if they proved to be inept when they did try? Relate your purpose statement to your audience. For example, suppose your listeners never considered playing golf because it seemed uninteresting. You could make the topic relevant and significant to your listeners this way:

> Mark Twain once said that golf was a good walk spoiled. For many of you that may seem true. Most members of my family tell me that watching golf on television is as exciting as watching mold form on rotting food. I beg to differ with these assessments. Golf can be a wonderful activity to watch and play. Golf is a good walk, but it is only spoiled if you lack knowledge of the strategy behind the game and your skill level is deficient. Understanding the strategy, and learning to play golf well can make for an extremely enjoyable few hours of recreation in the bright sun and fresh air. Also,

millions of dollars worth of business are negotiated on the golf links every day. By not learning to play golf, men and women have restricted their ability to compete in the business world. Learning how not to make a fool of yourself while swinging a driver or blasting out of a sand trap when your big business opportunity comes could save you tons of embarrassment and just might seal a deal. Even if you don't foresee a business deal on the horizon, it's never too early to begin learning the game in case your big chance comes unexpectedly. To put it succinctly, golf can be entertaining and it can enhance your life physically, psychologically, economically, and occupationally.

I can't teach you to play golf well in a 5-minute speech. You'll want to find a qualified golf instructor to help you do that. I can, however, briefly explain four qualities to consider when choosing a golf instructor.

Preview the Main Points   Previewing your main points is the final requirement of an introduction. A preview presents the coming attractions of your speech. A speech will normally have two to four main points that flow directly from the purpose statement. For example:

I want to explain how you can save money when purchasing a new car. There are three ways: First, you can save money by comparison shopping, second by lowering your interest payments, and third, by purchasing at the end of the year.

Although the purpose statement and the significance can be reversed in order, attention is always the first requirement. The preview is the final requirement of an introduction. Note how all four aspects of a competent introduction are present in this example:

[ATTENTION] Orville Delong, a 57-year-old Canadian maintenance worker, was playing golf on July 12, 1998, when a meteorite the size of a baseball whizzed by his ear at an estimated speed of 124 miles per hour. "At first we thought somebody was shooting at us," commented Delong. University of Toronto geology Professor John Rucklidge speculated that the meteorite probably originated in an asteroid belt between Mars and Jupiter. Is Delong's near-death experience with a meteorite merely a freak event, or do we all have something to fear from rocks falling out of the sky and imperiling life on earth? We are indeed imperiled. [PURPOSE STATEMENT] That is why I want to convince you that a space-based shield from meteorites is critical to our human survival.

Meteorites are fragments of meteoroids that reach earth before burning up in the earth's atmosphere. Meteoroids streaking through the earth's atmosphere are commonly referred to as shooting stars. [SIGNIFICANCE] Earth has already had many significant direct encounters with meteorites. In 1908 the famous Tunguska meteorite scorched a 20-mile area of Siberian forest and flattened trees. In 1947 a meteorite exploded into fragments in eastern Siberia leaving more than 200 craters. In 1992 a 27-pound meteorite crumpled the back end of a Chevrolet in Peekskill, New York. In June 1998 a one-ton meteorite smashed into Turkmenistan, south of Russia, leaving a 20-foot-wide crater.

The need to create a shield against meteorites is real and urgent. [PREVIEW] I will explore three points to convince you that this is true. First, the probability of earth experiencing a catastrophic collision with a meteoroid is very high. Second, current efforts to address this problem are woefully inadequate. Third, a space-based shield is the only sensible alternative.

This introduction satisfies all four requirements for an effective introduction. It presents a novel attention strategy. The purpose statement is clear and concise. Significance is clearly developed by making the entire audience feel imperiled by the threat. Finally, the preview is direct and concise and sets up the body of the speech.

Some speech experts suggest that there is a fifth requirement for a good introduction: establishing the credibility of the speaker. Mentioning to your audience that you have surfed for 10 years, worked as an auto mechanic for 3 years, or have a degree or certificate in computer science would likely induce your listeners to grant you credibility on those subjects. If you have expertise relevant to your purpose statement, don't hesitate to tell your audience. Student speakers and laypersons, however, often cannot establish their credibility in this way during the introduction to their speech. They may have no particular experience or expertise on a subject that would produce initial credibility with an audience. Speakers may simply have a strong viewpoint and an intense desire to affect decision making. Even informing an audience that you have conducted extensive research on the subject can sound self-serving. Why not let your evidence and command of the facts make that point obvious, and leave it at that?

Credibility is created primarily by developing your purpose with logic and supporting materials throughout the body of your speech. If you sound as if you know what you are talking about, listeners will be inclined to perceive you as credible. Establishing credibility in this way, however, takes an entire speech, not merely a few statements during the introduction. Credibility will be discussed in greater detail in Chapter 16. At this point, however, establishing credibility should be viewed as one possible element of an introduction, but not as an absolute requirement.

Requirements for Competent Conclusions

Conclusions should do what introductions do, except in reverse. You want your introduction to begin strongly, and you want your conclusion to end strongly. Do not end abruptly, apologize for running short on time, or ramble until you fizzle out like a balloon deflating. Be as organized about your conclusion as you are with your introduction.

Summarize the Main Points In your introduction you preview your main points as a final step. In your conclusion you summarize those main points, usually as a first step. Bond Benton (1995), a student at Wichita State University, began his conclusion this way:

> Today we have examined the problems of private policing, by first examining how these officers are unequipped for their roles as police and how this problem has become so widespread in society. We then examined some simple and pragmatic solutions to this problem at both the societal and, finally, at the personal level. (p. 33)

Summarizing your main points during your conclusion reminds the audience of the most important points in your speech.

Refer to the Introduction If you used a dramatic story or example to begin your speech, referring to that story or example in your conclusion provides closure. This is how Moorpark College student Tara Kubicka (1995) concluded her speech on tainted organ transplants:

> Clearly, by examining the problems associated with the unregulated organ industry and the factors leading to this tragedy, we can see that such steps are necessary. Only then can we insure that when the Ruth Glor's and Brian Clark's of the world receive their long awaited saving transplant that it is indeed life saving and not a death sentence. (p. 11)

She finishes by making reference to opening examples that she used to grab the attention of her audience.

Make a Memorable Finish   You begin your speech with an attention strategy, and you should end your speech in similar fashion. The same attention strategies that grab listeners' attention in your introduction will work as well in your conclusion. Erica Williams (1995), a University of Alaska, Anchorage student, gave a speech on the health dangers of margarine. She began her speech with a reference to Woody Allen in the movie *Sleeper*. This is how she finished her speech:

> Although Woody Allen's character wanted to continue to eat wheat bran instead of doughnuts, he learned to adapt to his new world. Just like his character adapted, so must we. We often resist the thing that is best for us. In this case it can lead to an early death. So far we have been taught to say, "I can't believe it's not butter." In the future don't find yourself saying, "I can't believe I've got heart disease." (p. 2)

She makes eating margarine a vital concern to her audience, and her finish is novel.

A clever quotation, a rhetorical question, a moving example, or a humorous statement make effective attention grabbers for introductions. They serve the same purpose for effective conclusions.

One final note about conclusions. They should be memorable, but don't make them memorable by rambling on and on until your audience wants to conclude your existence. Be concise and to the point when finishing your speech. Your conclusion should be about 5% of your total speech. Don't diminish the effect of a great speech with a bloated, aimless conclusion.

Competent Outlining and Organizing

Does a poorly organized speech make a speaker less effective with an audience? The answer is a resounding "yes." The quality of speech organization directly influences how well your listeners understand your key points (Thompson, 1960). A very disorganized speech arouses negative perceptions from your listeners. Speakers who are well organized impress listeners as more credible than speakers who are disorganized. A speaker who doesn't seem able to connect two thoughts together doesn't inspire confidence. Recall how frustrating it is to listen to a disorganized instructor present a rambling lecture. Note taking becomes chaotic. Learning is impaired. Mastering effective outlining methods and organizational formats is a significant skill for the competent public speaker.

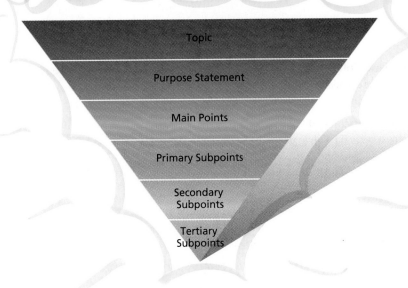

Figure 13-1 The Outlining Process of Organizing a Speech

Topic

Purpose Statement

Main Points

Primary Subpoints

Secondary Subpoints

Tertiary Subpoints

Competent Outlining

There is a standard form of outlining that has stood the test of time. Standard outlining follows a few basic criteria for appropriate format.

Symbols   Standard outlining form uses a specific set of symbols. Briefly, they are:

I. Roman numerals for *main* points
   A. Capital letters for *primary* subpoints
      1. Standard numbers for *secondary* subpoints
         a. Lowercase letters for *tertiary* subpoints

Each successive set of subpoints is indented to separate visually the main points from the primary, secondary, and tertiary subpoints. Thus, you would *not* format an outline as follows:

  I. Main point
  A. Primary subpoint
  1. Secondary subpoint
  a. Tertiary subpoint

You can readily see that lack of indentation merges all of your points and can easily lead to confusion for the speaker.

Coherence   Logical consistency and clarity are qualities of an effective outline. Your outline should flow from your purpose statement. When developing your outline, think of your speech as an inverted pyramid with the base on top and the apex on the bottom (Figure 13-1).

Begin with your topic, narrow the topic to your specific purpose statement, and develop main points from that purpose statement, which break down further into subpoints. Work from the most general to the most specific. For example:

[TOPIC] The aging U.S. population
[PURPOSE STATEMENT] To explain in what ways longer lifespans stress fragile
    support systems for elderly Americans.

  I. [MAIN POINT] Americans are living longer than ever before.
  II. [MAIN POINT] Longer lifespans stress fragile support systems for the elderly
    in three significant ways.

Coherence requires that main points flow directly from the purpose statement. Subpoints, however, should also flow from main points. For example, look at the development of Main Point I:

I. [MAIN POINT] Americans are *living longer* than ever before.
   A. [PRIMARY SUBPOINT] The average lifespan of an American is at its highest level in history.
   B. [PRIMARY SUBPOINT] Americans are living increasingly to 100 years old and beyond.

Each primary subpoint flows from the main point on "living longer."

Each primary subpoint can be further divided into secondary subpoints that flow from primary subpoints. For example:

   A. [PRIMARY SUBPOINT] The *average lifespan* of an American is at its highest level in history.
      1. [SECONDARY SUBPOINT] Average lifespan of an American is a record 77 years old.
      2. [SECONDARY SUBPOINT] Average lifespan of an American has increased from 69 years old just two decades ago.
   B. [PRIMARY SUBPOINT] Americans are living increasingly to *100 years old* and beyond.
      1. [SECONDARY SUBPOINT] A record 30,000 Americans are 100 years old or older.
      2. [SECONDARY SUBPOINT] There will be an estimated 800,000 Americans at least 100 years old by the year 2050.

Following this pattern of working from the most general to the increasingly specific will assure coherence.

If primary subpoints relate directly to a main point, secondary subpoints relate to primary subpoints, and tertiary subpoints relate directly to secondary subpoints, every point will then flow logically from the purpose statement.

Completeness Your first attempt to outline your speech will prove to be more successful if you use complete sentences. Complete sentences communicate complete thoughts. A word or phrase may suggest a thought without communicating it completely or clearly. For example:

PURPOSE STATEMENT: To explain hazing (initiation rituals).

I. Hazing
   A. Campus hazing
   B. Military hazing
   C. Corporate hazing

II. Solutions
   A. Laws
   B. Policies
   C. Penalties
   D. Education

This word and phrase outline creates informational gaps and questions that can't be answered by merely referring to the outline. The purpose statement provides no direction. What will be explained: How to do hazing? Why it is a problem? Ways it can be controlled? Why it shouldn't be controlled?

The main points and subpoints are no clearer. Main Point I is about hazing, and subpoints indicate three types: campus, military, and corporate. Still, no direction or complete thought is communicated. Are these three types of hazing serious problems? Should they be prevented? Should we find them amusing? Should we encourage hazing on campus, in the military, and in the corporate world? Main Point II suffers from the same problem. Solutions are suggested, but solutions imply a problem has been described when no problem is indicated in the previous main point or in the purpose statement. If a problem exists, what type of legal, policy, and educational solutions are offered? This remains unclear.

Consider how much more complete a full sentence outline is when compared to the incomplete and confusing word and phrase outline:

PURPOSE STATEMENT: To explain specific ways to prevent the problem of hazing.

I. Hazing is a growing problem in the United States.
   A. More than 50 deaths and numerous injuries have occurred from hazing in just the last decade.
   B. The number of hazing incidents requiring intervention by authorities has doubled in the last decade.

II. There are several ways to prevent hazing.
   A. Hazing could be outlawed in all states.
   B. College, corporate, and military policies could specifically ban hazing rituals.
   C. Penalties for violations of laws and policies could be increased.
   D. Students, employees, and soldiers could receive instruction on the dangers of hazing and the consequences of violating laws and policies banning the practice.

Balance Each main point deserves substantial development. This does not mean that you have to allot an equal amount of time during your speech to each main point. Nevertheless, you want a relatively balanced presentation. If you have three main points in the body of your speech, don't devote 4 minutes to the first main point and only a minute or less to your two remaining main points. Such a lopsided time allotment means either that your second and third main points aren't really main points at all or that you haven't developed your last two main points sufficiently. Increase the development of main points given insufficient treatment, or drop these points and replace them with more substantial points.

Division Main points divide into subpoints. Note the plural on subpoints. Logically, you don't divide something into one. You divide a pie into two or more pieces. Likewise, you divide main points into two or more subpoints.

Incorrect Version	**Correct Version**
I. Main point	I. Main point
A. Primary subpoint	A. Primary subpoint
	B. Primary subpoint
II. Main point	
A. Primary subpoint	II. Main point
1. Secondary subpoint	A. Primary subpoint
	B. Primary subpoint
	1. Secondary subpoint
	2. Secondary subpoint

[handwritten margin note: always have more than one subpoint or main point]

If you can't divide a point into at least two subpoints, this should signal to you that your point probably doesn't need division or that the point isn't substantial enough. It's time to rethink the development of your speech (Box 13-2).

Competent outlining requires proper use of symbols, coherence, completeness, balance, and appropriate division of points. An outline maps the flow of a speaker's ideas. A perfect outline, however, does not guarantee a perfect speech. A speaker's points may be clearly presented, but they may be incorrect, misleading, or distorted. Supporting materials (discussed in Chapter 14) must bolster a speaker's points. Nevertheless, clearly outlining your speech is an important step in the public speaking process.

Competent Organization

Taking a large, complex body of information and making it understandable to listeners is a big challenge. Finding an appropriate pattern for the information is a key to effective comprehension by your listeners. There are several patterns for organizing a speech. The most common ones used in U.S. culture are topical, chronological, spatial, causal, problem-solution, and problem-cause-solution.

 Topical Pattern   A topical pattern shapes information according to types, classifications, or parts of a whole. For example:

PURPOSE STATEMENT: To explain the three types of prisons in the United States.

  I. The first type is minimum security.

  II. The second type is medium security.

  III. The third type is maximum security.

A topical pattern doesn't suggest a particular order of presentation for each main point. You could begin with maximum security and work to minimum security prisons as easily as the reverse.

Chronological Pattern   Some speeches follow a time pattern. A chronological pattern suggests a specific sequence of events. When speeches provide a biographical sketch of an individual, explain a step-by-step process, or recount a historical event, chronological order is an appropriate pattern of organization. For example:

PURPOSE STATEMENT: To explain the renovation plan for our local downtown city center.

  I. The old Cooper House and Del Rio Theatre will be demolished.

  II. Main Street will be widened.

  III. A Cinemax theatre complex will replace the Del Rio Theatre.

  IV. A new, twice-as-large Cooper House will replace the old Cooper House.

Each main point follows a logical sequence. You don't replace buildings on the same sites until the old buildings are demolished. There is a sequence that must be followed.

 Spatial Pattern   Some speeches provide information based on a spatial pattern. This spatial pattern may be front to back, left to right, north to south, top to bottom,

Box 5-2   Sharper Focus

A Student Outline: Rough Draft and Revision

Constructing a competent outline can be a struggle, especially if appropriate outlining form and criteria are not well understood. Initial attempts to outline a speech may prove challenging, and first attempts may produce seriously flawed results. Don't despair. Outlining is a process that trains our minds to think in an orderly fashion. It takes time to learn such a sophisticated skill.

Compare this rough draft of a student outline to the revised outline constructed by the same student. (My comments appear in italics.)

Rough Draft Outline

PURPOSE STATEMENT: To eliminate the drug problem by making drug testing mandatory. (*Overstates the potential outcomes of mandatory drug testing. Try significantly reducing drug use, not "eliminating the drug problem." General purpose is only implied—will you try to convince us?*)

I. The drugs among society. (*No clear direction is provided. What do you want to say about "the drugs among society?" This is also not a complete sentence.*)
   A. The effects of drugs. (*Are you concerned with only negative effects? Unclear! This is not a complete sentence.*)
      1. The immediate effects of drugs.
      2. The permanent effects of drugs. (*1 and 2 are not complete sentences.*)
   B. The effects of using drugs. (*This seems to repeat A above. Do you have a different idea in mind? Unclear! This is not a complete sentence.*)
      1. Memory loss.
      2. Addicted babies.
      2. Brain damage.
      3. Physical harm. (*1–4 are not complete sentences.*)
II. Ways to solve drug abuse. (*Your purpose statement indicates only one solution—mandatory drug testing. Stay focused on your purpose statement.*)
   A. The first step is to be aware of the problem. (*"Awareness" doesn't seem related to mandatory drug testing. Let your purpose statement guide your entire outline.*)
      1. Establish drug testing in all companies.
      2. Establish stricter laws against drug users.
      3. Start more drug clinics. (*Good use of complete sentences. Subpoints 1–3 do not relate directly to "A"—they are not kinds of awareness. Subpoints 2 and 3 also seem unrelated to mandatory drug testing. These are coherence problems.*)

(*You have an A point without a B point—problem of division. Also, main point II is less developed than main point I—problem of balance.*)

Revised Version

PURPOSE STATEMENT: To convince my audience that every place of employment should start a mandatory drug testing program. (*This is a much improved purpose statement. "Every place of employment," however, seems a bit drastic. Try narrowing the application of your proposal to workers who might jeopardize the health and safety of others if drugs were used—airline pilots, bus drivers, etc.*)

I. Drug use in the workplace is a serious problem. (*Good clear main point.*)
   A. Drug use in the workplace is widespread.
      1. Many employees in large companies use drugs.
      2. Many employees in factories use drugs.
   B. Drug use in the workplace is dangerous.
      1. Workers injure even kill themselves.
      2. Customers have been injured and killed. (*Doesn't the risk go far beyond customers? If a plane crashes on a neighborhood because the pilot was loaded on drugs, dead and injured include far more than customers.*)

(*This entire main point with its subpoints is much improved. One question—are you focusing only on drugs used on the job or do you include drug use that occurs hours before starting work?*)

II. Mandatory drug testing in the workplace will reduce drug abuse. (*This is a solid second main point that flows nicely from your purpose statement.*)
   A. Drug testing will catch drug users.
      1. Testing is very accurate.
      2. Drug testing will provide absolute proof of drug use by workers. (*"Absolute proof" seems overstated. Try "solid proof."*)
   B. Drug testing will prevent drug use in the workplace.
      1. Workers will worry about getting caught using drugs.
      2. Drug testing can prevent drug users from being hired.

(*Second main point is coherent, balanced, divided appropriately, and complete sentences were used throughout. One final question: What do you propose should happen to employees who use drugs? Rehabilitation? Immediate job termination?*)

bottom to top, and so forth. Explaining directions to a particular place requires a spatial order, a visualization of where things are spatially. Explaining how the Brooklyn Bridge was built would necessitate starting the explanation at the base of the bridge and working up spatially.

PURPOSE STATEMENT: To explain how to load up a backpack for camping.

I. Certain items must go on the bottom of the pack.

II. Some items are best packed in the middle.

III. There are several items that pack well on top.

IV. A few items fit well lashed to the outside of the pack.

The outline focuses on segments of space. Actually loading a backpack while you explain your four points is an essential visual aid.

 Causal Pattern   Humans look for causes of events. A standard organizational pattern is causes-effects or effects-causes. The causes-effects pattern looks for why things happen and then discusses the consequences. For example:

PURPOSE STATEMENT: To explain the causes and effects of yearly flu viruses.

I. There are several causes of yearly flu viruses.

II. Flu viruses result in serious illness and death for millions of people worldwide.

Your speech can also begin with the effects of an event and then move to what caused the event. For example:

PURPOSE STATEMENT: To show that grading systems create learning deficiencies at the elementary school level.

I. There are serious deficiencies in student learning from grades 1 to 6.

II. Grading systems promote these learning deficiencies.

 Problem-Solution Pattern   The problem-solution organizational pattern explores the nature of a problem and proposes a solution or possible solutions for the problem.

PURPOSE STATEMENT: To argue for a flat income tax to replace the current graduated income tax.

I. The present income tax system has several serious problems.

II. A flat income tax will solve these problems.

 Problem-Cause-Solution Pattern   The problem-cause-solution organizational pattern expands on the problem-solution pattern by exploring causes of the problem and addressing these causes in the solution.

PURPOSE STATEMENT: To argue for a government-sponsored program to prevent hearing loss among teenagers and young adults.

I. Teenagers and young adults are suffering serious hearing loss.

II. There are several causes of this hearing loss.

III. A government-sponsored program to prevent hearing loss is critical.

All of the organizational patterns discussed here are commonly used in the predominant U.S. culture. Other cultures and co-cultures, however, may use additional patterns (Jaffe, 1998). Space does not permit an explanation of less standard, though valid, forms of speech organization. Learning the standard forms of outlining, however, is an excellent beginning for the novice public speaker.

Summary

Speech development is audience-centered. You begin developing a speech by analyzing your audience. Speech appropriateness and effectiveness are largely dependent on developing a speech that resonates with your specific audience. The first requirement for any speaker is to gain the attention of listeners. If no one pays attention to your speech, you might as well not give it. An effective introduction is vital to the success of your speech. The introduction establishes the basis for an audience to listen to the whole presentation. An effective conclusion is also important because you want to finish your speech in a memorable way. Outlining and organizing the body of your speech clearly and precisely is an essential part of the speech development process. An organized, clearly outlined speech will build your credibility as a speaker, and it will improve the comprehension of your message by an audience.

Suggested Readings

Noonan, P. (1998). *Simply speaking: How to communicate your ideas with style, substance, and clarity.* New York: HarperCollins. A highly readable work on how to develop a speech by Ronald Reagan's speechwriter.

Shachtman, T. (1995). *The inarticulate society: Eloquence and culture in America.* New York: The Free Press. The author presents a nice discussion of the progressive loss of eloquence in public speaking and why this has occurred.

Chapter 14

Presenting the Speech

Successful acting is largely a matter of presentation. Shakespeare's great literature, spoken by an inept actor, can sound like gibberish. A joke told badly produces a collective groan from an audience. Some people can butcher a terrific line, and others can make an ordinary line thigh-slappingly funny. Poetry read poorly can leave listeners preferring fingernails on a chalkboard; poetry presented skillfully can be a sublime experience. The greatest script, the wittiest joke, and the cleverest poetry are diminished or enhanced by how they are presented. Likewise, the effectiveness of a speech can depend largely on its presentation. Even ordinary ideas can seem extraordinary when said well. As James Russell Lowell notes poetically:

> Though old the thought and oft exprest,
> 'tis his at last who says it best.

The primary purpose of this chapter is to demonstrate how to present a speech effectively. There are three objectives:

1. to explain how to present supporting materials capably,
2. to discuss effective style, and
3. to learn what constitutes proficient delivery.

 ## Supporting Materials

A bridge is only as strong as its supporting structure. Provide a weak supporting structure and the bridge will collapse. Likewise, a speech without supporting materials is weak and risks failure. Supporting materials include examples, statistics, and testimony. In Chapter 6 you learned about the fallacious use of examples, statistics, and testimony of authorities. Before presenting a speech, briefly review this material. Having access to valid supporting materials doesn't necessarily mean, however, that you have used them effectively. The competent communicator presents supporting materials for a speech in the most effective manner possible. To understand how to present supporting materials effectively, let's take a closer look at the purposes and the presentation of supporting materials.

Purposes

We use supporting materials to accomplish four specific goals: to clarify points, to amplify ideas, to support claims, and to gain interest. This is an audience-centered process. Work with your listeners cooperatively, not against them competitively. You are trying to "win over" your listeners and gain allies with the help of your supporting materials.

Clarify Points   When we don't understand a point made by someone, a common practice is to ask "Can you give me an example?" An example can clarify your point. Consider this:

> Classifying "races" according to skin color is like categorizing books in a library by
> the color of their covers. What value would there be in such an artificial grouping?
> What would it tell us about the content and substance of the book itself? Skin color is a
> superficial human trait that reveals nothing significant about the content of the group.
> We might as well have a freckle-faced race, a short or tall race, maybe a bow-legged,

bald-headed, or protruding belly button race. No one seriously suggests that these inherited physical traits should be the basis of racial designations, yet who can be heard laughing at the suggestion that a Black, White, or Yellow race exists?

The speaker's point is clarified by the profusion of examples. Merely asserting that skin color makes a poor basis for differentiating human groups leaves listeners guessing as to the basis of such a claim. Providing clear examples lessens opportunities for misunderstanding by listeners.

Amplify Ideas Supporting materials can amplify ideas, producing a greater impact on an audience. A speaker, for example, could make a claim: "Obesity in the United States is a serious problem." That claim lacks power and impact without supporting evidence. Supporting evidence makes the point. Notice how supporting testimony, facts, and statistics gathered from the annual conference of the American Dietetic Association (as cited in Bavley, 1998) and the U.S. Agriculture Department's first conference on childhood obesity (Webb, 1998) amplify the claim, making it significant, even urgent. Here is a compilation of this information.

> U.S. residents, on average, are the fattest people on earth. If eating patterns continue unabated, every American will be obese by the year 2030. Sachiko Tokunaga de St. Jeor, director of the nutrition research and education program at the University of Nevada, notes: "We're the fattest we've ever been. Obesity is the No. 1 malnutrition problem in the United States." A record 55 percent of American adults are overweight or obese. A record 10 million U.S. children are overweight and a high percentage of these children will become obese. Agriculture Secretary Dan Glickman calls it a "quiet epidemic." Obesity causes 75 percent of all diabetes in the U.S., half the high blood pressure cases, and half the high cholesterol cases. The direct and indirect costs of treating obesity-related diseases is almost $100 billion annually.

Without the supporting materials, the claim that obesity is a serious problem can easily be ignored. Supporting testimony, facts, and statistics amplify the claim and encourage listeners to pay attention.

Support Claims A claim without evidence is like a haystack in a hurricane—it is blown apart from lack of support. Claims are generalizations that must be established with supporting evidence. Speakers who make claims without supporting evidence diminish their credibility. In the 1988 presidential campaign, televangelist Pat Robertson, a Republican candidate, seriously damaged his credibility when he made numerous unsupported claims that were wild in the extreme. Among those unsupported claims were that he knew an impotent man who gave AIDS to his wife, and "the only thing they did was kiss" ("Rivals Blast Robertson," 1988). He asserted that a person could catch AIDS from an infected person who sneezes in a crowded room. He further asserted that there were nuclear missiles in Cuba and that nine American hostages in Lebanon "could have been rescued" because their location was known ("Robertson Sets Off," 1988). All of these claims were false based on the evidence.

During an interview on NBC *Meet the Press* in October 1998, billionaire Ross Perot—Reform Party candidate for U.S. president in 1992 and 1996—accused President Clinton of "emotional instability" and "using cocaine." When pressed by interviewer Tim Russert for proof, Perot was unable to provide any evidence, but he repeated his assertions again. Such wild, unsubstantiated assertions are unethical because they are dishonest, unfair, and disrespectful. If you have the proof, provide it. If not, don't make the claim. George Bush said it well when he was accused by Pat Robertson of using dirty campaign tactics to win the Republican presidential nomination in 1988, "Stand up like a Southern gentleman with a little evidence. I'd like to see an apology or proof" (as cited in "Rivals Blast Robertson," 1988).

Quality evidence can establish a claim. Notice how Christy Kennedy, a student at Hastings College in 1995, bolsters her claim that breastfeeding babies is better than feeding infants formula milk:

> Scientists have discovered that no formula, no matter how intelligently devised comes close to the known and potential benefits of nursing. . . . *The American Journal of Public Health,* September 1994, is quick to note that breast milk reduces the risk of several infections including: infant gastrointestinal infection; respiratory tract infections; otitis media; bacteremia; and meningitis. The *New York Times* of April 6, 1994 reports it has long been known that breastfed infants have about one-fourth the risk of developing serious respiratory and gastrointestinal illnesses and one-tenth the risk of being hospitalized with a life-threatening bacterial infection.

Clearly, claims supported by quality evidence strengthen a speech.

Gain Interest   Clarifying, amplifying, and supporting the points made in your speech are important goals that can be satisfied by using supporting materials. Perhaps less significant, but still helpful, is the use of supporting materials to gain the interest of listeners. Much has already been said about gaining and maintaining the attention of an audience. The same characteristics of attention can be applied to using supporting materials. A startling quotation, a novel example, or a vital statistic, for instance, can keep an audience listening to your speech. Gaining the interest of your listeners is not the most important use of supporting materials. If you have two pieces of evidence that prove a claim, however, and one is dry and dull and the other is phrased in a novel way that will likely get notice from listeners, why not use the more attention-getting supporting material?

Effective Presentation

Using supporting materials effectively is a challenge. There are specific ways to make each type of supporting material effective with audiences (Figure 14-1).

Examples   The well-chosen example is often memorable for audiences and may have a great impact on listeners. There are two types of examples, hypothetical and real examples.

A **hypothetical example** describes an imaginary situation, one that is concocted to make a point, illustrate an idea, or identify a general principle. Hypothetical examples help listeners envision what a situation might be like or call up similar experiences listeners have had without having to cite a historically factual illustration that may not be readily available. *As long as the hypothetical example is consistent with known facts, it will be believable.* Note how this hypothetical example is consistent with known facts:

> Imagine that you are working at your desk at your place of employment. Suddenly the air is filled with noxious odors. You begin to cough and gasp for air. Your eyes become

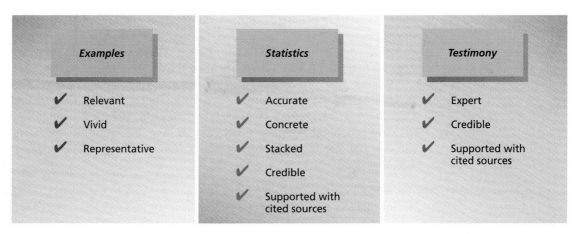

Examples	Statistics	Testimony
✔ Relevant	✔ Accurate	✔ Expert
✔ Vivid	✔ Concrete	✔ Credible
✔ Representative	✔ Stacked	✔ Supported with cited sources
	✔ Credible	
	✔ Supported with cited sources	

Figure 14-1 Making Supporting Materials Effective

irritated and begin to water. You are exposed to ammonia fumes, chemical acetate, hydrogen sulfide, methane gas, hydrogen cyanide, nitric oxide, formaldehyde, and dozens of other substances that are irritants, poisons, or carcinogens. Would you shrug your shoulders and endure these potentially lethal toxins? Would you support "smokers' rights" to pollute your air with such hazardous substances? Although laws have been passed across the United States banning smoking in the workplace, the one workplace where employees typically cannot escape the hazardous risks of second-hand smoke is the local bar. Bars and taverns across this country, with few exceptions, force their employees to endure second-hand smoke in total disregard of their health. Congress must ban smoking in all bars and taverns.

A hypothetical example can help an audience visualize what might occur. Imagine what it would be like to experience a hurricane, tornado, or tsunami. What would happen to you if you suddenly lost your job, were laid up in a hospital for 3 months, or became permanently disabled? These hypothetical examples help listeners picture what might happen and motivate them to take action that might prevent such occurrences.

Real examples are actual occurrences. Real examples are factual, so they are more difficult to discount than hypothetical examples. A real example can personalize a problem. Hypothetical examples can be discounted; real examples are not so easy to ignore. If a speaker talks about his or her personal experience, it can rivet an audience. There is an immediacy and a genuineness about real examples. Just picture the different response you would have to a speaker saying "I *could become* an alcoholic and so could all of you" and a speaker saying "I *am* an alcoholic, and if it happened to me it could happen to you." Real examples have more credibility than hypothetical examples.

There is a skill to using examples effectively. First, examples must be *relevant* to the point you make. A young Abraham Lincoln, acting as a defense attorney in a courtroom trial, explained what "self-defense" meant by using a relevant story to clarify his point. He told the jury a story about a man who, while walking down a country road with pitchfork in hand, was attacked by a vicious dog. The man was forced to kill the dog with his pitchfork. A local farmer who owned the dog asked the man why he had to kill his dog. The man replied, "What made him try to bite me?" The farmer persisted, "But why didn't you go at him with the other end of the pitchfork?" The man responded, "Why didn't he come at me with the other end of the dog?" (as cited in Larson, 1992, p. 181). Lincoln made his point that the degree of allowable force is dependent on the degree of force used by the attacker.

Second, examples should be *vivid*. A vivid example triggers feelings and provokes strong images (Pratkanis & Aronson, 1991). Ronald Reagan had an extraordinary gift for telling vivid stories to make his points. Reagan gave a speech vividly recounting "disabled" citizens carrying the Olympic Torch with pride through the streets of America on the way to the 1984 Olympic Games in Los Angeles:

> In Richardson, Texas, it was carried by a fourteen-year-old boy in a special wheelchair. In West Virginia the runner came across a line of deaf children and let each one pass the torch for a few feet, and at the end these youngsters' hands talked excitedly in their sign language. Crowds spontaneously began singing, "America the Beautiful" or "The Battle Hymn of the Republic."
>
> Then in San Francisco a Vietnamese immigrant, his little son held on his shoulders, dodged photographers and policemen to cheer a nineteen-year-old black man pushing an eighty-eight-year-old white woman in a wheelchair as she carried the torch. (as cited in Erickson, 1985, p. 107)

Reagan was making a speech of reconciliation. He ended this vivid recitation of heartwarming examples with the statement: "My friends, that's America" (p. 107).

Third, examples should be *representative*. Speakers often like to generalize from one or two vivid examples. If these examples are not truly representative, however, then the speaker makes a hasty generalization. A **hasty generalization** is a broad claim based on too few or unrepresentative examples. John Hinkley, who shot Ronald Reagan, successfully pleaded insanity. Dan White, who killed San Francisco mayor George Moscone and city supervisor Harvey Milk, successfully argued the "Twinkie Defense" (junk food made him murder two people). Based on these two high-profile cases, we easily leap to the conclusion that the insanity defense is widely used and often successful. A survey (Jeffrey & Pasework, 1983) of college students and nonstudent residents revealed that when asked to estimate how often the insanity plea is used by defendants in criminal trials they estimated 33% and 38%, respectively. Yet fewer than 1% of defendants attempt such a defense. These same survey participants were asked to estimate how often the insanity defense is successful when tried. Both groups estimated 45%, yet the truth is that only 4% of such pleas are successful (Jeffrey & Pasework, 1983). The Hinkley and White cases are vivid examples. They stick in our minds because they are dramatic, but they are not representative of what normally occurs in criminal trials.

Vivid examples can influence an audience far beyond their legitimacy as proof. Vivid examples that are unrepresentative have the power to distort the truth. *When using vivid examples, make sure that they are truly representative.*

Statistics Statistics are measures of what is true or factual expressed in numbers. A well-chosen statistic can amplify an idea quickly, support claims, show trends, correct false assumptions, validate hypotheses, and contradict myths, perhaps not as dramatically and memorably as a vivid example, but often more validly.

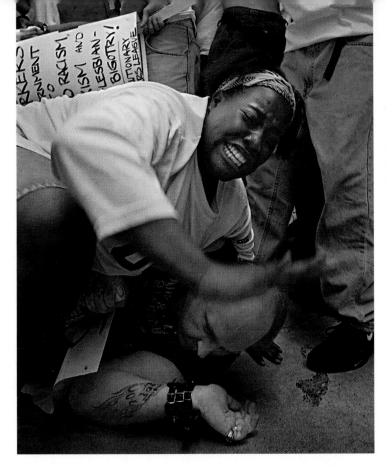

An African American woman protects a White Ku Klux Klan member from an angry mob. It is a vivid example that provokes a strong, memorable impression.

You've probably heard the now-famous remark of Prime Minister of England Benjamin Disraeli that "there are three kinds of lies—lies, damned lies, and statistics." Certainly statistics can be manipulated to distort truth. There are three ways to use statistics effectively, however, without being accused of lying with statistics.

First, *use accurate statistics accurately.* Bill Clinton claimed that 80,000 lobbyists were roaming the halls of Congress, a figure originated by a university professor who admitted he made up the statistic (Crossen, 1994). The statistic itself should be accurate, but the speaker should also *use* a statistic accurately. News media and even health care professionals commonly claim that a woman's chance of developing breast cancer is 1 in 9. That, however, is the cumulative probability of getting breast cancer if a woman lives to an age of 85 years or older. The chances of developing breast cancer by age 50, however, are about 1 in 52, or less than 2% (Paulos, 1994). The risk gradually increases beyond the age of 50. Scaring young women into getting mammograms every year when their chances of getting breast cancer are slim is an unnecessary expense and creates unreasonable fear.

Statistics that are inaccurate or inaccurately used can seriously jeopardize intelligent decision making. As Crossen (1994) notes,

> The consequences range from trivial to profound. Maybe they [consumers] bought the wrong car; unless it was a Corvair, what real difference did it make? . . . But maybe they elected the wrong mayor, governor or even president. Maybe they got the wrong treatment for their disease; maybe they did not stop smoking; maybe they starved themselves on diet pills; maybe they exonerated a polluter or acquitted a murderer; maybe they lost their life savings; maybe they could not solve their society's gravest problems. (p. 37)

Statistical accuracy can be a roadmap for decision making. Statistical inaccuracy can be like a 10 car pile-up.

Second, *make statistics concrete.* In 1991, when Pete Wilson was governor, the state of California faced a staggering $13 billion budget deficit. Wilson explained in a press conference what this meant: "We could close all our state universities, we could open the doors of all our prisons, we could eliminate our entire state workforce, and we still would not balance the budget" (as cited in Kershner, 1991). These examples made the statistics concrete, allowing the audience to easily understand the magnitude of the statistics. Dr. Dennis Mangano, head of the research team at San Francisco Veterans Affairs Medical Center, also used concrete examples to describe what it is like to undergo noncardiac surgery. Such surgery typically raises a patient's heart rate from a normal resting rate of 60 to 70 beats per minute to 90 to 110 beats per minute, often lasting for days: "It's like running 10 marathons in a row. It's like being on a treadmill for 100 hours" (as cited in Puzzanghera, 1996, p. A 28).

Large statistics don't always communicate meaning to listeners. L. R. Wilson (1998), Chairman and CEO of BCE, Inc., speaking to the Canadian Club Montreal, in Quebec, Canada on November 10, 1997, made his statistics concrete when discussing the phenomenal technological advances in the Canadian telephone system:

> Ten years ago, the biggest single inter-city trunks in Canada could transmit digital information at the rate of 565 megabits per second, sufficient to support 8,000 simultaneous voice calls. Today, those trunks run at 10,000 megabits per second and can handle 130,000 simultaneous calls. The latest equipment being installed by Nortel can carry a quarter million simultaneous conversations along a single pair of optical fibres, the width of a human hair. The next generation, which is already in the pipeline, is a 160 gigabit fibre, which would be able to transmit the text of 35,000 full length novels every second. (pp. 182–183)

Wilson doesn't just offer the statistics. He makes the statistics concrete to the average listener by translating the statistic into common human experience.

An effective way to make some statistics concrete is to use comparison to provide a point of reference. At the end of 1997, IBM announced a major breakthrough in the capacity of computer disk drives. IBM discovered a way to store 11.6 billion bits of data (11.6 gigabits), equivalent to 725,000 pages of double-spaced typewritten text, on a single square inch of a disk drive. This was more than double the previous world record capacity. In an effort to provide concrete perspective for this accomplishment, an article in the *San Jose Mercury News* provided a statistical comparison (Rae-Dupree, 1997). Storage on the first hard drive constructed in 1956—IBM's RAMAC—was able to store a mere 2,000 bits of data per square inch at a cost of $10,000 per megabyte (1 million bits of data). By 1988, the cost per megabyte had dropped precipitously to $11.54 per megabyte. Ten years later the cost had dramatically dropped again to 7 cents per megabyte and was projected to continue dropping into the new millennium. Comparison provides perspective.

Third, *stack statistics for impact.* Jon Celoria (1997), a student at William Carey College, effectively stacks statistics for maximum impact in a speech on counterfeit airline parts:

> Aviation Week & Space Technology of July 29, 1996, reports that since 1978, US air traffic has grown ten times faster than the inspector force employed by the FAA. As a

result, the FAA's nearly 3,000 inspectors currently have the unthinkable task of over-seeing 7,300 jets, 200,000 other planes, 4,700 repair stations, 650 pilot training schools, 190 maintenance schools, and nearly 700,000 active pilots. (p. 80)

This is an impressive stack of statistics supporting the point that thwarting the flood of bogus airline parts is an impossible task for current inspection teams.

Stacking statistics should be used only to create an impact on the central points in a speech. An audience will tune out if it becomes weary from the mountain of statistics you are stacking.

Fourth, *use credible sources* for your statistics to build believability among your listeners. As noted in Chapter 6, biased sources diminish the quality and the credibility of a statistic. National polling agencies such as Gallup, Harris, and Roper are credible sources of polling statistics. They have no vested interest in the outcome of their polls and surveys, and they have established a strong reputation for accuracy. *Objectivity* and *accuracy* are essential for sources to be credible.

Fifth, *cite credible sources for all statistics* used during your speech. Speakers often cite credible sources for some, but not all, statistics used. Make it an automatic practice that every time you use a statistic you cite a credible source for that statistic. Listeners should never be given the opportunity to say to themselves, "I wonder where the speaker got that statistic."

Testimony Testimony from experts provides important supporting material. Experts can help laypeople sort fact from fantasy. Expert testimony, however, must be credible. This requires a complete citation of the expert source. A complete source citation includes, as a minimum:

1. the name of the expert,
2. the expert's specific title or expertise, and
3. publication and date of the expert's statement.

All of these elements of a complete citation will establish the credibility of the expert testimony. You should be skeptical of any expert testimony that does not include such details.

The Internet is a rich source of expert testimony, but it is loaded with dubious testimony as well. Remember, the Internet itself is not an authority. It is a medium of communication. "According to the Internet . . ." is way too general a citation. Citing a specific NBC news program on TV, however, or a specific issue of a particular newspaper or magazine, is better. Quoting the actual experts on the program or in the articles is best.

The Internet is replete with examples of so-called experts who provide few if any details about themselves, oftentimes only a name, yet offer seemingly authoritative advice about all manner of controversial things. The October 1995 issue of *Self* magazine reports that a Dr. David Schiem of the National Institutes of Health was pushing unusual cancer cures over the Internet. When *Self* contacted Dr. Schiem, it turned out that he was a computer engineer at the NIH and that his doctorate was in mathematics. He was pushing tea, algae, and cow cartilage as cures for cancerous tumors. He let Internet users believe that he was a medical doctor. The Internet user must be wary of nonspecific credentials. If a so-called expert leaves out his or her specific expertise, be suspicious. The title "Dr." in front of a name doesn't tell you what kind of doctor. The same is true of titles such as "scientist," "professor," "attorney" (criminal or civil), "author," and a host of other authoritative sounding, but inadequate, references to experts.

Brian Eclov (1997), a student at Bartlesville Wesleyan College, in a speech on life insurance fraud, shows how to cite expert testimony: "In the August, 1996 *Money* magazine, the president of the Consumer Federation of America, Bob Hunter, comments, 'What we often have is the illusion of regulation'" (p. 108). The citation is concise, yet complete. You could easily find this reference if you wished.

Effective and Appropriate Style

British author Oscar Wilde once said that "one's style is one's signature always." Although he was referring to a person's writing style, the same can be said of an individual's speaking style. Your speaking style reveals an identity. It is part of who you are. A speech is a combination of substance and style. Your **style** is composed of the words you choose to express your thoughts and the ways you use language to bring your thoughts to life for an audience. A verbose style may tag you as boring. A clear and precise style may identify you in the minds of listeners as interesting or instructive. A vivid style may identify you as exciting, even inspiring. Take your style seriously because it is the picture that you project to your audience. Your style may leave a more lasting image with your audience than any specific points made in your speech. In this section you will learn about the differences between written and oral style and the primary elements of an effective and appropriate style.

Oral Versus Written Style

Oral speech and the written word have distinct differences, which should be considered when speaking to an audience. First, when we speak, we usually use simpler sentences than when we write. An audience must catch the speaker's meaning immediately. When you read a sentence, however, you can reread it several times if necessary to discern the correct meaning, even consult a dictionary if you do not know the meaning of certain words. In a speech, very complex sentence structure can confuse even the speaker, who may get entangled in a thicket of words and lose track of grammar and meaning. George Bush had such a tendency. In response to a reporter's question about tax cuts asked at a 1991 press conference, he stated:

> I think it's understandable, when you have a bad—economic numbers come in from time to time, mixed, I must happily say, with some reasonably good ones—other people get concerned. I'm concerned. But I don't want to do—take—I don't want to say to them, "Well, you shouldn't come forward with proposals." (as cited in Shachtman, 1995, p. 6)

Bush wanted to state the simple point that some people were too concerned about bad economic numbers but that he would still consider proposals to improve the economy. Unfortunately, what he did say was confusing rather than informative.

Second, oral style is more personal and less formal than written style. When speaking, you can look directly into the faces of your listeners. If you sense that they do not understand your point, you can adjust by rephrasing your point,

Elizabeth Taylor has an effective speaking style. Her speaking efforts on behalf of AIDS victims have raised millions of dollars for research.

adding an example, even asking your audience if they are confused. None of this can occur with the written word. Feedback is immediate from listeners, but feedback from readers is delayed and often nonexistent. The speaker and the audience influence each other directly. If you crack a joke and no one laughs, you may decide to dump other attempts at humor. Spelling errors only occur in written language. Grammar mistakes may go unnoticed when words are spoken but may jump off the page when words are written. More slang and casual forms of address creep into spoken language than appear in written form. We tend to be more conversational when we speak than when we write.

Audience expectations for speakers are different from those they have for writers. A speech is a cooperative, transactional effort of speaker and listeners. Speakers and listeners have to work together and make adjustments for a speech to be appropriate and effective. Speakers affect listeners, and listeners affect speakers. Cooperation is less of a factor with the written word. A writer must anticipate how readers will likely respond but can only hope his or her thoughts resonate with readers. A speech and an essay seem very similar, as hundreds of my students will attest when they write a manuscript speech. The two, however, can be quite different (Box 14-1).

Standards of Oral Style

Oral style is effective and appropriate when it fulfills certain criteria. In this section these criteria and some examples of effective oral style will be presented.

Clarity In Chapter 4 abstract language, connotation, jargon, euphemism, and gobbledygook were addressed. Language that conceals rather than reveals is stylistically weak because it confuses listeners. Oral style works more effectively

Box 14-1 Focus on Controversy

Women and Public Speaking: When Silence Isn't Golden

In the Middle Ages, women who dared speak in public risked "branking," a primitive form of humiliation where a metal bit and a muzzle were strapped into the offending woman's mouth. Thus encumbered, the poor woman was either tied to a post in the village square or paraded through the town for public derision. In 17th-century America, a woman who offended colonial society by speaking publicly could be dunked in any available body of water. When raised, sputtering and breathless, she was given two choices—agree to curb her offending tongue or suffer further dunkings. In Boston during the same century, women who gave speeches or spoke in religious or political meetings could be gagged (Jamieson, 1988). The mere presentation of a speech by a female in public was considered "unwomanly" and invited scorn, ridicule, and humiliation (Levander, 1998).

Historically, female speech has been pejoratively labeled to keep women silent. "Nags," "shrews," "fishwives," "gossips," and "magpies" are just some of the unflattering labels used to silence women. Prominent linguist Otto Jesperson (1924) characterized female speech as "languid and insipid" (p. 247). Societal institutions were mounted against women to curb their public speaking. As Jamieson (1988) explains:

> To hold speech of women in check, the clergy, the courts, and the keepers of the medical profession devised labels discrediting "womanly" speech. "Heretics!" said the clergy. "Hysterics!" yelled the doctors. "Witches!" decreed the judges. "Whores!" said a general chorus. "Harpies!" exclaimed those husbanding their power over women's names and property. These names invited the silence that in earlier times had been ensured by force. (p. 69)

So intent were men on silencing women that in the 18th and 19th centuries a ridiculous fiction was propagated that women who insisted on speaking in public would become sterile. Even as recently as the early 1970s, Congresswoman Patricia Schroeder felt it necessary to tell a hostile constituent, "Yes, I have a uterus and a brain, and they both work" (as cited in Tolchin & Tolchin, 1973, p. 87). Public speaking is significant for a lot of reasons, but contemporary men and women can only laugh scornfully at the nonsensical notion that public speaking could be a method of population control.

The relentless ridicule of female public speaking of the past, reaped from a dominance power perspective that accorded men rights and privileges not available to women, carries into more recent times. Madeleine Kunin, first female governor of Vermont and later assistant secretary of education and ambassador to Switzerland, comments on the most difficult part of her transformation from private citizen to public official—speech presentations: "The fearful idea that by speaking out I would no longer be a good girl, that my words might antagonize those who heard me, was deeply rooted. If I said the wrong thing at the wrong time, I risked punishment: I might not be liked. Worse yet, I would not be loved" (Kunin, 1994, p. 63). Kunin gives testimony to the power of society's constricting labels applied to the female voice. Women have had to fight a history of putdowns and punishment for daring to open their mouths and give voice to their ideas and perspectives.

The battle to legitimize the female voice continues even today. The weapons of opposition no longer include

when language is clear and understandable. When using abstract terms (e.g., freedom, rights, justice), operationalize them. Give them concrete, understandable referents. Try to avoid words that may trigger explosive connotations in the minds of listeners. Use jargon carefully. Avoid it when possible if your audience is likely to be unfamiliar with the terminology. Use euphemisms rarely. Euphemisms may be appropriate when sensitivity to the feelings of listeners is the central concern. When the prime concern is to camouflage wrongdoing or controversy, avoid euphemisms. Expunge gobbledygook from any speech. You gain nothing by speaking incoherently.

Clarity comes from a simple, concise style. John F. Kennedy asked his speechwriter, Ted Sorensen, to discover the secret of Lincoln's Gettysburg Address. Sorensen noted this: "Lincoln never used a two- or three-syllable word where a one-syllable word would do, and never used two or three words where one word

(continued)

gags, muzzles, and dunking, nor are the intimidating labels as frequent or brazenly offensive. The strategy to restrict female speech has become far more subtle. The "feminine style" of speaking, characterized as "personal, excessive, disorganized, and unduly ornamental" has been devalued in favor of the "masculine style," characterized as "factual, analytic, organized, and impersonal" (Jamieson, 1988, p. 76; see also Levander, 1998).

Exhibiting toughness by employing the rhetoric of fire and sword (masculine style) is the standard by which our society has judged political speech. When Congresswoman Geraldine Ferraro debated George Bush in the 1984 vice presidential debate, she felt it necessary to adopt the masculine style and appear tough and analytical. Female political candidates, until very recently, have adopted the masculine style of speaking traditionally favored in the male-dominated political arena. This can be problematic for women, however, who are often judged on a double standard. Former United Nations Ambassador Jeane Kirkpatrick explains the predicament:

> If I make a speech [in the United Nations], particularly a substantial speech, it has been frequently described in the media as "lecturing my colleagues," as though it were somehow peculiarly inappropriate, like an ill-tempered schoolmarm might scold her children. When I have replied to criticisms of the United States (which is an important part of the job), I have frequently been described as "confrontational." (as cited in Campbell & Jerry, 1987)

The marriage of television and politics offers a unique opportunity for women. Television, as we will explore in greater detail in the final chapter, favors a narrative, personal, self-disclosive, dramatic or feminine style of speech (Jamieson, 1988). The adversarial, competitive, data-driven, impersonal, aggressive masculine style can come across on television as abrasive, unfriendly, and sometimes bland. It can disconnect an audience, especially female viewers. Ironically, Ronald Reagan helped legitimize the feminine style. His was a personal, narrative, dramatic style more typically associated historically with female speech. Bill Clinton has blended the two styles, mingling narrative, self-disclosive, and dramatic elements with detailed explanations of policies and issues supported with copious amounts of data.

Women have had to learn the masculine style of speech to compete effectively in the political forum. Men have typically avoided, even derided, the feminine style. Women are in a unique position to combine the best of both styles. They can blend their acquired masculine style (analytical, organized, data-based) with their traditional feminine style (personal, narrative, dramatic) of speaking, thus exploiting positive aspects of both styles. Men are late to appreciate the feminine style and are thus likely to find television more challenging than women do.

Questions for Thought

1. If television is well suited to the feminine style of speaking, why should women blend both feminine and masculine styles?
2. How can men adopt the feminine style suitable for television without appearing awkward or weak?

would do" (National Archives, 1987, p. 1). He was simple and concise. Inexperienced speakers may think that big ideas require big words. When listeners start noticing the big words, however, the big ideas shrink into the dark shadows of obscurity. Don't try to impress an audience with a vocabulary that sounds as if you consulted a thesaurus on a regular basis. Remember, oral style requires greater simplicity than written style.

A clear style is a simple style, but simple doesn't mean simplistic. Abraham Lincoln spoke simply, yet profoundly. Lincoln's second inaugural address included this memorable line: "With malice toward none, with charity for all, with firmness in the right as God gives us to see the right." The words are simple, yet the meaning is profound, even moving. If your style is too simple, however, your sentences will sound choppy. Use variety in your style so your words flow. Including an occasional complex sentence or more challenging vocabulary can work well. Although Lincoln used a simple, clear style, his sentence structure and phrasing were not always simple. In his Gettysburg Address, he included several lengthy, complex sentences. He also included this sentence: "We cannot dedicate, we cannot consecrate, we cannot hallow this ground." He could have said, "We cannot set aside for the special purpose of honoring, we cannot make holy this ground." Always choosing simple vocabulary may cause wordiness. Sometimes more challenging vocabulary provides an economical use of language. By occasionally using more sophisticated vocabulary, Lincoln spoke more concisely, clearly, and eloquently. If in doubt, however, default to simple sentence structure and vocabulary.

Precision Baseball great Yogi Berra once observed this about the game that made him a household name: "Ninety percent of this game is half-mental." Yogi also said, "Toots Shore's restaurant is so crowded nobody goes there anymore." Yogi was not renowned for his precise use of the English language. Nor was Deborah Koons Garcia, wife of the Grateful Dead's Jerry Garcia, when she remarked, "Jerry died broke. We only have a few hundred thousand dollars in the bank" (as cited in White, 1998). You, however, should be precise in your use of language. Choose words that express precisely what you mean, not "sort of" what you mean.

A precise style is an accurate style. Adlai Stevenson, twice a candidate for president of the United States and a gifted public speaker, had just finished a speech before the United Nations when a woman approached him excitedly and said, "I really enjoyed your talk; it was without exception superfluous!" Before Stevenson could respond to the woman's unintended characterization of his speech as unnecessary, she continued, "Will it be published?" "Yes," replied Stevenson. "Posthumously." "Good," said the woman. "The sooner the better" (as cited in Rand, 1998, p. 282). Stevenson probably did not feel flattered by the woman's unintended encouragement that he die soon so his speech could be published after his demise. Using and understanding the precise denotative meaning of words is important if you want your style to build your credibility, not diminish it.

Precision is one strong reason sexist language should be avoided. Claiming so-called generic references such as "man," "mankind," "he," "him," and "his" include women stretches credulity and is imprecise. These generic uses of language ask women to believe that a statement such as "Man is the master of his own destiny" also means "Man is the master of *her* own destiny." Such an interpretation requires a mental two-step. First we gain an image of maleness, then we must add femaleness to the picture. Women can never know for sure whether they are included or excluded when these generic references are used. Until recently, women could rightly suspect that they were excluded. "All men are created equal" is a compelling statement from the Declaration of Independence. Women, however, clearly were not included in this statement. At that time women had no property rights, no voting rights, and no equal treatment in employment. In fact, the U.S. Supreme Court ruled in 1894 that it was reasonable for a lower court to rule that the Virginia bar could deny women the practice of law because a woman was not legally a person (*In re Lockwood* 154 U.S. 116 [1894]).

Desexing our language, thereby becoming more precise, is quite simple. Sexist references can be avoided by using plural forms. For example, "A doctor should treat *his* patients compassionately" could be rephrased as "Doctors should treat *their* patients compassionately." If using the plural form becomes too cumbersome, there are additional ways to desex our language with minimal effort. Here are some suggestions:

Sexist References	Nonsexist Alternatives
man, mankind	human, humankind
he, him, his	they, them, theirs
	he and she, him and her
	his and hers
chairman	chairperson, chair
businessman	businessperson, executive
policeman	police officer
postman	letter carrier
fireman	firefighter

Nonparallel Usage	Parallel Usage
men and girls	men and women
man and wife	husband and wife

Sex Stereotypes	Alternatives
housewife	avoid it or use homemaker
best man for the job	best person for the job
manhole	sewer lid

Trivializing Forms	Alternative Forms
lady lawyer	lawyer
male nurse	nurse
career girl	career woman
astronette, jockette	astronaut, jockey
poetess	poet

Linguist Otto Jesperson (1923) proudly proclaimed that English is "the language of a grown-up man, with very little childish or feminine about it" (p. 1). Using language to demean and exclude women, although once widely accepted even by many women, is no longer tolerated, and rightly so. Aside from the inherent bigotry, sexist language is imprecise and often inaccurate language usage. Where once business*man*, police*man*, fire*man*, and post*man* fairly accurately reflected a society with few female executives, police officers, firefighters, and letter carriers, that is no longer true. Use language precisely. Eliminate sexist language.

Vividness   Simple, concise, precise use of language doesn't mean using words in a boring fashion . A vivid style paints a picture in the minds of listeners and makes a speaker's ideas memorable. William Gibbs McAdoo, twice an unsuccessful candidate for the Democratic nomination for president, vividly described the speeches of President Warren G. Harding this way: "His speeches left the impression of an army of pompous phrases moving over the landscape in search of an idea. Sometimes these meandering words would actually capture a straggling thought and bear it triumphantly a prisoner in their midst, until it died of servitude and overwork." The words are simple and the point is clearly drawn. The style, however, is quite vivid.

Consider the difference vivid style makes by comparing the phrasing of several famous statements with a plainer version of the same statements:

Vivid:	"Friends, Romans, countrymen, lend me your ears." (Shakespeare's version of a speech by Mark Antony)
Plain:	"Friends, Romans, countrymen, may I please have your attention?"
Vivid:	"Don't fire until you see the whites of their eyes." (Colonel William Prescott at the Battle of Bunker Hill)
Plain:	"Don't shoot until they get really close."
Vivid:	"I have a dream." (Martin Luther King)
Plain:	"I have an idea."
Vivid:	"I have nothing to offer but blood, toil, tears and sweat." (Winston Churchill, The Battle of Britain)
Plain:	"I have nothing to offer but a struggle."

There are many ways to make your speech style vivid. Here are a few suggestions for you to consider.

Metaphor and Simile Figures of speech use words or phrases in a nonliteral sense or unusual manner to produce vividness. Metaphors and similes are two main figures of speech. A **metaphor** is an implied comparison of two seemingly dissimilar things. In a speech delivered on January 6, 1941, Franklin Roosevelt said that selfish men "would clip the wings of the American eagle in order to feather their own nests." Jesse Jackson, a candidate for the presidential nomination for the Democratic party in 1988, used vivid metaphors in his speech to the convention of delegates. In reference to the plight of poor children living in the Watts neighborhood of Los Angeles, he said, "Their grapes of hope have become raisins of despair." Referring

Rob Rogers reprinted by permission of United Features Syndicate, Inc.

to his own life, he said, "I was not born with a silver spoon in my mouth. I had a shovel programmed for my hand." Patrick Buchanan, a Republican candidate for president, in a speech at the Republican National Convention in 1992, characterized the Democratic National Convention held weeks before as a "giant masquerade ball [where] 20,000 radicals and liberals came dressed up as moderates and centrists in the greatest single exhibition of cross-dressing in American political history." You can differ with the point of view expressed by each of these speakers, but clearly both speakers created vivid images that brought their ideas to life.

Be careful not to mix your metaphors elsewise your vivid imagery may sound laughable. Famous movie producer Samuel Goldwyn once remarked, "That's the way with these directors. They're always *biting the hand* that *lays the golden egg*." Mixing incompatible metaphors can sound goofy, and just a little difficult to imagine.

A **simile** is an explicit comparison of two seemingly dissimilar things using the words *like* or *as*. Curt Simmons described what it was like pitching to Hank Aaron: "Trying to get a fastball past Hank Aaron is like trying to get the sun past a rooster." Bill Clinton, in a speech at Galesburg, Illinois, on January 23, 1995, used simile in an amusing way: "Being president is like running a cemetery; you've got a lot of people under you and nobody's listening."

Similes can enhance a speech, but not if the similes are shopworn phrases that were clever when first spoken but have become tired from overuse. "Naked as a jaybird," "dumb as a post," "dull as dishwater," "strong as an ox," and "smooth as a baby's butt" are picturesque phrases, but they have become clichés.

Create your own unique similes and metaphors, but don't create picturesque figures of speech that offend and insult listeners. Similes and metaphors can be offensive. Hitler once compared Jews to "maggots on rotting flesh." His point was ugly and so was his figurative language. Using figures of speech is your opportunity to play with language, but play with it carefully.

Alliteration When Spiro Agnew was vice president of the United States during the Nixon presidency, he became famous for phrases such as "nattering nabobs of negativism" and "pusillanimous pussyfooters." These were examples of **alliteration,** the repetition of the same sound, usually a consonant sound, starting each word. The problem with Agnew's use of alliteration, however, was that most listeners couldn't decipher what he had said because he loved to use silver dollar words when nickle and dime words would have been more effective.

Vice President Al Gore used alliteration to make his point that democracy is not well served by "going negative" during political campaigns: "We should not demean our democracy with the politics of distraction, denial, and despair." Former Chairman of the Joint Chiefs of Staff Colin Powell used alliteration in a speech on volunteerism delivered in Philadelphia on April 28, 1997, when he said, "As you've heard, up to 15 million young Americans today are at risk. They are at risk of growing up unskilled, unlearned or, even worse, unloved. They are at risk of growing up physically or psychologically abused. They are at risk of growing up addicted to the pathologies and poisons of the street." First Lady Hillary Clinton likewise used alliteration to enliven her point that hatred should be fought by everyone: "In a nation founded on the promise of human dignity, our colleges, our communities, our country should challenge hatred wherever we find it."

Alliteration can create a captivating cadence. Don't overuse alliteration, however. A little alliteration is appropriate. Frequent alliteration could become laughable.

Parallelism   A **parallel construction** has a similar arrangement of words, phrases, or sentences. This parallel construction creates a vivid rhythm. Here are some examples:

> The denial of human rights anywhere is a threat to human rights everywhere. Injustice anywhere is a threat to justice everywhere. (Jesse Jackson)

> Today, we have a vision of Texas where opportunity knows no race or color or gender. . . . Tomorrow, we must build that Texas.
> Today, we have a vision of a Texas with clean air and land and water. . . . Tomorrow, we must build that Texas.
> Today, we have a vision of a Texas where every child receives an education that allows them to claim the full promise of their lives. Tomorrow, we must build that Texas. (Ann Richards, Governor of Texas)

> We shall fight on the beaches.
> We shall fight on the landing grounds.
> We shall fight in the fields and in the streets.
> We shall fight in the hills.
> We shall never surrender. (Winston Churchill)

As is true of any stylistic device, a little goes a long way. Be careful not to overuse parallel constructions.

Antithesis   Charles Dickens began his famous novel, *A Tale of Two Cities,* with one of the most memorable lines in literature: "It was the best of times; it was the worst of times." This is an example of the stylistic device called **antithesis,** the use of opposites to create impact. Perhaps the most famous example of antithesis in public speaking is from John F. Kennedy's inaugural address in 1961: "Ask not what your country can do for you, ask what you can do for your country." The effectiveness of antithesis is in the rhythmic phrasing. Four months before his inaugural address, Kennedy made this statement: "The new frontier is not what I promise I am going to do for you. The new frontier is what I ask you to do for your country." This also used antithesis, but it wasn't memorable. The phrasing wasn't as easily remembered. It seems more verbose. Be concise when using antithesis.

The principal standards of stylistic effectiveness are clarity, precision, and vividness. You can learn much about style by examining competent speakers who follow these standards. Ultimately, however, your style must be your own. Trying to mimic the style of Jesse Jackson by copying his rhythmic phrasing would sound silly. Jesse Jackson's style is uniquely his own. Work on clarity, precision, and vividness by listening to successful speakers, but explore what fits you well. Metaphors and similes may come easily to you, but antithesis may seem artificial and awkward. Develop your own style by experimenting. Try including metaphors in your conversations with others. Play with language informally before incorporating stylistic devices in your formal speeches. Remember, style is your signature.

Delivery can be a critical element of public speaking. Jerry Seinfeld's delivery was essential to his success as a standup comedian.

Delivery

Cornell University psychology professor Stephen Ceci had been receiving average student evaluations of his teaching. He decided to change his delivery of class lectures. He spoke more loudly than usual, varied the pitch of his voice more dramatically, and gestured more emphatically than normal. The student ratings for his class and his instruction went up dramatically, from an average of between 2 and 3 on a 5-point scale to a 4-plus (Murray, 1997). Ceci was perceived by students to be more effective, knowledgeable, and organized because of the change in delivery. Surprisingly, students found the textbook more interesting to read and Ceci's grading policy (unchanged) more fair than in previous terms when he had used a more commonplace delivery. Students also believed they had learned more material even though their test scores were identical to those of previous classes where his delivery was commonplace. Does delivery make a difference? Unquestionably it does.

The next section begins with a brief discussion of common delivery problems. Then various methods of delivery that can be used by a speaker will be explored.

Common Delivery Problems

Inexperienced public speakers often fail to notice problems of delivery that interfere with the effectiveness of their message. Most are commonplace problems that are easily corrected with practice.

Weak Eye Contact Eye contact can be riveting. It is an important part of gaining and maintaining the attention of your audience. Direct, penetrating eye contact with listeners can be quite intense. If you doubt this, try staring at someone for a prolonged period of time. The intensity can be quite powerful. When you do not look directly at your audience, listeners' minds can easily wander. Inexperienced speakers have a tendency to look at the ground, above the heads of their listeners, at one side of their audience or the other but not both, or they bury their head in a manuscript. When you zero in on listeners by making eye contact, it is difficult for listeners to ignore you. When you rarely look at your audience, you allow your listeners' attention to drift.

Monotone Voice   Some individuals have very little range in their voices when giving a speech. Their voices sound flat and uninteresting. Strive for vocal variety, not a monotone voice. You can avoid attention-killing monotony by raising and lowering the pitch of your voice. The singing voice has a range of pitch from soprano to bass. Similarly, you can vary your speaking voice by moving up and down the vocal range from high sounds to lower sounds and back.

Monotony can also be avoided by varying the loudness or softness of your voice. A raised voice signals intense, passionate feelings. It will punctuate portions of your presentation much as an exclamation point punctuates a written sentence. Using vocal volume to gain attention, however, can be overdone. As Mark Twain noted, "Noise proves nothing. Often a hen who has merely laid an egg cackles as if she laid an asteroid." Incessant, unrelenting, bombastic delivery of a message irritates and alienates the audience. Speak loudly only when you have an especially important point to make. All points in your speech do not deserve equal attention.

Speaking softly can also induce interest. When you lower the pitch and loudness of your voice, the audience must strain to hear. This can be a nice dramatic twist to use in a speech, if used infrequently. Vocal variety signals shifts in mood and does not permit an audience to drift into the hypnotic, trance-like state produced by the white noise of the monotone voice.

Rapid Pace   Steve Woodmore of Orpington, England spoke 637.4 words per minute on a British TV program called *Motor Mouth*. Sean Shannon, a Canadian residing in Oxford, England, recited the famous soliloquy "To be or not to be . . ." from Shakespeare's *Hamlet* at a 650-words-per-minute clip. Most speakers, however, are unintelligible when speaking faster than 300 words per minute, and most audiences become twitchy when a speaker motors along at much above 200 words per minute. As mentioned in Chapter 6, a very slow speaking pace (about 125 words per minute) can induce a stupor in an audience. Speaking pace should be lively enough to keep attention but not so fast that you appear to have consumed too many cafe expressos. A speaking pace of 175 to 200 words per minute is usually appropriate. Without actually measuring your speaking pace, you can get a rough idea of the appropriate pace by enunciating your words carefully and pausing to take breaths without gasping for air.

Pausing not only slows your pace, it can be used for dramatic emphasis. Prolonged silence is intense for most people. Silence punctuates important points in your speech. A pregnant pause—silence held a bit longer than would be usual if you were merely taking a breath—interjects drama into your speech and spotlights what you are saying. It calls attention to an especially important point you want to make.

Awkward Body Movements A speaker stands before an audience, grabs the podium in a vise-like grip (white knuckles clearly visible to everyone), assumes an expressionless face reminiscent of a marble statue in a museum, and appears to have feet welded to the floor. This is an example of too little body movement that calls attention to itself and diminishes a speaker's effectiveness. Excessive body movement or variation, however, also detracts from a speech. Aimlessly pacing like a caged panther, wildly gesticulating with arms flailing in all directions, or awkwardly wrapping legs and arms around the podium is distracting. Strive for a balance between excessive and insufficient body movement. The general guideline is "everything in moderation." An animated, lively delivery can excite an audience, but you don't want to seem out of control.

Proper gesturing can be a concern for the inexperienced public speaker. Don't let it overly concern you. Unless you have adopted some really odd or distracting gestures while speaking, your gestures will rarely, if ever, torpedo your speech. Let gestures emerge naturally. You don't need to plan gestures. As Motley (1995) explains, gestures "are supposed to be non-conscious. That is to say, in natural conversation we use gestures every day without thinking about them. And when we do consciously think about gestures, they become uncomfortable and inhibited" (p. 99). Focus on your messages, and your audience and the gestures will follow.

Distracting Behaviors This is a catchall category. There are dozens of possible quirky behaviors that speakers can exhibit, often without realizing that they are distracting an audience's attention from the message. Playing with change in your pocket while speaking is one example. Playing with a pen or pencil is another. Sometimes a speaker will click a ballpoint pen and not even realize it. Sometimes a speaker will tap the podium while speaking. Distracting behaviors can easily be eliminated. Don't hold a pen in your hand and you won't play with it while speaking. Take change out of your pocket before speaking if you have a tendency to jiggle coins when you put your hand in your pocket. Distracting behaviors won't destroy a quality speech unless the behavior is beyond weird. Nevertheless, eliminating them will help create the impression of a polished presentation.

Methods of Delivery

There are several methods of delivery, each with its own pros and cons. The four methods discussed here are manuscript, memorized, impromptu, and extemporaneous speaking.

Manuscript Speaking Speakers often refer to "writing their speeches." In my lifetime I have delivered thousands of speeches. No more than a handful were written word for word. Remember that oral and written style have distinct differences. It is very difficult to write a speech for oral presentation that won't sound like an essay read to an audience. I often tell my students that I do not have to look at a speaker to know immediately that the speaker is reading his or her speech. A read manuscript has a distinct sound and rhythm. Effective speeches are not merely spoken essays. An essay read to an audience can sound stilted and overly formal.

A manuscript speech may be an appropriate method of delivery in certain situations. If you must be scrupulously precise in your phrasing for fear of being legally encumbered or causing offense, then a manuscript may be necessary. Political candidates spend millions of dollars for television and radio ads. They cannot tolerate mistakes in phrasing or wordy speeches. Their speeches are precisely written and delivered from a teleprompter, an electronic device that scrolls a manuscript speech, line by line, for the speaker to read while looking right at the audience or the television camera. A television audience does not see the manuscript scrolling in front of the speaker. Most speakers, however, neither need a teleprompter nor have access to one.

It takes extensive practice to present a manuscript speech in such a way that an audience is not aware that the speaker is using the manuscript. A chief drawback of manuscript speaking is that the speaker will get buried in the manuscript and fail to establish eye contact with an audience. Reading to an audience can disconnect the speaker from the listeners. Another drawback is that digressions from the prepared manuscript are difficult to make smoothly, yet such changes may be critical if the audience does not respond well to a portion of the speech. Generally, manuscript speaking should be left to professional speakers who have substantial experience using this delivery method.

 Memorized Speaking Some speakers attempt to memorize their speeches. This is nothing more than a manuscript speech delivered without the manuscript in front of the speaker. Aside from overcoming the problem of weak eye contact so prevalent with manuscript speaking, all of the limitations of manuscript speaking remain—and new problems arise. The obvious disadvantage of memorized speaking is that you may forget your speech. Awkward silences while you desperately attempt to remember the next sentence in your speech can cause great embarrassment for speaker and listeners alike. Generally, memorized speaking should be discouraged. Memorizing a few important lines in a speech may be useful, but memorizing an entire speech requires far too much energy. A memorized speech usually sounds memorized—artificial, not natural.

 Impromptu Speaking An impromptu speech is a speech delivered off the cuff, or so it seems. There is little or no obvious preparation. You are asked to respond to a previous speaker without warning, or to say a few words on a subject or issue without advance notice. Although impromptu speeches can be challenging, a few simple guidelines can help.

First, if you have any inkling that you might be called on to give a short speech on a subject, begin preparing your remarks. Don't wait until you are put on the spot. Anticipate impromptu speaking.

Second, draw on your life experience and knowledge for the substance of your remarks. F. E. Smith once remarked that "Winston Churchill has devoted the best years of his life to preparing his impromptu speeches." Churchill had clarified his ideas and points of view in his mind. When called on to speak in an impromptu fashion, he was already prepared to say what was on his mind. Life experience is preparation for impromptu speaking. Draw from that experience.

Third, formulate a simple outline for an impromptu speech. Begin with a short opening attention strategy—a relevant story, a humorous quip you've used successfully on other occasions, or a clever quotation you've memorized. State your point of view or the theme for your remarks. Then quickly identify two or three short points that you will address. Finally, summarize briefly what you said. You

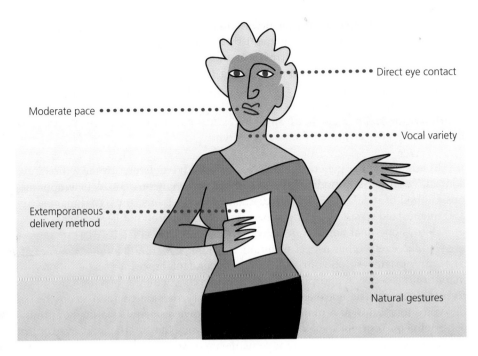

Figure 14-2 Elements of Effective Speech Delivery

Direct eye contact

Moderate pace

Vocal variety

Extemporaneous delivery method

Natural gestures

are not expected to provide substantial supporting material for your points during an impromptu speech, but if you have some facts and figures memorized, you will impress your audience with your ready knowledge. Impromptu speaking is usually more informal than a standard speech, so be conversational in tone and presentation.

Extemporaneous Speaking   Most public speaking classes stress extemporaneous speaking, usually called "extemp" speaking for short. An extemp speech is delivered from a prepared outline or notes. There are several advantages to extemp speaking (Figure 14-2). First, even though fully prepared in advance, an extemp speech sounds spontaneous because the speaker does not read from a manuscript but instead glances at an outline or notes, then puts his or her thoughts into words on the spot. In this sense, extemp speaking falls between impromptu and manuscript speaking. It sounds impromptu and has the detail and substance of a manuscript speech without being either.

Second, extemp speaking permits greater eye contact with the audience. The speaker isn't buried in a manuscript with his or her head down. Of course, an outline can take on the form of a manuscript if it is too detailed. It is possible to write an entire speech, word for word, on a 3 × 5 index card. In such cases, the manuscript is merely tiny.

Eye contact is easy when speaking from brief notes or a brief outline. Typically, a speaker prepares an extemp speech by constructing an outline composed of full sentences. The speaker delivers the speech, however, from an abbreviated outline composed of simple words or phrases that trigger complete thoughts and ideas. Extemp speaking appears more natural than manuscript speeches and is usually more organized and substantial than impromptu speeches.

Third, extemp speaking allows the speaker to respond to audience feedback as it occurs. You can adjust to the moment-by-moment changes in audience reactions much more so than with manuscript or memorized speeches.

The one drawback of extemp speaking is that learning to speak from notes or an outline takes practice. Inexperienced speakers tend to worry that they will forget important elements of their speech if it isn't all written down. There is no substitute for practicing extemp speaking. Once you learn how to do it, you may never want to use any other method of delivery.

In summary, the general guidelines for effective delivery are: use direct eye contact, vocal variety, moderate pace and body movement, and the extemporaneous method of speaking. Eliminate distracting mannerisms, and avoid manuscript and memorized speaking until you become an experienced public speaker.

Here is one final note about delivery: *Delivery should match the context for your speech.* Like every other aspect of public speaking, delivery is audience centered. The appropriateness of your delivery is dependent on certain expectations inherent to the occasion and purpose of your speech. A eulogy calls for a dignified, formal delivery. The speaker usually limits body movements and keeps his or her voice toned down. A motivational speech, however, requires a lively, enthusiastic delivery. Your voice may be loud, body movements are dramatic, eye contact is intense and direct, and facial movements are expressive. During a motivational speech, the podium is usually moved aside or ignored and the speaker moves back and forth across a stage, or even moves into the audience. An after dinner speech or "roast" calls for a lively, comic delivery. Facial expressions consist mostly of smiles, gestures may be gross or exaggerated for effect, and a speaker's voice may be loud, even abrasive, for effect. There is no one correct way to deliver a speech, but many effective ways. Match your delivery to the speech context.

Summary

How a speaker presents a speech can be as important as the substance of the speech. Three aspects of speech presentation were discussed in this chapter: using supporting materials effectively, developing an appropriate and effective style, and developing a competent delivery. The three primary supporting materials are examples, statistics, and testimony. Each can be made effective by following the guidelines provided. Effective and appropriate style should meet three standards: clarity, precision, and vividness. Finally, there are common problems of delivery that become more frequent with some methods of delivery and less frequent with others. The four main methods of delivery are manuscript, memorized, impromptu, and extemporaneous speaking. Most common problems of delivery occur with manuscript, memorized, and impromptu speeches. Extemporaneous speaking has many important advantages compared to the other three methods of delivery.

Suggested Readings

Crossen, C. (1994). *Tainted truth: The manipulation of fact in America.* New York: Simon & Schuster. This is an excellent treatment of the importance of credible use of evidence.

Gilovich, T. (1991). *How we know what isn't so: The fallibility of human reason in everday life.* New York: The Free Press. The author does a wonderful job of presenting common fallacies of reasoning and evidence in a very entertaining way.

Sagan, C. (1996). *The demon-haunted world: Science as a candle in the dark.* New York: Random House. Carl Sagan wrote this book just before his death. As usual, Sagan has written an articulate defense of science and human reasoning and a compassionate, yet direct, critique of magical thinking.

Chapter 15

Informative Speaking

The advent of electronic technologies has ushered in the Information Age. Richard Wurman (1989) contends that "information has become the driving force in our lives" (p. 32). We have greater access to information than at any time in human history. The ease with which we share information, and misinformation, is highlighted by a simple statistic: Americans send approximately 2.2 billion e-mail messages *every day* (Sklaroff, 1999).

Crawford and Gorman (1996) use the metaphors of surfing, swimming, and drowning to underline the need to manage information effectively. Although discussing information in the context of electronic technology, their metaphors seem applicable to informative speaking. An informative speech with too little information presented is unsatisfying to an audience. This is analogous to surfing, merely skimming the top of a subject without delving deeply. Presenting too much information is analogous to drowning, swamping an audience in a tidal wave of information too voluminous to appreciate or comprehend. An informative speech works best when the speaker swims in the information, finding the right balance between too little and too much information for the audience.

In Chapter 12 the issue of swimming, not drowning or surfing in information, was discussed in a general way when explaining the process of narrowing and researching a topic. This issue was further refined in Chapter 13 when outlining and organizing a speech were discussed. In this chapter the focus is on constructing and presenting a specific type of speech—the informative speech.

Informative speaking is a common event. A survey of graduates from five colleges in the United States found that informative speaking was ranked as the top skill most critical to job performance (Johnson & Szczupakiewicz, 1987). Another survey found that 62% of those surveyed claimed they used informative speaking "almost constantly" (Wolvin & Corley, 1984). Teachers spend the bulk of their time in the classroom speaking informatively. Managers speak informatively at meetings. Military officers give briefings. Religious leaders speak informatively when organizing fund drives, charitable activities, and special events. Students give informative presentations in a wide variety of courses and disciplines. Competent informative speaking is a valuable skill.

The principal purpose of this chapter is to discuss how to construct and present informative speeches competently. There are four objectives:

1. to distinguish between informative and persuasive speaking,
2. to explain the different types of informative speeches,
3. to present guidelines for competent informative speaking, and
4. to discuss ways visual aids can be used to enhance informative speeches.

 ## Distinguishing Informative From Persuasive Speaking

No clear line can be drawn distinguishing informative from persuasive speaking. In general, however, an informative speech focuses on *teaching* an audience something new, interesting, and useful. You want your listeners to learn. A persuasive speech focuses on *convincing* listeners to change their viewpoint and behavior. You want your listeners to act.

Don't think of informative and persuasive speeches as dichotomous. They differ more by degree than in kind. Nevertheless, several specific distinctions

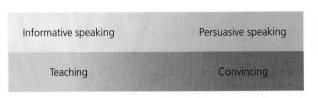

Figure 15-1 The Informative-Persuasive Speaking Continuum

between informative and persuasive speeches can help you understand where a speech falls on the informative-persuasive continuum (Figure 15-1).

Agenda-Setting Function

The news media perform an agenda-setting function. They don't tell us so much what to think as what to think *about*. We pay more attention to the stories carried on the news than to those that are ignored. In similar fashion, informative speeches direct an audience to think about a specific topic. If an informative speech is effective, it focuses a spotlight on subjects about which listeners may know little or nothing. Are you concerned about identity fraud? Ever heard of it? Imposters find your name and social security number by rummaging through your trash or in some other way, apply for credit cards using your name but a different address, and run up huge bills without your knowledge. It's fraudulent, but it can take years to clear your credit rating. If you didn't know about this fast-growing crime in the United States, you might be concerned after hearing an informative speech on the subject. The agenda has been set. You now think about the subject, maybe even take steps to protect yourself from such fraud.

The mere presentation of information to an audience may convince listeners to act differently. If you hear a speech informing you of the hazards of lax dental care, you might be encouraged without any prompting from the speaker to make an appointment with your dentist. If a speaker relates a personal story about the rewards he or she experiences teaching young children, you might begin to consider teaching as a profession, even though the speaker never makes such an appeal. It is a blurry line that separates informative from persuasive speeches.

Noncontroversial Information

Informative speeches do not usually stir disagreement and dissension. A speech describing several ways listeners could save money on textbook purchases won't likely arouse animated disagreement. Mostly, your audience will be thankful for the information. Still, some subjects ignite disagreement. Mention alternative medicine to some individuals and they have a signal reaction, displaying contempt and disgust. A recent study by Dr. David Eisenberg (as cited in "An Intense Look," 1998), an assistant professor of medicine at Harvard University, found that Americans visit alternative practitioners almost twice as often as medical doctors each year. Simply reporting this result to listeners already inclined to view alternative medical treatments with disdain might incite even stronger criticism. Nevertheless, presenting both sides on this and other issues, as most journalists report the news, focuses on teaching something new, interesting, or useful, not on advocating a point of view. This makes the speech essentially informative. If, however, conclusions are drawn regarding which side is correct after weighing the evidence, then an informative speech moves a bit more in the direction of persuasion, although it still retains its informative nature.

Precursor to Persuasion

An informative speech may arouse listeners' concern on a subject. This concern may trigger a desire to correct a problem. The informative speech may act as a precursor, or stepping stone, to a subsequent persuasive speech advocating strong action to correct the problem. According to the U.S. Census Bureau, almost 5 million Americans reported that they were too busy to vote in the 1996 presidential election, triple the number giving that reason for political apathy in 1980. Only 54.2 % of the voting age population cast ballots in the 1996 election ("More Americans," 1998). An informative speech detailing the serious consequences of such voter apathy might lead to a later speech, even by the same speaker, that calls for adoption of specific proposals to rectify this problem. Nevertheless, your speech is essentially informative if you make little or no attempt to move your listeners to act in a specific way.

If you are given an assignment by your speech teacher to present an informative speech to the class, are told by your boss to make a report to a committee or group, or are asked to explain a new software package to novice computer users, remember that your focus will be on teaching, not convincing your listeners. The more neutral and even-handed your presentation, the more essentially informative it is. When you take a firm stand, present only one side without critique, or advocate a change in behavior from your listeners, you have moved into persuasive territory.

The competent public speaker recognizes when persuasion is appropriate and when the specific context calls for a presentation more informative in nature. When teachers use the classroom as a platform for personal advocacy, they may step over the not always clear line between informative and persuasive speaking. Advocacy on issues directly relevant to the teaching role—such as advocating the scientific method as a means of critical thinking—is appropriate. Advocacy of "correct" political points of view, however, can run dangerously close to proselytizing, or converting the "unbelievers," not teaching. Again, it is a matter of degree.

Types of Informative Speeches

The issue of what constitutes an informative speech becomes clearer by looking at different types of informative speeches. Three types of informative speeches are reports, lectures, and demonstrations. There is some overlap between the types, but each type has its own unique qualities.

✳ Reports

A report is usually a brief, concise, informative presentation that fulfills a class assignment, updates a committee on work performed by a subcommittee, reveals the results of a study, provides recent findings, or identifies the latest developments in a current situation of interest. Students give reports in classes and during meetings of student government. Scientists give reports on research results. Press secretaries give reports, or briefings, to members of the mass media. Military officers give briefings to fellow officers and to the press, especially when an event such as the

An officer gives a military briefing to soldiers, for which the map is an essential visual aid.

1999 conflict in Kosovo occurs. Visual aids are sometimes useful when making a report. Videotape of laser-guided missiles striking targets in Iraq in 1991 and again in Yugoslavia in 1999 were used extensively during press briefings to detail the progress of these two wars fought by the United States. Maps and charts were used often to explain strategy and to assess the effectiveness of the air war campaigns.

Lectures

Students are most familiar with this type of informative speech, having heard hundreds of lectures from numerous instructors. A lecture is an informative speech whose principal purpose is to explain concepts and processes or to describe objects or events. Unlike reports, lectures can vary widely in length, from as little as 5 or 10 minutes to several hours. Also unlike most reports, lectures work best when they are highly entertaining. Attention strategies discussed extensively in Chapter 13 are extremely important to the success of a lecture. Maintaining the attention of a sometimes captive audience for long periods of time is a huge challenge. Celebrities, famous authors, politicians, consultants, and experts of all types use the lecture platform to share ideas. They often earn a fat check in the process.

Demonstrations

A demonstration is an informative speech that shows the audience how to use an object or perform a specific activity. Dance teachers demonstrate dance steps while explaining how best to perform the steps. A salesperson demonstrates how a product works. Cooking and home improvement television programs are essentially demonstration speeches. Demonstration speeches require the speaker to actually show the physical object or display the activity for the audience. A demonstration is not a mere description of objects or activities. If you are going to give a speech on martial arts, show the audience specific movements and techniques, don't just ask the audience to imagine them. A speech on how card tricks and magic are performed must actually demonstrate the trick slowly and clearly so the audience can understand.

These three types of informative speeches can overlap. A report may occasionally veer into a demonstration when listeners don't appear to understand what is reported. A teacher typically lectures for a majority of a class period, but the teacher may do demonstrations to add variety and make a point more memorable and meaningful. I have used a fairly lengthy demonstration of a polygraph, or lie detector machine, using student volunteers, to drive home several points related to nonverbal communication and connotative meaning related to words. It never fails to engender interest, even fascination, from the class. Years later students tell me they still remember that particular demonstration and what it showed.

Guidelines for Competent Informative Speaking

In general, informative speeches work best when the information presented is clear, accurate, and interesting. In this section the general criteria for competent informative speaking are explained.

Organize Carefully

Because the primary purpose of an informative speech is to teach, organization of the speech is vitally important. Any of the standard organizational patterns discussed in Chapter 13 can work well, depending on your topic and purpose statement. Several additional organizational tips are also useful.

Basic Structure The basic structure of most speeches, but especially informative ones, divides the speech into an introduction, body, and conclusion (Figure 15-2). The *introduction* grabs attention, explains the significance of the topic to the audience, provides a clear purpose statement, and previews the main points of the speech. The *body* of the speech, which takes the most time to present, develops the main points previewed in the introduction. The *conclusion* provides a quick summary of the main points, often makes reference to the introduction, and offers a memorable finish.

This basic structure may seem unusual to individuals from cultures or co-cultures accustomed to high-context communication patterns. In high-context cultures speakers typically do not provide such explicit organization when communicating messages to audiences. A purpose statement and main points won't

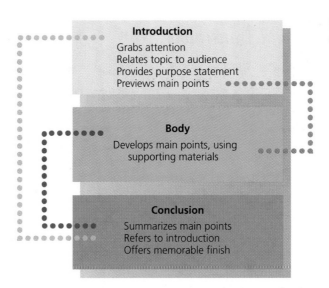

Figure 15-2 Basic Structure of an Informative Speech

normally be precisely stated. Listeners are expected to understand the principal message of a speech from the context. Previous knowledge about the speaker and the message help listeners interpret meaning.

The United States, however, is a low-context culture. There is a general expectation that messages will be communicated explicitly and that ambiguity will be kept to a minimum. Because of this prevailing expectation, individuals from high-context cultures will be more effective public speakers in the United States if they organize their speeches explicitly, fulfilling standard requirements for a competent introduction, body, and conclusion. Explicit organization by a speaker can also help listeners from cultures whose native language is not English to understand the speaker's message.

Definition of Key Terms Key terms, especially unfamiliar or technical ones, should be defined clearly and precisely. For example, do you know what hemochromatosis is? How about endocrine disruptors? Jennifer Bazil (1997), a student at West Chester University, gave an informative speech on hemochromatosis. She defined the term, unfamiliar to most listeners, in this way: "Hemochromatosis is a genetic blood disorder resulting in iron overload. It begins to take effect when an error in the metabolic system causes people to absorb too much iron from their diet" (p. 119).

Adam Childers (1997), a student at the University of Oklahoma, does an equally effective job when he defines endocrine disruptors as "human-made chemicals that have an uncanny ability to mimic some of the human body's most powerful hormones" (p. 103). Even though most people have a passing familiarity with the term *hormone,* many may have a difficult time giving a precise definition. Childers anticipates this and defines hormones as "little more than messengers of the endocrine system. They are released by the pituitary gland, and then they circulate throughout the body, telling different cells what to do. For example, the hormone adrenaline tells our heart when to beat faster" (p. 104). This is a nice definition of hormones. You can picture what hormones do in the body.

Box 15-1 Sharper Focus

Examples of Signposts and Transitions

Signposts		Transitions	
My first point is	The key points are	So what does this mean?	In similar fashion
My second point is	In summary	For example	Why should we care?
My principal concern is	In review	Nevertheless	Naturally
There are three points to explore	Next	Along the same lines	Of course
Let me begin by	Finally	Consequently	Therefore
Please note	Consider this point carefully	Consider the following	On the one hand
My final point	There are two ways	Afterwards	Accordingly
		Unfortunately	Yet
		Instead	In addition
		Therefore	Conversely
		Specifically	Hence
		Thus	In other words
		Once again	A better way

Signposts and Transitions Signposts and transitions both have the same purpose. They guide the listener during a speech. Although not unique to informative speeches, signposts and transitions are extremely important when the principal aim is to help listeners understand. They may be especially helpful to listeners whose native language is other than English. **Signposts** are organizational markers that indicate the structure of a speech and notify listeners that a particular point is about to be addressed. **Transitions** connect what was said with what will be said. They are bridges between points. Box 15-1 offers examples of typical signposts and transitions.

Internal Summaries When you say "summary," most people think of a final wrap-up to a speech or essay. There is another type, however, called an internal summary, which is useful for both informative and persuasive speeches. An **internal summary** restates a key point or points in a speech. It occurs in the body of the speech, not in the conclusion. Internal summaries help listeners follow the sequence of ideas, connecting the dots so the picture drawn by the speaker comes into focus. Lauren McGarity (1997), a student at Rice University, makes a nice internal summary of key points detailing a problem with medical privacy, or the right of patients to have their medical records protected from public scrutiny and use. "Thus, the powerful movement toward cost containment in health care, combined with the inadequacy of current legislation dealing with medical privacy, means that patients now face a privacy nightmare virtually every time they walk into a doctor's office" (p. 129). She then continues her speech by offering possible solutions to the problem.

Use Supporting Materials Competently

Much has been said in previous chapters about the use of supporting materials. In this section how to use supporting materials, not in general but in an informative speech, is discussed.

1. *Avoid fallacies.* This is a reminder to review the material in Chapter 6 on fallacies. No matter how interesting your informative speech might be, presenting misinformation to your audience is not competent public speaking.

2. *Cite sources completely for each supporting material.* Cite a credible source for each statistic used, unless the statistic is common knowledge and widely accepted (e.g., number of senators in the U.S. Congress). One of the most frequent mistakes made during informative speeches is that statistics are provided without a credible source, or any source at all. Also, sources may not be cited completely. Provide the source, the source's qualification if not immediately obvious, and the date of the citation. The same should occur for every authoritative source used to supply important factual information or to present expert testimony. Cite your source even if you are merely paraphrasing the expert's precise statement.

Karmen Kirtley (1997), a student at Sheridan College in Wyoming, presents these supporting materials in her speech on funerals.

> "The average funeral costs between $5,000 and $10,000; this means that most of us will spend 20 to 40 percent of our yearly income on an average funeral" (p. 155).
> "Every year in our country, two million people die; eighty percent of them are buried, occupying over 3,000 square miles of land each year" (p. 156).
> "A survey done by the *San Francisco Chronicle* showed that 85% of us want simple, inexpensive funerals . . ." (p. 155).

In the first two examples no source is offered for several important statistics. Although the statistics appear credible, why raise any doubt by failing to cite a quality source? In the last example no date is provided. There is no way to judge how current or out of date the information might be. Also, the survey from the *Chronicle* does not give a sample size—85% of how many people surveyed want inexpensive funerals? These are minor imperfections in an otherwise effective speech because they occur infrequently, but such minor flaws can become major if they are a frequent occurrence. Kirtley presented a strong speech, well organized and generally well supported, but the few instances of no source or incomplete source citations diluted the effectiveness of an otherwise high-quality speech.

The initial citation of a source should be complete, but subsequent references to the same source can be abbreviated to avoid tedious repetition, unless the abbreviation might cause confusion (e.g., two articles from the same magazine). Teresa Jascob (1997), a student at Ohio State University, does it this way: "According to the same Chicago Tribune article . . ." (p. 98). Sara Hefling (1997), a student at South Dakota State University, abbreviates the source as follows: "As *The Human Rights Watch* report tells us . . ." (p. 123). Jennifer Sunstrom, a student at University of Wisconsin-Eau Claire, offers this form of abbreviating a source: "According to the previously cited *ABA Journal* . . ." (p. 153).

3. *Cite sources in their field of expertise.* When sources are cited on a subject requiring expertise, make sure you provide the experts' qualifications so listeners know they are quoted in their field. Failure to do this gives listeners no reason to grant expertise to the source. Amy Cram (1997), a student at Casper College in Wyoming, cites many quality sources in her speech on high school sex education. An audience isn't able to determine the expertise of two sources she cites, however.

"According to Neil Bernstein in *Learning to Love,* 1995, three million teens acquire a sexually transmitted disease each year" (p. 157). This may appear to be an adequate citation of the source's expertise, but closer examination reveals that we have no idea who Neil Bernstein is aside from the author of a book. Did Bernstein do a study that produced the statistic cited? Listeners have no way of knowing. Is Bernstein an expert or merely someone interested in making a buck by writing a book? Cram also makes the following citation: "This quote from Lance Morrow, 1995 . . ." (p. 158). Who is Lance Morrow? We're never told. Unless every member of your audience is likely to know the expertise of your source already, provide that information.

Use sources that are clearly credible in a field central to your subject. Adam Childers (1997), a student at University of Oklahoma, does a nice job of citing scientific and medical sources on his topic of "hormone hell." He cites, among others, specific articles in *Environmental Health Perspectives, Nature, New England Journal of Medicine, Lancet,* and *British Medical Journal.* All of his sources are credible, respected, and authoritative on the subject of endocrine systems and hormones.

4. *Choose the most interesting of your credible supporting materials.* Learning doesn't usually occur when listeners are bored or uninterested in the subject matter. This doesn't mean substituting colorful but weak supporting material for strong but bland material. Your first consideration when choosing supporting materials should be their credibility and strength. Nevertheless, strong, credible, but interesting, supporting material is the best of all choices. Startling statistics, dramatic examples, and clever quotations by experts add interest to a speech that could become tiresome if supporting materials are dull and lifeless. Use the strategies explained in Chapter 14 for effective use of supporting materials to enliven an informative speech (Box 15-2).

Competent Use of Visual Aids

We can surf, swim, or drown in information. There is little reason to use visual aids if our information on a subject merely surfs the surface. A speech on apple farming doesn't require a picture of an apple split in half unless the speaker plans to present information at a much deeper level than merely identifying readily apparent parts of this common fruit (skin, core, seeds, and so forth). Visual aids can be exceedingly helpful, however, in preventing an audience from drowning in data. A simple chart or graph can make complex information readily understandable to listeners. Visual aids can help speakers and listeners swim, not surf or drown, in information. In this section the benefits and types of visual aids available as well as presentational media and the guidelines for competent use of visual aids are presented.

 Benefits of Visual Aids

Visual aids provide several benefits for a speaker. First, they can clarify difficult points or descriptions of complex objects. Actually showing an object to an audience can help listeners understand. Try explaining a motherboard for a computer or the internal combustion engine without a visual aid. Second, visual aids gain and maintain audience attention. A dramatic photograph of an anorexic teenager

Box 15-2 Sharper Focus

Outline and Text of an Informative Speech

Here is an outline and the text of an informative speech. Each incorporates the suggestions offered for constructing a competent informative speech.

Introduction

I. Attention strategy: Use startling examples.
   A. Describe the Spanish flu pandemic of 1918–1919.
   B. Refer to the 1957 Asian flu pandemic and 70,000 deaths.
   C. Mention the 1968 Hong Kong flu pandemic.

II. Significance: We should all be concerned about yearly flu viruses for two reasons.
   A. A serious flu epidemic could strike again.
   B. Everyone is susceptible to flu viruses each year.

III. Purpose statement: to inform my audience about the hazards of flu viruses and ways to combat them.

IV. Preview: Three main points will be discussed.
   A. Flu viruses pose serious health hazards to all of us.
   B. Flu viruses are difficult to combat.
   C. There are several ways to combat the flu now, and new weapons are on the horizon.

Body

I. Flu viruses pose serious health hazards to everyone.
   A. Ordinary, annual flu viruses are killers.
      1. On average, 20,000 Americans die each year from the flu.
      2. Between 10,000 and 30,000 individuals with diabetes die each year from flu complications.
   B. Flu viruses can make you very sick.
      1. Flu produces symptoms such as high fever, sore throat, aches, cough, and severe fatigue.
      2. "Stomach flu," however, is a misnomer.
   C. Flu viruses are highly contagious.
      1. Children easily catch the flu.
      2. Children infect adults.
      3. Adults spread flu to coworkers.
      4. A worldwide flu epidemic is a virtual certainty in the next 30 years.

II. Flu viruses are difficult to combat.
   A. "Influenza" was thought to be the "influence" of the stars, making it exceedingly difficult to combat.
   B. There are many strains of flu, even in a single flu season.
      1. The 1997–98 season had four strains— A/Wuhan, A/Bayern, B/Beijing, and A/Sydney

2. The 1998–99 flu season also had four strains, only one of which occurred in the previous year.
3. Occasionally a flu virus will mutate causing a pandemic.

III. Flu can be prevented and a cure is near.
   A. Flu can be prevented.
      1. Stay generally healthy.
      2. Flu vaccinations are the best preventive.
         a. Flu shots are 70–90% effective.
         b. Flu shots could prevent 80% of deaths and serious complications if everyone got immunized.
         c. Flu shots cannot cause the flu.
         d. FluMist, a flu vaccine sprayed up your nose, is an effective alternative for those who dislike shots.
   B. Cures for the flu are on the horizon.
      1. Flumadine, an antiviral medication, can shorten a bout with the flu.
      2. Neurominidase inhibitors show great promise in shortening the length of illness.
      3. Sambucol, the European elderberry available in some health food stores, appears to combat flu very effectively in early testing.

Conclusion

I. Provide summary of main points.
   A. Flu viruses can be hazardous to humans.
   B. Combatting flu viruses can be difficult.
   C. Most flus can be prevented and cures are on the horizon.

II. Make reference to the introductory example of Spanish flu.

III. Memorable finish—final cure for this annual plague.

Bibliography

Facts about flu. (1998, January 14). Press release, Centers for Disease Control.

Flu shots can be a life preserver for people with diabetes, CDC says. (1998, August 31). Press release, Centers for Disease Control.

Garrett, L. (1994). *The coming plague: Newly emerging diseases in a world out of balance.* New York: Penguin Books.

Haney, D. (1998, November 8). Researchers breaking new ground on flu front. *San Jose Mercury News*, p. 10A.

Recer, P. (1995, July 25). Experts warn of threat to humans posed by reinvigorated diseases. *Associated Press*, p. 1A.

Box 15-2 Sharper Focus

The Annual Plague

It killed 21 million people worldwide and sickened one billion more, according to Laurie Garrett, health and science writer for *Newsday* and the award-winning author of the 1994 book *The Coming Plague*. [CREDIBLE SOURCE] Garrett tells us that half-a-million Americans died of the disease in a single year, a greater loss of life than Americans suffered in all of the wars in the 20th century combined. [USE OF STARTLING STATISTICS GAINS ATTENTION; COMPARISON MAKES STATISTIC CONCRETE] The virus was so severe that some died from it within 1 day, a few within hours. Women who boarded the New York subway at Coney Island, feeling only mild fatigue, were found dead when the subway pulled into Columbus Circle 45 minutes later. [VIVID, REAL EXAMPLE MAKES STATISTICS MORE CONCRETE AND PROVOKES STRONG, MEMORABLE IMAGE] This lethal disease began in Europe and spread to every corner of the globe. Almost 20% of the population of Western Samoa died from the illness, and entire Inuit villages in isolated parts of Alaska were wiped out.

What was this killer disease? [TRANSITION] The Black Death of the 14th century revisiting the human species? Some biological warfare agent? Cholera, small pox, or diptheria? [RHETORICAL QUESTIONS INVOLVE AUDIENCE, CREATE CURIOSITY] None of these were the cause of this massive loss of life. The global killer was the flu! [STARTLING STATEMENT FOR MOST LISTENERS] That's right, the so-called Spanish flu of 1918–1919 caused this pandemic, or worldwide epidemic.

In 1957 a flu pandemic struck again. Laurie Garrett [ABBREVIATED SECOND REFERENCE TO SOURCE] notes that 70,000 Americans died from the Asian flu, and millions more were incapacitated for weeks by this illness. In 1968, yet another flu pandemic, the Hong Kong flu, felled the human population. The Hong Kong flu hit the United States with sledgehammer force, sickening a huge portion of the country. [USE OF COLORFUL LANGUAGE; EXAMPLES MAKE A NOVEL OPENING TO GRAB ATTENTION]

Why should we care about flu epidemics of the past? [RHETORICAL QUESTION INVOLVES AUDIENCE, MAKES TRANSITION] There are three good reasons to be interested in such notable events: (1) a flu pandemic could strike again, (2) less dramatic flu viruses can cause death and severe illness, and (3) everyone in this room is a potential victim of a deadly flu virus. [SIGNIFICANCE OF TOPIC TO THE AUDIENCE IS ESTABLISHED] Since every person here probably has suffered from the flu at least once, you'll want to listen carefully as I inform you about the hazards of flu viruses and ways to combat them. [CLEAR PURPOSE STATEMENT] I have three main points: I will show that flu viruses are a serious health hazard, that there are specific reasons flu viruses are diffi-

cult to combat, and that flu can be prevented and a cure is near. [CLEAR, CONCISE PREVIEW OF MAIN POINTS; PROBLEM-CAUSE-SOLUTION ORGANIZATIONAL PATTERN USED]

Let's begin by discussing the serious health hazards produced by a normal flu season. [SIGNPOSTING FIRST MAIN POINT] Even ordinary flu viruses that hit the United States every year between the months of October and April are killers. According to a press release from the Centers for Disease Control dated January 14, 1998, in an average flu season 20,000 people die from this disease. [STARTLING STATISTIC MAINTAINS ATTENTION AND INTEREST] An August 31, 1998, CDC press release notes that annually, 10 to 30 thousand people with diabetes die from complications, most commonly pneumonia, triggered by the flu. [USE OF CREDIBLE SOURCES FOR ALL STATISTICS] Annual flu, directly or indirectly, kills more people than AIDS. [COMPARISON MAKES STATISTIC CONCRETE]

Most of you won't die from a common flu virus, but you may wish you were dead. [TRANSITION] Typical flu symptoms include high fever, sore throat, intense muscle aches, congestion, cough, and severe fatigue. My friend, Terry, once described how he feels when he gets the flu, "Its like being suddenly hit by a speeding car, catapulted into a concrete wall, roasted in an oven, then forced to participate in the Iron Man marathon. Death by comparison seems pleasant." [VIVID USE OF SIMILES; INTENSITY USED TO MAINTAIN ATTENTION] Although nausea sometimes occurs with the flu, the "stomach flu" is a misnomer. According to the January 14, 1998, press release of the CDC, severe vomiting is rarely a prominent symptom of flu. [CREDIBLE SOURCE] The so-called stomach flu is actually a gastrointestinal illness caused by microorganisms that cause food poisoning. Symptoms of flu can last from a few days to several weeks. The flu can often lead to severe complications, such as bronchitis and pneumonia, which may require hospitalization.

In addition to the severity of its symptoms, [TRANSITION] flu is hazardous to humans because it is highly contagious. According to Daniel Haney, science reporter for the Associated Press, in a November 8, 1998, article in the *San Jose Mercury News*, young children are flu incubators. [CREDIBLE SOURCE] Haney continues, "In epidemiological terms, children are in the same category as ticks, rats, and mosquitos: They are vectors of disease." [COLORFUL QUOTE] This is not a very flattering portrait of our newest and most precious additions to the human population, but it's nevertheless true. Youngsters have not developed immunity to the flu, something that comes only from previous exposure or immunization. Day care centers and classrooms are flu breeding grounds where sick chil-

(*continued*)

dren spew the virus everywhere by coughing, sneezing, and wiping their runny noses. [VIVID DESCRIPTION CREATES ATTENTION] Children also bring the flu home and infect adult parents who pass it along to coworkers, and so it spreads throughout the population.

An average flu season can kill thousands and sicken millions in the United States. The threat of a not-so-average flu season, however, a full-blown flu pandemic, is real. Dr. Robert Webster, chair of St. Jude Hospital's Department of Virology and Molecular Biology, in an August 18, 1997, press release, claims that another worldwide flu epidemic is a near certainty. [CREDIBLE SOURCE; TESTIMONY OF EXPERT] No one can predict exactly when another severe flu outbreak will occur, but Dr. Joshua Lederberg, Nobel laureate from Rockefeller University, states in a July 25, 1995, Associated Press story that "We'll be fortunate if we get through the next 30 years without another pandemic." [CREDIBLE SOURCE; TESTIMONY OF EXPERT] So you can see that flu viruses pose a serious health hazard for all of us because flu can cause death and widespread suffering. [INTERNAL SUMMARY OF MAIN POINT]

Naturally, [TRANSITION] we're all interested in why flu is an annual event about as welcome as flies, frogs, and the other plagues God visited upon the ancient Egyptians in the biblical story of the Exodus. This brings me to my second main point, [SIGNPOSTING MAIN POINT] which is that flu viruses are difficult to combat for specific reasons.

Previous centuries produced many theories as to the cause of flu. Influenza, flu being the shortened version of this term, reflects the 15th-century astrological belief that the disease was caused by the *influence* of the stars. According to Laurie Garrett, [CREDIBLE SOURCE] prominent American physicians of the time thought the 1918 Spanish flu might have been caused by nakedness, fish contaminated by Germans, Chinese people, dirt, dust, unclean pajamas, open windows, closed windows, old books, or "some cosmic influence." [HISTORICAL EXAMPLES ARE NOVEL ATTENTION GETTER]

Unlike our predecessors, [TRANSITION] we know that a virus causes flu, but a flu virus is difficult to combat. There are many strains, not just a single type. For instance, during the 1997–98 flu season, the CDC [CREDIBLE SOURCE] announced that four strains—A/Wuhan, A/Bayern, B/Beijing, and A/Sydney—were circling the globe. Flu strains are divided into A and B types and designated by the principal city where the flu is first reported. The CDC identified four flu strains for the 1998–99 season, but only one, A/Sydney, was a repeat from the previous year. There are many strains of flu because flu

viruses continually change over time. Sometimes they change their genetic structure only slightly. This genetic "drift" means that your immune system's antibodies, produced to fight a previous flu, will not combat the disease as well when exposed to a slightly altered virus. Occasionally, a flu strain will mutate, altering the genetic structure of the virus so greatly that human antibodies from previous exposures to flu will be useless. According to Laurie Garrett, [CREDIBLE SOURCE] the pandemics of 1918, 1957, and 1968 were mutated flu strains. [REFERENCE TO EARLIER EXAMPLES PROVIDES CONTINUITY TO THE SPEECH; CREDIBLE SOURCE] The changing structure of flus and their many strains make finding a cure very challenging. [INTERNAL SUMMARY OF MAIN POINT]

So what can be done about the yearly flu? [USE OF RHETORICAL QUESTION TO INVOLVE AUDIENCE; TRANSITION] This brings me to my final main point, [SIGNPOSTING MAIN POINT] that flu can be prevented and a cure is close at hand. There are two primary ways to prevent getting the flu. First, [SIGNPOSTING SUBPOINT] stay generally healthy. Those in a weakened or vulnerable physical state, such as the very young, the elderly, those with chronic health conditions, and pregnant women are most likely to catch the flu. Magdalene Vulkovic, chief pharmacist at the University of Houston Health Center, on its Health Center home page, April 1999, states, "Exercise, proper diet, and plenty of rest will lessen your chances of catching the flu." [CREDIBLE SOURCE; TESTIMONY OF EXPERT] Also, avoid large crowds and confined spaces as much as possible where flu sufferers can spread the disease. Airplanes, classrooms, and offices are flu factories.

Second, [SIGNPOSTING SUBPOINT] a yearly flu shot is the best preventive. The CDC, in its January 14, 1998, press release, claims that flu shots are 70–90% effective in preventing flu among healthy adults, and close to 80% of deaths from flu and its complications could be prevented with mass immunization each year. [CREDIBLE SOURCE; CREDIBLE STATISTICS] Because flu viruses change, last year's vaccination won't protect you against this year's flu strains. Despite common belief, a flu shot cannot give you the flu because, as the CDC press release notes, flu shots contain no live virus. [CREDIBLE SOURCE CITATION; TESTIMONY OF EXPERT] The most frequent side effect is brief soreness at the site of the shot.

For those who get weak in the knees at the simple sight of a syringe, there is hope on the horizon. [COLORFUL LANGUAGE; USE OF ALLITERATION; TRANSITION] A November 8, 1998, article in the *San Jose Mercury News* identifies an alternative to a flu shot. [CREDIBLE SOURCE CITATION] FluMist is a vaccine that you spray up your nose. In one test, Flu-

Box 15-2 Sharper Focus

(continued)

Mist was 86% effective against A/Sydney, even though it did not specifically target that strain. Its side effects are minimal, especially when compared to some things people shoot up their noses. Side effects from FluMist consist of a cool, tingling sensation and a slight strawberry aftertaste. Pain phobics take note—it doesn't hurt! FluMist should be available for the 2000–01 flu season. It could be a breakthrough alternative for vaccinating children. As Dr. Michael Marcy of Kaiser Foundation Hospital notes in the same *Mercury News* article, "If we could vaccinate all children annually, we could go a long way toward stopping flu transmission in this country." [TESTIMONY OF EXPERT]

Of course, [TRANSITION] an outright cure for flu is what we all hope will occur. News on this front is encouraging. The CDC's January 14, 1998, press release notes that antiviral medications, such as Flumadine, shorten a bout with the flu for most people. [CREDIBLE SOURCE] Flumadine, if taken within 48 hours of the first flu symptoms, can make you feel better on the second day of treatment. It also stops the flu virus from reproducing in your body so you are no longer contagious.

There is also a new class of drugs called neuro-minidase inhibitors that are being tested. They block an essential protein that a flu virus needs to make copies of itself and spread through the human system. These drugs also shorten the length of illness if taken as soon as symptoms strike.

Those of you who prefer to avoid prescription drugs whenever possible, may find the answer to flu in your local health food store. Sambucol, a product derived from the European elderberry, shows promise as a flu fighter. Initial research on Sambucol conducted by Dr. Madeleine Mumcuoglu [mum-shu-glu], a virologist at Hadassah-Hebrew University Medical Center in Israel, [CREDIBLE SOURCE] shows it reduced fever, cough, and muscle pain in 20% of patients within 24 hours. Mumcuoglu's 1998 report, entitled "Flu Fighter Extraordinaire," claims that within 3 days a complete cure was achieved for 90% of patients taking Sambucol. Among a control group, most patients took 6 days to feel well. The sample size was too small to draw any clear conclusions, but the results are promising. [NOVEL INFORMATION IN THIS SECTION MAINTAINS ATTENTION]

In review, [SIGNPOST] I have shown that flu viruses can be hazardous to humans, that combatting flu can be difficult, but that most flus can be prevented and cures are on the horizon. [SUMMARY OF MAIN POINTS] I began with a reference to the 1918 Spanish flu. Nobody knows where the Spanish flu virus went or whether it will surface again. In 1976, 300 recruits at Fort Dix, New Jersey, became ill with flu, igniting a "swine flu" scare. Although this flu mimicked the structure of the Spanish flu, only one person died and no cases outside Fort Dix ever appeared. [REFERENCE TO THE SPANISH FLU EXAMPLE IN THE INTRODUCTION GIVES CLOSURE TO THE SPEECH] We had a near miss in 1976. Let's all hope that new medicines currently being tested will prove to be a final cure for this annual plague. [REFERENCE TO SPEECH TITLE, "ANNUAL PLAGUE," MAKES A MEMORABLE FINISH] can rivet attention during the opening of a speech on eating disorders. Third, visual aids can enhance speaker credibility. Presenting impressive statistics in a graph, chart, or table can drive home an important point in your speech. Fourth, visual aids can improve your delivery. Novice speakers find it difficult to stray from notes or a manuscript. A good first step to take toward an extemporaneous delivery is to make reference to a visual aid. When you are showing an object, a chart, a graph, or some other visual aid, you move away from reading your speech. You assume a more natural delivery when you explain your visual aid to your listeners. Fifth, visual aids can reduce speech anxiety. When you make reference to a visual aid, you shift the focus of your listeners from you to the visual aid. You don't feel so spotlighted when the audience shifts back and forth between looking at you and viewing the visual aid. Finally, visual aids are memorable. Demonstration speeches rely heavily on visual aids. We can remember a magic trick, a martial arts move, or the proper way to arrange flowers when we have actually seen them demonstrated.

Types of Visual Aids

There are several types of visual aids, each with its advantages and disadvantages. Both strengths and limitations of each type are discussed in this section.

Objects Sometimes there is no substitute for the actual object of your speech. A demonstration on tying different types of knots really requires a rope, not a mere drawing of knots in a rope. Tying knots is a process that is dependent on a specific object. "Imagine me tying a knot in a rope" just doesn't work for the audience. Giving a speech on how to pack the most camping supplies and necessities into a backpack can't be effectively demonstrated without the backpack and some supplies.

There are limitations, however, to the use of objects as visual aids. Some objects are too large to haul into a classroom or even an auditorium. Some objects are not available for show. A speech on building a bullet train in the United States similar to those in Europe and Asia may benefit from a visual aid, but you surely can't drive a real train into a classroom or auditorium. Students have given speeches in my class on surfing. A few have attempted to bring in surfboards as visual aids for their speeches. One student wanted to show how the size of surfboards has changed over the years, so he hauled in four different-sized surfboards. His immediate problem was that his longboard hit the ceiling when it was placed on its end, punching a hole in the ceiling tiles.

Some objects are illegal or dangerous or potentially objectionable to at least some audience members. One of my students long ago thought it was a good idea to bring in a live marijuana plant he had been cultivating as a "show-and-tell" object. Another student wanted to show students "how to roll a doobie." He began his speech by pulling out a plastic bag of marijuana and papers to roll a joint. In both cases, the speech had to be halted because the objects were illegal. Firearms, poisons, combustible liquids, or sharp objects are dangerous. One student wanted to give a speech on "the dangers of pornography." She asked me in advance, thank goodness, if she could bring in explicit pornographic photographs as a visual aid. I nixed her idea. Offending an audience with a visual aid, as abortion protesters often do with graphic pictures of aborted fetuses, can easily backfire and call into

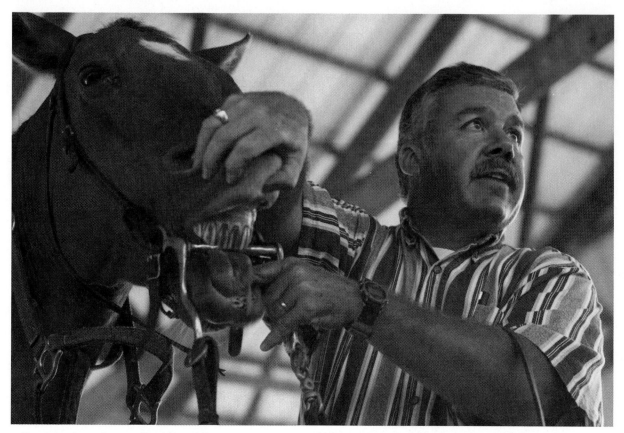

A live animal may be an effective visual aid in certain circumstances, but animals can be very difficult to control.

question a speaker's credibility and good taste. Simply exercise responsible judgment. Check for rules or laws that could invite trouble before using any visual aid that seems questionable.

Inanimate objects are usually preferable to living, squirming objects. Puppies are unfailingly cute and great attention grabbers, but they are also very difficult to control. One student brought a puppy to class for her speech. The puppy whined, barked, and howled throughout her presentation. At first it was cute. After 5 minutes the audience was thoroughly annoyed. Some living objects can frighten audience members. A live snake, especially one not in a cage, will make some audience members extremely uneasy, even agitated. One student brought a live tarantula to class for her speech. She let the spider walk across a table as she presented her informative speech. Audience members were transfixed—not by what she was saying but by the hairy creature moving slowly in front of them.

Models When objects relevant to your informative speech are too large, too small, expensive, fragile, rare, or unavailable, models can often act as effective substitutes. A speech on dental hygiene is an apt example. Speakers usually bring in a larger-than-normal model of a human mouth full of teeth. It isn't practical or effective to ask for a volunteer from the audience to open wide so the speaker can

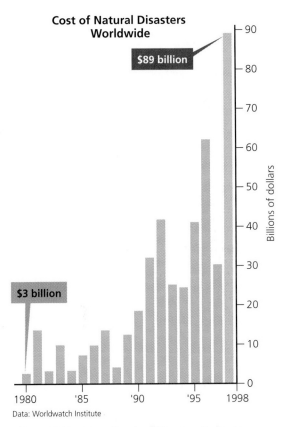

Cost of Natural Disasters Worldwide

$89 billion

$3 billion

Billions of dollars

1980   '85   '90   '95   1998

Data: Worldwatch Institute

Figure 15-3 A Bar Graph of Damage Estimates From Natural Disasters (Source: Associated Press)

Holiday Sales Nov.–Dec. '97

The following are percentages of annual sales that take place in November and December. The figures are based on actual 1997 sales.

Total retail **23.9%**

Chain department store **25.5%**

Discount department store **23.5%**

Apparel & accessories **23.05%**

Electronic store **22.73%**

Catalog/Internet **20.04%**

Jewelry store **33%**

Sporting goods **21.35%**

Data: National Retail Federation/U.S. Department of Commerce

Figure 15-4 A Bar Graph Illustrating the Impact of Holiday Sales on Annual Sales Figures (Source: San Jose Mercury News)

show the volunteer's teeth to everyone. The teeth will be too small to see well, especially for audience members in the back row. Such a demonstration will also be extremely awkward. The speaker may have to point out tooth decay, gum disease, and fillings in the volunteer's mouth—not something most people want others to notice, much less have spotlighted.

Demonstration speeches on cardiopulmonary resuscitation (CPR) require a model of a person. You can't ask for an audience member to serve as a victim for the demonstration. Pushing forcefully on a person's chest could be dangerous and potentially embarrassing.

 **Graphs** A **graph** is a visual representation of statistics in an easily understood format. There are several kinds. Figures 15-3 and 15-4 are bar graphs. A *bar graph* compares and contrasts two or more items or shows variation over a period of time. Bar graphs can make a dramatic visual impact. Figures 15-5 and 15-6 are line graphs. A *line graph* is useful for showing a trend or change over a lengthy period of time. A *pie graph* depicts a proportion or percentage for each part of a whole. Figure 15-7 is a pie graph.

Graphs are effective if they are uncluttered. Too much information in a graph makes it difficult for an audience to understand. A graph must be immediately understandable to an audience. More detailed graphs published in newspapers

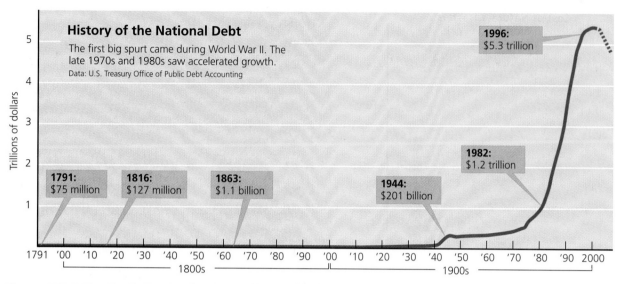

Figure 15-5 A Line Graph Showing the History of the National Debt (Source: San Jose Mercury News)

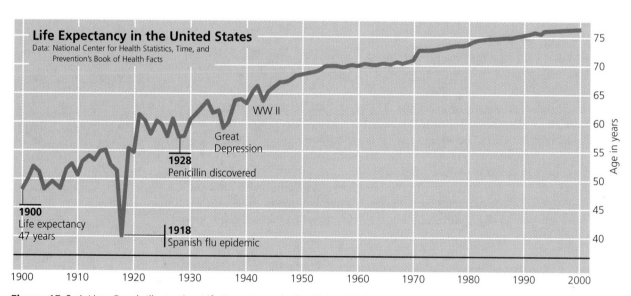

Figure 15-6 A Line Graph Illustrating Life Expectancy in the United States (Source: San Jose Mercury News)

Quantity of Smoking Among College Students

How many cigarettes?
For 1997 smokers, per day:

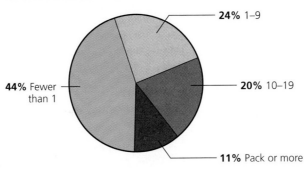

24% 1–9

20% 10–19

44% Fewer than 1

11% Pack or more

Data: Harvard School of Public Health

Figure 15-7 A Pie Graph Showing Smoking Rates Among College Students
(Source: Knight Ridder/Tribune Information Services)

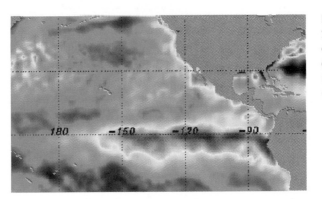

Figure 15-8 A Map That Shows the Effects of El Niño on Worldwide Weather
(Source: U.S. Navy Fleet Numerical Meteorology and Oceanography Center)

and other print media can be effective because readers can examine the graphs carefully. During a speech, this is not possible, nor desirable.

Maps   A map helps audience members see geographic areas to make important points. Commercial maps are normally too detailed to be useful as a visual aid for a speech. The most effective maps are large, simple, and directly relevant to the speaker's purpose. Figure 15-8 is an example of an effective map. Some speakers attempt to draw their own maps, but the proportions and scale of continents, countries, or bodies of water are often badly represented. A map should be exact to be effective. You don't want the United States to look three times bigger than Asia.

Tables   A **table** is an orderly depiction of statistics, words, or symbols in columns or rows. Figure 15-9 is an example of a table. A table can provide easy-to-understand comparisons of facts and statistics. Tables, however, are not as visually interesting as graphics. Tables can also become easily cluttered with too much information. Figure 15-10 is an example of a table with too much information for a speech. Two or three tables could be made from the information in this single table. For instance, a table with only the eight baseball teams that made the play-offs in 1998 and their total payrolls could be compared to the eight teams with the

The Highest Peaks

Mountain	Location	Elevation
Everest	Nepal-Tibet	29,028
K2	Kashmir	28,250
Kanchenjunga	India-Nepal	28,208
Lhotse	Nepal-Tibet	27,916
Makalu	Nepal-Tibet	27,766
Cho Oyu	Nepal-Tibet	26,906
Dhaulagiri	Nepal	26,795
Manaslu	Nepal	26,781
Nanga Parbat	Kashmir	26,660
Annapurna	Nepal	26,545
Gasherbrum I	Kashmir	26,470
Broad Peak	Kashmir	26,400
Shishapangma	China	26,397
Gasherbrum II	Pakistan	26,360

Data: Mountain Madness via the Seattle Times

Figure 15-9 A Table Comparing the Highest Mountain Peaks (Source: San Jose Mercury News)

worst records and their total team payrolls. This would make the point that player salaries correlate with team success or failure.

Tables will be a visual distraction if the headings are too small to read, the columns or rows are crooked, and the overall impression is that the table was hastily drawn. With readily available computer technology there is little excuse for amateurish looking tables.

Photographs   The many photographs included in this textbook underline the effectiveness of this visual aid to make a point, clarify a concept, and draw attention. When objects are too big or unwieldly, unavailable, or too fragile to use as visual aids, photographs may serve as effective substitutes. Instead of bringing the wiggling, fussing, barking puppy to class, perhaps several photographs of the cute pet will suffice. Instead of violating the law by displaying a real marijuana plant in class, show a photograph of the plant.

Photographs have some drawbacks. They may need to be enlarged, and this can be expensive. Postage-stamp-size photographs are worthless as visual aids for an informative speech. When a speaker says to his or her audience "So as you can see in this photograph," and no one can because the photograph is minuscule, the photo becomes not an aid but an embarrassment. The photograph should be large enough for everyone in the audience to see easily.

1998 Payrolls

*-team made playoffs

Team	Payroll	W-L	Pct.	Team	Payroll	W-L	Pct.
Baltimore	$71,860,921	79-83	.487	Seattle	43,698,136	76-85	.472
*N.Y. Yankees	65,663,698	114-48	.703	Kansas City	35,610,000	72-89	.447
Los Angeles	62,806,667	83-79	.512	Chicago White Sox	35,180,000	80-82	.493
*Atlanta	61,708,000	106-56	.654	Toronto	34,158,500	88-74	.543
*Texas	60,519,595	88-74	.543	Milwaukee	31,897,903	74-88	.456
*Cleveland	59,543,165	89-73	.549	Arizona	31,614,500	65-97	.401
Boston	59,497,000	92-70	.567	Philadelphia	28,622,500	75-87	.462
N.Y. Mets	58,660,665	88-74	.543	Tampa Bay	27,370,000	63-99	.388
*San Diego	53,066,166	98-64	.604	Minnesota	24,527,500	70-92	.432
*Chicago Cubs	49,816,000	90-73	.552	A's	22,463,500	74-88	.456
Giants	48,514,715	89-74	.546	Cincinnati	20,707,333	77-85	.475
Anaheim	48,389,000	85-77	.524	Detroit	19,237,500	65-97	.401
*Houston	48,304,000	102-60	.629	Florida	15,141,000	54-108	.333
Colorado	47,714,648	77-85	.475	Pittsburgh	13,695,000	69-93	.425
St. Louis	44,090,854	83-79	.512	Montreal	8,317,500	65-97	.401

Figure 15-10 An Ineffective Table With Too Much Information on Major League Baseball Team Payrolls, 1998 (Source: USA Today)

Drawings When photographs are unavailable, a careful drawing might be an effective substitute. Drawings of figures performing ballet moves or pole vaulting techniques could be instructive for an audience. If the drawings are sloppy, distorted, small, and appear to have been drawn by a 5-year-old with no artistic talent, find a different visual aid.

Visual Aids Media

There are many media, or means of communicating, with visual aids. The most frequently used media are discussed next.

Chalkboard Every student is familiar with the chalkboard. The chalkboard is a useful visual aid medium when time and resources don't permit the use of more sophisticated media. Chalkboards are widely available and allow great flexibility. Tables, drawings, and graphs all can be put on a chalkboard. Mistakes can be immediately, and easily, erased.

Chalkboards, however, do have several serious drawbacks. The quality of the table, drawing, or graph is usually inferior. Students are sometimes tempted to draw on a chalkboard during their speech, consuming huge portions of their allotted speaking time creating their visual aid. If a student uses the chalkboard prior to his or her speech, the class waits impatiently while the speaker creates the visual aid. It is too time-consuming. Most instructors discourage the use of chalkboards as a visual aid medium.

Poster Board   A poster board is a very simple medium for visual aids. Available in most college bookstores or stationery outlets, you can draw, stencil, and make graphs or tables using poster board. Making the poster appear professional, however, is a primary challenge. Posters are usually attached to an easel for display. Simply standing them on a chalktray, however, will usually result in the poster curling at the top and flopping onto the ground. Tape it to a wall if no better option exists.

Handouts   Distributing a handout is a popular form of visual aid. A table, map, drawing, or even a photograph can appear on a handout. One significant advantage of a handout is that the listeners can keep it long after the speech has been presented. It can serve as a useful reminder of the information presented.

Handouts have several potential disadvantages, however. Passing out a handout in the middle of your speech wastes time, breaks the flow of the speech, and can be a huge distraction when you try to regain audience attention. If your listeners are busy reading your handout while you're speaking, they will not be attending to your message. You may be speaking on a different point while audience members are still reading your handout on a previous point.

Distribute a handout just prior to giving your speech if the handout will be an integral part of your presentation. If the handout is necessary for explanation of important points throughout your speech, the handout will not distract but will assist audience members to maintain focus and increase understanding of your message. Sometimes a handout can be passed out after the speech has ended. A handout with names, e-mail addresses, and phone numbers of organizations or agencies that can provide additional information on your subject can be handed out after your speech (e.g., Dr. Dean Edell's website list of primary care physicians who prescribe acupuncture treatments). A handout can be distributed during a speech if you are lecturing for a long time (an hour or two). During short speeches (5–10 minutes), however, don't distribute a handout in the middle of your presentation.

Projection Equipment   There are several options available for projecting images onto a large screen. An opaque projector is a relic from another age that still has its uses. An opaque projector enlarges pictures from magazines, newspapers, and books, or it enlarges photographs onto a screen. Its greatest advantage is that no special preparation is necessary to use the equipment. You don't have to spend significant amounts of money to enlarge pictures that are too small to be effective visual aids. The opaque projector does the temporary enlargement.

The opaque projector does have several disadvantages. First, it is a clunky piece of equipment. It is awkward to use, especially if you have no experience with the projector. The bulb is very hot, so pictures placed in the projector can easily burn or curl if left in it too long.

Another piece of projection equipment is the slide projector. This takes preparation to use effectively. Slides must be developed and placed in a circular tray right side up. Slide projectors provide beautiful enlarged pictures on a screen. If you need a picture and none is available, a slide projector allows you to take your

Transparencies are an effective, low-tech visual aid.

own picture and blow it up on a screen for the audience. Slide projectors, however, are notorious for causing problems. Slides sometimes jam in the tray, bulbs burn out in the middle of a presentation, and the tray sometimes doesn't advance to the next slide for a variety of reasons.

Overhead projectors are yet another type of projector that can be used to display enlarged images. They are widely used because they are easy, relatively problem free, and are a flexible piece of equipment. Transparencies are placed on the overhead projector, enlarging a table, map, picture, graph, or drawing. Transparencies are very easy to prepare. Whatever can be photocopied can be made into a transparency. The relative ease with which this equipment can be used tempts speakers to overdo the number of transparencies used during a speech. Be careful not to substitute transparencies for an actual speech.

Videotape   A videotape excerpt from a movie or a segment from a videotape you shot yourself can be a valuable visual aid. Videotapes can be dramatic, informative, and moving. They often are great attention grabbers. Videotapes used during an informative speech, however, have several limitations. First, the sound on a videotape will compete with the speaker for attention. Shut off the sound when you are trying to explain a point while the tape is playing. Second, a videotape with its dramatic action can make your speech seem tame, even dull, by comparison. It is tough to compete with a Hollywood production. Third, a videotape isn't a speech. I have to remind my students of this often. There is a real temptation to play a videotape as a major portion of a student's speech without any narration or direct reference to the tape while it is rolling. A videotape should not be a substitute for your speech. If you use a videotape excerpt during your speech, be certain that it is properly cued so you won't have to interrupt the flow of your presentation by looking for the right place to start the tape. Use only very short video excerpts.

Computer-Assisted Presentations   By now you should be familiar with the many options available for computer-assisted presentations. Power Point is probably the most widely available and utilized example of this visual aid medium. Space does not allow a "how-to" explanation for using this technology. For relatively short presentations (5–10 minute speeches) this technology is probably overkill. For longer speeches (an hour-long lecture) computer-assisted presentations can be wonderful. The biggest drawbacks to these visual aids media are the availability of the technology, the time it takes to prepare the presentation using this technology, and the potential for glitches to occur during the actual speech.

Guidelines for Competent Use of Visual Aids

Poorly designed and clumsily presented visual aids will detract, not aid, your speech. Here are some guidelines for the competent use of visual aids.

Keep Aids Simple

Complex tables, maps, and graphics can work well in print media such as magazines and newspapers. Readers can closely examine a visual aid. Listeners do not have the same option. Complex visual aids do not work well for speeches, especially short ones, where the information needs to be communicated clearly and quickly. Your audience will be intent on figuring out a complex visual aid, not listening to you speak. Keep visual aids simple.

Make Aids Visible

The general rule for visual aids is that people in the back of the room or auditorium should be able to see your visual aid easily. If they can't, it is not large enough to be effective. Audience members should not have to strain to see words or numbers on your visual aid. Your audience will quickly grow uninterested in your visual aid if it is not large enough to be easily seen.

Make Aids Neat and Attractive

I had a student who realized 5 minutes before his speech that a visual aid was required for the speaking assignment. I actually saw him take his lunch bag, pour out the contents, take a black marker pen, and quickly sketch a drawing for his visual aid. When he gave his speech and showed his lunch bag drawing, audience members had to stifle their laughter. Don't embarrass yourself by showing a visual aid of poor quality. When you use a visual aid, you want it to look neat and attractive. This means you have to take time to prepare the visual aid. Sloppy, last-minute drawings, posters, tables, and the like won't suffice.

Don't Block the Audience's View

A very common mistake made even by professional speakers is that they block the audience's view of the visual aid. Standing in front of your poster, graph, drawing, or table while you talk to the visual aid, not to your audience, is awkward and self-defeating. You want your audience members to see the visual aid. Your audience should not have to stand and move across the room to see it, crane their necks, or give up in frustration because you're blocking their view. Simply stand beside your poster, drawing, graph, even videotape while you explain it to the audience. Point the toes of your shoes toward the audience and imagine that your feet are nailed to the ground. If you don't move your feet, you will continue to stand beside, not in front of, your visual aid. Talk to your audience, not to your visual aid.

Put the Aid Out of Sight When Not in Use

Cover your poster or drawing, graph, or photo when not actually referring to it. Simply leaving it open to view when you no longer make reference to it or showing it way before you actually use it distracts an audience. You want the focus on you. Shut off the overhead or slide projector, VCR, or opaque projector when you are finished using the visual aid. Turn them on only when actually referring to the slides, photos, drawings, and so forth.

Practice With Aids

Using visual aids competently requires practice. At first, using a visual aid may seem awkward, even unnatural. Once you have practiced your speech using a visual aid, however, it will seem more natural and less awkward. Practice will also help you work out any problems that might occur before actually giving your speech for real.

Don't Circulate Your Aids

Don't pass around photos, cartoons, drawings, objects, or anything that can distract your audience from paying attention to you while you're speaking. If audience members want to see your visual aid again, let them approach you after the speech for a second viewing.

Summary

Informative speaking is central to teaching, business, religious practice, and a host of other common events in our lives. Informative speaking teaches, whereas persuasive speaking primarily moves an audience to act. Reports, lectures, and demonstrations are the main types of informative speeches. Organization and use of supporting materials is vital to the success of an informative speech. Using visual aids competently will also enhance your informative speeches.

Suggested Reading

Mathews, J. (1998). *Escalante: The best teacher in America.* New York: Henry Holt. This is a nice biographical treatment of famous high school math instructor Jaime Escalante, subject of the movie *Stand and Deliver*. It shows informative speaking in action.

Chapter 16

Persuasive Speaking

During most of 1998 and part of 1999, Americans and others from around the globe witnessed the peculiar spectacle of presidential impeachment. Special prosecutor Kenneth Starr had charged President Clinton with "high crimes and misdemeanors" resulting from the president's sexual affair with intern Monica Lewinsky. House Judiciary Committee members voted along straight party lines for impeachment. The Republican members fought to impeach the president, and the Democratic members defended the president. Both sides battled to frame the issues to their advantage. Ultimately, the goal was to win the hearts and minds of the American people.

Representative Henry Hyde, Chairman of the House Judiciary Committee, in his opening speech before the committee, framed the issues in this case succinctly, "Do we still have a government of laws and not of men? . . . Do we have one set of laws for the officers and another for the enlisted?" (as cited in Trounstine, 1998). Representative John Conyers, the highest ranking Democrat on the Judiciary Committee and a staunch defender of the president, framed Clinton's defense this way in his opening speech: "The idea of a federally paid sex policeman spending millions of dollars to trap an unfaithful spouse . . . would have been unthinkable prior to the Starr investigation" (as cited in Abramson, 1998).

Persuasive speaking occupied center stage throughout the contentious proceedings in the House, and again in the climactic stage before the full United States Senate. The impeachment trial was a war of words, an oratorical duel between rival political parties. One of the most effective speakers was Cheryl Mills, a little-known White House deputy counsel. She became a brief sensation for her eloquent defense of the president on the obstruction of justice charge. Even Republicans who favored impeachment offered congratulations for her spirited and well-reasoned persuasive speech. Ultimately, senators and the American public found the case for impeachment unconvincing.

The battle to impeach Bill Clinton reaffirmed the importance of persuasive speaking in our democracy. When issues large and small are considered, those with persuasive speaking skills are an invaluable asset. One study (Bennett, 1995) found that when economists totaled the number of people whose jobs depend predominantly on persuading people—lawyers, counselors, managers, administrators, salespersons, and public relations specialists—persuasion accounts for 26% of the gross domestic product of the United States. Turn on the television and you will see persuasive speaking everywhere. CNN interviews individuals every day who engage in persuasive speaking before the cameras. Most talk shows display persuasive speaking from panelists and audience members, although many persuasive attempts are dismal efforts by unskilled and untrained speakers. Court TV and several "people's court" programs show average citizens defending themselves in court cases.

The primary purpose of this chapter is to explain how to construct and present a competent persuasive speech. There are two objectives:

1. to explain the foundations of persuasion, and
2. to discuss persuasive strategies that speakers can use effectively.

 Foundations of Persuasion

Almost 2,500 years ago, Aristotle systematically discussed persuasion in his influential *The Rhetoric*. The scientific study of persuasion, however, began little more than a half-century ago in the United States. Much has been learned from the

50-plus years of research on persuasion. In this section the foundations of persuasion, which have been derived from scientific research, will be explored. This will provide a basis for discussing specific persuasion strategies.

Defining Persuasion

Persuasion is a communication process of converting, modifying, or maintaining the attitudes, beliefs, or behavior of others. As a communication process, persuasion is transactional. This means that speakers influence listeners, but listeners also influence speakers. Thus, persuasive speaking is not merely a speaker motivating listeners in a linear, one-way manner. If it were, pointing a gun at your audience and threatening to shoot anyone who refuses to sign a petition or contribute money to a social or political cause would be persuasive. In such an instance the audience would have little or no influence on the speaker. Most people and scholars, however, would perceive threatening violence as coercion, not persuasion.

So what is the difference? The essential difference between coercion and persuasion is the *perception of free choice* (Strong & Cook, 1990). Those who coerce seek to *eliminate* choice by force or threats of force. Those who persuade seek to *limit* choice to the most acceptable options by using logical and emotional appeals. Logical and emotional appeals can influence listeners, but listeners are still free to choose what to believe and how to behave. As noted in Chapter 1, coercion raises serious ethical concerns because free choice is taken away.

Persuasive speaking is a communication process of convincing through open and honest means, not compelling by use of force. Coercion is the dominance form of power in action. When listeners can choose for themselves which attitude to accept or which behavior to perform, they are in charge of their decision making. This means that listeners have to cooperate with speakers for persuasion to occur. If listeners refuse to pay attention to the speaker, ignore the persuasion effort, or do not heed the speaker's advice or plea, persuasive speaking fails.

Goals of Persuasion

Persuasive speaking can have several goals. Choosing the appropriate goal for the situation will largely determine your degree of success or failure.

Conversion   Psychologist Muzafer Sherif and his associates (1965) developed the **social judgment theory** of persuasion to explain attitude change. Their theory states that when listeners hear a persuasive message they compare it with attitudes they already hold. The preexisting attitude on an issue serves as an anchor, or reference point. Surrounding this anchor is a range of possible opinions an individual may hold. Positions a person finds tolerable form his or her *latitude of acceptance*. Positions that provoke only a neutral or ambivalent response form the *latitude of noncommitment*. Those positions the person would find objectionable because they are too far from the anchor attitude form the *latitude of rejection*. Figure 16-1 depicts this range of possible opinions on an issue.

hardcore   Research by Sherif and his colleagues (1965) found that persuasive messages that fall within a person's latitude of rejection almost never produce a change in attitude. The further away a position is from the anchor attitude, the less likely persuasion will be successful. This is especially true when the listener has high ego

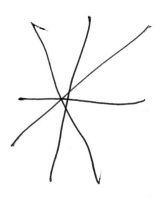

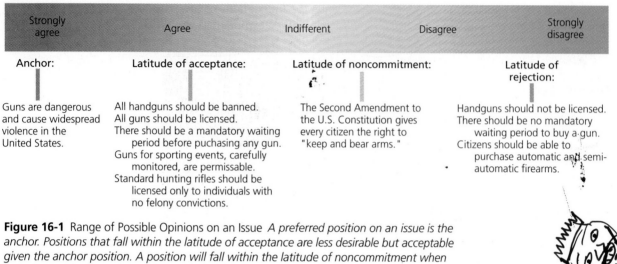

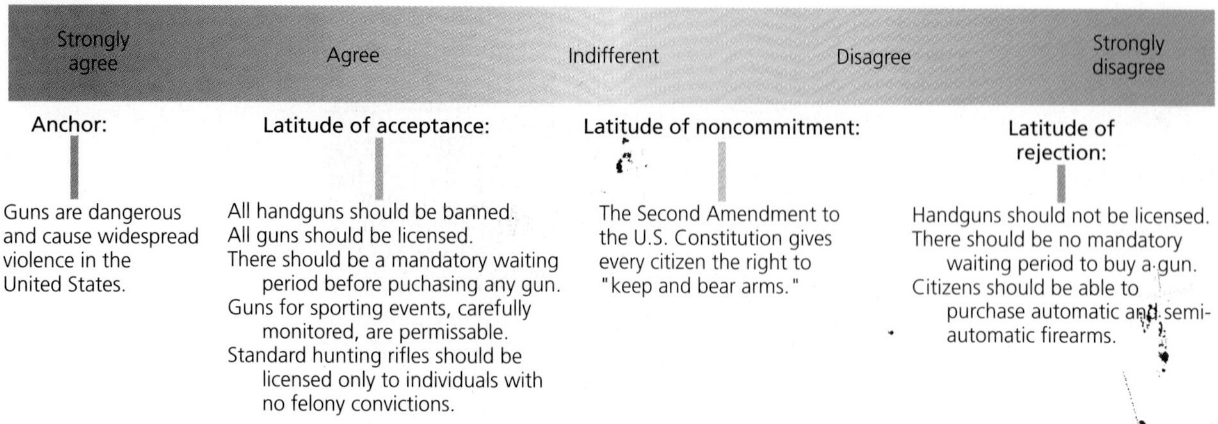
Strongly agree
Agree
Indifferent
Disagree
Strongly disagree
Anchor:
Guns are dangerous and cause widespread violence in the United States.
Latitude of acceptance:
All handguns should be banned.
All guns should be licensed.
There should be a mandatory waiting period before puchasing any gun.
Guns for sporting events, carefully monitored, are permissable.
Standard hunting rifles should be licensed only to individuals with no felony convictions.
Latitude of noncommitment:
The Second Amendment to the U.S. Constitution gives every citizen the right to "keep and bear arms."
Latitude of rejection:
Handguns should not be licensed.
There should be no mandatory waiting period to buy a gun.
Citizens should be able to purchase automatic and semi-automatic firearms.

Figure 16-1 Range of Possible Opinions on an Issue *A preferred position on an issue is the anchor. Positions that fall within the latitude of acceptance are less desirable but acceptable given the anchor position. A position will fall within the latitude of noncommitment when an individual has no opinion about the position because he or she lacks knowledge or information, or the individual has ambivalence (feelings pro and con simultaneously). Positions that fall within the latitude of rejection clearly contradict a person's anchor position.*

involvement with the issue. *Ego involvement* refers to the degree to which an issue is relevant or important to a person (Littlejohn, 1999).

Social judgment theory strongly suggests that setting conversion as your goal for persuasion is unrealistic. Conversion asks listeners to move from their anchor position to a completely contradictory position. This is especially unlikely when conversion is sought during a brief persuasive speech. Students often make the attempt to convert the "unbelievers" in speeches on abortion, religion, and other emotionally charged topics. Such efforts are doomed from the start. Unless a significant emotional event occurs, such as a death of a loved one, divorce, or winning the state lottery, conversion almost never happens from a single persuasive attempt. A staunch member of the National Rifle Association may become a convert to gun control when a son or daughter is killed by a handgun. Absent such an emotional event, however, an NRA member is unlikely to become a gun control advocate by hearing a 10-minute persuasive speech, no matter how eloquent. Conversion, then, is an unrealistic goal for most persuasive speeches. Attempting to convert an audience with a brief persuasive speech is inviting failure.

Modification A more realistic goal for persuasion is modification of an attitude or behavior. Positions that lie at the outer fringes of a listener's latitude of acceptance may become the new anchor position as a result of a persuasive speech. For example, very restrictive gun control legislation may be a person's anchor. A strong persuasive speech, however, may realistically modify this person's position to an outright ban on all handguns. Once this position is embraced, it may become the new anchor. Subsequent persuasive efforts may move the anchor incrementally until the person eventually accepts a complete ban on ownership of all guns. Notice that the change in attitude occurs bit by bit. It is rarely a one-shot effort. Modification of attitudes and behavior is an appropriate, realistic goal for a persuasive speech.

Louis Farrakhan speaks to his followers. One goal of persuasive speaking is maintenance of existing points of view.

Maintenance When most people think of persuasion, changing attitudes and behavior immediately come to mind. Much persuasion, however, does not aim to produce change. Most advertising of well-established products, such as Coke, McDonalds, or Toyota Camry aims to maintain buying habits of the public. The goal is to keep consumers purchasing products over and over. In political campaigns, initial persuasion is usually aimed at "securing the base." This means motivating Democrats to keep voting for Democratic candidates and to keep Republicans voting for Republican candidates. The message is "Do what you've been doing." Sunday sermons usually change few minds because most people who attend a church service require no change of heart. They already believe the religious truths articulated by the minister, priest, or rabbi. "Preaching to the choir," however, can inspire the faithful, energize believers, and reinforce preexisting attitudes. Maintaining current attitudes and behavior is a valid and realistic goal of persuasive speaking.

Part of maintaining current attitudes and behavior of an audience is inducing resistance to counterpersuasion, or attacks from an opposing side. Inducing resistance to counterpersuasion helps maintain current attitudes.

There are two principal ways to induce resistance to counterpersuasion. First, *forewarn* an audience that an attempt to change their attitudes, beliefs, or behavior will occur (Gass & Seiter, 1999). One study (Fukada, 1986) forewarned one group of participants that they would hear a message aimed at provoking fear about syphilis; another group received no such forewarning. The forewarned group was less likely to get tested for syphilis than the group that received no forewarning. Bob Dole forewarned voters in the 1996 presidential election that Bill Clinton would try to scare the elderly about the possible demise of Social Security. Prosecution and defense attorneys often use forewarning in their opening statements to juries. When we are very aware of persuasive attempts, psychological reactance emerges and produces resistance (Fukada, 1986).

A second way to induce resistance to persuasion is to *inoculate* your audience (McGuire, 1964). When we inoculate individuals against disease, we expose them to a weakened version of the virus to trigger an immune response. Likewise, inoculating an audience to counterpersuasion exposes listeners to a weakened version of counterarguments. Studies aimed at preventing teenagers from starting to smoke cigarettes found that merely mentioning arguments for smoking (e.g., smoking is cool; peers will like you) and then refuting these weakly presented arguments did induce resistance to peer persuasion to start smoking (Pfau & Van Bockern, 1994). The inoculation, however, must occur between elementary and high school, or it will be too late to prevent teen smoking.

Attitude-Behavior Consistency

An **attitude** is "a learned predisposition to respond favorably or unfavorably toward some attitude object" (Gass & Seiter, 1999, p. 41). An attitude sets our mind to draw certain judgments. Our attitudes and our behavior aren't always consistent. For example, energy conservation is socially desirable. Few people would argue that consumers should waste energy. One study found that 85% of those surveyed considered the energy crisis serious (Costanzo et al., 1986). This same study, however, found little relationship between stated attitudes on the energy crisis and actual conservation of energy. As the authors of this study conclude, "People who cite conservation as the single most important strategy for improving our energy future are no more likely than others to engage in energy-conserving behaviors. This finding is consistent with other research on the tenuous link between attitudes and behavior" (p. 522). Most Americans believe the Ten Commandments should guide our lives, yet everyone violates at least some of the commandments as if they were merely the Ten Suggestions.

Very often changing attitudes is not sufficient. It is behavior that needs to change. If 100% of the adult population believe voting in national elections is important, but barely half actually vote, then producing greater consistency between attitudes and behavior emerges as a key focus of attention. Attitudes without corresponding actions often give rise to cynicism. "Nothing's ever going to change" is the lament of those victimized by inaction. What good comes from a general consensus that teen pregnancy is a serious problem if few take steps to correct the problem? Will your behavior reflect your attitudes or will it contradict them?

Why the discrepancy between attitudes and behavior? Several variables affect how consistent our attitudes and behavior are likely to be.

 Personal Experience   Attitudes that are formed from personal experience usually conform closely to actual behavior (Fazio, 1986). Those that are shaped more indirectly by media images or what friends and others have told us tend to be inconsistently related to actual behavior. These "second-hand attitudes" (Gass & Seiter, 1999) usually serve as weak predictors of behavior because, when faced with actual situations, the attitudes are more borrowed than personal. You may steadfastly avoid drinking alcohol because you have experienced first-hand what alcoholism can do to a family. If your attitude about alcohol is mostly formed from watching public service announcements on the dangers of alcohol, however, when prodded to drink by friends and peers, you may cave in to the pressure more easily.

Personal Impact "How does this affect me personally?" is a common question that pops into listeners' minds while hearing a persuasive speech. In previous chapters, establishing the significance of a topic to an audience has been stressed. From the standpoint of persuasion, if you want your listeners to act, not just nod their heads in mindless agreement, make them feel personally affected by the problem you describe (M. Smith, 1982). Poverty may be a significant national issue, but if your audience has never experienced poverty directly, how do you get them to take action to address this issue? Connect it to their lives. Who pays for poverty? We all do—in blighted neighborhoods, increased crime, heavier taxes to pay for welfare, and embarrassment that the wealthiest nation on earth can't take care of its own people, especially our children.

Effort Required NBC News reported on April 8, 1999, that 60,000 children have died in car accidents in the 1990s. The backseats of cars are not "child friendly," according to this report, because car seats for children often are not used or are improperly installed. Parents may understand that car seats protect children from injury in accidents. They may uniformly agree that children should be strapped into car seats for their own protection. Nevertheless, parents often do not act in accordance with this belief. Why? The primary reason is that the car seats are difficult and time-consuming to install. This same NBC report noted that car manufacturers have developed a prototype car seat that folds down from the standard backseat. No installation is required, and strapping a child into this seat is quick and easy.

Despite the best intentions, attitudes and behavior will often be inconsistent because consistency may require too great an effort to perform the behavior (M. Smith, 1982). Recycling our cans, bottles, and newspapers is too labor intensive if we have to separate each item into separate bins, load them into the trunks of our cars, then drive to the nearest recycling center to unload the waste. Increasingly, however, communities around the country are recognizing the benefits of curbside recycling. Participation in recycling programs grows explosively when recycling is no more difficult than hauling a trash bin to the curb in front of our homes. In Santa Cruz, California the recycling bin looks the same as the garbage can, except it is a different color. Up and down the block recycling bins dot the landscape on trash day. The effort to recycle is minimal, so compliance is almost universal.

California began a program in July 1998 to assist low-income families in acquiring basic health insurance covering medical, dental, and eye care for as little as $3 a month. By the end of the year a mere 10% of the 400,000 eligible families had signed up (Kaplan, 1998). Clearly, the 90% who failed to enroll had no opposition to the program. It provided a huge benefit to all eligible families. The principal problem was that a 28-page application form was required to enroll. The state trimmed the application form to 4 pages in the spring of 1999 and increased the payments to nonprofit agencies who assist eligible families in filling out the forms, all to ease the burden of applying.

When trying to persuade an audience to act on a problem, find the easiest ways for listeners to express their support. Signing a petition or donating a dollar on the spot are easy ways to show support. Asking listeners to write a letter to members of Congress, however, will usually fail to produce much compliance. Most people do not have the time and energy to find the address of their congressperson, assuming they remember who that person is, write a letter, address an envelope, and mail the letter at a post office. (This is one reason members of Congress have established websites and e-mail addresses. E-mailing a member of Congress is easier than mailing a letter.) Asking listeners to canvass neighborhoods, call strangers on the phone to solicit support for a cause or a candidate, or raise money for a program are hampered by the effort required to perform the behavior. Far less participation in such activities should be expected as a result.

Consider how Sean McLaughlin (1996), a student at Ohio University, offers simple, yet effective, solutions for the problem of food poisoning:

> First, wash hands well and wash them often. . . . If you prefer to use sponges and dishcloths, be sure to throw them in the dishwasher two or three times a week. Also, try color coding your sponges—the red one for washing dishes and a blue one for wiping up countertops. . . . Experts also suggest using both sides of a cutting board—one side for meats and the other side for vegetables. And those who wash dishes by hand, be careful. Scrub dishes vigorously with an antibacterial soap and rinse with hot water. Air drying is preferred to drying with a towel. . . . Finally, and perhaps the best advice—don't become lax when it comes to food safety in your home. Don't write your congressperson, write your mom. As we have seen today, re-educating yourself and spreading the word on kitchen safety can significantly reduce chances of food poisoning. (p. 75)

The speaker provides several easy steps that will protect us from food poisoning. One step, air drying dishes, actually reduces labor. Towel drying requires effort; air drying requires merely waiting.

Solutions to serious problems cannot always be simple and easy to implement. Nevertheless, try to offer ways that even complex solutions can be implemented in relatively simple, straightforward steps.

Elaboration Likelihood Model

Throughout this textbook, mindful consideration of our communication with others is emphasized. The communication competence model gives prominence to appropriateness, which requires mindful, conscious attention to explicit and implicit, often subtle, communication rules within cultures. Sensitivity to cues from others during communication transactions is emphasized. Ethical considerations also require mindfulness. When faced with numerous persuasive messages bombarding us every day, however, it is difficult to be mindful about each message. The truth is, we can be persuaded when we are in a mindful or a mindless state.

Petty and Cacioppo (1986a, 1986b) developed the **elaboration likelihood model (ELM)** of persuasion to explain how attempts to persuade can be processed mindfully or relatively mindlessly. According to ELM, listeners cope with the bombardment of persuasive messages by sorting them into those that are important, or central, and those that are less relevant, or peripheral. The *central route* requires mindfulness. The content of the message is scrutinized for careful reasoning and substantial, credible evidence. Counterarguments are considered and weighed. Questions come to mind, and a desire for more information (elaboration) emerges.

"Surely not guilty. Next case."

The *peripheral route* is relatively mindless. Little attention is given to processing a persuasive message. The listener looks for mental shortcuts to make quick decisions about seemingly peripheral issues. Credibility, likability, and attractiveness of a persuader, how other people react to the message, and the consequences that might result from agreeing or disagreeing with the persuader are some of the shortcuts used in the peripheral route.

To illustrate the two routes to persuasion, let's say that you are on a date. You and your partner are about to order dinner at a nice restaurant. The waiter suggests several specials, all of them meat or fish. He even volunteers which one is his favorite. Your partner orders first. She is very careful to choose only vegetarian dishes from the menu. She asks the waiter whether an entrée is cooked in animal fat, is there any butter in the pasta, and does the sauce contain any dairy products? Your date turns to you and says with an animated delivery that you should eat vegetarian because it is healthier and reduces animal deaths. You have no strong opinion on the subject, but you are very attracted to your date. You tell the waiter, "I'll have what she ordered." Your date used the central route to decide her order. She was very mindful of her decision. She considered her decision very carefully because it was important to her. You, on the other hand, used the peripheral route. The decision was relatively unimportant to you so you based your order on a cue unrelated to the menu, the waiter's preference, or the arguments offered by your date. You ordered vegetarian because your date was attractive and you hoped to gain favor with her.

Listeners use both central and peripheral routes when processing persuasive messages. This is called *parallel processing* (Petty et al., 1987). Listeners will tend to choose one route over the other, however. Which route will most likely be favored depends on two things: (1) the individual's motivation to think about the persuasive message, and (2) the ability to process the information presented. Personal experience with an issue and its impact on us have already been discussed in relation to attitude-behavior consistency. These two factors, however, also influence whether central or peripheral routes will be chosen for processing persuasive messages.

The more personal the issue is to us and the greater the perceived impact on us, the more central will be the processing. Persuasive messages perceived by listeners to be tangential to their interests and largely inconsequential to their lives will usually receive peripheral processing. Also, some persuasive messages are too complex and require technical knowledge to evaluate. Do you really understand the Second Law of Thermodynamics when creationism and evolution are debated? In such cases, our ability to use central processing is limited. Typically, peripheral cues, such as how other audience members respond to the messages, will be used.

Clearly, central processing of persuasive messages should be encouraged (Pratkanis & Aronson, 1991). Central processing is what skeptics do when presented with a persuasive message. It fits the communication competence model snugly. Central processing also produces more long-lasting persuasion than peripheral processing does (Gass & Seiter, 1999). If you purchased an ionizing air filtering system primarily because you found the salesperson very attractive, the product may sit in a box unopened or you may return it later for a refund. If you purchased the ionizing air filtering system because you read the literature, pondered the scientific research, and received credible answers to your questions, however, you will want to try the product as soon as possible. Additional units might be purchased, especially if the ionizer performs as expected.

Central processing can be increased by making issues relevant to listeners' lives. Complex, technical issues can be simplified for lay audiences. If listeners understand the basic concepts, they can analyze arguments and evidence presented. Even highly involved listeners, however, will use both central and peripheral processing. Because of time constraints and information overload, we sometimes have no choice but to use peripheral processing. Persuasive strategies that typically trigger both central and peripheral routes to persuasion will be discussed in this chapter.

Culture and Persuasion

The scientific investigation of persuasive speaking is a peculiarly Western interest. In China and other Asian countries, for instance, spirited debates to influence decision making have been viewed as relatively pointless. Debates create friction and disharmony and usually end inconclusively (Jaffe, 1998). Persuasion works best when it is adapted to the cultural context. Persuasive strategies that may successfully change attitudes and behavior in an individualistic country such as the United States may not be so successful in collectivist countries.

One study (Han & Shavitt, 1994) examined slogans used in magazines for their cultural persuasiveness. Slogans such as these were considered (see also Gass & Seiter, 1999):

The art of being unique.
We have a way of bringing people closer together.

She's got a style all her own.
The dream of prosperity for all of us.
A leader among leaders.
Sharing is beautiful.

Which of these slogans do you think would work best in individualist cultures, and which would work best in collectivist cultures? When comparing the United States and Korea, it was found that slogans like the first, third, and fifth were used more in the United States and were more persuasive than the other slogans. These three appeal to individual success, personal benefits, and independence. Slogans like the second, fourth, and sixth were used more in Korea and were more persuasive than the others. They appeal to group harmony, cooperation, and collective benefit.

Another study (Wiseman et al., 1995) found that when attempting to convince roommates to quiet down, individuals from the United States preferred direct statements such as "Please be quiet," "You are making too much noise," or "If you don't quiet down, I'll be as noisy as possible when you are trying to study." These statements pay little attention to face saving or harmony. They address individual needs. Persons from China, however, used more indirect strategies of persuasion, such as hinting that less noise would be preferred or making statements invoking group awareness ("Your noisiness shows a lack of consideration for others").

Clearly, your choice of persuasive strategies should be influenced by the diversity of your audience. It is only one element of the complex persuasion equation, but it is an important element.

Persuasion Strategies

Consideration of all possible persuasive speaking strategies would require a lengthy book. In this section you will learn about a few of the most prominent and effective persuasive strategies.

Enhance the Speaker

Our first impression of a speaker may be our last. If the impression of a speaker drawn by listeners is unfavorable, all the crafty, carefully planned persuasive strategies won't matter. Persuasive speaking begins with enhancing the speaker. This can be accomplished in several ways.

Establish Identification With the Audience   Kenneth Burke (1950) wrote, "You persuade a man [or woman] only insofar as you can talk his language by speech, gesture, tonality, order, image, attitude, idea, identifying your ways with his" (p. 55). Burke considered **identification,** the affiliation and connection between speaker and listeners, the essence of persuasion. Larson (1992), revealing Burke's influence, defines persuasion as "the cocreation of a state of identification or alignment between a source and receiver" (p. 11).

A key element of identification is likability of the speaker. If we perceive the speaker as likable, compliance and assent are more probable than if we do not like the speaker (Cialdini, 1993). We tend to like people who are similar to us

Presidential candidate Lamar Alexander poses with some of his supporters. Stylistic similarity, in this case wearing plaid, creates identification.

(Cialdini, 1993). There are two primary ways a speaker can develop the perception of similarity to create identification with an audience.

Stylistic Similarity   We can dress, look, and speak similarly to our audience. This is called stylistic similarity. A bureaucrat from the Department of Agriculture visits farmers in Kansas wearing an expensive suit and carrying a briefcase. Do you think farmers will likely give this person a nanosecond of their time? He doesn't look, dress, or probably even speak like them. Repeatedly, Bill Clinton and Al Gore in the 1992 and 1996 presidential campaigns "dressed the part" when they visited farmers, factory laborers, and construction workers. When visiting midwest farmers, both Clinton and Gore wore jeans and casual shirts, sat on hay bales to chat informally with the folks that gathered, and played down the formality of the presidential office and campaign. Lamar Alexander, a Republican candidate for president in 1996, wore flannel shirts almost everywhere he campaigned in New Hampshire to create a folksy image in a mostly rural state. His supporters began wearing identical flannel shirts to show their solidarity with him. All these candidates attempted to identify with their audiences by dressing and acting similarly to their listeners.

Sometimes dressing the part, however, can make you look lame. The 1988 Democratic presidential candidate, Michael Dukakis, was persuaded by his advisers to climb aboard an army tank dressed in army fatigues and a tank commander's hat. This "photo opportunity" was supposed to create an image that Dukakis, despite his liberal credentials, was a strong supporter of the military. Actually, he looked like Snoopy from the "Peanuts" comic strip. This poor attempt to identify with more conservative elements of the electorate backfired. The more contrived dressing the part appears to be, the less likely it will connect with the audience. Dressing informally, for example, must be complemented by a relaxed, informal style of speaking and presenting oneself, or it will seem phoney.

When the situation is formal, dress and speak formally. Slang and verbal obscenity should be avoided. When the situation is informal, however, a persuader needs to shift styles and speak, dress, and act informally. Speaking, dressing, and acting very formally in an informal setting, such as a tavern or in a wheat field, disconnect a speaker from his or her audience. Speaking, dressing, and acting informally in a formal setting, such as a banquet dinner or a prestigious awards ceremony, may be viewed as insulting by an audience.

Substantive Similarity A second way to develop the perception of similarity between speaker and audience is by shaping the substance of your speech to highlight similarities in positions, values, and attitudes. This substantive similarity creates identification by establishing common ground between speaker and audience. If listeners can say "I like what I'm hearing," they can identify with the speaker. Often you are trying to change listeners' attitudes and behavior, but your point of view and proposed action may not be similar to your audience's. In such cases, it is helpful to build bridges with your audience by pointing out common experiences, perceptions, values, and attitudes before launching into more delicate areas of disagreement. Listeners will be more inclined to hear your more controversial viewpoints if they initially identify with you.

Notice how Geraldine Ferraro, the first female vice presidential candidate, tries to connect not merely with convention delegates but with the much larger television audience in her acceptance speech to the 1984 Democratic National Convention:

> Last week, I visited Elmore, Minnesota, the small town where Fritz Mondale [Ferraro's running mate] was raised. And soon Fritz and Joan will visit our family in Queens. Nine hundred people live in Elmore. In Queens, there are 2,000 people in one block. You would think we would be different, but we're not. Children walk to school in Elmore past grain elevators; in Queens, they pass by subway stops. But, no matter where they live, their future depends on education—and their parents are willing to do their part to make those schools as good as they can be. In Elmore, there are family farms; in Queens, small businesses. But the men and women who run them all take pride in supporting their families through hard work and initiative. On the Fourth of July in Elmore, they hang flags out on Main Street; in Queens, they fly them over Grand Avenue. But all of us love our country, and stand ready to defend the freedom that it represents. (Ferraro, 1992, pp. 365–366)

Ferraro takes what seem to be, on the surface, vast differences that separate her from her audience and finds commonalities in each instance to establish identification between herself and her listeners (Box 16-1).

Identification takes the peripheral path to persuasion. The appeal is based on liking the speaker and finding familiar themes, values, and perceptions. Yet identification can act as a precursor to central processing of persuasive messages. Audiences are more likely to concentrate on the message, analyze it carefully, and be moved by the arguments when they can identify with the speaker.

Build Credibility Tonya Harding endorsed Nike athletic equipment but was quickly dumped by the company when her involvement in the assault on fellow

Box 16-1 Sharper Focus

The "Spread Fred" Campaign

The 1998 campaign for the U.S. Senate in Vermont produced a striking example of how far identification can carry you. Fred Tuttle, a 79-year-old retired farmer, ran against a well-financed Republican named Jack McMullen. McMullen spent almost $500,000 trying to win the nomination and eventually run against incumbent Democrat Patrick Leahy. Tuttle spent $200. He held 5-*cent*-a-plate fund-raisers (4 cents for seniors). Tuttle defeated McMullen by 10 percentage points. How did he do this? Vermont voters identified with Tuttle but were turned off by McMullen, whom they saw as an outsider. McMullen had moved from Massachusetts to Vermont a year prior to the campaign so he could run for the Senate seat.

Tuttle's low-key style and straightforward message resonated with voters. His style of dress and campaign approach were uniformly casual. His message was simple and direct: "Vermont for Vermonters." He made developers and out-of-staters key issues in the campaign. As Paul Dreher, an architect and Vermont voter explained, "McMullen was an out-of-stater. A lot of people are coming in here and buying our land, and posting 'no hunting' signs, and a sense of community is being lost. They're trying to re-create the gated community, and we don't like it" (as cited in Higham, 1998).

Everywhere Tuttle campaigned crowds would ask for his autograph. "Spread Fred" bumper stickers were everywhere. Even Leahy, Tuttle's eventual opponent, found him attractive. Leahy had dinner with Tuttle and they campaigned together. Tuttle, in his open and honest style, divulged at one point, "I'll probably vote for Senator Leahy. He's a wonderful man. He's done a wonderful job" (as cited in Higham, 1998). Leahy won by a comfortable margin, but Tuttle demonstrated that identification can be a powerful persuasive strategy.

---

skating competitor Nancy Kerrigan was revealed. O. J. Simpson was a spokesman for Hertz rental cars until he was accused of killing his wife. Mike Tyson endorsed Pepsi until he was convicted of rape. The instant these celebrities lost credibility, they lost their endorsement contracts. The credibility of the speaker can make a huge difference when persuasion is attempted. Speakers who lack credibility persuade few. Credibility of a speaker is part of the peripheral route to persuasion. Listeners who are relatively uninvolved in an issue are more influenced by speaker credibility than listeners who are highly involved (Reardon, 1991).

O'Keefe (1990) defines **credibility** as "judgments made by a perceiver (e.g., a message recipient) concerning the believability of a communicator" (pp. 130–131). In *The Rhetoric* Aristotle identified the ingredients of credibility, or **ethos** in his terminology, as "good sense, good moral character, and good will." Recent research affirms Aristotle's observation and expands the list of dimensions somewhat. The primary dimensions of credibility are competence, trustworthiness, dynamism, and composure (Gass & Seiter, 1999; Strong & Cook, 1990). Let's take a closer look at each of these dimensions.

Competence refers to the audience's perception of the speaker's knowledge and experience on a topic. Competence addresses the question "Does this speaker know what he or she is talking about?" When speakers identify their background, experience, and training relevant to a subject, they can enhance their credibility (O'Keefe, 1990). Citing sources of evidence used, speaking fluently, and avoiding disfluencies ("uhm," "ah," "like," "you know") also enhance credibility (O'Keefe, 1990).

Trustworthiness refers to how truthful or honest we perceive the speaker to be. Trustworthiness addresses the question "Can I believe what the speaker says?" We don't feel comfortable hiring a dishonest plumber, electrician, or carpenter. We

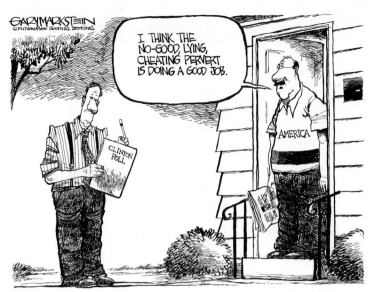

Milwaukee Journal Sentinel 9/16/98 by Gary Markstein. © 1998 Journal Sentinel, Inc.
Reproduced with permission.

hesitate to buy anything from a salesperson we perceive to be dishonest. Detective Mark Fuhrman repeatedly testified during the O. J. Simpson trial that he never uttered the "N-word." Later in the trial it was revealed that he had used the racist epithet dozens of times during tape-recorded interviews with Laura McKinney, a screenwriter. His credibility was destroyed by this revelation, and the prosecution's case suffered seriously from his apparent dishonesty.

Trustworthiness, however, may not be as important as competence in some situations. A Field poll of 1,005 Californians conducted 1 month after Bill Clinton was acquitted on impeachment charges showed an interesting interplay between competence and trustworthiness. Fifty-two percent of the respondents viewed Clinton as not very honest or not honest at all, and only 38% said they liked him (as cited in Ostrom, 1999). Sixty-eight percent of the same sample of Californians, however, approved of the job Clinton was doing. Poll director Mark DiCamillo interpreted the results by comparing Clinton to former president Jimmy Carter: "Jimmy Carter was well-liked as a person but wasn't seen as effective. And that's what you're hiring (a president) to do" (p. A10). Credibility is a constellation of dimensions. Trustworthiness is important in a president, but apparently not as important as doing the job competently and producing beneficial results for the American people.

One way to increase your trustworthiness is to argue against your self-interest. If you take a position on an issue that will cost you money, a job, a promotion, or some reward or benefit, most listeners will see you as presenting an honest opinion. They're more likely to trust what you have to say than to trust someone who stands to gain from arguing a particular position. Few people trust the explanations for rapid increases in gas prices provided by spokespeople for the oil companies. Quite simply, the oil companies make profits when gas prices are inflated. Their self-interest diminishes their credibility.

Dynamism is a third dimension of credibility. It refers to the enthusiasm and energy exhibited by the speaker. Sleepy, lackluster presentations by speakers lower credibility. If a speaker tries to convince an audience that a serious problem exists but seems almost uninterested in the subject, credibility will be a real issue. Hucksters on infomercials are invariably enthusiastic about the products they

Cheryl Mills, a relatively unknown attorney, built tremendous credibility with this carefully reasoned, composed speech defending Bill Clinton during the Senate impeachment.

sell. Sometimes they are overly enthusiastic, bordering on the berzerk. Too little dynamism can hinder persuasion, but too much can also turn off an audience.

Speakers who are dynamic inspire audiences. They seem self-confident, charismatic, and comfortable in front of an audience. They are articulate, powerful speakers. Mario Cuomo, Jesse Jackson, and Ann Richards are examples of dynamic speakers.

A final dimension of speaker credibility is *composure*. Audiences tend to be influenced by speakers who are composed, meaning they are emotionally stable, appear confident and in control of themselves, and remain calm even when problems arise during a speech. Clint Eastwood has made composure a trademark part of his image in films. During emergencies, we are more likely to listen and be influenced by a person who is composed than by someone shrieking or raging at us.

Former member of Congress Patricia Schroeder held a press conference to announce her candidacy for the 1992 presidential race. During that announcement she lost her composure and cried. Hers was the shortest-lived presidential candidacy in United States history. It was over as she announced it. Breaking down at a press conference when merely declaring your intent to run for public office doesn't inspire confidence from most listeners. Ross Perot lost his composure on a few occasions during the 1992 presidential race, becoming angry and attacking the press. His poll ratings dropped each time.

Displaying emotion overtly, however, does not always destroy a speaker's credibility. Too much composure may be perceived as hard-heartedness or insensitivity. Shedding tears at a funeral or expressing outrage at an atrocity may enhance your credibility with some listeners. The appropriateness of displaying composure depends on the context.

All four dimensions of credibility operate together. Strength in some dimensions may be overridden by weakness in even one dimension. A Gallup poll taken in May 1999 found that four out of five respondents thought Vice President Al Gore was a good husband and father, and most thought he was honest, trustworthy, caring, and experienced. Thus, Gore scored well in trustworthiness and competence. The majority of respondents, however, also felt that Gore was uninspiring, even dull (as cited in Jacobs, 1999b). Gore's perceived lack of dynamism became a key challenge in his pursuit of the presidency.

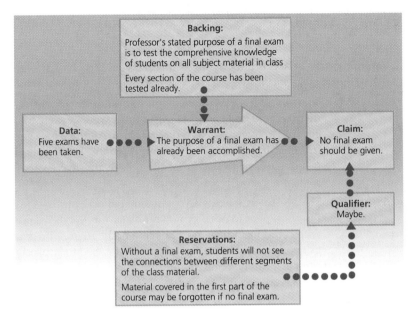

Figure 16-2 The Toulmin Structure of Argument

The figure shows boxes connected by dotted arrows:

Backing: Professor's stated purpose of a final exam is to test the comprehensive knowledge of students on all subject material in class

Every section of the course has been tested already.

Data: Five exams have been taken.

Warrant: The purpose of a final exam has already been accomplished.

Claim: No final exam should be given.

Qualifier: Maybe.

Reservations: Without a final exam, students will not see the connections between different segments of the class material.

Material covered in the first part of the course may be forgotten if no final exam.

Build Arguments

Much has already been said about the importance of logic and evidence to speakers and listeners. In this section, however, building arguments based on logic and evidence, what Aristotle called **logos,** will be addressed with a specific focus on persuading audiences.

Toulmin Structure of Argument Arguments are the essence of a strong persuasive speech. Audiences aren't persuaded just by logic and evidence, but weak reasoning and shakey evidence leave your claims open to challenge. The central path to persuasion travels through arguments. Mindful listeners will examine your arguments closely, looking for strengths and weaknesses. Strong, compelling arguments can be highly persuasive, especially to skeptics.

An argument or "train of reasoning" is composed of several parts (Toulmin et al., 1979):

1. *Claim*—that which is asserted and requires support.
2. *Data*—the grounds, or support, for the claim. Statistics, testimony of experts, and verifiable facts are data.
3. *Warrant*—the reasoning that links the data to the claim. It is usually implied, not stated explicitly.
4. *Backing*—the data that support the warrant.
5. *Reservations*—exceptions or rebuttals that diminish the force of the claim.
6. *Qualifier*—degree of truth to the claim (possible, plausible, probable, highly probable).

Everyday reasoning follows this pattern known as the Toulmin structure of argument (Figure 16-2; Freeley, 1996). For example, suppose you are a guy who wants to date a supermodel. Your train of reasoning might proceed as follows:

Claim: I can date supermodel Jasmine.

Data: I am a brainy, average looking, very nice guy with an average income.

> *Warrant:* She dates brainy, average looking, very nice, sensitive guys with average incomes.
>
> *Backing:* The last three guys she dated were brainy. Two of them had college degrees, and one had a Ph.D. All three were average looking according to five girls I asked at random. All three had very average incomes and drove 3- or 4-year-old sedans. I read interviews with Jasmine where she said that all of these guys were very nice and sensitive, caring human beings.
>
> *Reservations:* She's a supermodel who could date almost any guy she wanted. I'm a stranger to her. I don't know anyone who is friends with her who could introduce me. She has a body guard who could inflict grievous bodily harm on my person if I tried to approach her. I can't just call her. She might think I'm a stalker.
>
> *Qualifier:* *Possible* she would accept a date, but don't bet the farm.

Persuasive speeches incorporate a series of claims. The primary, overriding claim for a persuasive speech is called a **proposition.** The proposition becomes the essence of your persuasive purpose statement. Propositions define and focus the argument, limit the issues that are relevant, and set standards for what should be addressed (Inch & Warnick, 1998).

There are three types of propositions: fact, policy, and value. A *proposition of fact* alleges a truth ("Lax sex education is a primary cause of high teen pregnancy rates"). A *proposition of policy* calls for a significant change from how problems are currently handled ("Smoking should be banned from all public places"). A *proposition of value* calls for a judgment that assesses the worth or merit of an idea, object, or practice ("Capital punishment is immoral"). Main **arguments,** or the chief reasons offered to support a proposition, are secondary claims. When asked why smoking in public places should be banned, you might list several main reasons:

1. Second-hand smoke is dangerous to nonsmokers.
2. Second-hand smoke is annoying to nonsmokers.
3. Smokers violate nonsmokers rights to breath unpolluted air.
4. Employees in bars and restaurants cannot escape the smoke even if they so desire.

Quantity and Quality of Arguments The number and quality of arguments advanced for a proposition can be factors in persuasive speaking. One study (Petty & Cacioppo, 1984) tested to what degree students could be persuaded that completing comprehensive examinations as a condition of graduating from college is a good proposal. Student groups were told either that the exams would begin in one year (meaning they would have to take the exams) or in 10 years (meaning they would not have to take the exams). Presumably, those directly affected by the proposal (must take the exams) would scrutinize the persuasive message, whereas those unaffected by the proposal would see the message as peripheral and use the number of arguments, even if weak, as decision-making cues.

The quantity and quality of arguments made a big difference. Mindful students directly affected by the proposal were not persuaded by nine weak arguments. In fact, the more weak arguments they heard, the more they disliked the proposal.

They were persuaded only when strong arguments were used, especially when many strong arguments were used. Students unaffected by the proposal, however, used peripheral processing of the persuasive message. The quality of the arguments did not matter to this group. They were more persuaded that the proposal was a good idea when nine arguments were presented than when only three were offered, no matter how strong or weak the arguments.

When constructing your persuasive speech, pick the strongest arguments to support your proposition. Several strong arguments can be persuasive to listeners who process your message either peripherally or centrally. Weak arguments only have the potential to convince uninvolved listeners.

The strength of an argument depends primarily on the strength of your warrant, as indicated by the quality of your evidence and reasoning. In Chapter 6 fallacies in the use of evidence and reasoning were explained. Three criteria— credibility, relevance, and sufficiency—determine the quality of evidence and reasoning. We say that a claim is "unwarranted" when these standards are poorly met. When you present statistical evidence to support a claim, the underlying warrant is that the statistics are from credible sources, relevant to your claim, and sufficient to accept your claim. If this proves to be untrue, your argument is weak. When a speaker claims a causal relation from only a correlation, he or she provides an insufficient logical connection between the data and the claim.

In the supermodel example, the data at first may appear to be completely irrelevant to the claim. Why would a supermodel want to date a brainy, sensitive, average looking guy with a moderate income? The warrant tries to make the connection between the data and the claim. It is only partly successful. The claim is probably unwarranted. Review the specific fallacies that arise from failing to meet the criteria for use of evidence and reasoning.

You build a persuasive case by identifying your proposition (primary claim) and by establishing main arguments (secondary claims). All claims must be supported with evidence, or mindful, skeptical listeners will find your persuasion deficient and unconvincing. Several strong arguments will persuade listeners processing your message using either the peripheral or central route.

Induce Cognitive Dissonance

When we want to persuade others to change their attitudes or behavior, one of the most common strategies is to point out inconsistencies between two attitudes or between attitudes and behavior. A student asks her professor for more time on an assignment. The professor says no. The student retorts, "But you gave extra time to Jim. Why won't you give me the same extension?" The professor sees herself as a very fair-minded person. Faced with this apparent inconsistency in the treatment of two students, the professor feels tense and uncomfortable. Festinger (1957) called this unpleasant feeling produced by seemingly inconsistent thoughts **cognitive dissonance.**

Whenever a person holds two inconsistent ideas, beliefs, or opinions (cognitions) at the same time, or when an attitude and a behavior are inconsistent, dissonance occurs (Pratkanis & Aronson, 1991). Parents often confront this persuasive strategy from their children. "Why can't I stay up past midnight on weekends? You let Tommy when he was my age?" "Why do I have a curfew? You never gave a curfew to Billy or Caroline."

Festinger

We want to be perceived as consistent, not hypocritical or nonsensical, so dissonance emerges when inconsistencies are pointed out to us. If we view ourselves as unbiased but laugh at a sexist joke, some dissonance will likely surface. If we consider ourselves honest but use a copy machine at work for personal projects, we will likely experience some dissonance, especially if the inconsistency is pointed out to us.

Festinger (1977) claims that "cognitive dissonance is a motivating state of affairs. Just as hunger impels a person to eat, so does dissonance impel a person to change his opinions or his behavior" (p. 111). According to this theory, you have to awaken dissonance in listeners for persuasion to occur. Without dissonance, there is little motivation to change attitudes or behavior. Therefore, the strategy for the persuader is to induce dissonance in the audience, then remove the dissonance by persuading listeners to change their attitudes or behavior in the direction desired. Pratkanis and Aronson (1991) explain:

> The [persuader] intentionally arouses feelings of dissonance by threatening self-esteem—for example, by making the person feel guilty about something, by arousing feelings of shame or inadequacy, or by making the person look like a hypocrite or someone who does not honor his or her word. Next, the [persuader] offers one solution, one way of reducing this dissonance—by complying with whatever request the [persuader] has in mind. The way to reduce that guilt, eliminate that shame, honor that commitment, and restore your feelings of adequacy is to give to that charity, buy that car, hate that enemy, or vote for that leader. (p. 36)

Important decisions arouse more dissonance than less important ones (Gass & Seiter, 1999). Pointing out to a teacher that he or she was not consistent when grading a test could elicit varying degrees of dissonance. If the inconsistency involves a single point on a 100-point exam, the teacher can easily downplay the inconsistency as minor and inherent to any subjective grading system. If the inconsistency involves an entire grade difference and seems based on sex bias, however, the dissonance could be quite large.

Notice how Gary Allen (1996), a student at Northeastern State University, uses cognitive dissonance on the topic of drug testing in the military:

> The final problem is caused by a double standard, because a program is only as good as the goal it achieves. While alcohol is universally recognized as the most commonly abused drug, the military does not test for alcohol as regularly as for other drugs. . . . Soldiers caught drunk on the job are given 45 days extra duty, that is work that must be performed after the regular duty day, they have a letter put into their permament file, and they are returned to light duty. Yet the soldier who receives a positive [drug] test result is, currently, kicked out of the military with a dishonorable discharge. Let me say that again. Everyday soldiers are required to undergo a test of their innocence without suspicion of guilt. The soldier who is found guilty is kicked out and marked for life with a dishonorable discharge, while soldiers drunk on the job, endangering everyone's life, are returned to duty with a slap on the hand. (p. 82)

Here the speaker points out a glaring inconsistency to induce dissonance in the audience. Supporting such a "double standard" is hypocritical and unjust, so the speaker implies. Cognitive dissonance can be a very effective persuasive strategy.

Tall professional basketball players look small in contrast to the extremely tall Margaret Dydek. The contrast effect as a persuasive strategy works similarly. What appears to be a huge commitment may seem relatively small when contrasted to a much larger commitment.

Use the Contrast Effect

You're a salesperson and a woman comes into the dress store where you work. Most of your pay is based on commission, so you want to sell as much merchandise as you can at the highest prices possible. Do you show the woman the inexpensive dresses first, then gradually show her more expensive dresses, or do you begin with very expensive dresses probably outside of her price range, then show her less expensive dresses? Which will net you the biggest commission? According to research on the contrast effect, you'd make a better choice if you began expensive and moved to less expensive (Cialdini, 1993). The contrast effect says listeners are more likely to accept a bigger second request or offer when contrasted with a much bigger request or offer. If shown a really nice dress that costs $250, most shoppers will balk at purchasing it because it is "so expensive." If shown a $475 dress first, however, then shown the $250 dress, the second dress just seems less expensive by contrast with the first. Once the $250 dress is purchased, "accessorizing" it with $30 worth of jewelry, scarves, or whatever will seem like very little by contrast.

The contrast effect, sometimes referred to as the *door-in-the-face strategy*, is used in all types of sales. I once purchased a recliner for $250. It was regularly priced, not "on sale." About 2 months later I was browsing through a furniture store and spotted the same recliner advertised as part of a "giant blowout sale." The price tag showed $800 marked out, then $600 marked out, then $475 marked out, and

Box 16-2 Sharper Focus

An Exercise in Contrast

Although this example is a letter, you can easily see how this strategy could apply in a persuasive speech.

Dear Mother and Dad:

Since I left for college I have been remiss in writing and I am sorry for my thoughtlessness in not having written before. I will bring you up to date now, but before you read on, please sit down. You are not to read any further unless you are sitting down, okay?

Well, then, I am getting along pretty well now. The skull fracture and the concussion I got when I jumped out the window of my dormitory when it caught on fire shortly after my arrival here is pretty well healed now. I only spent two weeks in the hospital and now I can see almost normally and only get those sick headaches once a day. Fortunately, the fire in the dormitory, and my jump, was witnessed by an attendant at the gas station near the dorm, and he was the one who called the Fire Department and the ambulance. He also visited me in the hospital and since I had nowhere to live because of the burnt-out dormitory, he was kind enough to invite me to share his apartment with him. It's really a base-ment room, but it's kind of cute. He is a very fine boy, and we have fallen deeply in love and are planning to get married. We haven't set the date yet, but it will be before my pregnancy begins to show.

Yes, Mother and Dad, I am pregnant. I know how much you are looking forward to being grandparents and I know you will welcome the baby and give it the same love and devotion and tender care you gave me when I was a child. The reason for the delay in our marriage is that my boyfriend has a minor infection which prevents us from passing our premarital blood tests and I carelessly caught it from him. I know that you will welcome him into our family with open arms. He is kind and, although not well educated, he is ambitious.

Now that I have brought you up to date, I want to tell you that there was no dormitory fire, I did not have a concussion or skull fracture, I was not in the hospital. I am not pregnant, I am not engaged, I am not infected, and there is no boyfriend. However, I am getting a "D" in American History and an "F" in Chemistry, and I want you to see those marks in their proper perspective.

Your loving daughter,

SHARON

Source: Cialdini, 1993, p. 14.

finally the "sale price" of $400. A casual customer who hadn't shopped around might see this recliner as a super bargain. The price had been cut in half. Yet this store was asking $150 more than what I paid for the same recliner at regular price from another store. Cialdini (1993) provides an apt example of the contrast effect in action in parent-child persuasion (Box 16-2).

As a strategy to use in a persuasive speech, the contrast effect works well when presenting your solution to a problem. For example, say you have argued that injuries and deaths from guns pose a serious problem in the United States. You could begin the solution portion of your speech this way:

"Clearly, gun violence in the United States requires a major change. I propose that Congress ban all guns. All individuals who own guns must turn them in to local law enforcement agencies within 3 months from the implementation date of this proposal. Failure to do so will be a felony punishable by a year in prison and a $5,000 fine. Production of ammunition for guns of any sort will stop immediately. Banning guns and ammunition is the way to significantly reduce injuries and death from firearms. Britain has done it, so has Japan, with terrific results. Shouldn't we as a nation do likewise?

Although a total ban on private ownership of guns would be very beneficial, it probably isn't entirely practical in this country. Perhaps instead we should close the loopholes in the Brady bill, merely making guns more difficult to own. . . .

Peruse the sample speech at the end of this chapter for another example of the contrast effect.

Try Emotional Appeals

We are not like Spock or Data on *Star Trek*. Although logic and evidence can be enormously persuasive, especially for highly involved listeners, emotional appeals—what Aristotle termed **pathos**—are also powerful motivators. There isn't a pure distinction between reasoning and emotion; they overlap. Even logic and evidence can produce emotional reactions from listeners.

General Emotional Appeals   Appeals to freedom, pride, honor, patriotism, sex, guilt, and shame all have their place as persuasion strategies that ignite emotional reactions and change behavior (Gass & Seiter, 1999). Appeals to anger also may prove to be quite persuasive, although little research exists to prove this. Consider how Kristin Michael (1997), a student at the University of Northern Iowa, uses an anger appeal on the subject of corporate welfare:

> What is truly outrageous, though, is that according to the Cato Institute, a conservative think-tank, an estimated $85 billion in the form of direct federal subsidies and tax breaks is funneled into thriving, multi-billion dollar corporate giants each year. And where does this $85 billion a year go? The Walt Disney Corporation, whose profits in 1995 exceeded $1 billion, received $300,000 in federal assistance last year for fireworks. McDonalds continues to receive $2 million annually to market Chicken McNuggets in the Third World, and defense manufacturer Lockheed Martin billed the government for $20,000 worth of golf balls, an "entertainment" expense, according to the *Boston Globe*, July 7, 1996.

Citizens will attend public meetings in droves when angered by an increase in energy rates or a perceived injustice. Anger is a strong motivation to act. Unquestionably, however, fear is the number one emotional appeal used to persuade audiences to change attitudes and behavior.

Fear Appeals   "Don't put that in your mouth. It's full of germs." "You'll poke your eye out if you run with those scissors." "Don't ever talk to strangers. They may hurt you." "Never cross the street before looking both ways. You could be killed." From childhood we are all familiar with fear appeals. Our parents give us a heavy dose to keep us safe and out of trouble. Do fear appeals work? Yes, they do. In fact, despite earlier research that indicated that excessively intense fear appeals could backfire, more recent research (Dillard, 1994; Witte & Allen, 1996) indicates that the more fear is aroused in listeners, the more vulnerable they feel, and the more likely they will be convinced (Gass & Seiter, 1999).

Several conditions determine the likely effectiveness of a high fear appeal (Gass & Seiter, 1999). First, *listeners must feel vulnerable*. We don't all fear the same things. Teenagers may not be frightened by the risk of contracting lung cancer from smoking cigarettes, but they may fear social disapproval from their peers. Public service announcements presenting smokers as disgusting, uncool, and sickeningly smelly may trigger greater fear than any health threat. Some people are frightened by the ready availability of guns in the United States. Other people take comfort from having the security and protection of a Smith and Wesson.

This is a fear appeal on the dangers of cigarette smoking and an anger appeal against the tobacco industry. The combination of appeals can be highly persuasive.

Second, *a clear specific recommendation for avoiding or lessening the danger is important.* Vague recommendations (fight corruption) are not as effective as specific recommendations (vote for Proposition 45).

Third, *the recommendation must be perceived as effective.* The "Just Say No" campaign against drugs was a slogan, not a solution (Pratkanis & Aronson, 1991). Imagine kids being pressured by peers to take drugs. What would they likely fear most—the risk of the drugs or the threat of social disapproval from not going along with the peer group?

Fourth, *listeners must perceive that they can perform the actions recommended.* Again, the effort required to perform the behavior is a key variable. Giving up meat entirely for the rest of your life to avoid the danger of high cholesterol may not be possible for most people. The effort is too great. Cutting meat consumption in half, however, may be realistic.

Notice how Holly Sisk (1997), a student at George Mason University, uses a high fear appeal combined with an almost effortless solution:

> In 1994 over five hundred Washington state residents were stricken by the e-coli bacteria. The story you probably didn't read, however, was that 49 of those patients never ate the tainted meat. They merely touched someone who had. The February 5, 1996 *Wall Street Journal* estimates that every year food poisoning cases from poor hand washing results in over 32 million illnesses and nearly four thousand deaths. . . .
> Over the last few years, Americans have made changes in their health. We've stopped smoking, started having safer sex and changed our eating habits. But hand washing is a thirty second procedure that is the #1 daily thing you can do to protect your health. So if ten minutes of reasons haven't convinced you to spare those thirty seconds, my hands are clean. (pp. 143, 145)

Finally, studies have shown that *fear appeals are more persuasive when combined with high-quality arguments* (Gleicher & Petty, 1992; Rodriguez, 1995). The fear appeal becomes more believable when it is bolstered by credible arguments.

Use a Persuasive Organizational Pattern

How you organize your persuasive speech can have a major effect on its potential to convince listeners. There are two primary persuasive organizational patterns: two-sided speeches and Monroe's motivated sequence.

Two-Sided Speeches   Is it better to present arguments in favor of your proposition and ignore opposing arguments, or should you make your case, then refute opposing arguments? Until recently, this question produced contradictory research results, but studies by Allen (1991, 1993) provide a clear answer. Two-sided persuasive speeches are more effective than one-sided speeches in convincing listeners to change attitudes.

A two-sided organizational pattern begins with a presentation of main arguments supporting your proposition. After you have laid out your case, answer common objections, or opposing arguments, against your case. This, of course, means that you need to anticipate what an audience might question about your position. Answering opposing arguments is called **refutation.**

There are four steps to refutation. First, *state the opposing argument.* "A common objection to colleges shifting from a semester to a quarter system is that not as much subject matter will be covered each term" is a statement of an opposing argument. Second, *state your reaction to the opposing argument.* "This isn't true. Courses that meet 3 hours per week could meet 5 hours per week under the quarter system" is a statement of response to an opposing argument. Third, *support your response with reasoning and evidence.* Refutation requires the same standards of reasoning and evidence that are relevant to any claim asserted. Fourth, *indicate what effect, if any, opposing arguments have had on the strength of your case.* If some disadvantage will occur from your proposal, admit it, but weigh the damage against the claimed advantages of your proposal. "No quarter system is perfect. Yes, students will be pressured in some instances to work more intensely in a condensed period of time. Overall, however, the advantages of a quarter system — greater number and variety of courses, more diversity of instructors, better vacation schedules, and greater retention and success rates — far outweigh the minor objections to my proposal." The sample speech at the end of this chapter provides a detailed example of two-sided organization.

Monroe's Motivated Sequence   The **Monroe motivated sequence** was first designed for sales presentations. It is a persuasive organizational pattern with five steps (Gronbeck et al., 1998).

1. *Attention:* create interest; use attention strategies.
2. *Need:* present a problem to be solved, and relate it to your audience.
3. *Satisfaction:* provide a solution to the problem that will satisfy your audience.
4. *Visualization:* provide an image for your audience of what the world will look like if your solution is implemented.
5. *Action:* make a call to action; get the audience involved and committed.

The sample speech in Box 16-3 provides an extended example of the Monroe motivated sequence.

Box 16-3 Sharper Focus

A Sample Outline and Persuasive Speech

A sample outline and text of a persuasive speech are presented here. This is approximately a 15-minute persuasive speech. That is a longer speech than most in-class presentations but shorter than many public presentations. This somewhat lengthier speech is presented to provide a more comprehensive illustration of several persuasive strategies than could be included in a shorter version.

The speech presented here uses the Monroe motivated sequence organizational format. Steps in this sequence are identified in square brackets. Annotations identify specific persuasion strategies.

Introduction

I. [ATTENTION STEP] Begin with notable examples of big money in college sports.
   A. CBS paid NCAA $1.7 billion for TV rights for basketball championship.
   B. Notre Dame has $38 million television contract.
   C. Some universities have $30 million athletic budgets.
   D. The Rose Bowl pays $8.25 million to participating leagues.
   E. The Fiesta Bowl pays $12.5 million.
   F. Coors pays $5 million to University of Colorado, and Nike pays $5.6 million.

II. Proposition: to convince you that colleges and universities should significantly reduce the scale of their athletic programs.

III. Establish significance to the audience.
   A. All college students partially pay for athletic programs with fees and taxes.
   B. Student scholars must compete with student athletes for scholarships.
      1. Duke University gave $4 million to athletes, but $400,000 to students for academic merit.
      2. The University of North Carolina gave $3.2 million to athletes, but $636,000 to students for academic merit.

IV. Preview the main points.
   A. Athletic programs contradict the educational mission of colleges.
   B. A specific plan will be offered to solve this problem.
   C. Common objections to such a plan will be addressed.

Body

I. [NEED STEP] Big-time intercollegiate athletic programs contradict educational goals of colleges and universities.
   A. Athletic prowess, not academic ability, are often given priority.
      1. Athletes are given scholarships to play ball.
      2. Chris Washburn was a notable example.
      3. SAT scores for athletes are, on average, 200 points lower than for nonathletes.
   B. Student nonathletes and athletes alike are academically harmed by the contradiction.
      1. Student scholars may be bumped from academic admittance to make space for the student athlete with lower academic qualifications.
      2. Admitting marginal students because of their athletic ability is also harmful to the athlete and the college.
         a. Athletes struggle to survive academically.
         b. Colleges spend resources on tutors.
         c. Athletes often take "hide-away curricula."
   C. Colleges' primary mission is often diminished by athletic department deficits.
      1. Most colleges suffer big athletic department deficits.
         a. Almost half of Division I colleges averaged $628,000 deficits apiece.
         b. The deficit for 1997 was $200 million for NCAA colleges.
         c. Deficit figures do not include huge coaches salaries.
      2. Huge deficits threaten academic programs.
         a. Deficits siphon precious resources from academic programs.
         b. Tulane University is a notable example.

II. [SATISFACTION STEP] Take the money out of college sports.

(continued)

A. Drop all college sports entirely (contrast effect).
B. The real plan is as follows:
1. Provide no scholarships based on athletic ability.
2. Student athletes must maintain minimum 2.5 GPA.
3. Team practice sessions will be limited to 10 hours per week.
4. No corporate sponsorships, logos, names on arenas and so forth allowed.
5. No money from TV rights will go to college athletic programs.
6. College coaches will be paid instructor salaries.
7. Football and basketball must be self-supporting; no general college funds may be used.
8. NCAA will enforce these provisions using probation, suspension of sports program, or banishment from a league.
C. Three common objections to this proposal will be addressed.
1. Objection 1 is that disadvantaged student athletes will lose scholarships and be denied an education.
   a. This is true.
   b. Total number of student scholarships will not decrease.
   c. Student athletes will realize importance of academics.
2. Objection 2 is that career training for pros will be lost.
   a. This is also true, but colleges shouldn't be farm teams for sports corporations.
   b. A minuscule percentage go on to be professionals.
3. Objection 3 is that sports fans lose an entertainment source.
   a. There will still be college sports programs.
   b. There will still be gifted athletes entertaining us.
   c. There just won't be big money distorting academics.

III. [VISUALIZATION STEP] Imagine what it will be like when money is removed from college sports.

A. Colleges won't need to reduce or eliminate academic programs because of athletic department deficits.
B. More scholarship money will be available for academic merit.
C. Colleges will no longer contradict their mission.
D. Student tuition and fees will not be raised to pay for athletics.
E. Failure to implement this plan means increased deficits, hypocrisy, and reductions in academic programs.

Conclusion

I. [ACTION STEP] Take action now.
A. Summary of main arguments.
1. Big money has corrupted college sports, thwarting colleges' academic mission.
2. The proposed plan takes the money out of college sports.
3. Common objections were found to be meritless.
B. Take action.
1. Contact your student representatives.
2. Sign the petition to be sent to the NCAA.
C. Memorable finish: Begin the dialogue; stop the hypocrisy!

Bibliography

Byers, W. (1995). *Unsportsmanlike conduct: Exploiting college athletes.* Ann Arbor, MI: The University of Michigan Press.

Eitzen, D. (1997, December 1). Big-time college sports. *Vital Speeches,* pp. 122–126.

Gup, T. (1998, December 18). Losses surpass victories, by far, in big-time college sports. *Chronicle of Higher Education,* p. A52.

Simons, J. (1997, March 24). Improbable dreams. *U.S. News & World Report,* pp. 46–52.

Sperber, M. (1990). *College sports inc.: The athletic department vs. the university.* New York: Henry Holt.

Sperber, M. (1998). *Onward to victory: The crisis that shaped college sports.* New York: Henry Holt.

Box 16-3   Sharper Focus

(continued)

Get Big Money Out of College Sports

[ATTENTION STEP] College sports are big business. Sociology Professor Emeritus Stanley Eitzen of Colorado State University, in the December 1, 1997 issue of *Vital Speeches* cites the following facts to support this claim: In 1994 CBS agreed to pay the National Collegiate Athletic Association (NCAA) $1.7 *billion* for television rights for the men's national basketball tournament through the year 2002. Notre Dame University has a $38 million contract to televise its football games. Some university athletic budgets have surpassed $30 million a year, more than the entire budgets of many colleges. Pac-10 and Big-10 colleges received $8.25 million for participating in the 1997 Rose Bowl game. Teams that play in the Fiesta Bowl for the national college football championship each receive $12.5 million. Coors Brewing Company paid $5 million to the University of Colorado for naming its new field house "Coors Events Center." The university also receives $5.6 million in shoes, apparel, and cash from Nike.

Big-time college sports are seemingly awash in money. Is this increasing commercialization of college sports compatible with the educational mission of institutions of higher learning? Professor Eitzen in his 1997 speech observes: "Big-time college sport confronts us with a fundamental dilemma. Positively, college football and basketball offer entertainment, spectacle, excitement, festival, and excellence. Negatively, the commercial entertainment function of big-time college sport has severely compromised academia. Educational goals have been superseded by the quest for big-money. And, since winning programs receive huge revenues from television, gate receipts, bowl and tournament appearances, boosters, and even legislatures, many sports programs are guided by a win-at-any-cost philosophy." Let's be honest: college athletics, especially football and basketball programs, are a commercial entertainment venture far removed from the educational mission of colleges and universities. College sport has become so gigantic that it distorts the priorities of colleges and universities around the country. As Professor Ted Gup of Georgetown University, in a December 18, 1998, *Chronicle of Higher Education* article puts it, "The grossly disproportionate resources and attention given to big-time college sports infect our institutions with corruption, venality, and hypocrisy." Because this is a serious problem, I will try to convince you that colleges and universities should significantly reduce the scale of their athletic programs. [PROPOSITION OF POLICY]

Every college student listening to me speak today is affected by this commercialization of college sports. [PERSONAL IMPACT] It is you who partially pay for big-time athletic programs with student fees and taxes. Student scholars are forced to compete against student athletes for scholarships and resources. Murray Sperber, professor of English at Indiana University, in his 1998 book *Onward to Victory,* states that "many big-time sports schools spend much more money on grants for jocks than on academic merit scholarships." He cites two notable examples. Duke University awarded $4 million for 550 athletes, but only $400,000 in academic merit scholarships for its 5,900 other undergraduates. Likewise, the University of North Carolina gave $3.2 million to 690 athletes, but only $636,000 in merit scholarships for its 15,000 other students. In addition to competition for scholarships, academic programs central to your educational goals and dreams may be jeopardized by huge deficits incurred by athletic programs, especially those with losing records.

I can guess what some of you are thinking. "He wants to reduce college athletic programs because he hates jocks and was a geek who always lost at sports." Not true!

(continued)

Baseball and basketball were my two favorite sports, and I earned my share of trophies and accolades playing both. I am an avid 49ers fan, and I grew up worshipping the L.A. Dodgers. You may not appreciate the teams I chose to support, but clearly I do not propose reducing college athletics because I hate sports. [IDENTIFICATION] A college education, however, can open the doors of success for each and every one of you. It is your ticket to a better future. College sports should never serve as a substitute for academic success or impede any student's chance to acquire the best education possible, but it threatens to do just that. [PERSONAL IMPACT]

Let me make several arguments to support my proposal to significantly reduce college athletic programs. Please listen to these arguments before making a judgment. I will show how athletic programs contradict the educational mission of colleges. I will offer a specific plan to rectify this serious problem. Finally, I will respond to primary objections you may have to my proposal.

[NEED STEP] Returning to my first argument, that athletic programs contradict the educational mission of colleges, let me begin with what I think we all know is true. The principal mission of a college or university is to provide a quality education for all students. Excessive emphasis on sports programs, however, contradict this mission in three ways. [COGNITIVE DISSONANCE] First, athletic prowess, not academic ability, are often given priority by colleges. Athletes receive scholarships to attend colleges and universities, not to become great scholars or even to receive a quality education. They receive scholarships to play ball and entertain fans. Pursuing an education is often secondary at best, a time-consuming irritant that interferes with athletes' opportunity to practice their sport.

Chris Washburn, a future professional basketball player, entered North Carolina State University with a SAT score of 470. The average SAT score for the student body at N.C. State was 1,030 at the time. More than one hundred universities offered Washburn a scholarship to play basketball. Partly as a result of this widely publicized and embarrassing example, the NCAA tightened SAT score requirements. Nevertheless, marginal student athletes continue to receive special treatment. As Professor Eitzen notes, football and men's basketball players are six times as likely to be admitted below standard college entrance requirements as other students. SAT scores for athletes are, on average, more than 200 points lower than the rest of the student body. Clearly, athletic prowess, not academic potential, is what counts.

Second, student athletes and nonathletes alike are harmed by the emphasis placed on athletic ability. [CONTINUATION OF COGNITIVE DISSONANCE] Admitting marginal students because of their athletic abilities prevents other more academically qualified students from gaining entrance to some of the best colleges and universities. Some of you may have been denied entrance to the college of your choice and had to settle for a second, third, or even fourth choice because athletes with far weaker academic records were granted preferential admittance. [MILD ANGER APPEAL] Does this not seem unfair to you? I know it does because Professor Sperber reports results of his study on college sports in *Onward to Victory*. A huge majority, 83% of undergraduate respondents to the survey, agreed with the statement "Athletic scholarship winners should meet the same college entrance requirements as regular students."

In addition, admitting marginal students with athletic ability does no favors for the student athletes. Marginal students struggle to keep up in classes, often require tutors at college expense, and many never get a degree. Journalist Linda Seebach, editorial writer for *Inside Denver*, states in her December 14, 1997, editorial, "Athletes on scholarship . . . often have wall-to-wall tutors and major in 'hideaway curriculums'

Box 16-3   Sharper Focus

(*continued*)

designed solely for them." Professors of economics Robert Frank and Philip Cook, in their 1995 book *The Winner-Take-All Society* state that many football programs graduate fewer than 10% of their players. Big-money sports distort educational priorities.

Third, the primary mission of colleges and universities, to educate students, is often diminished by athletic department deficits. [CONTINUATION OF COGNITIVE DISSONANCE] As Professor Sperber explains in his 1990 book *College Sports, Inc.*: "If profit and loss is defined according to ordinary business practices, only 10 to 20 athletic programs make a consistent albeit small profit, and in any given year another 20 to 30 break even or do better. The rest—over 2300 institutions—lose anywhere from a few dollars to millions annually." The 1996 Annual Report of the NCAA showed almost half of Division I football programs alone had an average deficit of $628,000 apiece in the previous year. The 1997 NCAA Annual Report showed a total deficit of $200 million for Division I athletic programs in the United States. [USE OF PERSUASIVE EVIDENCE; STARTLING/UNUSUAL/STATISTICS] These figures are undoubtedly too low because coaches salaries, among other things, aren't included in the athletic budgets. They're listed as faculty salaries. Only a handful of athletic programs make a profit, yet as Walter Byers, former NCAA executive director in his 1995 book *Unsportsmanlike Conduct* notes, most colleges invest enormous resources trying to keep up with the few wealthy athletic programs.

These huge deficits threaten academic programs. [MILD FEAR APPEAL] Professor Eitzen notes that in 1996 Tulane University announced a sixfold increase in the athletic department budget from $550,000 to $3.4 million. Simultaneously, Tulane hacked $8.5 million from the general budget used to support academic programs. Student tuition was raised 4%, faculty and staff salaries were frozen for a year, 50 staff positions were cut, and funding for undergraduate and graduate financial aid and stipends was reduced. Athletic department deficits siphon precious resources from academic programs, possibly academic programs central to your educational and career goals. Big-money athletic programs clearly contradict the primary mission of institutions of higher education by admitting poorly prepared and under-qualified athletes, by valuing students for their athletic prowess not their academic potential, and by creating huge deficits that necessitate diminished resources for academic programs.

So what should be done about this problem? Clearly, since football and basketball programs are typically the source of all these problems, we should eliminate them from all colleges and universities. [CONTRAST EFFECT] If we were to eliminate football and basketball, less visible and far less costly sports such as baseball, golf, gymnastics, and field hockey could provide some athletic opportunities for students. Intramural football and basketball programs, at virtually no cost to the college, could be established for those students who prefer such sports. Let's face facts—getting the money out of college sport is essential if we are going to solve the problems I've outlined.

Total elimination of football and basketball except for intramural programs solves the problems I've underscored. Perhaps, however, we don't need such a radical solution. As a sports fan and former athlete I would be disappointed if colleges dumped their football and basketball programs, entirely. [IDENTIFICATION] I do strongly believe, however, that the big money must be taken out of college sports.

[SATISFACTION STEP] My plan to do this is simple:

1. There will be no scholarships for students based on athletic ability. Scholarships and grants must be based on academic potential and financial need.
2. Student athletes must be admitted according to the same standards as all other students. They must maintain a minimum 2.5 GPA to participate in athletic programs.

(continued)

3. Team practice sessions will be limited to no more than 10 hours per week. Professor Sperber notes that athletes are often required to spend 30 to 40 hours per week practicing their sport. This competes with time for academic pursuits.
4. Absolutely no corporate money goes to athletic programs. No corporate logos or names should appear on any sports facilities, equipment, or apparel of any kind.
5. No money from television rights or bowl games will go to college athletic programs.
6. College coaches must be paid instructor's salaries just like any professor. In a highly publicized story, Steve Spurrier, football coach at the University of Florida was given a contract averaging $2 million per year in salary, bonuses, and extras until the year 2002. No coach should earn 10 to 20 times what the college president earns. It sends a distorted message about college priorities.
7. Football and basketball must be self-supporting. Ticket sales and sports merchandise will be primary sources of funds.
8. The NCAA will enforce all provisions, using probation, suspension of a sports program, or banishment from a league as possible penalties.

This plan will substantially reduce college athletic programs without eliminating them. I have merely taken the big money out of college sports. Leagues, championships, and bowl games can continue, but without the huge financial incentives to distort the academic mission of colleges. Academic programs will no longer be threatened by huge athletic department debts. Without the big money, colleges can return to their primary mission—to provide a quality education for all students.

[SATISFACTION STEP CONTINUED] In case you're not completely convinced that my plan is a good idea, let me address common objections to my proposal. [TWO-SIDED PERSUASION] The first objection might be that disadvantaged student athletes will lose scholarships and be denied a college education. That's true. Athletic scholarships awarded each year, however, could be added to the general scholarship and grant pool at each college. The net effect on students as a group would be zero. The faces would change, but the same number of students could receive financial help. In addition, if student athletes realize that they cannot play college sports unless they qualify academically, this will provide an incentive for them to take their studies seriously or risk ineligibility.

A second objection [TWO-SIDED PERSUASION CONTINUED] might be that many academically unprepared student athletes will lose a training ground for a career in professional sports without scholarships. This may be true, but is it relevant? Should a college be a farm team for professional sports corporations? Journalist John Simons in his March 24, 1997, article in *U.S. News* notes that any high school athlete's chances of playing professional sports is remote—about 1 in 10,000. Yet according to the Northeastern University's Center for the Study of Sport in Society cited in the same article, 66% of all African American males between the ages of 13 and 18 believe they can make it to the professional ranks some day. Professors Frank and Cook note that 60% of NCAA Division I college basketball starters believe they will some day start for an NBA team. The actual figure is fewer than 5%. University of Chicago sports economist Allen Sanderson, quoted in the 1997 *U.S. News* article, says, "It's like pinning your hopes on the lottery."

These students are attending college to play ball as a way of auditioning for professional teams. Educational success often gets lost in the hoopla and hubbub over athletic accomplishment. Colleges should not be a party to such exploitation. [COGNITIVE DISSONANCE] As Professor Eitzen concludes, "When schools over-recruit minorities for their athletic skills and under-recruit minorities for their academic skills, they contradict the

Box 16-3   Sharper Focus

(*continued*)

fundamental reason for their existence." As John Simons notes in his 1997 *U.S. News* article, African Americans are vastly underrepresented in such important professions as medicine, law, journalism, and engineering, to name just a few. Colleges should be working hard to prepare minority students for these and other professions because that is their primary mission. They should stop serving as a farm team for professional sports corporations interested only in profit.

Finally, won't sports fans lose a key source of entertainment if my plan is implemented? [TWO-SIDED PERSUASION CONTINUED] This is not true. Notre Dame and USC will still remain arch rivals on the football field. Bowl games will still exist. Championships will still be contested, simply in scaled-down versions. The difference will be that academic programs will not be diminished because of huge deficits from athletic programs, and the academic mission of colleges will not be distorted to pay for a bloated athletic program. The scale of college athletics will be substantially reduced, but the excitement and spectacle can remain.

[VISUALIZATION STEP] Imagine what my plan will accomplish. No longer will colleges be tempted or forced to reduce or eliminate an academic program, perhaps a program in your major, to pay for deficits incurred by bloated athletic programs. Millions of dollars in scholarships and grants will be available for academically qualified and needy students. Colleges will no longer serve as farm teams for profit-motivated corporations. Colleges will no longer appear hypocritical, espousing an educational mission on one hand while undermining it on the other. Your student fees and tuition will not have to be raised to support a faltering, expensive sports program.

Imagine what will happen if this problem is ignored. Athletic budgets will continue to swell and deficits will rise. Your tuition and fees will increase, academic programs will be cut, and some programs and majors will be eliminated to cover the athletic department deficits. The quality of your education and your opportunities for academic success will be threatened. [MILD FEAR APPEAL]

[ACTION STEP] College sports have become too closely connected to corporate interests. Big money has corrupted college athletics. I have proposed a solution that will work by taking money out of college sports. I have responded to common objections raised against my plan, and these objections have been found meritless. I ask that you support my proposal to significantly reduce college athletic programs. Stop the erosion of academic values and quality. Speak to your Student Senate officers and representatives. Discuss the issues I have raised with the college administration. This college can be a beacon of light signaling the way for other colleges to follow. Change begins with us. Sign this petition that I will circulate in a moment that asks the NCAA to change the rules and remove big money from our college sports programs. [EFFORT REQUIRED IS MINIMAL] Begin the dialogue! Stop the hypocrisy.

Summary

Persuasion is the communication process of converting, modifying, or maintaining the attitudes, beliefs, and behavior of others. Changing attitudes alone may not change behavior. Personal experience, personal impact, and effort required to perform the behavior all affect how consistent attitudes and behavior will be. There are two primary paths to persuasion: peripheral and central. Uninvolved listeners are more easily influenced by peripheral factors such as the credibility of the speaker and how others react to the persuasive message. Involved listeners are more influenced by quality arguments and evidence. There are many persuasive strategies a speaker can use. Among these are establishing identification, building credibility, building solid arguments, inducing cognitive dissonance, making emotional appeals, using the contrast effect, and using persuasive organizational patterns. Competent public speakers will find success if they utilize some or all of these strategies to persuade others.

Suggested Readings

Cialdini, R. (1993). *Influence: The new psychology of modern persuasion.* Glenview, IL: Scott Foresman. This is a very well-written work on common persuasion strategies used in everyday life.

Pratkanis, A., & Aronson, E. (1991). *The age of propaganda: The everyday use and abuse of persuasion.* New York: W. H. Freeman. This title says it all. This is a very readable work on common persuasion strategies.

Chapter 17

Technology and Communication

We are awash in technology. Technology has become so much a part of our daily lives that communication cannot be easily separated from technology. Canadian English professor Marshall McLuhan (1964, 1967) was the focal point for intense debate over electronic media and its effects when television was still a relatively new invention. Derisively labeled the "Oracle of the Electronic Age," the "High Priest of Pop Culture," and the "Metaphysician of Media," McLuhan gained notoriety partly because of his gift for creating memorable phrases. "The medium is the message," "the medium is the massage," and "the global village" are all McLuhan creations. Despite criticisms of McLuhan's point of view (see especially Davis, 1993)—a view that was essentially optimistic about electronic media and its potential contributions to humankind—McLuhan did shift the debate from a focus on content in the media to media itself.

Meyrowitz (1997) notes, "The spread of printing, radio, television, telephone, computer networks, and other technologies have altered the nature of social interaction in ways that cannot be reduced to the content of the messages communicated through them" (p. 196). Consider a few simple examples that illustrate what a shift in focus from content of messages transmitted through communication media to the use of communication technologies themselves is like. Your partner sits at the breakfast table reading a newspaper while you try to engage him or her in a conversation. Does it matter what your partner is reading, or does the mere act of reading the newspaper interfere with interpersonal connection? Familes that eat dinner in front of the television rarely engage in conversation. In fact, conversation during a television program is considered rude and will often provoke a collective "shoosh" from family members. Does it matter what is being watched? The mere act of watching television can close off dialogue and opportunities for conversation. When children and parents spend hours alone in front of computer screens, does it matter whether they are playing video games, surfing the Internet, or catching up on office work? The mere use of communication technologies has the power to shape our lives in ways we may not notice.

The purpose of this chapter is to discuss the power of communication technologies to shape our lives. There are four objectives:

1. to examine trends in communication technologies,
2. to explain how the nature of each communication technology reveals a bias,
3. to discuss the consequences of these trends, and
4. to offer ways competent communicators can cope with the impact of communication technologies.

The content of messages transmitted via communication technologies does matter. Violent television programming and pornographic images on the Internet are subjects of heated debate and intense concern. You are probably familiar with the controversies surrounding these content issues. What you may not recognize, however, is how the mere use of communication technologies is changing our lives. The focus of this chapter, therefore, is on the use, not the content, of communication technologies.

Trends in Communication Technologies

Recognizing trends in communication technologies can help the competent communicator understand the latest developments in and anticipate the likely future of these technologies. There are three primary trends: (1) the pace of technological

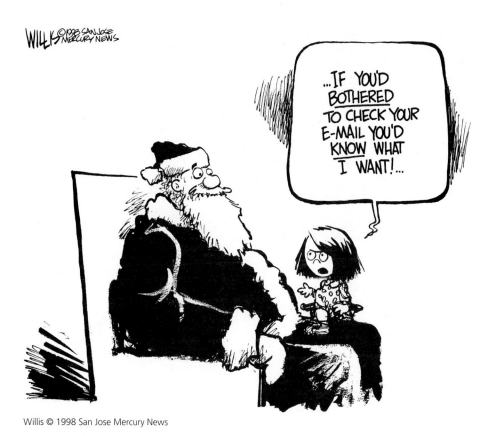

Willis © 1998 San Jose Mercury News

change and widespread use of communication technologies are accelerating, (2) communication technologies are merging, and (3) demassification is becoming an important force.

Accelerating Pace

The pace of technological change is accelerating. In the first half of the 20th century a new major communication technology might come along once in a decade or two. Now, with the digital world of computers, communication technology arrives more quickly and changes more rapidly. Computer processing speed, for example, doubles, on average, every 18 months (Klopfenstein, 1997). This means that the computer that cost you $1,000 or more will become obsolete in about the same amount of time. Shenk (1997) claims that by the year 2005 Americans will have dumped about 150 million computers into the garbage. Bill Seawick of computer software giant Oracle Corporation says, "Technology is coming at such a fantastic pace that people have to learn new technologies every three or four months" (as cited in Shenk, 1997, p. 86).

The pace of technological acceptance by the public has also accelerated. The Center for Policy Analysis notes that new communication technologies are reaching and being used by a significant portion of the U.S. population faster than ever. The telephone took 35 years to reach a quarter of the U.S. population; radio took 22 years, television 26 years, the PC only 16 years, the mobile phone 13 years, and

ENIAC, the first "full-service" electronic computer, was introduced in 1946. It weighed 60,000 pounds and was composed of 17,500 vacuum tubes and 500 miles of wire that consumed 150,000 watts of electricity. When it is compared to the palm pilot, a more powerful computer than ENIAC, the rapid pace of technological change can readily be seen.

the Internet just 7 years (as cited in "Reeling in the Years," 1998). By the mid-1990s the Internet, hardly recognized by most Americans at the start of the decade, had emerged as a dominant communication system used by people from a variety of backgrounds. In January 1999 Pew Research Center for the People and the Press reported that 41% of Americans use the Internet (as cited in Williams, 1999). The "information superhighway" is spreading rapidly around the world.

Technological Merging

"Digital technology, the basis of today's new media technologies, represents the translation of all forms of content (text, images, audio, video and other animation) into a form that is easily manipulated by computers. That sentence sums up developments in communication technologies for the last 20 years" (Klopfenstein, 1997, p. 22). Digitalization has permitted extensive merging of communication technologies. Until the arrival of the computer, communication technologies were typically analog. Turow (1999) offers a simple explanation of the differences between analog and digital.

An old-fashioned vinyl record that uses a turntable and a needle to reproduce sound is analog. A more modern CD is digital. Close examination of a vinyl record reveals grooves. When a singer or a band creates sound, the waves of sound create vibrations. In a recording studio, equipment reproduces these vibrations, which produce grooves that are pressed onto the vinyl platter. When the record player's needle travels over the grooves on the vinyl platter, sound is reproduced. This is a literal physical reproduction of the recording artists' sound—an **analog.**

A CD, by contrast, uses a very different process. There is no physical reproduction of sound. Instead, computers transform the sound of a singer's voice or a band's instruments into a pattern of **binary digits,** a code composed of the two digits 0 and 1. These patterns, or strings of zeros and ones, are called **bits.** These bits act as a symbolic representation of the sounds. Your CD player translates these bits by passing a laser beam over the code, sending the code to a computer chip programmed to recognize the strings of zeros and ones. The chip transforms the bits into electrical impulses that reproduce sound once these impulses travel through an amplifier and sound system.

The digital world of computers has merged with virtually all communication technologies, creating a communication revolution (DeFleur & Dennis, 1998). There are computer chips in televisions, radios, CD players, telephones, VCRs, and fax and copy machines. Digitalization has made possible the integration of communication technologies unparalleled in human history. We now talk of interactive television, an unprecedented combination of communication technology that would merge cable, television, telephone, and computer technology. The Internet, which merges computer and phone (modems) technology, can be a medium of print, graphics, photography, video, or sound. It can be linear, one-way communication, or it can be interactive with chatrooms and e-mail permitting interchange between users. This technological merging has created a far different world of communication than existed just two decades ago.

Demassification

As communication technologies develop rapidly, providing an increasing array of choices for the average consumer, competition for our attention has become fierce. Each new technology doesn't necessarily supplant an older technology. Radio didn't kill newspapers, television didn't replace radio, VCRs didn't destroy the motion picture industry, and the Internet hasn't replaced any of these technologies. Nevertheless, each new communication technology can pose challenges for the older media.

Newspapers, magazines, and radio all had to adapt to the challenge of television. They did so mostly by becoming specialized—aiming at small segments of the overall market instead of appealing to a national audience. Of the more than 12,000 newspapers in the United States, only three are truly national: the *Wall Street Journal, Christian Science Monitor,* and *USA Today.* General interest magazines such as the *Saturday Evening Post, Good Housekeeping, Life, Look,* and *Reader's Digest* all became very successful with a national audience. "Magazines were truly America's first national mass medium" (Baran, 1999, p. 127). With the advent of television following World War II, however, magazines fell on hard times. Forced to compete with this new national communication medium, magazines became more specialized to survive. Instead of appealing to a broad, general population, most magazines began targeting particular groups. Most of the more than 22,000 magazines published each year in the United States today are specialty magazines with a narrow audience (e.g., *Seventeen, Flyfishing, Muscle & Fitness, Wired*).

Radio was also forced to adapt when television emerged. Radio formats began targeting particular segments of the national audience instead of trying to appeal to an entire nation. Music programs became increasingly narrow in focus, talk shows increased in popularity, and all-news formats emerged.

This increasing specialization applied to communication technologies is called **demassification.** Although television was a primary cause of demassification of other technologies, it too has become demassified. Cable and satellite technology have expanded consumers' choices to as many as 500 television channels. The remote control permits easy channel surfing. What once was *broad*casting has become increasingly *narrow*casting. National networks have seen their audience shrink dramatically in recent years. There's a television channel for almost every conceivable interest, no matter how narrow the focus. Public access channels available on cable have some remarkably amateurish programming with very few viewers. The more specialized the audience, the more demassified the communication technology becomes.

The process of demassification doesn't necessarily replace the focus on a mass audience. Videotapes of popular movies, for example, aim for a national audience. Videotapes on gourmet cooking, hair restoration, and rock climbing, however, target very specialized interest groups. Internet websites have a similar mix of general and specialized emphases. The Internet has increased the trend toward demassification.

Bias of Communication Technologies

Put in its simplest form, a **technology** is a tool to accomplish some purpose, and a communication technology is a tool to communicate with others. Every technology has a bias. Each predisposes, or biases, us to view the world in a particular way. A person with a hammer looks for something to pound. Someone with a knife looks for something to slice. An individual with a camera looks for an image to capture on film. A person with an automobile looks for places to drive. Every technology has its capabilities and limitations.

Television and Computers

Neil Postman (1985, 1993), professor of media ecology at New York University, in his provocative books *Amusing Ourselves to Death* and *Technopoly,* argues that we are in the midst of a cultural shift. This shift is away from a reliance on print media and toward a dependence on electronic technology, primarily television and computers.

Postman argues that television, by its nature, is a visual medium. As such, television's pictures determine its effectiveness. Poor video images make poor television. "Talking heads" conducting a discussion on television is boring because the visual images are mostly static and uninteresting. This partly explains why many talk shows have gone for the sensational and bizarre to spice up the images projected on TV. Weird people that you wouldn't invite into your home verbally and physically abuse each other on these shows. Television is an action-oriented, fast-paced, visual medium. Slow, deliberate conversation on abstract topics doesn't grab a viewing audience because there is little to view—unless a fight breaks out.

Postman argues that television is essentially an entertainment medium. As he puts it:

> No matter what is depicted or from what point of view, the overarching presumption is that it [television] is there for our amusement and pleasure. That is why even on news shows which provide us daily with fragments of tragedy and barbarism, we are urged by the newscasters to "join them tomorrow." What for? One would think that several minutes of murder and mayhem would suffice as material for a month of sleepless nights. . . . A news show, to put it plainly, is a format for entertainment, not for education, reflection or catharsis. (pp. 87–88)

Calvin and Hobbes   by Bill Watterson

An apt example of Postman's point of view was the Fox News Channel presentation of Wilma Carroll, an "astrologer/psychic," on its August 18, 1998, newscast (Zurawik, 1998). She used tarot cards to predict "problems for the Clintons" and especially "female problems for Hillary." Clearly, this was not news but merely entertainment, not credible and not in particularly good taste at that.

Great video largely determines what gets on the nightly news. This is why a relatively inconsequential bank robbery in Denver, Colorado, made it on all the network news programs. Why?—because a news helicopter had live video coverage of the police chasing the bank robbers. The video was too exciting, immediate, and dramatic not to show as *national* news. In other words, the video was entertaining if not exactly momentous.

Sometimes the entertainment value of an event seems more voyeuristic than newsworthy. On April 30, 1998, Daniel V. Jones, a 40-year-old maintenance worker suffering with cancer, stood on a connector loop overlooking a Los Angeles freeway, placed a shotgun under his chin, and pulled the trigger. This grisly suicide was covered in the afternoon on live television. Two stations, the local WB Network and the Fox broadcasting affiliates, interrupted children's programs to cover the incident live.

When television tries to get serious or takes itself seriously by offering "important" programs such as televised "debates" between presidential candidates, according to Postman, it fails. Television demands immediacy, brevity, and entertainment. A rerun of the old *Perry Mason* TV show drew three times the viewers in the San Francisco area as the televised coverage of the Clinton impeachment trial's opening session (Kava, 1999). The trial was immediate, but it lacked drama because the outcome was preordained. Speakers droned on tediously about technical points of law. The proceedings were far removed from the more concise, dramatic scripting viewers are accustomed to in courtroom series such as *Law & Order* and *The Practice*.

Television does not allow a person to pause and carefully analyze an issue. A presidential candidate, a guest on a talk show, or an individual interviewed by a reporter cannot pause after a question during a telecast and say, "Let me think about that for a minute or two." Television can't permit dead-air time. TV requires active visual images that entertain, not static downtime. With remote controls at the ready, viewers quickly jump to another channel if there is a boring pause in the action.

Print media, unlike television, requires a sequence of thoughts and ideas, use of evidence and reasoning, and careful development of viewpoints. Readers can ponder, reflect, and even research points of view long after they have been read. Print media, from Postman's perspective, is therefore a more appropriate technology than television for serious discussion of issues and ideas. When television turns serious, it often becomes boring.

The bias of television as a communication medium has a wide reach. Postman (1985) explains:

> It is not merely that on the television screen entertainment is the metaphor for all discourse. It is that off the screen the same metaphor prevails. As typography [print] once dictated the style of conducting politics, religion, business, education, law and other important social matters, television now takes command. (p. 93)

Applied to education, the television metaphor could change teaching dramatically. Teachers are pressured to teach the way television is formatted by its nature—to provide a thrill a minute. This means that no difficult information should be presented because it might be boring and cause students to switch off their minds. Presentation of ideas and concepts should be entertaining and offered in bite-sized, easily digestible chunks. Teachers should be evaluated as television programs are rated—on their entertainment and interest—a kind of Nielsen ratings for instruction. Learning becomes secondary to having a good time in class.

Other technologies have also been affected by television. *USA Today* was launched in 1982. Postman (1985) claims it "is modeled precisely on the format of television. It is sold on the street in receptacles that look like television sets. Its stories are uncommonly short, its design leans heavily on picture, charts, and other graphics, some of them printed in colors. Its weather maps are a visual delight; its sports section includes enough pointless statistics to distract a computer" (p. 111).

USA Today was immediately criticized for its fluff journalism, superficial news coverage, and bite-sized length of stories. Dubbed "McPaper" by some critics, *USA Today* makes no apology for its style. Its first editor-in-chief, John Quinn, unapologetically stated early on, "We are not up to undertaking projects of the dimensions needed to win prizes. They don't give awards for the best investigative paragraph" (as cited in Postman, 1985, p. 112). Sold mostly at airports on a single-issue rather than subscriber basis, its daily circulation of 1.6 million makes it the second largest selling newspaper in the United States (Turow, 1999).

The advent of computer technology hasn't improved the situation from Postman's (1993) perspective. The nature of computers is speed of transmission and the ability to process large amounts of data. The bias that computers create, therefore, is for immediacy. We want huge amounts of information instantly, and are impatient with delay. Accessing huge amounts of information swiftly, however, does nothing to assist us in pondering, reflecting, and analyzing the information. Generating huge amounts of data quickly will not necessarily help us solve important problems. Postman (1993) explains:

> Our most serious problems are not technical, nor do they arise from inadequate
> information. . . . Where people are dying of starvation, it does not occur because of
> inadequate information. If families break up, children are mistreated, crime terrorizes a
> city, education is impotent, it does not happen because of inadequate information. . . .
> The computer is useless in addressing them. (p. 119)

As you will see in the section on the consequences of communication technologies, swift access to huge amounts of information has both a positive and a negative side.

Assessing the Postman Perspective

Postman makes some important points about communication technologies. First,
each communication technology is limited by its nature. Trying to make a technology perform in a way that contradicts its nature renders the technology ineffective.
A mime show on radio would be absurd. A long pause to meditate and reflect
during a television broadcast is silly. Trying to make computers process information more slowly defies their nature. Second, each new communication technology
changes our lives, not always for the better. We need to focus more on how technology alters our lives and less on the bells and whistles associated with the hype
that accompanies every technological change. Third, it is the technology itself, not
what content is transmitted, that should be our primary focus. Will computers in
the classroom necessarily improve student learning, or are we naively accepting
uncritically the hype from the computer industry? Several studies cast doubt
on the hype (see Gumz, 1997; Schmitt & Slonaker, 1996). If elaborate Power Point
demonstrations prove to be no more educational than a few video clips or some
color transparencies, then the expensive technology merely siphons scarce resources. The billions of dollars spent on computer technology means less money
is available for more traditional educational resources such as books, field trips,
musical instruments and art supplies, theatrical costumes and supplies for set
building, and so forth. Unless we know how to use the technology effectively, incorporating computers in the classroom may be counterproductive to the overall
educational experience of children.

Postman raises important points, but he also misses a significant point. What
effects result from technological merging? His analysis of technology focuses
too narrowly on the effects of television or computers as separate technologies.
Television has a clear visual bias, and computers have a speed of transmission and
storage of information bias. What happens, however, when television, computer,
and print technology all merge, as in the Internet? Does the Internet predispose us
to favor entertaining visual images or the sequential thought patterns of print
technology? Print technology has not been replaced by the Internet. If anything,
it has been enhanced. The written word is now more widely and easily available
to a mass audience than ever before in human history. Encarta makes an encyclopedia of knowledge more widely and easily accessible to a mass audience than
standard encyclopedias mostly found in libraries ever could. The print media,
especially newspapers and magazines, increasingly rely on computer databases
for up-to-the-minute information. Many newspapers and magazines have gone
online, creating websites with electronic versions of their daily papers. How do we
explain the widespread use of the Internet for scientific research and collaboration

that is mostly devoid of entertainment? Postman has raised important points about communication technologies, but his perspective seems somewhat disconnected from the reality of technological merging.

Consequences of Communication Technologies

The history of communication technologies appears to be a simple process of adding new technologies on top of old ones. It is far more complicated than this. As Postman (1993) explains:

> A new technology does not add or subtract something. It changes everything. In the year 1500, fifty years after the printing press was invented, we did not have old Europe plus the printing press. We had a different Europe. After television, the United States was not America plus television; television gave a new coloration to every political campaign, to every home, to every school, to every church, to every industry. (p. 18)

With the inherent bias of each communication technology interacting with accelerating technological change, technological merging, and increasing demassification, the consequences of communication technologies must be viewed primarily from a holistic perspective. The central question to ask isn't "What effects do television *or* computers as separate communication technologies have on us?" Television's effects on our communication with others cannot be analyzed in isolation from the effects of computer technology because the two technologies have become complementary and integral to each other. Television is becoming digitalized, and computer technology is incorporating some of the visual bias of television. The central question is: "What are the consequences of all these communication technologies working in tandem?"

Information Overload

The amount of information we are exposed to each day is staggering. Americans send 2.2 billion e-mail messages every day; there are 50,000 new books published each year in the United States; there are 12,000 newspapers, 22,000 magazines, 600 million radios, and at least one television set in 98% of U.S. homes; almost half of the population in the United States has access to the Internet (Baran, 1999; DeFleur & Dennis, 1998; Turow, 1999). Add to this millions of fax machines, pagers, copy machines, and cell phones. All this technology pumps out information at a staggering rate. We can produce gigaheaps of data too voluminous for processing. "More information is generated in a 24-hour period than you could take in for the rest of your life. And as more people go online and add information to the Internet, we will rapidly approach a situation in which more information is generated on earth in one hour than you could take in for the rest of your life" (Davidson, 1996, p. 496). De Moor (1996) concludes that "information chaos" is arising from this information overload.

Effects of Information Overload   Information chaos is the general result of information overload. Several specific consequences, identified by Shenk (1997), result from information overload. These consequences are discussed next.

Calvin and Hobbes

by Bill Watterson

IT USED TO BE THAT IF A CLIENT WANTED SOMETHING DONE IN A WEEK, IT WAS CONSIDERED A RUSH JOB, AND HE'D BE LUCKY TO GET IT.

NOW, WITH MODEMS, FAXES, AND CAR PHONES, EVERYBODY WANTS EVERYTHING INSTANTLY! IMPROVED TECHNOLOGY JUST INCREASES EXPECTATIONS.

THESE MACHINES DON'T MAKE LIFE EASIER—THEY MAKE LIFE MORE HARASSED.

SIX MINUTES TO MICROWAVE THIS?? WHO'S GOT THAT KIND OF TIME?!

IF WE WANTED MORE LEISURE, WE'D INVENT MACHINES THAT DO THINGS *LESS* EFFICIENTLY.

Impedes Critical Thinking Too much information "thwarts skepticism, rendering us less sophisticated as consumers and citizens" (Shenk, 1997, p. 31). We simply don't have time to process the pile of information. Buried in an avalanche of data from the myriad communication technologies, we have a hugely difficult time separating the garbage from the good stuff. Students recognize this immediately when they prepare research papers for class. Finding information on almost any subject these days is not the difficult part. Knowing when to stop searching and begin thinking about the organization of your paper and the points you want to make is the difficult part. You can become so engrossed in finding information for your paper that you don't leave yourself enough time to think about the information you have gathered.

Promotes Indecisiveness "The psychological reaction to such an overabundance of information . . . is to simply avoid coming to conclusions" (Shenk, 1997, p. 93). Bill Clinton is frequently accused of indecisiveness. "To listen to him speak extemporaneously about an issue is to witness a man able to grasp so much data, he frequently becomes engulfed in it" (p. 94). Clinton's seemingly endless hunger for facts and statistics could get him focusing on the trees not the forest. Journalist Elizabeth Drew (1994, p. 79) notes that White House staffers complained to her that Clinton was fond of delivering "an intense seminar on government minutiae" every chance he got.

The paradox of the new Technological Age is that our world is speeded up enormously, yet our ability to make decisions is slowed down by the easily accessible megamountains of information. It's tough to be decisive when you're never sure if some new fact or statistic available to everyone in an instant will suddenly emerge to invalidate your point of view.

Creates Normalization of Hyperbole Communication scholar Kathleen Hall Jamieson says that our society is experiencing a "normalization of hyperbole" (as cited in Janofsky, 1995). **Hyperbole** is exaggeration for effect not meant to be taken literally. As we become evermore swamped in information, gaining the attention of an audience becomes a bigger challenge. Hyperbole is the solution for many.

Information overload creates normalization of hyperbole. Marilyn Manson stretches the limits to get attention in the din created by communication technologies.

"Extreme measures to grab attention are not only condoned; they're admired. Outrageous behavior by individuals is rewarded with wealth and influence" (Shenk, 1997, p. 104). Dennis Rodman, Madonna, Roseanne, Rush Limbaugh, radio shock jocks Howard Stern and Don Imus all "pump up the volume" to get noticed and amply rewarded. "Historically, discourteousness and vulgarity have always signified a lack of sophistication; garishness was considered tasteless and degrading. In today's attention-deficit society, however, people have learned that churlish behavior is the key to headlines, profit, and power" (Shenk, 1997, p. 104).

If practically everyone is shouting at us, grossly overstating the importance of his or her message, and competing for our attention by being outrageous and sensational, how are we to take seriously any message that truly is urgent? If everything is made to be a crisis, how are we to cope? Regularly I receive junk mail with "URGENT" written repeatedly across the envelope. On the few occasions I have actually opened the envelope, I was invariably disappointed to find a rather routine message asking me to renew a magazine subscription.

During the Clinton impeachment, "legitimate" journalists anguished about the "tabloidization of journalism" where sensational stories about political figures' private lives become front-page headlines. "The fast-food part of the modern media diet—conflict, celebrities, and catastrophe—exists in part because of burgeoning technology. To be heard above the din of growing competition, much of journalism today finds itself in tabloid mode, shouting and trivializing to attract attention" (Fulton, 1999, p. 63). Amidst this din, how can voices of rationality and balance be heard? The answer: not easily.

Coping With Information Overload   Coping with information overload can't be done by turning back the clock. Brian Lamb, founder and chairman of C-SPAN, identifies the problem succinctly: "You can't stop the process. It's the American way. Which part of the library or the Internet do you want to shut down? Let me tell you something: If we can't survive all the information that we're going to develop, then we're in real trouble. Because no one is going to stop writing books. No one is going to stop creating information" (as cited in Shenk, 1997, p. 22). Coping with information overload is critically important, and there are several steps a competent communicator can take.

Screen Information   Be in charge of your own information environment. You can choose to ignore much of the flood of information that can drown you in pointless detail. E-mail can automatically be screened, or you can do it manually. Simply delete messages that are irrelevant or trivial. I regularly delete messages without opening them. On average I open about 20% of all the e-mail messages I receive by simply looking at the title of the message. Telephone messages can also be screened. Let them go to the message machine, listen to who is calling about what, and decide if you want to take the call or ignore it. This puts you in charge, and it screens out telemarketers, solicitors, and people who want to intrude on your private time at home.

Limit Your Exposure to Technology   Pagers, cell phones, fax machines, e-mail, and other electronic gadgets and toys can be wonderful communication technologies if kept under control. The cell phone and pagers working in tandem, for example, can be an electronic lasso that ties a family together. Stuck in traffic, you can call a family member and allay his or her fears or anxieties. Messages of endearment can be coded to a pager. Parents can "tuck in" their children by cell phone during a break in a late-night meeting. Communication technologies, however, can also be what Shenk calls "electronic leashes" if we can never escape their intrusiveness. They can definitely reduce the amount of uninterrupted quiet time available to us where we pause from the daily routine of processing information and making decisions.

If you find that communication technologies have become more of a leash than a lasso, plan for times during each day when you will have no access to any of these technologies. Turn off the pager or put it away. Shut off the computer, switch off the cell phone, and turn off the television set. Try simple conversation with another person with no technological distractions. Play a game, have a cup of coffee with a friend, take a walk, exercise, hike, shoot hoops, or just relax in a hot tub of water.

Narrow the Search   If you search the Internet without a specific target, you will be overwhelmed. Narrow your search for information by having a clear, specific purpose in mind. You can best narrow the search for information by finding relevant patterns. As Klapp (1978) notes, "Once a pattern is perceived, 90 percent of information becomes irrelevant" (p. 13). **Pattern recognition,** the process of piecing together seemingly unrelated information into a plan, design, or whole picture, narrows your search for information. Once a pattern is discerned, you immediately know what information is irrelevant and useless and what information is on target. An effective outline for a speech or research paper establishes a pattern, allowing you to weed out the useless from the useful information.

De-nichify Strive to be more of a generalist looking at the "big picture" rather than a specialist lost in an increasingly narrow world of detail. The more specialized we become to cope with information overload, the more limited our world becomes. *As we become ever more specialized, we learn more and more about less and less.* If everyone moves toward specialization, soon we will have very little to discuss with each other except maybe the weather.

Niches are specialized segments of an audience. Niche marketing targets radio, television, magazines, newspapers, the Internet, and books to a narrow segment of the total audience. Shenk (1997) suggests "de-nichifying." Instead of subscribing to many magazines on specialized topics, for example, subscribe to one or two that are broad based. *Time* and *Newsweek,* for example, are general news magazines that provide a general overview of world news and controversial issues of the week. Some specialization is necessary to remain current in your field of endeavor, but balance the specialization with a general knowledge of the world. This is the philosophy behind most colleges' mandatory general education requirements, which are meant to supplement students' major coursework.

Proliferation of Misinformation

On June 5, 1998, the Associated Press news service and several sources on the Internet announced that comedian Bob Hope had died. The announcement was then brought to the attention of House Majority Leader Dick Armey, who notified Rep. Bob Stump, a member of the House Veterans Affairs Committee. An obituary was read on the House floor. The speech by Stump was telecast live by C-SPAN. Reuters news service issued a bulletin. A national ABC radio report lamented Hope's demise. Presented with this startling piece of "news," the very alive Bob Hope quipped, "They were wrong, weren't they?" (as cited in Antonucci, 1998). Mark Twain once remarked that falsehood spreads halfway around the world before truth puts on its boots. In this age of electronic speed-of-light transmission, misinformation spreads more rapidly than Twain could ever have imagined.

In 1998 a rash of reckless news reports became national news. A CNN and *Time* story alleging that the U.S. military used lethal nerve gas in a 1970 attack on defectors in a small Laotian village during the Vietnam War was retracted, embarrassing both news organizations (Getlin, 1998). This inaccurate story followed close behind other prominent cases of inaccurate or fabricated stories in reputable news media. Patricia Smith, a *Boston Globe* columnist, was fired for inventing quotes in four of her articles. Stephen Glass, a writer for the *New Republic,* was also fired for fabricating 27 stories. The *Dallas Morning News* and the *Wall Street Journal* both apologized to readers for printing an erroneous story that Bill Clinton and Monica Lewinsky had been caught having sex in the Oval Office.

Newsweek columnist Jonathan Alter (1998) succinctly summarized the causes of this proliferation of misinformation reported to the public: "Hype, cyberspeed and 24-hour competition are bringing out journalism's worst this year" (p. 66). Competition comes not just from credible news organizations but also from the more peripheral and questionable outlets, such as gossip on Internet sites, tabloid papers, and talk radio. Robert Lichter, president of the Center for Media and Public Affairs in Washington, D.C., claims that there is too much use of unidentified sources and hearsay by the standard news media. Reporters aren't checking their

facts because of competition to be the first person breaking the story. As Lichter explains, "People are afraid to hold on to every detail for fear that it will show up in the (Internet gossip) Drudge Report or on talk radio" (as cited in Antonucci & Quinn, 1998, p. A12).

Facts should be checked before stories are written or broadcast to avoid reporting misinformation, but the combination of hypercompetitiveness in the news marketplace and the instant accessibility of information from an array of communication technologies has lowered journalistic standards. As Ben Bagdikian, former assistant managing editor for the *Washington Post* and professor of mass media at the University of California, Berkeley explains, "In the past, the degraded standards of non-serious media . . . would get into serious print and serious network news only after going through a careful editorial process. That filtering system has disappeared" (as cited in Antonucci & Quinn, 1998, p. A12).

Competition to break a story ahead of competitors has always been a driving force in the world of journalism, but it has taken on a new dimension. Combine the problems associated with information overload (diminished critical thinking, indecisiveness, and hyperbole) with the hypercompetitiveness in the world of news and you have a formula for the proliferation of misinformation as never before.

Figure 17-1 Competent Communication: Consuming Information

Competent consumer of information

So what can you do about this spread of misinformation? What you can't do reasonably is slow down the transmission of information, censor talk radio and tabloid papers, or reduce competition in the journalistic marketplace. Those are structural changes that bump against constitutional guarantees and consumer choice. The answer lies in becoming a more competent consumer of information (Figure 17-1).

1. *Seek credible sources of information.* Ignore websites from questionable sources. Pay no attention to tabloid stories unless they have been verified by more reputable news sources.
2. *Question the reliability of any story that quotes unidentified sources.* Reputable media increasingly use such dubious sources to compete with peripheral news outlets, but misinformation is easily spread when consumers can't determine the reliability of the information.
3. *Check several reputable sources on controversial or startling facts before drawing a conclusion.* The erroneous story of Bob Hope's death was not reported by all news organizations. CNN didn't report the initial announcement; neither did MSNBC. Reliance on a single source is always shaky.

The proliferation of misinformation will continue and perhaps grow worse in the future. Our only protection from the spread of falsehoods is to become more savvy about the increasing unreliability of even reputable news organizations. We don't have to believe everything we see and hear in the media.

Interpersonal Effects

Communication technologies markedly influence our relationships with others and our lives in general. There are those who argue that e-mail, Internet chatrooms, cell phones, pagers, and fax machines bring us closer together because they increase communication. Others argue that all this technology doesn't create community but disconnection. Let's examine the interpersonal effects of communication technologies.

Social Contact   Most research shows that television watching reduces social contact and involvement (Brody, 1990; Neuman, 1991). The time spent viewing television displaces time spent engaging in social activities with friends and family. Isolation and fragmentation can easily occur when households have more than one TV set. Family members disperse to separate rooms to watch different television programs. Even though television is sometimes viewed in the presence of others, the quality of the social interaction is generally weak (Kraut et al., 1998). Talking during television watching interrupts the viewing. Conversation during commercial breaks invariably gets unplugged once the TV program continues. The social interaction is usually secondary to the television viewing.

Social contact may also be diminished by the use of computers and the Internet. Kraut and his associates (1998) found that, like television viewing, the Internet displaces time that could have been spent with family members and friends in conversation and social activities. This time displacement is particularly serious when Internet use becomes excessive. On June 27, 1999, Kelli Michetti became enraged with her husband Robert for his excessive use of the Internet, especially his chats with women until 4 a.m. several days in a row. Kelli seized a meat cleaver and began whacking power cords on the computer, then started hacking at the computer terminal as her husband struggled with her. Kelli was arrested and charged with domestic violence ("Women Angry," 1999).

Internet addiction has become an increasing problem (Locke, 1998). Cyberaddicts comprise about 10% of Internet users. They average 38 hours a week online and about 4 hours of sleep a night (Baran, 1999). The University of Maryland in College Park began a counseling service for cyberaddicted students called "Caught in the Net." One study at the University of Glasgow in Scotland revealed that 16% of participants admitted they were irritable, restless, depressed, or tense if prevented from going online; 27% felt guilty about the time they spent online; 10% confessed that they neglected a partner, child, or a project at work because of their addiction (as cited in Locke, 1998).

The telephone is often used, especially by teenagers, for social connection. Even phones, however, can be a source of disconnection in ways similar to television and computers. When teens spend hours on the phone with friends, they disassociate themselves from family. When parents spend a great deal of time on the phone talking business, it is time not spent with children and partners. Phone addiction can be as serious a problem as cyberaddiction. The time spent using our technological toys is often time spent away from social contact with significant people in our lives. This can strain relationships and produce disconnection with those we count on for support, affection, and love.

The picture isn't all bad regarding the interpersonal effects of communication technologies. When distance prevents physical contact with friends and family, phones and e-mail are useful substitutes. Parents sometimes purchase computers and connect to the Internet just to remain in touch with a son or daughter at college. Almost 10% of those over age 55 are online (Marcus, 1999). Seniors are filling introductory computer classes. A 3-year study in Sweden, Portugal, Great Britain, and Ireland shows that seniors get a psychological boost from online communication (as cited in Marcus, 1999). They also get important health information. Family therapist Howard Adelman encourages his older patients to use e-mail to counteract loneliness and depression. "Seniors are often depressed, and with depression comes withdrawal. E-mail brings them back to the world" (as cited in Marcus, 1999, p. 62).

Young people also find e-mail particularly useful and engrossing. About 16 million youngsters under the age of 18 have Internet access, and e-mail is their principal online activity (Silver & Perry, 1999). They mostly gossip with friends. America Online offers "Instant Message," a popular service for kids. Users compile a list of friends, all of whom can chat online at the same time as their comments appear on screen. Fourteen-year-old Grace Doherty reveals, "I would totally say so many things online I would never say to someone's face" (as cited in Silver & Perry, 1999, p. 57). That can be good or bad depending on what is said.

Many studies also show that interpersonal relationships are formed online (see especially Park & Floyd, 1995). The depth of these relationships, however, certainly can be questioned, and since there is no physical proximity, you hardly know what is truth and what is fiction. These online friendships, however, are rare, and even if they prove to be quality relationships, they do not counteract the general decline in proximate communication with family and friends (Kraut et al., 1998). Those who are physically and personally close to us tend to suffer most from our overuse of communication technologies.

Conflict "E-mail, and now the Internet and the World Wide Web, are creating networks of human connection unthinkable even a few years ago. But at the same time that technologically enhanced communication enables previously impossible loving contact, it also enhances hostile and distressing communication" (Tannen, 1998, p. 239). A British study of more than a 1,000 office workers found that 46% had reduced their face-to-face communication at work by using e-mail. Thirty-six percent sent messages by e-mail purposely to avoid face-to-face communication (as cited in Locke, 1998). Using e-mail to avoid direct interpersonal contact may produce conflict.

Psychiatrist Esther Gwinnell, author of *Online Seductions*, notes: "E-mail is totally devoid of social cues. It lacks any . . . facial movement, body language, even dress or handwriting. You can learn more from two minutes at a party than from months of E-mail communication" (as cited in Herbert & Hammel, 1999, p. 56). Messages communicated by e-mail can be easily misinterpreted. Sarcasm, for instance, or teasing without the requisite tone of voice, facial expressions, and physical cues that signal how the message should be interpreted can be mistaken for serious personal attacks.

E-mail also reduces the natural constraints on incivility and hostility that come from facing a person directly. **Flaming** is a cyberterm for an abusive, attacking e-mailed message. The same British study just cited found that 51% of the respondents had received flames, 31% had responded with a flame of their own, and 18% revealed that their relationships with fellow workers had disintegrated permanently after the exchange of flaming e-mail messages. The absence of normal constraints on incivility and hostility that come with in-person transactions (such as implicit rules against ugly public displays of anger) coupled with the ease and swiftness of e-mail often combine to the detriment of relationships. As Brin (1998) explains:

> Electronic conversations seem especially prone to misinterpretation, suddenly and rapidly escalating hostility between participants, or else triggering episodes of sulking silence. When flame wars erupt, normally docile people can behave like mental patients. . . . Typing furiously, they send impulsive text messages blurting out the

first vituperation that comes to mind, abandoning the editing process of common courtesy that civilization took millennia to acquire. (p. 166)

Flaming is competitive, defensive communication. Those given to flaming often experience sender's regret—they wish they hadn't sent the angry, emotionally damaging message in the heat of the moment. Once it is sent, however, the damage is done.

So what can you do if using communication technologies severely reduces important social contact with others and increases hostile conflict? Here are two suggestions.

1. *Use communication technologies appropriately; don't overuse them.* Time spent on the Internet can be quite productive. Relationships can be strengthened, information can be shared, and groups with shared interests can be formed. Faculty members sometimes find that students more readily contribute points of view and ideas through e-mail than in class. They aren't intimidated by what their peers will think when the communication is directly between teacher and student. Nevertheless, time spent using communication technologies can severely limit more direct, personal contact with significant people in our lives. If you find that the reduction of personal contact with others has disconnected you from important people in your life and this bothers you, try monitoring your use of technologies. Turn off the computer, the TV set, the radio, or any communication technology that prevents you from engaging others in face-to-face transactions. Sometimes there simply is no substitute for personal, face-to-face contact, as anyone who has tried to conduct a long-distance relationship can attest. You can't hug, caress, and kiss a partner by e-mail, fax, or cell phone.

2. *Delay sending any e-mail message that has strong emotional content.* If you want to avoid sender's regret, delay sending any e-mail message written in the heat of the moment. I make it a standard practice never to send an angry message to anyone until I have reconsidered it at least overnight. I then reread the message the next day before deciding to send, edit, or delete it entirely. Usually, upon reflection, I have chosen to delete the message. Flaming e-mail messages should always be put aside overnight. Never send an angry response to someone else's flame until you have had time to cool down. If an immediate response is required, simply ask for time to reflect on what was said and the way it was said.

Cultural Effects

In 1991 I visited Holland. After a long plane ride and a trip through Customs, I was anxious to find my hotel and relax. Once I found my hotel room and put away some of my things, I switched on the television set. I was surprised to see an episode of *Cheers* playing with Dutch subtitles. I switched channels. CNN was reporting the news in English.

McLuhan talked about the global village created by communication technologies. Probably the biggest impact communication technologies have had on diverse cultures is a steady erosion of cultural integrity. It is difficult to maintain cultural values and viewpoints when an unending barrage of information and images are being transmitted from other cultures. This is sometimes referred to as **cultural imperialism**—"the invasion of an indigenous people's culture

Cultural imperialism, the invasion of an indigenous people's culture by powerful foreign countries through mass media is a real concern of nations worldwide. The Goddess of Liberty statue, remarkably similar to the Statue of Liberty, was made during a student protest in China in 1989. It shows the effect one culture can have on another when information is so readily available.

by powerful foreign countries through mass media" (Baran, 1999, p. 469). We see concern expressed by a wide variety of cultures that their cultural identity is eroding.

CNN transmits to 800 million people in 60 countries. The 1991 Gulf War and NATO's conflict in Yugoslavia in 1999 were viewed all over the world on CNN. The BBC broadcasts all over the world in 40 languages. Radio Beijing from China does likewise. American movies and television programs are widely available worldwide. This is a concern for many cultures bothered by the heavy diet of violence and sex in most U.S. movies and TV series.

Consider just one commonplace example that illustrates the concern other cultures have regarding the ubiquity of the media invasion from the United States. American TV crime programs such as *Law & Order* and *NYPD Blue* apparently are affecting French citizens' perception of proper courtroom procedure. According to a poll in France, most French people think a judge should be addressed as "Your Honor" instead of the customary French form of address, "Mr. President." Many are also demanding warrants when police try to search their homes, even though

Box 17-1   Sharper Focus

China and the Internet

China traditionally has been closed off from the outside world. Anxious to protect its cultural values and way of life, China has severely restricted access to information from both outside and within China. With the development of the Internet, however, China faces a new challenge. Recognizing the growing connection between the Information Age and economic vitality, China has gone online with enthusiasm. About 50 million Chinese have access to the Internet, and the Chinese government is investing $54 billion in the expansion of its telecommunications system (Rubin, 1999).

Chinese officials hope to join the information revolution while controlling access to information that challenges cultural values and political points of view. Security officials block websites of foreign media or dissident Chinese groups outside the country. A Chinese citizen who wishes to access a foreign website must register and pledge not to read or disseminate information that imperils state security (Rubin, 1999). Cyberpolice read e-mail and block websites in most large cities in China.

These attempts to interrupt the free flow of information on the Internet are only partly successful. Banned material can be acquired from within China by accessing "proxy servers," computers located outside of China. Dissident materials can be e-mailed out of the country to proxies who can then send them back to Internet users inside China. At the moment, there is no imminent peril of government collapse from the Internet. In a decade, however, about 100 million Chinese will have access to the Internet. According to Minxin Pei, a scholar at the Carnegie Institute, "Party control of information will totally collapse. There will be a critical mass of informed people penetrating all segments of society, not just the elite. There will be a popularization of the Internet, more communication between groups. Popular resentment will grow" (as cited in Rubin, 1999, p. P7).

What this will mean for China is difficult to predict. What it illustrates, however, is that the expansion and intrusion of communication technologies clearly disrupt cultural stability and the status quo.

---

no warrant is required under French law. These findings prompted a French official to exclaim, "It's a cultural catastrophe! French citizens don't even understand their own legal system anymore" (as cited in "France," 1997, p. 156).

Most countries impose quotas on media content from foreign countries. In 1989, for instance, the European Union mandated that 50% of all programming on European television had to be produced in Europe (Baran, 1999). Restrictions in China, Singapore, and a host of non-Western countries are even more rigid (Box 17-1).

Whether the global village will ultimately prove to be a boon or a bust for the people of the world remains to be seen. Unquestionably, our world will be a very different place as communication technologies become even more widely dispersed and utilized.

Summary

The history of communication technologies shows three trends: the pace of technological change is accelerating, communication technologies are merging, and specialization or demassification is increasing. The consequences of these trends are far reaching. Information overload has become a serious problem. The proliferation of misinformation has become widespread. Our relationships with others have been affected in both positive and negative ways, and cultural integrity has become an issue. The competent communicator still has control over technology.

Control requires monitoring your use of communication technologies, understanding how these technologies influence your daily life, and limiting your use of cell phones, fax machines, television, radio, and the Internet when social contact with family and friends becomes a problem. Communication technologies can solve problems or create new ones. It is ours to choose.

Suggested Readings

Brin, D. (1998). *The transparent society: Will technology force us to choose between privacy and freedom?* Reading, MA: Addison-Wesley. This is an interesting book on how communication technologies have diminished our privacy.

Locke, J. (1998). *The de-voicing of society: Why we don't talk to each other anymore.* New York: Simon & Schuster. The author shows the marked impact communication technologies have had on society and individuals.

Postman, N. (1985). *Amusing ourselves to death: Public discourse in the age of show business.* New York: Viking Penguin. This is a provocative book on the nature of television and its impact on U.S. society. Postman has a definite point of view.

Shenk, D. (1997). *Data smog: Surviving the data glut.* New York: HarperCollins. This is the best work on information overload and its consequences.

Appendix

Interviewing

Interviewing is a common communication event. We interview individuals as potential roommates or housemates. When gathering information for a speech, we may interview experts on the subject. Then, of course, there is the job interview.

In every instance, communication competence is a central element of effective interviewing. In a study by Peterson (1997), all 253 personnel interviewers at small and large businesses agreed that communication ability during an interview has a major effect on hiring decisions. Fewer than 60%, however, believed current job applicants demonstrate even adequate communication skills.

The principal purpose of this appendix is to offer ways to improve your interviewing skills. There are two objectives:

1. to identify common mistakes made during interviews, and
2. to present specific advice that can improve your interviewing skills.

Interviewing is defined as "a purposeful, planned conversation, characterized by extensive verbal interaction" (Peterson, 1997, p. 288). Two kinds of interviewing are discussed here: job interviews and informational interviews. The first type focuses primarily on how to communicate as an interviewee. The second type focuses on how to conduct an effective interview when gathering information.

Job Interviews

Few events are as anxiety-producing and as significant to our lives as a job interview. So much can be riding on such a brief encounter. Communicating competently during a job interview can be crucial to securing a job. In this section, common mistakes and effective communication strategies are addressed.

Interviewing Mistakes

There probably is no such thing as a perfect interview. Communication strategies that work in one interview may not work as well in another. Nevertheless, there are some behaviors that seem destined to torpedo any chance of success when interviewing for a job. Personnel executives have offered examples of actual interviewee communication behaviors that demolished the credibility of job applicants. Here are some examples in the words of the personnel executives (as cited in Miller, 1991):

> "Said if he was hired, he'd teach me ballroom dancing at no charge, and started demonstrating."
>
> "Took three cellular phone calls. Said she had a similar business on the side."
>
> "Applicant walked in and inquired why he was here."
>
> "After a difficult question, she wanted to leave the room for a moment to meditate."
>
> "Candidate was told to take his time answering, so he began writing down each of his answers before speaking."
>
> "Man brought in his five children and cat."
>
> "Wanted to borrow the fax machine to send out some personal letters."
>
> "Brought a mini tape recorder and said he always taped his job interviews."
>
> "Applicant handed me an employment contract and said I'd have to sign it if he was going to be hired."
>
> "She sat in my chair and insisted that I sit in the interviewee's chair."

These examples are clearly cases of clueless communication behavior on the part of interviewees. Peterson (1997), however, identified more typical, less extreme interviewing mistakes. They include weak eye contact, irrelevant response to topic, disorganized response to questions, poor listening skills, unclear response to questions, problems with response fluency, weak voice projection, inadequate volume control, and lack of preparation for the interview.

In addition to these mistakes, interviewees commonly err in general ways during the interview. First, they approach the interview as though it were a sales pitch and they are the product. Most people are mildly, sometimes profoundly, repelled by a hard sell no matter what the product. Using a hard sell to land a job will likely produce a similar response from an interviewer or employment committee. Second, interviewees sometimes attempt to relate their entire life story when answering a question. Too much detail can make interviewers weary and cause their attention to fade. Third, interviewees sometimes try to fake their knowledge and experience by inflating the importance of relatively minor background and accomplishments. If an interviewing committee senses that you are unreasonably padding your résumé, they may doubt your credibility across the board. Fourth, interviewees who are obviously unprepared to answer tough questions have little hope of being chosen for the job.

Competent Interviewing Skills

Anderson and Killenberg (1999) identify three qualities that are necessary for an interview to be a success: empathy, honesty, and respect. Empathy puts us in the position of seeing from the other person's perspective. This is a vital quality for an interviewee. Empathy allows you to anticipate questions that will be asked and to frame answers that will speak to the concerns of those interviewing you. Honesty is vital, because no one is likely to hire a person if the person is not perceived to be candid and straightforward. If a person lies on his or her résumé and the lie is discovered, it can be grounds for immediate dismissal from the position. Embellishing minor accomplishments walks close to the precipice of dishonesty. Respect, the final quality, shows sensitivity and concern. Respect, of course, is a two-way street. Interviewers should show the applicant respect by addressing him or her in a manner that is not demeaning. Similarly, interviewees should show respect for interviewers. Some of the previous examples of clueless behavior during interviews show disrespect for the interviewer. Taking cell phone calls during the interview and taking the interviewer's chair both show disrespect for those who might hire an applicant.

There are several ways to improve your interviewing skills. First, *be prepared.* Do research on the job you seek. Most job announcements specify what experience, skills, and knowledge are essential to the performance of the job. Be prepared to adapt your background to the specific requirements of the job. If the job calls for knowledge of specific software or computer technology, be prepared to list your experience with such software and technology. If the job announcement expressly identifies "effective interpersonal skills" as desirable in an applicant, have a list ready that speaks to this qualification directly. For example, if you have taken a college course in interpersonal communication, if communication is your college major or minor, if you have taken any workshops in conflict management or couples communication, or if you have conducted workshops or classes in interpersonal communication, list these on your résumé. Have these examples ready in case you are asked questions on such background during the interview.

Second, *rehearse for your interview.* Have a friend ask typical interview questions. Some examples might be:

What are your strengths and weaknesses?
Why did you apply for this particular job?
Why did you leave your previous job?
Have you ever had difficulty working for a boss or supervisor?
What problems did you encounter at your last position?
Where would you like to be professionally in 5 years?
What's the worst job you've ever had?
Would you have difficulty contradicting your boss if you thought he or
    she was about to make a bad decision?
Do you work well on a team?
Have you had good or bad experiences working in groups?

Frame your answers as positive learning experiences and positive reflections on your work ethic and determination to excel. For example, the question "Have you ever had difficulty working for a boss?" could be answered this way: "Yes, and it taught me a lot about how to deal with difficult people . . ." "Where would you like to be professionally in 5 years?" could be answered, "I'd like to have my work recognized and receive a promotion because of it." You certainly don't want to answer such a question by indicating that the job you are seeking is merely a stepping stone to a better position elsewhere. Honesty doesn't require an answer that wasn't sought.

Third, *look and act the part of a credible candidate for the job.* Professional jobs require professional attire. Show that you care about the position by arriving on time, appearing well-groomed, neat, and dressed in professional clothing. During the interview, speak so everyone can easily hear you. Listen carefully to all questions, and if in doubt, ask for clarification or elaboration. Answer questions directly, and eliminate nervous mannerisms (tapping fingers on the table, cracking knuckles, twirling hair, tapping a pen or pencil, or biting nails). Humor is often welcomed, but avoid sarcasm or ethnic humor. Self-deprecating humor often works well as long as it doesn't diminish your qualifications for the position. Establish direct eye contact with the interviewer. If a panel conducts the interview, establish initial eye contact with the panel member who asks you the questions, then gradually direct your eyes to all panel members as you develop your answer. Do not express anger or hostility for previous bosses that have "done you wrong." Interviewers are looking for composure as an indicator of credibility. Speak fluently. Avoid long vocal pauses and disfluencies (uhm, uh, you know, like). Don't be reticent to smile, look friendly, or demonstrate enthusiasm for the position.

Fourth, *provide sufficient elaboration when answering questions.* Very brief answers ("Yes, I did that") with no detail provided leave interviewers guessing about your qualifications for the position. Successful applicants for jobs use focused elaboration when asked questions (Anderson & Killenberg, 1999). This means they provide considerable detail when answering questions, and the detail is always directly relevant to the question asked. Unsuccessful applicants usually provide no elaboration, or their answers drift to irrelevant experiences, stories, or knowledge. When providing detail, look for signals from interviewers that indicate that you've answered the question sufficiently. When interviewers glaze over, fidget, glance around the room, stare at a pencil, look at the clock, or shift in their chair, it is usually time to wrap up your answer.

Fifth, *organize your answers.* If you have prepared sufficiently for the interview, most questions asked should elicit a clear, outlined answer. "What experience do you have working with individuals from diverse cultural backgrounds?" might be one question asked. A possible answer might be, "I've worked with three very diverse groups. At Datacom West, a third of the workers were Asian. When I worked at Silicon Software, several of the workers I supervised were from India and Pakistan. When I ran my own printing business, most of my workers were either African American or Jewish. As you can see, I've worked with a rich mixture of ethnic groups, and I feel such diversity has produced synergy."

Sixth, *provide sufficient evidence of your qualifications for the job.* Behavioral interviewing is becoming increasingly popular, especially in the business world. **Behavioral interviewing** occurs when interviewers ask for specific examples of behavior by an applicant that illustrates an answer (Eng, 1997). Here are some typical behavioral interviewing questions:

> Describe a time when you tried to persuade a person or group to do something they opposed.
> Give an example of a time when you faced many obstacles to achieving a goal and explain how you handled the situation.
> Identify a stressful experience and discuss how you dealt with it.
> Describe a conflict you've had with a fellow worker.
> Tell us about a time when you had to meet strict deadlines.
> Provide an example of a situation where you were forced to make an important decision without adequate information.

All of these questions seek evidence of your skills on the job. These behavioral questions reveal an applicant's knowledge of real-life situations. Be prepared to provide specific evidence of your talents and abilities. Brainstorm examples that illustrate your strengths. Use the **STAR interviewing method** for answering such behavioral questions. **ST** stands for situation/task, **A** is action, and **R** stands for result. Thus, you identify the situation or task, explain what action you took, and describe what resulted from that action.

Seventh, *be prepared to ask relevant questions of interviewers.* An interview is a conversation not an interrogation. Unlike a witness in a court trial, you have a right to ask questions of your interviewers. Your interviewers want to know if you are right for the job, but you also want to know if the job is right for you. Use the behavioral interviewing technique when asking questions of your interviewers. Don't ask "Do people get promoted in this company?" Instead ask "Can you give me an example of the last person to receive a promotion and how that person earned it?"

Informational Interview

You won't always be in the position of answering questions during an interview. There will be times when it is you who conducts the interview. You may need important information on a speech topic or group assignment, and the only way to acquire the information is to interview an expert on the subject. How you conduct that interview will determine how much useful information you gather.

Preparation

A newspaper reporter doesn't just walk into an interview with no idea what he or she hopes to gain from questioning someone. A reporter prepares in advance by doing background research and making a list of questions that can serve as a basis for the interview. Similarly, when you plan to interview someone to gather information for a speech assignment, prepare much as a newspaper reporter would prepare. Remember that this is a conversation, but a conversation with a specific focus.

Let's say that you are researching the parking problem on campus. You haven't been able to find much information on the subject other than anecdotal complaints from students and faculty about the difficulties finding a parking space. You decide that you need to interview several individuals who might be able to provide solid evidence of the problem and offer possible solutions. Research who might be the best, most knowledgeable individuals to interview on the subject. Know in advance what you hope to find out from the interview. Bring a list of thoughtful and relevant questions with you. Here are some questions that you might ask on the parking problem:

How many total parking spaces are there on campus?
How many parking permits have been issued?
How many additional parking spaces are needed on campus?
How do you determine the number of additional spaces required?
Are there alternatives to adding parking spaces? If so, what are they?
Why haven't these alternatives been implemented?

These questions are specific and focused directly on the problem. They, of course, do not constitute an exhaustive list of possible relevant questions you could ask on this subject. Answers you receive from the interviewee often trigger additional follow-up questions. You might finish the interview with an open-ended question such as, "Is there anything else you would like to add on this subject?"

Conducting the Interview

How you conduct the interview can be as important as the questions you ask. After scheduling an appointment with the person, there are several ways to conduct the interview so it will be productive. First, *remember that this is not an interrogation.* It is a conversation. You need information. You are not likely to get much information if you make the interviewee defensive. Review the differences between defensive and supportive communication patterns discussed in Chapter 8. You want to stay away from evaluation, blame, and criticism. You don't want to ask a question such as, "You're in charge of student services on campus. Why haven't you done something about the parking problem?" This puts the interviewee on the defensive and creates a competitive, uncomfortable interpersonal climate that is not conducive to gathering information. Instead, you might ask "As someone who has to deal with student complaints about parking on campus, what are some of the reasons the parking problem seems to grow worse each year?"

Second, *be warm and friendly during the interview.* Make the interview a cordial conversation. Most individuals are anxious to provide information in their area of expertise if they feel friendly toward the interviewer.

Third, *state your purpose at the beginning of the interview.* Make certain that the goal of the interview is clear to the interviewee. That will likely prevent irrelevant conversation on tangential issues.

Fourth, *remain attentive at all times during the interview.* If your attention fades during the interviewee's answer, you show indifference. This will produce defensiveness. Maintain direct eye contact, encourage elaboration from the interviewee, and demonstrate attentiveness by asking follow-up questions based on the interviewee's answers.

Fifth, *take notes during the interview.* Don't rely on your memory to recall facts and statistics. If your interviewee has a report or printed material on the subject that would be helpful, ask if you can have a copy. Sometimes you can tape the interview, but many people prefer an unrecorded conversation. A tape recorder can cause an interviewee to be more cautious and careful when responding to questions.

Sixth, *ask both open- and closed-ended questions.* Open-ended questions allow an interviewee room to discuss an issue. Closed-ended questions require only a yes or no response or a very specific answer and can seem like an interrogation, not a conversation. Both types of questions are useful. You do want to know how many parking spaces are on campus (closed-ended). You also want the interviewee to explore possible solutions to the parking problem (open-ended).

Seventh, *stay within time limits.* Try to specify the length of the interview before meeting with the person. If you need 15 minutes, ask for 15. If the interview needs to go beyond the agreed upon time limit, ask the interviewee for more time. This shows respect for the person interviewed.

Eighth, *thank the interviewee for his or her time.* The interviewee has done you a favor by granting the interview, so acknowledge that fact at the end.

Summary

Interviews are important events in our lives. The job interview is the most common type, but the informational interview is probably a close second. An interview is a purposeful, planned conversation characterized by extensive verbal interaction. Empathy, respect, and honesty should embue every interview. Preparation is a major element of an interview both from the standpoint of the interviewee and the interviewer. The interview should be focused. Questions and answers should be direct, relevant, and purposeful.

Glossary

abstracting Process of selective perception in which we leave out characteristics associated with objects, events, and ideas and focus on certain perceived common characteristics.

accommodating Communication style of conflict management characterized by yielding to the needs and desires of others during a conflict.

alliteration Repetition of the same sound, usually a consonant sound, starting each of several words.

analog Physical duplication of a sound or picture created by electrical signals that mimic the original.

antithesis Stylistic device that uses opposites to create impact.

appropriateness Avoiding violating social or interpersonal norms, rules, or expectations.

argument Chief reason offered to support a proposition.

assertiveness Ability to communicate the full range of thoughts and emotions with confidence and skill.

assimilation Absorption of one group's culture into the dominant culture.

attention Focused awareness on a stimulus at a given moment.

attitude Learned predisposition to respond favorably or unfavorably toward some attitude object.

avoiding Communication style of conflict management that sidesteps or turns away from conflict.

behavioral interviewing Interviewer asks for specific examples of a behavior by an applicant that illustrates an answer.

binary digits Zeros and ones sequenced to represent different meanings.

bits Strings of binary digits that serve as a code or symbolic representation of meaning.

brainstorming Creative problem-solving method characterized by encouragement of even zany ideas, freedom from initial evaluation of potential solutions, and energetic participation from all group members.

burden of proof Obligation of the claimant to support any claim he or she makes using evidence and reasoning.

by-passing Making an assumption that all parties share the same meaning for a word without determining whether this is true.

captive audience Listeners who gather to hear a speech because they are compelled to, not because they expect entertainment or intellectual stimulation.

casual audience Listeners picked to act as an audience because they happen to be milling about or passing by and hear a speaker, stop out of curiosity or casual interest, and remain until bored or sated.

channel Medium through which a message travels, such as oral or written channels.

charisma Constellation of personal attributes that people find attractive.

chilling effect Partner low in power avoids discussion of issues with his or her abusive partner that might trigger aggression.

claims Generalizations that require support.

co-culture Group of people who live in a dominant culture yet remain connected to another cultural heritage that may be quite different from the dominant culture.

coalition Temporary alliances of individuals to increase their power relative to others.

cognitive dissonance Theory of persuasion based on the view that unpleasant psychological tension that results from inconsistent beliefs or a contradiction between beliefs and behavior motivates us to become more consistent.

cohesiveness Degree of liking we have for members of a group, and the level of commitment to the group that this liking produces.

collaborating Communication style of conflict management characterized by parties working together to maximize the attainment of goals for all parties in a conflict.

commitment Conscious decision to invest in another person to nourish and sustain a relationship.

committed audience Listeners who voluntarily assemble to hear a speaker because they want to invest time and energy listening to the speaker's thoughts and being inspired by his or her words.

communication Transactional process of sharing meaning with others.

communication competence Ability to communicate in a personally effective and socially appropriate manner.

communication orientation Method for controlling speech anxiety that focuses on making the message clear and interesting while deemphasizing the performance aspects of giving a speech.

communication skill Successful performance of a communication behavior and the ability to repeat such a behavior.

communication style of conflict management Typical way a person addresses conflict.

competing style Communication style of conflict management that is a power-forcing effort to win a conflict by use of threats, criticism, contempt, hostile remarks, sarcasm, ridicule, intimidation, fault-finding, blaming, or denials of responsibility.

competition Process of mutually exclusive goal attainment.

compromising Communication style of conflict management where participants give up something to get something.

concerned audience Listeners who gather voluntarily to hear a speaker because they care about issues and ideas and want to learn from the speaker.

confirmation bias Psychological tendency to look for and listen to information that supports our beliefs and values and to ignore or distort information that contradicts our beliefs and values.

conflict Expressed struggle of interconnected parties who perceive incompatible goals and interference from one or more parties in attaining those goals.

conformity Inclination of group members to think and behave in ways that are consistent with group norms.

confrontation Overt recognition of conflict and the direct effort to find creative ways to satisfy all parties in a conflict.

connection Key dimension of conversation characterized by a desire to bond with others that encourages interdependence, cooperation, and empowerment.

connection-autonomy dialectic Dialectic that pushes us toward coming together with another person while simultaneously pulling us toward remaining apart, independent, and in control of our life.

connotation Volatile, private, subjective meaning of symbols.

consensus State of mutual agreement among members of a group where all legitimate concerns of individuals have been addressed to the satisfaction of the group.

constructive conflict Conflict characterized by a We-orientation, cooperation, and flexibility.

content dimension Dimension of a message that includes what is actually said and done.

content-only response Response by a listener who focuses on the content of a message but ignores the emotional side of the communication.

context Environment where communication occurs.

continuous change Extensions of previous decisions in teams.

control Communication that seeks to regulate or direct a person's behavior.

conventionality-uniqueness dialectic Dialectic that pushes us to want our relationship with another person to be viewed by outsiders as fitting societal norms yet pulled to have it viewed as special and unlike any other.

convergence Similarities that connect us to others.

conversational narcissism Tendency of listeners to turn the topics of ordinary conversations to themselves without showing sustained interest in the topics of others.

cooperation Process of mutually inclusive goal attainment.

correlation Consistent relationship between two variables.

credibility Judgments made by a perceiver concerning the believability of a communicator.

cue Anything that triggers meaning.

cultural imperialism Invasion of an indigenous people's culture by powerful foreign countries through mass media.

cultural relativism View that cultures are merely different and that these differences should not translate into perceptions of deficiencies.

culture Learned set of shared interpretations about beliefs, values, and norms that affect the behavior of a relatively large group.

cynics Individuals set on finding fault with others and tearing down and ridiculing the ideas and values of others.

dead-level abstracting Practice of freezing on one level of abstraction.

defensive response Reaction to a perceived attack on our self-concept, self-esteem, or self-identity.

defiance Overt, unambiguous, purposeful noncompliance.

demassification Increasing specialization applied to communication technologies.

demographics Characteristics of an audience such as age, gender, culture, ethnicity, and group affiliations.

denotation Objective meaning of symbols shared by members of a speech community.

descriptions Verbal reports that sketch what we perceive from our senses; also a supportive communication pattern.

destructive conflict Conflict characterized by escalation, retaliation, domination, competition, cross-complaining, and inflexibility.

dialectics Contradictory impulses in relationships with others that push and pull us in conflicting directions.

directive style Originally called autocratic, this leadership style puts heavy emphasis on the task dimension of groups with slight attention to the social dimension.

discontinuous change decisions Major changes that depart significantly from the direction a team is currently taking.

display rules Culture-specific prescriptions that dictate appropriateness of nonverbal cues such as facial expressions and gestures.

disruptive roles Roles that serve individual needs at the expense of group needs and goals.

divergence Differences that separate people.

dogmatism Belief in the self-evident truth of one's opinion.

dominance Exercise of power over others.

dysfunctional speech anxiety Intensity of the fight or flight response prevents an individual from performing appropriately.

effectiveness How well you progress toward achievement of goals.

elaboration likelihood model (ELM) Model that identifies two paths to persuasion, a central route that requires mindfulness or the careful scrutiny of reasoning and evidence and a peripheral route that is relatively mindless and given to considering credibility, likability, and attractiveness of a persuader and how others react to the message.

emblems Gestures that have precise meanings separate from verbal communication.

empathy Thinking and feeling what an individual perceives another person to be thinking and feeling.

empowerment Having enough power to accomplish your own goals or to help others attain theirs.

equivocation Using language that permits more than one plausible meaning.

ethics Application of a set of standards for judging the moral correctness of a communication behavior.

ethnocentrism View that one's own culture is central to perceptions of the world and that all other cultures should be judged in reference to it.

ethos Aristotle's term for credibility of a speaker composed of good sense, good moral character, and goodwill.

euphemism Kinder, gentler term that substitutes for words that hurt, cause offense, or create problems for us.

evaluations Value judgments made about individuals and their performance.

fallacy An error in evidence or reasoning.

false dichotomy An either-or choice stated in the language of opposing possibilities when more than two opposing possibilities clearly exist.

feedback Receiver's verbal and nonverbal responses to a message.

fields of experience Cultural background, ethnicity, geographic location, extent of travel, and general experiences accumulated over the course of a lifetime that influence the perception of messages.

flaming A cyberterm for an abusive, attacking e-mail message.

flooding When you can no longer think clearly because conflict triggers emotional reactions that clog the brain's ability to reason.

forgiveness Letting go of feelings of revenge and desires to retaliate.

formal roles Roles that assign a position such as president or chair.

framing Using language to shape meaning for others.

functional speech anxiety Fight or flight response is managed and stimulates an optimum performance.

fundamental attribution error Overestimating dispositional (traits) and underestimating situational (environment) causes of other people's behavior.

gender Social role behavior that differentiates men and women.

glass ceiling Invisible barrier of subtle discrimination that excludes women from top leadership positions in corporate and professional America.

gobbledygook Incomprehensible language used to confuse.

grammar Set of linguistic rules that specify how sound, structure, and meaning interrelate.

graph Visual representation of statistics in an easily understood format.

group Three or more individuals interacting for the achievement of some common purpose who influence and are influenced by one another.

grouphate Negative view of working in groups.

groupthink Process of group members stressing cohesiveness and agreement instead of skepticism and optimum decision making.

hasty generalization Broad claim based on too few or unrepresentative examples.

hearing Physiological activity of registering soundwaves as they hit the eardrum.

high-context style Implicit style of communication where the meaning of messages is determined largely from the unspoken cultural context.

hostile environment sexual harassment Atmosphere at work and sometimes in educational environments that creates the perception of insult, ridicule, or intimidation from sexual messages.

hyperbole Exaggeration for effect that is not meant to be taken literally.

hypercompetitiveness Excessive emphasis on beating others to achieve one's goals.

hypothetical examples Examples that describe an imaginary situation concocted to make a point, illustrate an idea, or identify a general principle.

identification Affiliation and connection between speaker and listeners.

illustrators Gestures that help explain what a person says to another person.

inclusion-seclusion dialectic Dialectic that pushes us to include outsiders in our lives while pulling us to spend time alone with our partner.

individual accountability Providing consequences for performance that ensure that everyone honors their agreements and commitments in relationships and groups.

individual achievement Realization of personal goals obtained without having to defeat an opponent.

individualism-collectivism dimension Continuum distinguishing cultures on the basis of their emphasis on the individual or the group.

inferences Statements about the unknown based on the known.

inferential error Assumption that inferences are factual descriptions of reality instead of interpretations made by individuals.

informal roles Roles that identify functions.

informational listening Listening for comprehension of a speaker's message.

integration Collaborative strategy that meets the goals of all parties in a conflict.

intensity Concentrated stimuli; an extreme degree of emotion, thought, or activity.

interdependence All parties rely on each other to achieve goals.

internal summary Restatement in the body of a speech of a key point or points made by a speaker.

interrupting One person stops speaking because another person starts speaking.

interviewing A purposeful, planned conversation, characterized by extensive verbal interaction.

jargon Specialized language of a profession, trade, or group.

judgments Subjective evaluations of objects, events, or ideas.

knowledge Understanding what is required by the communication context.

language Structured system of symbols that communicates meaning.

leadership Transactional influence process whose principal purpose is group goal achievement produced by competent communication.

legitimate authority Person who is perceived to have a right to direct others' behavior because of his or her position, title, role, experience, or knowledge.

lexicon Total vocabulary of a language.

listening Process of receiving, constructing (and reconstructing) meaning from, and responding to spoken or nonverbal messages.

logos Aristotle's term for the use of logic and evidence to persuade listeners.

low-context style Explicit style of communication where messages are clearly spelled out to avoid ambiguity.

maintenance roles Roles that address the social dimensions of small groups.

manipulators Gestures made by one part of the body, usually the hands, rubbing, picking, squeezing, cleaning, or grooming another part of the body.

message Stimulus that produces meaning.

metaphor Implied comparison of two seemingly dissimilar things.

mindfulness Paying attention to our thinking and behavior.

misattribution Attribution about the reason for an event given by a foreigner that differs from that typically given by a member of the host culture.

mislabeling Applying a verbal map to an incorrect territory; unconventional usage and application of words used to categorize people, objects, and events.

mixed message Inconsistency between verbal and nonverbal messages.

mondegreens Mishearing phonemes and constructing odd phrases and sentences, usually related to song lyrics.

Monroe's motivated sequence Persuasive organizational pattern with five steps: attention, need, satisfaction, visualization, and action.

morpheme Smallest unit of meaning in a spoken language such as words, prefixes, and suffixes.

Murphy's Law Anything that can go wrong likely will go wrong.

negative synergy Product of joint action of group members that produces a worse result than expected based on perceived individual abilities and skills of members.

negativity bias Strong tendency to weigh negative information more heavily than positive information.

neutrality Indifference toward others.

neutralizing Dialectical strategy where opposing impulses are both partially satisfied.

niches Specialized segments of an audience targeted by communication media.

noise Any interference with effective transmission and reception of a message.

nominal group technique Creative problem-solving technique where team members brainstorm without group participation and make decisions based on averaged rankings.

nonverbal communication Sharing meaning with others nonlinguistically.

norms Rules that indicate what group members have to do (obligation), should do (preference), or cannot do (prohibition) if they want to accomplish specific goals.

openness-closedness dialectic Dialectic that pushes us toward self-disclosure with a partner while pulling us toward keeping private and secret.

operational definition Specifies what to do or observe to bring the word into one's experience; observable or measurable definition of a term.

parallel construction The similar arrangements of words, phrases, or sentences.

paraphrasing Concise response to the speaker that states the essence of the other's content in the listener's words.

participative style Originally called democratic, this leadership style places emphasis on both the task and social dimensions of groups.

pathos Aristotle's term for emotional appeals used to persuade listeners.

pattern recognition Coping with information overload by piecing together seemingly unrelated information into a plan, design, or whole picture.

perception Process of selecting, organizing, and interpreting data from our senses.

perception checking Finding out whether our perceptions, influenced by gender, culture, sensory limitations, and sets, are accurate.

perceptual set Tendency to perceive a stimulus in a fixed way as the result of an expectation.

persuasion Communication process of converting, modifying, or maintaining the attitudes, beliefs, or behavior of others.

phonemes Sounds that make up a spoken language consisting of vowels, consonants, and blends of the two.

physical noise External distractions that interfere with the effective transmission and reception of messages, such as startling sounds or poorly heated rooms.

physiological noise Biological influences that interfere with the effective transmission and reception of a message, such as sweaty palms, pounding heart, or butterflies in the stomach.

power Ability to influence the attainment of goals sought by yourself or others.

power-distance dimension Dimension that distinguishes cultures on the basis of variations in the acceptability of unequal distribution of power in relationships, institutions, and organizations.

power resource Anything that enables individuals to achieve their goals.

predictability-novelty dialectic Dialectic that pushes and pulls us toward stability and change simultaneously.

prevention Efforts to keep others from exercising power over us.

primacy effect The tendency to perceive information presented first as more important than later information, especially when evaluating others.

primary groups Groups such as family and friends that can provide warmth, affection, support, and a sense of belonging.

principle of least interest The person who cares less about continuing a relationship has more power.

productivity Goal of the task dimension of groups; the degree to which the group accomplishes its work efficiently and effectively.

proposition Primary, overriding claim for a persuasive speech that defines and focuses the argumentation, limits the issues that are relevant, and sets standards for what should be addressed.

provisionalism Use of qualifiers to avoid absolute statements.

psychological noise Preconceptions, biases, and assumptions that interfere with the effective transmission and reception of messages.

psychological reactance Theory that the more someone tries to control our behavior and restrict our choices, the more we are inclined to resist or defy such efforts or to be attracted to that which is prohibited, especially if we feel entitled to choose.

purpose statement Concise, precise declarative statement phrased in simple, clear language that states both the general goal and the central idea of a speech.

quid pro quo sexual harassment The more powerful person requires sexual favors from the less powerful individual in exchange for keeping a job, getting a high grade in a class, landing an employment promotion, or the like.

random sample Portion of the population studied that is chosen in such a manner that every member of the entire population has an equal chance of being selected.

readiness Ability of group members, their motivation, and their experience with relevant tasks.

real examples Actual occurrences that a speaker can use to make a point, illustrate an idea, or identify a general principle.

receiver Decoder or "translator" of a message.

recency effect Tendency to evaluate others on the basis of the most recent information or evidence available.

referents That to which a symbol makes reference.

reframing Dialectical strategy that takes a seeming contradiction between two impulses and looks at it from a different frame of reference.

refutation Process of answering opposing arguments during a persuasive speech.

relationship dimension How the message defines or redefines the association between individuals.

resistance Covert, ambiguous noncompliance.

response styles Initial way a person reacts when another person comes to us with a problem.

revelation-concealment dialectic Dialectical dilemma concerning how much to let outsiders know about our personal relationships and how much to keep private.

rhetorical question Question asked by a speaker that the audience answers mentally but not out loud.

role fixation Group member plays a role rigidly with little or no inclination to try other roles.

roles Patterns of behavior that group members are expected to exhibit.

rule A followable prescription that indicates what behavior is obligated, preferred, or prohibited in certain contexts.

Sapir-Whorf hypothesis Language molds habits of thought and perception, and different languages steer speakers toward different perceptions of reality.

segmenting Dialectical strategy where partners categorize certain parts of their relationship for special treatment.

selecting Dialectical strategy where one contradictory impulse is given attention while the other impulse is ignored.

selective memory bias Tendency to remember information that supports our stereotypes but forget information that contradicts them.

self-concept Sum total of everything that encompasses the self-referential term "me."

self-disclosure Process of purposely revealing to others information about ourselves that they would not otherwise know.

self-esteem Individual's self-appraisal, perception of worth, attractiveness, and social competence.

self-help/support groups Groups whose purpose is to empower individuals to deal with addictive behavior, physical or mental illness, or make life transitions.

self-reflexiveness Using words about words, such as describing language functions by using language.

self-selected sample Population sample studied that comes from voluntary participation from anyone interested, aroused, or committed enough to contribute.

self-serving bias Tendency to attribute our successes or good fortune to ourselves but our failures or bad fortune to external circumstances.

semantic noise Word choice that is confusing or distracting, such as racist, sexist, or homophobic references that interfere with the effective transmission and reception of messages.

sender Initiator and encoder of a message.

sense experience What we perceive with our senses at the first level of the abstraction process.

sensitivity An aspect of communication competence characterized by an ability to pick up signals coming from others and treating others as you would have them treat you.

sensory acuity Level of sensitivity of our senses.

service groups Groups established to help others.

sex Biological differences between men and women.

shift response Competitive vying for attention and focus on self by shifting topics.

signal reaction Automatic and unreflective response to a symbol.

signposts Organizational markers that indicate the structure of a speech and notify listeners that a particular point is about to be addressed.

simile Explicit comparison of two seemingly dissimilar things using the words "like" or "as."

skepticism Process of examining claims, evaluating evidence and reasoning, and drawing conclusions based on probabilities.

smoothing Calming the agitated feelings of others during a conflict episode.

social dimension Relationships between group members and the impact these relationships have on a group.

social groups Hobby or special interest groups where members share a common purpose or pursue common goals.

social judgment theory Theory of persuasion that claims listeners compare a persuasive message to a preexisting attitude, or anchor and posits that the further away the persuasive message is from the anchor the less likely persuasion will occur.

social loafing Tendency of individuals to reduce their work effort when they join groups.

speech anxiety When an individual reports he or she is afraid to deliver a speech.

standardization Formal rules of correct grammar and pronunciation of a language.

STAR interviewing method Identify the situation or task, explain what action you took, and describe what resulted from that action.

status Key dimension of conversation characterized by hierarchical distinctions that encourage independence, competitiveness, and desire for control.

stereotypes Preconceived perceptions of others.

stonewalling Exhibiting stoney silence, monosyllabic mutterings, refusal to discuss problems, or physical removal when one partner is complaining.

strategic communication Manipulative attempt by one person to maneuver another toward the manipulator's goal.

study groups Groups of individuals who gather to share knowledge and understanding on topics of mutual concern.

style Speaker's choice of words to express thoughts and bring those thoughts to life for an audience.

support response Cooperative effort to focus attention on the other person.

symbol reaction Delayed, reflective response to words.

symbols Arbitrary representations of objects, events, ideas, and relations that can produce ambiguous meaning.

syndication Licensing TV programs to mass market stations on a program-by-program basis.

synergy Group process that occurs when group members work together that yields a greater total effect than the sum of the individual members' efforts could have produced.

syntax Grammatical rules that specify how words are combined to form meaningful sentences.

systematic desensitization A method for controlling speech anxiety that involves incremental exposure to increasingly threatening stimuli coupled with relaxation techniques.

table An orderly depiction of statistics, words, or symbols in columns or rows.

task dimension Work performed by the group and its impact on a group.

task roles Roles that advance the attainment of group goals.

team Small number of people with complementary skills who are equally committed to a common purpose, goal, and working approach for which they hold themselves mutually accountable.

teamwork Process of team members exercising competent communication.

technology Tool to accomplish some purpose.

testimonial Praising a product that you have used.

thinking Manipulation of mental representations to reach a conclusion, which includes mental imagery, concepts, problem solving, and decision making.

traits Relatively enduring characteristics of a person that exhibit differences between people.

transitions Words or phrases that connect what was said with what will be said.

true believer Person who willingly accepts claims by authorities or valued sources without question.

turning points Key changes that move a cross-cultural relationship forward, such as sharing an interest, disclosing a personal secret, or requesting a favor.

Twenty Percent Rule Discrimination decreases when at least 20% of the group is composed of women and minorities.

vividness effect Graphic, outrageous, shocking, controversial, and dramatic events that distort our perception of the facts.

work teams Self-managed groups that work on specific tasks or projects within an organization.

World Wide Web Graphical portion of the Internet that permits computer users with appropriate software to view photos, drawings, video, and text.

zero-sum contest Adversarial confrontation where the amount of your gain is equal to another's loss.

References

Abell, G. (1981). Astrology. In G. Abell & B. Seiger (Eds.), *Science and the paranormal*. New York: Charles Scribner's Sons.

Abramson, J. (1998, November 20). Starr: A man with two missions. *San Jose Mercury News*, p. A16.

Adelmann, P. (1995). Why don't men do more housework? A job characteristics exploration of gender and housework satisfaction. *Center for Urban Affairs and Policy Research*. (Working paper.)

Adler, J. E. (1998, January/February). Open minds and the argument from ignorance. *Skeptical Inquirer*, 41–44.

Adler, J., & Springen, K. (1999, May 3). How to fight back, *Newsweek*, 36–38.

Adler, M. J. (1983). *How to speak, how to listen*. New York: Macmillan.

Adler, R. (1977). *Confidence in communication: A guide to assertive and social skills*. New York: Holt, Rinehart & Winston.

Adler, R., & Towne, N. (1999). *Looking out, looking in*. Fort Worth, TX: Harcourt Brace.

Advertising is hazardous to your health. (1986, July). *University of California, Berkeley Wellness Letter*, 1–2.

Aguayo, R. (1990). *Dr. Deming: The American who taught the Japanese about quality*. New York: Simon & Schuster.

Ahrons, C. (1994). *The good divorce: Keeping your family together when your marriage comes apart*. New York: Harper Perennial.

Allen, G. (1996). Military drug testing. *Winning Orations*, 80–83.

Allen, M. (1991). Comparing the persuasiveness of one-sided and two-sided messages using meta-analysis. *Western Journal of Speech Communication, 55*, 390–404.

Allen, M. (1993). Determining the persuasiveness of one- and two-sided messages. In M. Allen & R. Preiss (Eds.), *Prospects and precautions in the use of meta-analysis*. Dubuque, IA: Brown & Benchmark.

Alter, J. (1998, July 13). Something in the coffee. *Newsweek*, 66.

Altman, I., & Taylor, D. (1973). *Social penetration: The development of interpersonal relationships*. New York: Holt, Rinehart & Winston.

Amato, P., & Loomis, L. (1995). Parental divorce, marital conflicts, and offspring well-being during early adulthood. *Social Forces, 73*, 895–915.

Amoral majority "fesses up." (1991, April 19). *San Jose Mercury News*, p. A1.

Amparano, J. (1997, January 23). Taking good care of workers pays off. *The Arizona Republic*, pp. E1, E3.

An intense look at alternative medicine. (1998, November 11). *San Jose Mercury News*, p. A5.

Anatomy of a massacre. (1999, May 3). *Newsweek*, 25–31.

Andersen, P. (1999). *Nonverbal communication: Forms and functions*. Mountain View, CA: Mayfield.

Andersen, P., Murphy, M., & Wendt-Wasca, N. (1985). Teachers' reports of students' nonverbal communication in the classroom: A development study in grades K–12. *Communication Education, 34*, 292–307.

Andersen, P., Todd-Mancillas, W., & Di-Clemente, L. (1980). The effects of pupil dilation on physical, social, and task attraction. *Australian Scan: Journal of Human Communication, 7 & 8*, 89–95.

Anderson, N. (1981). *Foundations of information integration theory*. New York: Academic Press.

Anderson, R., & Killenberg, G. (1999). *Interviewing: Speaking, listening, and learning for professional life*. Mountain View, CA: Mayfield.

Anderson, R., & Ross, V. (1994). *Questions on communications: A practical introduction to theory*. New York: St. Martin's Press.

Ansen, D. (1997, July 14). The all American hero: James Stewart, 1908–1997. *Newsweek*, 74–78.

Antonucci, M. (1998, June 6). Hope's alive and quipping. *San Jose Mercury News*, p. A1.

Antonucci, M., & Quinn, M. (1998, January 27). Media accused of reckless reporting. *San Jose Mercury News*, p. A12.

Aronson, E. (1976). *The social animal*. San Francisco: W. H. Freeman.

At the beep, USC fires Robinson. (1997, December 18). *San Jose Mercury News*, p. D2.

Ayres, J., & Hopf, T. (1995). *Coping with speech anxiety.* Norwood, NJ: Ablex.

Bach, G., & Goldberg, H. (1972). *Creative aggression.* New York: Avon.

Bahrick, H. P. (1984). Semantic memory content in permastore: Fifty years of memory for Spanish learned in school. *Journal of Experimental Psychology, 113,* 1–35.

Bailey, B. (1996, November 2). Perot says Clinton's promises are like vows of a bank robber. *San Jose Mercury News,* p. A21.

Balgopal, P., Ephross, P., & Vassil, T. (1992). Self-help groups and professional helpers. In R. Cathcart & L. Samovar (Eds.), *Small group communication: A reader.* Dubuque, IA: Wm. C. Brown.

Baran, S. (1999). *Introduction to mass communication: Media literacy and culture.* Mountain View, CA: Mayfield.

Barker, L., Edwards, C., Davis, K., & Holly, F. (1981). An investigation of proportional time spent in various communication activities by college students. *Journal of Applied Communication Research, 8,* 101–109.

Barnard, B. (1994, August 6). Could you cheer for the Denver Darkies? *Desert News,* p. A9.

Barnett, T. (1996, April 19). A clean slate, a fresh start. *Santa Cruz Sentinel,* p. A2.

Baron, R. A. (1988). Negative effects of destructive criticism: Impact on conflict self-efficacy, and task performance. *Journal of Applied Psychology, 73,* 199–207.

Baron, R. A. (1990). Countering the effects of destructive criticism: The relative efficacy of four interventions. *Journal of Applied Psychology, 75,* 235–243.

Barry, D. (1991). *Dave Barry's guide to life.* New York: Wings Books.

Bauer, B. (1996, February 24). Undue pride tied to violence. *San Jose Mercury News,* p. A20.

Baumeister, R., Smart, L., & Boden, J. (1996). Relation of the threatened egotism to violence and aggressions: The dark side of high self-esteem. *Psychological Review, 103,* 5–33.

Bavelas, J., Black, N., Choil, N., & Mullett, J. (1990). *Equivocal communication.* Newbury Park, CA: Sage.

Bavley, A. (1998, October 23). Girth of a nation. *Santa Cruz Sentinel,* p. A1.

Baxter, L. (1990). Dialectical contradictions in relationship development. *Journal of Social and Personal Relationships, 7,* 69–88.

Baxter, L. (1994). A dialogic approach to relationship management. In D. Canary & L. Stafford (Eds.), *Communication and relational maintenance.* New York: Academic Press.

Baxter, L., & Montgomery, B. (1996). *Relating: Dialogues and dialect.* New York: Guilford Press.

Bazil, J. (1997). The ferrous wheel of death. *Winning Orations,* 118–121.

Bechler, C., & Johnson, S. (1995). Leadership and listening: A study of member perceptions. *Small Group Research, 26,* 77–85.

Begley, S. (1998, July 13). You're OK, I'm terrific: Self-esteem backfires. *Newsweek,* 69.

Belbin, R. (1996). *Team roles at work.* London: Butterworth-Heinemann.

Bellamy, R., & Walker, J. (1996). *Television and the remote control.* New York: Guilford Press.

Benne, K., & Sheats, P. (1948). Functional roles of group members. *Journal of Social Issues, 4,* 41–49.

Bennett, A. (1995, January 10). Economics + meeting = a zillion causes and effects. *Wall Street Journal,* p. B1.

Bennis, W., & Biederman, P. (1997). *Organizing genius: The secrets of creative collaboration.* New York: Addison-Wesley.

Bennis, W., & Nanus, B. (1985). *Leaders: The strategies for taking charge.* New York: Harper & Row.

Benoit, W., & Benoit, P. (1987). Everyday argument practice of naive social actors. In J. Wenzel (Ed.), *Argument and critical practices.* Annandale, VA: Speech Communication Association.

Benton, B. (1995). Very fake badges, very real guns. *Winning Orations,* 31–33.

Berko, R. (1996, May). News and statistics in the world of education. *Spectra,* 9.

Berko, R., & Brooks, M. (1994). *Rationale kit: Information supporting the speech communication discipline and its programs.* Annandale, VA: Speech Communication Association.

Berko, R., Rosenfeld, L., & Samovar, L. (1997). *Connecting: A culture-sensitive approach to interpersonal communication competency.* Fort Worth, TX: Harcourt Brace.

Berlo, D. (1960). *The process of communication.* New York: Holt, Rinehart & Winston.

Billie, K., & Chatterjee, C. (1998, September/October). The new gender gap. *Psychology Today,* 22.

Bingham, S. (1991). Communication strategies for managing sexual harassment in organizations: Understanding message options and their effects. *Journal of Applied Communication Research, 19,* 88–115.

Birdwhistell, R. (1970). *Kinesis and context.* Philadelphia: University of Pennsylvania Press.

Black, K. (1990a, March). Can getting mad get the job done? *Working Women,* 86–90.

Black, K. (1990b, March). The matter of tears. *Working Women,* 88.

Black, K. (1993, October 31). Dennis: No longer a menace. *Newsday* [fanfare section], 12.

Blake, R., & Mouton, J. (1964). *The managerial grid.* Houston: Gulf Publishing.

Blakely, E., & Snyder, G. (1997). *Fortress America: Gated communities in the United States.* Washington, DC: Brookings Institute.

Bochner, S., & Hesketh, B. (1994). Power distance, individualism/collectiveness, and job-related attitude in a culturally diverse setting. *Journal of Cross-Cultural Psychology, 25,* 233–258.

Body builders thinking small. (1998, January 6). *San Jose Mercury News,* p. A4.

Boffey, P. (1985, May 30). Rise in science fraud is seen: Need to win cited as a cause. *New York Times,* p. B5.

Bok, S. (1978). *Lying: Moral choice in public and private life.* New York: Random House.

Bolton, R. (1979). *People skills: How to assert yourself, listen to others, and resolve conflicts.* New York: Simon & Schuster.

Bond, M., Wan, K., Leung, K., & Giacalone, R. (1985). How are responses to verbal insults related to cultural collectivism and power distances? *Journal of Cross-Cultural Psychology, 16,* 111–127.

Booknews. (1994, January 8). *San Jose Mercury News,* p. A2.

Bormann, E. (1990). *Small group communication: Theory and practice.* New York: Harper & Row.

Bostrom, R. (1970). Patterns of communicative interaction in small groups. *Speech Monographs, 37,* 257–263.

Bower, S., & Bower, G. (1976). *Asserting yourself.* Reading, MA: Addison-Wesley.

Bradley, B. (1991). *Fundamentals of speech communication: The credibility of ideas.* Dubuque, IA: W. C. Brown.

Brehm, J. (1972). *Responses to loss of freedom: A theory of psychological resistance.* Morristown, NJ: General Learning Press.

Brembeck, W., & Howell, W. (1976). *Persuasion: A means of social influence.* Englewood Cliffs, NJ: Prentice-Hall.

Bridge, K., & Baxter, L. (1992). Blended friendships: Friends and work associates. *Western Journal of Communication, 56,* 200–225.

Brin, D. (1998). *The transparent society: Will technology force us to choose between privacy and freedom?* Reading, MA: Addison-Wesley.

Brislin, R. (1993). *Understanding culture's influences on behavior.* Fort Worth, TX: Harcourt Brace Jovanovich.

Brody, G. (1990, April). Effects of television viewing on family interactions: An observational study. *Family Relations, 29,* 216–220.

Broeder, D. (1959). The University of Chicago jury project. *Nebraska Law Review, 38,* 760–774.

Brooks, L., & Perot, A. (1991). Reporting sexual harassment: Exploring a predicted model. *Psychology of Women Quarterly, 15,* 31–47.

Bross, I., Shapiro, P., & Anderson, B. (1972). How information is carried in scientific sub-language. *Science, 176,* 1303–1309.

Brown, D. (1999, January 16). Sex survey stumbles into political fray; medical editor fired. *San Jose Mercury News,* p. A1.

Brown, R. (1970). The sentences of child and chimpanzee. In R. Brown (Ed.), *Psychology.* New York: Free Press.

Brown, R. (1986). *Social psychology.* New York: Free Press.

Browne, A. (1993). Violence against women by male partners: Prevalence, outcomes, and policy implications. *American Psychologist, 48,* 1077–1087.

Brownell, J. (1990). Perceptions of listening behavior: A management study. *Journal of Business Communication, 27,* 401–416.

Bruch, H. (1978). *The golden cage: The enigma of anorexia nervosa.* Cambridge, MA: Harvard University Press.

Bruch, H. (1980). Preconditions for the development of anorexia nervosa. *American Journal of Psychoanalysis, 40,* 169–172.

Bruck, M., Ceci, S. J., & Heinbrook, H. (1998, February). Reliability and credibility of your children's reports. *American Psychologist, 53,* 136–151.

Bryson, B. (1990). *The mother tongue: English and how it got that way.* New York: William Morrow.

Buller, D., & Aune, K. (1992). The effects of speech rate similarity on compliance: Application of communication accommodation theory. *Western Journal of Communication, 56,* 37–53.

Burgoon, J. (1985). Nonverbal signals. In M. Krapps & G. Miller (Eds.), *Handbook of interpersonal communication.* Beverly Hills, CA: Sage.

Burgoon, J., Manusou, V., Mineo, P., & Hale, J. (1985). Effects of gaze on hiring, credibility, attraction, and relational message interpretation. *Journal of Nonverbal Behavior, 9,* 133–146.

Burke, K. (1950). *A rhetoric of motives.* New York: Prentice-Hall.

Burns, J. (1978). *Leadership.* New York: Harper & Row.

Burpitt, W., & Bigoness, W. (1997). Leadership and innovation among teams: The impact of empowerment. *Small Group Research, 28,* 414–423.

Bushman, B., & Baumeister, R. (1998). Threatened egotism, narcissism, self-esteem, and direct and displaced aggression: Does self-love or self-hate lead to violence? *Journal of Personality and Social Psychology, 75,* 219–229.

Cahn, D., & Lloyd, S. (1996). *Family violence from a communication perspective.* Thousand Oaks, CA: Sage.

Campbell, A. (1993). *Men, women, and aggression.* New York: Basic Books.

Campbell, K., & Jerry, E. (1987). Woman and speaker: A conflict in roles. In S. Brehn (Ed.), *Social roles and personal lives.* Westport, CT: Greenwood Press.

Canary, D. J., Cupach, W. R., & Messwong, S. J. (1995). *Relationship conflict: Conflict in parent-child, friendship, and romantic relationships.* Thousand Oaks, CA: Sage.

Canary, D., Emmers-Sommers, T. M., & Faulkner, S. (1997). *Sex and gender difference in personal relationships.* New York: Guilford Press.

Canary, D. J., & Spitzberg, B. H. (1987). Appropriateness and effectiveness of perception of conflict strategies. *Human Communication Research, 14,* 96.

Canary, D., & Stafford, L. (1994). Maintaining relationships through strategies and routine interaction. In D. Canary & L. Stafford (Eds.), *Communication and relational maintenance.* New York: Academic Press.

Canfield, J., Hansen, M. V., & Kirberger, K. (1997). *Chicken soup for the teenage soul.* Deerfield Beach, FL: Health Communications.

Caplan, M., & Goldman, M. (1981). Personal space violations as a function of height. *Journal of Social Psychology, 114,* 167–171.

Carnevale, A. (1996). *Workplace basics: The skills employers want.* Washington, DC: U.S. Department of Labor Employment and Training Administration.

Carnevale, P., & Probst, T. (1998). Social values and social conflict in creative problem solving. *Journal of Personality and Social Psychology, 74,* 1300–1309.

Celoria, J. (1997). The counterfeiting of airline safety: An examination of the dangers of bogus airline parts. *Winning Orations, 79*–81.

Charnofsky, H., Ching, R., Dufault, D., Kegley, J., & Whitney, D. (1998, December 16). Final report of Merit Pay Task Force, CSU Academic Senate [On-line]. Available: www.academicsenate.cc.ca.us

Chatman, J., & Barsade, S. (1995). Personality, organizational culture, and cooperation: Evidence from a business simulation. *Administrative Science Quarterly, 40,* 423–443.

Chen, G. (1993). *A Chinese perspective of communication competence.* Paper presented at the annual convention of the Speech Communication Association, Miami Beach, FL.

Chen, G., & Starosta, W. (1998b). *Foundations of intercultural communications.* Boston: Allyn & Bacon.

Chen, G., & Starosta, W. J. (1998a). Chinese conflict management and resolution: Overview and implications. *Intercultural Communication Studies, 7,* 1–16.

Chiarappo, M. (1996, June). I went bald at 33. *Ladies Home Journal,* 36–40.

Childers, A. (1997). Hormone hell. In L. G. Schnoor (Ed.), *Winning orations.* Northfield, MN: Interstate Oratorical Association.

Children labeled slow learners may be deaf instead. (1978, May 20). *Eugene Register-Guard,* p. C13.

Christensen, D., Farina, A., & Boudreau, L. (1980). Sensitivity to nonverbal cues as a function of social competence. *Journal of Nonverbal Behavior, 4,* 145–156.

Ciach, M. (1994). Hepatitis B—What every college student doesn't know. In L. G. Schnoor (Ed.), *Winning orations.* Northfield, MN: Interstate Oratorical Association.

Cialdini, R. (1993). *Influence: Science and practice.* New York: HarperCollins.

Clark, J., & Barber, B. (1994). Adolescents in postdivorce and always married families: Self-esteem and perceptions of father's interest. *Journal of Marriage and the Family, 56,* 608–614.

Clarke, C. (1995). Title unknown. In L. G. Schnoor (Ed.), *Winning orations.* Northfield, MN: Interstate Oratorical Association.

Clendenin, M. (1996, May 25). Buzz cut or bald? *San Jose Mercury News,* p. B1.

Cloven, D., & Roloff, M. (1991). Sense-making activities and interpersonal conflict: Communicative cure for the mulling blues. *Western Journal of Speech Communication, 55,* 134–158.

Coates, J. (1993). *Women, men and language.* New York: Longman.

Cohen, S., & Bailey, D. (1997). What makes teams work: Group effectiveness research from the shop floor to the executive suite. *Journal of Management, 23,* 239–291.

Coleman, D., & Straus, M. (1986). Marital power, conflict, and violence in a nationally representative sample of American couples. *Violence and Virtues, 1,* 141–157.

Colt, G. (1997, August). The magic of touch. *Life,* 53–62.

Conway, F., & Siegelman, J. (1995). *Snapping: America's epidemic of sudden personality changes.* New York: Stillpoint Press.

Coontz, S. (1997). *The way we really are: Coming to terms with America's changing families.* New York: Basic Books.

Cooper, L. (1960). *The rhetoric of Aristotle: An expanded translation with supplementary examples for students of composition and public speaking.* New York: Appleton Century Crafts.

Costanzo, M., Archer, D., Aronson, E., & Pettigrew, T. (1986). Energy conservation behavior. *American Psychologist, 41,* 521–528.

Cox, T., Lobel, S., & McLeod, P. (1991). Effects of ethnic groups' cultural differences on cooperative and competitive behavior on a group task. *Academy of Management Journal, 34,* 827–847.

Craig, K., & Rand, K. (1998). The perceptually "privileged" group member: Consequences of solo status for African Americans and Whites in task groups. *Small Group Research, 29,* 339–358.

Cram, A. (1997). High school sex education. In L. G. Schnoor (Ed.), *Winning orations.* Northfield, MN: Interstate Oratorical Association.

Crandall, C. (1988). Social contagion of binge eating. *Journal of Personality and Social Psychology, 55,* 588–598.

Crawford, W., & Gorman, M. (1996). Coping with electronic information. In J. Dock (Ed.), *The press of ideas: Readings for writers on print culture and the information age.* Boston: St. Martin's Press.

Crossen, C. (1994). *Tainted truth: The manipulation of fact in America.* New York: Simon & Schuster.

Crusco, A., & Wetzel, C. (1984). The Midas touch: The effects of interpersonal touch on restaurant tipping. *Personality and Social Psychology, 10,* 512–517.

Cupach, W. R., & Spitzberg, B. H. (Eds.). (1994). *The dark side of interpersonal communication.* Hillsdale, NJ: Lawrence Erlbaum.

Cytowic, R. (1993). *The man who tasted shapes.* New York: Warner Books.

Dale, P. (1972). *Language development: Structures and functions.* Hinsdale, IL: Dryden Press.

Davidowitz, M., & Myricm, R. D. (1984). Responding to the bereaved: An analysis of "helping" statements. *Death Education, 8,* 1–10.

Davidson, J. (1996, June 1). The shortcomings of the information age. *Vital Speeches, 62,* 495–503.

Davis, D. (1993). *The five myths of television power, or why the medium is not the message.* New York: Simon & Schuster.

De Moor, A. (1996). Toward a more structured use of information technology in the research community. *American Sociologist, 27,* 91–102.

DeBono, E. (1992). *Sur/petition: Going beyond competition.* New York: HarperCollins.

DeFleur, M., & Dennis, E. (1998). *Understanding mass communication: A liberal arts perspective.* Boston: Houghton Mifflin.

De Klerk, U. (1991). Expletives: Men only? *Communication Monographs, 58,* 156–169.

DePaulo, B., & Kasby, D. (1998). Everyday life in close and casual relationships. *Journal of Personality and Social Psychology, 74,* 63–79.

DePaulo, B., Kasby, D., Kirkendol, S., Wyer, M., & Epstein, J. (1996). Lying in everyday life. *Journal of Personal and Social Psychology, 70,* 979–995.

Derber, C. (1979). *The pursuit of attention: Power and individualism in everyday life.* New York: Oxford University Press.

Derlaga, U., & Chaikin, A. (1975). *Sharing intimacy: What we reveal to others and why.* Englewood Cliffs, NJ: Prentice-Hall.

Deutsch, M. (1985). *Distributive justice: A social-psychological perspective.* New Haven: Yale University Press.

DeVito, J. (1990). *Messages: Building interpersonal communication skills.* New York: Harper & Row.

Dewar, H. (1997, March 23). Nominees now face "trial by fire": Senate confirmation process has evolved into political warfare. *Washington Post,* p. A10.

Diamond, D. (1997, January 31). Behind closed gates. *USA Weekend,* pp. 4–5.

Diamond, R. (1997, August 1). Designing and assessing course and curricula, *Chronicle of Higher Education,* p. B7.

Dillard, J. (1994). Rethinking the study of fear appeals: An emotional perspective. *Communication Theory, 4,* 195–323.

Dillard, J. P., & Miller, K. I. (1988). Intimate relationships in task environments. In S. Duck (Ed.), *Handbook of personal relationships.* Sussex, UK: John Wiley.

Domagalski, T. (1998). *Experienced and expressed anger in the workplace.* Unpublished doctoral dissertation, University of South Florida.

Donohue, W. A., & Kolt, R. (1992). *Managing interpersonal conflict.* Newbury Park, CA: Sage.

Dorfman, P., & Howell, J. (1997). Managerial leadership in the United States and Mexico. In C. Granrose & S. Oskamp (Eds.), *Cross-cultural work groups.* Thousand Oaks, CA: Sage.

Downs, C., & Conrad, C. (1982). A critical incident study of effective subordinancy. *Journal of Business Communication, 19,* 27–38.

Dressler, C. (1995, December 31). Please! End this meeting madness! *Santa Cruz Sentinel,* p. D1.

Drew, E. (1994). *On the edge: The Clinton presidency.* New York: Simon & Schuster.

Drewnowski, A., & Yee, D. (1987). Men and body image: Are males satisfied with their body weight? *Psychosomatic Medicine, 49,* 626–634.

Driscoll, R., Davis, K., & Lipetz, M. (1972). Parental inference and romantic love: The Romeo and Juliet effect. *Journal of Personality and Social Psychology, 24,* 1–10.

DuBois, C. (1992, September/October). Portrait of the ideal MBA. *The Penn Stater,* p. 31.

Duck, S. (1991). Some evident truths about conventions in everyday relationships: All communications are not created equal. *Human Communication Research, 18,* 228–269.

Duck, S. (1994a). *Meaningful relationships.* Thousand Oaks, CA: Sage.

Duck, S. (1994b). Strategems, spoils, and a serpent's tooth: On the delights and dilemmas of personal relationships. In W. R. Cupach & B. H. Spitzberg (Eds.), *The dark side of interpersonal communication.* Hillsdale, NJ: Lawrence Erlbaum.

Dunlap, A. (1997). *Mean business: How I save bad companies and make good companies great.* New York: Simon & Schuster.

Eagly, A., Karau, S., & Makhijani, M. (1995). Gender and the effectiveness of leaders: A meta-analysis. *Journal of Personality and Social Psychology, 117,* 125–145.

Early, C. (1989). Social loafing and collectivism: A comparison of the United States and People's Republic of China. *Administrative Science Quarterly, 34,* 555–581.

Eclov, B. (1997). True peace of mind. In L. G. Schnoor (Ed.), *Winning orations.* Northfield, MN: Interstate Oratorical Association.

Edward, G. (1995). *Scuse me while I kiss this guy.* New York: Simon & Schuster.

Edwards, R. (1995, February). New tools help gauge marital success. *APA Monitor.*

Eisenhardt, K. (1989). Making fast strategic decisions in high-velocity environments. *Academy of Management Journal, 32,* 543–576.

Eitzen, S. (1996, January 1). Ethical dilemmas in American sport. *Vital Speeches of the Day,* 182–185.

Ekman, P. (1992). *Telling lies: Clues to deceit in the marketplace, politics, and marriage.* New York: W. W. Norton.

Ekman, P. (1993). Facial expression and emotion. *American Psychologist, 48,* 384–393.

Ekman, P. (1994). Strong evidence for universals in facial expressions: A reply to Russell's mistaken critique. *Psychological Bulletin, 115,* 268–287.

Ekman, P., & Friesen, W. (1969). The repertoire of nonverbal behavior: Categories, origins, usage, and coding. *Sanities, 1,* 49–98.

Ekman, P., & Friesen, W. (1987). Universal and cultural differences in the judgment of facial expressions of emotion. *Journal of Personality and Social Psychology, 53,* 712–717.

Ekman, P., Friesen, W., & Bear, J. (1984, May). The international language of gestures. *Psychology Today,* 64–69.

Elgin, S. H. (1989). *Success with the gentle art of verbal self-defense.* Englewood Cliffs, NJ: Prentice-Hall.

Emmert, P. (1996, Spring). President's perspective. *ILA Listening Post, 56,* 2–3.

Endicott, F. (1979). *The Endicott Report: Trends in the employment of college and university graduates in business and industry.* Evanston, IL: Placement Center, Northwestern University.

Eng, S. (1997, May 14). Cover story, *San Jose Mercury News,* [Getting Ahead section], pp. 1, 8.

Eng, S. (1999, February 9). Love among the workstations. *San Jose Mercury News,* pp. C13, C14.

Erickson, P. (1985). *Reagan speaks: The making of an American myth.* New York: New York University Press.

Ex-pal's tapes give Lewinsky voice. (1998, December 18). *San Jose Mercury News,* p. A15.

Fairhurst, G., & Sarr, R. (1996). *The art of framing: Managing the language of leadership.* San Francisco: Jossey-Bass.

Farmer, S., & Roth, J. (1998). Conflict-handling behavior in work groups: Effects of group structure, decision processes, and time. *Small Group Research, 29,* 669–713.

Farrell, W. (1993). *The myth of male power: Why men are the disposable sex.* New York: Simon & Schuster.

Feingold, A. (1992). Good-looking people are not what we think. *Psychological Bulletin, 111,* 304–341.

Female boss, bad review. (1997, September/October). *Psychology Today,* 24.

Ferraro, G. (1992). Acceptance of the democratic nomination for vice president. In J. Andrews & D. Zarefsky (Eds.), *Contemporary American Voices.* New York: Longman.

Festinger, L. (1957). *A theory of cognitive dissonance.* Stanford, CA: Stanford University Press.

Festinger, L. (1977). Cognitive dissonance. In E. Aronson (Ed.), *Readings about the social animal.* San Francisco: W. H. Freeman.

Fiedler, F. (1970). *Leadership.* Morristown, NJ: General Learning Press.

Fiedler, F., & House, R. (1988). Leadership theory and research: A report of progress. In C. Cooper & I. Robertson (Eds.), *International review of industrial and organizational psychology.* New York: Wiley.

Fields, G. (1998, June 16). The chain saw cuts both ways, CEO finds. *San Jose Mercury News,* p. C3.

Final report of the California task force to promote self-esteem and personal and social responsibility. (1990). Sacramento, CA: California State Department of Education.

Fisher, M. (1994, July 21). Moon landing? Don't believe it, the newspapers say. *International Herald Tribune,* p. 1.

Fisher, R., & Brown, S. (1988). *Getting together: Building a relationship that gets to yes.* Boston: Houghton Mifflin.

Fiske, E. (1990, March 5). How to learn in college: Group study, many tests. *New York Times,* p. A1.

Fletcher, G., & Fincham, F. (1991). Attribution in close relationships. In G. Fletcher & F. Fincham (Eds.), *Cognition in close relationships.* Hillsdale, NJ: Lawrence Erlbaum.

Folger, J., Poole, M., & Stutman, R. (1993). *Working through conflict: Strategies for relationships, groups, and organizations.* New York: HarperCollins.

Forsyth, D., Heiney, M., & Wright, S. (1997). Biases in appraisals of women leaders. *Group Dynamics: Theory, Research, and Practices, 1,* 98–103.

Foschi, M., Warriner, G., & Hart, S. (1985). Standards, expectations, and interpersonal influence. *Social Psychology Quarterly, 18,* 108–117.

Fourth-grader calls in a lawyer to fight the school cafeteria. (1999, March 13). *San Jose Mercury News,* p. A20.

Foushee, M. (1984). Dyads and triads at 35,000 feet: Factors affecting group process and aircraft performance. *American Psychologist, 39,* 885–893.

France. (1997, August). *Reader's Digest,* 156.

Frank, R., & Cook, P. (1995). *The winner-take-all society.* New York: Free Press.

Freed, A. (1992). We understand perfectly: A critique of Tannen's view. In *Locating power* [Proceedings of the 1992 Berkeley women and language conference]. Berkeley, CA: University of California.

Freeley, A. J. (1996). *Argumentation and debate: Critical thinking for reasoned decision making.* Belmont, CA: Wadsworth.

Freeman, K. (1996). Attitudes toward work in project groups as predictors of academic performance. *Small Group Research, 27,* 265–282.

Frerking, B. (1995, March 15). Question authority, parents say. *San Jose Mercury News,* p. A4.

Frymer, M. (1996, March 16). Controversy follows Dershowitz like cash follows O. J. lawyers. *San Jose Mercury News,* p. E1.

Frymier, A., & Shulman, G. (1996). The development of a learner empowerment measure. *Communication Education, 45,* 181–199.

Fucci, D., Harris, D., Petrosino, L., & Banks, M. (1993). Effects of preference for rock music on magnitude-production scaling behavior in young adults: A validation. *Perceptual and Motor Skills, 77,* 811–815.

Fukada, H. (1986). Psychological processes mediating the persuasion inhibiting effect of forewarning in fear arousing communities. *Psychological Reports, 58,* 87–90.

Gabrenya, W. (1985). Social loafing on an optimistic task: Cross-cultural differences among Chinese and Americans. *Journal of Cross-Cultural Psychology, 16,* 223–242.

Galanter, E. (1962). Contemporary psychophysics. In R. Brown, E. Galanter, E. H. Hess, & G. Mendler (Eds.), *New directions in psychology.* New York: Holt, Rinehart & Winston.

Galanter, M. (1989). *Cults: Faith, healing, and coercion.* New York: Oxford University Press.

Gallup, G., & Gallup, A. (1989, January 29). Communicating is critical to a satisfying relationship. *San Jose Mercury News,* p. A1.

Gammon, R., & Clarke, K. (1997, November 6). Kurek gets eight years. *Santa Cruz Sentinel,* pp. A1, A4.

Garcia, E. (1996, May 30). Tattoo-removal plan for ex-gang members. *San Jose Mercury News,* p. B1.

Gardner, L., & Leak, G. (1994). Characteristics and correlates of teacher anxiety among college psychology teachers. *Teaching of Psychology, 21,* 28–32.

Gardner, M. (1981). *Science: Good, bad, and bogus.* New York: Avon Books.

Gardner, M. (1997, July/August). Heaven's gate: The UFO cult of Bo and Peep. *Skeptical Inquirer,* 15–17.

Gardner, R., & Gardner, B. (1969). Teaching sign language to a chimpanzee. *Science, 165,* 664–672.

Garfield, C. (1986). *Peak performers.* New York: Avon Books.

Gass, R., & Seiter, J. (1999). *Persuasion, social influence, and compliance gaining.* Boston: Allyn & Bacon.

Gastil, J. (1994). A meta-analytic review of the productivity and satisfaction of democratic and autocratic leadership. *Small Group Research, 25,* 384–410.

Gates, D. (1993, March 29). White male paranoia. *Newsweek,* 48–53.

Gathright, A. (1990, February 18). Shots silence wife's secret terror. *San Jose Mercury News,* p. A1.

Gayle, B. (1991). Sex equity in workplace conflict management. *Journal of Applied Communication Research, 19,* 152–169.

Gebhardt, L., & Meyers, R. (1995). Subgroups influence in decision-making groups: Examining consistency from a communication perspective. *Small Group Research, 26,* 147–168.

Geertz, C. (1983). *Local knowledge.* New York: Basic Books.

Geier, J. (1967). A trait approach in the study of leadership in small groups. *Journal of Communication, 17,* 316–323.

Gelles, R., & Straus, M. (1988). *Intimate violence: The causes and consequences of abuse in the American family.* New York: Simon & Schuster.

Gerow, J. (1996). *Essentials of psychology: Concepts and applications.* New York: HarperCollins.

Gerstel, N., & Gross, H. (1985). *Commuter marriage.* New York: Guilford Press.

Getlin, J. (1998, July 3). CNN, Time pull nerve-gas story. *San Jose Mercury News,* pp. A1, A10.

Getter, H., & Nowinski, I. (1981). A free response test of interpersonal effectiveness. *Journal of Personality Assessment, 45,* 301–308.

Gibb, C. (1969). Leadership. In G. Lindzey & E. Aronson (Eds.), *The handbook of social psychology* (Vol. 4). Reading, MA: Addison-Wesley.

Gibb, J. (1961). Defensive communication. *The Journal of Communication, 11,* 141–148.

Gilovich, T. (1991). *How we know what isn't so: The fallibility of human reason in everyday life.* New York: Free Press.

Gilovich, T. (1997, March/April). Some systematic biases of everyday judgment. *Skeptical Inquirer,* 31–35.

Girl undergoes surgery for smile. (1995, December 16). *San Jose Mercury News,* p. B3.

Give Congress some credit for trying to find harmony. (1999, March 12). *San Jose Mercury News,* p. B6.

Givens, D. (1983). *Love signals: How to attract a mate.* New York: Pinnacle Books.

Glass ceiling intact, statistics show at hearing. (1994, September 9). *San Jose Mercury News,* p. E1.

Glassman, J. K. (1998, May 29). Put shootings in proper perspective. *San Jose Mercury News,* p. B7.

Gleicher, F., & Petty, R. (1992). Expectations of reassurance influence the nature of fear-stimulated attitude change. *Journal of Experimental Social Psychology, 28,* 86–100.

Goldberg, H. (1994, March 3). Yawning gulf of perceptions. *Sacramento Bee,* p. A12.

Goleman, D. (1991, September 17). Nonverbal cues are easy to misinterpret. *New York Times,* p. C1.

Goleman, D. (1995). *Emotional intelligence.* New York: Bantam.

Goleman, D. (1998). *Working with emotional intelligence.* New York: Bantam.

Goode, E. (1999, February 23). When people see a sound and hear a color. *New York Times,* p. D3.

Goodman, E. (1996, August 5). Why shave Shannon? *San Jose Mercury News,* p. B13.

Gottman, J. (1994a). *What predicts divorce? The relationship between marital processes and marital outcomes.* Hillsdale, NJ: Lawrence Erlbaum.

Gottman, J. (1994b). *Why marriages succeed and fail: And how you can make yours last.* New York: Simon & Schuster.

Gottman, J., & Carrere, S. (1994).Why can't men and women get along? Developmental notes and marital inequities. In D. Canary & L. Stafford (Eds.), *Communication and relational maintenance.* New York: Academic Press.

Gottman, J., & Silver, N. (1999). *The seven principles for making marriage work.* New York: Crown.

Gottschalk, M. (1996, May 12). Do's and don'ts of dressing down. *San Jose Mercury News,* p. A17.

Gould, S. J. (1981). *The mismeasure of man.* New York: W. W. Norton.

Green, W., & Lazarus, H. (1990). Are you meeting with success? *Executive Excellence, 7,* 1–12.

Griffin, E. (1994). *A first look at communication theory.* New York: McGraw-Hill.

Gronbeck, B., German, K., Ehninger, D., & Monroe, A. (1998). *Principles of speech communication.* New York: Longman.

Grusky, O., Bonacich, P., & Webster, C. (1995). The coalition structure of the four-person family. *Current Research in Social Psychology,* 16–29.

Gudykunst, W. (1991). *Bridging differences: Effective intergroup communication.* Newbury Park, CA: Sage.

Gudykunst, W. B., & Kim, Y. Y. (Eds.). (1992). *Readings on communicating with strangers.* New York: McGraw-Hill.

Gumz, J. (1997, November). Payoffs from technology in schools remain unproven. *Santa Cruz Sentinel,* p. Al.

Hackman, M., & Johnson, C. (1996). *Leadership: A communication perspective.* Prospect Heights, IL: Waveland Press.

Hahner, J. C., Sokoloff, M. A., & Salesch, S. L. (1997). *Speaking clearly: Improving voice and diction.* New York: McGraw-Hill.

Hall, E. (1959). *The silent language.* New York: Doubleday.

Hall, E. (1969). *The hidden dimension.* New York: Doubleday.

Hall, E. (1981). *Beyond culture.* New York: Doubleday.

Hall, E., & Hall, M. (1987). *Understanding cultural difference.* Yarmouth, ME: Intercultural Press.

Hall, J., & Watson, W. (1970). The effects of normative intervention on group decision making. *Human Relations, 23,* 299–317.

Hamachek, D. (1982). *Encounters with others: Interpersonal relationships and you.* Fort Worth, TX: Holt, Rinehart & Winston.

Hamachek, D. (1992). *Encounters with the self.* Fort Worth, TX: Harcourt Brace Jovanovich.

Han, S., & Shavitt, S. (1994). Persuasion and culture: Advertising appeals in individualistic and collectivistic societies. *Journal of Experimental Social Psychology, 30,* 326–350.

Harwood, B. (Ed.). (1982). *The pursuit of the presidency 1980.* New York: Berkeley Books.

Haslett, B. (1992). *The organization woman: Power and paradox.* Norwood, NJ: Ablex.

Hats off for bobbies in Manchester. (1996, February 7). *San Jose Mercury News,* p. A12.

Hawkins, K. (1995). Effects of gender and communication content on leadership emergence in small task-oriented groups. *Small Group Research, 26,* 234–249.

Heat's on to close wage gap. (1999, January 30). *San Jose Mercury News,* p. A1.

Hecht, M., Collier, M., & Ribeau, S. (1993). *African American communication: Ethnic identity and cultural interpretation.* Newbury Park, CA: Sage.

Hecht, M., Collier, M., & Ribeau, S. (1994). Love ways and relationship quality in heterosexual relationships. *Journal of Social and Personal Relationship, 1,* 25–44.

Hefling, S. (1997). Prison rape. In L. G. Schnoor (Ed.), *Winning orations.* Northfield, MN: Interstate Oratorical Association.

Heilman, M., & Stopeck, M. (1985). Being attractive, advantage or disadvantage? Performance-based evaluation and recommended personnel actions as a function of appearance, sex, and job type. *Organizational Behavior and Human Decision Process, 35,* 202–215.

Hellweg, S., Samovar, L., & Skow, L. (1994). Cultural variations in negotiation styles. In L. Samovar & R. Porter (Eds), *Intercultural communication: A reader.* Belmont, CA: Wadsworth.

Henley, N. (1995). Body politics revised: What do we know today? In P. Kalbfleisch & McCody (Eds.), *Gender, power, and communication in human relationships.* Hillsdale, NJ: Lawrence Erlbaum.

Hentoff, N. (1992). *Free speech for me, but not for thee.* New York: Harper Perennial.

Herbert, W., & Hammel, S. (1999, March 22). *U.S. News & World Report,* 57.

Herriot, J. (1973). *All things bright and beautiful.* New York: Bantam.

Hershey, P., & Blanchard, K. (1988). *Management organizational behavior: Utilizing human resources.* Englewood Cliffs, NJ: Prentice-Hall.

Heslin, R. (1974, May). Steps toward a taxonomy of touching. Paper presented to the annual convention of the Midwestern Psychological Association.

Hess, E., & Goodwin, E. (1974). The present state of pupilometrics. In M. Janice (Ed.), *Pupillary dynamics and behavior.* New York: Plenum Press.

Hess, E., Seltzer, A., & Schlien, J. (1965). Pupil response of hetero- and homosexual males to pictures of men and women: A pilot study. *Journal of Abnormal Psychology, 70,* 165–168.

Hetherington, E., Bridges, M., & Insabella, G. (1998, February). What matters? What does not? Five perspectives on the association between marital transitions and children's adjustment. *American Psychologist, 53,* 167–184.

Hickson, M., & Stacks, D. (1989). *Nonverbal communication: Studies and applications.* Dubuque, IA: Wm. C. Brown.

Higham, S. (1998, October 17). Ex-farmer's Senate bid resonates in Vermont. *San Jose Mercury News,* p. DD6.

Hirokawa, R. (1985). Discussion procedures and decision-making performance: A test of a functional perspective. *Human Communication Research, 12,* 203–224.

Hite, S. (1987). *Women in love.* New York: Alfred Knopf.

Hoban, P. (1998, July 11). The right direction. *TV Guide,* 41–42.

Hocker, J., & Wilmot, W. (1995). *Interpersonal conflict.* Dubuque, IA: Wm. C. Brown & Benchmark.

Hofstede, G. (1980). *Culture's consequences: International differences in work-related values.* Beverly Hills, CA: Sage.

Hofstede, G. (1991). *Cultures and organizations: Software of the mind.* New York: McGraw-Hill.

Hofstede, G. (1996). Gender stereotypes and partner preferences of Asian women in masculine and feminine cultures. *Journal of Cross-Cultural Psychology, 27,* 533–547.

Hollander, E. (1985). Leadership and power. In G. Lindzey & E. Aronson (Eds.), *Handbook of social psychology.* New York: Random House.

Hollander, E., & Offerman, L. (1990, February). Power and leadership in organizations. *American Psychologist,* 179–189.

Holmes, S. (1997, March 14). Census bureau predicts huge U.S. ethnic shift. *Sacramento Bee,* p. A1.

Home chores still a battle of the sexes. (1993, February 16). *San Jose Mercury News,* p. A5.

Hoover-Dempsey, K., Plas, J., & Wallston, B. (1986). Tears and weeping among professional women: In search of new understanding. *Psychology of Women Quarterly, 10,* 19–34.

Horner, T., Guyer, M., & Kalter, N. (1993). The biases of child sexual abuse experts: Believing is seeing. *Bulletin of the American Academy of Psychiatric Law, 21,* 281–292.

Howell, J. (1982). *A laboratory study of charismatic leadership.* (Working paper, University of Western Ontario.)

Hui, C. H., & Triandis, H. C. (1986). Individualism-collectivism: A study of cross-cultural research. *Journal of Cross-cultural Psychology, 17,* 225–248.

Hunt, M. (1982). *The universe within: New science explores the human mind.* New York: Simon & Schuster.

Huston, M., & Schwartz, P. (1995). Relationships of lesbians and gay men. In J. Wood & S. Duck (Eds.), *Understanding relationship processes, 6: Understudied relationships: Off the beaten track.* Thousand Oaks, CA: Sage.

In the blink of an eye. (1996, October 21). *Newsweek,* 6.

Inagaki, Y. (1985). *Jiko Hyogen No Gijutsu (Skills in self-expression).* Tokyo: PHP Institute.

Inch, E., & Warnick, B. (1998). *Critical thinking and communication: The use of reason in argument.* Boston: Allyn & Bacon.

Infante, D., Chandler, T. A., & Rudd, J. E. (1989). Test of an argumentative skill deficiency model of interpersonal violence. *Communication Monographs, 56,* 163–177.

Infante, D., Rancer, A., & Womack, D. (1997). *Building communication theory.* Prospect Heights, IL: Waveland Press.

Infante, D., Riddle, B., Horvatt, C., & Tumlin, S. (1992). Verbal aggressiveness: Messages and reasons. *Communication Quarterly, 40,* 116–126.

Infante, D., Sabourin, T., Rudd, J., & Sharron, E. (1990). Verbal aggression in violent and nonviolent marital disputes. *Communication Quarterly, 4,* 361–371.

Insurance policies offered against alien impregnation. (1996, August 24). *San Jose Mercury News,* p. A4.

Irvine, M. (1998, April 6). Coming out in the classroom. *Santa Cruz Sentinel,* p. A1.

Ishii, S., Klopf, D., & Cambra, R. (1984). The typical Japanese student as an oral communicator: A preliminary profile. *Otsuma Review, 17,* 39–63.

Ivins, M. (1992, August). The billionaire boy scout. *Time,* 38–39.

Jackson, D. (1997, November 24). It took way too long to lower the boom. *San Jose Mercury News,* p. B7.

Jackson, M. (1999, February 14). Office romance: More and more couples mix business, personal lives. *Santa Cruz Sentinel,* p. D2.

Jacobs, J. (1989, October 2). Designs for better education elude summiteers. *San Jose Mercury News,* p. B5.

Jacobs, J. (1996, January 4). Who will raise the children? *San Jose Mercury News,* p. 7B.

Jacobs, J. (1999a, February 1). Warning: Remove label before testing. *San Jose Mercury News,* p. B7.

Jacobs, J. (1999b, June 7). Gore's hope: Boring guys aren't losers. *San Jose Mercury News,* p. B7.

Jacobson, N., & Gottman, J. (1998, March/April). Anatomy of a violent relationship. *Psychology Today,* 61–65.

Jaffe, C. (1998). *Public speaking: Concepts and skills for a diverse society.* Belmont, CA: Wadsworth.

Jaksa, J., & Pritchard, M. (1994). *Communication ethics: Methods of analysis.* Belmont, CA: Wadsworth.

James, D., & Clarke, S. (1993). Women, men, and interruptions: A critical review. In D. Tannen (Ed.), *Gender and conversational interaction.* New York: Oxford University Press.

James, D., & Drakich, J. (1993). Understanding gender differences in amount of talk: A critical review of research. In D. Tannen (Ed.), *Gender and conversational interaction.* New York: Oxford University Press.

Jamieson, K. H. (1988). *Eloquence in an electronic age.* New York: Oxford University Press.

Jandt, F. (1995). *Intercultural communication: An introduction.* Thousand Oaks, CA: Sage.

Janis, I. (1982). *Groupthink: Psychological studies of policy decisions and fiascoes.* Boston: Houghton Mifflin.

Janis, I. (1989). *Crucial decisions: Leadership in policy-making and crisis management.* New York: Free Press.

Janofsky, M. (1995, October 23). Increasingly, political war of words is fought with Nazi imagery. *New York Times,* p. A12.

Jascob, T. (1997). Prescription drug counseling. *Winning Orations,* 97–100.

Jeffrey, R., & Pasework, R. (1983). Altering opinions about the insanity plea. *Journal of Psychiatry and Law,* 29–44.

Jelinek, P. (1998, December, 19). Korean school teaches smiling. *San Jose Mercury News,* p. A6.

Jensen-Campbell, L., Graziano, W., & West, S. (1995). Dominance, prosocial orientation, and female preferences: Do nice guys really finish last? *Journal of Personality and Social Psychology, 68,* 427–440.

Jesperson, O. (1923). *Language: Its nature, development and origins.* New York: Holt, Rinehart & Winston.

Jesperson, O. (1924). *Language: Its nature, development and origin.* New York: Henry Holt.

Johnson, D., & Johnson, R. (1989). *Cooperation and competition: Theory and research.* Edina, MN: Interaction Book Company.

Johnson, G. (1995, June 6). Chimps talk debate: Is it really language? *New York Times,* p. C1.

Johnson, J., & Szczupakiewicz, N. (1987). The public speaking course: Is it preparing students with work-related public speaking skills? *Communication Education, 36,* 131–137.

Johnson, S., & Bechler, C. (1998). Examining the relationship between listening effectiveness and leadership emergence: Perceptions, behaviors, and recall. *Small Group Research, 29,* 452–471.

Johnson, W. (1946). *People in quandries.* New York: Harper.

Johnstone, C. (1981). Ethics, wisdom, and the mission of contemporary rhetoric: The realization of human being, *Central States Speech Journal, 32,* 177–188.

Jones, E. (1979). The rocky road from acts to dispositions. *American Psychologist, 34,* 107–117.

Jones, S. (1994). *The right touch: Understanding and using the language of physical context.* Cresskill, NJ; Hampton Press.

Judge, C. (1997, November 21). Greatest victory: Saving a life. *San Jose Mercury News,* p. D7.

Judge, C. (1998, July 31). Rookie's father would be proud. *San Jose Mercury News,* p. D8.

Jurors' views differ on King beating trial. (1993, February 15). *San Jose Mercury News,* p. B3.

Kalb, C., & McCormick, J. (1998, September 21). Bellying up to the bar. *Newsweek,* 89.

Kalbfleisch, P., & Cody, M. (Eds.). (1995). *Gender, power, and communication in human relationships.* Hillsdale, NJ: Lawrence Erlbaum.

Kamprath, N. (1997) . [Personal letter summarizing results of study at UCSC.]

Kaplan, T. (1998, November 27). Few using health plan. *San Jose Mercury News,* p. B1.

Karau, S., & Williams, K. (1993). Social loafing: A meta-analytic review and theoretical integration. *Journal of Personality and Social Psychology, 65,* 681–706.

Kassin, S. (1998). *Psychology.* Upper Saddle River, NJ: Prentice-Hall.

Katayama, H. (1982). Koto Ni Hanei Sareta Nipponjin No Gengokan: Japanese views of language as reflected in proverbs. *Kyoiku Kiyo 8-go.* Matsudo, Chiba-ken: Matsudo Dental School, Nihon University, pp. 1–11.

Kato, D. (1996, May 13). Make-over dreams. *San Jose Mercury News,* pp. C1, C8.

Katzenbach, J., & Smith, D. (1993a). *The wisdom of teams.* Boston: Harvard Business School Press.

Katzenbach, J., & Smith, D. (1993b, March/April). The discipline of teams. *Harvard Business Review,* 111–120.

Kava, B. (1999, January 16). "Perry Mason" tops Clinton trial on TV. *San Jose Mercury News,* p. A11.

Keller, H. (1955). *Teacher: Anne Sullivan Macy.* Garden City, NY: Doubleday.

Kelley, H. (1979). *Personal relationships: Their structures and processes.* Hillsdale, NJ: Lawrence Erlbaum.

Kelley, H. (1984). Affect in interpersonal relations. *Review of Personality and Social Psychology, 5,* 89–115.

Kelsey, B. (1998). The dynamics of multicultural groups: Ethnicity as a determinant of leadership. *Small Group Research, 29,* 602–623.

Kendall, K. E. (1985). Do real people ever give speeches? *Spectra, 31,* 10.

Kershner, V. (1991, March 30). Budget "emergency" declared by governor. *Santa Cruz Sentinel,* p. A1.

Kiecolt-Glaser, J., Fisher, L., Ogrocki, P., & Stout, J. (1987). Marital quality, marital disruption and immune function. *Psychosomatic Medicine, 49,* 13–34.

Killion, A. (1996, July 5). VanDerveer ordeal proves worth it for well-drilled team. *San Jose Mercury News,* pp. D1, D3.

Killion, A. (1999, January 29). Pro football becoming a woman's game. *San Jose Mercury News,* pp. A1, A22.

Kilmann, R., & Thomas, K. (1977). Developing a force-choice measure of conflict handling behavior: The "mode" instrument. *Educational Psychological Measurement, 37,* 309–325.

Kilpatrick, W. (1975). *Identity and intimacy.* New York: Dell.

Kim, M. (1992). A comparative analysis of nonverbal expressions as portrayed by Korean and American print-media advertising. *Howard Journal of Communication, 3,* 321.

Kim, U., Triandis, H., Kagitcibasi, C., Choi, S., & Yoon, G. (1994). *Individualism and collectivism: Theory, method, and application.* Thousand Oaks, CA: Sage.

Kipnis, D. (1976). *The powerholder.* Chicago: University of Chicago Press.

Kirshmeyer, C., & Cohen, A. (1992). Multicultural groups: Their performance and reactions with constructive conflict. *Group and Organizational Management, 17,* 153–170.

Kirtley, K. (1997). Grave matter: The high cost of leaving. *Winning Orations,* 154–157.

Klapp, O. (1978). *Opening and closing: Strategies of information adaptation in society.* New York: Cambridge University Press.

Kleiman, C. (1991, July 28). A boost up the corporate ladder. *San Jose Mercury News,* p. PC1.

Klein, S. (1996). Work pressure as a determinant of work group behavior. *Small Group Research, 27,* 299–315.

Klopf, D. (1998). *Intercultural encounters: The fundamentals of intercultural communication.* Englewood, CO: Morton.

Klopfenstein, B. (1997). New technology and the future of the media. In A. Wells & E. Hakanen (Eds.), *Mass media and society.* Greenwich, CT: Ablex.

Knapp, M. (1980). *Essentials of nonverbal communication.* New York: Holt, Rinehart & Winston.

Knapp, M., & Vangelisti, A. (1992). Stages of relationships. In M. Knapp & A. Vangelisti (Eds.), *Interpersonal communication and human relationships.* Needham Heights, MA: Allyn and Bacon.

Kohn, A. (1987, October). It's hard to get left out of a pair. *Psychology Today,* 53–57.

Kohn, A. (1992). *No contest: The case against competition.* Boston: Houghton Mifflin.

Kohn, A. (1993). *Punished by rewards.* New York: Houghton Mifflin.

Kohn, A. (1994, December). The truth about self-esteem. *Phi Delta Kappan,* 272–283.

Korzybski, A. (1958). *Science and sanity*. Lakeville, CT: International Non-Aristotelian Literary Publishing Company.

Kouri, K., & Lasswell, M. (1993). *Black–White marriages*. Binghamton, NY: Hayworth Press.

Koury, R. (1998, June 9). Berkeley may strip down law on nudity. *San Jose Mercury News*, p. B1.

Kraut, R., Patterson, M., Lundmark, V., Kiesler, S., Mukopadhyay, T., & Scherlis, W. (1998). Internet paradox: A social technology that reduces social involvement and psychological well-being? *American Psychologist, 53*, 1017–1031.

Kristof, N. (1995, December 14). Sales pitch. *San Jose Mercury News*, p. A27.

Kroll, W., & Peterson, K. (1965). Study of values test and collegiate football teams. *The Research Quarterly, 36*, 141–147.

Krucoff, C. (1998, November 11). When winning becomes the reason. *San Jose Mercury News*, p. D3.

Kubicka, T. (1995). Traitorous transplants: The enemy within. *Winning Orations*, 9–11.

Kuiper, N., & Rogers, T. (1979). Encoding of personal information. *Journal of Personality and Social Psychology, 37*, 499–514.

Kunin, M. (1994). *Living a political life*. New York: Knopf.

Kurtz, L. (1997). *Self-help and support groups: A handbook for practitioners*. Thousand Oaks, CA: Sage.

Kushner, H. (1981). *When bad things happen to good people*. New York: Avon.

Kutner, L. (1994, February 20). Winning isn't only thing that counts. *Santa Cruz Sentinel*, p. D2.

Landers, A. (1995, February 25). Low income families need fire protection too. *Santa Cruz Sentinel*, p. D5.

Langer, E. (1989). *Mindfulness*. Reading, MA: Addison-Wesley.

Langer, E., & Abelson, R. (1974). A patient by any other name: Clinician group differences in labeling bias. *Journal of Consulting and Clinical Psychology, 42*, 4–9.

Langer, S. (1951). *Philosophy in a new key*. New York: New American Library.

Langfred, C. (1998). Is group cohesiveness a double-edged sword? An investigation of the effects of cohesiveness on performance. *Small Group Research, 29*, 124–143.

Langlois, J., Roggman, L., & Musselman, L. (1994). What is average and what is not average in attractive faces? *Psychological Science, 5*, 214–220.

Lanka, B. (1989). *I dream a world: Portraits of Black women who changed America*. New York: Stewart, Tabori, & Chang.

Lantz, D., & Stefflre, V. (1964). Language and cognition revisited. *Journal of Abnormal and Social Psychology, 49*, 454–462.

Lardner, G. (1997, August 25). Survey: Number of violent attacks underestimated. *San Jose Mercury News*, p. A6.

Lardner, G. (1998, July 27). Crime at work often unreported. *San Jose Mercury News*, p. A3.

Larson, C. (1992). *Persuasion: Reception and responsibility*. Belmont, CA: Wadsworth.

Larson, C., & LaFasto, M. (1989). *Teamwork: What must go right, what can go wrong*. Newbury Park, CA: Sage.

Larson, J. R. (1989). The dynamic interplay between employees' feedback-seeking strategies and supervisors' delivery of performance feedback. *Academy of Management Review, 14*, 408–422.

Last year's best. (1997, July 9). *San Jose Mercury News*, p. A4.

Latane, B., Williams, K., & Harkin, S. (1979). Many hands make light the work: The causes and consequences of social loafing. *Journal of Personality and Social Psychology, 37*, 822–832.

Lazar, J. (1991). Ensuring productive meetings. In R. Swanson & B. Knapp (Eds.), *Innovative meeting management*. Austin, TX: Minnesota Mining and Manufacturing.

Leathers, D. (1970). The process effects of trust-destroying behaviors in the small group. *Speech Monographs, 37*, 181–187.

Leathers, D. (1976). *Nonverbal communication systems*. Boston: Allyn & Bacon.

Leathers, D. (1979). The impact of multichannel message inconsistency on verbal and nonverbal decoding behavior. *Communication Monographs, 46*, 88–100.

Leathers, D. (1986). *Successful nonverbal communication: Principles and applications*. New York: Macmillan.

Leavitt, H. (1964). *Managerial psychology*. Chicago: University of Chicago Press.

Lederer, R. (1990). *Crazy English: The ultimate joy ride through our languages*. New York: Pocket Books.

Lee, B. (1997). *The power principle: Influences with honor*. New York: Simon & Schuster.

Lee, Y., Lee, J., & McCauley, C. R. (1995). *Stereotype occurring toward appreciating group differences*. Washington, DC: American Psychological Association.

Lefton, L. (1991). *Psychology*. Boston: Allyn & Bacon.

Leland, J., & Miller, M. (1998, August 17). Can gays 'connect?' *Newsweek*, 47–52.

Leung, K., Bond, M., Carment, D., Krishnan, L., & Liebrand, W. (1990). Effects of cultural femininity on preference for methods of conflict processing: A cross-cultural study. *Journal of Experimental Social Psychology, 26*, 373–388.

Levander, C. (1998). *Voices of the nation: Women and public speech in nineteenth-century American literature and culture*. Cambridge, UK: Cambridge University Press.

Levine, M., & Shefner, J. (1991). *Fundamentals of sensation and perception*. Pacific Grove, CA: Brooks/Cole.

Lewin, T. (1996, March 2). Child care in conflict with job. *New York Times*, p. 8.

Lewis, M. H., & Reinsch, N. L. (1988). Listening in organizational environments. *Journal of Business Communication, 25*, 49–67.

Lieberman, M., & Snowden, L. (1993). Problems in assessing prevalence and membership characteristics of self-help group participants. *Journal of Applied Behavioral Science, 29*, 166–180.

Lipstadt, D. (1993). *Denying the holocaust: The growing assault on truth and memory*. New York: Penguin.

Littlejohn, S. (1999). *Theories of human communication*. Belmont, CA: Wadsworth.

Littlejohn, S., & Jabusch, D. (1982). Communication competence: Model and application. *Journal of Applied Communication Research, 10*, 29–37.

Lloyd, S., & Emery, B. (1993). Abuse in the family: An ecological life-cycle perspective. In T. Brubacker (Ed.), *Family relations: Challenges for the future*. Newbury Park, CA: Sage.

Locke, J. (1998). *The de-voicing of society. Why we don't talk to each other anymore*. New York: Simon & Schuster.

Loftus, E., & Ketcham, K. (1994). *The myth of repressed memory.* New York: St. Martin's Press.

Loftus, E., & Palmer, J. (1974). Reconstruction of automobile destruction: An example of the interaction between language and memory. *Journal of Verbal Learning and Verbal Behavior, 13,* 585–589.

Loftus, E., & Zanni, G. (1975). Eyewitness testimony: The influence of the wording of a question. *Bulletin of the Psychonomic Society, 5,* 86–88.

Lubman, S. (1996, September 15). Volunteers bring schools more than they bargained for. *San Jose Mercury News,* pp. A1, A21.

Lubman, S. (1998a, February 22). Asian equation troubles UC. *San Jose Mercury News,* p. A1.

Lubman, S. (1998b, February 21). Culture clash crops up within families as Asian-American students assimilate. *San Jose Mercury News,* p. A20.

Lubman, S. (1998c, January 12). Majoring in pragmatism. *San Jose Mercury News,* p. A4.

Luchins, A. (1957). Primacy-recency in impression formation. In C. Hovland (Ed.), *The order of presentation in persuasion.* New Haven, CT: Yale University Press.

Lulofs, R. (1994). *Conflict: From theory to action.* Scottsdale, AZ: Gorsuch Scarisbrick.

Lund, M. (1985). The development of investment and commitment scale for prediction continuity of personal relationships. *Journal of Social and Personal Relationships, 2,* 3–23.

Luria, A. (1968). *The mind of a mnemonist.* New York: Basic Books.

Lustig, M., & Koester, J. (1993). *Intercultural competence across cultures.* New York: HarperCollins.

Lustig, M., & Koester, J. (1999). *Intercultural competence: Interpersonal communication across cultures.* New York: Longman.

Lutz, W. (1996). *The new doublespeak: Why no one knows what anyone's saying anymore.* New York: HarperCollins.

Lying in America. (1987, February 23). *U.S. News & World Report,* pp. 54–61.

Lying is part of everyday life, research confirms. (1996). [On-line]. Available: http://www.nando.net/newsroom/ntm/health/061096/health 16_10972.html

Maccoby, E., & Mnookin, R. (1992). *Dividing the child: Social and legal dilemmas of custody.* Cambridge, MA: Harvard University Press.

Mandal, M., Bryden, M., & Bulman-Fleming, M. (1996). Similarities and variations in facial expressions of emotions: Cross-cultural evidence. *International Journal of Psychology, 31,* 49–58.

Mandelbaum, D. (Ed.). (1949). *Selected writings of Edward Sapir.* Los Angeles: University of California Press.

Mansfield, M. (1990). Political communication in decision-making groups. In D. Swanson & D. Nimmo (Eds.), *New directions in political communication: A resource book.* Newbury Park, CA: Sage.

Marcel, A. (1983). Conscious and unconscious perception: An approach to the relation between phenomenal experience and perceptual processes. *Cognitive Psychology, 15,* 238–300.

Marcus, D. (1999, March 22). When granny goes online. *U.S. News & World Report,* 61–62.

Marshall, L. (1994). Physical and psychological abuse. In W.

Cupach & B. Spitzberg (Eds.), *The dark side of interpersonal communication.* Hillsdale, NJ: Lawrence Erlbaum.

Martin, J., & Nakayama, T. (1997). *Intercultural communication in contexts.* Mountain View, CA: Mayfield.

Matlin, M. (1992). *Psychology.* Fort Worth, TX: Harcourt Brace Jovanovich.

Matsumoto, D. (1990). Cultural influences on facial expressions of emotion. *The Southern Communication Journal, 56,* 128–137.

Matsumoto, D. (1994). Culture and emotion. In L. Adler & U. Gielan (Eds.), *Cross-cultural topics in psychology.* Westport, CT: Praeger.

Maugh, T. H. (1998, February 21). The secret to happy marriage: "Yes, dear." *San Jose Mercury News,* p. A1.

May, R. (1972). *Power and innocence: A search for the sources of violence.* New York: W. W. Norton.

McAleer, N. (1985). *The body almanac.* New York: Doubleday.

McCall, W. (1996, June 25). The hand that holds the remote rules the most. *San Jose Mercury News,* p. D1.

McCann, D., & Margerison, C. (1996). High-performance teams. In R. Cathcart, L. Samovar, & L. Henman (Eds.), *Small group communication: Theory and Practice.* Dubuque, IA: Brown & Benchmark.

McCroskey, J. C., Fayer, J. M., & Richmond, V. P. (1985). Don't speak to me in English: Communication apprehension in Puerto Rico. *Communication Quarterly, 33,* 185–192.

McCrum, R., Cran, W., & MacNeil, R. (1986). *The story of English.* New York: Penguin.

McCullough, M., Rochal, K. C., & Worthington, E. L. (1997). Interpersonal forgiving in close relationships. *Journal of Personality and Social Psychology, 73,* 321–336.

McDaniel, E., & Andersen, P. (1995, May). *Intercultural variations in tactile communication: An empirical field study.* Paper presented at the International Communication Association, Albuquerque, NM.

McGarity, A. (1997). Big brother goes to the doctor. *Winning Orations,* 127–130.

McGonagle, K. A., Kessler, R. C., & Gotlif, I. H. (1993). The effects of marital disagreement style, frequency, and outcome on marital disruption. *Journal of Social and Personal Relationships, 9,* 507–524.

McGuinnies, E., & Ward, C. (1980). Better liked than right: Trustworthiness and expertise as factors in credibility. *Personality and Social Psychology Bulletin, 6,* 467–472.

McGuire, W. (1964). Inducing resistance to persuasion: Some contemporary approaches. In L. Berkowitz (Ed.), *Advances in experimental social psychology.* New York: Academic Press.

McKay, M., Rogers, P., & McKay, J. (1989). *When anger hurts: Quieting the storm within.* Oakland, CA: New Harbinger.

McLaughlin, S. (1996). The dirty truth about your kitchen: Using common sense to prevent food poisoning. In L. G. Schnoor (Ed.), *Winning orations.* Northfield, MN: Interstate Oratorical Association.

McLuhan, M. (1964). *Understanding media: The extensions of man.* New York: McGraw-Hill.

McLuhan, M. (1967). *The medium is the massage.* New York: Random House.

McNutt, P. (1997, October/November). When strategic decisions are ignored. *Fast Company.*

Meacham, J. (1996, July 27). Revenge of the nerd. *San Jose Mercury News*, p. DD8.

Meg Ryan: The new Lombard? (1993, June 27). *Akron Beacon Journal*, p. D1.

Mehrabian, A. (1981). *Silent message: Implicit communication of emotion and attitude.* Belmont, CA: Wadsworth.

Menzel, K. E., & Carrell, L. J. (1994). The relationship between preparation and performance in public speaking. *Communication Education, 43,* 17–26.

Mere mention of "sex" makes woman faint. (1996, July 15). *San Jose Mercury News*, p. A9.

Mercer, G., & Benjamin, J. (1980). Spatial behavior of university undergraduates in double-occupancy residence room: An inventory of effects. *Journal of Applied Social Psychology, 10,* 32–44.

Merritt, A. (1998). Replicating Hofstede: A study of pilots in eighteen countries. [Online]. Available: http://www.psy.utexas.edu.psy.helmreich/hofrep.htm

Message of hope. (1998, July 24). *USA Weekend*, 9–10.

Metts, S., Cupach, N., & Imahori, T. (1992). Perceptions of sexual compliance resisting messages in three types of cross-sex relationships. *Western Journal of Communication, 56,* 1–17.

Meyrowitz, J. (1997). Shifting worlds of strangers: Medium theory and changes in "them" versus "us." In K. Massey (Ed.), *Readings in mass communication: Media literacy and culture.* Mountain View, CA: Mayfield.

Michael, K. (1997). Corporate welfare: A national injustice. In L. G. Schnoor (Ed.), *Winning orations.* Northfield, MN: Interstate Oratorical Association.

Milgram, S. (1974). *Obedience to authority.* New York: Harper & Row.

Miller, K. (1996, April). Together forever. *Life,* 44–56.

Miller, K., & Monge, P. (1986). Participation, satisfaction, and productivity: A meta-analytic review. *Academy of Management Journal, 29,* 727–753.

Mills, N. (1996, July). The (almost) born-again Dennis Quaid. *Cosmopolitan, 156,* 162.

Minister accidentally kills self. (1998, October 3). *San Jose Mercury News*, p. A13.

Mintz, H. (1998, April 18). The end of a 12-year nightmare. *San Jose Mercury News*, p. A1.

Misunderstood word costs D.C. official job in mayor's office. (1999, January 28). *San Jose Mercury News*, p. A2.

Moghaddam, F., Taylor, D., & Wright, S. (1993). *Social psychology in cross-cultural perspective.* New York: W. H. Freeman.

Mohamed, A., & Wiebe, F. (1996). Toward a process theory of groupthink. *Small Group Research, 27,* 416–430.

Montemayor, R. (1986). Family variation in parent-adolescent storm and stress. *Journal of Adolescent Research, 1,* 15–31.

Moody, F. (1996, June/July). Wonder women in the rude boys' paradise. *Fast Company,* 12–14.

More Americans "too busy" to vote. (1998, August 17). *San Jose Mercury News*, p. A7.

Morreale, S. (1999, March). Ability to communicate ranked no. 1 by employers. *Spectra, 35,* 10.

Morris, D. (1977). *Manwatching: A field guide to human behavior.* New York: Harry N. Abrams.

Morris, D. (1985). *Body watchers.* New York: Crown.

Morris, D., Collett, P., Marsh, P., & O'Shaughnessy, M. (1979). *Gestures: Their origins and distribution.* New York: Stein & Day.

Morris, T., & Gorham, J. (1996). Fashion in the classroom: Effects of attire on student perceptions of instructors in college classes. *Communication Education, 45,* 135–148.

Morse, S., & Gergen, K. (1970). Social comparison, self-consistency and the concept of self. *Journal of Personality and Social Psychology, 16,* 149–156.

Motley, M. T. (1995). *Overcoming your fear of public speaking: A proven method.* New York: McGraw-Hill.

Mudrack, P., & Farrell, G. (1995). An examination of functional role behavior and its consequences for individuals in group settings. *Small Group Research, 26,* 542–571.

Muehlenhard, C., Koralewski, M., Andrews, S., & Burdick, C. (1986). Verbal and nonverbal cues that convey interest in dating: two studies. *Behavior Therapy, 17,* 404–419.

Mulac, A., & Bradac, J. (1995). Women's style in problem solving interaction: Powerless, or simply feminine? In P. Kalbfleisch & M. Cody (Eds.), *Gender, power and communication in human relationships.* Hillsdale, NJ: Lawrence Erlbaum.

Mulac, A., Wiemann, J., Wideman, S., & Dibson, T. (1988). Male/female language differences and effects in same-sex and mixed-sex dyads: The gender-linked language effects. *Communication Monographs, 55,* 315–335.

Mullen, B., Anthony, T., Salas, E., & Driskill, J. (1994). Group cohesiveness and quality decision making: An integration of tests of the groupthink hypothesis. *Small Group Research, 25,* 189–204.

Mulshine, P. (1998, April 26). Statistics distort drunken-driving standards debate. *San Jose Mercury News*, p. F3.

Murphy, B., & Zorn, T. (1996). Gendered interaction in professional relationships. In J. Wood (Ed.), *Gendered relationships.* Mountain View, CA: Mayfield.

Murray, B. (1997, May). How important is teaching style to students? *APA Monitor,* 1–3.

Myers, S. (1999, January 23). Military discharging more gays, but why? *San Jose Mercury News*, p. A17.

Naked came the commencement speaker. (1998, July 18). *San Jose Mercury News*, p. A3.

Napolitan, D., & Goethals, G. (1979). The attribution of friendliness. *Journal of Experimental Social Psychology, 15,* 105–113.

Narcisco, J., & Burkett, T. (1975). *Declare yourself.* Englewood Cliffs, NJ: Prentice-Hall.

Nash, A. (1998, July). Marvelous Meg. *Good Housekeeping,* 96–99.

Natale, R. (1994, December). Megabucks megastar Meg Ryan. *Cosmopolitan,* 150–153.

National Archives and Records Administration. (1987). *Kennedy's inaugural address of 1961.* Washington, DC: U.S. Government Printing Office.

Neisser, A. (1983). *The other side of silence.* New York: Knopf.

Nelson, M. (1998). *Embracing victory: Life lessons in competition and compassion.* New York: William Morrow.

Neuman, S. (1991). *Literacy in the television age: The myth of the TV effect.* Norwood, NJ: Ablex.

New Pentagon manual focuses on cooperation. (1991, December 19). *San Jose Mercury News*, p. A2.

Nicotera, A., & Rancer, A. (1994). The influence of sex on self-perception and social stereotyping of aggressive communication predispositions. *Western Journal of Communication, 58,* 283–307.

Nishida, T. (1991). *Sequence patterns of self-disclosure among Japanese and North American students.* Paper presented at the conference on communication in Japan and the United States, California State University, Fullerton.

Noe, R. (1988). Women and mentoring. *Academy of Management Review, 13,* 65–78.

Noonan, P. (1998). *Simply speaking: How to communicate your ideas with style, substance, and clarity.* New York: HarperCollins.

Northouse, P. (1997). *Leadership: Theory and practice.* Thousand Oaks, CA: Sage.

O'Brien, T. (1995, November 5). No jerks allowed. *West,* 8–14.

Ofshe, R., & Watters, E. (1994). *Making monsters: False memories, psychotherapy, and sexual hysteria.* New York: Charles Scribner's Sons.

O'Keefe, D. (1990). *Persuasion: Theory and research.* Newbury Park, CA: Sage.

O'Leary, M., Curley, A., Rosenbaum, A., & Clarke, C. (1985). Assertion training for abused women: A potentially hazardous treatment. *Journal of Marital and Family Therapy, 11,* 319–322.

Orlick, T. (1978). *Winning through cooperation: Competitive insanity, cooperative alternatives.* Washington, DC: Acropolis Books.

Ornish, D. (1990). *Dr. Dean Ornish's program for reversing heart disease.* New York: Ballantine.

Orr, D. (1968). Time compressed speech—A perspective. *Journal of Communication, 18,* 272–282.

Orwell, G. (1949). *Nineteen eighty four.* New York: New American Library.

Osborn, M., & Osborn, S. (1997). *Public speaking.* New York: Houghton Mifflin.

Osgood, C., Suci, G., & Tannenbaum, P. (1957). *The measurement of meaning.* Urbana, IL: University of Illinois Press.

Ostrom, M. (1999, March 18). Poll: Clinton disliked, but effective as ever. *San Jose Mercury News,* p. A10.

Pacheco, T. (1995). Untitled. *Winning Orations,* 116–117.

Paetzold, R., & O'Leary-Kelly, A. (1993). Organizational communication and the legal dimensions of hostile work environment sexual harassment. In G. Kreps (Ed.), *Sexual harassment: Communication implications.* Creskill, NJ: Hampton Press.

Park, M., & Floyd, K. (1995). Making friends in cyberspace. *Online Journal of Computer Mediated Communication, 1*(4).

Parks, C., & Vu, A. (1994). Social dilemma of individuals from highly individualist and collectivist cultures. *Journal of Conflict Resolution, 3,* 708–718.

Patterson, D. (1996, February 4). Public speaking skills can give job seekers an edge. *Seattle Times,* p. B1.

Patterson, F. (1978, October). Conversations with a gorilla. *National Geographic,* 438–465.

Patterson, M., Powell, J., & Lenihan, M. (1986). Touch, compliance, and interpersonal affects. *Journal of Nonverbal Behavior, 10,* 41–50.

Paulos, J. (1994, March). Counting on Dyscalculia. *Discourse,* 30–36.

Paulos, J. A. (1988). *Innumeracy: Mathematical illiteracy and its consequences.* New York: Hill & Wang.

PC buyers influenced strongly by salespeople. (1996, October 21). *Investor's Business Daily,* p. A6.

Pendergrast, M. (1995). *Victims of memory: Incest accusations and shattered lives.* Hinesburg, VA: Upper Access, Inc.

Peterson, D. (1991). Physically violent husbands of the 1980s and their resources. *Journal of Family Violence, 6,* 1–15.

Peterson, M. S. (1997). Personnel interviewers' perception of the importance and adequacy of applicants' communication skills. *Communication Education, 46,* 287–291.

Pettigrew, T., & Martin, J. (1987). Shaping the organizational context for Black American inclusion. *Journal of Social Issues, 43,* 41–78.

Petty, R., & Cacioppo, J. (1984). The effects of involvement on responses to argument quantity and quality: Central and peripheral routes to persuasion. *Journal of Personality and Social Psychology, 46,* 69–81.

Petty, R., & Cacioppo, J. (1986a). The elaboration likelihood model of persuasion. In L. Berkowitz (Ed.), *Advances in experimental social psychology* (Vol. 19). New York: Academic Press.

Petty, R., & Cacioppo, J. (1986b). *Communication and persuasion: Central and peripheral routes to attitude change.* New York: Springer-Verlag.

Petty, R., Kasmer, J., Haugtvedt, C., & Cacioppo, J. (1987). Source and message factors in persuasion: A reply to Stiff's critique of the elaboration likelihood model. *Communication Monographs, 54,* 233–249.

Pfau, M., & Van Bockern, S. (1994). The persistence of inoculation in conferring resistance to smoking initiation among adolescents: The second year. *Human Communication Research, 20,* 413–430.

Phillips, E., & Cheston, R. (1979). Conflict resolution: What works? *California Management Review, 21,* 76–83.

Philpot, J. (1983). *The relative contribution to meaning of verbal and nonverbal channels of communication: A meta-analysis.* Unpublished master's thesis, University of Nebraska.

Pinker, S. (1994). *The language instinct: How the mind creates language.* New York: HarperCollins.

Pipher, M. (1994). *Reviving Ophelia: Saving the selves of adolescent girls.* New York: Ballantine.

Pipher, M. (1996). *The shelter of each other: Rebuilding our families.* New York: Ballantine.

Plotnik, R. (1996). *Introduction to psychology.* Pacific Grove, CA: Brooks/Cole.

Pogrebin, L. C. (1987). *Among friends.* New York: McGraw-Hill.

Poll: One in three aren't convinced Holocaust occurred. (1993, April 20). *San Jose Mercury News,* p. A1.

Postman, N. (1985). *Amusing ourselves to death: Public discourse in the age of show business.* New York: Viking Penguin.

Postman, N. (1993). *Technopoly: The surrender of culture to technology.* New York: Knopf.

Praise thy employees survey says. (1994, September 13). *San Jose Mercury News,* p. E1.

Pratkanis, A., & Aronson, E. (1991). *The age of propaganda: The everyday use and abuse of persuasion.* New York: W. H. Freeman.

Propp, K. (1995). An experimental examination of biological sex as a status cue in decision-making groups and its influence on information use. *Small Group Research,* 451–474.

Pruitt, D., & Rubin, J. (1986). *Social conflict: Escalation, stalemate, and settlement.* New York: Random House.

Purdy, M., & Borisoff, D. (1997). *Listening in everyday life.* Lanham, MD: University Press of America.

Put enjoyment ahead of achievement. (1994, February 20). *Santa Cruz Sentinel,* p. D2.

Puzzanghera, J. (1996, December 5). Drug helps high-risk patients survive surgery, study says. *San Jose Mercury News,* pp. A1, A28.

Quarttrone, G., & Jones, E. (1980). The perception of variability within in-groups and out-groups: Implications for the law of small numbers. *Journal of Personality and Social Psychology, 38,* 141–152.

Raban, J. (1997, November 24). What the nanny trial tells us about transatlantic body language. *New York Times,* p. 55.

Rae-Dupree, J. (1997, December 30). Disk-drive leap doubles capacity. *San Jose Mercury News,* p. A1.

Rand, H. (1998, February 15). Science, non-science and nonsense. *Vital Speeches of the Day,* 282–284.

Rath and Strong Inc. (1989). *Rath and Strong climax index.* Lexington, MA: Author.

Rathus, S. (1990). *Psychology.* Fort Worth, TX: Holt, Rinehart & Winston.

Reardon, K. (1991). *Persuasion in practice.* Newbury Park, CA: Sage.

Reeling in the years. (1998, April 13). *Newsweek,* 14.

Regan, D., & Totten, J. (1975). Empathy and attribution: Turning observers into actors. *Journal of Personality and Social Psychology, 32,* 850–856.

Remland, M., Jones, T., & Brinkman, H. (1995). Interpersonal distance, body orientation, and touch: Effects of culture, gender, and age. *The Journal of Social Psychology, 135,* 281–297.

Renzetti, C. (1991). *Violent betrayal: Partner abuse in lesbian relationships.* Newbury Park, CA: Sage.

Reyneri, A. (1984). The nose knows, but science doesn't. *Science, 84,* 26.

Rezendes, D. (1998, November 11). Medical information sites on the Web can be bad for your health. *San Jose Mercury News,* pp. A1, A5.

Richmond, V., & McCroskey, J. (1989). *Communication: Apprehension, avoidance, and effectiveness.* Scottsdale, AZ: Gorsuch Scarisbrick.

Ritts, V., & Patterson, M. (1992). Expectations, impressions, and judgments of physically attractive students: A review. *Review of Educational Research, 62,* 413–426.

Rivals blast Robertson talk about hostages. (1988, February 25). *San Jose Mercury News,* p. A8.

Robertson sets off furor on hostage. (1988, February 26). *Chicago Tribune,* p. C12.

Rodriguez, J. (1995). *Confounds in fear arousing persuasive messages: Do the paths less traveled make all the difference?* Unpublished doctoral dissertation, Michigan State University, East Lansing, MI.

Roediger, H., Capaldi, E., Paris, S., & Polivy, J. (1991). *Psychology.* New York: HarperCollins.

Rogers, C., & Roethlisberger, F. (1952, July/August). Barriers and gateways to communication. *Harvard Business Review,* 28–35.

Roloff, M. E., & Cloven, D. H. (1990). The chilling effect in interpersonal relationships: The reluctance to speak one's mind. In D. Cohen (Ed.), *Intimates in conflict: A communication perspective.* Hillsdale, NJ: Lawrence Erlbaum.

Romano, D. (1988). *Intercultural marriage: Promises and pitfalls.* Yarmouth, ME: Intercultural Press.

Romig, D. (1996). *Breakthrough teamwork: Outstanding results using structured teamwork.* Chicago: Irwin Professional Publishing.

Rosenbaum, L., & Rosenbaum, W. (1985). Morale and productivity consequences of group leadership style, stress, and type of task. *Journal of Applied Psychology, 55,* 343–358.

Rosenfeld, L. (1983). Communication climate and coping mechanisms in the college classroom. *Communication Education, 32,* 169–174.

Rosenhan, D. (1973). On being sane in insane places. *Science, 179,* 250–258.

Rosenthal, N. (1997, July 15). How to prevent that "us vs. them" feeling within the family. *San Jose Mercury News,* p. E4.

Rosenthal, R. (Ed.). (1979). *Skill in nonverbal communication: Individual differences.* Cambridge, MA: Gunn & Hain.

Roth and Strong, Inc. (1989). *Roth and Strong climate index.* Lexington, MA: Roth & Strong, Inc.

Rothwell, J. (1982). *Telling it like it isn't: Language misuse and malpractice.* Englewood Cliffs, NJ: Prentice-Hall.

Rothwell, J. (1998). *In mixed company: Small group communication.* Fort Worth, TX: Harcourt Brace.

Rubenstein, M. (1975). *Patterns of problem solving.* Englewood Cliffs, NJ: Prentice-Hall.

Rubin, L. (1985). *Just friends: The role of friendship in our lives.* New York: Harper & Row.

Rubin, T. (1999, March 21). China aims to have it both ways on the Net. *San Jose Mercury News,* p. P7.

Ruch, W. (1989). *International handbook of corporate communication.* Jefferson, NC: McFarland.

Ruggeiro, V. (1988). *Teaching thinking across the curriculum.* New York: Harper & Row.

Ryan, M. (1991, March 31). Another way to teach migrant students. *Los Angeles Times,* p. B20.

Rymer, R. (1993). *Genie: An abused child's flight from silence.* New York: HarperCollins.

Sagan, C. (1995, January/February). Wonder and skepticism. *Skeptical Inquirer,* 24–28.

Saint, S., & Lawson, J. (1997). *Rules for reaching consensus.* San Diego, CA: Pfeiffer.

Salazar, A. (1995). Understanding the synergistic effects of communication in small groups. *Small Group Research, 26,* 169–199.

Samovar, L., & Porter, R. (1995). *Communication between cultures.* Belmont, CA: Wadsworth.

Savage-Rumbaugh, S., & Lewin, R. (1994). *Kanzi.* New York: Wiley.

Schaef, A. (1985). *Women's reality: An emerging female system in a White male society.* New York: Harper & Row.

Schittekatte, M., & Van Hiel, A. (1996). Effects of partially shared information and awareness of unshared information on information sampling. *Small Group Research, 27,* 431–449.

Schlossler, E. (1997, September). A grief like no other. *The Atlantic Monthly,* 37–76.

Schmidt, S., & Kipnis, D. (1987, November). The perils of persistence. *Psychology Today,* 32–34.

Schmidt, W. (1991, October). *Oral communication across the curriculum: A critical review of literature.* Paper presented at the meeting of the Florida Communication Association Convention, Vero Beach, FL.

Schmitt, C., & Slonaker, L. (1996, January 14). High technology doesn't always equal high achievement. *San Jose Mercury News,* p. A1.

Schmitt, E. (1996, September 7). Minnesotans battle over a 5-letter word. *San Jose Mercury News,* p. A7.

Schneider, K. S. (1993, August 2). Educating Meg. *People Weekly,* 68–74.

Schneider, K., & Levitt, S. (1996, June 3). Mission impossible. *People,* 65–74.

Scholar, E. (1990, April 6). Americans a threat to planet. *Charlotte Observer.*

Scholtes, P. (1990). An elaboration of Deming's teachings on performance appraisal. In McLean, G., Damme, S., & Swanson, R. (Eds.), *Performance appraisal: Perspectives on a quality management approach.* Alexandria, VA: American Society for Training and Development.

Schultz, C. (1998, May 30). Message of peace from war photo. *San Jose Mercury News,* p. E3.

Schuster, M. (1984). The Scanlon Plan: A longitudinal analysis. *Journal of Applied Behavioral Science, 20,* 23–28.

Schwartz, S. (1995). Identifying culture-specifics in the context and structure of values. *Journal of Cross-Cultural Psychology, 26,* 92–116.

Sciolino, E. (1996, November 12). Subject of famous photograph lays wreath at Vietnam Memorial. *San Jose Mercury News,* pp. A1, A14.

Sedikides, C., Campbell, W., Reeder, G., & Elliott, A. (1998). The self-serving bias in relational context. *Journal of Personality and Social Psychology, 74,* 378–386.

Seipel, T. (1997, October 4). The spit felt round the world. *San Jose Mercury News,* pp. A1, A26.

Sessums, K. (1995, May). Maximum Meg. *Vanity Fair,* 104–111.

Sexton, J. (1993, September 21). Brave's second wind blows everyone away. *San Jose Mercury News,* p. C5.

Shachtman, T. (1995). *The inarticulate society: Eloquence and culture in America.* New York: Free Press.

Shackelford, S., Wood, W., & Worchel, S. (1996). Behavioral styles and the influence of women in mixed-sex groups. *Social Psychology, 59,* 284–293.

Shenk, D. (1997). *Data smog: Surviving the data glut.* New York: HarperCollins.

Sheridan, C., & King, R. (1972). Obedience to authority with an authentic victim. *Proceedings of the 80th Annual Convention: American Psychological Association, 7,* 165–166.

Sherif, M., Sherif, C., & Nebergall, R. (1965). *Attitude and attitude change: The social judgment-involvement approach.* Philadelphia: Saunders.

Sherman, S., & Lee, J. (1997, May 12). Levi's: As ye sew, so shall ye reap. *Fortune,* 104–111.

Shevlin, J. (1994). Wife abuse: Its magnitude and one jurisdiction's response. In A. Taylor & J. Miller (Eds.), *Conflict and gender.* Cresskill, NJ: Hampton Press.

Shimanoff, S. (1992). Group interaction via communication rules. In R. Cathcart & L. Samovar (Eds.), *Small group communication: A reader.* Dubuque, IA: Wm. C. Brown.

Shimanoff, S. B. (1980). *Communication rule: Theory and research.* Beverly Hills, CA: Sage.

Shimanoff, S., & Jenkins, M. (1996). Leadership and gender: Challenging assumptions and recognizing resources. In R. Cathcart, L. Samovar, & L. Henman (Eds.), *Small group communication: Theory and practice.* Dubuque, IA: Brown & Benchmark.

Shirley, D. (1997). *Managing creativity: Inventing, developing, and producing innovative products.* [Online]. Available: http://www.managingcreativity.com

Sillars, A. L., Coletti, S. G., Parry, D., & Rogers, M. A. (1982). Coding verbal conflict tactics: Nonverbal and perceptual correlates of the "avoidance-distributive-integrative" distinction. *Human Communication Research, 9,* 83–95.

Silva, J. (1982). *The current status of applied sport psychology: A national survey.* Paper presented at the American Alliance for Health, Physical Education, Recreation, and Dance convention, Houston, TX.

Silver, M., & Perry, J. (1999, March 22). Hooked on instant messages. *U.S. News & World Report,* 57–58.

Simons, L., & Zielenziger, M. (1996, March 3). Culture clash dims U.S. future in Asia. *San Jose Mercury News,* pp. A1, A22.

Singer, M. (1987). *Intercultural communication: A perceptual approach.* Englewood Cliffs, NJ: Prentice-Hall.

Singer, M. (1995). *Cults in our midst: The hidden menace in our everyday lives.* San Francisco: Jossey-Bass.

Singh, D. (1993). Adaptive significance of female physical attractiveness: Role of waist-to-hip ratio. *Journal of Personality and Social Psychiatry, 65,* 293–307.

Sisk, H. (1997). Dirty hands across America. In L. G. Schnoor (Ed.), *Winning orations.* Northfield, MN: Interstate Oratorical Association.

Sklaroff, S. (1999, March 22). E-mail nation. *U.S. News & World Report,* 54–55.

Sloan, A. (1998, June 6). Chainsaw massacre. *Newsweek,* 62.

Sloan, W., Stovall, J., & Startt, J. (1993). *Media in America: A history.* Scottsdale, AZ: Publishing Horizons.

Smedes, L. B. (1984). *Forgive and forget: Healing the hurts we don't deserve.* New York: Harper & Row.

Smith, D. (1997). Women and leadership. In P. Northouse (Ed.), *Leadership: Theory and practice.* Thousand Oaks, CA: Sage.

Smith, D., Gier, J., & Willis, F. (1982). Interpersonal touch and compliance with a marketing request. *Basic and Applied Social Psychology, 3,* 35–38.

Smith, M. J. (1982). *Persuasion and human interaction: A review and critique of social influence theories.* Belmont, CA: Wadsworth.

Smith, P., & Bond, M. (1994). *Social psychology across cultures: Analysis and perspective.* Boston: Allyn & Bacon.

Smith, P., Dugan, S., & Trompenaars, F. (1996). National culture and the values of organizational employees. *Journal of Cross-Cultural Psychology, 27,* 231–264.

Snyder, M., & Uranowitz, S. (1978). Reconstructing the past: Some cognitive consequences of person perception. *Journal of Personality and Social Psychology, 36,* 941–950.

Something about Meg. (1998, July). *Good Housekeeping,* p. 98.

Sorensen, S. (1981, May). *Grouphate.* Paper presented at the International Communication Association, Minneapolis, MN.

Spencer, L., & Spencer, S. (1993). *Competence at work: Models for superior performance.* New York: Wiley.

Spencer, T. (1994). Transforming relationships through ordinary talk. In S. Duck (Ed.), *Understanding relationship processes, 4: Dynamics of relationships.* Thousand Oaks, CA: Sage.

Spitzberg, B., & Cupach, W. (1989). *Handbook of interpersonal competence research.* New York: Springer-Verlag.

Spitzberg, B., & Hecht, M. (1984). A component model of relational competence. *Human Communication Research, 10,* 575–599.

Springen, K. (1997, June 3). The biology of beauty. *Newsweek,* 61–66.

Starr, T. (1991). *The natural inferiority of women: Outrageous pronouncements by misguided males.* New York: Poseidon Press.

Steil, L. K. (1980, May 26). Secrets of being a better listener. *U.S. News & World Report,* 65.

Steward, A., & Lupfer, M. (1987). Touching as teaching: The effect of touch on student's perceptions and performing. *Journal of Applied Psychology, 17,* 800–809.

Stewart, L., Cooper, P., Stewart, A., & Friedley, S. A. (1996). *Communication and gender.* Scottsdale, AZ: Gorsuch Scarisbrick.

Stiff, J., Dillard, I., Somera, H., & Sleight, C. (1988). Empathy, communication, and prosocial behavior. *Communication Monographs, 55,* 198–213.

Stoll, C. (1995). *Silicon snake oil: Second thoughts on the information highway.* New York: Anchor Books.

Straus, M., & Gelles, R. (1990). *Physical violence in American families.* New Brunswick, NJ: Transaction Publishers.

Straus, M. A., & Sweet, S. (1992). Verbal/symbolic aggression in couples: Incidence rates and relationship to personal characteristics. *Journal of Marriage and the Family, 54,* 346–357.

Street, M. (1997). Groupthink: An examination of theoretical issues, implications, and future research suggestions. *Small Group Research, 28,* 72–93.

Strong, W., & Cook, J. (1990). *Persuasion: Strategies for speakers.* Dubuque, IA: Kendall/Hunt.

Sudweeks, S., Gudykunst, W., Ting-Toomey, S., & Nishida, T. (1990). Developmental themes in Japanese-North American relationships. *International Journal of Intercultural Relations, 14,* 207–233.

Sunstrom, J. (1997). A child's last hope. *Winning Orations,* 151–154.

Survey: Violence in the workplace a universal issue. (1998, July 20). *San Jose Mercury News,* p. A12.

Sypher, B., & Sypher, H. (1984). Seeing ourselves as others see us. *Communication Rewards, 11,* 97–115.

Tannen, D. (1979). Ethnicity as conversational style. In *Working papers in sociolinguistics* (No. 55). Austin, TX: Southwest Educational Development Laboratory.

Tannen, D. (1990). *You just don't understand: Women and men in conversation.* New York: Ballantine.

Tannen, D. (1994). *Talking from 9 to 5.* New York: Avon.

Tannen, D. (1998). *The argument culture: Moving from debate to dialogue.* New York: Random House.

Taps, J., & Martin, P. (1990). Gender composition, attributional accounts, and women's influence and likability in task groups. *Small Group Research, 4,* 471–491.

Tavris, C. (1989). *Anger: The misunderstood emotion.* New York: Simon & Schuster.

Tavris, C. (1992). *The mismeasure of women.* New York: Simon & Schuster.

Tebbel, J. (1987). *Between covers: The rise and transformation of American book publishing.* New York: Oxford University Press.

The dress-down revolution. (1996, May 12). *San Jose Mercury News,* p. A17.

The ethics of American youth: A warning and a call to action. (1990). Marina Del Rey, CA: The Josephson Institute of Ethics.

The gate debate: How you voted. (1997, February 28). *USA Weekend,* 9.

The perils of geek speak. (1998, December 21). *Newsweek,* 77.

Thomas, J. (1998, November 8). A state ready to wrestle with the future. *San Jose Mercury News,* p. P3.

Thomas, K., & Velthouse, B. (1990). Cognitive elements of empowerment: An "interpretive" model of intrinsic task motivation. *Academy of Management Review, 15,* 666–681.

Thomma, S. (1996, February 4). Nostalgia for '50s surfaces. *Philadelphia Inquirer,* p. B1.

Thompson, E. (1960). An experimental investigation of the relative effectiveness of organization structure in oral communication. *Southern Speech Journal, 26,* 59–69.

Thompson, J. (1986, April). Larger than life: Many women see themselves as roundfaced and pudgy, even when no one else does. *Psychology Today,* 39–44.

Thourlby, W. (1978). *You are what you wear.* New York: New American Library.

Ting-Toomey, S. (1983). An analysis of verbal communication patterns in high and low marital adjustment groups. *Human Communication Research, 9,* 306–319.

Ting-Toomey, S., Gao, G., Yang, Z., Trubisky, P., Kim, H., Lin, S., & Nishida, T. (1991). Culture, face maintenance, and styles of handling interpersonal conflict: A study in five cultures. *International Journal of Conflict Management, 2,* 275–296.

Tolchin, M., & Tolchin, S. (1973). *Clout: Woman power and politics.* New York: Cowad, McCann & Georghepon.

Tomb, G. (1999, August 2). Boonters losing the lingo. *San Jose Mercury News,* pp. 1A, 12A.

Toulmin, S., Rieke, R., & Janik, A. (1979). *An introduction to reasoning.* New York: Macmillan.

Townsend, P. (1996, April 13). Face the truth. *Santa Cruz Sentinel,* p. D1.

Trenholm, S., & Jensen, A. (1988). *Interpersonal communication.* Belmont, CA: Wadsworth.

Triandis, H. (1975). Values, attitude, and interpersonal behavior. In R. Bushlin, S. Bochnerm & W. Lonner (Eds.), *Cross-cultural perspective on learning.* New York: Wiley.

Triandis, H. (1990). Cross-cultural studies of individualism and collectiveness. In J. Berman (Ed.), *Cross-cultural perspective.* Lincoln, Nebraska: University of Nebraska Press.

Triandis, H. (1995). *Individualism and collectiveness.* Boulder, CO: Westview Press.

Tropman, J. (1988). *Meetings: How to make them work for you.* New York: Van Nostrand Reinhold.

Tropman, J. (1996). *Making meetings work: Achieving high quality group decisions.* Thousand Oaks, CA: Sage.

Trounstine, P. (1998, November 20). Democrats, GOP battle in a tale of two inquiries. *San Jose Mercury News,* p. A1.

Turow, J. (1999). *Media today: An introduction to mass communication.* Boston: Houghton Mifflin.

Tutzauer, F., & Roloff, M. (1988). Communication processes leading to integrative agreements: Three paths to joint benefits. *Communication Research, 5,* 360–380.

Tziner, A., & Eden, D. (1985). Effects of crew composition on crew performance: Does the whole equal the sum of the parts? *Journal of Applied Psychology, 70,* 85–93.

Understanding culture: Don't stare at a Navajo. (1974, June). *Psychology Today,* 107.

Unger, R., & Crawford, M. (1992). *Women and gender: A feminist psychology.* New York: McGraw-Hill.

Ury, W. (1993). *Getting past no: Negotiating your way from confrontation to cooperation.* New York: Bantam.

U.S. Bureau of the Census (1998). *Statistical abstract of the United States.* Washington, DC: U.S. Government Printing Office.

U.S. Department of Labor. (1991). *Skills and the new economy.* Washington, DC: U.S. Government Printing Office.

Van Oostrum, J., & Rabbie, J. (1995). Intergroup competition and cooperation within autocratic and democratic management regimes, *Small Group Research, 26,* 269–295.

Vangelisti, A., Knapp, M., & Daly, J. (1990). Conversational narcissism: *Communication Monographs, 57,* 251–274.

Ventura: Keillor book "cheating." (1999, February 6). *San Jose Mercury News,* p. A2.

Verderber, R., Elder, A., & Weiler, E. (1976). *A study of communication time usage among college students.* Unpublished manuscript, University of Cincinnati.

Vitanza, S. (1991). *The relationship of stress, cognitive appraisal and dating violence.* Unpublished master's thesis, University of North Texas, Denton, TX.

Vitanza, S., & Marshall, L. (1993). *Dimensions of dating violence, gender and personal characteristics.* Unpublished manuscript.

Vobejda, B. (1998, July 27). Habit to cohabit increasing. *San Jose Mercury News,* p. A3.

Wachtel, P. (1983). *The poverty of affluence: A psychological portrait of the American way of life.* New York: Free Press.

Wade, C., & Tavris, C. (1990). *Psychology.* New York: Harper-Collins.

Wald, M. (1997, July 18). Highway violence surges with more traffic, fewer cops. *Santa Cruz Sentinel,* p. A1.

Walker, L. (1999). Psychology and domestic violence around the world. *American Psychologist, 54,* 21–29.

Waller, W., & Hill, R. (1951). *The family: A dynamic interpretation.* New York: Dryden.

Wallerstein, J., & Blakeslee, S. (1995). *The good marriage: How and why love lasts.* Boston: Houghton Mifflin.

Walters, E., & Kendler, K. (1995). Anorexia nervosa and anorexia-like syndromes in population-based female twin samples. *American Journal of Psychiatry, 152,* 64–71.

Watzlawick P., Beavin, J., & Jackson, D. (1967). *Pragmatics of human communication.* New York: W. W. Norton.

Wayne, M. (1974). The meaning of silence in conversations in three cultures. In *Patterns of communication in and out of Japan.* Tokyo: ICU Communication Department.

We met at the office. (1999, February 14). *Parade,* 25.

Webb, T. (1998, October). Obesity in kids at epidemic level. *San Jose Mercury News,* p. A11.

Webster, E. (1964). *Decision making in the employment interview.* Montreal, Canada: Industrial Relations Center, McGill University Press.

Weick, K. (1990). The vulnerable system: An analysis of the Tenerife air disaster. *Journal of Management, 16,* 571–593.

Weiner, B., Graham, S., Peter, D., & Zmuidinas, M. (1991). Public confession and forgiveness. *Journal of Personality, 59,* 281–312.

Weingarten, G. (1994, September 27). I'm absolutely sure: You need a marshmallow enema. *San Jose Mercury News,* p. B7.

Wener, R., Frazier, W., & Farberstein, J. (1987, June). Building better jails. *Psychology Today,* 40–49.

Wetzel, P. (1988). Are "powerless" communication strategies the Japanese norm? *Language in Society, 17,* 555–564.

What dictionaries say. (1999, January 30). *San Jose Mercury News,* p. A19.

White, D. (1998, December 30). Stupid things really said by famous people. *San Jose Mercury News,* p. E5.

Whitkin, R. (1987, September 19). FAA says Delta had poor policies on crew training. *New York Times,* p. 1.

Whorf, B. (1956). *Language, thought, and reality.* (J. B. Carroll, Ed.). Cambridge, MA: MIT Press.

Williams, E. (1995). Margarine. *Winning Orations,* 1–2.

Williams, L. (1999, January 15). Study shows rising diversity of Net users. *San Jose Mercury News,* p. A15.

Williams, R., & Williams, V. (1993). *Anger kills.* New York: Random House.

Wilson, L. R. (1998, January 1). The new frontier: Cyberspace and the telecosm. *Vital Speeches, 64,* 182–186.

Wilson, M. (1992). Say "AHA" to virtual reality. In L. G. Schnoor (Ed.), *Winning orations.* Northfield, MN: Interstate Oratorical Association.

Winch, P. (1959). Nature and convention. *Proceedings of the Aristotelian Society, 60,* 242.

Wiseman, R., Sanders, J., Congalton, J., Gass, R., Sueda, K., & Ruiqing, D. (1995). A cross-cultural analysis of compliance gaining: China, Japan, and the United States. *Intercultural Communication Studies, 1,* 1–18.

Witte, K., & Allen, M. (1996, November). *When do scare tactics work? A meta-analysis of fear appeals.* Paper presented at the annual meeting of the Speech Communication Association, San Diego, CA.

Witteman, H. (1993). The interface between sexual harassment and organizational romance. In Kreps, G. (Ed.), *Sexual harassment: Communication implications.* Cresskill, NJ: Hampton Press.

Wolf, N. (1994). *Fire with fire: The new female power and how to use it.* New York: Fawcett Columbine.

Wolf, S. (1979). Behavioral style and group cohesiveness as sources of minority influence. *European Journal of Social Psychology, 9,* 381–395.

Wolfram, W., & Fasold, R. (1974). *The study of social dialects in American English.* Englewood Cliffs, NJ: Prentice-Hall.

Wolvin, A. (1984). Meeting the communication needs of the adult learners. *Communication Education, 33,* 267–271.

Wolvin, A., & Coakley, C. (1996). *Listening.* Dubuque, IA: Brown & Benchmark.

Wolvin, A., & Corley, D. (1984). The technical speech communication course: A view from the field. *Association for Communication Administration Bulletin, 49,* 83–91.

Woman angry over online time attacked computer, cops say. (1999, July 1). *San Jose Mercury News,* p. A11.

Women can be violent, too, in relationships. (1998, August 4). *San Jose Mercury News,* p. F1.

Wood, J. (1994). *Gendered lives: Communication, gender, and culture.* Belmont, CA: Wadsworth.

Wood, J. (1996). She says/he says; communication, caring, and conflict in heterosexual relationships. In J. Wood (Ed.), *Gendered relationships.* Mountain View, CA: Mayfield.

Woodman, T. (1991). *The role of forgiveness in marital adjustment.* Unpublished doctoral dissertation, Fuller Graduate School of Psychology, Pasadena, CA.

Workers lack verbal skills, survey finds. (1992, September 21). *San Jose Mercury News,* p. A2.

Wright, R. (1993, July 1). Women are taking center stage in the worldwide political arena. *San Jose Mercury News,* p. A10.

Wurman, R. (1989). *Information anxiety.* New York: Doubleday.

Yerby, J., & Buerkel-Rothfuss, N. L. (1982, November). *Communication patterns, contradictions, and family functions.* Paper presented at the meeting of the Speech Communication Association, Louisville, KY.

Yoshitake, T. (1977). A Chinese stereotypic image of Japan and its people. *Communication, 6,* 18–28.

Yu, X. (1997). The Chinese "nature" perspective on mao-dun (conflict) and mao-dun resolution strategies: A qualitative investigation. *Intercultural Communication Studies, 7,* 63–82.

Zander, A. (1982). The psychology of removing group members and recruiting new ones. *Human Relations, 29,* 1–8.

Zillmann, D. (1993). Mental control of angry aggression. In Wegner, D., & Pennebaker, J. (Eds.), *Handbook of mental control* (Vol. 5). Englewood Cliffs, NJ: Prentice-Hall.

Zimbardo, P. (1992). *Psychology and life.* New York: HarperCollins.

Zurawik, D. (1998, August 18). On all-news cable channels, no news is bad news for the public. *San Jose Mercury News,* p. A8.

Credits

Photos

Chapter 1 p. 2, © Stephanie Diani/Photo 20-20; p. 8, © Reuters/Jim Bourg/Archive Photos; p. 13, © Bob Daemmrich/The Image Works; p. 20, © Brad Markel/Liaison Agency, Inc.; p. 22, © AP/Wide World Photos **Chapter 2** p. 30, © Rotolo/Liaison Agency, Inc.; p. 33, © Len Lahman/*San Jose Mercury News*; p. 49, © C. Gatewood/The Image Works; p. 50, © Tony Freeman/PhotoEdit; p. 53, © Bonnie Kamin/PhotoEdit **Chapter 3** p. 58, © Gary A. Conner/PhotoEdit; p. 61, © Ron Chapple/FPG International; p. 65L, © Charles & Josette Lenars/Corbis; p. 65R, © Billy Barnes/PhotoEdit; p. 69, © DPA/The Image Works; p. 75, © Bonnie Kamin/PhotoEdit **Chapter 4** p. 84, © Jonathan Nourok/PhotoEdit; p. 91, © Ronald Cohn/Gorilla Foundation/Koko.org; p. 106, © Jeff Greenberg/PhotoEdit; p. 112, © Crandall/The Image Works **Chapter 5** p. 116, © AP/Wide World Photos; p. 123, © Wally McNamee/Corbis; p. 124, © Wally McNamee/Corbis; p. 133TL, © Michael Newman/PhotoEdit; p. 133TM, © Michael Newman/PhotoEdit; p. 133TR, © Michael Newman/PhotoEdit; p. 133BL, © Bob Daemmrich/The Image Works; p. 133BM, © Michelle Bridwell/PhotoEdit; p. 133BR, © Myrleen Cate/PhotoEdit; p. 136, © AFP/Corbis **Chapter 6** p. 146, © David Young-Wolff/PhotoEdit; p. 155, © R. Lord/The Image Works; p. 156, © Michelle Gabel/The Image Works; p. 168, © Steve Liss/Sygma **Chapter 7** p. 180, © AP/Wide World Photos; p. 187, © Dorothy Littell/Stock Boston; p. 192, © Bruce Ayres/Tony Stone Images; p. 204, © Liaison Agency, Inc.; p. 211, © Kevin Jacobus/The Image Works **Chapter 8** p. 214, © Mark Richards/PhotoEdit; p. 223L, © Tony Freeman/PhotoEdit; p. 223R, © Tom McCarthy/PhotoEdit; p. 232, © Alison Wright/The Image Works; p. 241, © Steven Wewerka/Impact Visuals **Chapter 9** p. 246, © Robert Brenner/PhotoEdit; p. 257, © P. McCarten/PhotoEdit; p. 262, © 1996, The Washington Post. Photo by James A. Parcell. Reprinted with permission; p. 269L, © AP/Wide World Photos; p. 269R, © John Plummer **Chapter 10** p. 276, © Kevin T. Gilbert/Corbis; p. 283, © Jose Cabrillo/PhotoEdit; p. 291L, © Adam Woolfitt/Corbis; p. 291R, © Antman/The Image Works; p. 300, © Eric Miller/Liaison Agency, Inc. **Chapter 11** p. 306, © AP/Wide World Photos; p. 312, © David Burnett/Contact Press Images; p. 316, © David Butow/SABA; p. 320, © J. Greenberg/The Image Works; p. 325, © Mark Richards/PhotoEdit **Chapter 12** p. 332, © Roberto Soncin Gerometta/Photo 20-20; p. 335, © Mark Richards/PhotoEdit; p. 346, © Jeff Greenberg/PhotoEdit; p. 349, © Spencer Grant/PhotoEdit **Chapter 13** p. 358, © AP/Wide World Photos; p. 363, © J. Marshall/The Image Works; p. 365, © AFP/Corbis; p. 369, © David Wells/The Image Works **Chapter 14** p. 384, © AFP/Corbis; p. 391, © Andrew Cutraro; p. 395, © Neal Preston/Corbis; p. 403, © David Turney/Corbis **Chapter 15** p. 410, © Ulrike Welsch/PhotoEdit; p. 415, © Bob Mahoney/The Image Works; p. 426, © Steve Warmowski/Journal-Courier/The Image Works; p. 433, © Gary Walts/The Image Works **Chapter 16** p. 436, © Rick Bloom/SABA; p. 441, © M. Peterson/SABA; p. 448, © Brooks Kraft/Sygma; p. 452, © Reuters/Senate TV/Archive Photos; p. 457, © AP/Wide World Photos; p. 460, © Michael Newman/PhotoEdit **Chapter 17** p. 470, © Gilles Saussier/Liaison Agency, Inc.; p. 474L, © Alan Gallegos/AG Photograph; p. 474R, © Corbis/Bettmann; p. 482, © AP/Wide World Photos; p. 490, © Corbis/Peter Turnley

Text and Illustrations

Chapter 3 pp. 64, 68, and 71, Hofstede, G. (1991). *Cultures and organizations: Software of the mind*. New York: McGraw-Hill. Copyright © 1991 Geert Hofstede. Reproduced with permission.

Chapter 9 p. 272, Chen, G. and Starosta, W. J., *Foundations of Intercultural Communication*. Boston: Allyn and Bacon. Copyright © 1998 by Allyn and Bacon. Reproduced with permission.

Chapter 12 p. 344, Motley, Michael T., *Overcoming Your Fear of Public Speaking—A Proven Method*. Copyright © 1995 by McGraw-Hill, Inc. Reproduced with permission.

Chapter 15 p. 427L, reproduced by permission of the Associated Press. pp. 427R, 428, adapted from the *San Jose Mercury News*. Copyright © 1998 *San Jose Mercury News*. All rights reserved. Reproduced with permission. Use of this material does not imply endorsement of the *San Jose Mercury News*. p. 429T, reproduced by permission of Knight Ridder/Tribune Media Services. p. 429B, reproduced by permission of the Fleet Numerical Meteorology and Oceanography Center, Monterey, California. This is a Government published work and is not subject to copyright. p. 430, adapted from the *San Jose Mercury News*. Copyright © 1998 *San Jose Mercury News*. All rights reserved. Reproduced with permission. Use of this material does not imply endorsement of the *San Jose Mercury News*.

Chapter 16 p. 458 from *Influence: Science and Practice*, 2nd ed. by Robert B. Cialdini. Copyright © 1988, 1985 HarperCollins Publishers. Reprinted by permission of Addison-Wesley Educational Publishers, Inc.

Index